DIGITAL PRIVACY

DIGITAL PRIVACY

Theory, Technologies, and Practices

Edited by
Alessandro Acquisti • Stefanos Gritzalis
Costas Lambrinoudakis • Sabrina De Capitani di Vimercati

Auerbach Publications
Taylor & Francis Group
New York   London

CRC Press is an imprint of the
Taylor & Francis Group, an **informa** business

Auerbach Publications
Taylor & Francis Group
6000 Broken Sound Parkway NW, Suite 300
Boca Raton, FL 33487-2742

© 2008 by Taylor & Francis Group, LLC
Auerbach is an imprint of Taylor & Francis Group, an Informa business

No claim to original U.S. Government works
Printed in the United States of America on acid-free paper
10 9 8 7 6 5 4 3 2 1

International Standard Book Number-13: 978-1-4200-5217-6 (Hardcover)

Visit the Taylor & Francis Web site at
http://www.taylorandfrancis.com

and the Auerbach Web site at
http://www.auerbach-publications.com

Contents

Preface ix

Acknowledgments xiii

About the Editors xv

Contributors xix

PART I: THE PRIVACY SPACE

1 **Privacy-Enhancing Technologies for the Internet III: Ten Years Later** 3
   Ian Goldberg

2 **Communication Privacy** 19
   Andreas Pfitzmann, Andreas Juschka, Anne-Katrin Stange, Sandra Steinbrecher, and Stefan Köpsell

3 **Privacy-Preserving Cryptographic Protocols** 47
   Mikhail J. Atallah and Keith B. Frikken

PART II: PRIVACY ATTACKS

4 **Byzantine Attacks on Anonymity Systems** 73
   Nikita Borisov, George Danezis, and Parisa Tabriz

5 **Introducing Traffic Analysis** 95
   George Danezis and Richard Clayton

6   Privacy, Profiling, Targeted Marketing, and Data Mining ... 117
Jaideep Vaidya and Vijay Atluri

PART III: PRIVACY-ENHANCING TECHNOLOGIES

7   Enterprise Privacy Policies and Languages 135
Michael Backes and Markus Dürmuth

**8   Uncircumventable Enforcement of Privacy Policies
via Cryptographic Obfuscation** 155
Arvind Narayanan and Vitaly Shmatikov

**9   Privacy Protection with Uncertainty
and Indistinguishability** 173
X. Sean Wang and Sushil Jajodia

10 Privacy-Preservation Techniques in Data Mining 187
*Chunhua Su, Jianying Zhou, Feng Bao, Guilin Wang,
and Kouichi Sakurai*

PART IV: USER PRIVACY

**11 HCI Designs for Privacy-Enhancing Identity
Management** 229
*Simone Fischer-Hübner, John Sören Pettersson,
Mike Bergmann, Marit Hansen, Siani Pearson,
and Marco Casassa Mont*

**12 Privacy Perceptions among Members
of Online Communities** 253
Maria Karyda and Spyros Kokolakis

**13 Perceived Control: Scales for Privacy
in Ubiquitous Computing** 267
Sarah Spiekermann

PART V: PRIVACY IN UBIQUITOUS COMPUTING

14 RFID: Technological Issues and Privacy Concerns 285
Pablo Najera and Javier Lopez

15 Privacy-Enhanced Location Services Information 307
*Claudio A. Ardagna, Marco Cremonini,
Ernesto Damiani, Sabrina De Capitani di Vimercati,
and Pierangela Samarati*

16   **Beyond Consent: Privacy in Ubiquitous Computing (Ubicomp)** 327
Jean Camp and Kay Connelly

PART VI: THE ECONOMICS OF PRIVACY

17   **A Risk Model for Privacy Insurance** 347
*Athanassios N. Yannacopoulos, Sokratis Katsikas,
Costas Lambrinoudakis, Stefanos Gritzalis,
and Stelios Z. Xanthopoulos*

18   **What Can Behavioral Economics Teach Us about Privacy?** 363
Alessandro Acquisti and Jens Grossklags

PART VII: PRIVACY AND POLICY

19   **Privacy of Outsourced Data** 381
*Sabrina De Capitani di Vimercati, Sara Foresti,
Stefano Paraboschi, and Pierangela Samarati*

20   **Communications Data Retention: A Pandora's Box for Rights and Liberties?** 409
Lilian Mitrou

21   **Surveillance of Emergent Associations: Freedom of Association in a Network Society** 435
Katherine J. Strandburg

Index 459

Preface

Privacy Issues in the Digital Era

Privacy as a social and legal issue has been a concern of social scientists, philosophers, and lawyers for a long time. Back in 1890, two American lawyers, S. Warren and L. Brandeis, defined privacy as the right of an individual to be alone, and it has been recognized as a fundamental human right by the United Nations Declaration of Human Rights, the International Convenant on Civil and Political Rights, the Charter of Fundamental Rights of the European Union, and many other international treaties. Therefore, in democratic societies the protection of privacy is a crucial issue.

Meanwhile, the intensive development of information and communication technologies has resulted in numerous new electronic services that aim to improve people's lives by allowing them to communicate and exchange data through the Internet, advertise their ideas through the World Wide Web, and purchase goods and services. To a large extent, the raw material for most of these electronic services is the personal data of individuals. Alongside the benefits for the people, these developments have introduced new risks such as identity theft, discriminatory profiling, continuous surveillance, and fraud. According to recent surveys, privacy and (especially) anonymity, are the fundamental issues of concern for most Internet users, ranked higher than issues like ease-of-use, spam-mail, cost, and security. In view of the above, the OECD Declaration on the Protection of Privacy on Global Networks (for developing a culture of privacy in the Global Village) is especially well timed.

In this volume, privacy is considered as the indefeasible right of an individual to control the ways in which personal information is obtained, processed, distributed, shared, and used by any other entity.

The Chapters

This volume is divided into seven parts, including twenty-one chapters in total:

Part I: The Privacy Space. Ian Goldberg, in his chapter entitled "Privacy-Enhancing Technologies for the Internet III: Ten Years Later" deals with the advances in privacy-enhancing technologies (PETs), while suggesting four principles (usability, deployability, effectiveness, and robustness) that may guide system designers when selecting or/and employing PETs. Andreas Pfitzmann, Andreas Juschka, Anne-Katrin Stange, Sandra Steinbrecher and Stefan Köpsell in their chapter entitled "Communication Privacy" present a thorough overview of anonymyzing techniques. Mikhail J. Atallah and Keith B. Frikken deal with "Privacy-Preserving Cryptographic Protocols" that allow the collaboration outcome to be computed, while the personal information revealed for the participants is minimized.

Part II: Privacy Attacks. This part starts with Nikita Borisov, George Danezis and Parisa Tabriz who study "Byzantine Attacks on Anonymity Systems." George Danezis and Richard Clayton, in their chapter entitled "Introducing Traffic Analysis" present the key issues around traffic analysis, while Jaideep Vaidya and Vijay Atluri in "Privacy, Profiling, Targeted Marketing, and Data Mining" highlight the problems of profiling, targeted marketing, data mining, and privacy.

Part III: Privacy-Enhancing Technologies. Michael Backes and Markus Dürmuth in their chapter address the issue of "Enterprise Privacy Policies and Languages" while Arvind Narayanan and Vitaly Shmatikov in "Uncircumventable Enforcement of Privacy Policies via Cryptographic Obfuscation" deal with obfuscation in the personal and group privacy era. X. Sean Wang and Sushil Jajodia in "Privacy Protection with Uncertainty and Indistinguishability" discuss the metrics of uncertainty and indistinguishability. The last chapter of this part is by Chunhua Su, Jianying Zhou, Feng Bao, Guilin Wang, and Kouichi Sakurai, who deal with "Privacy-Prevention Techniques in Data Mining."

Part IV: User Privacy. Simone Fischer-Hübner, John Sören Pettersson, Mike Bergmann, Marit Hansen, Siani Pearson, and Marco Casassa Mont, in their chapter "HCI Designs for Privacy-Enhancing Identity Management" report results from the human–computer interaction research work on privacy and identity management. Maria Karyda and Spyros Kokolakis deal with "Privacy Perceptions among Members of Online Communities," while Sarah Spiekermann in the chapter entitled "Perceived Control: Scales for Privacy in Ubiquitous Computing" presents three scales for measuring people's perception of control over being accessed when moving in RFID-enabled environments.

Part V: Privacy in Ubiquitous Computing. Pablo Najera and Javier Lopez in their chapter, "RFID: Technological Issues and Privacy Concerns," identify the threats and privacy issues in RFID environments. Claudio A. Ardagna, Marco Cremonini, Ernesto Damiani, Sabrina De Capitani di Vimercati, and Pierangela Samarati, in "Privacy-Enhanced Location Services Information" review the main techniques employed for protecting the location privacy of users in electronic services. Jean Camp and Kay Connelly in "Beyond Consent: Privacy in Ubiquitous Computing (Ubicomp)" identify basic threats in ubiquitous environments and propose a particular approach for bringing PETs to home-based ubicomp.

Part VI: The Economics of Privacy. Athanasios N. Yannacopoulos, Sokratis Katsikas, Costas Lambrinoudakis, Stefanos Gritzalis, and Stelios Z. Xanthopoulos in their chapter, "A Risk Model for Privacy Insurance," introduce a risk model that can be utilized by an IT firm for modeling the risks that it is exposed to as a result of privacy violation or disclosure of personal data of its clients. Alessandro Acquisti and Jens Grossklags in "What Can Behavioral Economics Teach Us about Privacy?" discuss the role of uncertainty, ambiguity, and behavioral biases in privacy decision making.

Part VII: Privacy and Policy. Sabrina De Capitani di Vimercati, Sara Foresti, Stefano Paraboschi, and Pierangela Samarati, in "Privacy of Outsourced Data," deal with the security issues arising in database outsourcing scenarios, while Lilian Mitrou is her chapter deals with "Communications Data Retention: A Pandora's Box for Rights and Liberties?" Finally, Katherine J. Strandburg, in "Surveillance of Emergent Associations: Freedom of Association in a Network Society" considers how relational surveillance must be regulated in order to preserve the growing role of emergent associations in politics and civic society.

Acknowledgments

We would like to express our appreciation to the chapters' authors of this book for their contributions in preparing a really valuable volume. Moreover, we would like to express our gratitude to Ray O'Connell of Auerbach Publications, Taylor & Francis Group, for giving us the opportunity to prepare this volume, as well as for his patience, understanding, and professional effort during the publication process.

Alessandro Acquisti
Stefanos Gritzalis
Costas Lambrinoudakis
Sabrina De Capitani di Vimercati

About the Editors

Prof. Alessandro Acquisti is an Assistant Professor of Information Technology and Public Policy at the H. John Heinz III School of Public Policy and Management, Carnegie Mellon University, a Partner at Carnegie Mellon Cylab, and a Research Fellow at the Institute for the Study of Labor (IZA). His work investigates the economic and social impacts of IT, and in particular the interaction and interconnection of human and artificial agents in highly networked information economies. His current research focuses primarily on the economics of privacy and information security, but also on the economics of computers and AI, agents economics, computational economics, ecommerce, cryptography, anonymity, and electronic voting. His research in these areas has been disseminated through journals, books, and leading international conferences. Prior to joining CMU Faculty, Alessandro Acquisti researched at the Xerox PARC labs in Palo Alto, California, with Bernardo Huberman and the Internet Ecologies Group; at JP Morgan London, Emerging Markets Research, with Arnab Das; and for two years at RIACS, NASA Ames Research Center, in Mountain View, California, with Maarten Sierhuis and Bill Clancey. Alessandro has received national and international awards, including the 2005 PET Award for Outstanding Research in Privacy Enhancing Technologies and the 2005 IBM Best Academic Privacy Faculty Award. He is a member of the program committees of various international conferences and workshops. Alessandro Acquisti has lived and studied in Rome (Laurea, Economics, University of Rome), Dublin (M.Litt., Economics, Trinity College), London (M.Sc., Econometrics and Mathematical Economics, LSE), and in the San Francisco Bay area, where he worked with John Chuang, Doug Tygar, and Hal Varian and received a Master and a Ph.D. in Information Management and Systems from the University of California at Berkeley. http://www.heinz.cmu.edu/~acquisti/

Prof. Stefanos Gritzalis holds a B.Sc. in Physics, an M.Sc. in Electronic Automation, and a Ph.D. in Informatics all from the University of Athens, Greece. Currently he is an Associate Professor, the Head of the Department of Information and Communication Systems Engineering, University of the Aegean, Greece and the Director of the Laboratory of Information and Communication Systems Security (Info-Sec-Lab). He has been involved in several national- and EU-funded R&D projects in the areas of Information and Communication Systems Security. His published scientific work includes several books on Information and Communication Technologies topics, and more than 140 journal and national and international conference papers. He has served on program and organizing committees of national and international conferences on Informatics and is an editorial advisory board member and reviewer for several scientific journals. He was a Member of the Board (Secretary General, Treasurer) of the Greek Computer Society. He is a member of the ACM and the IEEE. Since 2006 he has been a member of the "IEEE Communications and Information Security Technical Committee" of the IEEE Communications Society. http://www.icsd.aegean.gr/sgritz

Costas Lambrinoudakis is an Assistant Professor at the Department of Information and Communication Systems of the University of the Aegean and a senior researcher of the Information and Communication Systems Security Laboratory. He holds a B.Sc. (Electrical and Electronic Engineering) degree from the University of Salford (U.K.), an M.Sc. (Control Systems) and a Ph.D. (Computer Science) degree from the University of London (U.K.). His current research interests include: Information Systems Security and Privacy, Smart Cards, and Telemedicine Services. He is an author of several refereed papers in international scientific journals and conference proceedings. He has served on program and organizing committees of national and international conferences on Informatics and is a reviewer for several scientific journals. From 1987 to the present he has collaborated with several organizations and companies. He has participated in many national- and EU-funded R&D Projects. He is listed in *"Who's Who in the World"* and he is a member of the Technical Chamber of Greece, the ACM and the IEEE Computer Society. http://www.icsd.aegean.gr/clam

Sabrina De Capitani di Vimercati received the Laurea and Ph.D. degrees both in Computer Science from the University of Milan, Italy, in 1996 and 2001, respectively. From November 1999 to December 2002 she has been an Assistant Professor at the University of Brescia, Italy. Since January 2003 she is an Associate Professor at the Information Technology Department, University of Milan, Italy. Her research interests are in the area of information security, databases, and information systems. She has investigated the following issues: protection of information in federated systems, information flow control in object-oriented systems, protection of information from inference attacks, protection of network infrastructure, access control policies composition, and XML security. She has published more than 100 technical papers in international journals and conferences in her areas of research interest. She has been an international fellow in the Computer Science Laboratory at SRI, California (U.S.A.). She has been a visiting researcher at the ISSE Department of George Mason University, Virginia (U.S.A.). She has served on the program committees of various conferences and workshops. She is co-recipient of the ACM-PODS'99 Best Newcomer Paper Award. http://www.dti.unimi.it/decapita/

Contributors

Alessandro Acquisti
H. John Heinz III School
   of Public Policy and
   Management
Carnegie Mellon University
Pittsburgh, Pennsylvania, U.S.A.

Claudio A. Ardagna
Dipart. di Tecnologie
   dell'Informazione
Universita' degli Studi di Milano
Crema, Italy

Mikhail J. Atallah
Department of Computer Science
Purdue University
West Lafayette, Indiana, U.S.A.

Vijay Atluri
Department of
   Management Science and
   Information Systems
Rutgers University
Newark, New Jersey, U.S.A.

Michael Backes
Department of Computer Science
Saarland University
Saarbruecken, Germany

Feng Bao
Cryptography & Security Department
Institute for Infocomm Research
Singapore

Mike Bergmann
University of Technology Dresden
Dresden, Germany

Nikita Borisov
Department of Electrical
   and Computer Engineering
University of Illinois at
   Urbana-Champaign,
Urbana, Illinois, U.S.A.

Jean Camp
Indiana University
Bloomington, Indiana, U.S.A.

Richard Clayton
Computer Laboratory
University of Cambridge
Cambridge, U.K.

Kay Connelly
Department of Computer Science
Indiana University
Bloomington, Indiana, U.S.A.

Marco Cremonini
Dipart. di Tecnologie
  dell'Informazione
Universita' degli Studi di Milano
Crema, Italy

Ernesto Damiani
Dipart. di Tecnologie
  dell'Informazione
Universita' degli Studi di Milano
Crema, Italy

George Danezis
Department of Electrical Engineering
Katholieke Universiteit Leuven
Leuven, Belgium

Markus Dürmuth
Department of Computer Science
Saarland University
Saarbruecken, Germany

Simone Fischer-Hübner
Department of Computer Science
Karlstads Universitet
Karlstad, Sweden

Sara Foresti
Dipart. di Tecnologie
  dell'Informazione
Universita' degli Studi di Milano
Crema, Italy

Keith B. Frikken
Department of Computer Science
  and Systems Analysis
Miami University
Oxford, Ohio, U.S.A.

Ian Goldberg
David R. Cheriton School
  of Computer Science
University of Waterloo
Waterloo, Ontario, Canada

Stefanos Gritzalis
Department of Information and
  Communication Systems
  Engineering
University of the Aegean
Karlovassi, Samos, Greece

Jens Grossklags
School of Information
University of California
Berkeley, California, U.S.A.

Marit Hansen
Independent Centre for
  Privacy Protection
Schleswig Holstein,
  Holstenstraße
Kiel, Germany

Sushil Jajodia
Center for Secure Information
  Systems
George Mason University
Fairfax, Virginia, U.S.A.

Andreas Juschka
Department of Computer
  Science
University of Technology Dresden
Dresden, Germany

Maria Karyda
Department of Information and
  Communication Systems
  Engineering
University of the Aegean
Karlovassi, Samos, Greece

Sokratis Katsikas
Department of Technology
  Education and Digital Systems
University of Piraeus
Piraeus, Greece

Spyros Kokolakis
Department of Information and
 Communication Systems
 Engineering
University of the Aegean
Karlovassi, Samos, Greece

Stefan Köpsell
Department of Computer Science
University of Technology Dresden
Dresden, Germany

Costas Lambrinoudakis
Department of Information and
 Communication Systems
 Engineering
University of the Aegean
Karlovassi, Samos, Greece

Javier Lopez
Computer Science Department
University of Malaga
Malaga, Spain

Lilian Mitrou
Department of Information and
 Communication Systems
 Engineering
University of the Aegean
Karlovassi, Samos, Greece

Marco Casassa Mont
Hewlett-Packard Labs
Stoke Gifford, Bristol, U.K.

Pablo Najera
Computer Science Department
University of Malaga
Malaga, Spain

Arvind Narayanan
Department of Computer
 Sciences
The University of Texas at Austin
Austin, Texas, U.S.A.

Stefano Paraboschi
Dipart. di Ingegneria
 dell'Informazione e Metodi
 Matematici
Universita' degli Studi di Bergamo
Dalmine, Italy

Siani Pearson
Hewlett-Packard Labs
Stoke Gifford, Bristol, U.K.

John Sören Pettersson
Department of Information
 Systems
Karlstads Universitet
Karlstad, Sweden

Andreas Pfitzmann
Department of Computer Science
University of Technology Dresden
Dresden, Germany

Kouichi Sakurai
Department of Computer
 Science and Communication
 Engineering
Kyushu University
Nishi-ku, Fukuoka, Japan

Pierangela Samarati
Dipart. di Tecnologie
 dell'Informazione
Universita' degli Studi di Milano
Crema, Italy

Vitaly Shmatikov
Department of Computer Science
The University of Texas at Austin
Austin, Texas, U.S.A.

Sarah Spiekermann
Institute of Information Systems
Humboldt-Universität zu Berlin
Berlin, Germany

Anne-Katrin Stange
Department of Computer
  Science
University of Technology Dresden
Dresden, Germany

Sandra Steinbrecher
Department of Computer
  Science
University of Technology Dresden
Dresden, Germany

Katherine J. Strandburg
DePaul University College of Law
Chicago, Illinois, U.S.A.

Chunhua Su
Department of Computer
  Science and Communication
  Engineering
Kyushu University
Nishi-ku, Fukuoka, Japan

Parisa Tabriz
Google
Mountain View, California, U.S.A.

Jaideep Vaidya
Management Science and
  Information Systems Department
Rutgers University
Newark, New Jersey, U.S.A.

Sabrina De Capitani di Vimercati
Dipart. di Tecnologie
  dell'Informazione
Universita' degli Studi di Milano
Crema, Italy

Guilin Wang
Cryptography & Security Department
Institute for Infocomm Research
Singapore

X. Sean Wang
Department of Computer Science
University of Vermont
Burlington, Vermont, U.S.A.

Stelios Z. Xanthopoulos
Department of Statistics and
  Actuarial-Financial Mathematics
University of the Aegean
Karlovassi, Samos, Greece

Athanassios N. Yannacopoulos
Department of Statistics
Athens University of Economics
  and Business
Athens, Greece

Jianying Zhou
Network Security Group
Institute for Infocomm Research
Singapore

THE PRIVACY
SPACE

I

Chapter 1

Privacy-Enhancing Technologies for the Internet III: Ten Years Later

Ian Goldberg

Contents

1.1   Introduction 4
1.2   E-mail Anonymity and Pseudonymity Systems 5
     1.2.1   Type-0 Remailers 5
     1.2.2   Type-I Remailers 5
     1.2.3   Type-II Remailers 6
     1.2.4   Type-III Remailers 7
1.3   Interactive Anonymity and Pseudonymity Systems 7
     1.3.1   Anonymizer.com 8
     1.3.2   Onion Routing 8
     1.3.3   The Freedom Network 8
     1.3.4   Java Anon Proxy 9
     1.3.5   Tor 9
1.4   Communication Privacy Systems 10
     1.4.1   PGP and Compatible Systems 11
     1.4.2   SSL and TLS 11
     1.4.3   Off-the-Record Messaging 11

1.5   Other Privacy-Enhancing Technologies 12
         1.5.1   Private Payments..12
         1.5.2   Private Credentials 13
         1.5.3   Anti-Phishing Tools 13
1.6   Useful Security and Privacy Technologies..........................14
1.7   Conclusion...15
References...16

1.1   Introduction

In 1997, with Wagner and Brewer, and again in 2002, we looked at the then-current state of privacy-enhancing technologies (PETs) for the Internet [26,27]. Now, in 2007, we are taking a third look. Technologies to help users maintain their privacy online are as important today as ever before—if not more so. Identity theft is the fastest-growing crime in the United States today [47] and it is all too easy for would-be identity thieves to harvest personal information from the online trails Internet users leave every day. Losses of large databases of personal information are an almost daily occurrence [2]; for example, retailers' servers are penetrated [44], databases are traded between government and private companies [36], and laptops containing Social Security numbers are stolen [35].

In 1997, we discussed the *dossier effect*: all available information about a person gets cross-referenced, and the resulting dossier ends up being used for many purposes, lawful and not. This practice has expanded over the years; the companies that compile and sell these dossiers are known as *data brokers*. Choicepoint is a prime example—in 2005, this data broker sold dossiers on over 150,000 Americans to a group of criminals [10]. The PETs we discuss here give people a way to control how much of their personal information is revealed when they use the Internet. By controlling the spread of this information, they can limit the size of the data brokers' dossiers about them.

In this chapter, we examine different classes of privacy-enhancing technologies. For each class, we look at the state of the technology in 2002 and see what has happened in the intervening five years. In Section 1.2, we look at a range of systems to protect the identities of senders and recipients of electronic mail. In Section 1.3, we examine systems that attempt to solve the more complex problem of protecting your identity when accessing interactive Internet services. Section 1.4 surveys a number of technologies that protect the contents of Internet conversations, as opposed to the identities of the participants. In Section 1.5, we look to the future and examine three particular technologies in which we hope to see progress in the next 5 years. Section 1.6 outlines the principles researchers should keep in mind when designing future security and privacy technologies in order to maximize their usefulness, and Section 1.7 concludes the chapter analysis.

1.2 E-mail Anonymity and Pseudonymity Systems

The first class of PETs we will examine are systems to provide *anonymity* and *pseudonymity* for electronic mail. E-mail anonymity systems allow a user to *send* e-mail without revealing his or her own personal information, such as identity, e-mail address, or Internet protocol (IP) address. E-mail pseudonymity systems also allow the user to set up a persistent pseudonym, or *nym*, which can be used to *receive* e-mail as well. With these pseudonymous systems, users can participate in ongoing e-mail conversations while maintaining their privacy.

1.2.1 Type-0 Remailers

The oldest and simplest e-mail anonymity systems were the *type-0 remailers*. The term *remailer* stems from the basic operation of these systems: A user sends e-mail to the remailer, which strips off the user's identifying information and remails the message to its intended recipient. The remailer also assigns a random pseudonym to the sender. By keeping a master list matching the pseudonyms to senders' real e-mail addresses, replies to remailed messages can be delivered to the original sender.

While these type-0 remailers provided some protection against casual observers, the master list provided a tempting target for attackers; anyone who could get his hands on the list could reveal the real e-mail addresses of all the users of the remailer. The most well-known of these remailers, anon.penet.fi, was shut down after its operator lost a legal fight that required him to turn over parts of the list [30].

1.2.2 Type-I Remailers

In order to better protect the privacy of e-mail users, the *type-I*, or *cypherpunk remailers*, were developed. They work on the same principle—a message arrives at a type-I remailer, which removes the sender's identifying information and then sends the message out. But these remailers add a number of key improvements. The first is *chaining*: a user sends his message to a remailer with instructions to send it, not to the intended recipient, but rather to a second remailer (run by an operator independent from the first). *That* remailer is instructed to send it to a third remailer, and so on. Only the last remailer in the chain receives the e-mail address of the intended final recipient. Therefore, compromising any one of the remailers or their operators does not allow linking the sender to the recipient. The first remailer knows only that the sender is a user of the remailer network, but not with whom he is communicating. The last remailer in the chain knows that somebody sent an anonymous message to a particular recipient, but cannot identify who it was. Remailers in the middle of the chain know only that they are forwarding anonymous e-mail, but do not know the sender or recipient. The goal is that *all* of the remailers in the chain need to be compromised in order for the privacy of the sender to be breached.

The second improvement made by the type-I remailers is *encryption.* Without encryption, the first remailer in the chain could simply read the instructions to the later remailers, including the address of the final recipient. Instead, the first remailer receives an encrypted message. When it is decrypted, it finds only the address of the second remailer and another encrypted message. This inner message, however, is encrypted to the *second* remailer, so the first remailer cannot read it. The first remailer sends that message to the second remailer, which decrypts it to find the address of the third remailer and another encrypted message (that only the third remailer can read), and so on. Finally, when the last remailer decrypts its message, it finds the address of the final recipient as well as the (unencrypted) message to send.

The third improvement made by the type-I remailers is *mixing*: incoming messages to any remailer are batched together and randomly reordered before being sent out. This was an attempt to prevent a passive observer of a given remailer from determining which outgoing message corresponds to which incoming message. An attacker could perform a *timing correlation attack* by comparing the order in which messages were received by the remailer to the order in which they were subsequently sent out. By introducing delays and reordering, this attack is hindered.

Unlike the type-0 remailers, technical sophistication is required to use the type-I remailers. Users have to either manually construct all of the encrypted parts of a message before sending it or install a tool such as premail [34] that automatically handles the message construction.

1.2.3   Type-II Remailers

Although the type-I remailers were, privacy-wise, a great improvement over the type-0 system, they were still vulnerable to *size correlation attacks* or *replay attacks.* In a size correlation attack, an adversary tries to match the messages sent by a given remailer to the messages it receives by matching the sizes of the messages. In a replay attack, the adversary makes a copy of one of the messages received by the remailer, and sends many copies of it to that same remailer. The adversary then observes which outgoing message from that remailer gets repeated many times.

Type-II or *Mixmaster remailers* were deployed to address these problems [41]. Type-II remailers divide all messages into a number of fixed-sized packets that are sent separately through the network of remailers in order to defeat size correlations. These remailers also employ more complex techniques to defeat replay attacks.

Messages for type-II remailers cannot be constructed manually in any reasonable way; users need specially customized software in order to send anonymous mail.

1.2.4   Type-III Remailers

Type-II remailers were the current state-of-the-art in 2002. What has happened in the past five years? A design for *type-III* or *Mixminion remailers* has been proposed [13], which improves privacy protection in a number of ways. First, type-III remailers provide a better system for handling replies to anonymous messages. Type-II remailers only support anonymity—not pseudonymity. In order to receive replies to a type-II message, senders have to set up a pseudonym with the older type-I remailer network.

Type-III remailers also provide improved protection against replay attacks and against *key compromise attacks*, where an attacker learns the private decryption key of one or more of the remailers. The type-III system has several different new features to prevent other forms of attack and to aid in the management of the network.

Unfortunately, support for type-III remailers is not yet widespread. The implementation of the published design has never been released past the testing stage, and, in the last year, has seen little work done on it. Although there are about thirty type-III remailers scattered around the world (about the same as the number of type-II remailers), the authors of Mixminion specifically warn users that "you shouldn't trust Mixminion with your anonymity yet" [14].

1.3   Interactive Anonymity and Pseudonymity Systems

Today's online communication is increasingly interactive and real-time, using technologies such as instant messaging. Protecting these types of communication, as well as other interactive Internet applications, such as the World Wide Web, remote logins, voice-over-IP, and games, poses a much more significant challenge than the corresponding problem for e-mail. Whereas remailers obtain much of their security from delaying and reordering messages, such delays are unacceptable in the context of low-latency interactive services, and tradeoffs often have to be made.

In 1995, Wei Dai presented a design of an anonymity system for low-latency traffic, which he called "PipeNet" [12]. The design of PipeNet emphasized security over all else: If the system detected any anomaly that could be an attacker trying to compromise privacy, the entire network would shut down. Of course, no realistic system could work this way; people simply wouldn't use it. There have been a number of systems that have been implemented and fielded over the years to provide practical security and privacy to users of interactive Internet applications. We examine several of these next.

1.3.1 Anonymizer.com

Anonymizer.com, a company we mentioned in the 2002 survey [26], continues to run the Anonymizer proxy service [1], a system we first mentioned in the 1997 survey [27]. They continue to be one of the few commercially successful anonymity technology providers. The Anonymizer works much like the type-0 remailers: A Web browser makes a request to the Anonymizer, which relays the request to the intended Web server. This service protects the user's privacy from that Web server, but not from Anonymizer.com itself, or from anyone watching the Internet near it. As we saw in 2002, by providing protection only against this simpler threat model, Anonymizer.com is able to keep costs and complexity down.

1.3.2 Onion Routing

The U.S. Naval Research Lab's Onion Routing project [28,45] was the first PipeNet-like system to be widely deployed. Although its primary use was for anonymizing Web traffic, it also allowed users to anonymously connect to any Transmission Control Protocol (TCP)/IP server on the Internet. A user configures his Internet applications to use the SOCKS proxy protocol [33] to connect to an *Onion Proxy*. Analogous to remailer systems, the Onion Proxy creates a path through several *Onion Routers* situated around the Internet.

Unlike remailer systems, however, this path is long-lived. Once it is created, any data sent through this path is anonymously delivered to the intended TCP/IP server. Any replies from that server are returned along the path to the Onion Proxy, and from there to the user's application. When the application is finished communicating with the server, the path is torn down, freeing the resources allocated for it at the Onion Routers.

The original deployed Onion Routing network was primarily a proof-of-concept; it later evolved into the Tor network (see Section 1.3.5 below).

1.3.3 The Freedom Network

The Freedom Network was a commercial venture by Zero-Knowledge Systems, Inc. [5]. Also a PipeNet-inspired system, it incorporated some of the ideas from the Onion Routing project, but its design differed in important ways. For example, while Onion Routing was a TCP/IP-based system that could anonymously transport any TCP/IP protocol, the Freedom Network was an IP-based system that could transport User Datagram Protocol (UDP)/IP as well. Unlike Onion Routing's pure anonymity, the Freedom Network provided a persistent pseudonymity service, enabling users to maintain separate online personas. It also used protocol-specific techniques to protect both the users of the network and the network itself. Importantly, Freedom removed the need for users to configure their Internet applications, which removed the potential for privacy-degrading mistakes.

The Freedom Network recruited operators from all over the world to run its *AIP nodes* (Anonymous Internet Proxies, again analogous to remailers), and paid them to do so. Unfortunately, as we mentioned in the 2002 survey [26], these costs proved to be prohibitive; there were not enough paid users to support the high-quality network that a commercial venture requires, and the network had already been shut down by that time.

1.3.4   Java Anon Proxy

Java Anon Proxy (JAP) is a project of Technical University Dresden [23]. It is one of the few privacy-enhancing technologies that was around in 2002 and still in use today. Unlike PipeNet-based systems, JAP is a Web-only anonymization tool that uses the techniques of type-II remailers to do its job. Web requests and replies are divided into fixed-sized chunks and sent through a series of mix nodes. Each node collects a batch of these chunks, encrypts or decrypts them as appropriate, reorders them, and sends them on to the next mix node.

As with Onion Routing, users protect their privacy with JAP by running the JAP client program, and configuring their Web browsers to use the JAP client as an HTTP proxy. In this way, each of the user's Web requests is sent to the JAP client, which divides it into chunks and sends these chunks through the mix network.

1.3.5   Tor

Tor [18,19] is a new system that has appeared since the publication of the 2002 article [26]. It is the next generation of the Onion Routing project, and it is the most successful (in terms of number of users) interactive anonymity tool to date. Hundreds of thousands of users send about 8 terabytes of traffic per day through hundreds of Tor nodes. As it is an extension of the Onion Routing project, it shares many of that project's characteristics: It only anonymizes TCP/IP protocols, it requires configuration of users' Internet applications, and so on.

Unlike the erstwhile Freedom Network, the Tor nodes are run by volunteers and all of the software is free and open-source. Although somewhat cumbersome for novice users to install and use on its own, graphical user interfaces such as Vidalia [21] and other helpful tools like Torbutton [43] greatly enhance Tor's ease of use.

Currently, one of Tor's biggest drawbacks is its noticeable degradation to Web browsing speeds. Ideally, Tor could be used in an "always on" mode, with users not even noticing its presence. Although Tor's sluggish performance prevents this today, work is being done to improve the situation. One possible way to accomplish this is to use peer-to-peer techniques to improve its scalability, as was suggested in 2002 [26]. A different project, MorphMix [40], proposed such a design, but not only was it never widely deployed for general use, it was later shown to contain flaws in its privacy protection [46].

In addition to protecting the users of TCP/IP-based Internet services, Tor also contains a facility to protect *providers* of such services. The most common *hidden services* are Web servers; a user runs a Web server somewhere in the world, which is only accessible through Tor, and Tor protects the identities of both the user and the provider of the service. In this way, Tor provides a *censorship-resistant publishing* service, which has been used by whistleblowers, for example, to distribute information of public importance [37]. Other censorship-resistant publishing services include the Free Haven [17], FreeNet [8], and Publius [48] projects mentioned in 2002 [26]. Of these latter three projects, however, only FreeNet is still being developed and used today. The Wikileaks project [50,51] uses both Tor and FreeNet in order to provide a censorship-resistant repository of leaked documents, which anyone can easily add to.

1.4   Communication Privacy Systems

When communicating over the Internet, the above technologies can help keep identity information private, possibly from third parties, and possibly also from other parties to the communication. In addition, correspondents may wish to keep the *contents* of the communication private from third parties. The technologies in this section allow you to do this. Note that it is usually the case that these technologies can be combined with those of the previous sections to protect both a user's identity and the contents of his communication.

It is important to note that with these technologies, all parties to the communication need to have the same (or compatible) systems installed. This is not the case with the technologies in the previous sections; those systems protect their users' privacy without requiring the other parties' cooperation.

1.4.1 PGP and Compatible Systems

Pretty Good Privacy (PGP) [25,39] has been available in one form or another for over 25 years. Although newer versions have many more features, PGP's fundamental purpose is to encrypt or digitally sign e-mail (and to decrypt it and verify the signatures at the other end, of course). PGP has evolved from a command-line-only program to one with a full-featured graphical user interface, and there are a number of compatible implementations, such as GNU Privacy Guard (GnuPG) [32] and Hushmail [31].

Users install some PGP-compatible software and use it to encrypt their e-mail messages before sending them. This can be done manually, but some e-mail programs, including Outlook, Eudora, mutt, and pine, have incorporated PGP support, which greatly improves its ease of use.

1.4.2 SSL and TLS

As the World Wide Web turned into a platform for e-commerce in the late 1990s, it became important to protect the contents of Web transactions. Netscape invented the Secure Sockets Layer (SSL) protocol, which in later versions was renamed Transport Layer Security (TLS) [16,24]. Though not without problems, SSL and TLS are the single most widely used privacy-enhancing technology to date. Their success stems from the fact that every major Web browser comes with support for these technologies built in and that their use is largely invisible to the user. That is, no special installation or configuration needs to be done by end users before they can benefit from these technologies. A Web browser will automatically encrypt Web requests when communicating with an SSL/TLS Web server, and the server will automatically encrypt its responses; no user intervention is needed at all. Later, we will come back to this theme when we examine properties of useful security and privacy technologies.

1.4.3 Off-the-Record Messaging

In the past five years, online communication has increasingly moved from e-mail to instant messaging, especially among younger users [7]. First released in 2004, Off-the-Record Messaging (OTR) [3,4] is a technology to protect the contents of these instant messaging communications. As the name implies, OTR provides instant messaging users with an "off-the-record" conversation. Much like conversing face-to-face, OTR users can communicate privately and can also repudiate any claims as to the content of their conversation.

Fundamentally, OTR allows instant messaging users to communicate in an encrypted and authenticated manner. When user Alice sends a message to her buddy Bob using OTR, she is assured that only Bob will be able to read it. In turn, Bob is assured that the message came from Alice and has not been modified en route.

Moreover, OTR offers *deniability*. If Bob tells his friend Charlie what Alice sent him, Bob is able to offer no *proof* of that assertion—Charlie just has to trust him. OTR avoids using traditional nonrepudiable digital signatures for authentication of messages; if messages from Alice had been digitally signed, Charlie could easily check the signatures for himself. Instead, OTR uses inherently repudiable message authentication codes to assure Bob that the message really came from Alice, but renders him unable to prove that fact to anyone else.

In addition, by taking advantage of the fact that instant messaging conversations are interactive, OTR is able to provide *perfect forward secrecy* to its messages. If Bob's computer is lost, is hacked into, gets a virus, or any such thing, and all of his secrets are stolen, any messages Alice had previously sent Bob would remain secret.

Users clearly cannot manually encrypt every instant message they send, so the OTR encryption must be handled in an automatic way. There are three ways that users can integrate OTR into their instant messaging. The first is by using a proxy: The user runs an OTR proxy on her computer and configures her instant messaging client to talk to that proxy instead of talking directly to the instant messaging server. This technique can be used by users of proprietary instant messaging clients like iChat and Trillian in order to obtain OTR functionality. The second method is by using a plug-in: Many instant messaging clients have the ability to have their functionality extended by third-party plug-in modules. There are OTR plug-ins available for the Gaim, Trillian, and Miranda instant messaging clients. The third method is to have OTR functionality built directly into the user's client. This is, of course, the best option, since, like SSL/TLS, the user does not have to install or configure anything special in order to gain some benefit from OTR. The popular Adium X instant messaging client for the OS X operating system has OTR built in.

1.5 Other Privacy-Enhancing Technologies

There are many other privacy-enhancing technologies that have been proposed, but are not yet in widespread use. In this section, we look at three particular technologies; we hope to see progress on these over the next five years.

1.5.1 Private Payments

In 2002, we discussed the disappointing lack of adoption of electronic cash [26]. Today, there are still no serious electronic cash services. It is important to fill this gap in the set of available privacy-enhancing technologies. Not only is it undesirable for there to be centralized records of everything one purchases online, but databases of payment records—including credit card numbers—are routinely stolen from merchants and from credit card processing firms [15]. These losses can lead to both credit card fraud and identity theft.

While alternatives to online credit card transactions, such as PayPal [38], are gaining popularity, a true privacy-protecting electronic cash solution remains elusive. Although, the last of the patents protecting DigiCash's original electronic cash protocol has recently expired, the patents were not the only barrier to entry for a potential electronic cash provider. As we mentioned in 2002, making a system widely accepted and interoperable with the "real" money system is a difficult task. In fact, PayPal itself may be in the best position to offer true privacy-friendly payments online; it already has the payment infrastructure, it could easily provide an interface between electronic cash and the rest of the financial system, and it has a large installed user base. Skype is also considering adding a payment system to its voice-and-chat offering [22], though no information is yet available about privacy properties that this system may or may not have.

1.5.2 Private Credentials

As we saw in 2002, private credentials [6] are a way to separate *authorization* from *authentication*. They allow users to prove that they are authorized to access a certain service or gain a certain benefit, while revealing no unnecessary personal information, such as their identities. Rather than Alice proving "I am Alice" to some server, and the server checking that Alice is on the approved access list, Alice instead proves "I am approved to access this server" without revealing who she is. This obviates any personal information about Alice being stored on the server, removing the possibility of that information being disclosed or stolen. Credentica [11] is expected to release a line of privacy-friendly Digital Credential products based on this technology in the near future.

1.5.3 Anti-Phishing Tools

A *phishing attack* occurs when a user is directed to a malicious Web site, often via a link in e-mail or chat. The site appears to be a common site, like a bank, eBay, or PayPal, but is really run by an attacker—the *phisher*. The message encourages the user to log in to the site to address an urgent problem with their account. When the user complies, the phisher captures the login name and password. From there the phisher can hijack the account, steal money, or mount an identity theft.

There are a number of tools available to help a user determine if he is looking at an authentic Web site or at a phishing site. These tools often appear as a toolbar in the user's Web browser that turns one of three colors: one color if the tool determines the site is probably genuine, one if it determines the site is probably a phishing site, and one if it cannot make a determination.

The way these tools make these determinations vary. Some, like eBay's Account Guard [20], compare the URL being visited to centrally maintained lists of good and bad sites. Users can suggest sites to be added to either list, and the list maintainers generally manually verify before adding them. Other tools, like the Cloudmark Anti-Fraud Toolbar [9], use the collective ratings of its users to automatically mark sites as "genuine" or "phishing." Some, like Google's Safe Browsing toolbar [29], use the fact that genuine sites generally have higher Google PageRank than phishing sites. Many tools use combinations of these techniques.

Zhang et al. [52] present an evaluation of ten of these anti-phishing toolbars and find that they "left a lot to be desired." They give some suggestions for further improvements to toolbars like these. We can only hope the state-of-the-art will advance in the next five years.

1.6 Useful Security and Privacy Technologies

Since 2002, we have seen a small amount of progress; there are a handful of new technologies that people are actually using in order to protect their privacy when they use the Internet. In comparison, *research* in privacy-enhancing technologies in the past five years has been booming. New technologies have been proposed in a number of different academic settings, but many do not make it out of the lab. Worse, some do not even make it from design into working code at all. These technologies do not improve people's security and privacy.

What would be more advantageous are security and privacy technologies that make a real difference to real people. We call such systems *useful security and privacy technologies*, and we have identified a number of properties such technologies must have.

> **Usability:** It has long been known that many security and privacy technologies are hard to use or hard to use correctly. Difficult-to-use technologies frustrate users, and can even put them in the unfortunate situation of believing they are being protected when they, in fact, are not [42,49]. In order for a technology to be useful, users need to be *able* to use it, and be able to use it properly. In addition, users have to *want* to use it; if a system protects their privacy at the expense of greatly slowing down their Internet experience, for example, users will simply turn it off.

Deployability: In order for a technology to be useful, it must be possible for everyday users doing everyday things to obtain it and benefit from it. This means it needs to be compatible with their preferred operating system, their preferred Web browser, their preferred instant messaging client, and so on. Ideally, the technology would be built right in so that the user doesn't even need to find and install separate software packages.

Effectiveness: Many designed, and even widely deployed, security and privacy technologies contain flaws that can render their ostensible protection moot. For a technology to be useful, it, of course, has to work and to give the user the benefit it promises. Open design and open implementation can help experts spot problems before too many users are left vulnerable.

Robustness: Some technologies will work as advertised, but only so long as things go "according to plan." But most technology designers' plans overlook the realities of users on the Internet today: Their computers contract worms and viruses, they forget their passwords, they get tricked by phishing attacks, they misunderstand (or just "click through") security-critical dialog boxes, and so on. A useful system needs to maintain as much protection as possible in these situations, since unfortunately they will often occur in practice.

In order to close the gap between the number of systems proposed by researchers and the number of systems giving benefit to users, developers of privacy-enhancing technologies should design with these principles in mind.

1.7 Conclusion

The past five years have seen a small increase in the availability of privacy-enhancing technologies for the Internet, including at least one, Tor, which is seeing significant use. This improvement over the previous half decade is encouraging, but much work remains. We need more technologies that move all the way from design to widespread use and we suggest that the four principles of useful security and privacy technologies—usability, deployability, effectiveness and robustness—may guide us in the right direction.

References

[1] Anonymizer.com. Anonymizer—Anonymous Proxy, Anonymous Surfing and Anti-Spyware. http://www.anonymizer.com. Accessed 11 January, 2007.

[2] Attrition.org. DLDOS: Data Loss Database—Open Source. http://attrition.org/dataloss/dldos.html. Accessed 11 January, 2007.

[3] Nikita Borisov and Ian Goldberg. Off-the-Record Messaging. http://otr.cypherpunks.ca/. Accessed 10 January, 2007.

[4] Nikita Borisov, Ian Goldberg, and Eric Brewer. "Off-the-Record Communication or Why Not To Use PGP." In *Proceedings of the Workshop on Privacy in the Electronic Society 2004*, Washington, D.C., pp. 77–84, October 2004.

[5] Philippe Boucher, Adam Shostack, and Ian Goldberg. Freedom Systems 2.0 Architecture. http://osiris.978.org/~brianr/crypto-research/anon/www.freedom.net/products/whitepapers/Freedom_System_2_Architecture.pdf. Accessed 10 January, 2007.

[6] Stefan Brands. *Rethinking Public Key Infrastructures and Digital Certificates—Building in Privacy*. MIT Press, Cambridge, MA, August 2000.

[7] Dan Carnevale. E-mail is for old people. *The Chronicle of Higher Education*, 53(7): A27, 6 October, 2006.

[8] Ian Clarke, Oskar Sandberg, Brandon Wiley, and Theodore W. Hong. Freenet: A distributed anonymous information storage and retrieval system. In *Designing Privacy Enhancing Technologies: Proceedings of the International Workshop on Design Issues in Anonymity and Unobservability*, Berkeley, CA, pp. 46–66, July 2000.

[9] Cloudmark, Inc. Cloudmark—Anti-Spam and Spam Blocker Solutions. http://www.cloudmark.com/desktop/howitworks. Accessed 10 January, 2007.

[10] Consumers Union of U.S., Inc. CR Investigates: Your privacy for sale. *Consumer Reports*, 71(10): 41, October 2006.

[11] Credentica. Credentica—Enterprise Solutions for Identity and Access Management. http://www.credentica.com/. Accessed 10 January, 2007.

[12] Wei Dai. PipeNet 1.1. http://www.weidai.com/pipenet.txt. Accessed 11 January, 2007.

[13] George Danezis, Roger Dingledine, and Nick Mathewson. Mixminion: Design of a Type III anonymous remailer protocol. In *Proceedings of the 2003 IEEE Symposium on Security and Privacy*, Oakland, CA, pp. 2–15, May 2003.

[14] George Danezis and Nick Mathewson. Mixminion—Type III Anonymity Client. Manual page, http://mixminion.net/manpages/mixminion.1.txt. Accessed 11 January, 2007.

[15] Eric Dash and Tom Zeller, Jr. "MasterCard Says 40 Million Files Put at Risk." *The New York Times*, A1, June 18, 2005.

[16] Tim Dierks and Eric Rescorla. The Transport Layer Security (TLS) Protocol Version 1.1. RFC 4346, http://www.ietf.org/rfc/rfc4346.txt.

[17] Roger Dingledine, Michael J. Freedman, and David Molnar. The Free Haven Project: Distributed Anonymous Storage Service. In *Designing Privacy Enhancing Technologies: Proceedings of the International Workshop on Design Issues in Anonymity and Unobservability*, Berkeley, CA, pp. 67–95, July 2000.

[18] Roger Dingledine and Nick Mathewson. Tor: Anonymity Online. http://tor.eff.org/. Accessed 10 January, 2007.

[19] Roger Dingledine, Nick Mathewson, and Paul Syverson. Tor: The second-generation onion router. In *Proceedings of the 13th USENIX Security Symposium*, San Diego, CA, August 2004.

[20] eBay, Inc. Using eBay Toolbar's Account Guard. http://pages.ebay.com/help/confidence/account-guard.html. Accessed 10 January, 2007.

[21] Matt Edman and Justin Hipple. Vidalia—Home. http://vidalia-project.net/. Accessed 10 January, 2007.

[22] Joris Evers. What Threats Does Skype Face? http://news.com.com/What + threats + does + Skype + face/2008-7350_3-6146092.html, 2 January 2007. Accessed 10 January, 2007.

[23] Hannes Federrath. JAP—Anonymity and Privacy. http://anon.inf.tu-dresden.de/index_en.html. Accessed 10 January, 2007.

[24] Alan O. Freier, Philip Karlton, and Paul C. Kocher. The SSL Protocol—Version 3.0. Internet draft, http://wp.netscape.com/eng/ssl3/draft302.txt.

[25] Simson Garfinkel. *PGP: Pretty Good Privacy*. O'Reilly, Santa Clara, CA, December 1994.

[26] Ian Goldberg. Privacy-enhancing technologies for the Internet, II: Five years later. In *Workshop on Privacy Enhancing Technologies 2002, Lecture Notes in Computer Science 2482*, pp. 1–12. Springer–Verlag, Heidelberg, Germany, April 2002.

[27] Ian Goldberg, David Wagner, and Eric A. Brewer. Privacy-enhancing technologies for the Internet. In *Proceedings of COMPCON '97*, the 42nd IEEE Computer Society International Conference, San Jose, CA, (4), 9 pp. 103–109, February 1997.

[28] David Goldschlag, Michael Reed, and Paul Syverson. Onion routing for anonymous and private Internet connections. *Communications of the ACM*, 42(2): 39–41, 1999.

[29] Google, Inc. Google Safe Browsing for Firefox. http://www.google.com/tools/firefox/safebrowsing/. Accessed 10 January, 2007.

[30] Sabine Helmers. A brief history of anon.penet.fi—The legendary anonymous remailer. *Computer-Mediated Communication Magazine*, 1997. http://www.december.com/cmc/mag/1997/sep/helmers.html.

[31] Hush Communications Corp. Hushmail—Free E-mail with Privacy. http://www.hushmail.com/. Accessed 10 January, 2007.

[32] Werner Koch. The GNU Privacy Guard. http://www.gnupg.org/. Accessed 10 January, 2007.

[33] Marcus Leech, Matt Ganis, Ying-Da Lee, Ron Kuris, David Koblas, and LaMont Jones. SOCKS Protocol Version 5. RFC 1928, http://www.ietf.org/rfc/rfc1928.txt.

[34] Raph Levien. Premail. http://www.mirrors.wiretapped.net/security/cryptography/apps/mail/premail/. Accessed 11 January, 2007.

[35] Michael Liedtke. "Stolen UC Berkeley Laptop Exposes Personal Data of Nearly 100,000." The Associated Press, 28 March 2005.

[36] Leslie Miller. "Report: TSA Misled Public on Personal Data." The Associated Press, 25 March 2005.

[37] MindFreedom International. Eli Lilly Targets Free Speech on MindFreedom's Web Site in Battle Over Zyprexa Documents. http://www.mindfreedom.org/know/psych-drug-corp/eli-lilly-secrets. Accessed 10 January, 2007.

[38] PayPal. Privacy—PayPal. https://www.paypal.com/cgi-bin/webscr?cmd=xpt/general/Privacy-outside. Accessed 10 January, 2007.

[39] PGP Corporation. PGP Corporation—Products—PGP Desktop E-mail. http://www.pgp.com/products/desktop_email/index.html. Accessed 10 January, 2007.

[40] Marc Rennhard and Bernhard Plattner. Introducing MorphMix: Peer-to-peer-based anonymous Internet usage with collusion detection. In *Proceedings of the Workshop on Privacy in the Electronic Society 2002*, Washington, D.C., pp. 91–102, November 2002.

[41] Len Sassaman and Ulf Möller. Mixmaster. http://mixmaster.source-forge.net/. Accessed 11 January, 2007.

[42] Steve Sheng, Levi Broderick, Colleen Alison Koranda, and Jeremy J. Hyland. Why Johnny Still Can't Encrypt: Evaluating the Usability of Email Encryption Software. Poster presented at the Symposium on Usable Privacy and Security, Pittsburgh, PA, July 2006.

[43] Scott Squires. Torbutton. http://freehaven.net/~squires/torbutton. Accessed 10 January, 2007.

[44] Marina Strauss and Sinclair Stewart. "Computer Breach Exposes TJX Shoppers to Fraud: Parent of Winners, HomeSense Targeted." *The Globe and Mail*, Toronto, Canada, B3, January 18, 2007.

[45] Paul F. Syverson, David M. Goldschlag, and Michael G. Reed. Anonymous connections and onion routing. In *Proceedings of the 1997 IEEE Symposium on Security and Privacy*, Oakland, CA, pp. 44–54, May 1997.

[46] Parisa Tabriz and Nikita Borisov. Breaking the collusion detection mechanism of MorphMix. In *Workshop on Privacy Enhancing Technologies 2006, Lecture Notes in Computer Science 4258*, pp. 368–383. Springer-Verlag, Heidelberg, Germany, June 2006.

[47] U.S. Postal Service. Identity Theft. http://www.usps.com/postalinspectors/idthft_ncpw.htm. Accessed 11 January, 2007.

[48] Marc Waldman, Aviel Rubin, and Lorrie Cranor. Publius: A robust, tamper-evident, censorship-resistant Web publishing system. In *Proceedings of the 9th USENIX Security Symposium*, Denver, CO, pp. 59–72, August 2000.

[49] Alma Whitten and J.D. Tygar. Why Johnny can't encrypt: A usability evaluation of PGP 5.0. In *Proceedings of the 8th USENIX Security Symposium*, Washington, D.C., August 1999.

[50] Wikileaks. wikileaks.org. http://www.wikileaks.org/index.html. Accessed 17 January, 2007.

[51] Elizabeth Williamson. "Freedom of Information, the Wiki Way: Site to Allow Anonymous Posts of Government Documents." *The Washington Post*, A13, January 15, 2007.

[52] Yue Zhang, Serge Egelman, Lorrie Cranor, and Jason Hong. Phinding phish: Evaluating anti-phishing tools. In *Proceedings of the 14th Annual Network and Distributed System Security Symposium (NDSS 2007)*, San Diego, CA, February 2007.

Chapter 2

Communication Privacy*

Andreas Pfitzmann, Andreas Juschka, Anne-Katrin Stange, Sandra Steinbrecher, and Stefan Köpsell

Contents

2.1   Introduction 20
2.2   Simple Proxies 22
    2.2.1   Web Site 22
    2.2.2   Local Proxies 22
    2.2.3   Proxy Chain...23
2.3   Crowds 24
2.4   Broadcast 25
2.5   RING-Network 27
2.6   Buses 28
2.7   DC-Network 31
2.8   Mixes 33
    2.8.1   Mix Topologies 33
    2.8.2   Basic Functionality 35
    2.8.3   Preprocessing: Transforming the Message.......................36
        2.8.3.1   Reordering: Batch, Pool Mixing 37
        2.8.3.2   Test-for-Replay 37
        2.8.3.3   Dummy Traffic 38

* This work was supported by the European FP 6 project FIDIS—Future of Identity in the Information Society (http://www.fidis.net/).

19

        2.8.3.4   Recipient Anonymity: Untraceable Return
                 Addresses 38
        2.8.3.5   Checking the Size of the Anonymity Set............40
        2.8.3.6   Mix Channels.......................................40
    2.8.4   Existing Systems 41
        2.8.4.1   High Latency 41
        2.8.4.2   Low Latency...42
2.9   Private Information Retrieval 43
2.10 General Principles among the Systems............................44
References...45

2.1   Introduction

Many people have a fallacious feeling of being anonymous when surfing the Internet. But, ordinary Internet communication on the network layer is by default not anonymous because of the usage of identifying characteristics like Internet Protocol (IP) or Media Access-Control (MAC) addresses. So, if no additional measures are taken, an adversary can easily observe which participants of a network communicate with each other. But, anonymity on the network layer of communication systems can be achieved by the use of anonymizing techniques. Based on anonymous communication on the network layer, necessary identification and authenticity of users can still be implemented on a higher layer, e.g., with privacy-enhancing identity management [8].

According to [18], anonymity of a subject is the state of not being identifiable within a set of subjects, the anonymity set. A sender may be anonymous only within a set of potential senders, his sender anonymity set, which itself may be a subset of all subjects worldwide who may send messages from time to time. This kind of anonymity is called *sender anonymity.* The same is true for the recipient who may be anonymous within a set of potential recipients, which form his recipient anonymity set. This kind of anonymity is called *recipient anonymity.* Both anonymity sets may be disjointed, be the same, or may overlap. The anonymity sets may vary over time. Beneath sender and recipient anonymity, a third type of anonymity for communication is *relationship anonymity*, which is the property that it is unlinkable—who communicates with whom. Here unlinkability means that within the system [18], these items (messages, senders, recipients) are no more and no less related than they are related concerning the *a priori* knowledge. Accordingly, sender/recipient anonymity can be defined as the properties that a particular message is unlinkable to any sender/recipient and that to a particular sender/recipient, no message is linkable. Relationship anonymity is the property that it is unlinkable, who communicates with whom.

Anonymity is the stronger; the larger the respective anonymity set is, the more evenly distributed the execution of actions by the subjects within that set is, i.e., not only the size of the respective anonymity set determines the anonymity of a certain subject, but also how likely a subject of the anonymity set might have executed the action.

This describes what anonymizing techniques for communication do: To collect an appropriate set of users, a particular user can be anonymous within when communicating with others.

Usually subjects cannot have the same anonymity against every possible participant and outsider who might attack the subject's anonymity. Depending on the attacker's knowledge, the above set of possible subjects and the likelihood with which they have caused an action can vary. For a specific attacker's view, anonymity only can decrease. After the attacker has had time to observe/influence the system, his knowledge might increase. A passive attacker only observes the system. Whether he also has the opportunity to become an active attacker and execute several types of attacks influencing the system, depends on the strength of the system.

This chapter will present an overview of anonymizing techniques that enable anonymity in a communication network. In addition to the anonymity techniques presented here, encryption schemes are used to protect not only the circumstances of communication, but also the content of communication.

We can differentiate anonymizing techniques by the following criteria:

1. **Protection goal:** Which type of anonymity can be provided (sender, recipient, or relationship anonymity)?
2. **Security level:** Which kind of security level can be achieved for the protection goal (information theoretic/unconditional or cryptographic/computational security)?
3. **Attacker model:** Which attackers does the technique (or not) protect against (outsiders, participants, network providers)?
4. **Trust model:** Who does the user trust (network providers, participants)?

In the following sections, a classification of anonymizing techniques following the criteria listed above is given.

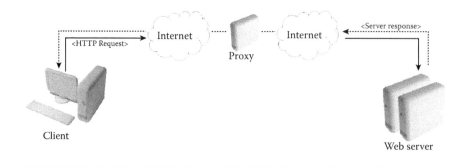

Figure 2.1   Using a proxy for surfing on the Internet.

2.2   Simple Proxies

One of the most popular concepts for anonymous surfing on the Internet is using proxies. The main idea behind this technology is that requests are not sent directly from the client computer to the Web server. Instead, the client is connected to another server, the so-called proxy server. The proxy server starts the HTTP request for the client (Figure 2.1) so that the Web server only gets the IP address of the proxy, but not the IP address of the client. In addition, some proxies also filter out information from the HTTP request, which could be used to identify the user. These include information such as cookies, the operating system, or browser used. "Active content" like JavaScript can be blocked as well. At the moment, there are two different possibilities to connect to a proxy, either via a Web site or by using a local proxy. These possibilities can also be combined to form proxy chains.

2.2.1   Web Site

A Web site-based proxy allows the use of the anonymizing service without installing any additional software.* On this Web site, a form usually can be found where the user fills in the address of the site he wants to surf. Now, the mechanism works as described above: The proxy sends a request to the Web server addressed by the user. After that, the server sends its answer to the proxy and then the requested data is transferred to the client. As an additional feature, the proxy also scans the HTTP content searching for any links. If there are links, they are transformed such a way so that they immediately can be used via the proxy. The user still remains anonymous to the provider of the Web sites when clicking on the links.

---

* This is also called the *Zero-Footprint* approach.

2.2.2 Local Proxies

The second method uses a local proxy. For this approach, a software is installed on the client's computer as a local proxy, which has to be registered on the browser as the one to be used when the user tries to connect to a Web site.

The local proxy software has a list of so-called *open proxies* that are proxies in the Internet that are—intentionally or mistakenly—left open for public use. This means that each Internet user can access and use an open proxy to hide his/her identity.

The manufacturer of the local proxy software scans the Internet automatically in order to discover new open proxies. The local proxy software randomly selects one of the open proxies it knows as proxy for anonymization (like in the Web site-based approach). Some of the local proxy software on the market also changes at a user selected time interval when the open proxy is used.

2.2.3 Proxy Chain

There also might be the possibility of using not only one proxy, but a chain of several proxies, which can be local or external, before the request is sent to a Web site. The combination of several proxies can be useful because different proxies have different pros and cons. By combining the single proxies, a proxy chain can be created. On the one hand, local proxies can provide a good filter for the HTTP requests and because of being local, the speed of surfing on the Internet does not slow down. On the other hand, by using different external proxies, the trust necessary in the single proxy providers becomes weaker because the proxy providers have to collaborate in order to recognize which Web site the client wants to surf.

> **Protection goal:** Sender anonymity against the recipient and relationship anonymity against all others.
> **Security level:** Unconditional security can be achieved.
> **Attacker model:**
> - Protection against the recipient.
> - No protection against a single proxy provider or a collusion of proxy providers in a chain.
> - No protection against outside attackers who could link incoming and outgoing messages of one user, e.g., by timing analysis.
>
> **Trust model:** The user has to trust in the proxy because it can record all transferred information and observe the user's activities. Some proxies insert additional information into the request of the client, e.g., x-forward-for, so that the Web server also might get the IP of the user.

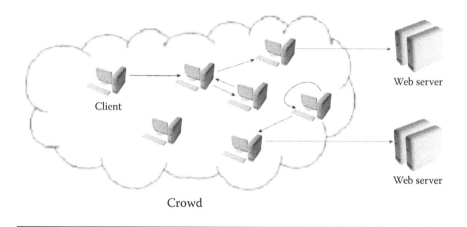

Figure 2.2   Sending request to a Web server via Crowds.

2.3   Crowds

The concept behind Crowds is that the activities of each single user can be hidden within the activities of many other users. So, the system consists of a dynamic collection of users called a *Crowd*. It was designed to provide sender anonymity and high performance.

As described in [20], a Web site request first passes a random number of participants of the Crowd before it is sent to the Web server. This means that when a member of the Crowd gets a message, it decides randomly whether to send the message directly to the destination server or forward it to another member of the Crowd. If the message is sent to another member, this member does the same until the message reaches its final destination—the Web site requested (Figure 2.2). Because of this mechanism, neither the server nor a member of the Crowd can decide if someone is the initiator of the request or if he is only forwarding the request. This means that plausible deniability is achieved.

If a user wants to take part in the Crowds network, he has to install additional software on his local computer, the so-called "jondo".* Furthermore, he has to register with a central server, the so-called blender. As one part of the registration procedure, the user must create a personal login and a password for personal authentication. The jondo software is a kind of local proxy, so it has to be configured in the browser before it can be used for surfing.

---

* Jondo is a pun on the name John Doe, used to hide the identity of a person.

When starting the system, the jondo first contacts the blender to request access to a Crowds network. For access, the blender sends back a list of Crowds' members (the crowd of the jondo) and keys for symmetric encryption. Further, the blender informs all other jondos in the network about the new member. The above-mentioned keys are necessary because all information (requests and responses) are encrypted from member to member on the Crowds network. Any Web request coming from the browser is now forwarded to the local jondo, which sends the request randomly to a member of the crowd (this can be another member or even the sender himself).

When a message is sent to or received from a member, a special path identification (ID) is stored. This ID makes it possible to forward a response of a server back to the requesting client. Each jondo saves pairs of path IDs (incoming and outgoing) in a local table. If a jondo receives a message from another jondo, it checks whether the received path ID is already stored in the table. If it is, the jondo forwards the message to the next jondo, depending on the second ID of the pair in the table. If the path ID is not in the table, a new destination jondo (or the server) is selected and the message is sent to it. Furthermore, a new pair of path IDs is stored in the table: The existing path ID from where the message has been received and the new path ID to where the message is sent.

> **Protection goal:** Sender anonymity against the recipient and relationship anonymity against all others.
>
> **Attacker model:** No protection against an outside attacker who monitors the entire network (because the jondos simply forward messages, but do not transform them). There is no protection for a jondo whose in- and outgoing links are all observed.
>
> **Security level:** Because this system does not use asymmetric cryptography, it is not based on cryptographic assumptions and, thus, unconditional security can be achieved.
>
> **Trust model:**
> - A central instance called a blender is used in this system and must be trusted.
> - The jondo that receives a message has to forward it to guarantee availability of the network.
> - The other members of one's Crowd should not collaborate.

2.4   Broadcast

Broadcast is a simple technique that already exists to distribute information in communication networks, e.g., for reception of radio and television. All participants of the network receive all information sent and select locally which information is relevant for them, e.g., by choosing a single television or radio channel. This makes it impossible for passive attackers to gain information about the recipient or recipients of particular information.

If a specific participant of a distribution network is addressed by a message, implicit addressing can be used. This means that there is no link between this implicit address and the physical receiver for anyone other than the recipient himself. The address can only be interpreted by the recipient (or more precisely, by his receiver) and so the sender does not get concrete information about the recipient. An implicit address, e.g., a large random number, has to be sent with the corresponding message and every station receiving the message compares it with its own implicit addresses to check whether it is the intended recipient of this message. If the address is visible for everyone, it is called a *visible implicit address*.

To avoid different messages to the same recipient from being linked by others, visible addresses should be changed for each message. The message itself should be encrypted to prevent other receivers of the broadcast from reading it. If the address also is encrypted, this is called *invisible implicit addressing*. But, this encryption forces every station to decrypt all messages to check if it is the recipient.

In a switched network, where each station only receives what the participant requested or another participant sent to him, a multicast can be produced. This kind of partial broadcasting means that not every participant in a network receives a message, only a subset of them. This reduces the bandwidth needed; however, the anonymity set decreases as well.

It is possible to use a satellite broadcasting network for surfing on the Internet [1]. This kind of broadcast can also be used for anonymous file sharing. The broadcast approach allows distribution by sending files via satellite back to the sender. In which case, all participants would have an easy opportunity to receive files.

Protection goal:
- Recipient anonymity by using implicit addresses.
- Recipient unobservability for outsiders if dummy traffic is sent.
- Unlinkability of different messages to the same recipient by changing visible implicit addresses or using invisible implicit addresses.

Security level: If the system does not use asymmetric cryptography (e.g., for implicit addresses), unconditional security can be achieved.

Attacker model: Regarding anonymity and unlinkability, there is protection against observing insiders and outsiders. Regarding unobservability, there is protection against outsiders.

Trust model: If dummy traffic and invisible implicit addressing is used, no trust in any other participant or provider is needed.

2.5 RING-Network

In a RING-Network, the stations are circularly cabled (Figure 2.3a). Therefore, this mechanism is only suitable for local or regional networks.

If a station sends a message, this message is sent in succession at least once to every station in the RING. By using digital signal regeneration in each participating station, each message is—regarding the analogue characteristics—independent of the original sender. Every station regenerates the message so that it looks like the original station initiated it. This method provides anonymity of the sender from attackers who observe or control stations or connections of the RING-Network, as long as this is not directly before *and* directly after the sender. By forwarding the message around the entire RING, the recipient becomes anonymous and unobservable as well. A further precondition to guarantee anonymity of the sender is that the sending permission is appropriately granted.

If two stations of a RING-Network try to observe the station between them without collaborating, they will not observe anything significant because outgoing messages are encrypted and, if implicit addresses are used, they cannot be interpreted. So, an attacker must encircle a single station and compare the incoming and outgoing messages. If the attacker cannot do this, it can only infer that someone in a group of directly connected stations sent a message, but the exact station is not specified.

In order to ensure that messages are received by the intended stations, it is sufficient if the sender gets the message back unmodified after one circulation.

Because of the serial connection of the stations, all connections and stations have to work properly for communication between two stations to be possible. Defective stations have to be removed from the RING-Network.

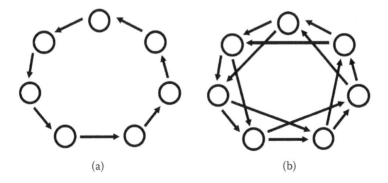

(a) (b)

Figure 2.3   (a) Ring topology, (b) braided ring.

A braided ring is a possible solution to avoid interferences. As presented in Figure 2.3b, two RING-Networks are interdigitated into each other. The first ring connects neighboring stations and the second ring connects the odd ones. This not only doubles the transmission capacity, but also compensates for a malfunction or breakdown in a station or connection. In this case, the braided ring is reconfigured so that the anonymity of the participants remains protected.

In conclusion, a ring topology with digital signal regeneration and a technique for anonymous multiaccess provides sender and recipient anonymity against an attacker who controls some stations.

> **Protection goal:**
> - Sender anonymity.
> - Recipient anonymity by sending messages around the entire ring.
>
> **Security level:** If the encryption used for outgoing messages is based on cryptographic assumptions, only computational security can be achieved. If the encryption is not based on such assumptions, unconditional security can be achieved.
>
> **Attacker model:**
> - Protection against an attacker who controls some stations just as long as the stations before and after the sending user do not collaborate.
>
> **Trust model:** The neighboring stations of a user must not collaborate against him.

2.6 Buses

Beimel and Dolev presented in [2] a mechanism for anonymous communication based on so-called buses. In their approach, each user is modeled as a bus station, while the messages between the users are transferred with the buses. The anonymity of the system is based on the premise that a person who goes by bus in an urban city can hardly be traced by an observer, especially, if the person uses different buses along the way.

If a user wants to send a message to another user, he first has to wait until the bus arrives at his station. Then he puts the message in one of the seats of the bus. Beimel and Dolev introduced three types of the system, each with different advantages and disadvantages.

The first type is based on a ring topology and uses only one single bus. As shown in Figure 2.4, the bus always moves in one direction. Furthermore, the bus has a seat for each pair of senders and recipients. If, for example, station A wants to send a message to station B, it encrypts the message with the public key of B and puts it into the seat AB of the bus. To ensure that an attacker cannot decide whether a station wants to send

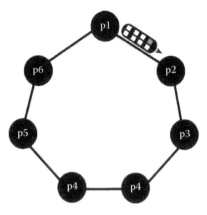

Figure 2.4 Ring network with only one bus present.

a message or not, every station has to send messages to all other stations, i.e., if the station currently has the bus. The attacker cannot decide if there is any "real" communication between the stations. To receive messages, a station has to decrypt and check all messages in its seats because the others could have put a message there.

This has an optimal communication complexity if we only count the number of messages, i.e., buses, because only one bus is necessary. But messages need a lot of time to be transferred from their sender to their recipient since, first, the length of each message grows quadratically with the number of stations, and, second, each message has to be passed around the ring station by station.

A modification of the system uses variable seats instead of fixed seats. In this case, the sender encrypts his message in an onion-like manner with all public keys of the stations, which the bus will pass on the way to the recipient. The message is encrypted first with the public key of the recipient and after that with the public keys of the stations between the sender and recipient in the reverse direction. Now, every station decrypts the incoming message and checks it to see if the content is meaningful or not. If it is meaningful, the station is the recipient of this message and so the message can be deleted or exchanged by dummy traffic. Otherwise, the message is forwarded to the next station. Having no confirmed seats increases the probability of collisions. Therefore, the number of the provided seats for the bus has to be suitably calculated.

The second type introduced by Beimel and Dolev uses two buses (one for each direction) on each connection between two stations. This leads to a good time complexity, but a bad communication complexity. In order to provide a system, with both a good time complexity and a small

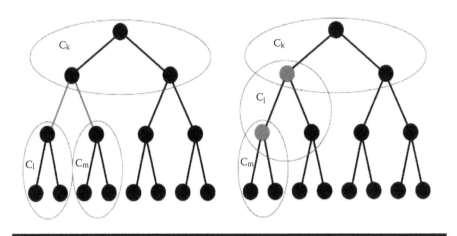

Figure 2.5   Network divided into clusters.

communication complexity, a cluster concept is introduced as the third type. As shown in Figure 2.5, the nodes or stations are integrated in clusters with nearly equal size. Every cluster has its own bus to transfer the messages.

In conclusion, buses enable one to use the technique of the RING-Networks in a higher communication layer for any network topology. On the one hand, the approach allows a flexible configuration between communication complexity and time complexity in contrast to ordinary RING-Networks. But, on the other hand, an implementation as realized in [15] has shown that the system is only usable for relatively small networks and also needs a high amount of dummy traffic to hide meaningful interactions.

> **Protection goal:**
> - Sender anonymity
> - Recipient anonymity
> - Relationship anonymity
>
> **Security level:** Only computational security can be achieved because the asymmetric encryption used for outgoing messages is based on cryptographic assumptions.
>
> **Attacker model:** Two types of attackers were described: an attacker who can read messages on the network and control some of the stations, and attackers who can create, manipulate, or delete messages.
>
> **Trust model:** As shown in [2], the system is not secure against DoS (denial of service) attacks. So, steps must be taken to guaranteed that such attacks do not happen. The other members of a given bus route should not collaborate.

2.7 DC-Network

The term *DC-Network* can stand for *Dining Cryptographers* network—an example used by its inventor, David Chaum, to describe the idea of DC-Networks [6,7]. But it is also possible that DC are for his initials. The technique is designed to provide sender anonymity on a variety of communication network topologies.

In order to explain the idea behind the DC-Network, the following example is presented. Three cryptographers eat at their favorite restaurant. After finishing dinner, the waiter informs the three that the bill has already anonymously been paid. The cryptographers respect this, but want to know whether one of them paid the bill or if it was the National Security Agency. In order to resolve this uncertainty, they use the following method: Every cryptographer flips a coin and shows the outcome to the cryptographer on his right. This means that every result is only known by two of them and each cryptographer knows two results. Each compares the two known results and discloses to the others only whether the results are equal or unequal. If one of the cryptographers is the payer, he would negate his result; that means, if it is unequal, he tells the others that it is equal. When the number of the unequal results is uneven, this indicates that a cryptographer has paid the bill. Otherwise, none of them is the payer.

By translating this principle in a communication network, it is called *superposed sending*. This technique realizes that every station sends its message or a meaningless one at a fixed point in time and the superposition (the sum within an Abelian group) of these messages will be received by all stations.

At first a station generates secret random keys* and communicates each key to exactly one other station in the network. These keys have to be transferred via a channel that guarantees secrecy. In the limiting case, this procedure will be repeated for every station in the network. Then, every station has $n-1$ keys (where n is the number of stations in the network) and keeps them secret.

If a station wants to send a message, it takes all known keys and the message and superposes them. Superposing means that all characters are the message, all keys generated, and the inverse of all keys received are added up. This is called *local superposing*. All stations that do not want to send a message have to send an empty message (i.e., the neutral element of the Abelian group) superposed with all known keys.

Each station sends the result of its local superposition—its output. All the outputs that are sent are now being superposed globally. That means

---

* The characters of the keys as well as the characters of the messages have to be elements of an Abelian group.

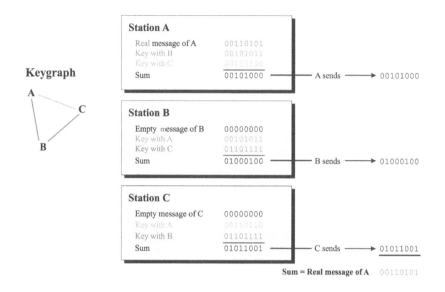

Keygraph

Figure 2.6 Superposing in a DC-Network with three stations.

they are added up.** The resulting sum is distributed to every station in the network. Because each key and its inverse were added exactly once the keys erase each other after the global superposition. Therefore, the result of the global superposition is the sum of all messages sent. If no member station wants to send a message, the sum is the message, which corresponds to the neutral element of the group. If exactly one member station wants to send a message, the sum is equal to its message.

If the binary digits 0 and 1 are chosen as the elements of the Abelian group, then this yields—for important practical purposes—the special case of binary superposed sending, which was specified by Chaum. In this case, one does not need to distinguish between addition and "subtraction" of the exclusive or (XOR), but uses keys operation. In Figure 2.6, the local and global superposing is shown for such a binary coded system.

Each key must only be used once, i.e., keys have to be changed for each round of the DC-Network. Otherwise, the output of a station that sends an empty message would stay identical. The exchange of keys can be reduced by using a generator for generating keys pseudorandomly.

Superposed sending may cause collisions if two or more stations of the network want to send simultaneously. All stations then will receive the sum of the simultaneously sent messages; however, the result will be a meaningless message. Collisions are a common problem in distribution

---

** More precise: The group operation is applied to the local outputs.

channels with multiaccess. It can be solved by access methods that preserve the anonymity of the sender and also preserve the impossibility to link sending events.

Every participant of the system gets to know the global sum and, consequently, the original message. To keep the message content secret (as for every anonymizing technique), an encryption system should be used. Implicit addressing preserves recipient anonymity.

The DC-Network is very susceptible to denial of service attacks. This means that if one station breaks down or has malfunctions, only meaningless messages would be transmitted. So, the concerted rules have to be abided by all. Only if everyone transfers the local sum and everyone gets the global sum, a DC-Network works fine. Additionally, it is a very expensive technique regarding network traffic because, with an increasing number of participants, the number of transferred messages and key characters increases linearly.

Protection goal:
- Sender anonymity.
- Recipient anonymity by using broadcast and implicit addresses.
- Relationship anonymity.
- Sender and recipient unobservability by using dummy traffic

Attacker model: Anonymity and unobservability even against insider attackers, but the system is vulnerable to denial of service attacks, but attackers can be traced and excluded from the DC-Network [21,22].

Trust model: A majority of all participants has to abide by the concerted rules.

2.8 Mixes

The idea of Mixes was described by Chaum in [5]. The method uses public key cryptography and was designed for e-mail systems to provide sender anonymity, recipient anonymity, and relationship anonymity without the need of a central trusted service.

In general, Mixes can be understood as a chain of proxies following one after another. So far, the idea is similar to proxy servers described in Section 2.1. In contrast to regular proxies, Mixes consider an attacker who can eavesdrop on all communications in the network as well as control all Mixes but one. Mixes have a number of mechanisms, which are described in the following sections.

2.8.1 Mix Topologies

The concept of Mixes works with only one single Mix present, but in this case the user has to completely trust this Mix. Therefore, not only one Mix, but typically a chain of Mixes is used. As stated, it is sufficient that one Mix of the chain is trustworthy. There are different methods to organize the cooperation within the network. One possibility is that each Mix exists independently in the network and the participants freely decide which route their messages should take. Thus, each node can communicate to all other nodes in the network. This topology is called *Mix network.*

Another possibility is defining a specific chain of Mixes that has to be used. This chain is called a *Mix cascade.* Besides these two extremes, a number of variations of hybrid systems exist, e.g., sparse expander graphs [10].

As mentioned in [3], there is a controversial discussion on which of the two Mix topologies, Mix networks or Mix cascades, is the better one.

Following is a discussion of some advantages and disadvantages of Mix networks and Mix cascades, according to [3] and [10].

In a Mix network, the user can decide which Mixes he wants to use for the interaction. This approach provides good scalability and flexibility. Furthermore, by users selecting the Mixes randomly, an attacker does not know which Mixes he has to control in order to observe a message. So, the attacker has to control large parts of the network.

In contrast, an attacker of a Mix cascade knows exactly which Mixes he has to control in order to observe the user messages. Furthermore, Mix cascades are vulnerable to denial-of-service attacks because disabling one Mix in the cascade will stop the entire system. It is also mentioned in [10] that cascades provide small anonymity sets in the general case and do not scale well to handle big traffic.

On the other hand, the authors of [3] found out that Mix networks (but not Mix cascades) are vulnerable to powerful attackers, who control all Mixes but one. Also Mix networks are weak against blending attacks. As argued by Dingledine et al. [13], this kind of attack does not depend on network topology, but does on nonsynchronous batching. Another disadvantage of Mix networks is that some Mixes can be used marginally while others are overloaded. In the first case, it is necessary to produce a lot of dummy traffic or to wait a long period of time to increase the anonymity set.

Protection goal:
- Sender anonymity.
- Relationship anonymity.

Attacker model:
- Protection against powerful attackers who can observe the whole network and control many Mixes (big brother).
- Susceptible to denial-of-service attacks and $(n-1)$ attacks.

Trust model: At least one Mix in a path used in a Mix network or in a Mix cascade has to be trusted.

2.8.2   Basic Functionality

As stated above, in this approach the clients do not send their requests directly to the server (or to another destination), but to a so-called Mix. In order to hide which participants communicate with which, the Mix does not send the incoming messages to the destination server instantly. Instead, the Mix stores several messages from different clients for a defined time, transforms the messages (thus, the name Mix), and then forwards them to the destination server or to another Mix, simultaneously. Therefore, even a global eavesdropper, who can observe all incoming and outgoing messages of the Mix, cannot decide which incoming message belongs to which outgoing message.

There are a number of building blocks (Figure 2.7) that ensure the security of the Mix. In almost every approach that deals with Mixes, the basic ideas are used. Only specific implementations vary from system to system.

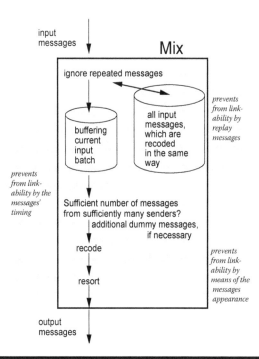

Figure 2.7   Building blocks of a Mix.

2.8.3 Preprocessing: Transforming the Message

The overall goal of transforming (recoding) the message hop by hop is to hinder an attacker from tracking a message simply by comparing the bit patterns of incoming and outgoing messages.

In order to send a message, the client has to prepare a message. First, it has to decide which way the message will take through the network. That means it has to specify to which Mix the message will be forwarded before it is sent to the destination server. In order to improve the security of the system, it is appropriated to use not only one Mix, but several. In this case, it is also important to configure in which order the message will be forwarded. As a next step, the client uses the provided public keys of the Mixes to encrypt its message. In this context, attention must be paid to the order of the encryptions. This depends on the order in which the Mixes will get the message. The whole process is like putting a letter in an envelope, addressing this envelope, and then putting it again in an envelope, and so on. So, when the first Mix gets the thus prepared message, the Mix will open (or better decrypt) the message and will find an address inside to where the decrypted message has to be send next. This process is shown in Figure 2.8.

The encryption scheme explained above can be more precisely described as follows:

$A_1, \ldots, A_n$ may be the sequence of the *a*ddresses and $c_1, \ldots, c_n$ the sequence of the *c*ipher keys that are publicly known as the Mix sequence $Mix_1, \ldots, Mix_n$ that was chosen by the sender, whereby c_1 also can be a secret key to a symmetric encryption system. A_{n+1} may be the address of the recipient who is called Mix_{n+1} for simplification, and c_{n+1} is its cipher key. $z_1, \ldots, z_n$ may be a sequence of random bit strings. If c_1 is a secret key of a symmetric system of secrecy, then z_1 can be an empty bit string. If c_1 is a cipher key of an asymmetric encryption system that encodes indeterministically, then z_1 can be an empty bit string as well. The sender creates messages N_i that will be received by Mix_i, on the basis of the

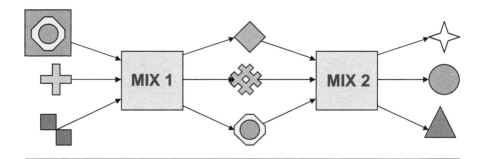

Figure 2.8   Mix cascade with two Mixes.

message N, which the recipient (Mix_{n+1}) is supposed to receive:

$$N_{n+1} = c_{n+1}(N)$$

$$N_i = c_i(z_i, A_{i+1}, N_{i+1}) \quad (\text{for } i = n, \ldots, 1)$$

The sender sends N_1 to Mix_1. After the decoding, each Mix receives the address of the next Mix and the message that is dedicated for the next Mix.

Note: The additional encoding of random bit strings is necessary for the application of asymmetric encryption systems that are deterministic because an attacker would be able to guess and test (by encrypting them) not only short standard messages with the publicly known cipher key, but also the entire output of the Mix (completely without guessing).

To ensure that an attacker cannot trace a message through a Mix, it is necessary that input–output pairs of messages have no identifying characteristic—one could be their size. One solution is to define a fixed size for all messages, which means short messages have to be filled up with meaningless information and long messages have to be split into pieces.

2.8.3.1 Reordering: Batch, Pool Mixing

When a Mix operates in batch mode, it collects a fixed number n of messages, and encrypts and reorders them before all stored messages are forwarded at once. In contrast to that, a Mix that operates in pool mode has always n messages stored in its buffer called pool. If a new message arrives, one of the stored messages is randomly picked and forwarded (see also [16]). The number n is the batch respective pool size.

2.8.3.2 Test-for-Replay

An often discussed type of attack is the replay attack. An attacker could copy a message he has eavesdropped on beforehand and send copies to the Mix. These messages would take the same way through the network as the original message because the decryption and the sending algorithms both work deterministically. By observing the network, a characteristic pattern of the copied message can be found. These patterns could easily be traced. In order to prevent such an attack, copies of messages have to be identified and filtered out.

One possibility to identify such invalid messages is by using time stamps. When the Mix gets a message, it also receives a tag that tells the Mix in which timeframe the message is valid. If the message arrives too late at the Mix, the forwarding will be denied. Another possibility is that the Mixes store a copy of every message they have already sent. Hence, new messages can be compared to this database. For performance and security reasons, it is best to restrict the volume of the database to a minimum. Messages should be stored only a short period of time before they are deleted.

2.8.3.3 Dummy Traffic

The information that specific participants send or receive messages can already be seen as a threat to anonymity. But, convincing an eavesdropper that no messages were sent on the network is not possible. Instead of this, it is possible to send messages on the network even when no information is being transferred. This has the same effect as sending no messages because an eavesdropper cannot decide if a meaningful message is sent or if the message contains only meaningless data.

The sending of such meaningless data on the network is called *dummy traffic*. According to the idea of Mixes, this means that a Mix could randomly forward dummy traffic to another Mix on the network. This mechanism also has a benefit for Mixes working in batch mode: Normally these Mixes have to wait until a certain number of messages have arrived at the Mix before all stored messages can be forwarded at once. This strategy can tend to create long delays when not enough messages were sent to the Mix. With the help of dummy traffic, it is possible to solve this problem. The Mix simply creates dummy messages to fill up the buffer.

2.8.3.4 Recipient Anonymity: Untraceable Return Addresses

So far, only the principle of anonymous sending of messages was described. To allow the recipient to also stay anonymous, a so-called untraceable return address can be used. This return address is a special message that has to be created by the recipient and used by the sender to send his message to the anonymous recipient.

The basic idea of untraceable return addresses is that not the sender but the recipient defines which Mixes in which order have to be used to deliver a certain message to him. The return address prepared by the recipient contains for each Mix on the path a symmetric key that the Mix will use to *encrypt* the message sent by the sender. Finally, the recipient will receive a message that is encrypted multiple times with symmetric keys as specified by the recipient. Because the recipient knows all of these symmetric keys (and the order of their application), he can decrypt the message. As the symmetric keys are unknown to the sender and the coding of the message changes from Mix to Mix (due to the encryption), the sender cannot trace his message to the recipient.

The scheme explained above can more precisely be described as follows:

$A_1, \ldots, A_m$ may be the sequence of the addresses and $c_1, \ldots, c_m$ may be the sequence of the publicly known cipher keys of the Mix sequence

$\text{Mix}_1, \ldots, \text{Mix}_m$, which was chosen by the recipient, whereby c_m can be a secret key of a symmetric encryption system as well. The message that is appended to the return address will pass these Mixes in ascending order depending on their indices. A_{m+1} may be the address of the recipient, who is called Mix_{m+1} for simplification. Likewise, for simplification, the sender will be called Mix_0. The recipient creates an untraceable return address (k_0, A_1, R_1) whereby k_0 is a key of a symmetric encryption system generated just for this purpose (an asymmetric encryption system would be possible, too, but more costly). Mix_0 is supposed to use this key k_0 to encode the content of the message in order to guarantee that Mix_1 is unable to read this message. R_1 is part of the return address, which is transmitted by Mix_0 containing the message content that was generated and encoded (by using key k_0). R_1 is created by starting with a randomly chosen unique name e of the return address in a recursive scheme described in the following:

■ R_j designates the part of the return address that will be received by Mix_j.
■ k_j designates the key of a symmetric encryption system (an asymmetric encryption system would be possible, too, but more costly) with which Mix_j encodes the part of the message that contains the message content.

$$R_{m+1} = e$$

$$R_j = c_j(k_j, A_{j+1}, R_{j+1}) \quad \text{for } j = m, \ldots, 1.$$

These return address parts R_j and the (already several times encoded, if necessary) message content I generated by the sender, called *message content part* I_j, are constituting the messages N_j. These messages N_j are created by Mix_{j-1} and sent to Mix_j according to the following recursive scheme. They are created and sent by the sender Mix_0 and then, in sequence, are passed through Mixes $\text{Mix}_1, \ldots, \text{Mix}_m$:

$$N_1 = R_1, I_1; \quad I_1 = k_0(I)$$

$$N_j = R_j, I_j; \quad I_j = k_{j-1}(I_{j-1}) \quad \text{for } j = 2, \ldots, m+1$$

Thus, the recipient Mix_{m+1} receives e, $N_{m+1} = e$, $k_m(\ldots k_1(k_0(I))\ldots)$ and is able to decrypt without any problems and to extract the message content I because he knows all secret keys k_j (in case of an asymmetric encryption system, all decryption keys) assigned to the unique name e of the return address part in the right order.

Note: The encryption of random bit strings if using deterministic encryption systems is not necessary because the encoded parts of messages R_j, which were encoded with publicly known cipher keys of the Mix, contain information the attacker does not get to know. According to the change of encoding by keys that are unknown to the attacker, he has no possibility to test.

2.8.3.5 Checking the Size of the Anonymity Set

If an attacker blocks the message of a specific participant, this message is isolated from the anonymity set. The same would happen if a message from a specific participant is surrounded by manipulated or generated messages from the attacker. This type of attack is known as an $(n - 1)$ attack. No general solution exists to prevent this type of attack in open environments, i.e., in environments where participants may join and leave in an uncoordinated fashion. One basic protection is to provide a mechanism that enables the Mix to identify each participant. Thus, a trustworthy Mix can check if the buffered messages were sent by a sufficient number of different users.

2.8.3.6 Mix Channels

Mix channels are used to handle a continuous stream of data in real-time or with only a small delay through a chain of Mixes.

A partitioning of the available bandwith is needed: a signaling part for establishing a channel and a data part for the actual transmission of messages. In the following we assume a static partition in a signaling channel and several data channels.

In order to establish the channel, a channel-establishing message is sent over the signaling channel, which sends the key k_i that should be used between the sender and Mix_i asymmetrically encrypted with Mix_i's public key. Therewith a channel, over which the actual message could be transmitted, now is defined by all Mixes, by mixing the channel-establishing message. A channel can be used as sending channel or as receiving channel.

A sending channel is the precise analogue of hybrid encryption: the sender establishes the channel, encodes continuously his information N as message $k_1(k_2(\ldots k_m(N)\ldots))$ and transfers it to Mix_1. Each Mix Mix_i $(i = 1, \ldots, n - 1)$ decodes the messages received continuously using k_i and transfers the result to Mix_{i+1}. Mix_m creates the plain text message N at the end. This allows the sender to send messages anonymously while the recipient is not anonymous.

A receiving channel is a sending channel that is used "backward": The recipient establishes the channel. The sender sends to Mix_m the information stream N which is not encoded specifically (but of course end-to-end encoded) for the Mix_m, encodes it using the key k_m and leads $k_m(N)$ "back" to M_{m-1}. The other Mixes, s do the same, i.e., Mix_1 puts out the encoded stream $k_1(\ldots k_m(N)\ldots)$. Since the receiver knows all keys k_i he is able to decrypt N. This allows the recipient to receive messages anonymously while the sender is not anonymous.

To reach both sender and recipient anonymity Pfitzmann et al. [19] suggested creating Mix channels as links of sending and receiving channels. The sender establishes a sending channel that ends at a Mix Mix_m and the recipient establishes a receiving channel that starts at Mix_m. Mix_m diverts the information stream that arrives at the sending channel to the receiving channel. The channels that are supposed to be linked are specified by a common channel flag that is received consistently in both channel establishing messages by Mix_m.

The data transfer is coordinated with an asymmetrically encrypted Mix-input-message that contains information about the Mix_m connecting the two channels, and whether the user sending the Mix-input-message acts as a sender or a recipient. Every Mix in the chain can decrypt this Mix-input-message and at the end the plain text is broadcasted to all subscribers. Now the channels can be established using establishment-messages of both participants. They choose the Mixes for the data transfer channel to the Mix_m and keep them private. So everyone only knows half of the way and Mix_m relays the incoming data of the Mix-sending-channel to the Mix-receiving-channel. The two halves of the Mix-channel are necessary to reach anonymity of the two participants against each other.

Every sender/recipient must have the same number of sending/receiving channels otherwise they are observable. So the usage of dummy channels is appropriate.

2.8.4   Existing Systems

In this section, several existing Mix systems are presented that are or have been available for practical use. They are listed under low latency and high latency systems.

2.8.4.1   High Latency

Mixminion: Mixminion is based on the specification of the Type-III Remailer protocol. As described in [11], it enables users to send and receive e-mails anonymously and thereby take part anonymously in news groups. This same anonymity set is shared to forward and reply messages. This also means that a remailer cannot distinguish between these two types. A message that is transferred is conformed to a fixed size by cutting it into pieces or padding it with dummy data. Mixminion is for asynchronous e-mail conversation, so it requires little synchronization and coordination between the nodes. Each packet is sent through a network of Mixminion servers where users can choose a route.

Mixmaster: Mixmaster was designed for the purpose of anonymous e-mail conversation. Its functionality is based on the Type-II Remailer as described in [17]. By sending an e-mail, packets of fixed size are created and each packet can be sent through the Mix network via another route. But, the last Mix, which will send the message to the recipient, has to be identical for all packets of an e-mail message. Only this Mix can reassemble the e-mail. A mixmaster server collects messages in a pool and forwards them in random order. If the traffic data is insufficient, the mixmaster creates dummy messages automatically. The mixmaster system provides anonymity for sending or receiving e-mails and communication relationships.

2.8.4.2 Low Latency

AN.ON project: AN.ON* provides a system that uses the topology of Mix cascades. The user installs on his computer a client software called JAP. After that, he can choose between different fixed routes of Mixes for anonymous Internet surfing. All packets that are transferred through a Mix cascade have the same size and are sent in a batch from Mix to Mix. In order to secure from traffic analysis dummy traffic also is used. This provides sender anonymity to users regarding their Web surfing.

Tor: Tor [12] is a circuit-based anonymous communication service that uses onion routing. It provides support of anonymity for services based on the Transmission Control Protocol (TCP) like Web browsing, instant messaging, e-mail, and peer-to-peer. The Tor network consists of several hundred nodes called Tor servers. A client chooses a random route of nodes through the network and builds a circuit. Each node in the circuit only knows its predecessor and its successor. The data through this circuit can leave the circuit at the end or in midstream so that the observation of the circuit's end is unprofitable. The traffic is divided into fixed size cells. Filter mechanisms for privacy enhancement are not provided by Tor. Therefore, proxies like Privoxy are recommended. The goal of Tor is to maximize anonymity and reduce the latency to an acceptable level.

Tarzan: Tarzan [14] is an anonymous peer-to-peer network based on the IP protocol. By providing a kind of IP tunnel, it is independent of a concrete application. It is decentralized and uses an open-ended, Internet-wide pool of nodes. Each peer in the network can act as a Mix. A message initiator selects a route of peers pseudorandomly through a restricted topology. At the end of the Mix chain is the network address translator who changes the origin of the

---

* http://anon.inf.tu-dresden.de/

packets and communicates directly with the recipient. Therefore, a bridge between the sender and the recipient is created. The sender of a message can be concealed because each participant could have generated a message or merely relayed traffic for others. Tarzan also makes use of dummy traffic to protect the data against traffic analysis. It protects against network edges analysis as well because a relay does not know whether it is the first of a Mix path. Because of the large number of possible peers, the significance of targeted attacks is reduced. Tarzan provides anonymity against malicious nodes and global eavesdroppers.

2.9   Private Information Retrieval

Private information retrieval (PIR) allows users to retrieve an item from another party (e.g., by querying a database or a news server) without revealing which item he is interested in (privacy for the item of interest) the IP address, which users normally leave behind while downloading messages from a service provider. In order to achieve this, interest of users can be observed; it is theoretically feasible that every user downloads any news on a news server and makes a local news selection. But, this may overstrain the news server and it would increase the amount of data that has to be transferred. In order to reduce the bandwidth needed private information retrieval was developed as an alternative. The idea behind this is [9] some kind of superposing of information such as that explained in the section on DC-Networks.

For this technique, several servers with identical databases (composed of n records) are queried. To each database an n-bit vector is sent. Each bit in the vector represents one record of the database. If the bit is 1 then the record is selected otherwise not. All selected records are superposed, e.g., the XOR operation is applied to them (as explained in Section 2.7 describing the DC-network). The result is sent back to the user. The superposition of all results from the databases gives the requested information. Note that the communication between the user and the database servers is encrypted.

In order to achieve this, the user has to create the query vectors according to the following scheme: All but one vector are generated randomly. The remaining vector is calculated as the superposition of the random vectors. Additionally the bit representing the record of interest needs to be filpped.

However, it must be pointed out that this is only possible with many servers that receive and store each message in the intended order and that adding new messages must take place simultaneously. So, updating news is complex and difficult. By using this approach, an attacker and even a news server would be unable to determine which position in memory is being read and, consequently, cannot spy on the information the user is interested in. If only one of the servers does not cooperate with an attacker, it will not be possible to determine the information a user is interested in.

> **Protection goal:** Unlinkability between a user and the item of interest.
>
> **Attacker model:**
> - Protection against the provider of news services.
> - Protection against passive attacks.
>
> **Security level:** Depending on the cryptography used for encryption of the messages sent between the user and the database servers, unconditional security can be achieved.
>
> **Trust model:** A collaboration of all news servers has to be excluded.

2.10 General Principles among the Systems

Based on the presented systems, some basic functionalities can be recognized that are reused in different approaches. In order to provide communication privacy, the following mechanisms are used:

> **Sender Anonymity**
> - Requests are not sent directly from sender to recipient, they are first transferred to other nodes of the system before they are sent to the recipient.
>
> **Recipient Anonymity**
> - A large number or even all participants of the system get the messages that are sent.
> - The recipient is not addressed explicitly. Each participant decides locally whether the received message is intended for him.
>
> **Hiding the Communication between Sender and Recipient**
> - By sending dummy traffic, meaningful communication messages can be concealed.
> - The creation of an anonymity set can hide the activities of a single user within the activities of many other users.

In conclusion, anonymity can be improved by combining the presented mechanisms and systems. But, one has to be careful to make a good trade-off between attacker/trust model, anonymity, and efficiency. The number of anonymizing services used in a chain (e.g., Mixes) should be chosen carefully because each service incurs transfer and computing time. The same holds for the number of users in the anonymity set using the same anonymizing service because usually each user either causes some additional delay or requires some additional computing power and/or transmission capacity.

References

[1] Andre Adelsbach and Ulrich Greveler. Satellite communication without privacy—attacker's paradise. In Hannes Federrath, Ed., *Sicherheit 2005 LNI Proceedings P-62*, LNI, German Informatics Society, Bonn, pp. 257–268. 2005.

[2] Amos Beimel and Shlomi Dolev. Buses for anonymous message delivery. *Journal of Cryptology*, 16(1): 25–39, 2003.

[3] Oliver Berthold, Andreas Pfitzmann, and Ronny Standtke. The disadvantages of free MIX routes and how to overcome them. In Hannes Federrath, Ed., *Designing Privacy Enhancing Technologies (PET'00)*, LNCS 2009, pp. 30–45. Springer-Verlag, Heidelberg, Germany, 2001.

[4] Philippe Boucher, Adam Shostack, and Ian Goldberg. Freedom systems 2.0 architecture. White paper, Zero Knowledge Systems, Inc., Montreal, Canada, December 2000.

[5] David Chaum. Untraceable electronic mail, return addresses, and digital pseudonyms. *Communications of the ACM*, 4(2), February 1981.

[6] David Chaum. Security without identification: Transaction systems to make big brother obsolete. *Communication of the ACM*, 28(10): 1030–1044, 1985.

[7] David Chaum. The dining cryptographers problem: Unconditional sender and recipient untraceability. *Journal of Cryptology*, 1: 65–75, 1988.

[8] Sebastian Clauß and Marit Köhntopp. Identity management and its support of multilateral security. *Computer Networks 37* (2001), special issue on Electronic Business Systems, Elsevier, North-Holland, 2001, 205–219.

[9] David A. Cooper and Kenneth P. Birman. Preserving privacy in a network of mobile computers. In *IEEE Symposium on Research in Security and Privacy*. IEEE Computer Society Press, Los Alamitos, CA, 1995.

[10] George Danezis. Mix-networks with restricted routes. In Roger Dingledine, Ed., *Proceedings of Privacy Enhancing Technologies Workshop (PET 2003)*. Springer-Verlag, Heidelberg, Germany, LNCS 2760, March 2003.

[11] George Danezis, Roger Dingledine, and Nick Mathewson. Mixminion: Design of a Type III anonymous remailer protocol. In *Proceedings of the 2003 IEEE Symposium on Security and Privacy*, IEEE Computer Society, Washington, D.C., May 2003.

[12] Roger Dingledine, Nick Mathewson, and Paul Syverson. Tor: The second-generation onion router. In *Proceedings of the 13th USENIX Security Symposium*, August 2004.

[13] Roger Dingledine, Vitaly Shmatikov, and Paul Syverson. Synchronous batching: From cascades to free routes. In *Proceedings of Privacy Enhancing Technologies Workshop (PET 2004)*, vol. 3424 of *LNCS*, May 2004.

[14] Michael J. Freedman and Robert Morris. Tarzan: A peer-to-peer anonymizing network layer. In *Proceedings of the 9th ACM Conference on Computer and Communications Security (CCS 2002)*, Washington, D.C., November 2002.

[15] Andreas Hirt, Michael J. Jacobson, Jr., and Carey Williamson. A practical buses protocol for anonymous internet communication. In *Proceedings of the Third Annual Conference on Privacy, Security and Trust*, October 12–14, 2005, St. Andrews, New Brunswick, Canada.

[16] Dogan Kesdogan, Jan Egner, and Roland Büschkes. Stop-and-go MIXes: Providing probabilistic anonymity in an open system. In *Proceedings of Information Hiding Workshop (IH 1998)*. Springer-Verlag, Heidelberg, Germany, LNCS 1525, 1998.

[17] Ulf Möller, Lance Cottrell, Peter Palfrader, and Len Sassaman. Mixmaster Protocol–Version 2. December 29, 2004. http://www.letf.org/internet.draft.sassa.man-mixmaster-03.txt.

[18] Andreas Pfitzmann and Marit Hansen. Anonymity, unobserveability, pseudonymity and identity management: A proposal for terminology. Available from http://dud.inf.tu-dresden.de/Anon_Terminology.shtml (current version 0.28–29 May, 2006; version 0.01 published in *Designing Privacy Enhancing Technologies (PET'00)*, LNCS 2009, Springer-Verlag, Heidelberg, Germany, 2001).

[19] Andreas Pfitzmann, Birgit Pfitzmann, and Michael Waidner. ISDN-mixes: Untraceable communication with very small bandwidth overhead. In *Proceedings of the GI/ITG Conference on Communication in Distributed Systems*, pp. 451–463, February 1991.

[20] Michael Reiter and Aviel Rubin. Crowds: Anonymity for Web transactions. *ACM Transactions on Information and System Security*, 1(1), June 1998.

[21] Michael Waidner and Birgit Pfitzmann. Unconditional sender and recipient untraceability in spite of active attacks—some remarks. Fakultt fr Informatik, Universitt Karlsruhe, Karlsruhe, Germany, Interner Bericht 5/89, March 1989.

[22] Michael Waidner and Birgit Pfitzmann. The dining cryptographers in the disco: Unconditional sender and recipient untraceability with computationally secure serviceability. In *Proceedings of EUROCRYPT 1989*. Springer-Verlag, Heidelberg, Germany, LNCS 434, 1990.

Chapter 3

Privacy-Preserving Cryptographic Protocols

Mikhail J. Atallah and Keith B. Frikken

Contents

3.1 Definition of Privacy-Preserving Cryptographic Protocols...........48
3.2 Applying Privacy-Preserving Cryptographic Protocols
to Real Problems 50
   3.2.1 Database Querying 50
   3.2.2 Distributed Voting 51
   3.2.3 Bidding and Auctions 51
   3.2.4 Data Mining..52
   3.2.5 Collaborative Benchmarking and Forecasting...............52
   3.2.6 Contract Negotiations 53
   3.2.7 Rational and Selfish Participants 54
3.3 Overview of General Results 55
   3.3.1 Two-Party Honest-But-Curious Scrambled
       Circuit Evaluation...55
   3.3.2 Extending Scrambled Circuit Evaluation.....................56
3.4 General Techniques for Privacy-Preserving Protocols 57
   3.4.1 Splitting Techniques..57
       3.4.1.1 Additive Splitting....................................57
       3.4.1.2 Encoding-Based Splitting 58
   3.4.2 Homomorphic Encryption and Computing
       with Encrypted Values.......................................58
   3.4.3 Input Quality Problems 59

3.5 Specific Applications 60
    3.5.1 Scalar Product 60
    3.5.2 Nearest Neighbor 60
    3.5.3 Trust Negotiation/Attribute-Based Access Control 62
    3.5.4 Computational Outsourcing....................................64
3.6 Summary 65
Acknowledgment 65
References..65

3.1 Definition of Privacy-Preserving Cryptographic Protocols

Online collaboration in its general form is the computation of some function over inputs that are distributed among different participants (i.e., organizations, individuals, etc.). As an example, consider an online auction: The inputs are the bidder's bid values and the outcome is the winner of the auction along with the required payment. A simple way to achieve such collaborations is to collect all of the inputs at a single location and to compute the desired outcome. However, this poses many confidentiality and privacy concerns, including (1) the shared information may be used against a participant at a later time; (2) sharing information makes security vulnerabilities greater because break-ins, spyware, and insider threats at one of the collaborator's sites will now reveal other collaborators' information; and (3) it may be illegal to share some of the participant's inputs (e.g., medical records cannot be shared under HIPAA legislation).

These privacy concerns lead to one of the following outcomes: (1) the collaboration does not occur and, thus, the potential benefit of such a collaboration goes unrealized, (2) the collaboration occurs and the participants have to absorb the cost of the privacy loss, or (3) the collaboration occurs and participants lie about their inputs. Note that in many cases the main privacy concern is not the outcome of the collaboration, but rather the revelation of the participants' inputs. In this chapter, we discuss secure protocols for such collaborations, that is, cryptographic protocols that allow the collaboration outcome to be computed, while revealing as little information as possible about the participants' inputs. With such protocols it is possible to obtain the benefit of the collaboration, while minimizing the cost of the privacy loss.

Computing functions without revealing the inputs is trivial if there is a party, which we call Trent, that every participant fully trusts with their information. The participants send their values to Trent and, after he has received all of the inputs, he computes the desired function. He then sends the results to the participants. Assuming that Trent is fully trusted, this does not reveal anything other than the result of the collaboration; of course, a participant may try to learn information about other inputs by trying to invert the function, but this is unavoidable. While this third party solution does not leak information other than the computed answer, the main problem with such an approach is the difficulty of finding a fully trusted party who is acceptable to every participant. Furthermore, even if such a party could be found, this party would be a lucrative target for outside attacks, and may become a performance and reliability bottleneck (a single point of failure).

While the above Trent-based approach for private collaboration is not possible in most environments, the level of security provided by the approach should be a goal for protocols that do not rely on a trusted third party. That is, a protocol is called privacy-preserving if it reveals only the result of the collaboration and what can be deduced from this result when given a group of participant's inputs. For example, suppose we wanted to compute the intersection of two sets, where each set was the input of a different party. According to the above definition of a privacy-preserving protocol, the revelation that "Alice" is the first (in terms of alphabetical order) item in the intersection would be acceptable because this information can be computed from the intersection of the two sets. However, the revelation of items that are in the first set but not the second set is unacceptable.

The goal of Secure Multiparty Computation (SMC) and Secure Function Evaluation (SFE) is to provide a privacy-preserving protocol for any possible function. This may seem like an impossible task; however, there are general results that state that any function that is computable in polynomial time can be computed securely with polynomial communication and computation under various adversary models. The earliest work in this regard was Yao [45,46], and it was shown that any function can be computed securely in the honest-but-curious adversary model for two participants. In the honest-but-curious model, an adversary will follow the prescribed protocol exactly, but after the protocol has finished, the adversary will try to learn additional information by using its local transcript of the protocol's execution. Clearly, this adversary model is contrived, but it is an important first step toward more realistic adversary models. In Goldreich et al. [23], this result was extended to multiple parties and to a malicious adversary model where the participants deviate arbitrarily from the prescribed protocol to gain advantage. More specifically, it was shown that as long as a strict majority of the participants are honest, then any function that is computable in polynomial time can be computed securely with polynomial communication and computation. There have been many other results in SMC that have given similar results for more complex adversary models and have made such protocols more efficient, but the general results are believed to be unusable for many interesting problems because of efficiency reasons. Thus, it has been suggested that domain-specific protocols be developed for important problem domains that are more efficient than the protocol obtained by using the generic results [24].

The remainder of this chapter is organized as follows: In section 3.2, we discuss the usefulness of SMC for various application domains. In section 3.3, we give a brief summary of the general results in SMC. In section 3.4, we outline many techniques that are used when creating domain-specific, privacy-preserving protocols, and in section 3.5, we give several specific applications of these techniques. Finally, we summarize the chapter in section 3.6.

3.2   Applying Privacy-Preserving Cryptographic Protocols to Real Problems

We begin with a brief (and nonexhaustive) sampling of typical application areas. The literature in some of these is quite voluminous and we, therefore, refrain from doing a literature survey of each—we merely give a brief description of each application area. For convenience, we shall use the term *privacy* both for individuals and for other entities (such as government and corporate entities), even though the term *confidentiality* is more suitable for the latter. Finally, to avoid duplication, in this section we do not go over the applications that are covered in section 3.5.

3.2.1   Database Querying

A query is often too revealing or subject to misinterpretation. For example, someone inquiring about a specific disease may leave the impression of either having it, being prone to it, or engaging in behavior that makes it possible (possibly with adverse consequences on the insurability or even the employability of the individual). This superficial inference from the query can, of course, be dramatically wrong (e.g., the person may be helping his child write a school paper on the disease), but it remains a possibility from which an individual may want to protect himself. A corporate entity considering making an acquisition (purchase of land, takeover of another firm, etc.) has more tangible reasons for wanting to cover its tracks—the mere suspicion of its interest can move the target's price (and, possibly, its own quoted stock price). The ability to query a database without revealing one's query would be quite valuable. The literature related to this topic is often abbreviated as PIR (private information retrieval).

As an illustration of the kinds of problems considered in this area, following is a formal definition of a rather simple version of the problem. The client has a string q, and the server has a database of strings $T = \{t_1, \ldots, t_N\}$; the client wants to know whether there exists a string t_i in the server's database that matches q. The match could be an exact match or an approximate (closest) match. The privacy requirement is that the server cannot know the client's secret query q or the response to that query, and the client cannot know the server's database contents, except for what could be derived from the query result.

An important version of this problem is in the framework of location-dependent query processing where the answer to the query depends on the position of the client; yet the client desires to hide its location from the server that will process the query. This is important because, while pervasive computing and communication have many benefits, one of their more chilling side effects is the extent to which they enable invasive and detailed tracking of individuals. The goal of a privacy-preserving protocol between the client and database is for the client to learn the answer to its location-dependent query without revealing to the remote database anything about its location. This framework may allow the database to know the answer to the query, if what it can infer from that answer is acceptably vague (e.g., revealing the location of the nearest gas station is much less intrusive than revealing the client's exact position).

3.2.2 Distributed Voting

Many protocols have been proposed for distributed voting in a manner that preserves voter privacy and prevents cheating. These protocols come in two broad classes: protocols that make use of a central tabulating facility, and protocols that involve only the n voters and no one else. The latter do not scale to large numbers of voters (not surprisingly). The preservation of privacy and prevention of cheating are the major challenges of these protocols (especially combined with the usual requirements of efficiency). Here the meaning of cheating is broad and includes the obvious notions of double voting, preventing others from voting, destroying their vote after they have voted, etc. But there are other less obvious notions of what constitutes cheating, so these protocols have other requirements, such as preventing voters from selling their vote (i.e., the technology should not enable voters to prove that they voted for a certain candidate).

3.2.3 Bidding and Auctions

The privacy requirements depend on the type of auction. In the sealed bid, first-price auction, all bidders simultaneously and independently submit their bids, and the highest bidder wins and pays the price it submitted. In this case, there is no need to reveal bids other than the highest bid, and that would be the goal of the protocol. Of course, the protocol must keep the participants honest (e.g., prevent them from trying to do ex-post facto modification of their bids).

In the Vickrey auction, all bidders also simultaneously and independently submit their bids, and the highest bidder wins, but now pays the *second highest* price submitted (not the price it submitted). In that case, there is no need to reveal bid values other than the second highest bid.

3.2.4   Data Mining

Data mining is an important technology that is used for identifying patterns and trends from massive amounts of data. Traditional data mining has used a data warehousing model in which the data is collected in one site and is subsequently analyzed using various algorithms. However, the privacy of many important kinds of records (e.g., health and financial records for individuals, proprietary data for corporations) can prevent the use of this centralized approach. Privacy-preserving data-mining addresses this issue along two main lines. One approach consists of sanitizing the data before making it available for centralized data mining—altering the data in such a manner that its release no longer compromises privacy, while preserving its usefulness for data-mining purposes. Another approach consists of using the technologies surveyed in this chapter, by assuming that the data is distributed among multiple entities who cooperatively mine it so that only the result is revealed (and not the data at each participant's site). The second approach was introduced to the data-mining community relatively recently, through the Lindell–Pinkas method [33] that makes it possible for two parties to build a decision tree without either party learning anything about the other party's data (other than what can be inferred from the resulting decision tree). The area has grown rapidly since then, with papers on techniques for association rules, clustering, classification, and many others.

In such a distributed data-mining framework, the partitioning of the data among the different sites can be either horizontal or vertical. In horizontal partitioning, each party has a subset of the rows, i.e., some of the records (but each in its entirety). In vertical partitioning, each party has a subset of the columns (hence, no party has an entire record). See [41] for a more extensive survey and bibliographic references.

3.2.5   Collaborative Benchmarking and Forecasting

Suppose several hospitals in a geographic area want to learn how their own heart surgery unit is performing compared with the others in terms of mortality rates, subsequent complications, or any other quality metric. Similarly, several small businesses might want to use their recent point-of-sales data to cooperatively forecast future demand and, thus, make more informed decisions about inventory, capacity, employment, etc. These are simple examples of cooperative benchmarking and (respectively) forecasting that would benefit all participants as well as the public at large. This is because they would make it possible for participants to avail themselves of more precise and reliable data collected from many sources, to assess their own local performance in comparison to global trends, and to avoid many of the inefficiencies that currently arise because of having less information available for their decision making. And yet, in spite of all these advantages, cooperative benchmarking and forecasting typically do not take place because of the participants' unwillingness to share their information with others. Their reluctance to share is quite rational and is due to fears of embarrassment, lawsuits, weakening their negotiating position (e.g., in case of overcapacity), revealing corporate performance and strategies, etc. The recent developments in private benchmarking and forecasting technologies hold the promise of allowing such collaborations to take place without revealing any participants' data to the others, thus, reaping the benefits of collaboration while avoiding the drawbacks. Moreover, this can empower organizations that could then cooperatively base decisions on a much broader information base.

3.2.6 Contract Negotiations

Suppose two entities (Alice and Bob) are negotiating a joint contract, which consists of a sequence of clauses (i.e., terms and conditions). Alice and Bob are negotiating the specific value for each clause. Example clauses include:

- How will Alice and Bob distribute the revenue received for jointly performing a task?
- Given a set of tasks, where Alice and Bob each have a set of tasks they are willing and able to perform, who performs which tasks?
- Given a set of locations to perform certain tasks, in which locations does Alice (and Bob) perform their tasks?

Alice and Bob will each have private constraints on the acceptability of each clause (i.e., rules for when a specific term is acceptable). A specific clause is an agreement between Alice and Bob that satisfies both of their constraints. In a nonprivate setting, Alice and Bob can simply reveal their constraints to one another. However, this has two significant drawbacks. (1) If there are multiple possible agreements, how do Alice and Bob choose a specific agreement (some are more desirable to Alice, others more desirable to Bob)? (2) The revelation of one's constraints and preferences is unacceptable in many cases (e.g., one's counterpart in the negotiation can use these to infer information about one's strategies or business processes or even use them to gain an information advantage for use in a future negotiation). This second problem is exacerbated when Alice and Bob are competitors in one business sector, but cooperate in another sector. The goal of a

privacy-preserving protocol for this problem is to facilitate contract negotiation without revealing either party's private constraints. There are two
components to such a negotiation: (1) the ability to determine whether
there is a contract that satisfies both parties' constraints (without revealing anything other than yes/no), and (2) if there is a contract that satisfies
both parties' constraints, the selection of a contract that is valid (acceptable
to both parties), fair (when many valid and good outcomes are possible,
one of them is selected randomly with a uniform distribution without either party being able to control the outcome), and efficient (no clause is
replaceable by another that is better for both parties).

3.2.7   Rational and Selfish Participants

In the evolution of the models of participant behavior, the honest-but-
curious model and the malicious model (both of which were described
in section 3.1) were chronologically the earliest. It was later realized that,
while these models are important, they do not accurately model many
important interactions that take place over the Internet. This is because
both of these models assume some of the parties are well behaving and
are to be protected from a subset of ill-behaving participants. In reality it
is often the case that *all* participants will misbehave if it is in their interest
to do so. This led to considerations of incentive issues, i.e., economics
and game theory: A model of participants who are rational and selfish
and who will maximize their expected utility whether it means following
the protocol or deviating from it. Thus, the growing activity in mechanism
design, which combines cryptographic protocols with the rational-selfish
model of participants (i.e., Homo economicus).

The economic notions of equilibrium play a central role in such designs.
For example, a *dominant equilibrium* exists if a participant's self-interest
dictates that he or she follows the protocol whether the other participant
follows the protocol or not; by "follow the protocol" we mean not only
electronically, but also as far as providing truthful inputs. On the other
hand, a Nash equilibrium exists if a participant's self-interest dictates that he
follow the protocol when the other participant also follows the protocol—if
Bob follows the protocol, then it is in Alice's best interest to follow, and
vice versa.

A further refinement of participant behavior goes beyond the unbounded
Homo economicus model. It is inspired by 1978 Nobel Prize winner Herbert
Simon's observation that people are only partly rational and, occasionally,
irrational, a fact later rigorously confirmed by some landmark experiments
that document rather puzzling irrationality (like irrational risk aversion)
whereby participants make choices that decrease the expected utility that
they get out of an interaction. This extension of participant behavior to the
bounded rationality model is handled in a rigorous and formal way through

two methods, one of which consists of modifying the utility function itself (including the possibility that it is no longer single-valued), while the other consists of placing limitations or imposing costs on the participant's ability to compute that function.

3.3 Overview of General Results

In this section we briefly describe many previous results for SMC. This section will not describe many of the technical details of these approaches, but we refer the reader to [21,22] for a thorough description of these details. The basic approach used for most papers in SMC is to build a logical circuit for computing the desired function f. Then, using cryptographic encodings, the circuit is evaluated in a scrambled fashion. More specifically, the values of the intermediate results are hidden, but the output results can be understood. Now, as long as the communication and computation to encode and evaluate a gate and wire are constant, the complexity of evaluating the function f in a privacy-preserving manner will be proportional to the size of the circuit that evaluates f (although in many cases the constant is very large). Thus, any function computable in polynomial time can be evaluated securely with polynomial communication and computation. In the remainder of this section, we give an overview of how scrambled circuit evaluation can be achieved with two participants in the honest-but-curious adversary model. We then give a summary of how this can be extended to multiple participants and to more complex and realistic adversary models.

3.3.1 Two-Party Honest-But-Curious Scrambled Circuit Evaluation

In this section is a summary of an honest-but-curious two-party scrambled circuit protocol that was introduced in Yao [46]. This protocol is also very useful for computing intermediate results when creating domain-specific protocols. Recently, there has been an implementation of this approach that is described in [34], and this implementation shows that this protocol is practical for some problems.

In this protocol, one party is a *generator* of a scrambled circuit and the other party is an *evaluator*. The generator creates a scrambled circuit where each wire of the circuit has two encodings (one for each possible value of the wire), and the gates contain information that allows an evaluator to obtain the encoding of the gate's output wire when given the encodings for the gate's input wires. What makes this a private circuit evaluation is that the evaluator learns the encoding corresponding to his input for each input wire and, thus, learns only one encoding per wire. Following is a description of a protocol for scrambled circuit evaluation in more detail.

- **Circuit Generation:** For each wire in the circuit $w_1, \ldots, w_n$, the generator creates random encodings for the wires. We denote the encodings of 0 and 1 for wire w_i, respectively, by $w_i[0]$ and $w_i[1]$. To create a 2-ary gate for a function f with input wires w_i and w_j and output wire w_k, the gate information consists of the following four messages in a randomly permuted order: $(m||w_k[f(0, 0)]) \oplus H(w_i[0], w_i[0])$, $(m||w_k[f(0, 1)]) \oplus H(w_i[0], w_j[1])$, $(m||w_k[f(1, 0)]) \oplus H(w_i[1], w_i[0])$, and $(m||w_k[f(1, 1)]) \oplus H(w_i[1], w_j[1])$. Note that m is a publicly agreed upon marker and that H is a pseudorandom function (PRF). Note that a PRF can be efficiently implemented using HMAC [4] or CBC MAC constructions.

- **Learning Input Wires:** In order to evaluate a circuit, the evaluator must know the values of the input wires. For input wires corresponding to the generator's inputs, the generator simply sends the evaluator the encoding of each of his inputs. For input wires corresponding to the evaluator's inputs, the two parties engage in a 1-out-of-2 Chosen Oblivious Transfer protocol [38] where the two "messages" are the generator's encodings of 1 and 0, and the evaluator gets the encoding corresponding to his input for that wire.

- **Evaluating the Circuit:** To evaluate a gate, the evaluator decrypts each message in the gate with the keys that it has for the input wires. Only one of these decrypted messages will contain the marker m (the others will look random) and, thus, the evaluator will learn exactly one encoding for the output wire.

- **Learning the Result:** If the goal is to have the evaluator simply learn the result, then it is enough for the generator to tell the evaluator both encodings and the meanings of the output wires.

3.3.2 Extending Scrambled Circuit Evaluation

There have been several schemes that extend SMC to multiple participants and to the malicious adversary model; the first such scheme was presented in [23]. The malicious model schemes all assume that a strict majority of the participants or two-thirds of the participants (the actual number depends on the assumptions being made) are honest. Such an assumption is unavoidable, due the to impossibility results of Byzantine agreement [16]. Most protocols for the malicious model use some form of zero-knowledge proof (for a detailed overview of zero-knowledge proofs, see [21]) in order to make sure that the participants are following the protocol correctly. We will now describe a brief summary of the protocol described in [35] that was an extension of Yao's scrambled circuit evaluation approach to multiple parties and to the malicious model. Instead of computing the desired function f, the participants jointly compute Yao's encoded circuit for f (where no minority of the parties would learn the encodings). The circuit is then revealed to all participants and they then evaluate the circuit to learn the result. While this approach computes any function in a privacy-preserving manner in a constant number of communication rounds, it is not believed that this approach nor other approaches for the malicious model are efficient enough to be used in practice (because of a very large constant). Recently, a scheme was proposed [12] that is a promising approach for efficient malicious model SMC for some problems. As a final note, general results for SMC have been proposed for other adversary models that are stronger than the malicious model, including [8] and [9].

3.4 General Techniques for Privacy-Preserving Protocols

3.4.1 Splitting Techniques

As already explained, in privacy-preserving distributed computations, the input is partitioned among the participants (Alice has some, Bob has the rest) and the output is to be revealed to Alice or Bob or both. But, software has more than just inputs and outputs, it has intermediate values that are computed as steps along the way to the desired output. Who has these intermediate values as the computation proceeds? They are usually *split* between the participants; this splitting can take many forms, of which we briefly review two.

3.4.1.1 Additive Splitting

A value x is additively split between A and B if A has a random x_A and B has a random x_B, such that $x_A + x_B = x$ where addition is modular. If y is split in a similar manner ($= y_A + y_B$) then A and B can compute the sum of x and y by adding their respective shares of x and y, that is, if $z = x + y$, then A computes $z_A = x_A + y_A$ and B computes $z_B = x_B + y_B$. Of course, computing $z = x * y$ in split form is considerably more complicated if x and y are additively split. In every intermediate step of the computation, the split inputs are used to compute the resulting intermediate value also in split form. In some papers, the addition is not modular and, in such a case, secrecy can be compromised because hiding a value v by adding a random r to it leaks information about it. However, the leakage of information about v is negligible if r is much larger than v.

Multiplicative splitting is similar to additive except that the roles of addition and multiplication are interchanged in the above.

3.4.1.2 Encoding-Based Splitting

Another commonly used form of splitting is to encode all intermediate values so that only one party (say, A) generates and knows the encoding, while the other party B actually carries out the computations and sees the encoded intermediate values, but does not know what they mean (A would know, but A does not see them). To illustrate this with an example, suppose that u is an intermediate Boolean variable in a program. Then, in this approach, A would generate an encoding of the possible values of each of these variables as follows. A random $r_u[0]$ is generated by A as the encoding of the value 0 for variable u, and another random $r_u[1]$ is generated by A as the encoding of the value 1 for that variable. As the computation proceeds, it is B that gets to see the encoded intermediate value of u (B sees either $r_u[0]$ or $r_u[1]$), but without knowing what it means.

3.4.2 Homomorphic Encryption and Computing with Encrypted Values

A useful tool for constructing privacy-preserving protocols is a public key, semantically secure [25] additively homomorphic encryption scheme, such as [11,36]. We denote the encryption and decryption functions of a homomorphic scheme by E_{pk} and D_{sk}, respectively. Given such a scheme, it is possible to add the plaintexts of two encrypted values by multiplying the ciphertexts; that is, when given the encryptions $E_{pk}(x)$ and $E_{pk}(y)$, we can compute $E_{pk}(x+y)$ by computing $E_{pk}(x) * E_{pk}(y)$. Also, when given $E_{pk}(x)$ it is possible to compute $E_{pk}(c*x)$ for any constant c by computing $E_{pk}(x)^c$. It is worth noting that the arithmetic for homomorphic schemes is modular. Finally, with homomorphic schemes, it is possible to re-encrypt a ciphertext value to generate another ciphertext with the same plaintext value.

Homomorphic encryption allows us to have another form of split values. More specifically, one party chooses a homomorphic encryption scheme, publishes the public key, and then sends its values to the other participant(s) encrypted with the homomorphic scheme. The participants without the encryption scheme's private key cannot learn any significant information about the encrypted values (because the encryption scheme is semantically secure). This homomorphic splitting technique works well with additively split values. If values are additively split modularly with the same modulus as the homomorphic scheme, then it is trivial to convert values between the additively split representation and homomorphically split representation. If the values are additively split in a non modular fashion, then it is usually possible to convert to and from a homomorphic-split fashion, but one has to prevent the calculations from getting larger than the modulus.

3.4.3 Input Quality Problems

One of the daunting issues that has delayed the widespread adoption of modern cryptographic privacy-preserving protocols is that when the inputs provided by a participant to a protocol are not revealed to any other participant, there is a temptation to gain an advantage by lying. A number of approaches have been proposed to mitigate this problem, of which we briefly review two. But, before we do so, let us stress that this issue goes beyond worries about the well-formedness of the inputs. That is, this is not a concern by A that an integer input by B is supposed to satisfy some constraint (like being in the range 1 to 10), and that B may input something outside of that range. This kind of mischief can be taken care of through the use of zero-knowledge proofs: B can convince A that its input is well-formed (in this case, is in the required range) without revealing to A anything else about that input. The real concern here is that B's true value is 8, but that B may lie and input 5 instead because of B's belief that something may be gained by this lie. People sometimes lie about their age, their salary, or their status when they believe they will gain from the lie.

One approach to resolving this has already been touched upon earlier: Design the interaction in such a way that B cannot gain anything through such a lie. A process in which no participant can gain anything by lying is said to be *incentive compatible*; more precisely, in an incentive-compatible interaction no participant can increase their expected utility by being untruthful about their inputs, or by deviating from the protocol. By way of example, the earlier mentioned sealed bid, first-price auction is not incentive-compatible, whereas the Vickrey auction is incentive-compatible (i.e., no participant can decrease what they pay by bidding a value that differs from what the item is truly worth to them); presumably this is why eBay uses the Vickrey auction mechanism.

While mechanism design can incentivize participants to be truthful about their private inputs, this is not possible in several situations, including the important problems of access control, trust negotiations, credit checking, and others where being untruthful may secure the desired access (or loan, service, etc.). One approach used in such situations is to have the participants' inputs certified offline by a third party certification authority. The solution must not require online involvement of the certifying authority in every subsequent certified-inputs transaction, as the third party would then become a bottleneck in the system. Such offline certification not only makes the resulting protocols more practical by reducing the burden on the certifying authority, it also makes them more similar to the state of the current practice where a credential (like a driver's license) is issued once and then used repeatedly without bothering the issuer, and it enhances privacy in that the issuer need not be alerted to every instance where the certificate is used (e.g., to prove the age is over 21). The technical challenge in such protocols is how each party can verify the other party's certified inputs without learning what they are. This approach of certified inputs is central to trust negotiations and attribute-based access control, which are covered in the next section.

3.5 Specific Applications

In this section, we introduce specific results for four different applications, including scalar product, nearest neighbor, trust negotiation, and computational outsourcing.

3.5.1 Scalar Product

Suppose Alice has a vector $\vec{a} = (a_1, \ldots, a_n)$, and Bob has a vector $\vec{b} = (b_1, \ldots, b_n)$. Further suppose that they want to learn the scalar product of $\vec{a}$ and $\vec{b}$. Given the scalar product, it is not possible to determine the other participant's exact vector (unless the vectors have size 1), but this may reveal a single entry in a vector. For example, suppose Bob's vector is all zeros except for one entry. In this case, Bob will learn exactly one entry of Alice's vector. There are many applications where this small amount of information is an acceptable leak and so a secure protocol for scalar product makes sense. Protocols for scalar product have been proposed in [13,40], but these protocols were shown to leak information in some cases in [20]. However, [20] also introduced a protocol that was proven secure for scalar product for the honest-but-curious adversary model, which is summarized below:

1. Alice chooses a homomorphic encryption scheme with E_{pk} and D_{sk} as the respective encryption and decryption functions. She gives Bob the public key along with the values $E_{pk}(a_1), \ldots, E_{pk}(a_n)$.
2. Bob computes the following: $\prod_{i=1}^{n} E_{pk}(a_i)^{b_i}$, which is equivalent to $E_{pk}(\sum_{i=1}^{n}(a_i b_i))$ (by the additive homomorphic properties of the encryption scheme). He sends this value to Alice.
3. Alice decrypts the value from Bob and learns the scalar product.

In the above protocol, Alice learns the scalar product. It is straightforward to construct a protocol where Bob learns the scalar product or where the product is additively split between Alice and Bob. The latter protocol is useful in situations where the scalar product is an intermediate result that should not be revealed.

3.5.2 Nearest Neighbor

We already discussed earlier the issue of location privacy in location-dependent query processing, where it is desired for the mobile client to learn the answer to its location-dependent query without revealing to the remote database anything about its location, other than what the database can infer from the answer it gives to the query. This section discusses the instance of this problem in which the queries are of the nearest-neighbor variety, i.e., the remote database has to return the address of the post office (or gas station or Chinese restaurant) that is nearest to the mobile unit without knowing precisely the location of that mobile unit.

We begin with simple solutions that do not require the use of complex protocols, but whose advantage of simplicity is balanced by drawbacks that range from a degraded quality of the answer returned by the server to an increased amount of communication between the client and server.

One simple solution that does not require the database to modify the way it does its query processing is for the client to lie about its position by a distance δ applied in a random direction from its real position. The client can choose a δ that is large enough for its own notion of how much it wants to hide its location. That δ is not known to the database, and may vary from one query to the next even for the same client (because the privacy/accuracy tradeoff for that client may change over time, or from one query to the next). The damage done to the quality of the server's answer is the distance between the post office returned and the true nearest post office, and is a function of δ. In the worst case, it is 2δ and this bound is tight. Assuming that post offices are uniformly distributed in the plane, it can be proven that the expected damage is $\leq \delta$.

A variation on the above scheme avoids the loss of accuracy in the answer, but it potentially requires more communication. The idea behind this variation is to "grid" the plane, covering it with tiles of dimensions $\lambda \times \lambda$; after this gridding of the plane, the client queries the database with the tile that contains the client's location. The database answers the query with all sites that are closest to at least one point in the query tile; that is, if v is any point of the query tile (not necessarily a site) and site w is the closest site to v, then w is a part of the answer that the database will return to the client (note that w could be inside the query tile, or outside of it, and that a site inside the query tile is always chosen as a part of the answer). Upon receiving these sites the client determines which of them is closest to his actual location. The disadvantage of this scheme is that the client may receive many sites in response to the query—the expected number received depends on λ, but also on the average density ρ of sites per unit area (the two determine the expected number of sites per tile, which is $\lambda^2\rho$). A further refinement of this basic tiling-based scheme is to have the database treat the answers that would be returned by the basic scheme merely as "candidates" for the one site that is returned as an answer: The site that has the largest number of "votes" from within the tile. In other words, if v and w are as above, then the winning candidate w is the one with the largest number of vs in the tile that "choose it" as the nearest site to them. This variant does not have the increased communication because a single site is returned as the answer, but it does have an accuracy tradeoff: The worst-case damage to a query's answer is no greater than the tile diameter D (and that bound is tight), whereas the expected damage is $0.27D$ assuming uniformly distributed sites and client locations.

The cryptographic protocol-based solution satisfies both the privacy requirement (not revealing anything to the server other than what it can infer from the answer it returns), and the quality of answer requirement (the answer returned is as good as if the server knew the client's exact position). This solution requires the server to organize its database in such a manner that it can support the query-processing protocol with the remote client, and then update it (additions/deletions of sites) incrementally later on. If n is the number of sites, then the database takes $O(n \log n)$ time to initially construct, and then polylogarithmic update time for a site insertion or deletion. Each nearest-neighbor query takes $O(\log n)$ amount of communication for its processing by the protocol.

The data structure used is Kirkpatrick's hierarchical search directed acyclic graph (DAG) for query point location in a planar subdivision [27], where the planar subdivision is a Voronoi diagram [14, 28, 37] of the sites at the database. The use of this DAG search structure is constrained by the strict privacy requirement, namely, that the database should not learn anything other than what it can infer from the query's answer. This rules out revealing such things as whether the query point is closer to one nonanswer site than to another, or revealing the specific reason for which the query point is outside of a Voronoi cell (only yes/no is allowed), etc. The processing of a query makes use of a cryptographic protocol that allows the server to determine whether a query point p (that is known to the client, but not to the server) is inside a planar subdivision's cell that is known to the server, but not to the client. This is done without revealing to the server anything other than the yes/no answer to the question of whether the client's query point is in the cell or not. The protocol is used repeatedly at each level of the search DAG, and the leaf at which this process ends gives the site that is the answer to the query (the Voronoi cell in which the query point lies provides the server no more information than the site returned as answer).

3.5.3 Trust Negotiation/Attribute-Based Access Control

In traditional access control systems, access is granted to a user based on that user's identity. Unfortunately, this does not scale to open systems, such as the Internet. A different access control approach that has been proposed is attribute-based access control [5, 15, 32]. In these systems the access control policy is stated as a function of a set of attributes. For example, a policy might be that a user must have secret clearance and work for the

CIA. For such a system to be secure, there must be a way to verify whether a user has an attribute. Digital credentials are a tool for doing this verification; a third party, which can verify the status of an attribute for a user, digitally signs a statement stating that the user has the attribute in question. It is worth pointing out that this notion of using attributes to grant access to a user mimics a common way that access control is done in the physical world, e.g., you must show your driver's license to prove your age.

A simple system for attribute-based access control is to have a user reveal all of his credentials to the resource holder. Clearly, this scheme has privacy problems, e.g., revealing one's age, employment status, or security clearance to everyone is not desirable. Furthermore, the credentials are not the only resource that has privacy concerns; more specifically, the policies themselves may be private. The motivation for hiding the policy is not necessarily protection from an evil adversary. For example, the policy may be a commercial secret and revelation of the policy would invite imitators. As another example, revealing a policy may encourage users to game the system, e.g., to find the path of least resistance for obtaining access to a resource.

There have been many attempts to resolve the privacy problems that are outlined above. For example, in trust negotiation [39,42–44,47–49], the approach is to assign a release policy to every credential, e.g., Bob will reveal his secret clearance credential to Alice only if Alice has a secret clearance credential or is a government employee. The participants then reveal a credential only when they know that the other party satisfies the release policy for that credential. An example revelation strategy is the eager strategy [44]. In the eager strategy, the participants take turns revealing credentials and, as soon as a credential's release policy is satisfied, the credential is revealed. This strategy guarantees that a credential is not revealed until its release policy is satisfied. Of course, the credentials are still revealed in this scheme and so there have been many schemes that protect the credentials further, including hidden credentials [7,19,26], secret handshakes [3], oblivious signature-based envelope [31], oblivious attribute certificates [29,30], policy-based cryptography [2], and many other schemes. In what follows, we outline the results of two such approaches.

In [17] secure protocols for attribute-based access control were introduced. Specifically, the requester would input a set of credentials (the credentials used identity-based encryption [6,10]) and the resource owner would input the access policy for the resource. At the end of the protocol the requester obtains the resource if the requester satisfied the access policy, but would learn little information if it did not satisfy the policy. Furthermore, the resource owner would not learn whether access was granted (and so the credentials were protected). The different protocols in [17] show a tradeoff between efficiency and privacy (as the more efficient protocols revealed more information). While it may seem that the previous solution reveals minimal information, there are some problems with this approach. In many environments, a resource owner must keep track of every user that has accessed a particular resource (perhaps for auditing purposes) or they learn this information from other sources. In such systems, it is possible for a resource owner to probe the client's credential set by using different policies for different accesses. To counteract this, protocols were introduced in [18] that integrated the ideas of trust negotiation with secure protocols. More specifically, the client inputs a set of credentials along with a set of release policies for those credentials, and the server does the same and also inputs an access policy for the resource in question. In this system, a credential was used only when the other party satisfied the release policy for the item. An additional benefit of this approach was that the scheme supported arbitrary policy cycles. For example, many other systems will deadlock if Alice and Bob both have a policy that states that they will reveal their secret clearance credential only to someone with secret clearance.

3.5.4 Computational Outsourcing

Outsourcing is a general procedure employed in the business world when one entity (call it A) chooses to farm out (*outsource*) a certain task to another entity (call it B). Computational outsourcing is the special case where A gets B to do a computational task for them. The possible reasons why A might want to outsource their computation to B include: A may be computationally weak (a sensor or inexpensive card); B may have superior computing power (possibly a supercomputing center); or B may have some other special capabilities, such as better software, more expert staff, or lower costs. The secure (i.e., privacy-preserving) version of the problem is when B doesn't learn either A's inputs or the output of the computation. If that was the only goal of the outsourcing protocol, then this would be the special case of the general problem described above in which A has all the inputs and B has none of the inputs. But the outsourcing protocol has another goal: To place most of the computational burden on B and as little of it as possible on A; placing such a deliberately unbalanced computational burden on the participants was previously not a design goal.

More formally, if we let $T(n)$ be the time complexity of the algorithm that will be used for solving the (presumably intensive) computational problem at hand, and if we let $S(n)$ be the space complexity of the input, then the protocol should place the $O(T(n))$ time computational burden on B, and the computational burden on A should be $O(S(n))$ (which is unavoidable because A has to at least read the input it has). For example, if A has two $n \times n$ matrices M_1 and M_2, and A wishes to securely outsource to B the task of computing their product $M = M_1 * M_2$ using the usual $O(n^3)$ time algorithm for matrix multiplication, then the protocol should be such that A has a computational burden of $O(n^2)$ time and it is the computational burden of B that has the $O(n^3)$ time complexity. Of course, A should learn the product M, and B should not learn anything about M_1, M_2, or their product M.

To illustrate an integrity problem associated with computational outsourcing, consider a situation where A is outsourcing to B a sequence of n computational tasks that A cannot afford to do on its own local machine (A could locally afford to do a small number of them, but not all n of them). For the sake of definiteness, assume that each task consists of an expensive dynamic programming computation that compares two biological sequences for similarity, and returns a similarity score for each such pair. If B was unscrupulous, B could collect A's money for carrying out the computational job, but without providing the full computational service: B could do only a fraction of the n tasks (say, 80 percent of them) and skimp on the remaining tasks by returning to A random answers for them. The problem of how A could detect such cheating with a high enough probability, and with minimal local computation by A, has received increasing attention.

Elegant negative results exist about the impossibility of securely outsourcing computationally intractable problems [1].

3.6   Summary

We have briefly described the framework of privacy-preserving protocols, surveyed some of the issues and results in it, and described a sampling of its applications. A brief chapter such as this can serve as a starting point for initial inquiries into this deep and complex area, but it cannot possibly go into in-depth overage of all its major theoretical issues—that would take a book. In fact, there is an excellent two-volume book by Goldreich for the reader interested in a more in-depth treatment of this material [21,22].

Acknowledgment

Portions of this work were supported by Grants IIS-0325345 and CNS-0627488 from the National Science Foundation, and by sponsors of the Center for Education and Research in Information Assurance and Security. The viewpoints expressed in this work are those of the authors, and do not necessarily reflect those of the National Science Foundation or of the other above-mentioned sponsors.

References

[1]   Martin Abadi, Joan Feigenbaum, and Joe Kilian. On hiding information from an oracle. In *Proceedings of the Nineteenth Annual ACM Conference on Theory of Computing,* pp. 195–203. ACM Press, New York, 1987.

[2] Walid Bagga and Refik Molva. Policy-based cryptography and applications. In *Proceedings of the 9th International Conference on Financial Cryptography and Data Security,* Roseau, Dominica, February 2005.

[3] Dirk Balfanz, Glenn Durfee, Narendar Shankar, Diana Smetters, Jessica Staddon, and Hao-Chi Wong. Secret handshakes from pairing-based key agreements. In *Proceedings of the IEEE Symposium on Security and Privacy,* Oakland, CA, pp. 180–196, May 2003.

[4] M. Bellare, R. Canetti, and H. Krawczyk. Keying hash functions for message authentication. In *Advances in Cryptology — CRYPTO '96,* vol. 1109, pp. 1–15, 1996.

[5] Matt Blaze, Joan Feigenbaum, and Jack Lacy. Decentralized trust management. In *Proceedings of the 1996 IEEE Symposium on Security and Privacy,* pp. 164–173. IEEE Computer Society Press, Los Alamitos, CA, May 1996.

[6] Dan Boneh and Matt Franklin. Identity-based encryption from the Weil pairing. In *Proceedings of CRYPTO 2001,* vol. 2139 of *Lecture Notes in Computer Science,* pp. 213–229. Springer-Verlag, Cambridge, U.K., 2001.

[7] Robert Bradshaw, Jason Holt, and Kent Seamons. Concealing complex policies with hidden credentials. In *Proceedings of 11th ACM Conference on Computer and Communications Security,* Washington, D.C., October 2004.

[8] Ran Canetti, Ivan Damgård, Stefan Dziembowski, Yuval Ishai, and Tal Malkin. On adaptive vs. non-adaptive security of multiparty protocols. *Lecture Notes in Computer Science,* Springer, Cambridge, U.K., 2045: 262+, 2001.

[9] Ran Canetti, Yehuda Lindell, Rafail Ostrovsky, and Amit Sahai. Universally composable two-party and multi-party secure computation. In *Proceedings of the Thirty-Fourth Annual ACM Symposium on Theory of Computing,* pp. 494–503. ACM Press, New York, 2002.

[10] Clifford Cocks. An identity-based encryption scheme based on quadratic residues. In *8th IMA International Conference on Cryptography and Coding,* vol. 2260, pp. 360–363. Springer-Verlag, Cambridge, U.K., December 2001.

[11] Ivan Damgård and Mads Jurik. A generalisation, a simplification and some applications of paillier's probabilistic public-key system. In *PKC '01: Proceedings of the 4th International Workshop on Practice and Theory in Public Key Cryptography,* pp. 119–136. Springer-Verlag, Cambridge, U.K., 2001.

[12] Ivan Damgård and Yuval Ishai. Constant-round multiparty computation using a black-box pseudorandom generator. In *Proceedings of Advances in Cryptology — CRYPTO '05,* vol. 3621 of *Lecture Notes in Computer Science,* pp. 378–411, Springer-Verlag, Cambridge, U.K., 2005.

[13] W. Du and M.J. Atallah. Privacy-preserving statistical analysis. In *Proceedings of the 17th Annual Computer Security Applications Conference,* pp. 102–110, New Orleans, LA, December 10–14, 2001.

[14] H. Edelsbrunner. *Algorithms in Combinatorial Geometry.* Springer-Verlag, Heidelberg, Germany, 1987.

[15] Carl Ellison, Bill Frantz, Butler Lampson, Ron Rivest, Brian Thomas, and Tatu Ylonen. SPKI certificate theory. IETF RFC 2693, September 1999.

[16] Paul Feldman and Silvio Micali. Optimal algorithms for byzantine agreement. In *Proceedings of the Twentieth Annual ACM Symposium on Theory of Computing*, pp. 148–161. ACM Press, New York, 1988.

[17] K. Frikken, M.J. Atallah, and J. Li. Attribute-based access control with hidden policies and hidden credentials. *IEEE Transactions on Computers*, 55(10): 1259–1270, 2006.

[18] K. Frikken, M. Atallah, and J. Li. Trust negotiation with hidden credentials, hidden policies, and policy cycles. In *Proceedings of 13th Annual Network and Distributed System Security Symposium (NDSS)*, San Diego, CA, pp. 152–172, 2006.

[19] Keith B. Frikken, Mikhail J. Atallah, and Jiangtao Li. Hidden access control policies with hidden credentials. In *Proceedings of the 3rd ACM Workshop on Privacy in the Electronic Society*, Washington, D.C., October 2004.

[20] B. Goethals, S. Laur, H. Lipmaa, and T. Mielikainen. On private scalar product computation for privacy-preserving data mining. In *The 7th Annual International Conference on Information Security and Cryptology (ICISC 2004)*, Seoul, Korea, 2004.

[21] Oded Goldreich. *Foundations of Cryptography: Volume I Basic Tools*. Cambridge University Press, Cambridge, U.K., 2001.

[22] Oded Goldreich. *Foundations of Cryptography: Volume II Basic Application*. Cambridge University Press, Cambridge, U.K., 2004.

[23] Oded Goldreich, Silvio Micali, and Avi Wigderson. How to play any mental game. In *Proceedings of the Nineteenth Annual ACM Conference on Theory of Computing*, New York, pp. 218–229, May 1987.

[24] Shafi Goldwasser. Multi party computations: past and present. In *Proceedings of the Sixteenth Annual ACM Symposium on Principles of Distributed Computing*, El Paso, TX, pp. 1–6. ACM Press, New York, 1997.

[25] Shafi Goldwasser and Silvio Micali. Probabilistic encryption. *Journal of Computer and System Sciences*, 28(2): 270–299, 1984.

[26] Jason E. Holt, Robert W. Bradshaw, Kent E. Seamons, and Hilarie Orman. Hidden credentials. In *Proceedings of the 2nd ACM Workshop on Privacy in the Electronic Society*, Washington, D.C., October 2003.

[27] D.G. Kirkpatrick. Optimal search in planar subdivisions. *SIAM Journal on Computing*, 12: 28–35, 1983.

[28] D.T. Lee and R.L. Drysdale, III. Generalization of Voronoi diagrams in the plane. *SIAM Journal on Computing*, 10, 73–87, 1981.

[29] Jiangtao Li and Ninghui Li. OACerts: Oblivious attribute certificates. In *Proceedings of the 3rd Conference on Applied Cryptography and Network Security (ACNS)*, vol. 3531 of *Lecture Notes in Computer Science*. Springer-Verlag, Cambridge, U.K., June 2005.

[30] Jiangtao Li and Ninghui Li. Policy-hiding access control in open environment. In *Proceedings of the 24nd ACM Symposium on Principles of Distributed Computing (PODC)*. ACM Press, New York, July 2005.

[31] Ninghui Li, Wenliang Du, and Dan Boneh. Oblivious signature-based envelope. In *Proceedings of the 22nd ACM Symposium on Principles of Distributed Computing (PODC)*. ACM Press, New York, July 2003.

[32] Ninghui Li, John C. Mitchell, and William H. Winsborough. Design of a role-based trust management framework. In *Proceedings of the 2002 IEEE Symposium on Security and Privacy*, pp. 114–130. IEEE Computer Society Press, Los Alamitos, CA, May 2002.

[33] Yehuda Lindell and Benny Pinkas. Privacy preserving data mining. In *Advances in Cryptology—CRYPTO 2000*, pp. 36–54. Springer-Verlag, Heidelberg, Germany, August 20–24, 2000.

[34] Dahlia Malkhi, Noan Nisan, Benny Pinkas, and Yaron Sella. Fairplay— secure two-party computation system. In *Proceeding of the 13th USENIX Security Symposium*, pp. 287–302. USENIX, Boston, MA, 2004.

[35] Silvio Micali and Phillip Rogaway. Secure computation (abstract). In *CRYPTO '91: Proceedings of the 11th Annual International Cryptology Conference on Advances in Cryptology*, pp. 392–404. Springer-Verlag, Cambridge, U.K., 1992.

[36] Pascal Paillier. Public-key cryptosystems based on composite degree residuosity classes. In *Advances in Cryptology: EUROCRYPT '99*, vol. 1592 of *Lecture Notes in Computer Science*, pp. 223–238. Springer-Verlag, Cambridge, U.K., 1999.

[37] F.P. Preparata and M.I. Shamos. *Computational Geometry: An Introduction.* Springer-Verlag, Heidelberg, Germany, 1993.

[38] Bruce Schneier. *Applied Cryptography: Protocols, Algorithms, and Source Code in C.* John Wiley & Sons, New York, 2nd ed., 1995.

[39] Kent E. Seamons, Marianne Winslett, and Ting Yu. Limiting the disclosure of access control policies during automated trust negotiation. In *Proceedings of the Symposium on Network and Distributed System Security (NDSS'01)*, San Diego, CA, February 2001.

[40] J. Vaidya and C. Clifton. Privacy preserving association rule mining in vertically partitioned data. In *KDD '02: Proceedings of the Eighth ACM SIGKDD International Conference on Knowledge Discovery and Data Mining*, pp. 639–644. ACM Press, New York, 2002.

[41] Jaideep Vaidya and Chris Clifton. Privacy-preserving data mining: Why, how, and when. *IEEE Security & Privacy*, 2(6), 19–27, 2004.

[42] William H. Winsborough and Ninghui Li. Towards practical automated trust negotiation. In *Proceedings of the Third International Workshop on Policies for Distributed Systems and Networks (Policy 2002)*, pp. 92–103. IEEE Computer Society Press, June 2002.

[43] William H. Winsborough and Ninghui Li. Safety in automated trust negotiation. In *Proceedings of IEEE Symposium on Security and Privacy*. IEEE Computer Society Press, Los Alamitos, CA, May 2004.

[44] William H. Winsborough, Kent E. Seamons, and Vicki E. Jones. Automated trust negotiation. In *DARPA Information Survivability Conference and Exposition*, vol. I, pp. 88–102. IEEE Press, Los Alamitos, CA, January 2000.

[45] Andrew C. Yao. Protocols for secure computations. In *Proceedings of the 23th IEEE Symposium on Foundations of Computer Science*, pp. 160–164. IEEE Computer Society Press, Los Alamitos, CA, 1982.

[46] Andrew C. Yao. How to generate and exchange secrets. In *Proceedings of the 27th IEEE Symposium on Foundations of Computer Science,* pp. 162–167. IEEE Computer Society Press, Los Alamitos, CA, 1986.

[47] Ting Yu, Xiaosong Ma, and Marianne Winslett. Prunes: An efficient and complete strategy for trust negotiation over the internet. In *Proceedings of the 7th ACM Conference on Computer and Communications Security (CCS-7),* pp. 210–219. ACM Press, New York, November 2000.

[48] Ting Yu and Marianne Winslett. A unified scheme for resource protection in automated trust negotiation. In *Proceedings of IEEE Symposium on Security and Privacy,* pp. 110–122. IEEE Computer Society Press, Los Alamitos, CA, May 2003.

[49] Ting Yu, Marianne Winslett, and Kent E. Seamons. Interoperable strategies in automated trust negotiation. In *Proceedings of the 8th ACM Conference on Computer and Communications Security (CCS-8),* pp. 146–155. ACM Press, New York, November 2001.

PRIVACY ATTACKS

Chapter 4

Byzantine Attacks on Anonymity Systems

Nikita Borisov, George Danezis, and Parisa Tabriz

Contents

4.1   Introduction 74
4.2   Anonymity Systems 74
4.3   Attack Models 75
    4.3.1   Common Threat Models 76
    4.3.2   A Participating Adversary 77
4.4   Path Compromise Attacks 78
4.5   Adversary Angels and Adversary Facades...........................79
4.6   Affecting Node Discovery 80
    4.6.1   Attacking Path Construction in MorphMix...................81
    4.6.2   The Attack 82
4.7   Simulation 82
    4.7.1   Attack Execution 82
    4.7.2   Countermeasures 83
4.8   Selective DoS...84
    4.8.1   Attacks on Tor 84
    4.8.2   Attacks on Mixminion 86
        4.8.2.1   Increasing Path Lengths (l) 87
    4.8.3   Systems Designed to Improve Reliability 88
4.9   Countermeasures..89
4.10   Conclusion 91
References..91

4.1 Introduction

In the study of anonymous systems, research into new designs for anonymity has been balanced by analysis of attack strategies for violating anonymity. Such strategies shed light on how well systems will defend users' privacy and suggest new directions for research and development. Any analysis of attacks, however, must be parameterized by a model of adversary capabilities. The choice of model has been evolving over the years; for example, as the scale of anonymous systems has grown, the popular global passive adversary becomes less realistic and a more limited adversary may be more appropriate [36]. At the same time, with more loose dynamics connecting the participants of today's anonymous networks, the likelihood that a large number of participants may be compromised and colluding together is perhaps higher than it used to be. This motivates deeper study of attacks that such participating adversaries can pose.

In this chapter, we consider how participating adversaries can attack anonymity systems both by observing traffic in the system and by behaving maliciously in order to confuse other participants to gain an advantage. Such Byzantine behavior can give attackers a significant advantage over following the protocol and can greatly reduce the levels of privacy provided by an anonymity system.

In particular, we look at attacks that compromise the path of a message as it travels through the anonymous system. There are several ways this attack can work, either by presenting misinformation about the network in order to make traffic pass through malicious participants, or by making malicious participants appear more desirable (or honest ones less so) for routing traffic, once again biasing path selection toward compromised hosts. The attacks apply to a wide range of deployed and proposed anonymity systems and can have a significant impact on the levels of privacy they provide.

Discussed below are countermeasures to both the path compromise attacks and the general problem of Byzantine participating adversaries. It turns out that general techniques for addressing Byzantine behavior in distributed systems do not easily apply to anonymous networks, and effective defense against Byzantine attackers remains elusive. This highlights the importance of the Byzantine adversary model for further study.

4.2 Anonymity Systems

The study and deployment of anonymous systems was kicked off by David Chaum's seminal paper on mix networks [7]. In his original proposal, anonymous messages are relayed by mixes that batch messages from different sources, permute them, and send them out to their destinations. Messages are also cryptographically transformed by the mix in order to hide the correspondence between inputs and outputs. The output of a mix may be sent to another mix for further mixing, creating a *chain* of mixes; layered encryption is used to ensure that each mix can only know the previous and next mix in the chain. The sequence of mixes chosen can also be called a *relay path.*

Chaum's design is quite influential and to this day forms the basis of most high latency anonymous communication systems [10,19,22]. For low latency communications, Chaum's design was modified to eliminate batching of messages and was called onion routing [37]; this traded off susceptibility to traffic analysis attacks for improved performance. The current generation low latency communication system, Tor [12], uses a similar design though it optimizes the cryptographic operations used to protect data transmissions.

The above networks usually construct relay paths chosen uniformly at random from the set of all mix nodes. Berthold et al. have argued [3] that a collection of static paths—a *mix cascade*—can better defend against some attacks, though the relative merits of mix cascades and free routes have been the subject of some debate [13]. More recently, peer-to-peer (P2P) structures for selecting mix nodes have been proposed [18,33] in order to increase the scale of mix-based networks.

Some alternatives to the mix design do exist, such as DC-Nets [8]. Our discussion of path compromise attacks below will, of course, not be applicable to such systems. Nevertheless, the adversary model and the general observations about Byzantine attacks are equally applicable to such systems and mix networks.

4.3 Attack Models

Any anonymous system must be evaluated for resistance to various types of attacks. An important decision predicating this analysis is what kind of adversary is to be considered. A too weak adversary model will lead to an overly optimistic outlook on the security of the system despite it being susceptible to attacks. A conservative adversary model, therefore, is preferred in the security community; yet defending from a very powerful adversary typically requires very significant costs that few users or operators are willing to pay. The experience of the Tor network [12] is that a somewhat weaker adversary model can help improve usability and attract larger numbers of users, which in itself improves the anonymity of a system. Therefore, a *realistic* adversary model is very important for anonymous system design.

4.3.1 Common Threat Models

Table 4.1 lists the adversary models and Table 4.2 lists systems that have been analyzed with each model. The most common model is a *global passive adversary*, who can observe all messages sent between all participants. Although such an adversary is quite powerful, most high latency anonymous systems, such as Babel [19], DC-Nets [8], and Mixminion [10], are designed to resist such an adversary, since this model subsumes all less powerful but more realistic adversaries. The requirements of low latency communication, however, make most practical systems susceptible to traffic analysis techniques [29], such that a global passive adversary is easily able to compromise anonymity. Therefore, adversaries that are considered by systems such as Tor are usually assumed to be more limited and can observe only a fraction c of the network.

An *active* adversary can additionally disrupt communication by inserting, deleting, delaying, or modifying messages on any communication link, generally following the Dolev–Yao model [14]. Some attacks available to such adversaries are trickle and flood attacks [35], where the volume of traffic on a link is increased or decreased to watch the effects on other parts of the network. Adversaries can also modify ("tag") messages in transit or replay past messages; in both cases, monitoring for corresponding errors or duplicates in other parts of the network to recover the path that messages travel on. Mixmaster [22] and Babel are both susceptible to tagging attacks; Mixminion, however, uses hashes to verify the integrity of message headers and cryptographic checksums to verify the payload. Other forms of active attacks may exploit the cryptographic primitives used by the anonymous systems [28] or the bandwidth limitations of low latency systems [24].

Active adversaries, like passive ones, may be either global or local; most of the attacks described above will succeed even if only a limited number of links are controlled by attackers. To some extent, active attacks can be mitigated by link-layer encryption and authentication of messages,

Table 4.1 Adversary Classifications in Anonymous Networking Systems, Their Influence on the Network (Where c Is the Proportion of Dishonest Users in the Network and $0 < c < 1$), and Their Behavior

Adversary	% of Network Affected	Behavior
Global passive adversary	100%	Observes traffic
Local passive adversary	c	Inserts, delays, modifies traffic
Global active adversary	100%	Observes traffic
Local active adversary	c	Inserts, delays, modifies traffic
Participating adversary	c	Participates in network by running mixes

Table 4.2 Adversary Classifications and Systems That Have Been Analyzed with That Threat Model

Adversary	Systems
Global passive adversary	Babel, DC-Nets, Mix-Nets, Mixmaster, Mixminion, Tarzan
Local passive adversary	Crowds, Mix-Nets
Global active adversary	Mix-Nets
Local active adversary	Hydra-Onions, Mixminion, Tor
Participating HBC adversary	Cashmere, Crowds
Participating Byzantine adversary	MorphMix, Tarzan, Tor

but absent a public key infrastructure (PKI), it may still be possible to compromise such link-layer protections.

4.3.2 A Participating Adversary

The final adversary model is what we call a *participating adversary*. Most anonymous communication systems are designed as a network of nodes. The participating adversary model supposes that some of these nodes belong to attackers. This may be achieved by compromising existing nodes or contributing new ones to an existing system. Since anonymous networks are usually run with volunteer contributions, these networks will readily accept (and welcome) new participants who help increase the capacity of such networks. The only requirement on an attacker is a computer with a reasonably reliable Internet connection. Therefore, such an adversary is much easier to set up than, say, a global passive adversary, and yet it can yield better attack possibilities due to a better vantage point.

We can subclassify the participating adversary into two categories. The first is an "honest, but curious" (HBC) participant who behaves according to the anonymity protocols but tries to learn as much as possible about the communication through observation. Though passive, this adversary may be able to learn more information since he can observe the private state of some of the participants. For example, in both the original mix system designed by Chaum [7] and its successors, observing the internal state of the mix will reveal the permutation connecting the inputs to the outputs, compromising the anonymity provided by this mix in a way that an outside observer would not be able to do. Chaum's design was concerned about such participating adversaries, motivating the approach of mix chains, where the presence of participating adversaries can be counteracted by honest mixes in the chain. More recent systems, such as Cashmere [41] and Crowds [30], have also been analyzed from the point of view of an HBC participating adversary.

An alternative participating adversary is one who may violate the protocol and behave in an arbitrary fashion. We call this the Byzantine participating adversary, after the Byzantine failure model [21]. Byzantine adversaries may lie about their capabilities or knowledge of the network, or disrupt communications, but they may also follow the protocol when that best suits their needs. In particular, Byzantine adversaries can actively try to avoid detection, making it difficult to isolate misbehaving nodes.

Recent research into anonymity systems, especially those using peer-to-peer designs, has considered some attacks that fall under the Byzantine adversary model. Most prominently, the Sybil attack [15] is an example of Byzantine behavior where a node violates the protocol by pretending to be multiple disparate node instances in order to gain undue influence on the network. However, Byzantine behavior is generally underexplored and new types of attacks can have a significant impact on the anonymity of existing designs. This situation is perhaps not surprising because the Byzantine model places few restrictions on attacker behavior and, therefore, makes it difficult to analyze the full range of possibilities. Yet the possibility of such attacks, and the low resource requirement to carry them out, means that it is important to carry out analysis of Byzantine adversaries in order to have confidence in the anonymity of a system.

We next describe several examples of attacks that can be mounted by Byzantine adversaries to demonstrate that they are a realistic threat before returning to the discussion of the Byzantine adversary problem in general. The attacks considered will all be of the *path compromise* type.

4.4 Path Compromise Attacks

Both mix networks and onion routing rely on hiding the complete relay path that a message follows from its source to the destination. An attacker who knows the entire path can easily link source and destination, compromising the unlinkability [27] that such systems aim to provide. These are called *path compromise* attacks to distinguish them from other types of attacks on unlinkability.

Path compromise attacks can be mounted by any participating adversary in a mix or onion-routing network. If relay paths through the network are selected randomly by users, each path will be compromised with some probability: c^l for mix networks, where l is the length of the relay path, or c^2 for onion-routing networks. The reason that onion-routing networks are more susceptible to path compromise is that the first and last node on a relay path can use traffic analysis to link traffic routed through them, eliminating the need to compromise the entire path. Wright et al. [39] demonstrate that an HBC adversary will succeed at path compromise after $0/c \log 1/c$ path creations with high probability, where n is the number of nodes in the network.

A Byzantine adversary can be even more successful at path compromise; for example, an attack on a hidden service in Tor [25] causes the service to repeatedly create new paths, enabling eventual compromise.* To address this issue, guard nodes [40] have been introduced in Tor to reduce the variety of constructed paths.

A Byzantine adversary may also use other techniques to make path compromise more successful. We consider three possible strategies: making paths that use compromised nodes appear more attractive, affecting the discovery process used to form paths, or impacting the reliability of "honest" paths, thereby driving traffic toward compromised nodes. Each of these approaches are discussed below.

4.5 Adversary Angels and Adversary Facades

Many anonymity systems have mechanisms to improve the efficiency and reliability of network routing. For example, MorphMix and Tor favor the inclusion of nodes with higher bandwidth capabilities in relay paths. As the performance of a relay path is bounded by the slowest node in the path, it is reasonable to improve performance by avoiding nodes on, say, modem connections in favor of nodes that have a digital subscriber line (DSL) or faster connectivity.

However this creates an easy avenue for adversaries to produce path compromise attacks by making themselves appear more attractive than other nodes in the system. In this way, they are selected more often as relay nodes and have a higher chance of succeeding. Adversaries can simply lie about their capabilities, thereby creating an *adversary facade*. Alternately, they, in fact, can provide extra capabilities by, for example, placing nodes in well-connected parts of the Internet. We call this second situation an *adversary angel*.

Systems that do not verify node capabilities are easily susceptible to adversary facades; for example, neither Tor nor MorphMix verify the stated bandwidth of nodes that nevertheless is used in selecting better-performing paths. Therefore, there is an incentive for attackers to overstate their capacity to drive more traffic their way [1].

Verification of capabilities could address this issue, but it is in itself difficult to implement. Using a central verification point may present undue load in a network like Tor and is simply impractical in a completely decentralized design, such as MorphMix. Further, reliable verification of capabilities

---

* To be more precise, this attack actually combines an active nonparticipating adversary who initiates connections with an HBC participant, who logs traffic; but, of course, a Byzantine adversary can easily simulate this attack.

such as bandwidth is difficult due to both variance in network conditions and the possibility of active deception on the part of the attackers when they are probed.

But even when validation is possible, there is still the concern of adversary angels, who are actually better performing than other nodes in the system. The incentive to contribute to the network is higher for an adversary trying to compromise anonymity than for a volunteer; hence, adversaries may be able to dedicate more resources to the task. This may take the form of buying extra bandwidth, dedicating extra central processing unit (CPU) resources, or ensuring high availability of nodes, making them more attractive for relaying traffic. (In many P2P systems, long-lived nodes will tend to be better connected than ones that have a shorter lifetime.)

Therefore, the drive to improve performance by biasing path selection must be carefully balanced by the possibility of such adversary attacks and any performance-optimizing mechanism must be designed and analyzed carefully with considerations of a Byzantine adversary, or even adversary angels.

4.6 Affecting Node Discovery

Anonymous networks such as Tor or Mixminion rely on the existence of a central directory listing all of the participating relay nodes in the network. All users consult this directory when paths are created; however, as the number of nodes grows, the directory becomes a limiting point of scalability. It is also a central point of failure and trust in an otherwise decentralized design, so there is some motivation for removing the centralized directory and using a P2P architecture to let mix nodes discover each other.

Developing effective node discovery mechanisms is an ongoing challenge in P2P networking. Node discovery must enable discovery of all the nodes that are currently live in the system and it must function correctly even in the face of an attack. It is important that all nodes may be discovered by all other nodes, since a node that picks relay nodes from a more limited pool may be fingerprinted based on its selections [9]. But, even if a protocol is designed to find all other nodes, Byzantine adversaries may disrupt such a protocol and force one to make choices toward a limited set to enable path compromise.

The most prevalent concern about Byzantine attacks has to do with Sybil attacks [15], where dishonest nodes are able to present multiple identities to control a larger proportion of the system than their individual numbers would otherwise allow. Methods to counter Sybil attacks include limiting participation based on IP addresses or resource verification techniques, such as solving computational puzzles [4].

But even when Sybil attacks are addressed, there is still the possibility of Byzantine attacks during node discovery. Since nodes learn about other nodes through their neighbors, these neighbors could misrepresent the state of the network and make path compromise easier. One approach, implemented in Tarzan [18], is to distribute a full directory of all nodes to all other nodes; however, this quickly runs into scaling issues as the number of participating nodes increases. Another approach is to use redundant information to validate data presented by neighbors. This is the approach used in MorphMix [33] and is discussed in more detail below.

4.6.1   Attacking Path Construction in MorphMix

MorphMix is a P2P onion-routing network, where all clients act as peers in the system, both routing their own traffic through the network as well as forwarding traffic for other peers. The peers are connected in an overlay topology through virtual links via transmission control protocol (TCP) connections between neighbor nodes in the system. Anonymous communication is performed by forming relay paths along this overlay structure. Each peer only knows about its own neighbors and learns about the possible next nodes to extend the relay path from previous nodes in the path. Therefore, a Byzantine participating adversary could lie about its connections to other nodes and ensure that all subsequent nodes in a path were colluding adversaries, leading to path compromise.

To avoid this attack, MorphMix incorporates a collusion detection mechanism (CDM). When a node is asked to extend a relay path, it provides a selection of its neighbors, along with their IP addresses. The initiator evaluates the selection for collusion by correlating the distribution of the IP address prefixes in the selection with past selections stored in a selection cache. The idea is that colluding attackers will be forced to choose from a small set of IP address prefixes and the colluding selections will have high correlations to each other, whereas honest nodes will provide a more random sampling of address prefixes. If a selection is deemed honest, a node is picked out of the selection as the next node in the path. For more details on the MorphMix path construction algorithm, refer to [31].

Notice that the CDM is designed specifically to resist a Byzantine adversary. It has been evaluated through simulation against two adversary strategies: providing selections consisting entirely of colluding nodes, or providing a mix of honest and colluding nodes in selections. In the former case, the CDM detects malicious selections; in the latter case, the selections are more likely to be marked as honest, but path compromise correspondingly is less likely [31].

However, a different, more "intelligent" attacker strategy can effectively defeat the CDM. This example demonstrates both the difficulty in fully analyzing all possible Byzantine adversary strategies and the importance of doing so.

4.6.2 The Attack

The attack is based on this simple intuition: Because each node's CDM and collusion threshold are based on only local knowledge, attackers can model and manipulate the local state of a node to avoid being detected. In particular, colluding attackers can maintain for each honest node a list of past selections consisting of colluding nodes that have been sent to that node. Then, when a new selection is requested, it is formed from colluding nodes that have the least overlap with past selections. In this way, the correlation with past selections is kept at a minimum and the CDM is fooled. More details about how intelligent selections are created can be found in [38].

4.7 Simulation

Because MorphMix does not have a substantial user base, we were unable to execute the attack on a live system. Instead, we simulated many tunnel constructions using the CDM from the MorphMix client prototype [32] and investigated the effects of the attack on one node, the victim node. We evaluated how successful the attack was based on how many tunnels we could compromise, what proportion of all tunnels constructed could be compromised, and how long the attack could run successfully.

Similar to the analysis in [31], we simulated 5,000 tunnel constructions consisting of only honest selections from a node distribution based on traffic traces taken from the Overnet/eDonkey file-sharing system [16]. The Overnet data gives us an approximation of what IP address distribution would be like in a deployed MorphMix system.

4.7.1 Attack Execution

We executed the attack during 5,000 tunnel construction attempts by a single victim node and calculated how many successful tunnels are constructed. In MorphMix, a node creates, on average, a new anonymous tunnel every 2 minutes. Therefore, creating 5,000 tunnels is roughly equivalent to 1 week of constant MorphMix usage. In Table 4.3, we can see that the attack results in a significant portion of anonymous tunnels being compromised using intelligent selections. If colluding adversaries control nodes in more than 15 percent of the represented subnets in MorphMix, they are able to compromise at least that percentage of tunnels constructed by

Table 4.3   Tunnel Construction for Range of Attackers

C	Honest Tunnels	Malicious Tunnels	Percentage Compromised
	(a) Uninterrupted attack execution		
5%	3,337.9	6.8	0.2% ($\sigma = 0.1$%)
10%	2,951.4	33.8	1.1% ($\sigma = 0.2$%)
15%	2,283.2	470.1	17.1% ($\sigma = 1.5$%)
20%	1,930.0	860.4	30.8% ($\sigma = 1.1$%)
30%	1,171.5	1,384.0	54.2% ($\sigma = 2.4$%)
40%	450.9	1,847.5	80.4% ($\sigma = 2.3$%)
	(b) Optimized attack execution		
5%	4,251.9	51.8	1.2% ($\sigma = .2$%)
10%	4,161.2	146.9	3.4% ($\sigma = .2$%)

victims. Attacking levels above 30 percent result in the majority of all constructed tunnels being compromised by an attacker. While adversaries that control nodes in fewer unique subnets cannot claim quite as high statistics, by slightly adjusting the attack (Table 4.3b), they can still successfully compromise more than the c^2 anonymous tunnels that are compromised using an HBC participating adversary.

4.7.2   Countermeasures

An immediate countermeasure to the above attack might be to increase the number of nodes in the tunnel and increase the number of entries in the selection cache. Unfortunately, increasing the size of the tunnel will increase connection latency and require greater storage and computation time for each execution of the CDM algorithm. Alternatively, one might introduce variable length tunnels into MorphMix; however, even with this change, attackers can still estimate the distribution of tunnel lengths and probability of compromise. New users to MorphMix are especially vulnerable to the intelligent selection attack. Since new users enter the system with an empty selection cache, attackers are guaranteed to successfully compromise a significant portion of a new user's initial tunnels, regardless of the cache size. This type of initial behavior in MorphMix would be an impediment to recruiting new users into the system.

The general limitation of the MorphMix CDM is that a node only considers its local knowledge when detecting collusive behavior. This local knowledge is limited, and too easy for attackers to model and exploit. A more global information flow could be used to better detect colluding attackers; for example, nodes could exchange statistics based on past selections. However, such solutions would need to address the questionable validity of information received from neighbors, so that adversaries would not use this information channel to their benefit by, for example, spreading misinformation about honest nodes so that they are considered malicious. An effective collusion detection mechanism that resists all manner of Byzantine attacks remains an open challenge.

4.8 Selective DoS

Another way that a participating adversary can attack the anonymity of a system is through a denial-of-service (DoS) attack. DoS has traditionally not been part of the threat model considered by designs for anonymous communication because privacy was seen as the most important security property. More recently, considerations of availability and usability have emerged, as an unusable or unavailable system cannot successfully protect users' privacy. However, there is a more direct connection between privacy and availability that can be exploited by attackers.

Most anonymous systems have a spectrum of more and less secure states. As seen above, in mix networks, paths that consist entirely of compromised nodes do not provide privacy protection and, similarly, in onion routing, paths that begin and end at compromised nodes are insecure. Participating adversaries can use a selective denial-of-service attack to reduce the availability and usability of more secure, paths in order to force users to use insecure alternatives. In this section, we will discuss how these attacks apply to two common systems—Tor [12] and Mixminion [10]—and consider some countermeasures. A more in-depth discussion of selective DoS can be found in [2].

4.8.1 Attacks on Tor

The Tor network is a widely used system for low latency anonymous Internet communication. The network has enjoyed quick growth since its initial deployment in 2003; as of November 2006, Tor is composed of approximately 800 active routers supporting hundreds of thousands of users.

Since Tor is an onion routing network, paths are compromised when the first and last routers in a tunnel are malicious, with probability c^2. To increase their odds, participating adversaries can perform a denial-of-service-attack on any tunnels that they cannot compromise. This attack is easy to implement: If the adversary acts as a first or last router in a tunnel, the tunnel is observed for a brief period of time and matched against all other tunnels where a colluding router is the last or first router, respectively. If there is a match, the tunnel is compromised; otherwise, the adversary

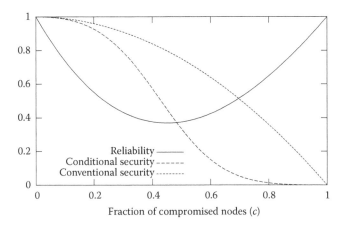

Figure 4.1   Reliability and security analysis of Tor under the selective DoS attack.

stops forwarding traffic on the tunnel, effectively killing it. The adversary also kills all tunnels where it is the middle node, unless both the previous and the next hop are also colluding.

Under this attack, a tunnel will be reliable only if the first and last nodes are compromised, or if it is composed of only honest nodes. So, the overall reliability of Tor in this case is:

$$R_{\text{DoS}} = c^2 + (1 - c)^3$$

Figure 4.1 plots the reliability of Tor under the selective DoS attack as a function of c. The reliability decreases as the number of compromised nodes grows, until it reaches a minimum at $c = 0.45$, at which point it starts to rise again. This is because at that point, the c^2 component starts to dominate; that is, the dishonest nodes start to perform DoS on fewer tunnels because they can now compromise more of them.

Figure 4.1 also shows the number of secure tunnels, as a fraction of reliable ones; i.e., the conditional probability of a tunnel being secure given that it is reliable. This is a useful calculation because the Tor software faced with a nonfunctioning tunnel, will create a new one in its place and will repeat this until a working tunnel is constructed. The conditional probability states how likely it is that this final tunnel will be secure. For low values of c, the line closely matches the conventional security figure of c^2, but with higher numbers of compromised nodes it quickly diverges. For example, with $c = 0.5$, conventional analysis suggests that 75 percent of all paths should be secure, whereas under the selective DoS attack, only 33 percent of the successful paths are uncompromised. Even if $c = 0.5$

is an unlikely fraction of colluding attackers (though perhaps not entirely unrealistic, given the volunteer nature of Tor participants), the main point is that a participating active adversary can have a much greater impact on Tor security than is shown by conventional analysis.

4.8.2 Attacks on Mixminion

Mixminion [10] and other high latency mix networks differ from Tor in their strategy for achieving anonymity in that the individual mixes perform delays and batching of incoming messages in order to frustrate traffic analysis. Therefore, it is usually not sufficient to compromise only the entry and exit points of a message, but rather the entire path of forwarders for a message must be compromised to link the source and the destination. This means that for a fraction c of compromised nodes and paths of length l, c^l messages end up being compromised. This feature of mix networks motivates the choice of longer paths for routing messages, with $l = 5$ being frequently used. Such long paths ensure that, for example, even if 50 percent of all mixes are compromised, only 3 percent of all messages can be linked. Cautious users may choose even higher values of l so that their messages remain secure even under the most pessimistic assumptions about the number of compromised mixes.

However, selective denial of service is just as easy to perform in the case of mix networks as in Tor. The goal of attackers is once again to disrupt any communication they cannot compromise; in this case, any time a message is to be either received from an honest node by a dishonest one, or sent from a dishonest one to an honest one, the message is dropped. This way, the attackers only forward messages when the path consists entirely of compromised nodes. Of course, when only honest nodes participate in forwarding a message, it is delivered as well, so the reliability of message delivery can be computed as:

$$R_{DoS} = c^l + (1 - c)^l$$

Mix networks usually lack end-to-end acknowledgments of a forwarding path; to improve reliability, Mixminion and other networks can send multiple copies of a message along multiple paths. This technique is used to address the inherent unreliability of (honest) mix nodes, but the same defense can be applied to address this selective denial-of-service attack. In both cases, redundant messages will increase the probability of a message being successfully delivered, but at the same time allow for more chances of compromise:

$$P[\text{compromise}] = \left(1 - (1 - c)^l\right)^w$$

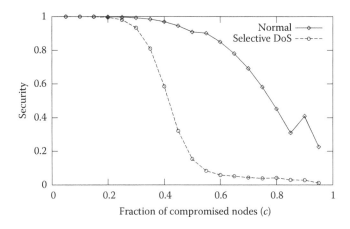

Figure 4.2   Reliability and security analysis of Mixminion under the selective DoS attack.

If we denote by f the fraction of honest nodes that are expected to fail during a single message delivery round, and by w the number of copies of a message that are sent (the "width" of a path), we can computed the revised reliability of message delivery as:

$$R_{DoS} = 1 - \left(1 - \left[c^l + ((1-c)(1-f))^l\right]\right)^w$$

It is easy to see that this figure grows with w, so the decrease in reliability due to the selective denial-of-service attack can be mitigated by sending more copies of a message. Figure 4.2 shows the effect of this defense on performance and security. In this figure, nodes tune their sending parameters w to achieve a reliability of 95 percent, with fixed $l = 5$ and $f = 0.1$. The parameters f and l are chosen to mimic the observed behavior of Mixminion nodes. We then calculate the fraction of messages that are sent through the networks that remain secure. We include the fraction also for a scenario without a selective DoS attack for comparison. It is clear that an attacker who denies service has an advantage, depicted as the gap between the two lines.

4.8.2.1   Increasing Path Lengths (l)

One response to increase security under the DoS attack may be to use longer paths. Conventional analysis suggests that higher values of l provide exponentially higher security, so nearly arbitrary security levels can easily be achieved by increasing l. Can the same approach work under the DoS strategy?

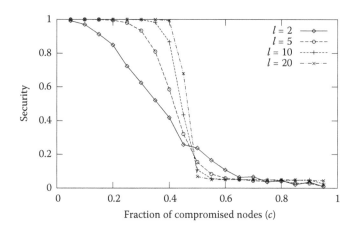

Figure 4.3   Effect of increasing path lengths.

Figure 4.3 shows the security achieved for varying values of l using the same parameters as in Figure 4.2 under the DoS strategy. For low values of c, increased values of l have the expected effect of increasing security. However, as c grows, longer paths not only do not help the security, but, in fact, are a detriment. This is because long paths make it easier for adversaries to perform DoS on paths, and the values of w required to achieve 95 percent reliability become so high that there are more opportunities for compromise.

The results show that in the presence of an active participating adversary, there is a fundamental limit on the number of compromised mixes that Mixminion and similar mix networks can withstand. When a majority of nodes are compromised, no increase in path length can avoid compromise. This limit is contrary to the conventional wisdom regarding mix network chains and demonstrates the importance of considering the Byzantime participating adversary threat model.

4.8.3   Systems Designed to Improve Reliability

Several anonymous communication systems have been designed with the explicit goal of improving reliability. We consider whether they can be used to reduce the threat of the selective DoS attack. The systems considered are Cashmere [41] and Hydra-Onions [20].

Cashmere uses the structured overlay Pastry [34] to improve reliability of anonymous communication. Briefly, instead of sending a message to a single mix, it is sent to a relay group consisting of several nodes. Particular features of Pastry routing are used to deliver the message in an anycast [26] fashion to the closest live member of the relay group, so that even if all but one of the group members are unavailable, the message will still be delivered.

Unfortunately, while this design handles nodes that fail in a fail-stop fashion, it does not handle potential Byzantine behavior of participating nodes. In particular, if the recipient of the anycast message simply drops the message, the forwarding path is broken. Therefore, the reliability of Cashmere is no better in the face of selective DoS than Mixminion with a single copy of the message. Furthermore, Cashmere uses a complicated PKI scheme that allows any member of the relay group to decrypt a message and forward it to the next group. This means that the probability of insecure paths is much higher in Cashmere than in Mixminion, since a single compromised node in each relay group compromises the entire path.

Unlike Cashmere, Hydra-Onions were engineered with Byzantine faults in mind. Hydra-Onions are similar in nature to mix networks that send multiple copies of a message along multiple paths, but Hydra-Onions introduce mixing between the multiple paths. A mix node that receives a message forwards it to the next node on the current path, as well as another node on a random other path. Thus, if a message on some path has been lost due to a failing or malicious mix router, it may be resurrected at the next step by a copy sent from another path.

Hydra-Onions, therefore, are more resilient than multiple paths used by Mixminion. They are also more vulnerable to attack: As in Cashmere, a single compromised node at each step is sufficient to compromise the entire path, whereas in Mixminion an entire path must be compromised:

$$P[\text{compromise}] = \left(1 - (1 - c)^w\right)^l$$

As can be seen in Figure 4.4, the extra vulnerability to path compromise more than compensates for the extra reliability and Hydra-Onions are no better at protecting privacy in the face of a selective-DoS attack than simple Mixminion.

4.9 Countermeasures

Recent years have seen the development of practical and generic techniques for Byzantine fault tolerance (BFT) [6]. We might hope that such techniques could be used to address Byzantine faults in anonymous systems as well. However, there are two fundamental difficulties in applying BFT to anonymity systems.

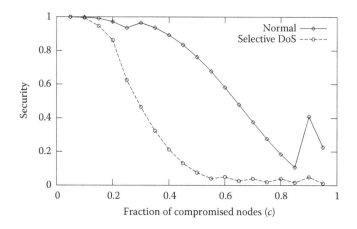

Figure 4.4 Security of Hydra-Onions under a selective DoS attack.

First, BFT algorithms rely on replicated state machines that implement the same function. But, fundamentally, a mix node is difficult to replicate because its operation relies on private state. For example, all replicas would need to be able to decrypt incoming messages and carry out the same permutation. Such replication would significantly decrease the security of the system, similar to what happened in Cashmere and Hydra-Onions. (In fact, Cashmere and Hydra-Onions both try to achieve fault tolerance through replication, though without rigorous BFT techniques.)

Second, even if replication problems could be overcome, problems of node discovery cannot be addressed with BFT techniques because they assume a static set of participating nodes, at most 1/3 of which are compromised. However, without reliable node discovery, it seems impractical to be able to create such a BFT group in the first place—a sort of "chicken and egg" problem.

There is some hope that reputation systems can help defend against Byzantine adversaries. A reputation system must accomplish two tasks: detect misbehavior and distribute information about past misbehavior among nodes in the system. Under selective DoS, for example, nodes could lose reputation whenever they are involved in a failing path; although some honest nodes would also be flagged, compromised nodes would appear more frequently among failing paths (unless half of all nodes are compromised) and could eventually be avoided. However, a robust mechanism for spreading such reputation is needed. As we saw with the MorphMix CDM, a local history is unlikely to be sufficient to effectively combat the DoS attack, but a more global reputation system creates the possibility of false reports by malicious nodes causing the reputation of honest nodes to fall. For smaller networks, a centralized solution with a globally trusted directory and verifiers may be appropriate [11], but robust reputation systems for large-scale P2P networks are still an open problem.

4.10 Conclusion

Byzantine attacks are an important consideration for anonymity systems. Given the volunteer dynamic of present and likely future anonymity networks, inserting a number of Byzantine adversaries into a network is well within reach of many attackers. And, adversaries that violate a protocol can be significantly more effective than honest-but-curious adversaries, or the traditional global passive adversary. Therefore, proposed and fielded systems must be evaluated against the Byzantine model.

At the same time, such evaluation is currently difficult, since the space of possible Byzantine behaviors is vast and analysis of some Byzantine strategies may miss other, more successful ones, as was the case with MorphMix. We, therefore, close with two important research challenges: effective countermeasures to the path compromise attacks we describe, and a systematic approach to verifying a system's resistance to Byzantine attacks.

References

[1] Kevin Bauer, Damon McCoy, Dirk Grunwald, Tadayoshi Kohno, and Douglas Sicker. Low-resource routing attacks against Tor. In *ACM Workshop on Privacy in Electronic Society*, Alexandria, VA. ACM Press, October 2007.

[2] Steven M. Bellovin and David A. Wagner, Eds. *2003 IEEE Symposium on Security and Privacy*, Berkeley, CA. IEEE Computer Society, May 2003.

[3] Oliver Berthold, Andreas Pfitzmann, and Ronny Standtke. The disadvantages of free MIX routes and how to overcome them. In Federrath [17], pp.30–45.

[4] Nikita Borisov. Computational puzzles as Sybil defenses. In Montresor and Wierzbicki [23], pp.171–176.

[5] Nikita Borisov, George Danezis, Prateek Mittal, and Parisa Tabriz. Denial of service or denial of security? How attacks on reliability can compromise anonymity. In *ACM Conference on Computer and Communications Security*, Alexandria, VA. ACM Press, October 2007.

[6] Miguel Castro and Barbara Liskov. Practical byzantine fault tolerance. In *USENIX Symposium on Operating Systems Design and Implementation (OSDI)*, New Orleans, LA. USENIX Association, 1999.

[7] David Chaum. Untraceable Electronic Mail, Return Addresses, and Digital Pseudonyms. *Communications of the ACM*, 24(2):84–88, 1981.

[8] David Chaum. The dining cryptographers problem: Unconditional sender and recipient untraceability. *Journal of Cryptology*, 1(1):65–75, 1988.

[9] George Danezis and Richard Clayton. Route fingerprinting in anonymous communications. In Montresor and Wierzbicki [23], pp. 69–72.

[10] George Danezis, Roger Dingledine, and Nick Mathewson. Mixminion: Design of a type III anonymous remailer protocol. In Bellovin and Wagner [2], pp. 2–15.

[11] Roger Dingledine, Michael J. Freedman, David Hopwood, and David Molnar. A reputation system to increase MIX-Net reliability. In Ira S. Moskowitz, editor, *Information Hiding*, vol. 2137 of *Lecture Notes in Computer Science*, pages 126–141, Cambridge, MA: Springer, 2001.

[12] Roger Dingledine, Nick Mathewson, and Paul F. Syverson. Tor: The Second-Generation Onion Router. In *USENIX Security Symposium*, pp. 303–320, 2004.

[13] Roger Dingledine, Vitaly Shmatikov, and Paul F. Syverson. Synchronous batching: From cascades to free routes. In David Martin and Andrei Serjantov, editors, *Privacy Enhancing Technologies*, volume 3424 of *Lecture Notes in Computer Science*, pp. 186–206, Pittsburgh, PA: Springer, 2004.

[14] D. Dolev and A. Yao. On the security of public key protocols. *IEEE Transactions on Information Theory*, 9(2):198–208, March 1983.24

[15] John Douceur. The Sybil Attack. In *International Workshop on Peer-to-Peer Systems (IPTPS)*, Cambridge, MA: Springer, March 2002.

[16] eDonkey File Sharing System, 2003.

[17] Hannes Federrath, Ed. *Designing Privacy Enhancing Technologies: Workshop on Design Issues in Anonymity and Unobservability*, Springer-Verlag, July 2000.

[18] Michael J. Freedman and Robert Morris. Tarzan: A peer-to-peer anonymizing network layer. In *9th ACM Conference on Computer and Communications Security*, Washington, DC. ACM SIGSAC, 2002.

[19] Ceki Gülcü and Gene Tsudik. Mixing E-mail with Babel. In *Network and Distributed Security Symposium (NDSS)*, pp. 2–16, San Diego, CA, February 1996.

[20] Jan Iwanik, Marek Klonowski, and Miroslaw Kutylowski. Duo–onions and hydra–onions – failure and adversary resistant onion protocols. In *IFIP TC-6 TC-11 Conference on Communications and Multimedia Security*, September 2004.

[21] Leslie Lamport, Robert Shostak, and Marshall Pease. The byzantine generals problem. *ACM Transactions on Programming Languages and Systems (TOPLAS)*, 4(3):382–401, July 1982.

[22] Ulf Möller, Lance Cottrell, Peter Palfrader, and Len Sassaman. Mixmaster Protocol — Version 2. Draft, available at: http://www.abditum.com/mixmaster-spec.txt, July 2003.

[23] Alberto Montresor and Adam Wierzbicki, editors. *Sixth IEEE International Conference on Peer-to-Peer Computing*, Cambridge, United Kingdom. IEEE Computer Society, 2006.

[24] Steven J. Murdoch and George Danezis. Low-cost traffic analysis of Tor. In *IEEE Symposium on Security and Privacy*, pages 183–195, Berkeley, CA. IEEE Computer Society, 2005.

[25] Lasse Øverlier and Paul Syverson. Locating hidden servers. In *IEEE Symposium on Security and Privacy*, Berkeley, CA. IEEE Computer Society, May 2006.

[26] C. Partridge, T. Mendez, and W. Milliken. Host anycasting service. RFC1546, November 1993.

[27] Andreas Pfitzmann and Marit Hansen. Anonymity, unlinkability, unde-tectability, unobservability, pseudonymity, and identity management — a consolidated proposal for terminology. Version 0.29, available at: http://dud.inf.tu-dresden.de/Anon Terminology.shtml, July 2007.

[28] Birgit Pfitzmann and Andreas Pfitzmann. How to break the direct RSA-implementation of MIXes. In *Advanced in Cryptology — EUROCRYPT '89*, Houthalen, Belgium. Springer-Verlag, April 1989.

[29] Jean-Francois Raymond. Traffic Analysis: Protocols, Attacks, Design Issues, and Open Problems. In Federrath [17], pp. 10–29.

[30] Michael K. Reiter and Aviel D. Rubin. Crowds: Anonymity for Web trans-actions. *ACM Transactions on Information and System Security TISSEC*, 1(1):66–92, 1998.25.

[31] Marc Rennhard. *MorphMix—A Peer-to-Peer-based System for Anonymous Internet Access.* PhD thesis, Swiss Federal Institute of Technology Zurich, 2004.

[32] Marc Rennhard. MorphMix prototype v0.1, 2004.

[33] Marc Rennhard and Bernhard Plattner. Introducing MorphMix: Peer-to-peer based anonymous Internet usage with collusion detection. In *Workshop on Privacy in the Electronic Society (WPES)*, Washington, DC, November 2002.

[34] Antony Rowstron and Peter Druschel. Pastry: Scalable, distributed object location and routing for large-scale peer-to-peer systems. In *IFIP/ACM International Conference on Distributed Systems Platforms (Middleware)*, pp. 329–350, Heidelberg, Germany. Springer, November 2001.

[35] Andrei Serjantov, Roger Dingledine, and Paul Syverson. From a trickle to a flood: Active attacks on several mix types. In Fabien Petitcolas, editor, *Information Hiding Workshop (IH)*. Springer-Verlag, October 2002.

[36] Andrei Serjantov and Steven J. Murdoch. Message splitting against the par-tial adversary. In *Privacy Enhancing Technologies Workshop (PET)*, Cavtat, Croatia. Springer, May 2005.

[37] Paul Syverson, Gene Tsudik, Michael Reed, and Carl Landwehr. Towards an Analysis of Onion Routing Security. In Federrath [17], pp. 96–114.

[38] Parisa Tabriz and Nikita Borisov. Breaking the collusion detection mecha-nism of MorphMix. In *Workshop on Privacy Enhancing Technologies (PET)*, Cambridge, United Kingdom. Springer, June 2006.

[39] Matthew Wright, Micah Adler, Brian Neil Levine, and Clay Shields. An analy-sis of the degradation of anonymous protocols. In *Network and Distributed Security Symposium (NDSS)*. Internet Society, February 2002.

[40] Matthew Wright, Micah Adler, Brian Neil Levine, and Clay Shields. Defend-ing anonymous communication against passive logging attacks. In Bellovin and Wagner [2].

[41] Li Zhuang, Feng Zhou, Ben Y. Zhao, and Antony Rowstron. Cashmere: Resilient anonymous routing. In *USENIX Symposium on Networked Systems Design and Implementation (NSDI)*, Boston, MA. USENIX Association, May 2005.

Chapter 5

Introducing Traffic Analysis

George Danezis and Richard Clayton

Contents

5.1   Introduction 95
5.2   Military Roots...96
5.3   Civilian Traffic Analysis 99
5.4   Contemporary Computer and Communications Security 101
      5.4.1   The Traffic Analysis of SSH 102
      5.4.2   The Traffic Analysis of SSL 103
      5.4.3   Web Privacy 103
      5.4.4   Network Device Identification and Mapping..............104
      5.4.5   Detecting Stepping Stones 106
5.5   Exploiting Location Data...106
5.6   Resisting Traffic Analysis on the Internet 107
5.7   Data Retention 110
5.8   Conclusion 112
References..112

5.1   Introduction

In World War II, traffic analysis was used by the British at Bletchley Park to assess the size of Germany's air force, and Japanese traffic analysis countermeasures contributed to the surprise of the 1941 attack on Pearl Harbor. Nowadays, Google uses the incidence of links to assess the relative importance of Web pages, credit card companies examine transactions to spot fraudulent patterns of spending, and amateur plane spotters revealed the CIA's "extraordinary rendition" program. Diffie and Landau, in their book on wiretapping, went so far as to say that "traffic analysis, not cryptanalysis, is the backbone of communications intelligence" [1]. However, until recently the topic has been neglected by computer science academics. A rich literature discusses how to secure the confidentiality, integrity, and availability of communication content, but very little work has considered the information leaked from communications "traffic data" and how these compromises might be minimized.

Traffic data records the time and duration of a communication, and traffic analysis examines this data to determine the detailed shape of the communication streams, the identities of the parties communicating, and what can be established about their locations. The data may even be sketchy or incomplete—simply knowing what "typical" communication patterns look like can be used to infer information about a particular observed communication.

Civilian infrastructures, on which state and economic actors are increasingly reliant, are ever more vulnerable to traffic analysis: Wireless and Groupe Spécial Mobile (GSM) telephony are replacing traditional systems, routing is transparent, and protocols are overlaid over others—giving plenty of opportunity to observe and take advantage of the traffic data. Concretely, an attacker can make use of this information to gather strategic intelligence or to penetrate particular security protocols and, thus, violate traditional security properties.

In this short introduction to the topic, we will highlight the key issues around traffic analysis. We start with its military roots and present the defenses that the military has developed. We then consider how traffic analysis is being used in modern civilian contexts. We move on to specific "computer science" issues, and provide an overview of the relevant research literature on attacks and defenses in contemporary networks. Finally, we discuss some of the current, rather contentious, policy issues relating to the retention of traffic data.

5.2 Military Roots

Traffic analysis is a key component of signal intelligence and electronic warfare. In his book, *Intelligence Power in Peace and War* [2], Michael Herman, who has served as chair of the U.K. Joint Intelligence Committee, discusses how information about messages (which he calls "nontextual" to distinguish it from the message content) is capable of establishing "targets' locations, order-of-battle and movement." He goes on to make the comparison that even when messages are not being deciphered, traffic analysis "provides indications of his [the enemy's] intentions and states of mind, in rather the same way as a neurologist develops insights about a silent patient by studying EEG traces from the brain."

Traffic analysis was used by the military even before the invention of wireless communications, but it was the broadcast nature of radio, permitting anyone to listen in, that transformed its usefulness. The first naval action of World War I, on August 5, 1914, was the cutting of Germany's trans-Atlantic cables by the British cable ship *Telconia* [3], so that wireless telegraphy would have to be used instead of hard-to-intercept cable communications. Traffic analysis became an extremely potent source of intelligence as wireless communication became more widespread, particularly in naval and air operations. Ships at sea had to balance the value of communicating against the threat of being detected via direction finding if they transmitted. When transmitting, strict standards, governing call signs and communication procedures, had to be adhered to in order to minimize the information that traffic analysis could provide.

Another example of traffic analysis providing valuable intelligence [2] is the British reconstruction in 1941 of the structure of the German air force radio network. This confirmed that a unit was composed of nine and not twelve planes, which led to a more accurate estimate of total strength. Identification of radio equipment was also used for accurate detection of redeployments: each transmitter can be "fingerprinted" by characteristics such as unintentional frequency modulations, the shape of the transmitter turn-on signal transient, the precise center of frequency modulation, and so on. These fingerprints can be used to track the device even though the messages it is transmitting are in an unbreakable code. Similar techniques can be used today to identify GSM phones [4]. In World War II, radio operators became skilled at recognizing the "fist" of other operators, i.e., the characteristic way in which they typed their Morse code. Indeed, prior to Pearl Harbor, the Japanese transferred their aircraft carrier radio operators ashore and took replacement crews, in order to persuade any eavesdropping Americans that the Japanese fleet was still in port. Even in more modern times, as the Desert Storm campaign began in 1991, the British Operation Rhino replayed radio traffic from an exercise a few weeks earlier and, thereby, misled the Iraqi forces as to where they were attacking [5].

Intelligence does not necessarily come from radio communications. The recording of aircraft identification numbers by amateur plane-spotting enthusiasts the world over permitted the reconstruction of recent CIA activities, and helped to prove the existence of their "extraordinary rendition" program, which transferred terrorist suspects to third countries for imprisonment and interrogation [6].

Why is traffic analysis so valuable to the military? The technique, although impressive in what it can determine, provides lower quality information when compared with cryptanalysis and recovery of message content. However, it is both easier and cheaper to extract and process traffic data than content. It is easier because ciphers need considerable effort to break (when they break at all). It is cheaper because traffic data can be automatically collected and processed to provide high level intelligence. Computers can collect traffic data and map out structures and locations, while a skilled human operator is needed to listen to every radio transmission (often in a foreign language) in order to extract intelligence. For these reasons, traffic analysis is often used to perform "target selection" for further intelligence gathering (such as more intensive and expensive surveillance), jamming, or destruction. Given the enormous amount of communication and information on public networks we can expect these "economics of surveillance" to be ever more relevant and applicable.

An insight into the power of traffic analysis in the military setting, and its relationship with code breaking techniques, can be obtained by working through the Zendian Problem [7]. This is a series of problems concerning a fictitious operation against the totalitarian island of Zendia that were used on a course taught to U.S. National Security Agency (NSA) cryptanalysts in the late 1950s, and that have now been declassified.

Signals Intelligence (or Sigint), the military term for techniques that include traffic analysis, is an arms race, and many "low probability of intercept and position fix" communication methods have been devised by the military to minimize exposure to traffic analysis and jamming (see [4]). Their principles of operation are simple: scanning many frequencies can only be done at some maximal rate and a great deal of power is necessary to jam a wide part of the frequency spectrum. Therefore, the first technique used to evade interception and foil jamming was "frequency hopping," now used in commercial GSM communications to improve reliability in the face of environmental noise. The basic technique is for Alice and Bob to share a key that determines, for each given time period, the frequency at which they will transmit. Eve, on the other hand, does not know the key and has to observe or jam the entirety of the frequency spectrum that may be used. In practice, hopping is cheap and easy to implement, and makes it difficult to jam the signal (given that the hop frequency is high enough), but it is poor at hiding the fact that communication is taking place. It is mainly used for tactical battlefield communications, where the adversary is unlikely to have very large jammers on hand.

A second technique is called Direct Sequence Spread Spectrum (DSSS). This transforms a high-power, low-bandwidth signal into a high-bandwidth, low-power signal, using a key that is shared between Alice and Bob. It is easy for them to pick out the transmitted signal, using their key, but an adversary will have to try to extract the signal from the noise, a difficult task given its low power (that will ideally be under the noise floor). DSSS has also inspired commercial communication systems and is now used in

Asymmetric Digital Subscriber Line (ADSL) and cable modems as Code Division Multiple Access (CDMA). Its most significant implementation problem is synchronization, and the availability of a reference signal (such as the Global Positioning System (GPS)) is of great help when implementing a practical system.

The final technique in the arsenal against interception is "burst communication." The key idea is to communicate in a very short burst, so as to minimize the probability that the adversary is monitoring the particular frequency being used at the relevant time. A cute variant of this is meteor scatter communications, which uses the ionization trail of small meteorites hitting the atmosphere to bounce transmissions between special forces troops in the field and a base station. Meteor scatter can also be used in civilian applications when low bandwidth, high latency, but very low cost and high availability communications are required.

5.3   Civilian Traffic Analysis

Contemporary sociology models groups of individuals, not as a mass or a fluid, but in terms of their positions within a "social network." The paradigm that underpins much of this research is that the position of an agent in the social network is in many ways more characteristic of them than any of their individual attributes. This position determines their status, but also their capacity to mobilize social resources and act (social capital). This position can also be determined via traffic analysis, yielding a map of the social network, and the position of each actor within it.

Social Network Analysis [8], and experimental studies, have recently gained popularity and led to interesting results that are of use not only to traffic analysis, but also to network engineering more generally. It was first noted by Milgram [9] that typical social networks present a "small world" property, in that they have a low diameter (experimentally determined to be about six hops between any two members) and are efficiently navigable. In other words, there are short paths (i.e., intermediaries) between you and anyone else in the world, and you can find them efficiently, for example by using hints from location and profession. This work has been used to build efficient peer-to-peer networks, but remains underused in security and trust analysis. Another key finding is that weak links—people you do not know all that well—are instrumental in helping you with activities that are not commonplace, but still very important. A well-studied example is finding a job, where people using "far links" are, on average, more successful than those who limit themselves to their local contacts [10].

The first mathematical studies [11] of social networks (or "power law networks" as they are often described because of the degree distribution of their edges) tell us a lot about their resilience to failure. It turns out that they are extremely resistant to random node failures, meaning that they stay connected and maintain a low diameter even when many random nodes have been removed. On the other hand, such networks are very sensitive to the targeted removal of the nodes with high degree. After a few nodes have been removed, the network will become disconnected and, well before that, the diameter increases substantially. An equally effective attack is for an adversary to remove nodes according to their "between-ness," i.e., how many other nodes they are connected to in the network. Traffic analysis can be used to select the appropriate targets to maximize communication degradation and disruption.

Carley et al. [12] proposed using network tools to disrupt networks of terrorists, and addressed the issues raised when multiple agents were involved, so that removing a single leader would be effective. Garfinkel [13] considers the Leaderless Resistance model of self-organizing independent cells without any central control. He notes that it is "a desperate strategy employed by movements that do not have broad popular support and that fear infiltrators" and makes a number of policy suggestions for combating it. More recent research by Nagaraja and Anderson [14] tries to find strategies for a peer-to-peer network of nodes to resist node deletion attacks. The intuition behind these defensive strategies is that nodes connect to other random nodes in order to get resilience, while connecting according to a power law strategy to get efficient routing. When under attack the network regenerates links to maximize fault tolerance, and when things are calmer, it reconfigures itself to be efficient.

Social network analysis is starting to be used for criminal intelligence [15,16]. Investigators try to map out criminal organizations by the use of traffic analysis techniques on telephone or network traffic and location data. This can be used to select targets for more intensive surveillance, and also to select appropriate targets for arrest and prosecution. Often these arrests are aiming to maximally disrupt the organization targeted. It is not always appropriate to arrest the most central or the most well-connected member—this would merely serve as a promotion opportunity for smaller crooks to take up the position. It is found to be more effective to arrest the specialists, i.e., those people in the organization that have a unique position or skills that others would find difficult to fill. Examples include those who can forge papers or crooked customs officials.

Similar techniques were used by the U.S. military to locate Saddam Hussein in 2003. Tribal and family linkages were used to identify particular individuals with close ties to him, and these were selected for closer surveillance [17]. The latest (December 2006) U.S. Army Counterinsurgency Manual now specifically deals with social network analysis, and discusses the Saddam Hussein operation as an example [18]. The ties between the 9/11 conspirators have also been mapped and these connections clearly pick out Mohamed Atta as the central figure [19]. Additionally, Dombrowski et al. [20] show how it is possible to predict the shape of a social network only some of whose members and links are known.

Moving away from social links, in the 1970s the German police searched for Baader-Meinhof safe houses by analyzing gas and electricity records, looking for rented apartments with spikes in fuel usage where the bills were paid by transfers from banks in different parts of the country. Thirty years later, the United Kingdom police searched for cannabis farms (where the plants are kept warm in artificial sunlight) by looking for unusually heavy usage of electricity or, if the meter has been overridden, a mismatch between the power consumed in a locality and that which is billed for. An infrared scan from a helicopter will then locate the house that is warmer than its neighbors. In more academic work, Fawcett and Provost [21] show how data-mining techniques can be used to detect cellular phone fraud, with their automated approach proving better than handcrafted detection rules.

Traffic analysis-inspired techniques can also be used to protect systems and build trust. Advogato [22] is a social network-based system that provides a community for free software developers. The fact that they are introduced to each other allows the system to establish whether an author is likely to be a spammer and filter their messages out. Gibson et al. [23] observed that the apparently anarchic structure of Web page links could be seen to comprise many communities with central "authoritative" pages linked by "hub pages." Google's PageRank [24] uses techniques that are very similar to Web page and social network profiling—it considers pages that are more central in the network (with more links pointing to them) as more authoritative. Techniques have also been devised [25] to automatically detect and extract Web communities. These results can be used both to assist and to attack users.

In a different milieu, Renesys Corporation monitors the Internet's global routing table and analyses the Border Gateway Protocol (BGP) traffic sent by service providers as they announce the blocks of Internet Protocol (IP) addresses for which they will carry traffic. Analysis of this data permits Renesys to generate market intelligence indicating when major Internet Service Provider (ISP) customers are starting to move to new providers, when ISP market share is changing, or the impact of mergers or acquisitions on customer numbers [26].

5.4 Contemporary Computer and Communications Security

Traffic analysis techniques can naturally be applied to Internet communications. Secured systems can be successfully attacked and sensitive information extracted. However, a key difference to keep in mind when studying civilian traffic analysis research is that the attackers are generally far from omnipotent. It is not military powers with large budgets and the ability to intercept most communications that worry us, but commercial entities, local governments, law enforcement, criminal organizations, and terrorist networks that have become the adversary. Therefore, research has focused on attacks and solutions that can be deployed at low cost and provide tangible tactical benefits (a pass phrase, a record of Web accesses, etc.). Beyond this, more strategic work is beginning to be done on the ways in which Internet traffic analysis can be of use to law enforcement, along with practical approaches for ensuring that routine surveillance can be evaded.

So what can we do if we are not allowed to look at the plaintext content?

5.4.1   The Traffic Analysis of SSH

The Secure Shell (SSH) protocol permits users to log into remote terminals in a secure fashion. It does this by performing authentication using a public keyring, with the private keys accessed locally via a passphrase. It subsequently encrypts all information transmitted or received, guaranteeing its confidentiality and integrity. One would think that any subsequent password entry (that might be required to log into further remote services), over an SSH connection, should be safe. However, Song et al. [27] show that there is a lot of information still leaking. In interactive mode, SSH transmits every key stroke as a packet and, hence, the password length is trivially available.

However, because keyboard layouts are not random and passwords are often based upon real words, the exact timing of the keystrokes is related to how quickly one particular character can be typed after another. Hence, more advanced techniques, using hidden Markov models, can be used to extract further information from interpacket timing and lower the effective entropy of the passwords, thereby making brute force guessing far easier.

It turns out that you do not need to measure the typing abilities of the person entering the password and another user can be used to build a profile because the similarities between users are exploitable. This links in with subtly different results from Monrose and Rubin's [28] research on identifying and authenticating users using keystroke dynamics. Although their focus was on biometrics and authentication, their results have a clear relevance to the traffic analysis of SSH. They show that there can be enough variability in typing patterns between users to be able to identity them, particularly after a long sequence has been observed. As a result, not only the content of your communications may be leaked, but also your identity—despite all of the confidentiality that SSH apparently affords.

5.4.2   The Traffic Analysis of SSL

The Secure Sockets Layer (SSL), and its close friend Transport Layer Security (TLS), were introduced primarily to provide private Web access. HTTP protocol requests and replies are encrypted and authenticated between clients and servers to prevent information from leaking. Yet there is plenty of research [29–33] to suggest that information is leaking out of this shell.

The key weaknesses come down to the shape of traffic that is inadequately padded and concealed. Browsers request resources, often HTML pages, that are also associated with additional resources (images, stylesheets, etc.). These are downloaded through an encrypted link, yet their size is apparent to an observer, and can be used to infer which pages are accessed (e.g., it would be possible to tell which specific company reports were being downloaded by an investment banker, with consequent possibilities for profitable stock trading). There are many variants of this attack: some attempt to build a profile of the Web site pages and guess which pages are being accessed, while others use these techniques to overcome naive anonymizing SSL proxies. In the latter cases, the attacker has access to the cleartext input streams and he tries to match them with encrypted connections made to the proxy.

It should be noted that latent structure and contextual knowledge are of great use when extracting information from traffic analysis. Levene and Loizou [34] provided a theoretical basis for computing the entropy of Web navigation and demonstrated that this "surfing" should not be seen as just random. Danezis [32] assumed that users will usually follow links between different Web resources. By learning merely the approximate lengths of the resources that were accessed, he showed that a hidden Markov model can be used to trace the most likely browsing paths a user may have taken. This approach provides much faster and more reliable results than considering users that browse at random, or Web sites that have no structure at all.

5.4.3   Web Privacy

Can a remote Web server that you are accessing tell if you have also been browsing another site? If you were looking at a competitor's site, then maybe giving you a better price might be in order.

Felten et al. [35] show that it is possible to use the caching features of modern Web browsers to infer information about the Web sites that they have been previously browsing. The key intuition is that recently accessed resources are cached and, therefore, will load much more quickly than if they had to be downloaded from the remote site. Thus, by embedding some foreign resources into a served page, the attacker's Web server can perform some timing measurements and infer particular previous browsing activity.

Note that this attack can be performed even if the communication medium is anonymous and unlinkable. Most anonymization techniques work at the network layer making it difficult to observe network identities, but perform only minimal filtering in higher layers. The presence of caches leads to the Felten attack, but doing away with any caching would be a major problem for anonymous communication designers, since it is important to use any efficiency improvements possible to make the already slow browsing more usable.

5.4.4 Network Device Identification and Mapping

Can you tell if two different addresses on the Internet are, in fact, the same physical computer? Kohno et al. at CAIDA [36] have devised a technique that allows an attacker to determine if two apparently different machines are the same device. They note that the clock skew (the amount by which the clock drifts per unit of time) is characteristic of a particular machine, differing even amongst otherwise identical models from the same manufacturer. Therefore, if the clock drift of two remote machines seems to match for a long time, it is possible to conclude that there is just one machine present. The technique they use is resistant to latency and can be applied remotely, even if the target machine synchronizes its clock with Network Time Protocol (NTP).

The technique can be used in forensics to link visiting machine identities together, and to determine if two Web sites are hosted on the same consolidated server. Equally, it can be used by hackers to detect if the multiple machines they are accessing are merely different versions of a virtualized honey-pot machine.

Murdoch [37] has extended this work by observing that the clock skew will change as the temperature changes. He has shown that, by modulating the amount of traffic sent to a machine, he can affect the amount of work it must do, and he can detect the resultant changes in system temperature by examining variations in the clock skew. Hence, if he accesses a "hidden" machine via an anonymizing overlay network (such as Tor [38]) and varies how much traffic he sends to it, then it will heat up and cool down as the workload changes. If he can observe a corresponding pattern of clock skew change on a candidate machine to which direct access is possible, this is sufficient to link that machine to the hidden identity—and the anonymization scheme is overcome.

The opposite question is often of interest—are machines physically different? Given two connections originating from the same network address, have they actually been initiated by one or multiple machines? It can be of particular relevance to count the number of machines behind NAT (Network Address Translation) gateways and firewalls. Bellovin [39] noted that the TCP/IP stack of many operating systems provides a host specific signature that can be detected and used to estimate the number of hosts behind a gateway. To be exact, in many operating systems at that time, the field identifier (IPID), used as a unique number for each IP packet, was a simple counter that was incremented every time a packet is transmitted. By plotting the IPID packets over time and fitting lines through the graph, one could estimate the number of unique Windows hosts. However, this technique is becoming less effective because many systems now scramble the IPID field to prevent "idle scanning" (as discussed further below) and so more complex analysis would now be necessary.

In IPv6 (the latest Internet protocol version) device addresses consist of a 64-bit network prefix and a 64-bit network identifier. This identifier needs to be unique, and initial proposals were for it to be constructed from the 48-bit Ethernet media access control (MAC) address for the interface. However, this provides a way for remote systems to link visits from the same mobile machine, despite them coming from different network locations. Narten and Draves (RFC3041) [40] developed a "privacy extension" for allocating identifiers randomly, and Aura (RFC3972) [41] documented a method of creating IPv6 addresses that are bound to a public key, so that machines could formally demonstrate address ownership without disclosing their identity to remote systems. However, Escudero Pascual [42] criticizes these schemes, particularly because it is possible for remote machines to determine that visitors are using privacy preserving addresses, which may in itself be sufficient to make their traffic stand out.

Finally, many network mapping techniques have been introduced in the applied security world and included in tools such as **nmap** [43]. The key operations that such tools perform are scanning for network hosts, scanning for open network ports on hosts, and identifying the operating systems and services running on them. This information is then used to assess whether they might be vulnerable to attack. The degree of sophistication of these tools has increased with the deployment of network intrusion detection system (IDS) tools, such as the open source **snort** [44] that can detect the scanning activities. **nmap** now can be configured to detect hosts and open ports using a variety of techniques, including straightforward **ping**, TCP connect, TCP SYN packet, as well as indirect scans. For example, idle scanning involves forging a TCP open (SYN) packet claiming to be from a third-party machine and destined to the target. It is possible to determine whether the target was prepared to accept the connection (it will send SYN/ACK) or if the port is "closed" (it will send RST or nothing). This is done by determining if the IPID value of the third-party machine has been altered by the sending of a RST in response to the unexpected (to it)

SYN/ACK. The obvious advantage is that any IDS at the target will believe that the third-party machine is the instigator of the scan. The full **nmap** documentation is well worth a read [45].

5.4.5 Detecting Stepping Stones

Much work has been done by the intrusion detection community to establish if a host is being used as an attack platform [46,47]. The usual scenario involves a firewall that sees incoming and outgoing connections, and tries to establish if a pair of them may be carrying the same stream. This might mean that the internal machine is compromised and used to attack another host, i.e., it is a "stepping stone" for the attacker to hide his identity.

The two main classes of techniques for detecting stepping stones are passive, where the firewall only observes the streams, and active, where the stream of data is modulated (often called "watermarked"). Since an adversary is controlling the content of the stream, and may be encrypting it, both types of detection rely on traffic data—usually the correlation between packet inter arrival times—to match incoming and outgoing streams. The family of traffic analysis techniques that arise are similar to those that are used to attack anonymous communication channels.

The key result in this area [48,49] is that, if the maximum latency of the communication is bounded, there is no way of escaping detection in the long run. This result is, of course, tied to a particular model (the adversary can match packet for packet, which is not obvious if the streams are encrypted under different keys or mixed with other streams), and covert channels out of its scope may prove it wrong and escape detection. It is worth observing that an arbitrary set of active detectors is extremely difficult (maybe even impossible) to defeat.

5.5 Exploiting Location Data

Wireless communication equipment often leaks location data to third parties, or wireless operators. The extent to which this data can be used to degrade security properties is still to be seen, but some experiments have already been performed, and their results are a precursor of a much richer set of attacks to come.

Escudero Pascual [50] describes an experiment he set up at the Hacker's-at-Large (HAL) summer camp. The camp had multiple wireless LAN access points, which recorded the wireless MAC address of the users whose traffic they handled. This provided a time-map of users' movements throughout the event, including clues about which talks they attended (the access points were related to the venues). Even more striking were the inferences that could be drawn about the relationship between users: random pairs of users could be expected to have a low probability of using the same access point at any time and access point usage between them should be uncorrelated over time. As a result, any above average correlation between two users is indicative of a social relationship between the users, i.e., they are consistently moving together at the same time around the camp.

Intel Research at Cambridge U.K., designed a similar experiment. Members of staff were issued Bluetooth devices that would record when another transmitting Bluetooth device was in range. The idea was to measure the ambient Bluetooth activity, not only to tune ad hoc routing protocols for real world conditions, but also to establish how often a random pair of devices meet, thereby establishing how effective the ad hoc communication infrastructure would be for two-way communications. To the surprise of the researchers analyzing the data, the devices of two members of staff were found to be meeting each other rather often at night, which led them to draw conclusions about their, otherwise undisclosed, relationship.

This is completely in line with evidence gathered by the MIT Reality Mining project [51]. The project distributed about one hundred mobile phones to students and staff of the Media Lab under the condition that all their traffic data (GSM, Bluetooth, and location data) could be used for analysis. The users were also asked to fill in forms about themselves and who they considered to be their friends or colleagues. The traffic data and questionnaires were then used to build classifiers. It turned out that calling or being with someone at 8 p.m. on a Saturday night is a very good indicator of friendship.

They also uncovered location signatures that could differentiate a student from a member of the staff. What is even more impressive is that they did not use the physical locations to draw inferences, but instead the frequency at which they were found to be at places designated as "work" or "home." Students tended to have a more uncertain schedule, while members of the staff were much more predictable in their habits. This, of course, led to research about the amount of entropy that location data provides and, as might be expected, for some individuals (if one is given a set of locations and time), it is possible to predict with high probability their next move and new location.

So, the evidence from these preliminary studies is highly suggestive that whatever the wireless medium used—mobile phone, wireless LAN, or Bluetooth—sensitive information about your identity, your relations to others, and your intentions can be inferred merely though traffic analysis.

5.6 Resisting Traffic Analysis on the Internet

A relatively old, but only recently mainstream, subarea of computer security research is concerned with "anonymous communications" and, more generally, communications that do not leak any residual information from their meta data. The field was started by Chaum [52], introducing the Mix as a basic building block for anonymity, and has continued since, adapting the techniques to provide private e-mail communications and more recently Web browsing. A thorough overview of the field and key results is available in two recent Ph.D. theses by Danezis and Serjantov [53,54].

Fielded anonymous communication systems that are the direct products of twenty years of research, include Mixmaster [55] and Mixminion [56] for e-mail, and JAP [57] and Tor [38] for Web browsing. They all increase the latency of communication and its cost in terms of traffic volumes.

A range of traffic analysis attacks has been used to degrade the security of anonymous communications networks. Long-term intersection attacks (also referred to as disclosure attacks) exploit long-term observations of input and output messages to detect communicating parties. These attacks [58–61] consider the anonymity network as a black box, and only observe parties sending and receiving messages. The key observation is that for anonymous communications to be usable, the latency of messages has to be bounded. As a result, the act of sending a message is correlated in time, albeit not exactly, with observing the corresponding message being received. An adversary, therefore, can observe the anonymity system for a sufficiently long period to obviate the lack of exactness, and infer the communication relationships between different users, and in turn de-anonymize the messages. Since this family of attacks in not concerned with the internals of the anonymity network, it is considered to represent a fundamental limit on how well any such technology can protect users against traffic analysis.

Stream traffic analysis has been used to trace Web requests and replies through low latency networks. Such attacks make use of the timing of the packet streams transferred by each anonymizing relay to follow the connection between the communicating parties. Packet counting is the simplest variant—an adversary simply counts the number of packets in a certain time interval and tries to match it with the number of packets on another network link [54]. Low latency anonymity systems are required to transport packets so quickly that this attack is often possible. A slightly more sophisticated method involves creating a template (a probabilistic model) of the stream to be traced, and matching it with other streams [53]. Unless a very strict traffic regime is imposed, with the side effect of slowing down data transfer or adding large amounts of dummy traffic, such attacks will always be successful in the long run. As a result, stream tracing attacks also represent a fundamental limit on the anonymity of low latency systems.

Finally, the attacker can infiltrate the network or try to influence the way in which honest nodes chose paths to anonymize their traffic. An important study of the effect of insiders on the security of anonymity systems is presented by Wright et al. [62], along with the predecessor attack on the crowds anonymity system. Crowds implements a simple pass-the-parcel algorithm to anonymize traffic: Messages are passed from one node to the other, until one of them—with some preset probability—sends it out onto the network. Only link encryption is used, and the intention is that anonymity will be achieved because although nodes will know the content of messages, they will not be able to tell who the initial sender of the message was. The predecessor attack relies upon nodes having persistent patterns of communications. This means that the actual initiator will appear as the predecessor of a particular message or request rather more often than other random nodes (that merely relay the communications).

Lately, attacks have focused on weaker adversaries, such as those considered by the Tor system, and it has been shown that some forms of traffic analysis can be performed without even having any access at all to the actual data streams to be traced. In particular, remote network monitoring techniques have been used to lower the anonymity of Tor [63]. Streams travelling over the same infrastructure influence each other's timing and, therefore, can be used by an adversary to perform traffic analysis on remote hosts. Similarly, as already mentioned, covert channels based on the effects of temperature on clock drift can be used to de-anonymize servers [37]. The fact that even such minuscule phenomena can be used to perform traffic analysis against hardened systems illustrates how difficult the task of securing systems against traffic analysis is. It also illustrates that so little importance has been paid to securing public networks against traffic analysis that the information leaked can be detected and abused far, far away from its source.

Source and destination network addresses are not the only raw material for traffic analysis: The timing characteristics of encrypted traffic on a link, such as its frequency or particular bursts, may also reveal information to a third party (as seen with the examples of SSL and SSH). Military and diplomatic circles have long been avoiding this problem by using line encryptors that fill a leased line with ciphertext, no matter if any information is being transmitted. This prevents an enemy noticing that traffic has either increased (or indeed decreased) as the result of an event (as, apocryphally, it is said that the volume of late-night Pentagon pizza orders changes when hostilities are imminent [64,65]).

Fixed-rate encryption equipment is expensive to purchase (and operate), so there is a temptation to move to off-the-shelf routers, software encryption, and the use of general purpose wide-area network links. Very little research has been done on protecting encrypted IP links against traffic analysis despite warnings concerning the threat posed against standard protocols like IPSec [66] and transport layer security (TLS). Venkatraman and Newman-Wolfe [67,68] have looked at imposing traffic schedules to minimize information leaked as well as covert channels. Ways to analyze the cost and anonymity provided by such systems is presented in [69].

The earliest mention of this problem can be found in 1983 [70], with the conclusion that "beyond the host level, further limitation on information release becomes increasingly expensive and are probably not necessary in a nonmilitary environment."

A related problem, of concern in military circles, is that an enemy could observe a network and even though all the traffic was encrypted, determine the function of each node through traffic analysis. A weather station would generate reports on an hourly basis, but the more interesting target of the military headquarters could be distinguished by the multiple flows in and out of its node. The U.S. DARPA Agency set this problem as one of its challenges in 1998 [71] and it has been addressed, albeit only for fairly limited network topologies, in a number of papers from Guan et al. [72–74] that consider adding extra traffic (padding) and rerouting some of the traffic along alternative network paths.

5.7 Data Retention

For some time, law enforcement officers (the police, secret services, etc.) have been using telephone call traffic data to identify criminals. Initially, very simple enquiries were made—determining who made the last call that the murder victim received, tracking the source of a ransom demand, and so on. However, there has been a growing use of genuine traffic analysis techniques to develop "friendship trees" and, thereby, identify the roles of individuals within a conspiracy [13]. However, the denationalization of incumbent fixed-line telephone companies has broken their close ties with the police, and the growth of mobile telephone usage has led to a fragmentation of the market and fierce price competition, so that collection and storage of traffic data is now seen as an expensive burden. At the same time, new flat-rate business models have made the business justification for call traffic data disappear. This has led to considerable anxiety within law enforcement agencies that a valuable source of information will cease to be available.

In parallel, criminals have started to use the Internet for their communications and law enforcement has found that within this open system, with an extremely disparate set of service providers, the traceability of communications can be problematic, and traffic analysis almost impossible. In particular, there has been concern that voice traffic will migrate from the closed and ordered telephony world to Voice over IP (VoIP) running on the open and anarchic Internet.

In response, particularly after the terrorist attacks in Madrid (2004) and London (2005), interest grew in mandatory data retention, requiring communications service providers to retain their traffic data logs for a fixed period, often far longer than their business needs would require. The term *data retention* should be contrasted with a "data preservation" regime, where data is preserved specially in response to a specific request from law enforcement personnel.

The United States has long had a data preservation regime, but in 2006 Congress started being pressured to consider moving to a data retention regime, with online child exploitation being cited as unnecessarily hard to investigate [75]. At much the same time, the 1994 Communication Assistance for Law Enforcement Act (CALEA) requirements on traditional telephony (call data provision, wiretapping capability) were extended to VoIP providers [76].

Meanwhile, the European Union (EU) adopted the Data Retention Directive (2006/24/EC) in March 2006 [77]. This provides for telephone companies to implement data retention by September 2007 and Internet companies by March 2009 at the latest. There is some doubt over the legal status of the directive, which is being challenged (early 2007) by Ireland on the basis that it should have been implemented under Third Pillar procedures for Police and Judicial Cooperation in Criminal Matters rather than as a First Pillar Directive for Market Harmonization. In practice, even though it is a directive, there is little harmonization, with EU member states free to decide on retention periods of anything between six months and two years, and with such technically incompetent definitions having been chosen that it they could refer to every point-to-point connection made over the Internet, or merely to records of e-mails passing through major servers. It looks like being several years before any clarity emerges, and it is very likely indeed that retention regimes will differ markedly in different countries.

Notwithstanding all this technical confusion, there has been very little informed debate on the types of information that will be capable of being extracted from the retained data. As should be apparent from even the limited survey we have presented in this chapter, there is significant scope for drilling down to reveal the most private of information about activities, habits, interests, and even opinions. Storing this data, in an easily accessible manner, represents a systemic vulnerability that cannot be overstated enough.

In order to make balanced judgments between the needs of law enforcement agencies and the entitlement of law-abiding citizens to privacy, policymakers must become far more aware of the wealth of information that could be extracted from such data about every aspect of the networked society. Even the extraction of apparently anonymous profiles from traffic databases would greatly facilitate privacy violations and routine surveillance. We believe that resistance to traffic analysis must be perceived of as a public good—the more that any attacker knows about the habits of your neighbors the more they can tell about you.

5.8 Conclusion

We have seen how traffic analysis has been used by the military and how broadly similar techniques are beginning to be seen in civilian life. Much activity still remains classified, but more is entering the public domain, not least because of a wish to reduce costs by having a broad range of commercial off-the-shelf (COTS) equipment available.

However, our understanding of the threat that traffic analysis attacks represent on public networks remains somewhat fragmented, although the active research in this field has led to considerable improvement. The results we have presented in this chapter, from what we know so far, should act as a warning against ignoring this threat. Traffic analysis not only can be used to reveal what is going on, but can also be used to bypass apparently robust security mechanisms.

References

[1] Diffie, W. and Landau, S., *Privacy on the Line: The Politics of Wiretapping and Encryption*, MIT Press, Cambridge, MA, 1998.

[2] Herman, M., *Intelligence Power in Peace and War*, Cambridge University Press, London 1996.

[3] Kahn, D., *The Codebreakers*, Scribner, New York, 1967.

[4] Anderson, R., *Security Engineering*, John Wiley & Sons, New York, 2001.

[5] Fullerton, J., British Ruse Held Iraqi's Attention While Real Invasion Came Elsewhere, *The Philadelphia Inquirer*, 3 March 1991.

[6] Paglen, T. and Thompson, A.C., Planespotting: Nerds with binoculars bust the CIA's torture taxis, *The Village Voice*, 15 October, 2006.

[7] Callimahos, L.D., *Traffic Analysis and the Zendian Problem*, Aegean Park Press, Walnut Creet, CA, 1989.

[8] Wasserman, S. et al., *Social Network Analysis: Methods and Applications (Structural Analysis in the Social Sciences)*, Cambridge University Press, London, 1994.

[9] Travers, J. and Milgram, S., An experimental study of the small world problem, *Sociometry*, 32, 1969.

[10] Lin, N. and Smith, J., *Social Capital: A Theory of Social Structure and Action*, vol. 19 of *Structural Analysis in the Social Sciences*, Cambridge University Press, London, 2002.

[11] Reed, W.J., A brief introduction to scale-free networks, *Technical report*, Department of Mathematics and Statistics, University of Victoria, British Columbia, 2004.

[12] Carley, K.M., Lee, J.S., and Krackhardt, D., Destabilizing networks, *Connections*, 22, 79, 2002.

[13] Garfinkel, S.L., Leaderless resistance today, *First Monday*, 3, 2003.

[14] Nagaraja, S. and Anderson, R., The topology of covert conflict, *Technical Report UCAM-CL-TR-637*, University of Cambridge, Computer Laboratory, 2005.

[15] Sparrow, M.K., The application of network analysis to criminal intelligence: An assessment of the prospects, *Social Networks*, 13, 251, 1991.

[16] Klerks, P., The network paradigm applied to criminal organisations, *Connections*, 24, 53, 2001.

[17] Hougham, V., Sociological skills used in the capture of Saddam Hussein, *Footnotes, Newsletter of the American Sociological Association*, 33, 2005.

[18] U.S. Army Headquarters Department, *Field Manual 3-24: Counterinsurgency*, U.S. Army, Washington, D.C., 2006.

[19] Krebs, V.E., Uncloaking terrorist networks, *First Monday*, 7, 2002.

[20] Dombroski, M., Fischbeck, P., and Carley, K., Estimating the shape of covert networks, in *Proceedings of the 8th International Command and Control Research and Technology Symposium*. National Defense War College, Washington D.C. *Evidence-Based Research, Track 3, Electronic Publication*, Vienna, VA., CCRP, 2003.

[21] Fawcett, T. and Provost, F., Adaptive fraud detection, *Journal Data Mining and Knowledge Discovery*, 1, 291, 1997.

[22] Levien, R., Attack resistant trust metrics, 2003, http://www.levien.com/thesis/compact.pdf.

[23] Gibson, D., Kleinberg, J., and Raghavan, P., Inferring web communities from link topology, in *Proceedings of the 9th ACM Conference on Hypertext and Hypermedia*, ACM Press, New York, 1998.

[24] Page, L. et al., The pagerank citation ranking: Bringing order to the web, *Technical report*, Stanford Digital Library Technologies Project, 1998.

[25] Kleinberg, J.M., Hubs, authorities, and communities, *ACM Computing Surveys*, 31, 5, 1999.

[26] Renesys Corporation, Market intelligence provides objective analysis of the service provider market, http://www.renesys.com/products_services/market_intel/.

[27] Song, D.X., Wagner, D., and Tian, X., Timing analysis of keystrokes and timing attacks on SSH, in *Tenth USENIX Security Symposium*, USENIX, Washington, D.C., 2001.

[28] Monrose, F., Reiter, M.K., and Wetzel, S., Password hardening based on keystroke dynamics, in *ACM Conference on Computer and Communications Security*, 73, ACM Press, New York, 1999.

[29] Cheng, H. and Avnur, R., Traffic analysis of SSL encrypted web browsing, 1998, http://www.cs.berkeley.edu/~daw/teaching/cs261-f98/projects/final-reports/ronathan-heyning.ps.

[30] Hintz, A., Fingerprinting websites using traffic analysis, in R. Dingledine and P.F. Syverson, Eds., *Privacy Enhancing Technologies*, vol. 2482 of *Lecture Notes in Computer Science*, 171, Springer-Verlag, Heidelberg, Germany, 2002.

[31] Sun, Q. et al., Statistical identification of encrypted web browsing traffic, in *IEEE Symposium on Security and Privacy*, 19, IEEE Computer Security Press, Los Alamitos, CA, 2002.

[32] Danezis, G., Traffic analysis of the HTTP protocol over TLS, 2003, http://www.cl.cam.ac.uk/~gd216/TLSanon.pdf.

[33] Bissias, G.D. et al., Privacy vulnerabilities in encrypted HTTP streams, in G. Danezis and D. Martin, Eds., *Privacy Enhancing Technologies*, vol. 3856 of *Lecture Notes in Computer Science*, 1, Springer-Verlag, Heidelberg, Germany, 2005.

[34] Levene, M. and Loizou, G., Computing the entropy of user navigation in the web, *International Journal of Information Technology and Decision Making*, 2, 459, 2003.

[35] Felten, E.W. and Schneider, M.A., Timing attacks on web privacy, in *ACM Conference on Computer and Communications Security*, 25, ACM Press, New York, 2000.

[36] Kohno, T., Broido, A., and Claffy, k.c., Remote physical device fingerprinting, in *IEEE Symposium on Security and Privacy* [?], IEEE Computer Society Press, Los Alamitos, CA, 211.

[37] Murdoch, S.J., Hot or not: Revealing hidden services by their clock skew, in A. Juels, R.N. Wright, and S.D.C. di Vimercati, Eds., *13th ACM Conference on Computer and Communications Security (CCS)*, Alexandria, VA, 27, ACM Press, New York, 2006.

[38] Dingledine, R., Mathewson, N., and Syverson, P., Tor: The second-generation onion router, in *Proceedings of the 13th USENIX Security Symposium*, USENIX, San Diego, CA, 2004.

[39] Bellovin, S.M., A technique for counting NATted hosts, in *Internet Measurement Workshop*, 267, ACM Press, New York, 2002.

[40] Narten, T. and Draves, R., *Privacy Extensions for Stateless Address Autoconfiguration in IPv6*, RFC3041, IETF, 2001.

[41] Aura, T., *Cryptographically Generated Addresses (CGA)*, RFC3972, IETF, 2005.

[42] Pascual, A.E., Privacy extensions for stateless address autoconfiguration in IPv6—"requirements for unobservability," in *RVP02, Stockholm*, Stockholm, 2002.

[43] Fyodor, Nmap—free security scanner for network exploitation and security audit, http://www.insecure.org/nmap/.

[44] Snort team, Snort, http://www.snort.org/.

[45] Fyodor, Nmap manual, 2006, http://www.insecure.org/nmap/man/.

[46] Wang, X. and Reeves, D.S., Robust correlation of encrypted attack traffic through stepping stones by manipulation of interpacket delays, in S. Jajodia, V. Atluri, and T. Jaeger, Eds., *ACM Conference on Computer and Communications Security*, 20, ACM Press, New York, 2003.

[47] Blum, A., Song, D.X., and Venkataraman, S., Detection of interactive stepping stones: Algorithms and confidence bounds, in E. Jonsson, A. Valdes, and M. Almgren, Eds., *RAID*, vol. 3224 of *Lecture Notes in Computer Science*, 258, Springer-Verlag, Heidelberg, Germany, 2004.

[48] Wang, X., Reeves, D.S., and Wu, S.F., Inter-packet delay-based correlation for tracing encrypted connections through stepping stones, in D. Gollmann, G. Karjoth, and M. Waidner, Eds., *ESORICS*, vol. 2502 of *Lecture Notes in Computer Science*, 244, Springer-Verlag, Heidelberg, Germany, 2002.

[49] Peng, P., Ning, P., and Reeves, D.S., On the secrecy of timing-based active watermarking trace-back techniques, in *S&P 2006* [?], IEEE Computer Society Press, Los Alamitos, CA, 334.

[50] Pascual, A.E., *Anonymous untraceable communications: Location privacy in mobile internetworking*, Ph.D. thesis, Royal Institute of Technology–KTH/IMIT, Stockholm, Sweden, 2001.

[51] MIT Media Lab Human Dynamics Group, Reality mining, http://reality.media.mit.edu/.

[52] Chaum, D., Untraceable electronic mail, return addresses, and digital pseudonyms, *Communications of the ACM*, 24, 84, 1981.

[53] Danezis, G., Designing and attacking anonymous communication systems, *Technical Report UCAM-CL-TR-594*, University of Cambridge, Computer Laboratory, 2004.

[54] Serjantov, A., On the anonymity of anonymity systems, *Technical Report UCAM-CL-TR-604*, University of Cambridge, Computer Laboratory, 2004.

[55] Langley, A., Mixmaster Remailers. In A. Oram, Ed., *Peer-to-Peer: Harnessing the Benefits of a Disruptive Technology*, O'Reilly, Sevastapol, CA, 2001.

[56] Danezis, G., Dingledine, R., and Mathewson, N., Mixminion: Design of a type III anonymous remailer protocol, in *IEEE Symposium on Security and Privacy*, IEEE, Berkeley, CA, 2003.

[57] Berthold, O., Federrath, H., and Köpsell, S., Web MIXes: A system for anonymous and unobservable Internet access, in H. Federrath, Ed., *Designing Privacy Enhancing Technologies*, vol. 2009 of *LNCS*, 115, Springer-Verlag, Heidelberg, Germany, 2000.

[58] Agrawal, D. and Kesdogan, D., Measuring anonymity: The disclosure attack, *IEEE Security and Privacy*, 1, 27, 2003.

[59] Kesdogan, D. and Pimenidis, L., The hitting set attack on anonymity protocols, in Fridrich, 326.

[60] Danezis, G. and Serjantov, A., Statistical disclosure or intersection attacks on anonymity systems, in Fridrich, 293.

[61] Kesdogan, D. et al., Fundamental limits on the anonymity provided by the mix technique, in *S&P 2006* [?], IEEE Computer Society Press, Los Alamitos, CA, 86.

[62] Wright, M. et al., An analysis of the degradation of anonymous protocols, in *NDSS*, The Internet Society, 2002.

[63] Murdoch, S.J. and Danezis, G., Low-cost traffic analysis of Tor, in *S&P 2005* [?], IEEE Computer Society Press, Los Alamitos, CA, 183.

[64] Gray, P., And bomb the anchovies, *Time*, 13 August, 1990.

[65] Warinner, A., Security clearances required for Domino's, 1996, http://home.xnet.com/~warinner/pizza.html.

[66] Bellovin, S.M., Probable plaintext cryptanalysis of the IP security protocols, in *NDSS*, IEEE Computer Society Press, Los Alamitos, CA, 1997.

[67] Newman-Wolfe, R. and Venkatraman, B., High level prevention of traffic analysis, *Seventh Annual Computer Security Applications Conference*, 102, 1991.

[68] Venkatraman, B. and Newman-Wolfe, R., Transmission schedules to prevent traffic analysis, *Proceedings of the Ninth Annual Computer Security Applications Conference*, IEEE, New York, 108, 1993.

[69] Newman, R.E. et al., Metrics for trafic analysis prevention, in R. Dingledine, Ed., *Privacy Enhancing Technologies*, vol. 2760 of *Lecture Notes in Computer Science*, 48, Springer-Verlag, Heidelberg, Germany, 2003.

[70] Voydock, V. and Kent, S., Security mechanisms in high-level network protocols, *ACM Computing Surveys (CSUR)*, 15, 135, 1983.

[71] Defense Advanced Research Projects Agency, Research challenges in high confidence networking, U.S. Department of Defense, Washington, D.C., 1998.

[72] Guan, Y. et al., Preventing traffic analysis for real-time communication networks, in *Proceedings of The IEEE Military Communication Conference (MILCOM) '99, November 1999*, IEEE Computer Society Press, Los Alamitos, CA, 1999.

[73] Guan, Y. et al., Efficient traffic camouflaging in mission-critical QoS-guaranteed networks, in *Proceedings of IEEE Information Assurance and Security Workshop, West Point, June 2000*, 143, IEEE Computer Society Press, Los Alamitos, CA, 2000.

[74] Guan, Y. et al., Netcamo: Camouflaging network traffic for QoS-guaranteed mission critical applications, *IEEE Transactions on Systems, Man, and Cybernetics, Part A*, 31, 253, 2001.

[75] Petersen, R., Towards a U.S. data-retention standard for ISPs, *Educause Review*, 41, 78, 2006.

[76] Federal Communications Commission, Second report and order and memorandum opinion and order, Washington, D.C., 2006.

[77] European Union, Directive 2006/24/EC of the European Parliament and of the Council of 15 March 2006 on the retention of data generated or processed in connection with the provision of publicly available electronic communications services or of public communications networks and amending Directive 2002/58/EC, *Official Journal of the European Union*, L 105, 54, 2006.

Chapter 6

Privacy, Profiling, Targeted Marketing, and Data Mining

Jaideep Vaidya and Vijay Atluri

Contents

6.1 Introduction 117
6.2 Privacy-Preserving Profiling 118
6.3 Ensuring Privacy in Targeted Marketing 122
    6.3.1 Ensuring Privacy of Static Users 122
    6.3.2 Ensuring Privacy of Mobile Users........................... 125
6.4 Privacy-Preserving Data Mining 127
References... 128

6.1 Introduction

With the ubiquitous collection and availability of data, there is significant pressure to actually analyze and correlate the collected data to turn it into a valuable resource. While it is clear that data can be significantly leveraged for great gains, the use of this data cannot be allowed at the cost of individual privacy. Too often, privacy is an afterthought and this can cause problems. For example, while a terminally ill HIV/AIDS patient may be happy to receive notice of experimental drugs that he may be unaware of, he definitely would not like his health information broadcast or even leaked to others. Similarly, laws like the Patriot Act may be necessary for security, but could represent a significant breach of privacy rights.

However, the purpose of this chapter is to show that data analysis is not necessarily antithetical to privacy. This chapter explores the problems of profiling, targeted marketing, data mining, and privacy. Today, there are significant advances in the field of cryptography that can be leveraged so that "we can have our cake and eat it, too." We start out by showing what is implied by privacy-preserving profiling and then describe technical ways to achieve it. We then explore the concept of targeted marketing for both static as well as mobile users, and describe technical ways to achieve privacy while still allowing clustering analysis. Finally, we show how all of these problems fall under the umbrella of privacy-preserving data mining, and provide a brief overview of it. All together, the chapter should convince you that there are technological solutions for privacy, which may yet enable safe and beneficial use of distributed data.

6.2 Privacy-Preserving Profiling

Profiling is defined as recording a person's behavior and analyzing psychological characteristics in order to predict or assess their ability in a certain sphere or to identify a particular group of people. To profile is to generalize or to typecast. In profiling, based on certain characteristics, a person is typecast into a certain category. Profiling works better if the characteristics profiled are accurate. For example, when pulled over by a police officer, if slurry speech is a good indication of intoxication, then that is a good characteristic for the police officer to ask for a breathalyzer test. Similarly, if furtively looking around a store or wearing a trench coat on a hot day is a good indication that the person is a shoplifter, then those are good characteristics for a store owner to pay attention to. But, if wearing baggy trousers and having a mohawk isn't a good indication that the person is a shoplifter, then the store owner is going to spend a lot of time paying undue attention to honest people with an unorthodox fashion sense.

Computerization greatly simplifies profiling. In the first place, computerization increases the amount of data available for people to create profiles. Also, instead of a person doing the profiling, a computer can look the profile over and provide some sort of rating. Generally, profiles with high ratings are further evaluated by people, although sometimes countermeasures kick in based solely on the computerized profile. However, since computers do not have any intuition nor can they adapt like humans, pure computerization can lead to false positives as well as false negatives.

One of the main drivers of profiling is security. For example, after 9/11, there has been a major push to increase checking at airports to reduce the chances of terrorists hijacking a flight. However, the manpower and resources required to comprehensively check every passenger are inordinate and would make it impossible. Instead, the Federal Aviation Administration

(FAA) has been trying in recent years to employ information technology to boost the overall efficiency of security screening. The basic idea behind the approach is to be more intelligent about which passengers are selected for rigorous inspections. Instead of searching all passengers, a whole lot of effort can be saved if you identify the suspicious ones and concentrate only on them. Of course, this only works if you can develop a good profile describing likely terrorists. However, once (or if) you have such a profile, it makes a lot of sense to apply it and concentrate your security efforts only on the people matching the profile.

Based on this intuitive premise, the Department of Homeland Security and the FAA would like to implement a computer-assisted passenger prescreening system (CAPPS & CAPPS II). The FAA contends that since CAPPS uses profiles to pinpoint potential terrorists for closer inspection, it not only results in the apprehension of more criminals, but also makes security screening more expedient for well-meaning citizens. However, there are several problems with deploying such a system. Chakrabarti and Strauss [11] identified a problem with CAPPS, such as nonrandom checking where an adaptive attacker can figure out the profiles used through several nonviolent runs through the system and then consciously vary from those profiles at the time of the real attack. Even more significantly, there has been a severe backlash due to privacy concerns. In order to match against the profiles, passenger information would be collated from a variety of sources and compared without regard to privacy. This is a significant problem and has caused the deferment of implementation for both CAPPS systems.

Following is a description of how this restriction can be lifted through technical means. We regard the profile matching as a classification task where the profiles define rules that, when matched, describe a particular behavioral class (target). Here, privacy-preserving profiling is possible through cryptographic means, though an efficient solution requires some trust. In order to perform privacy-preserving profiling, three conflicting privacy/security requirements must be met: (1) the data must not be revealed, (2) the classifier must not be revealed, and (3) the classifier must be checked for validity. Kantarcıoğlu & Clifton [21] proposed methods to apply a classification model without having to reveal it. This can be used for privacy-preserving profiling. Thus, the methods proposed have the following property:

1. The classification result is revealed only to a designated party.
2. No information about the classification result is revealed to anyone else.
3. Rules used for classification can be checked for the presence of certain conditions without revealing the rules (it is important to check, for example, that race is not being used as a deciding characteristic).

Formally, the problem can be defined as follows: Given an instance x from site D with v attributes, we want to classify x according to a rule set R provided by the site G. Let x_i denote the *ith* attribute of x. We assume that each attribute of x has n bits, and that each given classification rule $r \in R$ is of the form $(L_1 \wedge L2 \wedge \ldots \wedge L_v) \longrightarrow C$, where C is the predicted class if $(L_1 \wedge L2 \wedge \ldots \wedge L_v)$ evaluates to true. Each L_i is either $x_i = a$, or a "don't care" (always true). While one may argue that "don't care" clauses are redundant in the problem definition, if they are eliminated, one could potentially learn the number of clauses in each rule. This may, in itself, be sensitive information. Therefore, the "don't care" clauses are included explicitly in the protocol to mask the number of *true* clauses in each rule. Now, no party can gain extra information about the number of clauses in a rule. In addition, D has a set F of rules that are not allowed to be used for classification. In other words, D requires $F \cap R = \phi$. The goal is to find the class value of x according to R while satisfying the following conditions:

- D will not be able to learn any rules in R.
- D will be convinced that $F \cap R = \phi$ holds.
- G will only learn the class value of x and what is implied by the class value.

All of the above goals are easily achievable if there is a trusted third party asked to perform the computation. In this case, D and G would give their respective data (x, F, and R) to the trusted party T and ask it to check all the conditions and return the evaluation result to G. However, the main problem with this is to find such a trusted third party acceptable to all participants. The general methods for secure multiparty computation could be used. Yao first postulated the two-party comparison problem (Yao's Millionaire Protocol—two millionaires want to know who is richer without either disclosing their net worth) and developed a provably secure solution [42]. This was extended to multiparty computations (for any computable functionality) by Goldreich et al. [16] (as long as trap door permutations exist) and to the malicious model of computation by Ben-Or et al. [8]. The generic circuit-based technique can be used, but is highly restrictive in terms of the overall computation/communication cost.

Thus, in order to be efficient, the method assumes that an untrusted noncolluding site is used. The site is untrusted in the sense that it does not learn anything without active collusion with one or more of the data sites. Also, neither data site learns any extra information about the other site's data without active collusion with the untrusted third party. This assumption is not unreasonable—there are many examples of such collaboration in the real world (e.g., the auction site eBay is trusted by both sellers and buyers to not collude with the other).

The key tool used in the protocol is Commutative Encryption. A plain text data item enciphered with multiple encryption keys in any arbitrary order will have the same enciphered text if the encryption algorithm is commutative. Formally, an encryption algorithm is commutative if the following two equations hold for any given encryption keys $K_1, \ldots, K_n \in K$, any data item to be encrypted $m \in M$, and any permutations of $i, j : \forall m_1, m_2 \in M$, such that $m_1 \neq m_2$:

$$E_{K_{i_1}}(\ldots E_{K_{i_n}}(m)\ldots) = E_{K_{j_1}}(\ldots E_{K_{j_n}}(m)\ldots) \qquad (6.1)$$

and for any given $k, \epsilon < 1/2^k$

$$Pr(E_{K_{i_1}}(\ldots E_{K_{i_n}}(m_1)\ldots) = E_{K_{j_1}}(\ldots E_{K_{j_n}}(m_2)\ldots)) < \epsilon \qquad (6.2)$$

The order invariance property of commutative encryption can be used to easily check if two items are equal. Thus, if two values are encrypted by two keys (from a commutative public key system), then irrespective of the order of encryption, the two ciphertexts will be exactly the same as long as the original values are exactly the same. Thus, if two organizations wish to check if their local inputs are exactly the same, they can each generate a key and use it to encrypt their inputs. Now the two can encrypt each other's input and, simply by checking the encrypted ciphertexts, determine the equality of the original values. Pohlig and Hellman [29] is one example of a commutative encryption scheme (based on the discrete logarithm problem). This or any other commutative encryption scheme would work well for our purposes.

Using commutative encryption, it is easily possible to solve the problem of privacy-preserving profiling between the sites D and G as defined above along with an untrusted noncolluding site S. At the end of the protocol, S will only learn the number of attributes, the number of rules, and the number of literals satisfied by each rule for a given instance. The basic idea is that sites D and G send synchronized streams of encrypted data and rule clauses to site S. The order of attributes are scrambled in a way known to D and G, but not S. This prevents S from learning anything about the attributes. Each attribute is also given two values, one corresponding to "don't care," the other to its true value. Finally, each clause also has two values for each attribute. One possibility is an "X" or invalid value (masking the real value). The other is the desired result, either the actual value or the agreed upon "don't care" value. S compares to see if either the first or second values match. If so, then either the attribute is a match or the clause is a "don't care." If there is a match for every clause in a rule, then the rule is true.

While this is good, there exists one problem. If all the encryptions are the same, then S could correlate across rules and instances. However, the key is that the "don't care," true, and invalid values are encrypted directly for each data/rule pair in the stream in a way shared by D and G, but unknown to S. The order (is the first attribute the value or the "don't care" value?) also changes, again in a way known only to D and G. Since all values are encrypted (always with at least one key unknown to S) the noncolluding site S learns nothing except which rule matches. Since the rule identifier is also encrypted, this is useless to S. With all of these precautions, S can no longer learn even the class distribution of different instances over multiple runs through the protocol. Finally, the results are split and sent to the two sites. Checking for forbidden rules is possible using the commutative property of the encryption system. Having a third party is actually an advantage in the sense that, with collusion (perhaps under court order), it is possible to expose the entire working of the protocol and ensure that no one cheated. However, one large drawback of this work is that negative clauses are not supported and the entire protocol is not yet implemented. Nevertheless, this indeed shows that privacy-preserving profiling is technically possible.

6.3 Ensuring Privacy in Targeted Marketing

We now look at how to ensure privacy while still enabling targeted marketing. Depending on whether the customers are static or mobile, there are two distinct cases. Both have completely different requirements and solution approaches. Both are covered below.

6.3.1 Ensuring Privacy of Static Users

Effective marketing requires identification of the right target audience. In this sense, targeted marketing serves as one of the most efficient forms of marketing. The accepted way of doing this is through clustering. Clustering and cluster analysis is identified as a critical step in effective marketing. Malhotra [27] identifies the following critical applications of cluster analysis (or clustering) in marketing:

- *Segmenting the Market:* For example, consumers can be clustered depending on the benefit they seek from the purchase or obtain from it. Each cluster would then consist of consumers who are relatively homogeneous in terms of the benefits they seek.
- *Understanding Buyer Behavior:* Buyer behavior can be better understood if we group similar buyers together. This allows us to analyze the buying behavior of each homogeneous subgroup as opposed to looking at them as a whole. This can provide far more relevant factors for all of the subpopulations instead of simply getting a generic profile.

- *Identifying New Product Opportunities:* By clustering brands and products, competitive sets within the market can be determined. Brands in the same cluster compete more fiercely with each other than with brands in other clusters. Thus, a firm can examine its current offerings compared to those of its competitors to identify potential new product opportunities.
- *Selecting Test Markets:* By grouping locations into homogeneous clusters, it is possible to select comparable locations to test various marketing strategies.
- *Reducing Data:* In general, by identifying homogenized clusters, one can represent the entire cluster by a representative (sample). In this sense, the overall size of the dataset is reduced. Subsequent multivariate analysis can be conducted on the clusters rather than on the individual observations.

In general, any clustering algorithm can be applied to form the clusters. Traditionally, all clustering algorithms assume complete access to the underlying data. However, if the data is collected at several different sites (perhaps even remaining with the data owner, i.e., end consumer), privacy and security concerns restrict the sharing of this data. Thus, the key question is whether we can still create clusters and analyze them without complete access to the underlying data. However, this brings up the issue of exactly what is private and what are the results? For complete security, one should only learn the number of clusters and their composition, while receiving no other information. However, this depends on the clustering algorithm and the way data is shared.

Depending on the specific clustering algorithm used, several algorithms have been proposed to perform the clustering in a privacy-preserving manner. Vaidya and Clifton [33] proposed the privacy-preserving k-means algorithm for vertically partitioned data. Vertically partitioned data implies that the data for a single entity is split across multiple sites, and each site has information for all the entities for a specific subset of the attributes. Here, the security requirements would imply that the existence of an entity in a particular site's database may be revealed; however, it is the values associated with an entity that are private. Therefore, the goal is to cluster the known set of common entities without revealing any of the values that the clustering is based on. K-means clustering is a simple, iterative technique to group items into k clusters: k clusters centers are chosen at random, each item is assigned to the closest cluster, and then the cluster centers are recomputed based on the data placement. This procedure repeats until the clustering converges (or a certain number of iterations are done). The goal is to generate a solution that minimizes the intracluster variation while maximizing the intercluster distance. The results come in two forms—assignments of entities to clusters and the cluster centers themselves. Since the data is vertically partitioned, all parties need to know the cluster assignment of an entity (since all jointly own the data for that entity), but the cluster centers are semiprivate. Each party knows the cluster centers for the attributes that it owns. However, when data is horizontally partitioned (i.e., all sites collect the same features of information but for different entities, like different banks collecting credit card information for different customers), the results are quite different. The cluster assignment of an entity should be known only to the owning site, while the cluster centers may be private (not known to anyone) or be public (known completely to everyone) depending on the security requirements. Thus, the overall security requirements are quite different based on the data distribution.

The privacy-preserving k-means of Vaidya and Clifton [33] follows the basic k-means algorithm very closely. Starting means can be randomly generated together by all of the parties. The cluster assignment of each item needs to be decided via a secure protocol. Once all entities are assigned to clusters, recomputing the cluster means can be done locally by all of the parties. Finally, the termination test needs to be done securely as well. For the closest cluster computation, each party can independently calculate the local distance of its entity from each of the k clusters. What remains is to find the globally closest cluster. This is done via a secure addition and permutation procedure so that only the closest cluster index is revealed (neither distances to clusters nor cluster ordering is revealed).

When to terminate is decided by comparing the improvement to the mean approximation in each iteration to a threshold. If the improvement is sufficient, the algorithm proceeds, otherwise it terminates. Each party locally computes the difference between its share of the old mean and the new mean for each of the k clusters. Now, the parties must figure out if the total sum is less than the threshold. This looks straightforward, except that to maintain security (and practicality) all arithmetic takes place in a field and is, thus, modular arithmetic. This results in a nonobvious threshold evaluation at the end, consisting of a secure addition/comparison. *Intervals* are compared rather than the actual numbers. Further details can be found in [33]. Jagannathan and Wright [20] extend this idea to performing the k-means clustering over arbitrarily partitioned data.

Lin et al. [25] proposed a secure method to perform expectation maximization (EM)-clustering over horizontally partitioned data. This is simple if the (intermediate) cluster centers are public information. It is easy for each party to assign its points to the closest clusters. Recomputation of the cluster centers only requires secure summation across parties. There have been other methods proposed for secure clustering [19]. Any of these could be used.

6.3.2 Ensuring Privacy of Mobile Users

In recent years, mobile phones and wireless personal digital assistants (PDAs) have evolved into wireless terminals that are global positioning system (GPS) enabled. With the expected revenues of mobile commerce to exceed $88 billion by 2009 [1], mobile commerce will soon become a gigantic market opportunity. The market for location-aware mobile applications, often known as *location-based services* (LBS), is very promising. LBS is to request usable, personalized information delivered at the point of need, which includes information about new or interesting products and services, promotions, and targeting of customers based on more advanced knowledge of customer profiles and preferences, automatic updates of travel reservations, etc. For example, a LBS provider can be designed to present users with targeted content, such as clothing items on sale, based on prior knowledge of their profile, preferences, and knowledge of their current location, such as proximity to a shopping mall [39]. Additionally, LBS can provide nearby points of interests based on the real-time location of the mobile customer, advising of current conditions, such as traffic and weather; and deliver personalized, location-aware, and context-sensitive advertising, again based on the mobile customer profiles and preferences.

In order to implement such services, customization, and personalization based on the location information, customer profiles and preferences, and vendor offerings is required. This is because, to be effective, targeted advertising should not overwhelm the mobile consumers and only push information to a certain segment of mobile consumers based on their preferences and profiles, and based on certain marketing criteria. Obviously, these consumers should be targeted only if they are in the location where the advertisement is applicable at the time of the offer.

There are a number of security and privacy concerns in such a location-based service environment. First, effective delivery of a location-based mobile service may mean locating a mobile customer. Location information has the potential to allow an adversary to physically locate a person. As such, wireless subscribers carrying mobile devices have legitimate concerns about their personal safety if such information should fall into the wrong hands. Second, the location-based service should not be able to track a mobile customer and maintain a profile of the customer's spatiotemporal patterns. For example, learning that a user would typically be in a certain location during a certain time may potentially have similar adverse effects as those of locating a person. And finally, the identity of the individual should be kept confidential primarily because the services being requested by a user should not be traced by the LBS.

A privacy-preserving technique based on requiring a pseudo-ID has been proposed by Beresford and Stajano [9], which employs the notion of mix zone. This essentially is to prevent tracing a user if multiple requests originate from the user. Another significant approach is to employ the notion of location k-anonymity. The proposed approaches essentially enlarge the spatiotemporal region of an LBS request to include k-1 users [15,17,28]. The notion of k-anonymity has been extended to historical k-anonymity [10] to ensure k-anonymization of a trace of LBS requests.

Another important privacy requirement is protecting the user profile information, which may include both sensitive and nonsensitive attributes, such as name, address, linguistic preference, age group, income level, marital status, education level, etc. Whether LBS is delivered in a "push" or "pull" fashion, service providers require access to customers' preference profiles either through a proprietary database or then use an arrangement with an LBS provider, who matches customer profiles to vendor offerings [4]. Certain segments of mobile consumers are willing to trade off privacy by sharing such sensitive data with selective merchants, either to benefit from personalization or to receive incentives offered by the merchants. Therefore, it is important that the sensitive profile information is revealed to the respective merchants only on the need-to-know basis. For example, a security policy may specify that a customer is willing to reveal his age in order to enjoy a 20 percent discount coupon offered on sports clothing. But, he is willing to do this only during the evening hours and while close to the store. As a result, the security policies in such an environment are characterized by spatial and temporal attributes of the mobile customers (location and time), as well as their profile attributes.

One main challenge is in addressing the issue of overhead when enforcing security, as it may degrade the performance. One way to alleviate this problem and to effectively serve access requests is to efficiently organize the mobile objects as well as access control policies where users can specify which service providers can access their location/profile information based on the time and the users' location. Toward this end, an index scheme for moving object data and user profiles has been proposed in Atluri et al. [5]. However, this does not consider authorizations. An index structure has been proposed to index authorizations ensuring that the customer profile information be disclosed to the merchants based on the choice of the customers [43]. However, this provides separate index structures for data and authorizations. Atluri and Guo [6] have proposed a unified index structure called ^{S}TPR-tree in which authorizations are carefully overlaid on a moving object index structure (TPR-tree) [31], based on their spatiotemporal parameters. One main limitation of the ^{S}TPR-tree is that it is not capable of maintaining past information. As a result, it cannot support queries contingent on past location and security policies, which are based on the *tracking* of mobile users. More recently, Atluri and Shin [7] presented an index structure, called

S^{PPF}-tree, which maintains past, present, and future positions of the moving objects, along with authorizations, by employing the *partial persistent storage*.

6.4 Privacy-Preserving Data Mining

In general, most of the work discussed above falls under the umbrella of privacy-preserving data mining (PPDM). Privacy-preserving data mining deals with the problem of mining data without seeing it. While this may sound counterintuitive, as seen above, secure computation makes this possible. Agrawal and Srikant [3] introduced the idea of perturbing the local data to protect privacy while recovering the distribution to enable mining. For example, if we add a random number chosen from a Gaussian distribution to the real data value, the data miner no longer knows the exact value. However, important statistics on the collection (e.g., average) will be preserved. Special techniques are used to reconstruct the original distribution (not the actual data values). The mining algorithm is modified to work while taking this into consideration. Their seminal paper applied this idea to perform ID3 classification. Agrawal and Aggarwal [2] proved a convergence result for a refinement of this algorithm. The perturbation approach has also been applied to other data-mining tasks, such as association rule mining [14,30,44]. Zhu and Liu [45] studied the problem of optimal randomization for privacy-preserving data mining and demonstrated the construction of optimal randomization schemes for density estimation.

The perturbation approach is especially well suited to cases where individual users have access to their data and care about the privacy of certain attributes. A "perturber" could be deployed at each user that modifies the local values according to some known distribution and then sends them to a global site to collate and mine. However, the big drawback with the perturbation approach is that their security is not well established. Knowing the bounds on a value with some confidence level is often sufficient to breach privacy. For example, you may not need to know that your coworker Tom makes exactly $84,720. It is sufficient if you find out that his salary is between $80,000 to $85,000 with 95 percent confidence. Unfortunately, with perturbation, it is difficult to avoid such problems without severely degrading the data. Kargupta et al. and Huang et al. [18,23] pointed out several security problems with perturbation.

The alternative cryptographic approach is more secure, but often less efficient. It is well suited to situations with a small number of parties owning a large amount of data that needs to be jointly analyzed. This approach is characterized by the formal proofs of security that clearly show exactly what information is revealed through the secure protocol. Lindell and Pinkas [26] introduced this concept (of secure computation) to data mining by proposing a secure method to do ID3 classification over horizontally partitioned data. Since then there has been a lot of work on association rule mining [22,37], clustering [20,25,33], classification [13,34,36,41], outlier detection [35], and regression [12,24,32].

An excellent survey of all of this work can be found in [38,40]. In general, this shows that privacy-preserving data mining is here to stay. However, there are still several major research challenges open. First, it is still necessary to implement such methods and create a toolkit to establish the efficiency of such methods for deployment in real life. Also, result analysis needs to be carried out to establish exactly what information is revealed through multiple use of various different data-mining methods. Finally, much of this work has been method specific—more general methods enabling broad types of analysis would be much more useful.

References

[1] Mobile Commerce (M-Commerce) and Micropayment Strategies. Technical report, Juniper Research (http://www.juniperresearch.com/), August 2004.

[2] D. Agrawal and C.C. Aggarwal. On the design and quantification of privacy preserving data mining algorithms. In *Proceedings of the Twentieth ACM SIGACT-SIGMOD-SIGART Symposium on Principles of Database Systems,* pp. 247–255, Santa Barbara, CA, May 21–23, 2001, ACM.

[3] R. Agrawal and R. Srikant. Privacy-preserving data mining. In *Proceedings of the 2000 ACM SIGMOD Conference on Management of Data,* pp. 439–450, Dallas, TX, May 14–19 2000, ACM.

[4] V. Atluri. Mobile commerce. In *The Handbook of Computer Networks, Volume III Distributed Networks, Network Planning, Control, Management and Applications, Part 3: Computer Network Popular Applications.* John Wiley & Sons Inc., New York, 2007.

[5] V. Atluri, N.R. Adam, and M. Youssef. Towards a unified index scheme for mobile data and customer profiles in a location-based service environment. In *Workshop on Next Generation Geospatial Information (NG2I'03),* 2003, Boston, MA.

[6] V. Atluri and Q. Guo. Unified index for mobile object data and authorizations. In *ESORICS,* pp. 80–97, 2005, Milan, Italy.

[7] V. Atluri and H. Shin. Efficient enforcement of security policies based on the tracking of mobile users. In *DBSec,* pp. 237–251, 2006, Sophia Antipolis, France.

[8] M. Ben-Or, S. Goldwasser, and A. Wigderson. Completeness theorems for non-cryptographic fault-tolerant distributed computation. In *Proceedings of the Twentieth Annual ACM Symposium on Theory of Computing,* pp. 1–10, Chicago, IL, May 2–4, 1988.

[9] A.R. Beresford and F. Stajano. Mix zones: User privacy in location-aware services. In *IEEE Conference on Pervasive Computing and Communications Workshop,* pp. 127–131, 2004, Orlando, FL.

[10] C. Bettini, X.S. Wang, and S. Jajodia. Protecting privacy against location-based personal identification. In *Secure Data Management,* pp. 185–199, 2005.

[11] S. Chakrabarti and A. Strauss. Carnival booth: An algorithm for defeating the computer-assisted passenger screening system. *First Monday,* 7(10), 2002.

[12] W. Du, Y.S. Han, and S. Chen. Privacy-preserving multivariate statistical analysis: Linear regression and classification. In *2004 SIAM International Conference on Data Mining,* Lake Buena Vista, FL, April 22–24, 2004.

[13] W. Du and Z. Zhan. Building decision tree classifier on private data. In C. Clifton and V. Estivill-Castro, Eds., *IEEE International Conference on Data Mining Workshop on Privacy, Security, and Data Mining,* vol. 14, pp. 1–8, Maebashi City, Japan, Dec. 9, 2002. Australian Computer Society.

[14] A. Evfimievski, R. Srikant, R. Agrawal, and J. Gehrke. Privacy preserving mining of association rules. In *The Eighth ACM SIGKDD International Conference on Knowledge Discovery and Data Mining,* pp. 217–228, Edmonton, Alberta, Canada, July 23–26, 2002.

[15] B. Gedik and L. Liu. Location privacy in mobile systems: A personalized anonymization model. In *ICDCS,* pp. 620–629, Columbus, OH, 2005.

[16] O. Goldreich, S. Micali, and A. Wigderson. How to play any mental game—a completeness theorem for protocols with honest majority. In *19th ACM Symposium on the Theory of Computing,* pp. 218–229, 1987.

[17] M. Gruteser and D. Grunwald. Anonymous usage of location-based services through spatial and temporal cloaking. In *MobiSys,* 2003.

[18] Z. Huang, W. Du, and B. Chen. Deriving private information from randomized data. In *Proceedings of the 2005 ACM SIGMOD International Conference on Management of Data,* Baltimore, MD, June 13–16, 2005.

[19] G. Jagannathan, K. Pillaipakkamnatt, and R.N. Wright. A new privacy-preserving distributed *k*-clustering algorithm. In J. Ghosh, D. Lambert, D.B. Skillicorn, and J. Srivastava, eds., *SDM.* SIAM, 2006.

[20] G. Jagannathan and R.N. Wright. Privacy-preserving distributed *k*-means clustering over arbitrarily partitioned data. In *Proceedings of the 2005 ACM SIGKDD International Conference on Knowledge Discovery and Data Mining,* pp. 593–599, Chicago, IL, Aug. 21–24, 2005.

[21] M. Kantarcıoğlu and C. Clifton. Assuring privacy when big brother is watching. In *The 8th ACM SIGMOD Workshop on Research Issues in Data Mining and Knowledge Discovery (DMKD'2003),* pp. 88–93, San Diego, CA, June 13, 2003.

[22] M. Kantarcıoğlu and C. Clifton. Privacy-preserving distributed mining of association rules on horizontally partitioned data. *IEEE Transactions on Knowledge and Data Engineering,* 16(9): 1026–1037, September 2004.

[23] H. Kargupta, S. Datta, Q. Wang, and K. Sivakumar. On the privacy preserving properties of random data perturbation techniques. In *Proceedings of the Third IEEE International Conference on Data Mining (ICDM'03),* Melbourne, FL, November 19–22, 2003.

[24] A.F. Karr, X. Lin, A.P. Sanil, and J.P. Reiter. Secure regressions on distributed databases. *Journal of Computational and Graphical Statistics,* 14: 263–279, 2005.

[25] X. Lin, C. Clifton, and M. Zhu. Privacy preserving clustering with distributed EM mixture modeling. *Knowledge and Information Systems,* 8(1): 68–81, July 2005.

[26] Y. Lindell and B. Pinkas. Privacy preserving data mining. In *Advances in Cryptology—CRYPTO 2000,* pp. 36–54. Springer-Verlag, Heidelberg, Germany, August 20–24, 2000.

[27] N. Malhotra. *Marketing Research.* 4th ed., Prentice-Hall, Upper Saddle River, NJ, 2004.

[28] M.F. Mokbel, C.-Y. Chow, and W.G. Aref. The new casper: Query processing for location services without compromising privacy. In *VLDB,* Seoul, Korea, pp. 763–774, 2006.

[29] S.C. Pohlig and M.E. Hellman. An improved algorithm for computing logarithms over GF(p) and its cryptographic significance. *IEEE Transactions on Information Theory,* IT-24: 106–110, 1978.

[30] S.J. Rizvi and J.R. Haritsa. Maintaining data privacy in association rule mining. In *Proceedings of 28th International Conference on Very Large Data Bases,* pp. 682–693, Hong Kong, August 20–23, 2002.

[31] S. Saltenis, C.S. Jensen, S.T. Leuteneggerz, and M.A. Lopez. Indexing the positions of continuously moving objects. In *ACM SIGMOD International Conference on Management of Data,* pp. 331–342, San Diego, CA, 2000.

[32] A.P. Sanil, A.F. Karr, X. Lin, and J.P. Reiter. Privacy preserving regression modelling via distributed computation. In *KDD '04: Proceedings of the Tenth ACM SIGKDD International Conference on Knowledge Discovery and Data Mining,* pp. 677–682, New York, 2004. ACM Press.

[33] J. Vaidya and C. Clifton. Privacy-preserving *k*-means clustering over vertically partitioned data. In *The Ninth ACM SIGKDD International Conference on Knowledge Discovery and Data Mining,* pp. 206–215, Washington, D.C., August 24–27, 2003.

[34] J. Vaidya and C. Clifton. Privacy preserving naïve Bayes classifier for vertically partitioned data. In *2004 SIAM International Conference on Data Mining,* pp. 522–526, Lake Buena Vista, FL, April 22–24, 2004.

[35] J. Vaidya and C. Clifton. Privacy-preserving outlier detection. In *Proceedings of the Fourth IEEE International Conference on Data Mining (ICDM'04),* pp. 233–240, Los Alamitos, CA, November 1–4, 2004. IEEE Computer Society Press.

[36] J. Vaidya and C. Clifton. Privacy-preserving decision trees over vertically partitioned data. In *The 19th Annual IFIP WG 11.3 Working Conference on Data and Applications Security,* Storrs, CN, August 7–10, 2005. Springer-Verlag, Heidelberg, Germany.

[37] J. Vaidya and C. Clifton. Secure set intersection cardinality with application to association rule mining. *Journal of Computer Security,* 13(4): 593–622, November 2005.

[38] J. Vaidya, C. Clifton, and M. Zhu. *Privacy-Preserving Data Mining,* vol. 19 of *Advances in Information Security,* 1st ed., Springer-Verlag, 2005.

[39] V. Venkatesh, V. Ramesh, and A.P. Massey. Understanding usability in mobile commerce. *Communications of the ACM,* 46(12), 2003.

[40] V.S. Verykios, E. Bertino, I.N. Fovino, L.P. Provenza, and Y. Saygin. State-of-the-art in privacy preserving data mining. *SIGMOD Record*, 33(1): 50–57, March 2004.

[41] R. Wright and Z. Yang. Privacy-preserving Bayesian network structure computation on distributed heterogeneous data. In *Proceedings of the 10th ACM SIGKDD International Conference on Knowledge Discovery and Data Mining*, Seattle, WA, August 22–25, 2004.

[42] A.C. Yao. How to generate and exchange secrets. In *Proceedings of the 27th IEEE Symposium on Foundations of Computer Science*, pp. 162–167. IEEE, 1986.

[43] M. Youssef, N.R. Adam, and V. Atluri, Ed. Preserving mobile customer privacy: An access control system for moving objects and customer information, mobile data management, *6th International Conference, MDM*, Lecture Notes in Computer Science. Springer-Verlag, Heidelberg, Germany, 2005.

[44] N. Zhang, S. Wang, and W. Zhao. A new scheme on privacy-preserving association rule mining. In *The 8th European Conference on Principles and Practice of Knowledge Discovery in Databases (PKDD 2004)*, Pisa, Italy, September 20–24, 2004.

[45] Y. Zhu and L. Liu. Optimal randomization for privacy preserving data mining. In *KDD '04: Proceedings of the Tenth ACM SIGKDD International Conference on Knowledge Discovery and Data Mining*, pp. 761–766, New York, 2004. ACM Press.

PRIVACY-ENHANCING TECHNOLOGIES

Chapter 7

Enterprise Privacy Policies and Languages

Michael Backes and Markus Dürmuth

Contents

7.1 Introduction 135
    7.1.1 Motivation and Overview 136
    7.1.2 Enterprise Privacy Policies 136
    7.1.3 Suitably Working with Enterprise Privacy Policies 137
7.2 Syntax and Semantics of EPAL Enterprise Privacy Policies 139
    7.2.1 Hierarchies, Obligations, and Conditions.................. 139
    7.2.2 Syntax of EPAL Policies 141
    7.2.3 Semantics of EPAL Policies................................. 142
7.3 Refinement and Equivalence of EPAL Policies 144
7.4 Composition of EPAL Policies 147
    7.4.1 Defining Conjunction and Disjunction
         of Privacy Policies 148
    7.4.2 Algebraic Properties of the Operators 151
Acknowledgments 152
References.. 152

7.1 Introduction

This chapter illustrates some basic issues in the study of enterprise privacy policies and the underlying languages, namely the treatment of purposes, conditions, and obligations under which personal data is collected and can be accessed, as well as the derivation of a suitable toolkit for refining policies and for combining them according to several policy operations. These operations ideally yield an expressive algebra over enterprise privacy policies together with suitable algebraic laws that allow for conveniently using such policies in common business scenarios. This chapter uses IBM's Enterprise Privacy Authorization Language (EPAL) for illustrating these concepts.

7.1.1 Motivation and Overview

The past decades have come with a dramatic intensification in the social practices of gathering, storing, manipulation, and sharing information about people. Various new practices have aroused suspicion, indignation, and protest not only among legal experts and privacy advocates, but also in the popular media and among the general public, which in turn led to an increasing privacy awareness. As a consequence, the proper incorporation of privacy considerations into business processes has rapidly gained importance. Regulatory measures, such as the Children's Online Privacy Protection Act (COPPA), the Health Insurance Portability and Accountability Act (HIPAA), the Sarbanes–Oxley Act, and the European Union Directive on Data Privacy, serve as additional evidence that avoiding violations of privacy regulations is becoming a crucial issue. Adhering to such regulations, in particular, requires the development of an expressive and easily usable method for dealing with privacy concerns of Web site users that ensures law-compliant usage of personal data within enterprises as well as in general business-to-business matters. While the Platform for Privacy Preferences Project (P3P) [1] constitutes a valuable tool for dealing with privacy issues of Web site users, the fine-grained treatment of privacy concerns in business-to-business matters is still not settled satisfyingly, e.g., a language for the internal privacy practices of enterprises and for technical privacy enforcement must offer more possibilities for fine-grained distinction of data users, purposes, etc., as well as clearer semantics.

7.1.2 Enterprise Privacy Policies

To live up to these requirements, enterprise privacy technologies have emerged and rapidly gained momentum. One approach for capturing the privacy requirements of an enterprise—without already specifying the implementation of these requirements to retain sufficient flexibility—is the use of formalized enterprise privacy policies, see, e.g., [2–4] for first occurrences of this concept, which nowadays are widely considered to constitute a salient approach for providing such a method. Informally speaking, the aim of a privacy policy is to define by whom, for which purposes, and in which way collected data can be accessed. Further, a privacy policy may impose obligations on the organization using the data. Privacy policies formalize privacy statements, such as "we use data of a minor for marketing purposes only if the parent has given consent" or "medical data can only be read by the patient's primary care physician." In business-to-business matters, enterprise privacy policies often reflect different legal regulations, promises made to customers as well as more restrictive internal practices of the enterprise. Further, they may allow customer preferences. Technically, enterprise privacy policies closely resemble traditional policies for access control (see, e.g., [5–8]) augmented with privacy-specific characteristics, such as purposes, conditions, and obligations.

Although the primary purpose of enterprise privacy policies is enterprise-internal use, many factors speak for standardization of such policies. For example, it would allow certain technical parts of regulations to be encoded into such a standardized language once and for all, and a large enterprise with heterogeneous repositories of personal data then could hope that enforcement tools for all these repositories become available and allow the enterprise to consistently enforce at least the internal privacy practices chosen by the CPO (chief privacy officer).

For these reasons, IBM has proposed EPAL [3,4,9,10] as an XML specification, which has been submitted to World Wide Web Constorium (W3C) for standardization. We will illustrate the underlying ideas of enterprise privacy policies by means of EPAL in the following, since EPAL contains several central concepts of privacy languages in an easily understandable form. EPAL, in particular, allows for a fine-grained description of privacy requirements in enterprises and has the potential to become a valuable tool for (business) processes that span several enterprises or different parts of a larger organization.

7.1.3 Suitably Working with Enterprise Privacy Policies

Enterprise privacy policies often reflect different legal regulations, promises made to customers, as well as more restrictive internal practices of the enterprise. Further, they may allow customer preferences. Hence, they may be authored, maintained, replaced, and audited in a distributed fashion. In other words, it is highly desirable to offer a life-cycle management system for the collection of enterprise privacy policies. In the early days of privacy policy languages, approaches were based on monolithic and complete specifications, which is very restrictive given that several policies might have to be enforced at once while being under control of different authorities. Having in mind actual use cases where sensitive data obeying different privacy regulations has to be merged or exchanged, this situation calls for a composition framework that allows for integrating different privacy policies while retaining their independence.

The first operation constituting a fundamental notion for many situations in policy management is policy refinement. Intuitively, one policy refines another if using the first policy automatically also fulfills the second policy. Refinement enables verification that an enterprise privacy policy fulfills regulations or adheres to standards set by consumer organizations or a self-regulatory body, assuming only that these coarser requirements are once and for all also formalized as a privacy policy. Similarly, it enables verification that a detailed policy for a part of the enterprise (defined by responsibility or by technology) refines the overall privacy policy set by the company's CPO. The verification can be done in the enterprise or by external auditors, such as [11,12].

Composition is the notion of constructively combining two or more policies; often the goal is that the resulting policy refines them all. For instance, an enterprise might first take all applicable regulations and combine them into a minimum policy. A general promise made to customers, e.g., an existing P3P policy translated into the more general language, may be a further input. In enterprise parts that support detailed preferences of individuals, such preferences may be yet another policy to be composed with the others, yielding one final policy per individual. (In contrast, simple preferences may be represented as a set of Boolean opt-in or opt-out choices, and treated as context data by conditions within a single policy.) Typical applications where detailed preferences are needed are wallet-style collections of user data for the purpose of transfer to other enterprises, and collaborative tools, such as team rooms. Motivated by successful applications of algebraic tools in access control [5–8,13], privacy policy languages soon aimed at offering operators for composing and restricting policies as part of an expressive algebra over enterprise privacy policies together with its formal semantics and suitable algebraic laws that allow for a convenient policy management. Policy conjunction and disjunction serve as the core building blocks for constructing larger policies. For instance, an enterprise might first take all applicable regulations and combine them into a minimum policy by means of the conjunction operator. As one expects, these operators are not a simple logical AND and OR, respectively, for expressive enterprise privacy policies because of the treatment of obligations, different policy scopes, and default values.

Additional operators usually comprise scoping and master-slave compositions. While scoping allows for confining the scope of a policy to subhierarchies of a policy, master–slave composition allows for giving priority to one master policy while only evaluating the slave policy if the master policy does not care about the outcome. Both operators are of major use in practice as they enable managing, respectively reasoning about privacy requirements that involve only certain parts of an organization and that reflect hierarchical decision structures of enterprises.

7.2 Syntax and Semantics of EPAL Enterprise Privacy Policies

Informally speaking, the aim of an enterprise privacy policy is to define by whom, for which purposes, and in which way collected data can be accessed. Further, a privacy policy may impose obligations onto the organization using the data. This section shows the abstract syntax and semantics of IBM's EPAL privacy policy language [9,10,14,15] up to some augmentations needed to achieve the desired algebraic properties, e.g., that obligations are already structured in a suitable way (see [15]).

7.2.1 Hierarchies, Obligations, and Conditions

For conveniently specifying rules, the data, users, etc., are categorized in EPAL as in many access-control languages. The same applies to the purposes. To allow for structured rules with exceptions, categories are ordered in hierarchies; mathematically they are forests, i.e., multiple trees. For example, a user "company" may group several "departments," each containing several "employees." The enterprise can then write rules for the entire "company" with exceptions for some "departments."

Definition 7.1 (Hierarchy) *A hierarchy is a pair* $(H, >_H)$ *of a finite set* H *and a transitive, nonreflexive relation* $>_H \subseteq H \times H$, *where every* $h \in H$ *has at most one immediate predecessor (parent). As usual, we write* $\geq_H$ *for the reflexive closure.*

For two hierarchies $(H, >_H)$ *and* $(G, >_G)$, *one defines*

$$(H, >_H) \subseteq (G, >_G) \; :\Longleftrightarrow \; (H \subseteq G) \wedge (>_H \subseteq >_G) \; and$$

$$(H, >_H) \cup (G, >_G) \; := \; (H \cup G, (>_H \cup >_G)^*),$$

where $(\cdot)^*$ *denotes the transitive closure. Note that the union of hierarchies is not always a hierarchy again.*

As mentioned above EPAL policies can impose obligations, i.e., duties for an organization/enterprise. Typical examples are to send a notification to the data subject after each emergency access to medical data, or to delete data within a certain time limit. Obligations are not structured in hierarchies, but by an implication relation. For example, an obligation to delete data within thirty days implies that the data is deleted within two months. The overall obligations of a rule in EPAL are expressed as sets of individual obligations that must have an interpretation in the application domain. As multiple obligations may imply more than each one individually, the implication relation (which must also be realized in the application domain) is specified on these sets of obligations. The following definition also defines how this relation interacts with vocabulary extensions.

Definition 7.2 (Obligation Model)   *An* obligation model *is a pair* $(O, \to_O)$ *of a set O and a transitive relation* $\to_O \subseteq \mathfrak{P}(O) \times \mathfrak{P}(O)$, *spoken* implies, *on the powerset of O, where $\bar{o}_1 \to_O \bar{o}_2$ for all $\bar{o}_2 \subseteq \bar{o}_1$, i.e., fulfilling a set of obligations implies fulfilling all subsets. For $O' \supset \mathfrak{P}(O)$, we extend the implication to $O' \times \mathfrak{P}(O)$ by $((\bar{o}_1 \to_O \bar{o}_2) : \iff (\bar{o}_1 \cap O \to_O \bar{o}_2))$.*

To define the AND and OR composition of privacy policies in a meaningful way, we moreover assume that $\mathfrak{P}(O)$ is equipped with an additional operation $\vee$, such that $(\mathfrak{P}(O), \vee, \cup)$ is a distributive lattice; the operator $\vee$ reflects the intuitive notion of OR (in analogy to the set-theoretical union $\cup$, which corresponds to AND). In particular, we require the following:

- *For all $\bar{o}_1, \bar{o}_2 \subseteq O$, we have $\bar{o}_1 \to_O (\bar{o}_1 \vee \bar{o}_2)$.*
- *For all $\bar{o}_1, \bar{o}_2, \bar{o}'_1, \bar{o}'_2 \subseteq O$, we have $(\bar{o}_1 \to_O \bar{o}_2) \wedge (\bar{o}'_1 \to_O \bar{o}'_2)$ implies both $(\bar{o}_1 \vee \bar{o}'_1) \to_O (\bar{o}_2 \vee \bar{o}'_2)$ and $(\bar{o}_1 \cup \bar{o}'_1) \to_O (\bar{o}_2 \cup \bar{o}'_2)$.*

Finally, we assume that all occurring obligation models $(O, \to_O)$ are subsets of a fixed (super) obligation model $OM_0 = (O_0, \to_{O_0})$ such that $\to_O$ is the restriction of $\to_{O_0}$ to $\mathfrak{P}(O) \times \mathfrak{P}(O)$.

While EPAL's obligation model and implication relation constitute a course-grained abstraction of the relationship between obligations, they have given rise to various works on how to suitably define and work with obligations [16, 17].

The decision formalized by a privacy policy can depend on context data, such as the age of a person. In EPAL, this is represented by conditions over data in so-called containers [9]. The XML representation of the formulas is taken from XACML [13], which corresponds to a predicate logic without quantifiers. Containers are formalized as a set of variables with domains; conditions are formalized as formulas over these variables.

Definition 7.3 (Condition Vocabulary)   *A* condition vocabulary *is a pair* $Var = (V, Scope)$ *of a finite set V and a function assigning every $x \in V$, called a* variable, *a set $Scope(x)$, called its* scope.

Two condition vocabularies $Var_1 = (V_1, Scope_1)$, $Var_2 = (V_2, Scope_2)$ are compatible *if $Scope_1(x) = Scope_2(x)$ for all $x \in V_1 \cap V_2$. For that case, we define their* union *by $Var_1 \cup Var_2 := (V_1 \cup V_2, Scope_1 \cup Scope_2)$.*

One may think of extending this to a full signature in the sense of logic, i.e., including predicate and function symbols—in EPAL, this is hidden in user-defined functions that may occur in the XACML conditions. A given universe of predicates and functions with fixed domains and semantics is assumed.

Definition 7.4 (Condition Language) *Let a condition vocabulary Var =* (*V, Scope*) *be given.*

■ *The* condition language *C(Var) is the set of correctly typed formulas over V using the assumed universe of predicates and functions, and in the given syntax of predicate logic without quantifiers.*
■ *An* assignment *of the variables is a function $\chi : V \to \bigcup_{x \in V} Scope(x)$ with $\chi(x) \in Scope(x)$ for all $x \in V$. The set of all assignments for the set Var is written $\mathfrak{Ass}(Var)$.*
■ *For $\chi \in \mathfrak{Ass}(Var)$, let $eval_\chi : C(Var) \to \{true, false\}$ denote the evaluation function for conditions given this variable assignment. This is defined by the underlying logic and the assumption that all predicate and function symbols come with fixed semantics.*
■ *For $\chi \in \mathfrak{Ass}(Var)$, we denote by $c_\chi \in C(Var)$ some fixed formula such that $eval_\chi(c_\chi) = true$ and $eval_{\chi'}(c_\chi) = false$ for all $\chi' \in \mathfrak{Ass}(Var) \setminus \{\chi\}$.*

7.2.2 Syntax of EPAL Policies

An EPAL policy contains a vocabulary, a set of authorization rules, and a default ruling. The vocabulary defines element hierarchies for data, purposes, users, and actions, as well as the obligation model and the condition vocabulary. Data, users, and actions are as in most access-control policies (except that users are typically called "subjects" there, which in privacy policies would lead to confusion with data subjects), and functions are an important additional hierarchy for the purpose binding of collected data.

Definition 7.5 (Vocabulary) *A vocabulary is a tuple Voc = (UH, DH, PH, AH, Var, OM) where UH, DH, PH, and AH are hierarchies called user, data, purpose, and action hierarchy, respectively, Var is a condition vocabulary, and OM an obligation model.*

As a naming convention, we assume that the components of a vocabulary *Voc* are always called as in **Definition 7.5** with $UH = (U, >_U)$, $DH = (D, >_D)$, $PH = (P, >_P)$, $AH = (A, >_A)$, $Var = (V, Scope)$, and $OM = (O, \to_O)$, except if explicitly stated otherwise. In a vocabulary Voc_i, all components also get a subscript i, and similarly for superscripts.

Definition 7.6 (Ruleset and Privacy Policy) *A ruleset for a vocabulary Voc is a subset of $\mathbb{Z} \times U \times D \times P \times A \times C(Var) \times \mathfrak{P}(O) \times \{+, -\}$.*

A privacy policy or EPAL policy is a triple (Voc, R, dr) of a vocabulary Voc, a ruleset R for Voc, and a default ruling $dr \in \{+, \circ, -\}$. The set of these policies *is called EPAL, and the subset for a given vocabulary EPAL(Voc). Moreover, we call (Voc, R, dr) $\in$ EPAL well formed, if for all rules $(i, u, d, p, a, c, \bar{o}, r)$, $(i, u', d', p', a', c', \bar{o}', r') \in R$ with identical precedences i and for all assignments $\chi \in \mathfrak{Ass}(Var)$ the implication $(eval_\chi(c) = true = eval_\chi(c')) \Rightarrow (r = r')$ holds.*

Intuitively, a privacy policy is *well formed* if rules that allow for contradicting rulings do not have identical precedences. The rulings $+$, $\circ$, and $-$ mean "allow," "don't care," and "deny;" the value $\circ$ is special in the sense it can only be assigned to the default ruling of a policy. As a naming convention, we assume that the components of a privacy policy called *Pol* are always called as in **Definition 7.6**, and if *Pol* has a sub- or superscript, then so do the components.

7.2.3 Semantics of EPAL Policies

An EPAL request is a tuple (u, d, p, a), which should belong to the set $U \times D \times P \times A$ for the given vocabulary. Note that EPAL requests are not restricted to "ground terms" as in some other languages, i.e., minimal elements in the hierarchies. This is useful if one starts with coarse policies and refines them because elements that are initially minimal may later get children. For instance, the individual users in a "department" of an "enterprise" may not be mentioned in the CPO's privacy policy, but in the department's privacy policy. For similar reasons, we also define the semantics for requests outside the given vocabulary. We assume a superset S in which all hierarchy sets are embedded; in practice, it is typically a set of strings or valid XML expressions.

Definition 7.7 (Request) *For a vocabulary Voc, we define the set of valid requests as $Req(Voc) := U \times D \times P \times A$. Given a superset S of the sets U, D, P, A of all considered vocabularies, the set of all requests is $Req := S^4$.*

For valid requests $(u, d, p, a), (u', d', p', a') \in Req(Voc)$ we set

$$(u, d, p, a) \leq (u', d', p', a') : \Longleftrightarrow u \leq_U u' \text{ and } d \leq_D d' \text{ and } p \leq_P p' \text{ and } a \leq_A a'.$$

Moreover, we set $(u, d, p, a) <_1 (u', d', p', a')$ if and only if there is exactly one $x \in \{u, d, p, a\}$ such that x' is the parent of x and for all $y \in \{u, d, p, a\} \setminus \{x\}$ we have $y = y'$. Finally, we refer to a valid request $(u, d, p, a) \in Req(Voc)$ as leaf or leaf node if $u, d, p,$ and a are leaves in the respective hierarchy. We denote the set of all leaves of $Req(Voc)$ by $L(Voc)$ and for $q \in Req(Voc)$, we set $L(q, Voc) := \{q' \in L(Voc) \mid q' \leq q\} \setminus \{q\}$.

The semantics of a privacy policy *Pol* is a function $eval_{Pol}$ that processes a request based on a given assignment. The evaluation result is a pair $(r, \bar{o})$ of a ruling (also called *decision*) and associated obligations; in the case of a "don't care" ruling ($r = \circ$), we necessarily have $\bar{o} = \emptyset$, i.e., no obligations are imposed in this case. There further exists the exceptional ruling *scope_error*, which indicates that a request was out of the scope of the policy.

The semantics is defined by a virtual preprocessing that unfolds the hierarchies followed by a request processing stage. Note that this is only a compact definition of the semantics and not an efficient real evaluation algorithm.

Definition 7.8 (Unfolded Rules)   *For a privacy policy Pol = (Voc, R, dr), the unfolded rule set UR(Pol) is defined as follows:*

$$URD(Pol) := \{(i, u', d', p', a', c, \bar{o}, r) \in R \mid \exists (i, u, d, p, a, c, \bar{o}, r) \in R$$

$$\text{with } u \geq_U u' \wedge d \geq_D d' \wedge p \geq_P p' \wedge a \geq_A a'\};$$

$$UR(Pol) := URD(Pol)$$

$$\cup \{(i, u', d', p', a', c, \bar{o}, -) \in R \mid \exists (i, u, d, p, a, c, \bar{o}, -) \in URD(Pol)$$

$$\text{with } u' \geq_U u \wedge d' \geq_D d \wedge p' \geq_P p \wedge a' \geq_A a\}.$$

A crucial point in this definition is the fact that "deny" rules are inherited both downward and upward along the four hierarchies, while "allow" rules are inherited downward only. The reason is that the hierarchies are considered groupings: If access is forbidden for some element of a group, it is also forbidden for the group as a whole. If upward inheritance of deny rules is not considered, individuals may bypass their restrictions by instead posing the desired query on their whole group, which might possess additional rights (see [18]).

Next, we define which rules are applicable for a request given an assignment of the condition variables.

Definition 7.9 (Applicable Rules)   *Let a privacy policy Pol = (Voc, R, dr), a request q = (u, d, p, a) ∈ Req(Voc), and an assignment $\chi \in \mathfrak{Ass}(Var)$ be given. Then the set of applicable rules is*

$$AR(Pol, q, \chi) := \{(i, u, d, p, a, c, \bar{o}, r) \in UR(Pol) \mid eval_\chi(c) = true\}.$$

To formulate the semantics, it is convenient to define the maximum and minimum precedence of a policy.

Definition 7.10 (Precedence Range)   *For a privacy policy Pol = (Voc, R, dr), let max(Pol) := max\{i \mid \exists (i, u, d, p, a, c, \bar{o}, r) \in R\} and min(Pol) := min\{i \mid \exists (i, u, d, p, a, c, \bar{o}, r) \in R\}.*

We can now define the actual semantics, i.e., the result of a request given an assignment.

Definition 7.11 (Semantics) *Let a well-formed privacy policy Pol = (Voc, R, dr), a request q = (u, d, p, a) ∈ Req, and an assignment* $\chi \in \mathfrak{Ass}(Var)$ *be given. Then the* evaluation result $(r, \bar{o}) := eval_{Pol}(q, \chi)$ *of policy Pol for q and* χ *is defined by the following algorithm, where every "return" is understood to abort the processing of the algorithm.*

1. Out-of-scope testing: *If* $q \notin Req(Voc)$, *return* $(r, \bar{o}) := (scope\_error, \emptyset)$.
2. Processing by precedence: *For each precedence level* $i := max(Pol)$ *down to* $min(Pol)$:
   - Accumulate obligations: $\bar{o}_{acc} := \bigcup_{(i,u,d,p,a,c,\bar{o},r) \in AR(Pol,q,\chi)} \bar{o}$.
   - Normal ruling: *If some rule* $(i, u, d, p, a, c, \bar{o}, r) \in AR(Pol, q, \chi)$ *exists, return* $(r, \bar{o}_{acc})$.
3. Default ruling: *If this step is reached, return* $(r, \bar{o}) := (dr, \emptyset)$.

We also say that policy Pol rules $(r, \bar{o})$ *for q and* χ, *omitting q and* χ *if they are clear from the context.*

7.3 Refinement and Equivalence of EPAL Policies

Basically, refining a policy *Pol* means adding more details to it, i.e., enriching the vocabulary and the set of rules without changing the meaning of the policy with respect to its original vocabulary. When a policy is first designed, refinement may be achieved in a constructive way, e.g., by starting with the coarse policy and only adding details by certain provably refining syntactic means. However, if a regulation changes or the enterprise extends its operation to new sectors or countries, the enterprise has to verify that its existing policy still complies with the new or additional regulations. Hence, a definition of refinement between two arbitrary policies is needed. Sticky policies are another application of general refinement: Here data is transferred from the realm of one policy into another (where the transfer, of course, must be permitted by the first policy), and the second realm must enforce the first policy. However, the enforcement mechanisms (both organizational and technical) in the second realm often will not be able to deal with arbitrary policies for each obtained set of data. In this case, one realm must perform a refinement test before the data is transferred, i.e., one has to verify that the policy of the second realm refines the policy of the first, at least for the restriction of the first policy to the data types being transferred.

To be useful for actual use cases, it is essential that operators defined on privacy policies behave in a well-specified and "intuitive" manner with respect to refinement relations. Thus, before we can make concrete statements about the refinement properties of the operators introduced in the next section, we need some additional terminology.

Definition 7.12 (Compatible Vocabulary)   *Two vocabularies Voc_1 and Voc_2 are compatible if their condition vocabularies are compatible and $UH_1 \cup UH_2, DH_1 \cup DH_2, PH_1 \cup PH_2, AH_1 \cup AH_2$ are hierarchies again.*

The notion of compatible vocabularies is a technicality that turns out to be necessary to specify operations that combine different policies, which are not necessarily formulated in terms of identical vocabularies.

Definition 7.13 (Union of Vocabularies)   *The union of two compatible vocabularies Voc_1 and Voc_2 is defined as $Voc_1 \cup Voc_2 := (UH_1 \cup UH_2, DH_1 \cup DH_2, PH_1 \cup PH_2, AH_1 \cup AH_2, Var_1 \cup Var_2, OM)$, where $OM = (O, \rightarrow_O)$ is the obligation model with the lattice $(\mathfrak{P}(O), \vee, \cup)$ being generated by $\mathfrak{P}(O_1)$ and $\mathfrak{P}(O_2)$, and $\rightarrow_O$ being the restriction of $\rightarrow_{O_0}$ to $\mathfrak{P}(O) \times \mathfrak{P}(O)$.*

Next, we need the refinement of obligations whose definition requires some care, as a refined policy may well contain additional obligations, whereas at the same time some others have been omitted. Consequently, the definition of refinement of obligations makes use of both obligation models—that of the original (coarser) policy and that of the refined policy.

Definition 7.14 (Refinement and Equivalence of Obligations)   *Let two obligation models $(O_i, \rightarrow_{O_i})$ and $\bar{o}_i \subseteq O_i$ for $i = 1, 2$ be given. Then $\bar{o}_2$ is a refinement of $\bar{o}_1$, written $\bar{o}_2 \prec \bar{o}_1$ if and only if the following holds:*

$$\exists \bar{o} \subseteq O_1 \cap O_2 : \bar{o}_2 \rightarrow_{O_2} \bar{o} \rightarrow_{O_1} \bar{o}_1.$$

We call $\bar{o}_1$ and $\bar{o}_2$ equivalent, written $\bar{o}_1 \equiv \bar{o}_2$, if and only if $\bar{o}_1 \prec \bar{o}_2$ and $\bar{o}_2 \prec \bar{o}_1$. For $r_1, r_2 \in \{+, -, \circ, scope\_error\}$, we further define $(r_1, \bar{o}_1) \equiv (r_2, \bar{o}_2)$ if and only if $r_1 = r_2$ and $\bar{o}_1 \equiv \bar{o}_2$.

We can now formalize the notion of (weak) refinement of well-formed policies.

Definition 7.15 (Policy Refinement)   *Let two well-formed privacy policies $Pol_i = (Voc_i, R_i, dr_i)$ for $i = 1, 2$ with compatible vocabularies be given, and set $Pol_i^* = (Voc_i^*, R_i, dr_i)$ for $i = 1, 2$ where $Voc_i^* := (UH_1 \cup UH_2, DH_1 \cup DH_2, PH_1 \cup PH_2, AH_1 \cup AH_2, Var_i, OM_i)$.*
Let $r_1, r_2 \in \{+, -, \circ, scope\_error\}$ and $\bar{o}_i \subseteq O_i$ for $i = 1, 2$ be arbitrary. We say that $(r_2, \bar{o}_2)$ refines $(r_1, \bar{o}_1)$ (in OM_1 and OM_2), written $(r_2, \bar{o}_2) \prec (r_1, \bar{o}_1)$,

if and only if one of the following two conditions holds

$$(1) \quad (r_1, \bar{o}_1) \in \{(scope\_error, \emptyset), (\circ, \emptyset)\}$$

$$(2) \quad r_1 \in \{+, -\}, r_2 = r_1, \bar{o}_2 \prec \bar{o}_1.$$

We say that $(r_2, \bar{o}_2)$ *weakly refines* $(r_1, \bar{o}_1)$ *(in* OM_1 *and* OM_2*), written* $(r_2, \bar{o}_2) \precsim (r_1, \bar{o}_1)$, *if and only if one of the following three conditions holds:*

$$(1) \quad (r_2, \bar{o}_2) \prec (r_1, \bar{o}_1)$$

$$(2) \quad r_1 = +, r_2 = -$$

$$(3) \quad (r_1, \bar{o}_1) = (+, \emptyset), r_2 = \circ.$$

We call Pol_2 *a* refinement *of* Pol_1, *written* $Pol_2 \prec Pol_1$ *if and only if for every assignment* $\chi \in \mathfrak{Ass}(Var_1 \cup Var_2)$ *and every authorization request* $q \in Req$, *we have* $eval_{Pol_2^*}(q, \chi) \prec eval_{Pol_1^*}(q, \chi)$. *We call* Pol_2 *a* weak refinement *of* Pol_1 *if the same holds with* $\prec$ *replaced by* $\precsim$.

Intuitively, a privacy policy that weakly refines another policy is at least as restrictive as the coarser one: Even if the original policy rules "allow" for a certain request, after a weak refinement the same request may be denied, or (provided that no obligations get lost) an "allow" can be transformed into a "don't care."

Finally, the equivalence of two well-formed privacy policies is defined in the obvious manner.

Definition 7.16 (Policy Equivalence)   *Two well-formed privacy policies* Pol_1 *and* Pol_2 *are called* equivalent, *written* $Pol_1 \equiv Pol_2$, *if and only if they are mutual refinements, i.e.,* $Pol_1 \equiv Pol_2 : \Longleftrightarrow (Pol_1 \prec Pol_2 \wedge Pol_2 \prec Pol_1)$.

While this notion of policy equivalence is rather intuitive, it turns out that in some situations only a weaker form of equivalence can be achieved and we, therefore, conclude this section with the definition of weak policy equivalence.

Definition 7.17 (Weak Policy Equivalence)   *Two well-formed privacy policies* Pol_1 *and* Pol_2 *are called* weakly equivalent, *written* $Pol_1 \approx Pol_2$, *if and only if they are equivalent on their joint vocabulary, i.e., if and only if* $(Voc_1 \cup Voc_2, R_1, dr_1) \equiv (Voc_1 \cup Voc_2, R_2, dr_2)$.

7.4 Composition of EPAL Policies

Basically, defining symmetric operations on privacy policies reflecting the intuitive notions of conjunction (AND) and disjunction (OR) looks rather simple. Unfortunately, with a straightforward yet intuitive approach, it happens that the conjunction or disjunction of two privacy policies might no longer constitute a syntactically correct privacy policy. From a practical point of view, such a behavior is not desirable. First, available tools to enforce a (EPAL) privacy policy are designed to handle privacy policies only. Thus, to handle compositions of privacy policies, these tools had to be modified or new tools had to be developed. The obvious solution to this problem—making use of a wrapper program that queries several policies by means of existing tools and combines their results appropriately—is not always acceptable. In particular, such a workaround might violate conditions that were necessary to pass some (expensive) certification process.

Second, the combined privacy policies can originate in rather different sources, which are separated through significant geographical distances. Consequently, in larger, say, multinational, projects where policies of many different organizations have to be combined, it can be infeasible or at least very inconvenient to store all (component) policies that contribute to the ruling of the composition. To circumvent these problems, it is desirable to work in a subset of EPAL that is on the one hand closed under conjunction and disjunction as well as other suitable algebraic operations, and on the other hand is still expressive enough to capture typically used privacy policies. This subset is the set of so-called *well-founded* privacy policies [15]. The intuition underlying the notion of well-founded policies can be described as follows:

- Suppose the ruling specified for some group is "deny," but none of the group members is denied from accessing the respective data. Then this contradicts the idea that in EPAL the group ruling is to reflect ("to group") the rulings of the individual group members.
- If each member of a group is permitted to perform some action, then intuitively the group as a whole is permitted to perform this action, too.
- Assume that both the ruling specified for a group and for a member of this group is "allow," and assume further that the obligations of the group are not a superset of the obligations of the group member. Then the group member may be able to avoid certain obligations by submitting a query where the user is specified to be the group as a whole. Typically, the availability of such a "workaround" is not desirable. On the other hand, if the obligations of the group are

stricter than the union of the obligations of the group members and we (re)define the group obligations to be the union of the individual obligations, then no harm (in the sense that a group member can gain additional privileges) is caused by querying the group.

Formally, well-founded policies are captured as follows.

Definition 7.18 (Well-Founded Policy)   *Let Pol be a well-formed policy. Then we call Pol* well-founded *if and only if for all* $(q, \chi) \in Req(Voc) \times \mathfrak{Ass}(Var)$ *the following conditions are fulfilled:*

- *If q is no leaf node and* $eval_{Pol}(q, \chi) = (-, \bar{o})$, *then there exists* $q' <_1 q$ *such that* $eval_{Pol}(q', \chi) = (-, \bar{o}')$ *for some* $\bar{o}'$.
- *If* $eval_{Pol}(q', \chi) = (+, \bar{o}_{q'})$ *for each* $q' <_1 q$ *and arbitrary* $\bar{o}_{q'}$, *then* $eval_{Pol}(q, \chi) = (+, \bar{o})$ *for some* $\bar{o}$.
- *If* $eval_{Pol}(q, \chi) = (r, \bar{o})$, *then* $\bar{o} = \bigcup_{q' <_1 q, eval_{Pol}(q', \chi) = (r, \bar{o}')} \bar{o}'$.

Up to equivalence, well-founded policies are already uniquely determined by the rulings of the leaf nodes.

Lemma 7.1   Let Pol_1, Pol_2 be well-founded privacy policies with $Voc_1 = Voc_2$ and let $eval_{Pol_1}(q, \chi) = eval_{Pol_2}(q, \chi)$ for every $q \in L(Voc_1)$ and every $\chi \in \mathfrak{Ass}(Var_1)$. Then $Pol_1 \equiv Pol_2$.

Actually, the predetermined allow and deny rulings for the set of leaf nodes can be chosen arbitrarily. In addition, a well-founded policy can explicitly be transformed algorithmically into a form that is consistent with any predetermined set of rulings for all leaf nodes.

7.4.1 Defining Conjunction and Disjunction of Privacy Policies

Unlike in typical access control settings, defining the conjunction and disjunction of privacy policies requires taking care of the "don't care" ruling o, whose semantics is different from both "allow" and "deny." Motivated by the intuition behind the ruling o, definitions are given in analogy to the conjunction and disjunction in a three-valued Lukasiewicz logic L_3. To handle the obligations, use the operator $\vee$ provided by the obligation model. Intuitively, one does not want to give a positive answer to a request if one of the two policies that are to be combined by AND denies the access. Further on, if one policy allows the access and the other one "does not care," then returning a "don't care" seems plausible and is indeed needed to ensure the distributivity of the operators AND and OR. Similarly, for OR we allow an access if at least one of the two involved policies allows the request. Moreover, we "do not care," if one of the operands "does not care"—except if the other operand explicitly "allows" the request.

Conjunction and disjunction of two well-founded privacy policies can now be defined. **Lemma 7.1** implies that it is sufficient to define the operations for those requests that are leaves of the considered hierarchies since once the evaluations on the leaves are fixed, the corresponding privacy policy is (up to equivalence) uniquely determined. In addition, a policy can then be explicitly computed that is consistent with the given evaluations of the leaf nodes. However, to make definitions of the operators independent of an algorithmic specification, the actual definitions are formulated in such a way that the result of a conjunction/disjunction of two privacy policies constitutes an equivalence class of policies—not a specific privacy policy.

The motivation for defining an AND operation on privacy policies is rather straightforward. Assume that an enterprise takes part in some project for which data has to be accessed and processed that is controlled by some external project partner. Then the access to and processing of such data shall only be allowed as long as none of the individual privacy policies of the participating enterprises is violated.

Definition 7.19 (Policy Conjunction)   *Let Pol_1, Pol_2 be two well-founded privacy policies such that $Pol_i^* = (Voc_i^*, R_i, dr_i)$ for $i = 1, 2$ with $Voc_i^* := (UH_1 \cup UH_2, DH_1 \cup DH_2, PH_1 \cup PH_2, AH_1 \cup AH_2, Var_i, OM_i)$ are also well-founded privacy policies.*

Then the conjunction *of Pol_1 and Pol_2 is the equivalence class ($w.\,r.\,t. \equiv$) of all well-founded privacy policies Pol on the joint vocabulary $Voc := Voc_1 \cup Voc_2$ such that for all leaf nodes $q \in L(Voc)$ and for all assignments $\chi \in \mathfrak{Ass}(Var)$ we have $(r_1, \bar{o}_1) \equiv (r_2, \bar{o}_2)$, where*

$$(r_1, \bar{o}_1) := eval_{Pol}(q, \chi) \text{ and}$$

$$(r_2, \bar{o}_2) := eval_{Pol_1^*}(q, \chi) \text{ AND } eval_{Pol_2^*}(q, \chi),$$

where AND *is defined as in Table 7.1.*

By Pol_1 & Pol_2, we denote any representative of this equivalence class.

Note that this definition only imposes conditions on the leaf nodes; hence, the question arises to what extent "inner" queries obey the defining table for AND as well. Indeed, the desired relations are fulfilled for arbitrary queries.

Lemma 7.2   Let Pol_1, Pol_2 be well-founded privacy policies that satisfy the requirements of **Definition 7.19** and let $Pol = Pol_1$ & Pol_2. Then for all

Table 7.1   Definition of *AND* and *OR* Operators

AND	$(+,\bar{o}')$	$(-,\bar{o}')$	$(\circ,\emptyset)$
$(+,\bar{o})$	$(+,\bar{o}\cup\bar{o}')$	$(-,\bar{o}')$	$(\circ,\emptyset)$
$(-,\bar{o})$	$(-,\bar{o})$	$(-,\bar{o}\cup\bar{o}')$	$(-,\bar{o})$
$(\circ,\emptyset)$	$(\circ,\emptyset)$	$(-,\bar{o}')$	$(\circ,\emptyset)$
OR	$(+,\bar{o}')$	$(-,\bar{o}')$	$(\circ,\emptyset)$
$(+,\bar{o})$	$(+,\bar{o}\vee\bar{o}')$	$(+,\bar{o})$	$(+,\bar{o})$
$(-,\bar{o})$	$(+,\bar{o}')$	$(-,\bar{o}\vee\bar{o}')$	$(\circ,\emptyset)$
$(\circ,\emptyset)$	$(+,\bar{o}')$	$(\circ,\emptyset)$	$(\circ,\emptyset)$

requests $q \in Req(Voc)$ and for all assignments $\chi \in \mathfrak{Ass}(Var)$ we have the equivalence $eval_{Pol}(q, \chi) \equiv eval_{Pol_1^*}(q, \chi)$ AND $eval_{Pol_2^*}(q, \chi)$ with Pol_i^* as in **Definition 7.19**.

Similar to conjunction, the disjunction of privacy policies is essential for a variety of use cases. For example, consider two departments of an enterprise that cooperate in some project. For carrying out this project, it should then be possible to access data items whenever one of the individual privacy policies of the two departments grants such an access. This idea of "joining forces" is captured by the following definition.

Definition 7.20 (Policy Disjunction)   *Let Pol_1, Pol_2 be two well-founded privacy policies such that $Pol_i^* = (Voc_i^*, R_i, dr_i)$ for $i = 1, 2$ with $Voc_i^* :=$ $(UH_1 \cup UH_2, DH_1 \cup DH_2, PH_1 \cup PH_2, AH_1 \cup AH_2, Var_i, OM_i)$ are also well-founded privacy policies.*

Then the disjunction of Pol_1 and Pol_2 is the equivalence class (w.r.t. $\equiv$) of all well-founded privacy policies Pol on the joint vocabulary $Voc := Voc_1 \cup Voc_2$ such that for all leaf nodes $q \in L(Voc)$ and for all assignments $\chi \in \mathfrak{Ass}(Var)$ we have $(r_1, \bar{o}_1) \equiv (r_2, \bar{o}_2)$ where

$$(r_1, \bar{o}_1) := eval_{Pol}(q, \chi) \ and$$

$$(r_2, \bar{o}_2) := eval_{Pol_1^*}(q, \chi) \ OR \ eval_{Pol_2^*}(q, \chi),$$

where OR is defined as in Table 7.1.

By $Pol_1 + Pol_2$, we denote any representative of this equivalence class.

Unfortunately, for the disjunction of privacy policies, we have no analogue to **Lemma 7.2**, i.e., in general, we cannot achieve an equivalence of the form $eval_{Pol}(q, \chi) \equiv eval_{Pol_1^*}(q, \chi)$ OR $eval_{Pol_2^*}(q, \chi)$ for arbitrary requests q and assignments χ. In fact, it is not difficult to construct examples where imposing such a "node-wise equivalence" yields a contradiction to well-foundedness. Fortunately, also for the "inner nodes," the policy obtained by disjunction is still rather close to what one would expect intuitively.

Lemma 7.3 Let Pol_1, Pol_2 be well-founded privacy policies that satisfy the requirements of **Definition 7.19** and let $Pol = Pol_1 + Pol_2$. Then for all $q \in Req(Voc)$ such that $eval_{Pol}(q, \chi) = (-, \bar{o})$ or $eval_{Pol_1^*}(q, \chi)$ OR $eval_{Pol_2^*}$ $(q, \chi) = (+, \bar{o})$ holds for some $\bar{o}$, we have $eval_{Pol_1^*}(q, \chi)$ OR $eval_{Pol_2^*}$ $(q, \chi) \prec eval_{Pol}(q, \chi)$.

Additional operators that suitably complement conjunction and disjunction are *scoping* and *master–slave composition* (see [15]). Scoping essentially means restricting large policies to smaller parts. Use cases for scoping are omnipresent in practical policy management, e.g., deriving a department's privacy policy from the enterprise's global privacy policy, or considering only those rules that specifically deal with marketing purposes. Master–slave composition essentially means first applying one (master) policy, and if this policy gives a "don't care" ruling, then the other (slave) policy is applied. Master–slave composition constitutes the central tool for dealing with hierarchical structures of an enterprise, e.g., a privacy policy written by the CPO of a company and containing only a few regulations that have to be adhered to under all circumstances would be a master policy that can be master–slave composed with a more fine-grained department policy.

7.4.2   Algebraic Properties of the Operators

Since the operator definitions proposed in the previous section are quite intuitive, one would not expect any unpleasant surprises when using these operators to form more complex privacy policies involving three, four, or more operands. As actual use cases often involve more than only one or two different privacy policies, one has to ensure that the operators do not yield nonintuitive behaviors in such scenarios. Fortunately, this is not the case, and the usual algebraic laws apply.

Lemma 7.4 Let Pol_1, Pol_2, Pol_3 be well-founded EPAL policies such that the following expressions are well-defined, i.e., the respective requirements in **Definition 7.19** and **Definition 7.20** are met. Then the following holds:

$$\text{Idempotency}: \quad Pol_1 \,\&\, Pol_1 \equiv Pol_1, \tag{7.1}$$

$$Pol_1 + Pol_1 \equiv Pol_1,$$

$$\text{Commutativity}: \quad Pol_1 \,\&\, Pol_2 \equiv Pol_2 \,\&\, Pol_1, \tag{7.2}$$

$$Pol_1 + Pol_2 \equiv Pol_2 + Pol_1,$$

Associativity : Pol_1 & $(Pol_2$ & $Pol_3) \equiv (Pol_1$ & $Pol_2)$ & $Pol_3,$ (7.3)

$$Pol_1 + (Pol_2 + Pol_3) \equiv (Pol_1 + Pol_2) + Pol_3,$$

Distributivity : $Pol_1 + (Pol_2$ & $Pol_3) \equiv (Pol_1 + Pol_2)$ & $(Pol_1 + Pol_3),$ (7.4)

$$Pol_1 \text{ \& } (Pol_2 + Pol_3) \equiv (Pol_1 \text{ \& } Pol_2) + (Pol_1 \text{ \& } Pol_3),$$

Strong Absorption : $Pol_1 + (Pol_1$ & $Pol_2) \prec Pol_1.$ (7.5)

It is worth noting that the proof of the strong absorption property relies on both **Lemma 7.2** and **Lemma 7.3** and, although it may look tempting, one cannot simply switch the roles of conjunction and disjunction in the proof to derive a "dual" strong absorption law with the roles of & and + being exchanged.

In addition to purely algebraic properties of the operators, one can also establish several refinement results. In particular, the following relations, which from the intuitive point of view are highly desirable, hold true.

Lemma 7.5 Let Pol_1, Pol_2 be well-founded privacy policies such that the respective requirements of **Definition 7.19** and **Definition 7.20** are met. Then we have

Weak Multiplicative Refinement : Pol_1 & $Pol_2 \precsim Pol_i$ $(i = 1, 2),$ (7.6)

Weak Additive Refinement : $Pol_i \precsim Pol_1 + Pol_2$ $(i = 1, 2).$ (7.7)

Acknowledgments

We would like to thank Adam Barth, Günter Karjoth, John C. Mitchell, Rainer Steinwandt, Birgit Pfitzmann, Matthias Schunter, and Michael Waidner for interesting discussions on enterprise privacy languages.

References

[1] The platform for privacy preferences 1.0 (P3P1.0) specification, W3C recommendation. Available at http://www.w3.org/TR/P3P, 2003.

[2] Fischer-Hübner, S. IT-security and privacy: Design and use of privacy-enhancing security mechanisms, vol. 1958, *LNCS* Journal. Springer Heidelberg, Germany, 2002.

[3] Karjoth, G., Schunter, M., and Waidner, M. The platform for enterprise privacy practices—privacy-enabled management of customer data. In *Proc.*

Privacy Enhancing Technologies Conference, vol. 2482 of *LNCS*, 69–84. Springer, Heidelberg, Germany, 2002.

[4] Karjoth, G. and Schunter, M. A privacy policy model for enterprises. In *Proc. 15th IEEE Computer Security Foundations Workshop (CSFW)*, 271–281, Cape Breton, Nova Scotia, 2002.

[5] Bonatti, P.A., De Capitani di Vimercati, S., and Samarati, P. A modular approach to composing access control policies. In *Proc. 7th ACM Conference on Computer and Communications Security*, 164–173. ACM Press, New York, 2000.

[6] Wijesekera, D. and Jajodia, S. Policy algebras for access control—the propositional case. In *Proc. 8th ACM Conference on Computer and Communications Security*, 38–47, Philadelphia, 2001.

[7] Bonatti, P.A., de Capitani di Vimercati, S., and Samarati, P. An algebra for composing access control policies. *ACM Transactions on Information and System Security*, 5(1), 1–35, 2002.

[8] Wijesekera, D. and Jajodia, S. A propositional policy algebra for access control. *ACM Transactions on Information and System Security*, 6(2), 286–325, 2003.

[9] Ashley, P., et al. Enterprise Privacy Authorization Language (EPAL 1.2), 10 Nov 2003. www.w3.org/Submission/SUBM-EPAL-20031110/.

[10] Backes, M., Pfitzmann, B., and Schunter, M. A toolkit for managing enterprise privacy policies. In *Proc. 8th European Symposium on Research in Computer Security (ESORICS)*, vol. 2808 of *LNCS*, 162–180. Springer, Heidelberg, Germany, 2003.

[11] TRUSTe. Privacy Certification. Online at www.truste.com.

[12] Sentillion: Identity and access management for healthcare. Online at http://www.sentillion.com/.

[13] eXtensible Access Control Markup Language (XACML). OASIS Committee Specification 1.0, 2002. www.oasis-open.org/committees/xacml.

[14] Ashley, P., et al. E-P3P privacy policies and privacy authorization. In *Proc. 1st ACM Workshop on Privacy in the Electronic Society (WPES)*, 103–109, Washington, D.C., 2002.

[15] Backes, M., Dürmuth, M., and Steinwandt, R. An algebra for composing enterprise privacy policies. In *Proc. 9th European Symposium on Research in Computer Security (ESORICS)*, vol. 3193 of *LNCS*, 33–52, Springer, Heidelberg, Germany, 2004.

[16] Hilty, M., Basin, D., and Pretschner, A. On obligations. In *Proc. 10th European Symposium on Research in Computer Security (ESORICS)*, *LNCS*, 98–117, Springer, Heidelberg, Germany, 2005.

[17] Irwin, K., Yu, T., and Winsborough, W.H. On the modeling and analysis of obligations. In *Proc. 13th ACM Conference on Computer and Communications Security*, 134–143. ACM Press, New York, 2006.

[18] Barth, A. and Mitchell, J.C. Enterprise privacy promises and enforcement. In *Proc. of the 2005 Workshop on Issues in the Theory of Security (WITS05)*, 58–66, ACM Press, New York, 2005.

Chapter 8

Uncircumventable Enforcement of Privacy Policies via Cryptographic Obfuscation

Arvind Narayanan and Vitaly Shmatikov

Contents

8.1 Obfuscation and Its Uses 156
    8.1.1 Obfuscation for "White-Box" Cryptography 156
    8.1.2 Obfuscation for Copy Protection and Digital
        Rights Management... 157
    8.1.3 Obfuscation for Data Privacy 158
8.2 Cryptographic Obfuscation 159
8.3 Applications of Obfuscation to Digital Privacy 162
8.4 Obfuscation for Access Control 164
8.5 Obfuscation for Group Privacy 167
    8.5.1 Group Privacy Policy...................................... 168
    8.5.2 Tradeoff between Privacy and Utility...................... 169
References... 170

8.1 Obfuscation and Its Uses

Obfuscation, when used as a technical term, refers to hiding information "in plain sight" inside computer code or digital data. The history of obfuscation in modern computing can be traced to two events that took place in 1976. The first was the publication of Diffie and Hellman's seminal paper on public-key cryptography [DH76]. This paper is famous, of course, for introducing the first (or, at any rate, first publicly known) public-key cryptosystem. It also appears to be the first paper to describe *software obfuscation*. Diffie and Hellman suggested that making the encryption program incomprehensible might be a good way of converting a symmetric cryptosystem into a public-key one. Such a program would be an example of "white-box" cryptography because it would remain secure—in the sense that it would be hard for the adversary to invert the encryption function or to extract the symmetric key from it—even if the program were executed on a computer completely controlled by the adversary. This was the first instance of *obfuscation for "white-box" cryptography*.

Also in 1976, Bill Gates wrote "An Open Letter to Hobbyists" [Gat76], in which he argued against the hobbyist software market and for the importance of remunerating software authors for their work. The futility of this appeal to the morality of software users soon became apparent. Software manufacturers, concerned about protecting their revenues and anxious to prevent free-for-all copying of their code, soon launched their quest for copy prevention technologies, which led to the first uses of *obfuscation for copy protection and digital rights management*.

A more recent line of research has focused on *obfuscation for access control and data privacy*. In a typical application, a data owner wants to distribute a database to potential users. Instead of hiding individual data entries, he wants to obfuscate the database so that only certain queries can be evaluated on it, i.e., the goal is to ensure that the database, after it has been made public, can be accessed only in ways permitted by the "privacy policy."

8.1.1 Obfuscation for "White-Box" Cryptography

"White-box" cryptography aims to hide cryptographic material inside the code of a software application. This is a very challenging task because the attacker is assumed to have complete access both to the executable code of the application and to the computer on which the code is executing. A typical problem in "white-box" cryptography is to take an encryption program (e.g., a symmetric block cipher like DES or AES) and embed the encryption key in it in such a way that the attacker is unable to extract the key and/or to convert the encryption program into a decryption program.

Tamper-resistant software has generally been a failure from the security viewpoint, and obfuscated software ciphers are no exception. For example, Chow et al.'s obfuscated implementation of the DES cipher [CEJvO02], commercialized by Cloakware, was completely broken by Jacob et al. [JBF02] using standard cryptanalysis techniques, such as fault injection and differential cryptanalysis. Recent theoretical results suggest that there may exist symmetric cryptosystems that can be obfuscated (and, thus, turned into public-key cryptosystems) in a provably secure way [HMLS07], but no concrete examples are known as of this writing. It is also not clear whether theoretical "obfuscatability" implies the existence of practical obfuscated implementations because the polynomial increase in size and decrease in performance permitted by the theoretical definitions of security may not be acceptable in many usage scenarios.

8.1.2 Obfuscation for Copy Protection and Digital Rights Management

The most common application for "white-box" cryptography is *digital rights management* (DRM), i.e., protecting digital information from unauthorized uses. Unauthorized copying of software applications and digital content, including audio and video files, has been a long-standing concern of software manufacturers and content creators who deployed a variety of DRM technologies over the years to prevent copying of programs and media files.

A simple copy protection mechanism for "shareware" software might work as follows. A try-before-you-buy version checks the computer's clock to see if it is more than 30 days since the day of installation and, if so, refuses to run until a product key is paid for, obtained from the vendor and input to the program. The key is usually dependent on the user's name, computer ID, and so on. Clearly, one can circumvent this by perpetually resetting the computer's clock, and different people can share product keys if they pretend to be the same person. Doing so, however, presumably degrades the functionality of the computer to the extent that most users may prefer to pay the nominal price for the software.

A more creative attack involves modifying the binary code of the software to disable the date check. In general, this is a serious risk for any DRM technology: The user may try to separate the part of the program that is responsible to checking access rights, licenses, and so on from the "functional" part of the program, which is responsible for executing the actual application or playing back digital content. Therefore, software manufacturers and content vendors aim to design their programs in such a way that it is difficult to remove the DRM enforcement mechanism without crippling the product's functionality and performance.

Despite the best efforts of content and software vendors, DRM technologies have a dismal track record, and are often subject to "zero-day cracks," i.e., they are successfully attacked on the same day they are published. Few survive determined circumvention efforts launched by the hacker community. The Content Scrambling System (CSS) used to protect the first generation of DVDs was broken in several different ways [DeC04,Ste99]. The Advanced Access Content System (AACS), used to protect high-definition DVDs in HD-DVD and Blu-Ray formats, has also been broken [Sto07]. DRM protection has been cracked in Adobe eBooks [Pla01], as well as in Apple's FairPlay technology used to protect iTunes/iPod music files [BBC06]. Some CD protection technologies can be disabled simply by holding down the `shift` key to prevent the DRM program from loading [Hal03]. The list goes on and on.

In short, while DRM technologies in the marketplace appear to be reasonably successful in deterring casual users, obfuscation has failed to prevent reverse engineering and cracking. It is also worth mentioning that some DRM technologies, such as the notorious XCP from Sony-BMG, introduce serious security vulnerabilities into computers on which they are installed [HF06].

8.1.3 Obfuscation for Data Privacy

Conventional privacy mechanisms usually provide all-or-nothing privacy. For example, secure multiparty computation schemes enable two or more parties to compute some joint function while revealing no information about their respective inputs except what is leaked by the result of the computation [Yao86,GMW87]. Privacy-preserving data mining aims to completely hide individual data records while computing global statistical properties of the database.

In many scenarios, however, privacy of individual records is neither necessary, nor sufficient. What matters is *how* the record is accessed. For example, consider a credit-reporting bureau whose data records contain information on credit worthiness of individual consumers. Clearly, forbidding employees of the bureau from accessing any record is unacceptable: They may need to correct an individual's data, respond to reports of fraudulent transactions, and so on. Nevertheless, consumers may want to restrict the bureau's ability to compile a list of customers' addresses and sell it to a third party.

Online directories are another example. For instance, a college alumni directory may need to be protected in such a way that someone who already knows a person's name and year of graduation is able to look up that person's e-mail address, yet spammers cannot indiscriminately harvest addresses listed in the directory.

Cryptographic obfuscation provides technological support for this concept of privacy. Given a *privacy policy*, it effectively transforms the database so that only the queries permitted by the policy can be feasibly evaluated on it. This concept of privacy is incomparable to conventional definitions because, depending on the policy, a permitted query may or even *should* reveal individual data entries. One may think of this form of privacy enforcement as "embedding" access control into the data.

An important feature of cryptographic data obfuscation is that it is *provably* secure and, unlike ad-hoc DRM mechanisms based on code obfuscation, cannot be circumvented by the attacker or malicious user. Therefore, data owners need not assume that users access their data only via trusted, "tamper-proof" software or hardware.

Password hashes are perhaps the most common use of cryptographic obfuscation for data security purposes. For example, the UNIX operating system does not store user passwords in the clear. Instead, each password is hashed, and only the hash is stored in the password file. The only operation that can be feasibly computed on a password hash is to compare it for equality with another hash. If the hash function is cryptographically strong (and, thus, collision-resistant), with an overwhelming probability two hashes will be equal if and only if the inputs of the hash function are equal. Therefore, storing the password hash is equivalent to enforcing the following access control policy: "Given a stored user password, it may be compared for equality with a candidate password; no other operations on it are permitted."

What about guessing attacks? Great question. The password may indeed be very easy to guess, but even in this case the access control policy is enforced. To verify his password guess, the attacker must still comply with the policy, that is, hash the guess and compare it for equality with the stored password. Note that the privacy policy in this case does *not* say that the password should be hard to guess. Even in the case of a successful guessing attack, the only operation that the attacker is performing on the guessed password is comparing it for equality. The fact that users might choose passwords that are easy to guess may be a flaw of the overall authentication approach, but it is not a flaw of the mechanism that controls access to stored passwords.

8.2 Cryptographic Obfuscation

The rigorous study of cryptographic obfuscation began, or at least greatly accelerated, with the publication in 2001 of the paper by Barak et al. entitled "On the (Im)possibility of Obfuscating Programs" [BGI+01]. This paper received wide attention as the seminal work on formal definitions and cryptographic techniques for obfuscation. Its relevance to "real-world" obfuscation is not entirely clear, however, and the negative results established in the paper do not apply to many practical applications.

One of the main contributions of the Barak et al. paper is its use of the notion of a *virtual black box* in defining obfuscation. As is often the case in cryptography, defining a task turns out to be half the problem of solving it. For a program P that we want to obfuscate, we define an "ideal functionality" I_P as a "black box" that has the same input–output behavior as P. Intuitively, I_P is perfectly secure because it hides *everything* about the internals of P. I_P is an abstraction; it is how P would behave had it been implemented in tamper-proof hardware, which does not allow the user to separate P into parts, observe its internal values, learn anything about the implementation details, and so on. The goal is to achieve the same level of security simply by obfuscating P, i.e., transforming it into a hard-to-understand program that has the same input–output behavior.

We say that an obfuscated version O_P of P is secure if O_P "behaves like" I_P. But what does it mean for O_P to behave like I_P? The answer uses the standard cryptographic methodology: For any efficient *adversarial algorithm* A that interacts with O_P and produces some output, there should exist a *simulator* that interacts with I_P and produces the same output. Thus, O_P behaves as if it were a black box with P inside, hence, the name.

This is a fairly subtle concept. The virtual black box definition specifies what it means for a given program P to be securely obfuscated only indirectly, by reference to the ideal functionality. In the password-checking example, the ideal functionality is a black box, which accepts a candidate password, and responds "yes" if it is equal to the password inside the box, "no" otherwise. A password is securely obfuscated if the attacker is limited to performing equality tests in order to determine whether his guess of the password is correct. It does *not* say whether it is hard or easy to guess a password in response to which the box will answer "yes." Regardless of how easy it is to come up with a candidate password, the attacker must try all candidates one by one.

The real strength of the virtual black box definition of security is that it guarantees that there is no other feasible way to access the stored password. Even if the attacker is interested only in recovering, say, the first character of the password, he can do no better than come up with candidates for the *entire* password and try them one by one. This is important for practical security because a flawed implementation of password-based authentication may enable the attacker to recover parts of the password without guessing it in its entirety [Ope06].

Barak et al. showed that there is no *single* obfuscator that works for all programs. In particular, this means that the dream of creating a piece of software with a copy-protection check, and obfuscating it as the final step before public release, is not possible. At the very least, the software engineering cycle must include specifying which aspects of the program need to be obfuscated; the obfuscation method must be specific to the program being obfuscated.

Furthermore, there are fundamental classes of programs for which there is no single obfuscator, including encryption schemes and pseudorandom number generators. (The definition of Barak et al. might have been too strong, however; we will return to this issue momentarily.) Therefore, any program obfuscator must exploit the specific properties of the pseudorandom number generator or encryption scheme it is obfuscating, making obfuscation much harder and requiring an even tighter integration with the software design cycle.

As a consequence of the impossibility results demonstrated by Barak et al., their paper has often been misinterpreted as a conclusive proof that cryptographic obfuscation, in all its forms and manifestations, is impossible. This is not, however, the case because the paper does *not* rule out the use of obfuscation in many digital privacy scenarios.

It is worth bearing in mind that obfuscation is merely a cryptographic tool; it can be used for tasks that outwardly have little to do with each other. Recall the three classes of obfuscation applications surveyed above. Progress has been made toward the first class of applications, white-box cryptography. The main idea that makes this possible is the following: Normally, cryptographic algorithms must operate under the assumption that their input comes from a malicious adversary who is trying to attack the system. In many applications of obfuscation, however, the obfuscator has the luxury of knowing that his input is another cryptographic algorithm, parameterized by a key, which is guaranteed to be selected uniformly at random.*

Two recent papers considered such relaxations of the virtual black box property. Hofheinz et al. [HMLS07] argue that their definition is achievable because it gives simpler obfuscators and/or proofs of security for "point functions," which we discuss below. At the same time, their definition preserves the important property that an obfuscation of a symmetric encryption algorithm is an asymmetric encryption algorithm. Hohenberger et al. [HRSV07] introduce a similar relaxed definition of security, and actually construct an obfuscator for *re-encryption*. A re-encryption program takes a message encrypted with one person's public key and transforms it into a message encrypted under another person's public key. This is useful, for instance, in secure e-mail forwarding.

The crucial difference that will enable us to bypass the impossibility results of Barak et al. is that security in the case of data hiding is based on

---

* A system designer must be extra careful when an algorithm requires this guarantee for security because the failure of the other algorithm to ensure randomness of the key can be catastrophic.

the adversary's ignorance of one or more pieces of data and, therefore, this task resembles traditional encryption much more than the "magical" hiding that one hopes to achieve with software obfuscation.

Let us explore the encryption analogy further. A naive definition of security for encryption might say that the adversary shouldn't be able to recover the plaintext given the ciphertext. But this is virtually useless because the adversary may be able to recover all but a few bits of the plaintext, for instance, and the algorithm would still be "secure" according to this definition. Instead, the standard notion of security for encryption is *semantic security*, which states, very roughly, that anything that can be computed by the adversary with access to the ciphertext can be computed by the adversary simulator who does not have the ciphertext (therefore, the ciphertext does not leak any useful information). Note the similarity with the virtual black-box property.

Unlike the naive definitions of security, both semantic security and the virtual black-box property describe what the adversary can do instead of trying to describe what he cannot do. This is generally recognized as the right approach. A designer of a secure system who proves that the adversary cannot do A, B, or C, always has to worry that there is some computation D overlooked during the design phase, which the adversary can perform (since it is not ruled out by the definition of security), potentially breaking the system. By contrast, if the designer proves that the adversary is limited to a well-defined set of operations, he does not have to worry about overlooking some unexpected way of accessing the system.

8.3 Applications of Obfuscation to Digital Privacy

The simultaneous emergence of ubiquitous Internet access and public, Internet-accessible databases containing vast amounts of information about individuals and organizations has created a serious threat to privacy. U.S. Census tables, online directories, property tax appraisals, and all kinds of other databases can now be searched online by anyone with a personal computer and Internet connection. Even when the data stored in these databases do not directly violate individuals' privacy, they can be used— often in conjunction with other sources—to reveal sensitive information about them. Enforcing privacy policies in public databases is one of the critical challenges in privacy research today.

A typical scenario involves a database owner releasing some database for public use (perhaps in a sanitized form) or allowing public access to it through a Web front-end or similar interface. In either case, the owner has little or no control over the database once it has been released. Even if the initial query is audited or monitored, the user, after he or she has obtained some subset of the data, can distribute it further or perform additional queries on it at will. From the viewpoint of privacy, "the horse has left the barn" the moment the database has been made public.

The problem of protecting privacy in public databases is often interpreted as protecting *secrecy of individual records*. For example, consider a statistical database containing a sample of some population. Much research has been devoted to the so-called *census problem*: How to sanitize the database so that (1) the result of the sanitization does not violate privacy of any individual whose data is included in the sample, yet (2) the sanitized database allows accurate estimation of the statistical characteristics of the underlying population. This conflict between privacy and utility is inherent in public databases.

Conventional solutions to the census problem perturb individual data entries by adding random noise to them, while preserving certain statistical characteristics of the entire database [AS00,EGS03,CDM+05]. As a result, the user of the perturbed database can estimate its statistical properties, but privacy of the individual elements is preserved.

In many scenarios, however, the goal is not to hide individual entries, but to control *how* they are accessed. Statistical perturbation of the data does not address this problem at all. For example, if a company outsources its technical support, the support staffers must have access to the *unperturbed* individual records in the customer database. The objective is not confidentiality of database records, but access control. For example, users of the database should not be able to execute queries that return all information contained in the database. Some records should not be accessible unless the user provides a password; in other situations (e.g., preventing the user from harvesting records for spamming) the user must be able to describe precisely what he is looking for before access is granted. In all of these cases, the database must have a built-in access control mechanism that enforces the database owner's access policy.

Enforcing access control policies in public databases is a very challenging problem. The user accesses the database *after* it has been released. The underlying data is stored on the user's medium, and the query is evaluated in the user's computing environment where both the software and the hardware are controlled by the user. There is no trusted intermediary to monitor the user's queries and reject those that do not satisfy the database owner's policy. The database owner may attempt to "wrap" the database into a DRM program enforcing the desired policy. Unfortunately, the track record of DRM technologies is exceptionally poor, and none have been able to withstand determined attacks. The data is usually extracted even from allegedly "tamper-proof" access control programs in a matter of weeks, if not days.

We envision a different approach to the problem, which relies on cryptographic obfuscation. The goal is to transform the database in such a way that all queries that are not explicitly permitted by the owner's access control policy become *computationally infeasible*. This approach is crypto-graphically secure and *uncircumventable* in the following sense: Breaking the access control mechanism, i.e., accessing the data in any way other than those permitted by the access control policy, is equivalent to breaking a cryptographic primitive. Unlike ad hoc access control and DRM technologies that are routinely broken by attackers, the cryptographic primitives underlying our approach have withstood many years of intense scrutiny.

In our approach, the data owner defines the set of queries that the user of the database is permitted to evaluate. The database is then "obfuscated" so that these and *only* these queries can be computed on the obfuscated database. Evaluating any other query is not computationally feasible. In this way, the access control policy becomes an inseparable part of the database, which can then be publicly released to the users. Even though the database owner has no further control over the data, he can be sure that the users are accessing it only via policy-compliant queries.

Not every access control policy can be enforced in this way. As we explain below, only certain classes of queries can be securely obfuscated. In some cases, obfuscation imposes a heavy performance and storage cost. Nevertheless, for many scenarios—such as securing public directories against address harvesting—cryptographic obfuscation offers an efficient, provably secure alternative to ad hoc access control schemes.

8.4 Obfuscation for Access Control

One of the first observations that cryptographic obfuscation may be used for access control was made by Lynn et al. in [LPS04], who noted that the standard Unix password-hashing procedure* can be viewed as "point function obfuscation." A *point function* is a function that produces a special output on a single input, which may be thought of as a key or a password.

Instead of storing each user's password in the clear, Unix stores a hash of the password. The security objective is to protect against server compromise: If an attacker breaks into the system, he shouldn't be able to learn the users' passwords right away. Originally, Unix used a hash function based on the DES cipher, but modern versions of Unix use a true cryptographic hash function, such as MD5 or SHA-1.

To prove Unix password hashing secure, Lynn et al. invoke the so-called *random oracle model*, which is a proof technique that allows the algorithm designer to treat hash functions as if they behaved like true random

---

* By this, we mean the password-hashing procedure originally deployed in the Unix operating system starting in the late 1970s; before long, most systems using password authentication made use of some variant of this procedure.

functions, i.e., as if they mapped each input to a truly random value. While this model is somewhat controversial, cryptographers have had qualified success in building functions that sufficiently scramble their input so that they are difficult to distinguish from a random function.*

Lynn et al. observe that if the hash function is treated as a random oracle, then storing a hashed password is equivalent to obfuscating the original password. More precisely, storing a hashed password is essentially equivalent to giving the user access to an "oracle," which allows him to test any candidate password for equality with the original password. This is clearly the strongest security property one can hope for in a password authentication system: It is not feasible to do anything with the stored password other than compare it for equality with the user's input.

Let H be a cryptographic hash function, which is modeled as a "random function" with an n-bit output. If p is the password, we store the value $H(p)$. The security proof is based on the intuition that no matter how many times you evaluate H on inputs different from p, it is going to tell you nothing about p because H is independently random on every input; but if you ever query it on p, that means you knew or guessed p in the first place (in other words, $H(p)$ did not leak any useful information about p). You can then confirm the guess by asking the oracle whether it is equal to p.

On the other hand, the chance that you can successfully authenticate with an incorrect password $p' \neq p$ is negligibly small because this can happen only if $H(p) = H(p')$ for some p' different from p. For each p', the chance that this happens is only 2^{-n} because $H(p')$ is picked at random from a set of size 2^n.

Technically, an obfuscator outputs a *program* that verifies whether a password is correct or not. It is conceptually simpler, however, to think of the obfuscator as outputting simply the hash and having a separate program (which is independent of the password) to verify the user's input by hashing it and comparing for equality with the hash produced by the obfuscator.

Lynn et al. also observe that essentially the same construction can be used to obfuscate a "lookup function." If p is the password that unlocks some secret s, then the obfuscation consists of $H(p) \oplus s$, where $\oplus$ represents the XOR operation, as in a one-time pad. This can be thought of, intuitively, as encrypting s with p as the key.

This technique can be extended to obfuscating access control in public databases [NS05], by composing multiple lookup functions in parallel. A *directed-access database* is a database in which some attributes are

---

* Subsequent to the publication of [LPS04], Wee came up with a construction for a point function obfuscator and proved it secure under a set of assumptions that are closer to traditional cryptographic assumptions [Wee05].

designated as *query attributes*, and the rest as *data attributes*. The database is securely obfuscated if, for any record, it is infeasible to retrieve the values of the data attributes without supplying the values of the query attributes, yet a user who knows the query attributes can easily retrieve the corresponding data attributes.

To illustrate by example, a directed-access obfuscation of a telephone directory has the property that is easy to look up the phone number corresponding to a particular name and company or a name–address pair, but queries such as "retrieve all phone numbers stored in the directory" or "retrieve all names," are computationally infeasible. Such a directory is secure against abusive harvesting, but still provides useful functionality.

As mentioned before, our goal is to limit the attacker to a particular set of queries. It is up to the database owner to decide what these queries should be. For example, if he does not want query attributes, such as the name–address pair, to be easily guessable, he can require the user to supply additional information about the record before the record can be retrieved from the database. Cryptographic obfuscation provides the data owner with a technical mechanism for enforcing the desired policy.

The directed-access property of a single database record can be modeled as a point function. The input is the set of query attributes. The point function returns a special output on exactly one input, which is the set of correct values for the query attributes. In this case, the special output consists of the data attributes of that record.

Informally, we encrypt the data attributes with a key derived from the hashed query attributes. Directed-access obfuscation guarantees that the only computationally feasible way to retrieve the data attributes is to supply the corresponding query attributes; if the retriever does not know the right query attributes, no information can be extracted at all. Furthermore, the data attributes are themselves protected from mass harvesting, except possibly by guessing.

There are two subtleties in this construction. Suppose the user supplies the correct query attributes for some record, and retrieves a set of data attributes or what looks like data attributes. How does he know that the lookup succeeded? One answer is that if it is the wrong record, or if the wrong query attributes were supplied, the answer is going to "look random" (which is required by the virtual black-box definition of security) and, therefore, not meaningful to the user. This approach is fraught with danger, however, because it assumes that it is always possible to distinguish a correct data value from a random-looking one. For example, telling the difference between a random nine-digit value and a credit card number is possible, but may be difficult for an uneducated user. Attempting to define what qualifies as a well-formed piece of data is generally seen as both futile and unnecessary in cryptography. For instance, it is recommended to compress the data before encrypting (except in very special circumstances), and the encryption algorithm does not need to worry about trying to exploit redundancy in the data.

We follow the same approach, and in addition to the lookup functionality, we include "verification" functionality in the obfuscated database. The verification functionality is another point function obfuscation; this one will output YES on the correct input and NO everywhere else. The user first checks the verification functionality, and if it returns YES, proceeds to the actual lookup function. Note that correctness here holds with overwhelming probability, and we don't need to make any assumptions about the data.

This brings us to the issue of *composition*. Consider what happens when two records have the same query attributes. The hashes of the two sets of query attributes are going to be the same, revealing the fact that the attributes are equal. Depending on the circumstances, this may or may not be a privacy leak, but it is certainly a violation of the virtual blackbox definition of security. It is easy to prevent this from happening using the well-known technique of "salting," or adding a random value to each hash. We concatenate a random "salt" to the query attributes before hashing them, and publish the salt along with the hash. Technically, this is known as "self-composing" obfuscation.

8.5   Obfuscation for Group Privacy

Let us now turn to more complex privacy policies that possibly allow the user to retrieve more than one record at a time. The set of query attributes is no longer fixed; the user can base his query on different sets of attributes for different records. How can privacy be enforced? How can the database owner prevent the user from issuing the equivalent of a `"SELECT * FROM tablename"` query *after* the database has been publicly released?

Our solution is to allow a record to be retrievable if the user can "name" it precisely. Enforcing or even formulating what this means is difficult. Do we rule out all queries that return more than one record? This seems like a natural thing to do if we are concerned about not leaking information about a record to a user who cannot identify this record in advance. For example, consider the difference between someone who is looking up an old classmate in a college alumni directory and can describe precisely the person's name and year of graduation, and a spammer who wants to indiscriminately harvest all addresses listed in the directory.

To prevent abusive information harvesting from public databases, our approach differentiates legitimate and abusive queries by the number of records they return. A legitimate query "knows what it wants," and is matched by a relatively small number of records. An abusive query tries to extract as much information as possible, and is matched by a large number of records.

We adopt the general principle of *pricing via processing*, which has been used, for example, by the "hashcash" system for combatting spam and denial of service [Bac02]. In the hashcash scheme, the sender of an e-mail must compute a moderately hard, but not prohibitively expensive, function in order to send the e-mail. This deters abuse (as the amount of work to be done goes up linearly with the number of messages to send, even if they are all copies of each other), but does not affect legitimate, occasional usage. We will adopt a similar approach to database privacy by forcing the user to perform a very difficult computation if the number of records matching his query is large.

8.5.1 Group Privacy Policy

Defining a *group privacy* policy where the answers to queries with more and more matching records are harder and harder to obtain. Recall that we define privacy policies by specifying a black-box "ideal functionality," which describes how the database would behave had it been implemented in perfectly secure tamper-proof hardware. One way to do this would be for the ideal functionality to delay the response for a while before returning answers that contain multiple records. For technical reasons, however, it is not possible to incorporate temporal behavior into the ideal functionality, so we instead make the ideal functionality more and more error-prone as the number of records goes up.

The ideal functionality for group privacy is as follows: If there are t records matching query q, the ideal functionality returns them with probability 2^{-t}, otherwise it returns a special symbol $\perp$. If there are no records that match, it simply returns $\perp$. With access to this functionality, a user can evaluate a query matched by t records by repeating the query, on average, 2^t times.

In databases obfuscated to satisfy this policy, the user is forced to guess t bits before he can access the data attributes in any matching record. (If $t = 1$, i.e., the record is unique, the user still has to guess 1 bit, but this simply means that with probability $1/2$ he has to repeat the query.) The policy that requires the retriever to uniquely identify a single record, i.e., forbids any query that is satisfied by multiple records, can also be easily implemented using our techniques.

For example, consider an airline passenger database in which every record contains the passenger's name, flight number, date, and ticket purchase details. After the database has been obfuscated, if the user knows the name and date that uniquely identify a particular record (e.g., because this information was supplied in a court-issued warrant), he (almost) immediately learns the key that encrypts the purchase details in the obfuscated record. If the passenger traveled on k flights on that date, the retriever learns the key except for k bits. Since k is small, guessing k bits is still feasible. If, however, the retriever only knows the date and the flight number, he learns the key except for m bits, where m is the number of passengers on the flight, and retrieval of these passengers' purchase details is infeasible.

A database obfuscated using this method has the *group privacy* property in the following sense. It can be accessed only via queries permitted by the group privacy policy. The probability of successfully evaluating a permitted query is inversely exponential to the number of records that satisfy the query predicate. In particular, to extract a large number of records from the database, the retriever must know *a priori* specific information that uniquely identifies each record, or small subsets of records. The obfuscated database itself does not help him obtain this information. (The cryptographic details of obfuscation for group privacy can be found in [NS05].)

We still have not addressed the question of what kind of queries are permitted by the data privacy policy. If arbitrary queries are permitted, then it can be shown that the user can extract the entire database even under the most restrictive privacy policy, i.e., one where the ideal functionality responds to a query only if there is only a single record matching it. Therefore, we restrict the user to the following class of queries: Each attribute can only be tested for equality with a given candidate value; the results of testing can be combined in any manner whatsoever.

For example, query

```
e-mail = "johndoe@bigcorp.com" OR
e-mail = "jdoe@bigcorp.com" OR
e-mail = "doe.john@bigcorp.com"
```

is allowed, whereas the following query is forbidden:

```
e-mail LIKE "@bigcorp.com"
```

8.5.2 Tradeoff between Privacy and Utility

Much research still needs to be done on understanding the tradeoffs between utility, privacy, and efficiency in using cryptographic obfuscation for digital privacy. The cryptographic community generally views privacy as paramount and posits that if a given release of data does not achieve a "proper," cryptographically strong definition of security, then the data should not be released at all. The statistical database community, which tends to work with practical privacy problems in actual databases, adopts heuristics to protect privacy, and regards utility and efficiency as paramount. We propose a middle ground: While our provably secure constructions are not always feasible for large databases, we also describe practical heuristic methods that considerably improve efficiency [NS05]. In terms of utility, our query language is clearly less expressive than one might hope for, but it is not clear whether expressiveness can be improved without significantly sacrificing privacy.

Finally, our construction for group privacy has the security weakness that it is possible to launch a dictionary attack on individual fields, even when the privacy policy requires multiple fields to match in order to look up the corresponding records (technically, there is an individual verification oracle for each attribute). It is unclear if this weakness can be avoided while preserving the user's ability to retrieve records by supplying an arbitrary subset of query attributes.

References

[AS00] R. Agrawal and R. Srikant. Privacy-preserving data mining. In *Proc. of the 2000 ACM SIGMOD International Conference on Management of Data*, pp. 439–450. ACM Press, New York, 2000.

[Bac02] A. Back. Hashcash—a denial of service counter-measure. http://hashcash.org/, 2002.

[BBC06] BBC. iTunes copy protection 'cracked.' http://news.bbc.co.uk/2/hi/6083110.stm, Oct. 25, 2006.

[BGI+01] B. Barak, O. Goldreich, R. Impagliazzo, S. Rudich, A. Sahai, S. Vadhan, and K. Yang. On the (im)possibility of obfuscating programs. In *Proc. of Advance in Cryptology—CRYPTO 2001*, vol. 2139, *LNCS*, pp. 1–18. Springer, Heidelberg, Germany, 2001.

[CDM+05] S. Chawla, C. Dwork, F. McSherry, A. Smith, and H. Wee. Towards privacy in public databases. In *Proc. of the 2nd Theory of Cryptography Conference*, vol. 3378, *LNCS*, pp. 363–385. Springer, Heidelberg, Germany, 2005.

[CEJvO02] S. Chow, P. Eisen, H. Johnson, and P. van Oorschot. A white-box DES implementation for DRM applications. In *Proc. of the ACM Workshop on Security and Privacy in Digital Rights Management*, vol. 2696, *LNCS*, pp. 1–15. Springer, Heidelberg, Germany, 2002.

[DeC04] DeCSS Central. http://www.lemuria.org/DeCSS/, 2004.

[DH76] W. Diffie and M. Hellman. New directions in cryptography. *IEEE Trans. Info. Theory*, 22: 644–654, 1976.

[EGS03] A. Evfimievski, J. Gehrke, and R. Srikant. Limiting privacy breaches in privacy-preserving data mining. In *Proc. of the 22nd ACM SIGACT-SIGMOD-SIGART Symposium on Principles of Database Systems*, pp. 211–222. ACM Press, New York, 2003.

[Gat76] B. Gates. An open letter to hobbyists. http://www.digibarn.com/collections/newsletters/homebrew/V2_01/homebrew_V2_01_p2.jpg, 1976.

[GMW87] O. Goldreich, S. Micali, and A. Wigderson. How to play any mental game. In *Proc. of the 19th Annual ACM Symposium on Theory of Computing*, pp. 218–229. ACM Press, New York, 1987.

[Hal03] J. Halderman. Analysis of the MediaMax CD3 copy-prevention system. Technical Report TR-679-03, Princeton University, Computer Science Department, New Jersey, 2003.

[HF06] J. Halderman and E. Felten. Lessons from the Sony CD-DRM episode. In *Proc. of the 15th USENIX Security Symposium*. USENIX, Vancouver, British Columbia, 2006.

[HMLS07] D. Hofheinz, J. Malone-Lee, and M. Stam. Obfuscation for cryptographic purposes. In *Proc. of 4th Theory of Cryptography Conference*, vol. 4392, *LNCS*, pp. 214–252, Springer Amsterdam, the Netherlands, 2007.

[HRSV07] S. Hohenberger, G. Rothblum, A. Shelat, and V. Vaikuntanathan. Securely obfuscating re-encryption. In *Proc. of the 4th Theory of Cryptography Conference*, vol. 4392, *LNCS*, pp. 233–252, Springer, Amsterdam, the Netherlands, 2007.

[JBF02] M. Jacob, D. Boneh, and E. Felten. Attacking an obfuscated cipher by injecting faults. In *Proc. of the ACM Workshop on Security and Privacy in Digital Rights Management*, vol. 2696, *LNCS*, pp. 16–31. Springer, Heidelberg, Germany, 2002.

[LPS04] B. Lynn, M. Prabhakaran, and A. Sahai. Positive results and techniques for obfuscation. In *Proc. of Advances in Cryptology—EUROCRYPT 2004*, vol. 3027, *LNCS*, pp. 20–39. Springer, Heidelberg, Germany, 2004.

[NS05] A. Narayanan and V. Shmatikov. Obfuscated databases and group privacy. In *Proc. of the 12th ACM Conference on Computer and Communications Security*, pp. 102–111. ACM Press, New York, 2005.

[Ope06] Open Source Vulnerability Database. TENEX page fault race condition password prediction weakness. http://osvdb.org/displayvuln.php?osvdb_id=23199/, 2006.

[Pla01] Planet PDF. Index of Elcomsoft, Dmitry Sklyarov, Adobe, U.S. Government and DMCA-related coverage. http://www.planetpdf.com/mainpage.asp?webpageid=2365, 2001.

[Ste99] F. Stevenson. Cryptanalysis of Contents Scrambling System. http://www.cs.cmu.edu/dst/DeCSS/FrankStevenson/analysis.html, 1999.

[Sto07] B. Stone "A DVD Copy Protection Is Overcome By Hackers." *The New York Times*, Jan. 17, 2007.

[Wee05] H. Wee. On obfuscating point functions. In *Proc. of the 37th Annual ACM Symposium on Theory of Computing*, pp. 523–532. ACM Press, New York, 2005.

[Yao86] A. Yao. How to generate and exchange secrets. In *Proc. of the 27th Annual IEEE Symposium on Foundations of Computer Science*, pp. 162–167. IEEE Computer Society, Los Alamitos, CA, 1986.

Chapter 9

Privacy Protection with Uncertainty and Indistinguishability

X. Sean Wang and Sushil Jajodia

Contents

9.1 Introduction 173
9.2 Uncertainty 176
9.3 Indistinguishability 178
9.4 Technical Challenges and Solutions 181
9.5 Other Related Works 182
9.6 Conclusion 183
References... 183

9.1 Introduction

In many data systems, it is important to protect individual privacy while satisfying application requirements. To provide such protection, privacy disclosure must be measured in some quantitative manner, as absolute privacy is usually not a practical proposition. Privacy measurement metrics have appeared in the literature, but they are either for single table scenarios (e.g., [17, 22, 23]), or for a more theoretical purpose (e.g., [20]). This chapter introduces two data privacy measures that can be used for general relational data releases and that are amenable to practical applications, and outlines challenges and possible solutions in using these measures in applications.

Privacy metrics in general have two aspects. One aspect of privacy measure is based on uncertainty of private property values, i.e., the uncertainty of an individual's private value. The idea is that if the published data lacks the certainty of what private value an individual has, then the privacy of the individual is protected. The metrics of this type can be classified into two categories: nonprobabilistic and probabilistic. The nonprobabilistic metrics are based on whether the private value of an individual can be uniquely inferred from the released data [1,6,8,14,15,18] or whether the cardinality of the set of possible private values inferred for an individual is large enough [24,27]. The probabilistic metrics are based on some characteristics of the probability distribution of the possible private values inferred from the released data [2–4,10,11,13]. In this chapter, we concentrate on different metrics that are applicable on general relational query results [28].

However, uncertainty alone does not provide adequate protection. For example, we may reveal employee John's salary to be in a large interval (say, 100,000 to 300,000 annually). This large interval provides great uncertainty. However, if we also reveal that the salaries of all other employees are in ranges that are totally different from John's (say, all are subranges of 50,000 to 100,000), then John's privacy may still be violated. In this example, the privacy breach can be viewed as due to the fact that from the published data, an individual is different from all other individuals in terms of his possible private values. In other words, the example shows the violation of a privacy requirement, namely, the "protection from being brought to the attention of others" [12]. To adequately protect privacy, we need to consider the other aspect of privacy, what we call *indistinguishability* [26].

Indistinguishability is inspired by the notion of *k*-anonymization [5,16,19,22,23]. Given a positive integer *k*, *k*-anonymization is to recode, mostly by generalization, publicly available quasi-IDs in a single released table, so that at least *k* individuals will have the same recoded (or generalized) quasi-IDs. (Quasi-IDs are values on a combination of attributes that can be used to identify individuals through external sources [22,23].) In our view, this is an effort to provide indistinguishability among the *k* individuals, since the recoding makes the individuals indistinguishable from each other.

The indistinguishability notion used in this chapter applies to general query results, not just the single generalized table as in *k*-anonymity. Conceptually, each individual needs to belong to a group of individuals who are indistinguishable from each other in terms of their possible private values derived from the released data. In this way, an individual is hidden in a crowd that consists of individuals who have similar/same possible private values. For instance, in the above salary example, to protect John's privacy, one wants to make sure that any attacker can only derive from the published data that a large group of employees have the same range of salary as John.

Uncertainty and indistinguishability are two independent aspects for providing privacy; one does not imply the other. From the above examples, one can see that uncertainty cannot ensure good indistinguishability. Likewise, good indistinguishability cannot ensure enough uncertainty. For instance, if in the released data many employees have the same single, possible salary value, then these employees are indistinguishable from each other in terms of their salaries, but there is not enough uncertainty to protect their privacy (all their salaries are the same and revealed). This phenomenon was noted in [17], indicating that k-anonymity (a type of indistinguishability) alone is not enough to protect privacy, and l-diversity (a kind of uncertainty) is needed.

To set the stage for a technical discussion in this chapter, the scenario is formally defined here. We consider releasing data from a single private relational table Tbl with schema D, where D is a set of attributes. The attributes in D contain a set of ID attributes and a single P attribute. The ID attributes can be used to trace back to an individual, while P is the private attribute of the individual. These assumptions are for simplicity. Indeed, ID may consist of multiple attributes that together identify individuals, or ID may be quasi-IDs that can be used in combination of external sources to identify individuals. Also, in the table, there may be multiple secret attributes. However, this simplification makes an easier presentation without loss of generality.

It is assumed that the projection on ID, $\Pi_{ID}(Tbl)$, is publicly known. In the salary example, this means that the list of employees is publicly known. This assumption is realistic in many situations. In other situations where this is not true, one may take this approach as providing a conservative privacy measure. Assuming the attackers know more than they actually do is always a safe assumption, i.e., a conservative assumption.

Relational operations are considered on Tbl. A relational operation is a mapping that maps one or more input relations to an output relation. Traditional relational algebra operations, namely selection (π), projection (σ), join ($\bowtie$), and set operations ($\cup$, $\cap$, $-$) are typically used to derive query results from Tbl. Also included in the discussion are deterministic anonymization methods that map an input relation to a generalized relation (see, e.g., [5,16,19,22]). A query Q is a composition of relational operations on Tbl, and we assume all data releases are in the form of queries and the corresponding query results. This is a rather flexible data publication mechanism. In this chapter, V is used to denote a set of queries, v the set of corresponding query results, and the pair (V, v) a *view set* (a query with its result is usually called a *view*). Also, v is used alone to denote the view set (V, v) when V is understood.

Included in the following text is a formal definition of uncertainty and indistinguishability metrics for a view set (V, v) on the private table Tbl. We then outline basic ideas on how to achieve practical methods to check if a set of query results satisfies the uncertainty and indistinguishability metrics.

The rest of this chapter is organized as follows. In Sections 9.2 and 9.3, we formally define the privacy metrics uncertainty and indistinguishability, respectively. We then discuss in Section 9.4 technical challenges, and related solutions, in measuring relational query results against these two metrics. In Section 9.5, we provide pointers to other related works not mentioned elsewhere in the chapter. We conclude with a summary and a brief discussion of further research directions in Section 9.6.

9.2 Uncertainty

The example in Figure 9.1 is used to motivate the notion of uncertainty. In general, we assume that secret and private information takes the form of associations, that is, pairs of values appearing in the same tuple. For example, the association of "Bill" with "HIV" in the base table P_1 in Figure 9.1 is private information. Note that neither "Bill" nor "HIV" alone is a secret, but the association of the two values is. In Figure 9.1, the secret associations are all the pairs in $\pi_{Name, Problem}(P_1)$, where P_1 is the base table *Tbl*. In this case, *Name* is the *ID* attribute, while *Problem* is the *P* attribute in the general setting. We call $\pi_{ID, P}(Tbl)$ the *secret view*.

Also in Figure 9.1 are two queries and their results. By examining the queries and their results, there is no direct link between people and their problems. However, a simple deduction can show that Bill has HIV. In the same example, one can only deduce that George may have a cold or be obese. We will say that the two queries and their results provide

Name	Job	Salary	Problem
George	Manager	70K	Cold
John	Manager	90K	Obesity
Bill	Lawyer	11K	HIV

Base table P_1

$v_1 = \Pi_{Name,Job}(P_1)$

Name	Job
George	Manager
John	Manager
Bill	Lawyer

$v_2 = \Pi_{Job,Problem}(P_1)$

Job	Problem
Manager	Cold
Manager	Obesity
Lawyer	HIV

Figure 9.1   Base table and two releasing views.

1-uncertainty for Bill (which is no uncertainty at all), while providing 2-uncertainty for George (and John as well).

Before defining the uncertainty metric, we give one further notation and one auxiliary definition: Given a view set (V, v), we denote $\mathcal{I}^v$ to be the set of allowable relation tables on schema D, such that for each r in $\mathcal{I}^v$, we have $V(r) = v$. This means that $\mathcal{I}^v$ consists of all possible relational tables that give the same result v when the queries V are applied. The auxiliary definition is as follows.

Definition 9.1 (Association Cover) *Each binary tuple on (ID, P) is called an* association. *Given a view set v, a set A of associations on (ID, P) is called an* association cover *w.r.t. v if all the binary tuples in A have the same ID value and for each r in $\mathcal{I}^v$, $\pi_{ID, P}(r) \cap A \neq \emptyset$.*

Each association cover has the same value on *ID*. An association cover of size k is called a *k-association cover*. An association cover is *minimal* if none of its proper subsets are association covers.

Intuitively, a minimal association cover is a set of associations such that just by looking at the view set, one cannot tell which association in the association cover actually appears in the original base table *Tbl*. In Figure 9.1, {*(John, Cold), (John, Obesity)*} is an association cover. Indeed, *John* is a manager from v_1 while a manager has either *Cold* or *Obesity*, or both from v_2. Hence, for any base table instance r that yields v_1 and v_2, either *(John, Cold)* or *(John, Obesity)*, or both are in $\pi_{ID, P}(r)$. By definition, {*(John, Cold), (John, Obesity)*} is an association cover. This cover is minimal because neither {*(John, Cold)*} nor {*(John, Obesity)*} is an association cover. The fact that {*(John, Cold)*} is not an association cover is clear since *(John, Cold)* is not in P_1, but we know P_1 is in $\mathcal{I}^v$, where $v = \{v_1, v_2\}$. To see why {*(John, Obesity)*} is not an association cover, we only need to change P_1 slightly by switching the *Problem* values of *John* and *George*. In this changed table, the same two queries will yield the same results as applied to the original P_1, and, hence, the changed table is in $\mathcal{I}^v$, but *(John, Obesity)* is not in this changed table. All this really says is that by just looking at v_1 and v_2, one cannot tell in the original base table whether *John* is associated with *Cold* or *Obesity*. Minimal association covers provide us with a formal basis for defining uncertainty.

Definition 9.2 (k-uncertainty) *Given a view set v and integer $k \geq 2$, we say v violates k-uncertainty if there exists an association cover w.r.t. v of size less than k.*

Intuitively, if a view set does not violate *k*-uncertainty (for a user-specified, sufficiently large *k*), then we would say that all the secret associations are "protected." This definition requires that for each value *a* on *ID* an association cover of size less than *k* with *ID* being *a* does not exist; in other words, it requires *k*-uncertainty for *each a* on *ID*.

By definition, if a view set violates *k*-uncertainty, then there exists an *n*-association cover such that $n < k$. An extreme case is when 2-uncertainty is violated and, in this case, a binary tuple on (ID, P), the one in the association cover, is a secret association, i.e., it must be in the secret view on *Tbl* (actually, in any allowable instance that yields *v*). In Figure 9.1, the view set of v_1 and v_2 violates 2-uncertainty, since {*(Bill, HIV)*} is a 1-association cover. This means *(Bill, HIV)* must be a secret association.

9.3   Indistinguishability

In order to define indistinguishability, notation and assumption are extended a bit further. Given a relation r_{ID} on ID, we will use $\mathcal{I}^{ID}$ to denote the set $\{r|\pi_{ID}(r) = r_{ID}\}$, i.e., the set of the relations on D whose *ID*-projection coincide with r_{ID}. The domain of P, the private attribute, is denoted by $Dom(P)$. A tuple is an instance of $\mathcal{I}^{ID}$ is denoted by t or (a, p), where *a* is in $\pi_{ID}(Tbl)$ and *p* is in $Dom(P)$. The set $\mathcal{I}^{ID}$ corresponds to all possible private table instances by only knowing $\pi_{ID}(Tbl)$, which is assumed to be public information. Furthermore, we assume *ID* is a key in D, which means that each composite value on *ID* appears, at most, once in the private table. This last assumption can be easily dropped, but we choose to keep it to simplify our presentation.

We use the example in Figure 9.2 to explain our definition. The *ID* attributes are *Zip, Age, Race, Gender*, and *Charge*. We use $t_1, \ldots, t_{12}$ to denote the tuples in the table. Our assumption has been that for each *i*, $t_i[ID]$ can trace back to a particular individual. In the sequel, the $t_i[ID]$ value are used and the individual identified by $t_i[ID]$ interchangeably. The private attribute is *Problem*. Here, *Problem* is drawn from a finite discrete domain. (In general the private attribute also can be drawn from an infinite or a continuous domain, but it should not be difficult to extend the study to infinite discrete or continuous domains.)

Similar to section 9.2, when a view set (V, v) is released, $\mathcal{I}^v$ is denoted by the subset of possible instances in $\mathcal{I}^{ID}$ that yield *v*. The definition of indistinguishability, thus, is based on $\mathcal{I}^v$.

Definition 9.3 (Symmetricity)   *Given a view set v and two tuples a_i and a_j in $\pi_{ID}(Tbl)$, we say a_i and a_j are symmetric w.r.t. v if the following condition is satisfied: For each instance r in $\mathcal{I}^v$ containing (a_i, p_i) and (a_j, p_j) there exists another instance r' in $\mathcal{I}^v$ such that $r' = (r - \{(a_i, p_i), (a_j, p_j)\}) \cup \{(a_i, p_j), (a_j, p_i)\}$.*

Symmetricity is abbreviated as *SYM*. This definition requires that for each possible instance in $\mathcal{I}^v$, if two symmetric *ID* values swap their private

	Zip	Age	Race	Gender	Charge	Problem
t_1	22030	39	White	Male	1K	Cold
t_2	22030	50	White	Male	12K	AIDS
t_3	22030	38	White	Male	5K	Obesity
t_4	22030	53	Black	Male	5K	AIDS
t_5	22031	28	Black	Female	8K	Chest Pain
t_6	22031	37	White	Female	10K	Hypertension
t_7	22031	49	Black	Female	1K	Obesity
t_8	22031	52	White	Male	8K	Cold
t_9	22032	30	Asian	Male	10K	Hypertension
t_{10}	22032	40	Asian	Male	9K	Chest Pain
t_{11}	22033	30	White	Male	10K	Hypertension
t_{12}	22033	40	White	Male	9K	Chest Pain

Figure 9.2   A patient table (Tbl).

values while keeping all other tuples unchanged, the resulting new instance can still yield v. In the sequel, we say *two ID values $t_1[ID]$ and $t_2[ID]$ can swap their private values in an instance*, or simply $t_1[ID]$ *swaps with* $t_2[ID]$, if the resulting instance can still yield v.

Note that such a swap is required for all the instances yielding v, hence, this definition is in terms of v, not the current table Tbl (although we used the projection $\Pi_B(Tbl)$ in the definition, this projection is not Tbl itself and is assumed to be publicly known). In other words, for two ID values to be SYM is to be able to swap their corresponding private values in all possible instances, including Tbl.

For example, consider the released view v in Figure 9.3 on the table in Figure 9.2. The two ID values $t_9[ID]$ and $t_{10}[ID]$ are SYM because they can

	Zip	Problem
t_9	22032	Hypertension
t_{10}	22032	Chest Pain
t_{11}	22033	Hypertension
t_{12}	22033	Chest Pain

Figure 9.3   A released view $\Pi_{Zip,Problem}(Tbl)$ $\sigma_{Zip='22032'or'22033'}(Tbl)$ provides 2-SIND.

swap their *Problem* values in any instance to yield v while still yielding the same v. Similarly, the two *ID* values $t_{11}[ID]$ and $t_{12}[ID]$ are also SYM. However, $t_9[ID]$ and $t_{11}[ID]$ are not SYM, even though they have the same *Problem* value (*Hypertension*) in the current private table. To show this, consider an instance obtained by swapping the *Problem* values of t_9 and t_{10} in *Tbl* (while other tuples remain unchanged). Now t_9 has *Chest Pain* while t_{10} has *Hypertension*. Denote the new instance *Tbl'*. Clearly, *Tbl'* also yields the view v and, therefore, *Tbl'* is in $\mathcal{I}^v$. However, in *Tbl'*, if we swap the *Problem* values of t_9 (i.e., *Chest Pain*) with that of t_{11} (i.e., *Hypertension*), then both t_9 and t_{10} will have *Hypertension*. Therefore, the new instance obtained from *Tbl'* does not yield v and, hence, $t_9[ID]$ and $t_{11}[ID]$ are not SYM.

The definition of SYM requires a complete symmetry between two *B* tuples in terms of their private values. The sets of possible private values of the SYM tuples are the same because in each possible instance two SYM *ID* values can swap their private values without changing the views. Furthermore, the definition based on swapping makes SYM between two *ID* values independent on other *ID* values. That is, even if attackers can guess the private values of all other *ID* values, they still cannot distinguish between these two *ID* values because the two *ID* values still can swap their private values without affecting the views.

The binary relation SYM is *reflexive, symmetric,* and *transitive*. That is, SYM is an *equivalence* relation. It is easy to see that it is reflexive and symmetric. The transitivity is shown as follows. If an *ID* value a_1 can swap with another *ID* value a_2, and a_2 can swap with a_3, then a_1 can swap with a_3 by the following these steps: a_1 swaps with a_2, a_2 swaps with a_3, a_2 swaps with a_1, by the definition of SYM, the final instance still yields v.

Thus, the equivalence relation SYM partitions the *ID* values in $\pi_{ID}(Tbl)$. Each set in the partition, which is called a *SYM set*, is the "crowd" that provides individual privacy. The sizes of these crowds reflect how much protection they give to the individuals in the crowd, thus, we have the following metric.

Definition 9.4 (*k*-indistinguishability) *Given view set v, if each SYM set has a cardinality of at least k, we then say v provides k-indistinguishability.*

That is, if we can partition the individuals into SYM sets while each SYM set is at least of size k, then we have k-indistinguishability for each individual, providing a sizeable crowd (size $= k$) for each individual for protection.

In [26], it is shown that k-anonymity is a special case of k-indistinguishability in the single table release situation. This reveals the generality of the indistinguishability notion. On the other hand, in the above definition, one requires "perfect" indistinguishability, i.e., it requires complete symmetry in terms of the private attribute values between individuals. It is possible to relax this to allow a degree of symmetry. This is a topic worthy of future research.

9.4 Technical Challenges and Solutions

In this section, we discuss some technical challenges one faces when one needs to measure a given view set against the two privacy metrics. Specific practical solutions also are pointed out.

Given a view set (V, v), the uncertainty provided by the view set is measured on the associated association covers. From a theoretical perspective, the question is to determine "if there exists an interger k such that all the association covers are of at least size k." When we are dealing with relational view sets, the question in general is computable, but the time complexity can be rather high.

The basic approach to check for the sizes of the association covers has two steps: (1) from the query expressions and the basic assumptions (that are public knowledge), design a compact, symbolic representation of all the association covers, and (2) algorithmically check if there is any association cover in the symbolic representation smaller than k.

Summarized below are the general complexity results of [28].

■ When there are no functional dependencies in the original table (that are known to the public/attackers), then the checking can be done in polynomial time in the number of tuples in the view set. In this result, we take the number of queries and the size of the queries in the view set as constants, as they are insignificant in practice when compared with the number of tuples in the view set.

■ When there are functional dependencies, then the checking complexity is in general Σ_2^p-hard, which is intractable in practice. Special subcases exist in which there are still polynomial time algorithms [28].

The above complexity results apply to what we call the "accurate" checking problem, i.e., when the algorithm says "violate," then the view set does violate the k-uncertainty, while if the algorithm says "doesn't violate," then the view set does not violate the k-uncertainty. Even when the time complexity is polynomial, in practice, it may not be practical to apply these accurate algorithms especially when the number of tuples in the view set is large.

Conservative checking is only to check the necessary condition for the violation of k-uncertainty. That is, we only want to make sure that if a view set violates the k-uncertainty, then the algorithm *must* say "violate," while we allow the algorithm to make mistakes in the other direction, i.e., if the algorithm says "violate," the view set may or may not actually violate k-uncertainty. We can say such an algorithm only checks a *necessary condition* for k-uncertainty violation. Thus, the key to come up with conservative checking algorithms is to find necessary conditions for k-uncertainty violation.

Turning to indistinguishability, we know in general that it is intractable to check if a view set provides k-indistinguishability. We have the following [26]:

■ Given a view set v, whether v provide k-indistinguishability is coNP-hard.

The basic reason for this intractability is due to the fact that it is difficult to know if a particular tuple (a, p) is in any instance $r \in \mathcal{I}^v$ when the queries in the view set contains selection operations. When the selection conditions used in the view set are only on the *ID* attributes, then the problem is much easier, and we do have a polynomial algorithm.

As in the case of checking k-uncertainty, we can turn to conservative checking algorithms. That is, the algorithms must discover violation of k-indistinguishability by the view set, but may make mistakes when the view set actually does not violate k-indistinguishability. Again, we look for necessary conditions for k-indistinguishability violation [26].

9.5   Other Related Works

Earlier in this chapter, we mentioned some related works. In this section, we briefly discuss these works. Without attempting to provide a comprehensive survey, we concentrate on privacy metrics.

Other than the k-anonymity and l-diversity metrics mentioned earlier, a recent work [25] suggests the use of a combined metric, so-called (α, k)-anonymity. The idea is to "protect both identifications and relationships to sensitive information in data" [25]. This metric combines k-anonymity and l-diversity into one framework. However, the metric only applies to a single table, instead of a general relational view scenario as the uncertainty and indistinguishability discussed above.

Prior work exists that studies the privacy or secrecy disclosure by general database views. The conditions of perfect secrecy are studied in [9, 20] using a probability model, and in [29] using query conditional containment. With uncertainty and indistinguishability, we address the case where we intend to release data if some partial disclosure by database views is tolerated, and, hence, the disclosure requires measurement.

A related field is inference control. Authors have studied the information disclosure that resulted from FDs or other constraints at the tuple level.

One of the recent works is Brodsky et al. [6]. With uncertainty and indistinguishability, we concentrate on intuitive metrics for data privacy instead of general inference control.

Another related field is privacy-preserving data mining, first proposed in Agrawal and Srikant [3]. Most work in privacy-preserving data mining uses probability-based metrics, e.g., [2, 10, 11, 21]. A recent interesting work is Chawla et al. [7] that uses indistinguishability based on a probability "distance" as a privacy metric.

9.6 Conclusion

In this chapter, we defined two independent metrics that complement each other and are both important for privacy protection. The metrics apply to general scenarios where data is released as mutliple query results. We pointed out the computational intractability involved in checking the uncertainty and indistinguishability in a general view set; we also mentioned our research results in attacking the problem both for special tractable cases and in using efficient conservative methods.

A number of interesting research directions are worthy of attention. The most important one perhaps is to study methods that modify views to a user requirement in terms of uncertainty and indistinguishability, when the views do not satisfy already satisfy the requirement, perhaps in a similar way as in Machanavajjhala et al. [17]. Another interesting direction is to study additional special cases where tractable algorithms exist.

References

[1] Nabil R. Adam and John C. Wortmann. Security-control methods for statistical databases: A comparative study. *ACM Computing Surveys,* 21(4): 515–556, December 1989.

[2] Dakshi Agrawal and Charu C. Aggarwal. On the design and quantification of privacy-preserving data mining algorithms. In *Proceedings of the ACM SIGACT-SIGMOD-SIGART Symposium on Principles of Database Systems (PODS),* Santa Barbara, CA, 2001.

[3] Rakesh Agrawal and Ramakrishnan Srikant. Privacy-preserving data mining. In *Proceedings of the ACM SIGMOD International Conference on Management of Data (SIGMOD Conference),* pp. 439–450, Dallas, TX, 2000.

[4] Shipra Agrawal and Jayant R. Haritsa. A framework for high-accuracy privacy-preserving mining. In *Proceedings of the 21st International Conference on Data Engineering (ICDE),* pp. 193–204, Toyko, Japan, 2005.

[5] Roberto J. Bayardo Jr. and Rakesh Agrawal. Data privacy through optimal *k*-anonymization. In *Proceedings of the 21st International Conference on Data Engineering (ICDE),* pp. 217–228, Tokyo, Japan, 2005.

[6] Alexander Brodsky, Csilla Farkas, and Sushil Jajodia. Secure databases: Constraints, inference channels, and monitoring disclosures. *IEEE Transactions on Knowledge and Data Engineering*, 12(6): 900–919, 2000.

[7] Shuchi Chawla, Cynthia Dwork, Frank McSherry, Adam Smith, and Hoeteck Wee. Toward privacy in public databases. In *Theory of Cryptography, Second Theory of Cryptography Conference (TCC)*, pp. 363–385, Cambridge, MA, 2005.

[8] Harry S. Delugach and Thomas H. Hinke. Wizard: A database inference analysis and detection system. *IEEE Transactions on Knowledge and Data Engineering*, 8(1): 56–66, 1996.

[9] Alin Deutsch and Yannis Papakonstantinou. Privacy in database publishing. In *Database Theory— ICDT 2005, 10th International Conference*, pp. 230–245, Edinburgh, Scotland, 2005.

[10] Alexandre V. Evfimievski, Johannes Gehrke, and Ramakrishnan Srikant. Limiting privacy breaches in privacy-preserving data mining. In *Proceedings of the ACM SIGACT-SIGMOD-SIGART Symposium on Principles of Database Systems (PODS)*, San Diego, CA, pp. 211–222, 2003.

[11] Alexandre V. Evfimievski, Ramakrishnan Srikant, Rakesh Agrawal, and Johannes Gehrke. Privacy-preserving mining of association rules. In *Proceedings of the Eighth ACM SIGKDD International Conference on Knowledge Discovery and Data Mining (KDD)*, pp. 217–228, Edmonton, Alberta, Canada, 2002.

[12] Ruth Gavison. Privacy and the limits of the law. In Deborah G. Johnson and Helen Nissenbaum, Eds., *Computers, Ethics, and Social Values*, pp. 332–351. Freeman, San Francisco, 1995.

[13] Murat Kantarcioglu, Jiashun Jin, and Chris Clifton. When do data mining results violate privacy? In *Proceedings of the Tenth ACM SIGKDD International Conference on Knowledge Discovery and Data Mining (KDD)*, pp. 599–604, Seattle, WA, 2004.

[14] Krishnaram Kenthapadi, Nina Mishra, and Kobbi Nissim. Simulatable auditing. In *Proceedings of the ACM SIGMOD-SIGACT-SIGART Symposium on Principles of Database Systems (PODS)*, Baltimore, MD, pp. 118–127, 2005.

[15] Jon M. Kleinberg, Christos H. Papadimitriou, and Prabhakar Raghavan. Auditing Boolean attributes. In *Proceedings of the Nineteenth ACM SIGMOD-SIGACT-SIGART Symposium on Principles of Database Systems (PODS)*, pp. 86–91, 2000.

[16] Kristen LeFevre, David J. DeWitt, and Raghu Ramakrishnan. Incognito: Efficient full-domain k-anonymity. In *Proceedings of the ACM SIGMOD International Conference on Management of Data (SIGMOD Conference)*, pp. 49–60, Baltimore, MD, 2005.

[17] Ashwin Machanavajjhala, Johannes Gehrke, Daniel Kifer, and Muthuramakrishnan Venkitasubramaniam. l-diversity: Privacy beyond k-anonymity. In *Proceedings of the 22nd International Conference on Data Engineering (ICDE)*, pp. 24–35, Atlanta, GA, 2006.

[18] Donald G. Marks. Inference in MLS database systems. *IEEE Transactions on Knowledge and Data Engineering*, 8(1): 46–55, 1996.

[19] Adam Meyerson and Ryan Williams. On the complexity of optimal k-anonymity. In *Proceedings of the ACM SIGACT-SIGMOD-SIGART Symposium on Principles of Database Systems (PODS)*, Paris, France, pp. 223–228, 2004.

[20] Gerome Miklau and Dan Suciu. A formal analysis of information disclosure in data exchange. In *Proceedings of the ACM SIGMOD International Conference on Management of Data (SIGMOD Conference)*, pp. 575–586, Paris, France, 2004.

[21] Shariq Rizvi and Jayant R. Haritsa. Maintaining data privacy in association rule mining. In *Proceedings of 28th International Conference on Very Large Data Bases (VLDB)*, pp. 682–693, Hong Kong, China, 2002.

[22] Pierangela Samarati. Protecting respondents' identities in microdata release. *IEEE Transactions on Knowledge and Data Engineering*, 13(6): 1010–1027, 2001.

[23] Latanya Sweeney. Achieving *k*-anonymity privacy protection using generalization and suppression. *International Journal on Uncertainty, Fuzziness and Knowledge-Based Systems*, 10(5): 571–578, 2002.

[24] Lingyu Wang, Duminda Wijesekera, and Sushil Jajodia. Cardinality-based inference control in sum-only data cubes. In *Proceedings of 7th European Symposium on Research in Computer Security (ESORICS)*, pp. 55–71, Zurick, Switzerland, 2002.

[25] Raymond Chi-Wing Wong, Jiuyong Li, Ada Wai-Chee Fu, and Ke Wang. (α, k)-anonymity: An enhanced *k*-anonymity model for privacy-preserving data publishing. In Tina Eliassi-Rad, Lyle H. Ungar, Mark Craven, and Dimitrios Gunopulos, Eds., *Proceedings of the Twelfth ACM SIGKDD International Conference on Knowledge Discovery and Data Mining*, Philadelphia, *PA*, August 20–23, 2006, pp. 754–759. ACM Press, New York, 2006.

[26] Chao Yao, Lingyu Wang, Xiaoyang Sean Wang, and Sushil Jajodia. Indistinguishability: The other aspect of privacy. In Willem Jonker and Milan Petkovic, Eds., *Secure Data Management, Third VLDB Workshop, SDM 2006, Seoul, Korea, September 10–11, 2006, Proceedings*, vol. 4165 of *Lecture Notes in Computer Science*, pp. 1–17. Springer-Verlag, Heidelberg, Germany, 2006.

[27] Chao Yao, Xiaoyang Sean Wang, and Sushil Jajodia. Checking for *k*-anonymity violation by views. In *Proceedings of the 31st International Conference on Very Large Data Bases (VLDB)*, pp. 910–921, Trondheim, Norway, 2005.

[28] Chao Yao, Xiaoyang Sean Wang, and Sushil Jajodia. Checking for *k*-anonymity violation by views. In Klemens Böhm, Christian S. Jensen, Laura M. Haas, Martin L. Kersten, Per-Åke Larson, and Beng Chin Ooi, Eds., *Proceedings of the 31st International Conference on Very Large Data Bases, Trondheim, Norway, August 30–September 2, 2005*, pp. 910–921. ACM Press, New York, 2005.

[29] Zheng Zhang and Alberto O. Mendelzon. Authorization views and conditional query containment. In *Database Theory—ICDT 2005, 10th International Conference*, pp. 259–273, Edinburgh, Scotland, 2005.

Chapter 10

Privacy-Preservation Techniques in Data Mining

Chunhua Su, Jianying Zhou, Feng Bao,
Guilin Wang, and Kouichi Sakurai

Contents

10.1 Introduction 188
    10.1.1 What Is Data Mining? 188
    10.1.2 Privacy-Preserving Techniques in Data Mining 190
10.2 Random Data Perturbation Methodologies 192
    10.2.1 A Brief Review of Random Data Perturbation
             Techniques 192
    10.2.2 Privacy-Preserving Clustering Based on RDP
             Techniques 193
             10.2.2.1 Introduction and Primitives 193
             10.2.2.2 Our Proposal Based on Random Data
                      Perturbation 195
             10.2.2.3 Robustness against Filtering Attack 198
             10.2.2.4 Experimental Analysis 198
10.3 Cryptography-Based Methodologies 199
    10.3.1 Privacy-Preserving k-Means Clustering
             over Two Parties 201
             10.3.1.1 Brief Review of k-Means Clustering 201
             10.3.1.2 Known Results and Their Problems 203

10.3.1.3 General Description of Our Proposed
Method 205
10.3.1.4 The Details of the Proposed Protocols 207
10.3.1.5 Analysis of the Proposed Scheme 210
10.3.2 Privacy-Preserving Document Clustering 213
10.3.2.1 Background Introduction 213
10.3.2.2 Privacy-Preserving Document Clustering
Protocol 214
10.3.2.3 Implementing the Privacy-Preserving
Protocol 217
10.3.2.4 Security Analysis of the Whole Protocols 222
10.4 Concluding Remarks 223
References 224

10.1 Introduction

10.1.1 What Is Data Mining?

In today's information age, data collection is ubiquitous, and every transaction is recorded somewhere. The resulting data sets can consist of terabytes or even petabytes of data, so efficiency and scalability is the primary consideration of most data-mining algorithms. Data mining is becoming increasingly common in both the private and public sectors. Industries, such as banking, insurance, medicine, and retailing, commonly use data mining to reduce costs, enhance research, and increase sales. In the public sector, data-mining applications initially were used as a means to detect fraud and waste, but have grown to also be used for purposes, such as measuring and improving program performance.

Data mining is an analytic process designed to explore data (usually large amounts of data—typically business or market related) in search of consistent patterns and/or systematic relationships between variables, and then to validate the findings by applying the detected patterns to new subsets of data. The ultimate goal of data mining is prediction, and predictive data mining is the most common type and one that has the most direct business applications. The process of data mining consists of three stages: (1) the initial exploration, (2) model building or pattern identification with validation/verification, and (3) deployment (i.e., the application of the model to new data in order to generate predictions).

Inductive Learning: Induction is the inference of information from data and inductive learning is the model building process where the environment, i.e., database, is analyzed with a view to finding patterns. Similar objects are grouped in classes and rules formulated whereby it is possible to predict the class of unseen objects. This process of classification identifies classes such that each class has a unique pattern of values that forms the class description. The nature of the environment is dynamic, hence, the model must be adaptive, i.e., should be able to learn. Generally it is only possible to use a small number of properties to characterize objects, so we make abstractions, in that objects, which satisfy the same subset of properties, are mapped to the same internal representation.

Inductive learning, where the system infers knowledge itself from observing its environment, has two main strategies:

1. Supervised Learning: This is learning from examples where a teacher helps the system construct a model by defining classes and supplying examples of each class. The system has to find a description of each class, i.e., the common properties in the examples. Once the description has been formulated, the description and the class form a classification rule, which can be used to predict the class of previously unseen objects. This is similar to discriminate analysis as in statistics.
2. Unsupervised Learning: This is learning from observation and discovery. The data-mine system is supplied with objects, but no classes are defined, so it has to observe the examples and recognize patterns (i.e., class description) by itself. This system results in a set of class descriptions, one for each class discovered in the environment. Again this is similar to cluster analysis as in statistics.

Induction therefore is the extraction of patterns. The quality of the model produced by inductive learning methods is such that the model could be used to predict the outcome of future situations, in other words, not only for states encountered, but rather for unseen states that could occur. The problem is that most environments have different states, i.e., changes within, and it is not always possible to verify a model by checking it for all possible situations. Given a set of examples, the system can construct multiple models some of which will be simpler than others. The simpler models are more likely to be correct if we adhere to Ockhams razor, which states that if there are multiple explanations for a particular phenomenon, it makes sense to choose the simplest because it is more likely to capture the nature of the phenomenon.

Statistics: Statistics has a solid theoretical foundation, but the results from statistics can be overwhelming and difficult to interpret because they require user guidance as to where and how to analyze the data. Data mining, however, allows the expert's knowledge of the data and the advanced analysis techniques of the computer to work together. Statistics have a role to play and data mining will not replace such analyses, but rather they can act upon more directed analyses based on the results of data mining.

For example, statistical induction is similar to the average rate of failure of machines.

Machine Learning: Machine learning is the automation of a learning process and learning is tantamount to the construction of rules based on observations of environmental states and transitions. This is a broad field, which includes not only learning from examples, but also reinforcement learning, learning with teacher, etc. A learning algorithm takes the data set and its accompanying information as input and returns a statement, e.g., a concept representing the results of learning as output. Machine learning examines previous examples and their outcomes and learns how to reproduce these and make generalizations about new cases.

10.1.2 Privacy-Preserving Techniques in Data Mining

Generally when people talk of privacy, they request that information about themselves be unavailable to others. However, their real concern is that their information should not be misused. The fear is that once information is released, it will be impossible to prevent misuse. To do this, we need technical solutions that ensure data will not be released.

1. Protection of personal information: One should not sacrifice the privacy of individuals if doing so would not improve security. For example, consider the security-relevant question of whether a particular individual has been at a particular location. Monitoring the identities of every individual in that location will reveal whether a particular individual has been there, but unnecessarily reveals the whereabouts of every individual there. A privacy-preserving solution would answer only the question regarding the particular individual, rather than revealing everyone's identity. For example, insurance companies will be concerned about sharing this data. Not only must the privacy of patient records be maintained, but insurers will be unwilling to release rules pertaining only to them.

2. Protection of sensitive information: Suppose an airline wants to compare its passenger lists against a database of suspected individuals. Obviously, the contents of the database must be protected. Less obviously, it is also desirable to protect the passenger lists and the answers to the database queries, since this could be useful information to potential terrorists. Privacy-preserving techniques would allow an airline to interact with a law enforcement database to determine whether any passengers of a particular flight are on a list of suspicious individuals, without revealing any information

to intruders eavesdropping on the communication or revealing any additional information about the database to the airline.

3. Collaboration among different agencies: As has been well documented, different federal and local agencies do not always cooperate to the degree necessary to provide the highest security. Using privacy-preserving techniques, such agencies could collaborate in order to determine security-relevant outcomes based on their joint data without requiring any agency to reveal its data to the others or to a trusted third party. For example, photographic databases owned by two different agencies could be compared for potential matches. The ability to collaborate without revealing information could be instrumental in fostering interagency collaboration. A classical example of where privacy-preserving data-mining solutions can be of great importance is in the field of medical research. Consider the case where a number of different hospitals want to jointly mine their patient data for the purpose of medical research; the hospitals are reluctant to release their data unless there is a privacy-preserving solution.

Until recently, many papers about privacy-preserving data mining are coming out. Because the data-mining technology can be implemented in many practical methods, there is no universal solution for privacy-preserving data mining. They technologian can be divided into two methodologies generally: the data randomization technique and the cryptography-based technique, especially secure multiparty computation (SMC).

Organization of This Chapter. Section 10.2 describes random data perturbation methodologies. In this section, we propose a distributed data clustering scheme using the random data perturbation (RDP) technique, which has been widely used for preserving the privacy of individual records in statistical databases. Our privacy-preserving clustering algorithm is based on kernel density estimation, which takes into account the issues of both privacy and communication costs that arise in a distributed environment. We show that our scheme is more secure and robust against the random matrix-based filtering attack. Section 10.3 describes cryptography-based methodologies. In section 10.3.1, we present a new scheme to solve *k*-means in the security scenario of two-party. Furthermore, we show our scheme also deals with data standardization to make the result more reasonable. Finally, we show that our scheme is secure and more efficient. In section 10.3.2, we propose a framework to do the privacy-preserving document clustering among the users under the distributed environment: two parties, each having his private documents, want to collaboratively execute agglomerative document clustering without disclosing their private contents. Finally, we summarize our conclusions in section 10.4.

10.2   Random Data Perturbation Methodologies

10.2.1   A Brief Review of Random Data Perturbation Techniques

The random perturbation techniques, which are often used in disclosure control of statistical databases, have been studied by researchers in statistics, algorithms, and, more recently, data mining. It is to add the random noise to confidential numerical attributes. Thus, even if a snooper is able to attain an individual value of a confidential attribute, the true value is not disclosed. One of the key requirements of RDP methods is that they should provide the appropriate level of security against attackers who attempt to obtain information on confidential attributes through some mathematical techniques.

Estimation of Distribution Function from the Perturbed Dataset.
The random value perturbation method attempts to preserve privacy of the data by modifying values of the sensitive attributes using a randomized process [1]. Data miners explore two possible approaches. Value-class membership and value distortion and emphasize the value distortion approach. In this approach, the owner of a dataset returns a value $u_i + v$, where u_i is the original data, and v is a random value drawn from a certain distribution. Commonly used distributions are the uniform distribution over an interval $[-\alpha, \alpha]$ and Gaussian distribution with mean $\mu = 0$ and standard deviation σ. The n original data values $u_1, u_2, \ldots, u_n$ are viewed as realizations of n independent and identically distributed (i.i.d.) random variables $U_i, i = 1, 2, \ldots, n$, each with the same distribution as that of a random variable U. In order to perturb the data, n independent samples $v_1, v_2, \ldots, v_n$ are drawn from a distribution V. The owner of the data provides the perturbed values $u_1 + v_1, u_2 + v_2, \ldots, u_n + v_n$ and the cumulative distribution function $F_V(r)$ of V. The reconstruction problem is to estimate the distribution $F_U(x)$ of the original data from the perturbed version.

The authors [1] suggest the following method to estimate the distribution $F_U(u)$ of U, given n independent samples $w_i = u_i + v_i, i = 1, 2, \ldots, n$ and $F_V(v)$. Using Bayes' rule, the posterior distribution function $F'_U(u)$ of U, given that $U + V = w$, can be written as

$$F'_U(u) = \frac{\int_{-\infty}^{u} f_V(w - z) f_U(z) dz}{\int_{-\infty}^{\infty} f_V(w - z) f_U(z) dz}$$

which upon differentiation with respect to u yields the density function

$$f'_U = \frac{f_V(w - u) f_U(u)}{\int_{-\infty}^{\infty} f_V(w - z) f_U(z) dz}$$

where $f_U(\cdot)$, $f_V(\cdot)$ denote the probability density function of U and V respectively. If we have n independent samples $u_i + v_i = w_i, i = 1, 2, \ldots, n,$

the corresponding posterior distribution can be obtained by averaging:

$$f'_U(u) = \frac{1}{n} \sum_{i=1}^{n} \frac{f_V(w_i - u) f_U(u)}{\int_{-\infty}^{\infty} f_V(w_i - z) f_U(z) dz}$$

For sufficiently large number of samples n, we expect the above density function to be close to the real density function $f_U(u)$. In practice, since the true density $f_U(u)$ is unknown, we need to modify the right-hand side of the above equation. The authors suggest an iterative procedure where at each step $j = 1, 2, \ldots$, the posterior density $f_U^{j-1}(u)$ estimated at step $j-1$ is used in the right-hand side of above equation. The uniform density is used to initialize the iterations. The iterations are carried out until the difference between successive estimates becomes small. In order to speed up computations, the authors also discuss approximations to the above procedure using partitioning of the domain of data values.

10.2.2 Privacy-Preserving Clustering Based on RDP Techniques

10.2.2.1 Introduction and Primitives

Density Estimation-Based Clustering. In density estimation (DE)-based clustering, the search for densely populated regions is accomplished by estimating a so-called probability density or cumulative distribution function from which the given data set is assumed to have arisen. Many techniques for DE-based clustering are proposed [10,28]. The proposed clustering methods require the computation of a nonparametric estimation of the density function from the data. One important family of nonparametric estimates is known as kernel estimators. The idea is to estimate a density function by defining the density at any data object as being proportional to a weighted sum of all objects in the dataset, where the weights are defined by an appropriately chosen kernel function.

Our Contributions. Here, we study the random data perturbation techniques and propose a privacy-preserving, density-based clustering scheme using the RDP techniques.

■ We show that random noise addition methods can be used to preserve the data privacy in density estimation-based clustering; it is possible for a user of the masked data to estimate the distribution of the original data.
■ We make an extension of our scheme for the distributed clustering with the masking parameters published in order for estimates obtained from the masked data to be adjusted for consistency and unbiasedness.
■ Moreover, we show that our scheme is secure and it can prevent the random matrix-based filtering attack.

Problem Setting. In this section, we deal with the privacy problem of distributed data clustering (DDC). We assume that there are n parties wanting to cooperate on the joint databases $D_1 \cup D_2 \cup \ldots \cup D_n$ without revealing the private information of the databases. And we assume the standard synchronous model of computation in which n parties communicate by sending messages via point-to-point channels. Let $A(\cdots)$ be a clustering algorithm mapping any dataset S to a clustering of S, that is, a collection of pair-wise disjoint subsets of S. We define the problem of homogeneous distributed data clustering for clustering algorithm A as follows. Let $S = \{x_i | i = 1, \ldots, N\} \in R_n$ be a dataset of objects. Let L_j, $j = 1, \ldots, M$, be a finite set of sites. Each site L_j stores one dataset D_j, and it will be assumed that $S = \cup_{j=1}^{M} D_j$. The DDC problem then is to find for $j = 1, \ldots, M$, a site clustering C_j residing in the data space of L_j, such that

- $C_j = \{C \cap D_j : C \in A(S)\}$ (correctness requirement).
- Time and communications costs are minimized (efficiency requirement).
- At the end of the computation, the size of the subset of S, which has been transferred out of the data space of any site L_j, is minimized (privacy requirement).

Viewing all of the published data as encoded bits $z_1, \ldots, z_n$, the goal of the privacy-breaking adversary is to efficiently *decode* this encoding to get the original value. In our setting, the *decoding* algorithm is given access to a data matrix that is perturbed by adding some random noise. We want to provide a privacy scheme such that the *a priori* probability of original data X is the same as the *a posteriori* probability of original data X given the corresponding perturbed data Z.

Primitive Tools. *Random Data Perturbation:* Random data perturbation (RDP) methods are often used to protect confidential, numerical data from unauthorized queries while preserving a certain accuracy of original information to legitimate queries. This methodology is adding the random noise to confidential numerical attributes. One of the key requirements of RDP methods is that they should provide the appropriate level of security against an attacker who attempts to obtain information on confidential attributes through some mathematical techniques. To provide accurate information, it is desirable that perturbation does not result in a change in relationships between attributes. Therefore, database administrators have to balance the trade-off for confidentiality against the needs of legitimate users for easy access and analysis of organizational data. This method is also called simple additive noise masking. Let's assume that the vector of original data x_j for the j-th variable of the original dataset X_j is replaced by a vector $z_j = x_j + \epsilon_j$. Where the random variable $\epsilon_j \sim N(0, \sigma_{\epsilon_j}^2)$ such that the covariance $Cov(\epsilon_t, \epsilon_l) = 0$ for all $t \neq l$. Noise that satisfies these conditions is the uncorrelative noise.

Verifiable Secret Sharing (VSS) Scheme: A player might lie about his own share to gain access to other shares. A VSS scheme allows players to be certain that no other players are lying about the contents of their shares, up to a reasonable probability of error. Such schemes cannot be computed conventionally; the players must collectively add and multiply numbers without any individuals knowing what exactly is being added and multiplied.

10.2.2.2   Our Proposal Based on Random Data Perturbation

In this section, our cluster algorithm is based on Klusch et al.'s proposal [20]. Using kernel-based density estimation, it is straightforward to decompose the clustering problem into six steps as follows:

1. Choose a window width h and a kernel function f_K.
2. Form the data as a matrix with h columns.
3. Perturb the data and then make a linear transformation.
4. Reconstruct the density of the perturbed data.
5. Compute the kernel-based density estimate $\psi_{f_K, w}[S](\tilde{x})$ from the given dataset.
6. Detect regions of the data space where the value of the estimate is high and group all data objects of space into corresponding clusters.

To meet the privacy concern, we make a linear transformation on the original data before the clustering computation. In this section, we show how to implement the privacy-preserving protocol using the RDP technique.

Random Data Perturbation Based on Linear Transformation. A linear transformation between two vector spaces V and W is a map $T : V \longrightarrow W$ such that the following holds: $T(v_1 + v_2) = T(v_1) + T(v_2)$ for any vectors v_1 and v_2 in V, and $T(\alpha v) = \alpha T(v)$ for any scalar α. Our purpose is to perturb the original data while maintaining the unbiased value of summary statistics for the density estimation clustering. The basic idea is adding random noise to the original data and then make a linear transformation. And the linear transformation doesn't affect the accuracy of the clustering because the distances between variables don't change. Moreover, this type of transformation leads to a simple application of the change of variable theorem. Suppose that X is a random variable taking values in $S \in R$, where R is a set of real number, and that X has a distribution on S with probability density function f. Let $Y = ax + b$ where $a \in R \backslash 0$ and $b \in R$. And note that Y takes values in $T = \{ax + b : x \in S\} \subseteq R$. Apply the change of variables theorem to show that Y has probability density function $g(Y) = \frac{1}{|a|} f(\frac{y-b}{a})$, $y \in T$.

We model the database as a matrix that has h columns, where h is the window width. We then make a linear transformation on the original data matrix. Here, we denote the original data as x_i and noise added to original data as y_i. At first, we generate a perturbed data as $Z_j = x_j + y_i$. The random noise y_i can be generated from Gaussian distribution.

We apply the linear transform to the perturbed data Z_j to make them more secure against the random matrix-based filtering technique. We can do the linear transformation as: $D_j = aZ_j + b_j$. After this step, we can get a matrix:

$$D = aZ + B = a(X + Y) + B,$$

where B is a matrix whose j-th column contains the scalar b_j in all rows. Parameters a and b_j are determined under the restrictions that $E(D_j) = E(X_j)$ and $Var(D_j) = Var(X_j)$ for $j = 1, \ldots, n$, where E and Var denote the estimation and variance, respectively.

Due to the restrictions used to determine a, this method preserves expected values and covariances of the original variables and is quite good in terms of analytical validity. Namely, a new dataset D is reconstructed from the perturbed data using certain algorithms, and the difference between D and the actual original dataset X indicates how much private information can be disclosed. The farther apart D is from X, the higher level of the privacy preservation is achieved. Therefore, the difference between D and X can be used as the measure to quantify how much privacy is preserved. By fixing the perturbation of an entity, it can prevent the estimates of the value of a field in a record by repeating queries.

Density Reconstruction. The goal of density reconstruction is to estimate the means and standard deviations for each cluster so as to maximize the likelihood of the observed data (distribution). Put another way, the expectation maximization (EM) algorithm attempts to approximate the observed distributions of values based on mixtures of different distributions in different clusters. The EM algorithm is used to estimate the probability density of a set of given data. In order to model the probability density of the data, Gaussian Mixture Model is used. The probability density of the data modeled as the weighted sum of a number of Gaussian distributions.

The n original records $x_1, x_2, \ldots, x_n$ are modeled as realizations of n independent, identically distributed, random variables $X_1, X_2, \ldots, X_n$, each with the same distribution as a random variable X. To hide these records, n independent, p-variant variables $Y_1, Y_2, \ldots, Y_n$ are used, each with the same distribution as a random variable Y. The published data Z set will be $z_1 = x_1 + y_1$, $z_2 = x_2 + y_2, \ldots, z_n = x_n + y_n$. The purpose of our algorithm is to estimate the density function of the dataset X from our knowledge of the published data Z and the density function f_Y.

Here, we can reconstruct the possibility density function f_X from the perturbed data and get the approximated result f'_X. We approximate the density function f_X with the average of the density function over the interval in which x lies. Let $I(x)$ denote the interval in which x lies. Let $N(I_p)$ be the number of points that lie in interval I_p (i.e., number of elements in the set $\{z_i | z_i \in I_p\}$, since $m(z_i)$ is the same for points that lie within the same interval. The problem is to reconstruct the probability density function of each distribution, thus we can use the algorithm in Agrawal et al. [1] to reconstruct it for density estimation-based clustering.

Extending to Distributed Environment. We can apply this scheme to a distributed environment with n participants sites L_j, $j = 1, \ldots, n$ by using the VSS scheme [4]. A VSS scheme allows any processor to distribute shares of a secret, which can be verified for consistency. If the shares verify, the honest processors can always reconstruct the secret regardless of the adversary's behavior. Moreover, the curious processors by themselves cannot learn any secret information.

The Gaussian noise and the linear transformation parameter a and b_j can be generated and all the participants cooperatively verify that the shared values are legitimate. Finally, each party site L_j, $j = 1, \ldots, n$ can cooperatively reconstruct the original data density by using the reconstruction technique of the verifiable secret-sharing scheme and the density reconstruction algorithm such as in Agrawal et al. [1].

Here, we apply Dwork et al.'s [8] Gaussian noise generation to get the noise b_i that is mentioned in Section 10.3.1.

Distributed Protocol of Noise Generation

1. **Share Summands:** On query f, the holder of d_i, the data in row i of the database, computes $f(d_i)$ and shares out this value using a nonmalleable verifiable, secret-sharing scheme, $i = 1, \ldots, n$. The bits are represented as 0/1 values in $GF(q)$, for a large prime q. We denote this set $\{0, 1\}_{GF(q)}$ to make the choice of field clear.

2. **Verify Values:** Cooperatively verify that the shared values are legitimate (i.e., in $\{0, 1\}_{GF(q)}$, when f is a predicate).

3. **Generate Noise Shares:** Cooperatively generate shares of appropriately distributed random noise.

4. **Sum All Shares:** Each participant adds together all the shares that it holds, obtaining a share of the noisy $\sum_i f(d_i) + noise$. All arithmetic is in $GF(q)$.

5. **Reconstruction:** Cooperatively reconstruct the noisy sum using the reconstruction technique of the verifiable secret-sharing scheme.

The results from Dwork et al. [9] give us a good example of how to generate Gaussian distributions noise for which the noisy sums provide the indistinguishability against the adversary. Because, as usual in the Byzantine literature, we assume that at least 2/3 of the participants will survive, the total variance for the noise would be sufficient (but not excessive).

10.2.2.3 Robustness against Filtering Attack

In [18], Kargupta et al. showed that random matrices have predictable structures in the spectral domain and it developed a random matrix-based spectral filtering technique (SPF) to retrieve original data from the dataset distorted by adding random values. Let U be an $m \times n$ data matrix and V be a noise matrix with the same dimensions. The random value perturbation technique generates a modified data matrix $U_p = U + V$. What we want to do is to extract U from U_p. Let U_p be the covariance matrix and we get

$$U_p^T U_p = (U + V)^T (U + V) = U^T U + V^T U + U^T V + V^T V$$

As the data random vector and noise random vector are uncorrelated, we have $E[U^T V] = E[V^T U] = 0$. Then the equation can be simplified as $U_p^T U_p = U^T U + V^T V$. Since the correlation matrices $U^T U$, $U_p^T U_p$, $V^T V$ are symmetric and positive semidefinite, let $U^T U = Q_u \Lambda_u Q_u^T$, $U_p^T U_p = Q_p \Lambda_p Q_p^T$, $V^T V = Q_v \Lambda_v Q_v^T$, where Q_u, Q_p, Q_v are orthogonal matrix whose column vectors are eigenvectors of $U^T U$, $U_p^T U_p$, $V^T V$, respectively, and Λ_u, Λ_p, Λ_v are diagonal matrices with the corresponding eigenvalues on their diagonal. So, the attacker can get $\Lambda_p \approx \Lambda_u + \Lambda_v$ with this information; he also can get an approximation of original data.

To attack this ϵ-Gaussian distribution perturbation method, first we have to compute the eigenvalues of covariance matrix Y from the perturbed data, such as $\lambda_1 \leq \lambda_2 \leq \cdots \leq \lambda_n$. After that, we can estimate the noise eigenvalues and the theoretical bounds λ_{max} and λ_{min}, then we can identify the noisy eigenstates $\lambda_i \leq \lambda_i + 1 \leq \cdots \leq \lambda_j$ such that $\lambda_i \geq \lambda_{min}$ and $\lambda_j \leq \lambda_{max}$. The remaining eigenstates can be considered as the ones corresponding to the actual data.

Let Λ_v be the noise-related diagonal matrix and Λ_u be the actual data-related diagonal matrix. Then we decompose the covariance matrix into two parts, with $Y = Y_s + Y_r = A_u \Lambda_u A_u^T + A_v \Lambda_v A_v^T$. After that, we can separate the original data from the added noise by computing the estimate $\hat{U} = U_p A_u A_u^T$.

Our proposed scheme can guard against the random matrix-based filtering technique. After the linear transformation, the eigenvalues of original data are changed. The noise and actual data-related eigenvalues will be more difficult to analyze by the random matrix-based filtering technique because they are altered by the linear transformation. But, a shortcoming of the linear transform method is that it does not preserve the univariate distributions of the original data and it cannot be used in discrete variables.

10.2.2.4 Experimental Analysis

This section presents results for experiments with random numeric data, and show how our proposals can make the eigenvalues more noncorrelative,

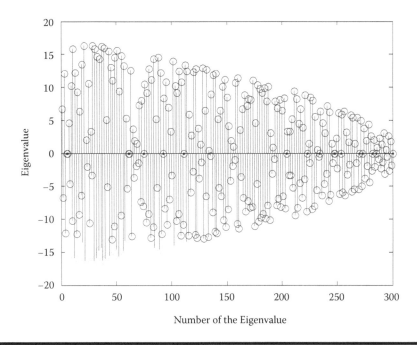

Figure 10.1   Eigenvalue distribution of original data with Gaussian noise added.

which can avoid the random matrix-based filtering attack. At first, we generate a random data 300×300 matrix, and then analyze the eigenvalue distribution. As we can see in Figures 10.1 and 10.2, the first figure shows the eigenvalues distribution of original data with Gaussian noise added, which can be attacked with a random matrix-based filtering technique. The second figure shows the eigenvalues distribution of linear transformation.

In Figure 10.2, we show that after a linear transformation, the distribution of the eigenvalues converges faster. That means its eigenvalues become more difficult to use in reconstructing the original data.

As indicated earlier in related works, while perturbation methods guarantee that complete disclosure will not occur, they are susceptible to partial disclosure. In our proposal, all the original data and their eigenvalue distribution are covered by the linear transformation. There is no way for a random matrix-based filtering attack to succeed.

10.3   Cryptography-Based Methodologies

Privacy Definition under Secure Multiparty Computation. The construction of our protocol is based on secure multiparty computation, which was introduced by Yao [32] and extended by Goldreich, Micali, and

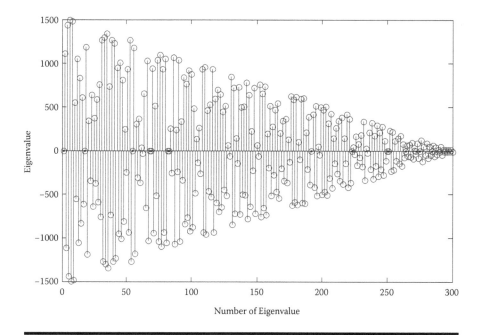

Figure 10.2 The eigenvalue distribution after the linear transformation.

Wigderson [14]. It allows a set of n players to securely compute any agreed function on their private inputs and the corrupted players do not receive any information concerning the other players' inputs. In secure multiparty computation, we always assume that all parties are *semihonest*. The first paper to take the classic cryptographic approach to privacy preserving data mining was presented by Lindell and Pinkas [22]. They present an effficient, secure multi-party protocol for the problem of distributed decision tree learning.

Privacy in the Semihonest Model: A semihonest party follows the rules of the protocol giving its correct input, but it is very curious and it only tries to deduce information on the inputs of the honest parties by inspecting all the information available to the corrupted parties. This is somewhat realistic in the real world because parties who want to mine data for their mutual benefit will follow the protocol to get correct results. Also, a protocol that is buried in large, complex software cannot be easily altered, so we always believe that a semihonest party will never cheat in the protocol's process. In the secure computation setting, there are two models. In the ideal model, every party sends inputs to a trusted party, who computes the document clustering and sends the outputs. In the real model, every party runs a real private document clustering protocol with no trusted help. A real protocol that is run by the parties (in a world where no trusted party exists) is secure, if no adversary can do more harm in a real execution than in an execution that takes place in the ideal world.

Let $f : \{0, 1\}^* \times \{0, 1\}^* \longrightarrow \{0, 1\}^* \times \{0, 1\}^*$ be a function. A two-party protocol is defined by a pair of probabilistic, polynomial, time-interactive algorithms $\pi = (\pi_A, \pi_B)$. The protocol π is executed as follows. Initially, Alice, who operates according to π_A, receives an input a and a random input r_A, and Bob, who operates according to π_B, receives an input b and a random input r_B. The execution then proceeds by synchronous rounds, where, at each round, each party may send to the other party a message as specified by π, based on Alice's input, her random input, and messages received in previous rounds. At each round, each party may decide to terminate and output some value based on Alice's entire view consisting of her input, random input, and received messages.

Consider the probability space induced by the execution of π on input $x = (a, b)$ (induced by the independent choices of the random inputs r_A, r_B). Let $view_A^\pi(x)$ (resp., $view_B^\pi(x)$) denote the entire view of Alice (resp., Bob) in this execution, including her input, random input, and all messages she has received. Let $output_A^\pi(x)$ (resp., $output_B^\pi(x)$) denote Alice's (resp., Bob's) output. Note that the above four random variables are defined over the same probability space. We say that π privately computes a function f if there exist probabilistic, polynomial time algorithms S_A and S_B such that:

$$\{(S_A(a, f_A(x)), f_B(x))\}_{x=(a,b)\in X} \equiv \{(VIEW_A^\pi(x), OUPUT_B^\pi(x))\}_{x\in X} \quad (10.1)$$

$$\{(f_A(x), S_B(b, f_B(x)))\}_{x=(a,b)\in X} \equiv \{(OUPUT_A^\pi(x), VIEW_B^\pi(x))\}_{x\in X} \quad (10.2)$$

where $\equiv$ denotes computational indistinguishability, which means there is no probabilistic polynomial algorithm A that can distinguish the probability distribution over two random strings. This chapter only considers the semi-honest adversaries. In this model, every party is assumed to act according to their prescribed actions in the protocol.

10.3.1   *Privacy-Preserving k-Means Clustering over Two Parties*

10.3.1.1   *Brief Review of k-Means Clustering*

K-means algorithm was introduced by J. MacQueen in 1967 [24]. The k-means algorithm is an iterative improvement algorithm for the k-means clustering problem, which groups data with similar characteristics or features together. It assigns each point to the cluster whose center (also called centroid) is nearest. The center is the average of all the points in the cluster, i.e., its coordinates are the arithmetic mean for each dimension separately over all the points in the cluster. It starts with an initial k-means clustering and then iterates to move each representative point to the centroid of each

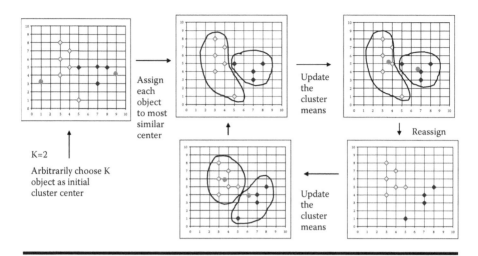

Figure 10.3   Example of *k*-means clustering.

cluster generated by the current representative points, until a local minimum solution is found. (see Figure 10.3) The algorithm can be described by a pseudo-program as follows:

```
Initialize k-clustering C₁,..., Cₖ for n points
xᵢ (i = 1,..., n) to 0;
Randomly select k starting cluster points C′₁,.., C′ₖ
repeat
   for all data points xᵢ do
   Compute the centroid x̄(Cⱼ) of each cluster;
   Assign data point xᵢ to cluster Cⱼ if distance
   d(xᵢ, Cⱼ) is the minimum over all j.
   end for
   Calculates new means C′₁,.., C′ₖ.
until the difference between C′₁,.., C′ₖ and C₁,...,
Cₖ is acceptably low.
```

Distance Measuring: To evaluate how well the cluster C_i works, we have to use mathematical definitions. Many applications of *k*-means clustering are used to measure the similarity of the two data objects. There are mainly two kinds of distance measuring methods, given vector $x_1, .., x_m$ and $y_1, ..., y_m$:

Euclidean Distance:

$$Dist_E(X, Y) = \sqrt{\sum_{i=1}^{m}(x_i - y_i)^2}$$

Correlation Distance:

$$Dist_C(X, Y) = 1 - \frac{(x_i - \bar{x})(y_i - \bar{y})}{\sum_{i=1}^{m}(x_i - y_i)^2}$$

If $Dist(x_i, C_m) \leq Dist(x_i, C_j)$ for all $j \neq m$, then x_i is in cluster m.

10.3.1.2 Known Results and Their Problems

There are some published papers that propose a number of solutions based on cryptographic techniques. The one by Vaidya and Clifton [31] introduced a solution based on Okamoto and Uchiyama homomorphism cryptosystem [26], which is not secure without random padding and the entire scheme is not collusion-resistant. Jagannathan and Wright's proposal [16] is based on Pallier's homomorphism cryptosystem [27], but there is a security weakness in the update computation, which applies an insecure scheme [2]. Thus the whole protocol is inefficient. In Jha et al.'s solution [17], two parties compute their k-means local clustering respectively, and then use oblivious polynomial devaluation to construct a private update computation of clusters to join the $2k$ clusters into k ones. It is known that the algorithm is very sensitive to initiative clusters, so the proposal has the correctness problem because the result is not based on two parties' joint databases. In [15], a secure scalar production protocol [7] is used as a subprotocol, which has a serious weakness. A leakage of some database entries can reveal the whole vector (database) and is very inefficient when the database is large. Beyond the security and correctness problem, all proposals above do not consider data standardization, which is frequently used in practical application to deal with different variables. The security, correctness data standardization, and efficiency improvement are what we want to solve in this chapter.

Our Improvements.

- In this section, we provide an interactive protocol with data standardization to execute a private two-party k-means clustering without security and correctness problems based on the homomorphic cryptosystem of Pailier's paper [27].
- Our solution can be divided into three parts: private data standardization, private distance measuring, and private update computation. We apply secure scalar production protocol [13] to do private distance measuring and oblivious polynomial evaluation to construct a secure two-party approximation protocol for private data standardization and private update computation.
- Our proposal is more efficient with less communication and computational complexity compared to existing proposals.

Problem Formulation and Notions. Below, we assume that there are two parties who possess private databases. They want to get the common benefit for doing clustering analysis in the joint databases. For the privacy concerns, they need a private preserving system to execute the joint k-means clustering analysis. The concern is solely that values associated with an individual entity not be released (e.g., personal or sensitive information); the techniques must focus on protecting such information.

We assume a multivariate database $D = \{d_1, .., d_n\}$, which consists of n objects, each data object d_i has m attributes. So, we take each d_i object as a vector set $d_i = x_{i,1}, \ldots, x_{i,m}$, where x denotes the attribute variable. That is, each d_i is partitioned into disjoint subsets d_i^A and d_i^B such that Alice knows d_i^A and Bob knows d_i^B. We assume that database Party A holds some data objects in the relational database $D = \{d_1, .., d_n\}$ mentioned above denoted by $D_A = \{d_1^A, .., d_n^A\}$, and Party B holds the other left data objects $D_B = \{d_1^B, .., d_n^B\}$. What we want to do is to attain the final result, which is output clusters computed over Party A and Party B's joint data, without revealing and invading any privacy of both parties. We have to prevent the $D = d_1, .., d_n$ from being acquired by the adversaries who are curious to learn the private data held by the other when the k-means clustering algorithm over the two parties is being executed.

Cryptographic Primitives. Following is a brief review of the cryptographic primitives based on public key cryptosystem. In modern terms, a public-key encryption scheme on a message space M consists of three algorithms (K, E, D):

- The key generation algorithm $K(1^k)$ outputs a random pair of private/public keys (sk, pk), relative to a security parameter k.
- The encryption algorithm $E_{pk}(m, r)$ outputs a ciphertext c corresponding to the plaintext $m \in M$, using random value r.
- The decryption algorithm $D_{sk}(c)$ outputs the plaintext m associated to the ciphertext c.

We will occasionally omit the random coins and write $E_{pk}(m)$ in place of $E_{pk}(m, r)$. Note that the decryption algorithm is deterministic. We require a homomorphic encryption scheme satisfying $E(a) * E(b) = E(a + b)$, where E is a cryptosystem, $*$ and $+$ denote modular multiplication and addition, respectively. It also follows that $E(a)^c = E(a * c)$ for $c \in N$. The Paillier cryptosystem [27] is a proper scheme, which has this property and is the cryptosystem of our choice to construct a secure protocol.

Oblivious Polynomial Evaluation (OPE) is one of the fundamental cryptographic techniques. It involves a sender and a receiver. The sender's input is a polynomial $Q(x)$ of degree k over some field F and the receiver's input is an element $z \in F$. The receiver learns $Q(z)$. It is quite useful to construct some protocols that enable keyword queries while providing privacy for both parties, namely, (1) hiding the queries from the database (client privacy) and (2) preventing the clients from learning anything but the results of the queries (server privacy).

Oracle-aided protocol is interactive and the input of queries are supplied by both parties. An oracle-aided protocol using the oracle functionality f is said to privately compute a function g if there exist polynomial time algorithms S_1 and S_2 that satisfy the definition of privacy in semi-honest model (1) and (2) mentioned at the beginning of Section 10.3 (from Definition of Privacy), respectively, where the corresponding views of the oracle-aided protocol g are defined in the natural manner.

10.3.1.3   General Description of Our Proposed Method

Our Security Goal. A secure protocol construction is actually a compiler that takes any polynomial-time functionality f, or actually a circuit C that computes f, and constructs a protocol for securely computing f in the presence of semihonest adversaries. In a secure protocol, the only value learned by a party should be his input and the final output. This means that the semihonest adversaries cannot get any useful information even if they have the simulator to simulate the protocol with the help of intermediate outputs as in Section 10.3.

This section considers the semihonest adversaries as mentioned in section 10.3. Our protocol is to preserve both parties' privacy against such adversaries during the execution of the protocol. We use the semihonest model for the secure computation in our protocol; we assume that the two participants (both Party A and B) are semihonest, i.e., they follow the protocol, but they want to reveal the other party's privacy. Our goal is to execute the k-means clustering over the two parties and protect the individual data and intermediate values from leaking to other parties. Each party learns nothing about the other's data, except the output results. Both privacy and correctness need to be preserved.

Initialization. At first, the two parties should agree on the same database schema for the nonnumeric data. Before they release the data and do the computation, they should remove the identifiers, such as the user name and customers' ID numbers from the databases. After that, both parties initialize the k cluster randomly. Party A holds a private share of clustering center as $\rho_1^A, \ldots, \rho_k^A$, while Party B holds $\rho_1^B, \ldots, \rho_k^B$. We use $(C_1, C_2, \ldots, C_k) = (\rho_1^A + \rho_1^B, \rho_2^A + \rho_2^B, \ldots, \rho_k^A + \rho_k^B)$ as the clustering centers. As we mention in Section 10.3.2, we assume that every data object has m attributes, so for one, cluster C_i is also m-attribute and consists of $C_i^1, \ldots, C_i^m$. We can see that for Party A, the share cluster ρ_i^A consists of $\rho_i^{A,1}, \ldots, \rho_i^{A,m}$, respectively, Party B holds ρ_i^B, which consists of $\rho_i^{B,1}, \ldots, \rho_i^{B,m}$.

Privacy-Preserving Two-Party Clustering Protocol. Here, we use existing cryptographic primitives to construct a secure protocol to execute the *k*-means algorithm to get a global result over two participant parties, with respect of the privacy of both parties.

Data Standardization: Correlation distance $Dist_C$ measures trends or relative differences $Dist_C(x, y) = Dist_C(ax + b, y)$ if $a > 0$, where a and b are real numbers. We can overcome this by standardizing the variables. And Euclidean distance measures absolute differences between vectors. The choice of distance measure should be based on the application area and what sort of similarities you would like to detect. In a multiattribute database, if the values of the variables are in different attributes, then it is likely that some of the variables will take very large values. Hence, the distance between two cases, on this variable, can be a large number. Other variables may be small in value, or not vary much between cases, in which case the difference in this variable between the two cases will be small. Thus, the distance metrics considered above are dependent on the choice of units for the variables involved. The variables with high variability will dominate the metric. So, we need the data standardization to force the attributes to have a common value range.

Let $\bar{x}$ be the mean and σ be the standard deviation of the data, then we can do the standardization and get the standardized data x'_i by computing $x'_i = \frac{x_i - \bar{x}}{\sigma}$, Euclidean and correlation distance are equivalent: $Dist_E(x, y)^2 = 2nDist_C(x, y)$. After that, the *k*-means clustering will go on. Following is the general description of our solution for the privacy-preserving *k*-means clustering.

The Description of Our Solution

Notions: C_i denotes the clustering center, which is a sum of A and B's shares. A has her own share cluster ρ^A and B has his own share cluster ρ^B, where $C_i = \rho_i^A + \rho_i^B$. x_i is a data object that is used as a private input in the protocol to be clustered into a group. x_i can be held by Party A or Party B.

Input: (1) Database D_A and D_B, which are owned by Party A and Party B, respectively, consisting of n object. (2) The total number of clusters k.

Output: The k proper clusters to which data objects belong with assignment.

1. Two parties execute the private data standardization protocol.
2. Randomly, Party A selects k objects from her database as random share $\rho_1^A, \ldots, \rho_k^A$. Symmetrically, Party B selects $\rho_1^B, \ldots, \rho_k^B$ randomly. And let $C_1, \ldots C_k = (\rho_1^A + \rho_1^B, \ldots, \rho_k^A + \rho_k^B)$ as the initial cluster.

3. Repeat the following steps:
   - Compute the distance of the numeric privately with the private distance measuring protocol.
   - Assign the data objects to the closest cluster.
   - Run the update computation and reassign the data to the closest clusters with private update computation protocol.
4. Stop when the difference between the clusters $C_1, \ldots, C_k$ and the former ones is minor.

Secure Approximation Construction: Secure approximation is quite useful in securing multiparty computation to construct an efficient and secure computation with the private inputs. We give an approximation to a deterministic function f. Feigenbaum et al. [12] report some important concepts about the secure approximation between parties. We need an approximation function $\hat{f}$ with respect to the target function f without revealing any input information of f. Let $f(x)$ be as above and $\hat{f}(x)$ is its randomized approximation function. Then $\hat{f}$ is functionally t-private with respect to f if there is an efficient randomized algorithm S, called simulator, such that for every x and $1 \leq i_1, \ldots, i_t \leq m$, $S((i_1, x_{i_1}), \ldots, (i_t, x_{i_t}), f(x))$ is identically distributed to $\hat{f}(x)$.

We use the secure approximation technique below to do the private data standardization and update computation. We say that $\hat{f}$ is functionally private with respect to f if there exists a probabilistic, polynomial time algorithm S such that $S(f(x_1, x_2)) \equiv \hat{f}(x_1, x_2)$, where $\equiv$ denotes computational indistinguishability. We define when to compute a deterministic functions f. We report that $\hat{f}$ is an ϵ-approximation of f if, for all inputs (x_1, x_2), $|f(x_1, x_2) - \hat{f}(x_1, x_2)| < \epsilon$.

10.3.1.4 The Details of the Proposed Protocols

Private Standardization Protocol. In this protocol, we have to solve the problem of private computation for mean and standard deviation. We assume that Party A has n_1 data entries in the database and Party B has n_2. Let the data held by Party A be $d_A = \sum_{i=1}^{n_1} d_i^A$ and data held by Party B be $d_A = \sum_{i=1}^{n_1} d_i^A$.

The mean is computed as $M = \frac{d^A + d^B}{n_1 + n_2}$, so that the standard deviation is computed as:

$$\sigma = \sqrt{\frac{1}{n_1 + n_2} \left\{ \sum_{i=1}^{n_1} (d_i^A - M)^2 + \sum_{i=1}^{n_2} (d_i^B - M)^2 \right\}}$$

So, if we can compute the mean M privately, the privacy-preserving problem will be solved. Here, we use a oracle-aided protocol proposed by Kiltz et al. [22] to compute the mean M, it can give a secure approximation of the standard deviation. After that, the standardized data can be used in the following computation.

Private Distance Measuring Protocol. For the standardization of the multiattribute data, we can compute the distance function using the Euclidean distance as follows: $\sum_{j=i}^{k} \sum_{i=1}^{n} ||x_i - C_j||^2$. The major computation in this step is to compute the distance function with respect to both parties' privacy. We break down the distance function into $x_i^2 - 2x_i * C_i + C_i^2$, and then we can apply the secure multiparty computation techniques to compute this function.

Let the data objects from Party A and Party B be $d_i = (x_{i,1}, \ldots, x_{i,m})$; we compute the distance:

$$Dist^2(d_i, \rho_j) = (x_{i,1} - \rho_j)^2 + (x_{i,2} - \rho_j)^2 + \cdots (x_{i,m} - \rho_j)^2$$

$$= \sum_{t=1}^{l} x_{i,t}^2 + \sum_{t=1}^{l} (\rho_{j,t}^A)^2 + \sum_{t=1}^{l} (\rho_{j,t}^B)^2 + 2\sum_{t=1}^{l} \rho_{j,t}^A \rho_{j,t}^B - 2\sum_{t=1}^{l} \rho_{j,t}^A x_{i,t}^B - 2\sum_{t=1}^{l} \rho_{j,t}^B x_{i,t}^A$$

$\sum_{t=1}^{m} x_{i,t}^2, \sum_{t=1}^{m} (\rho_{j,t}^A)^2, \sum_{t=1}^{m} (\rho_{j,t}^B)^2$ can be computed locally and privately by Party A or Party B because it does not involve the other's data. The computation $\sum_{t=1}^{l} \rho_{j,t}^A \rho_{j,t}^A, \sum_{t=1}^{l} \rho_{j,t}^A x_{i,t}^B$, and $\sum_{t=1}^{l} \rho_{j,t}^B x_{i,t}^A$ need the cooperative information, so we have to preserve the privacy for both parties.

We take a semantically secure homomorphic public-key cyptosystem $\Pi = $ *Gen, Enc, Dec*, and the plain space will be included in Z_m for some large m. We set $\mu := \lfloor \sqrt{m/N} \rfloor$ and assume that all the vector $\rho \in Z_\mu^N$ are possessed by Party A or Party B. Below, we show how to do the secure product computation.

Secure Scalar Product Protocol

Private Input: Private vectors $x, y \in Z_\mu^N$, we assume that x is held by Party A and y held by Party B.
Output: Shares $S_A + S_B \equiv x \cdot y \bmod m$, where S_A (resp., S_B) is the random share A (resp., B).

1. Party A chooses a homomorphic public cryptosystem; *Enc* denotes the encryption algorithm while *Dec* denotes the decryption algorithm. Party A generates a public and private key pair (pk, sk). Party A sends pk to Party B.
2. Party A sends $u_i = Enc_{pk}(x_i)$ (for $i \in 1, \ldots, N$) to Party B.
3. Party B sets $v \longleftarrow \prod_{i=1}^{N} u_i^{y_i}$. Generate his random share S_B. Send $v' = v \cdot Enc_{pk}(-S_B)$ to Party A.
4. A computes the $S_A = Dec_{sk}(v') = x \cdot y - S_B$, she sends S_A to B.
5. B knows the random S_B, he computes $S_A + S_B = x \cdot y$.

After executing this protocol, the result of $\sum_{t=1}^{m} \rho_{j,t}^{A} \rho_{j,t}^{A}$, $\sum_{t=1}^{m} \rho_{j,t}^{A} x_{i,t}^{B}$, and $\sum_{t=1}^{m} \rho_{j,t}^{B} x_{i,t}^{A}$ can be computed without violating the privacy of each other and output the final results.

Clustering Update Computation. In this step, we assign the data points to their nearest centroids according to the minimum distance rule. With this step, we can update the k-means clusters. There are two conditions that have to be satisfied: (1) data x_i must be encoded by its nearest center, and (2) each clustering must be at the centroid of points it owns. When iteration is finished, both Parties A and B know their own share. We want to find out the proper clustering center for each data object. For this purpose, we have to do the iteration of the mean value computation. For the privacy leakage point of view, using the homomorphic cryptosystem may cause some privacy leakage (according to [13]). From the security and efficiency point of view, we use the secure approximation protocol.

The distances that are used to update computation are the means of every attribute. For generality, we assume that Party A holds data objects, which are assigned to the closest cluster: $d_{i_1}^{A}, \ldots, d_{i_p}^{A}$ and Party B has data objects $d_{i_1}^{B}, \ldots, d_{i_q}^{B}$ for each cluster where $1 \leq i \leq k$. For the data objects' values in j-th attribute belonging to i-th cluster center is given by $d_{i,j}$, $1 \leq j \leq p$ (or q). Party A calculates her sum of the j-th attribute in i-th cluster as $s_j^{A} = \sum_{r=1}^{p} d_{i_r,j}^{A}$ and the number of data objects as n_j. Similarly, Party B calculates $s_j^{B} = \sum_{r=1}^{q} d_{i_r,j}^{B}$ and sets his total number of data objects as q.

We apply the secure mean computation protocol to do the mean calculation for the cluster update privately. The new i-th cluster for j-th attribute is: $C_{i,j} = (s_j^{A} + s_j^{B})/(n_j + m_j)$. It can be computed privately using the Oracle-aided protocol to compute a private 2^t-approximation protocol over the finite filed F_p proposed by Kiltz et al. [19]. We will use this protocol to make a secure computation.

For the cluster update computation, we use the result proposed in [19] and the OPE, which is proposed in [25] to do the clustering update computation. The input of the sender is a polynomial P of degree k over some field F. The receiver can get the value $P(x)$ for any element $x \in F$ without learning anything else about the polynomial P and without revealing to the sender any information about x. With the protocol, we can compute the approximated $\hat{M}$ with $\left| \frac{s_j^{A} + s_j^{B}}{n_j + m_j} - \hat{M} \right| \leq 2^{-t}$ for the clustering update privately, where t is an approximation and secure parameter.

Theorem 10.1 The correctness of the approximation protocol: The approximation of the two-party k-means clustering with a 2^{-t} approximation is achieved in our protocol.

Proof: The whole scheme for k-means clustering computing consists of two subprotocols. At first, the two parties execute private distance measuring protocol interactively, both parties can get the accurate results of the distance between their own data and the clustering centers. We can see that the output of the whole scheme will fall within a certain interval with a overwhelming probability if the other subprotocol for clustering center update can output acceptable approximation of the updated clustering centers. We can see that it doesn't cause too much bias in the data assignment to the clusters. In the clustering center update computation, we can get the approximated statistical mean result, it is a 2^{-t} approximation, as in Kiltz et al.'s proof [19]. So, we can say that the protocol can get 2^{-t} approximation.

Criterion for Iteration Stopping. Because the k-means clustering algorithm is iterative, we have to stop it when the output satisfies our requirements. For this step, we set a threshold value ϵ. The k-means clustering algorithm is doing the iteration until the difference of Euclidean distance between two consequent calculation is smaller than ϵ. That is $Dist(C_j, C_{j+1}) = Dist(\rho_j^{A,i+1} + \rho_j^{B,i+1}, \rho_j^{A,i} + \rho_j^{B,i}) < \epsilon$. We can see that the difference is minor, so we can transform the distance function into $(\rho_j^{A,i} + \rho_j^{B,i}) - (\rho_j^{A,i+1} + \rho_j^{B,i+1}) < \epsilon'$, where ϵ' is also a threshold value.

For justifying the stop criterion with respect to both Party A and Party B's privacy, we can use the homomorphic cryptosystem as follows: Party A locally computes $Enc(\rho_j^{A,i} - \rho_j^{A,i+1})$ using her and B's public key, and Party B locally computes $Enc(\rho_j^{B,i} - \rho_j^{B,i+1})$ using his and A's public key. Then they can do the multiplication with their encrypted intermediate results and do the decryption using a secret key and pass it to the other, then the other party also does the decryption using a secret key, after which we get the result: $T := Dec[Enc(\rho_j^{A,i} - \rho_j^{A,i+1}) \cdot Enc(\rho_j^{B,i} - \rho_j^{B,i+1})]$. If $T < \epsilon'$, they can stop the iteration of clustering update computation.

10.3.1.5 Analysis of the Proposed Scheme

Security Analysis

We have constructed an interactive style scheme to execute the k-means clustering algorithm. Our protocol is constructed under the semihonest model and we will prove them secure.

Private Distance Measuring: Clearly, the protocol is correct if the participants are honest. The security is based on the security of the homomorphic encryption scheme.

Lemma 10.1. Privacy is preserved in the private distance measuring protocol.

Proof: We denote π as the modified protocol, according to the definition in section 10.2.2. The view of Party B during the execution of $\pi(x, y)$ is $VIEW_B^\pi(x_i, y_i) = \{y_i, Enc_{pk}(x_i), S_B\}$, and the view of Party A is $VIEW_A^\pi(x_i, y_i) = \{x_i, \prod_{i=1}^N Enc_{pk}^{y_i} \cdot Enc_{pk}(-S_B), S_A\}$ (where $i \in 1, \ldots, N$). Since the cryptosystem we use is semantically secure, the two parties only see the random ciphertexts in the execution of our protocol, for which they cannot guess the plaintexts. In particular, even when B has given two candidate vectors x_1 and x_2 to A and A has randomly chosen one of them, $x := x_b$. Even after a polynomial number of protocol executions with A's input, B will gain only an insignificant amount of information about x_b that will not help him in guessing the value of b. On the other hand, A only sees a random encryption of $s_A = x \cdot y - s_B$, where s_B is random. But A has the key anyway, so she can decrypt this message. Thus, A obtains no information at all.

Private Data Standardization and Private Clustering Update Computation: Formally, an oracle computation accessed an oracle to get a result. Suppose that function g is privately reducible to f and that there exists a protocol for privately computing f, as well as a protocol for privately computing g.

Lemma 10.2. Privacy is preserved in private data standardization and private clustering update computation.

Proof: We employ oracle-aided secure mean computation protocol [19]. To prove privacy, we must define simulators S_A and S_B as in the definition in section 10.3.1. Party A takes the simulator $S_A(S_j^A, n_j, M_A, \hat{M})$ and Party B takes the simulator $S_A(S_j^B, m_j, M_B, \hat{M})$, each party performs divisions of their shares locally; parties output their shares at this point. The result will be identical. It can be readily checked that the statistical difference between simulators S_A and S_B and final output $\hat{M}$ is about 2^{-t} cooperative work.

Suppose that a simulator given $M = \frac{x_1 + x_2}{n_1 + n_2}$ adds uniform random noise R_1 and R_2 in the range $[-2^{-t}, 2^{-t}]$ and outputs $S(M) = M + R_1 + R_2$ with precision 2^{-2t}. When checked, the statistical difference between $S(M)$ and $\hat{M}$ is about 2^{-t}. This implies that the function computed by the protocol is functionally private with respect to the mean. The protocol satisfies the security in the semihonest model.

Criterion for Iteration Stopping: For computing the iteration stopping criterion, we use the homomorphic encryption scheme. The security is dependent on the cryptosystem we use; the security parameters, such as the length of public key, are very important for the implementation. The cryptosystem is considered semantically secure if it is not possible for a computationally bounded adversary to derive significant information under the chosen plaintext attack.

Theorem 10.2. Security of approximation protocol: Our scheme is secure under the semihonest model.

Proof: During the interactive protocol, we assume that there is adversary Adv to simulate the computation. In Section 10.2.3, we define the security under the semihonest model. Recall that there are two models of secure computation, ideal model and real model, so if we can prove the adversary cannot get any useful information to reveal any party's privacy in an ideal model, the protocol is secure. According to the security definition, the adversary plays a role of a third party who can get the output of any one of the parties during the protocol executed process.

In the distance computation of numeric attributes, the adversary's simulator S can get output of the secure scalar product protocol $OUTPUT_{SSP}$. Above we have shown that the secure scalar product protocol is secure, which means that the adversary's $VIEW$ is computational indistinguishable with $S(OUTPUT_{SSP})$. In the cluster update computation, we assume the information that simulator has attained is $VIEW_{mean}$. The view of the simulator cannot get any party's privacy because of the indistinguishability between the $S(VIEW_{mean}, OUTPUT_{SSP})$ and the output of protocol $\hat{M}$. At the last step, to decide whether the update computation iteration should stop, at i-th iteration, the view of simulator is $VIEW_{mean}^{i+1}$. The simulator's view during this process will be $S(VIEW_{mean}^{i+1} - VIEW_{mean}, OUTPUT_{SSP})$, for the security proof of the homomorphic encryption scheme, the simulator's view is also computational indistinguishable to the protocol final output. This means that during the whole protocol, the adversary's simulator cannot get any useful information to violate both two parties' privacy.

Complexity Analysis

In this section, we will analyze the communication and computation complexity and show our scheme is proper for the practical implementation. First, let's analyze the complexity.

The private distance computation is the most complex. If Party A sends n ciphertexts x_i, the overhead is N/μ, where N is the size of each ciphertext in bits. The data object d_i is m–attributes, which is represented by n; the homomorphic encryption complexity is $O(knm)$ encryptions.

For the cluster update computation, our solution for the cluster update computation clearly runs in a constant number of communication rounds between the two parties. The complexity of our protocol depends chiefly on the accuracy of the results. Given probabilistic polynomial time functionality is given as a binary circuit with N inputs and G gates. The computation complexity will be $O(N+t)$ exponentiations and a communication cost of $O((N+t)^2 N)$, where t is a secure parameter. Comparing to Jagannathan et al. [16], they use Yao's protocol or [2] for the mean computation. Without going into details, Yao's protocol requires a communication of $O(G)$ times the length of the output of a pseudo-random function. According to Kiltz et al.'s proof in [19], their solution complexity is higher.

Finally, for the iteration stopping criterion, we only need $O(km)$ bits communication complexity, better than the same computation in [16]'s proposal. Finally, for the iteration stopping criterion, we only need $O(nm)$ bits communication complexity, which is better than the same computation in [31] and [16]'s proposals, which require $O(knm)$.

10.3.2 Privacy-Preserving Document Clustering

10.3.2.1 Background Introduction

The document clustering problem is a kind of textual data-mining technique. Different from regular data mining, in textual mining, the patterns are extracted from natural language text rather than from structured databases of facts. This technique can enable the cross-enterprise document sharing over a similar topic. One solution is to show that the terms in a query are related to the words in the document. It is very helpful when a party, who holds some documents that belong to a discovered cluster with the description "security, privacy, database," wants to do a coresearch with other parties who hold the similar documents. Here, we concentrate more on agglomerative document clustering, since this method provides us more illustrations about the partitions of the clusters. The main idea is to find which documents have the most words in common and place the documents with the most words in common into the same groups. We then build the hierarchy bottom-up by iteratively computing the similarity between all pairs of clusters and then merging the most similar pairs. In the past few years, a lot of different document clustering algorithms have been proposed in the literature, including Scatter/Gather [5] and SuffixTree Clustering [33]. Bisecting k-means is proposed by Steinbach et al. [29] based on an analysis of the specifics of the clustering algorithms and the nature of document data. The above methods of text-clustering algorithms do not really address the special challenges of text clustering, and do not provide an understandable description of the clusters. This has motivated the development of new special text clustering methods, which are not based on the vector space. Some frequent term-based methods have been proposed, such as Beil et al. [3].

Problem Definition. Our protocol is a two-party frequent term-based clustering protocol with a divide-and-merge process. At first, we get the minimum overlap clusters and their descriptions and then build an agglomerative tree model for these clusters. Unlike the partitional algorithms that build the hierarchical solution for top to bottom, agglomerative algorithms build the solution by initially assigning each document to its own cluster and then repeatedly selecting and merging pairs of clusters to obtain a single all-inclusive cluster. We have defined a flat clustering as a subset of the set of all subsets of the database D, described by a subset of the set of all frequent term sets that covers the whole database. To discover a clustering with a minimum overlap of the clusters, we follow a greedy approach. After that, we employ agglomerative algorithms to build the tree from the bottom toward the top. The root is the whole database $D_A \cup D_B$ while the leaves are the minimum overlapping cluster.

Preliminaries. Let $D_A = \{Doc_A^1, \ldots, Doc_A^m\}$ be a database of m text documents held by Alice (D_B is held by Bob, respectively). Each document Doc_A^j is represented by the set of terms occurring in D_A. Let *minsupp* be a real number, $0 \leq minsupp \leq 1$, which is agreed by both Alice and Bob. Let $w_i = \{w_i^1, \ldots, w_i^k\}$ be the set of all frequent term sets in D_i ($i = A\,or\,B$) with respect to *minsupp*, the set of all term sets contained in at least *minsupp* of the D_i documents. Let $cov(w_i)$ denote the *cover* of w_i, the set of all documents containing all terms of w_i; more precisely, $cov(w_i) = \{Doc_i^j \in D_i \mid w_i \subseteq Doc_i^j\}$. The cover $cov(w_i)$ of each element w_i is a cluster candidate. A cluster can be any subset of the set of all subsets of two parties' database $D = D_A \cup D_B$ such that each document of D is contained in at least one of the sets (clusters). We define a clustering description CD as a subset of $w_1, \ldots, w_n$. We determine a cluster with a minimum overlap of the cluster candidates. The overlap can be measured by the mutual entropy.

Cryptographic Primitives: To construct a secure documents clustering protocol, we apply the following cryptographic primitives.

Homomorphic Encryption and *Oblivious Polynomial Evaluation (OPE)* (see section 10.3.2).

Oblivious Transfer (OT): A 1-out-of-N Oblivious Transfer protocol refers to a protocol where, at the beginning of the protocol, one party (Party B) has N inputs $x_1, \ldots, x_N$ and, at the end of the protocol, the other Party (A) learns one of the inputs x_i for some $1 \leq i \leq N$ of her choice, without learning anything about the other inputs and without allowing B to learn anything about x_i. Recently, Lipmaa et al. [23] proposed an efficient solution for 1-out-of-N oblivious transfer protocol with communication complexity $\Theta(\log^2 N)k$.

10.3.2.2 Privacy-Preserving Document Clustering Protocol

We proposed a privacy-preserving document clustering protocol [30]. There are two phases in our protocol, divide phase and merge phase. It works by breaking down the distributed documents clustering problem into two subproblems and the solutions to the subproblems are then combined to give a solution to the original problem. In our protocol, divide-and-merge algorithms are implemented in a nonrecursive way and the computation is interactive, so both parties play roles of both client and server, called client party and server party, respectively. At first, every local party makes a keyword list, and then he makes a private intersection computation with the other parties' keyword list. After that, two parties will make local clustering according his keyword list to get the local minimum overlapping clusters. Finally, both Alice and Bob can merge the two clusters into one according to similarity of every two clusters. The output will be a tree construction with a set of all documents as the root, and cluster descriptions will be the intersection of two keyword sets.

Privacy-Preserving Document Clustering Protocol

Input: Alice's document database D_A and Bob's document database D_B.
Output: The clusters and their descriptions based on $D_A \cup D_B$.
1. The two parties execute the document clustering in the *divide phase* and get the minimum overlapping clusters, respectively.
2. The two parties execute the interactive agglomerative clustering computation in the *merging phase.*
3. Both parties get agglomerative clusters and their descriptions.

In our protocol, all the computation of agglomerative document clustering is based on each document's frequent term, without revealing any unnecessary content of the document. What a party learns during the execution of the protocol is the common frequent term with the other party and the final output.

Initialization. Each party should do the precomputation on his own text data in every individual document. Each party should form his database, which contains N frequent terms as $X = (x_i, num_i)$ with $1 \le i \le N$. In every document held by the participant party, x_i is a keyword and num_i is the document number where the keyword x_i occurs in one document whose frequency is larger than *minsupp*. Two parties number all their own documents from 1 to m, where m is the number of total documents held by a party. For example, Alice can give numbers to her documents as $Doc_A^1, \ldots, Doc_A^m$.

Divide Phase of Document Clustering. At first, Alice and Bob have to predetermine the common threshold minimum support *minsupp* and the function for calculating the mutual overlap of frequent sets. After that, two parties execute the privacy-preserving frequent term query scheme interactively and get the frequent term sets for document clustering. In this phase, we apply the algorithm proposed by Beil et al. [3], which works in a bottom–up fashion. Starting with an empty set, it continues selecting one more element (one cluster description) from the set of remaining frequent term sets until the entire database is contained in the cover of the set of all chosen frequent term sets (the clustering), setting the database formed by selected documents. In each step, the party selects the remaining frequent term set with a cover having the minimum overlap with the other cluster candidates local.

Clustering Algorithm of Divide Phase

Input: Party P's (can be Alice or Bob) frequent keyword w_i of databases D_i, where $1 \leq i \leq n$ and the threshold minimum support *minsup*.

Output: The clusters and their descriptions based on frequent terms in w_i.

1. Party P locally finds out all frequent keywords whose frequency is larger than *minsupp*, denoted by w.
2. Perform the private keyword queries with w and get the IDs of the other party's documents, which have the common keywords.
3. Calculate entropy overlap for w and let $Candidate_w := $ element of w with minimum entropy overlap.
4. Remove all documents in $cov(Candidate_w)$ from D and from the coverage of all of the remaining documents.
5. Let $Selected_w := Selected_w \cup \{Candidate_w\}$ and $Remain_w := w - \{Candidate_w\}$.
6. Remove all documents in $cov(Candidate_w)$ from D and from the coverage of all of the $Remain_w$.
7. Party P updates the clusters until all the clusters are minimum overlap.
8. Return the keyword sets of $Selected_w$ as cluster descriptions and the cover of the sets $Selected_w$ as clusters.

Each party executes the clustering algorithm of the divide phase and gets local clusters. The algorithm returns clustering description and clusters, which is nonoverlapping. After this local computation, each party can continue the agglomerative clustering: Merging the cluster to build a agglomerative clustering tree.

Merge Phase of Document Clustering. In the divide phase, every party gets the local nonoverlap clusters based on the frequent terms of their own documents and other parties' document with common frequent keywords. The agglomeration algorithm creates hierarchical clusters. At each level in the hierarchy, clusters are formed from the union of two clusters at the next level down. In the merge step, each party starts with his own cluster and gradually merges clusters until all clusters have been gathered together in one big cluster. There are two steps for clusters merging computation

1. *Cluster Inclusion Merging Step:* A smaller cluster that is included by the larger one will be merged into the larger one.
2. *Agglomerative Step:* The two similar clusters will be merged as a new cluster according to the similarity computation. At the same time, the description of a new cluster will be the intersection of the two clusters' descriptions.

Algorithm of the Merge Phase

1. Initially, each party uses his clusters to do a private inclusion test with other parties' clusters. Merge the two clusters if one cluster is included in the other cluster. Stop when every included subset of clusters is merged.
2. Among all remaining clusters, pick the two clusters to do the private similarity computation.
3. Replace these two clusters with a new cluster, formed by merging the two original ones with the most similarities.
4. Repeat step 2 and step 3 until there is only one remaining cluster, which covers all parties' databases.

Note that in the algorithm, we can preserve the privacy by only outputting the cluster description. The merged cluster description CD is an intersection of two original cluster descriptions, not the union of the two. Because the coverage $Cov(CD)$ can cover all the documents whose frequent terms are included in CD, with the output of the protocol, the clients can match their documents with the cluster descriptions CD and assign them to the proper cluster with a subset relationship between each cluster and its predecessors in the hierarchy privately. This produces a binary tree or dendrogram, of which final agglomerative cluster is the root and each cluster is a leaf. The height of the bars indicates how close the clusters and their descriptions are.

10.3.2.3 Implementing the Privacy-Preserving Protocol

In this section, we show how to implement the privacy-preserving protocol using the cryptographic techniques, which we have mentioned in Section 10.3.2.1. Our constructions use a semantically secure public-key encryption scheme that preserves the group homomorphism of addition and allows multiplication by a constant.

Private Document Selection. When a party gets the local frequent keywords, he has to construct some queries to select the documents, which contain the same frequent term with respect to the privacy. In this section, we construct a protocol using oblivious polynomial evaluation (OPE) from Freedman et al. [12] scheme and apply the zero knowledge proof to avoid the malicious inputs of the client party. The basic idea of the construction is to encode database D's entries in $\{X = (x_1, num_1), \ldots, (x_n, num_n)\}$ as values of a polynomial, i.e., to define a polynomial Q such that $Q(x_i) = (num_i)$, where x_i denotes the keyword and num_i denotes the document number for clustering. Note that this design is different from previous applications of OPE, where a polynomial (of degree k) was used only as a source for $(k+1)$ wise independent values.

Document Selection with Private Keyword Search

Input: Client party inputs his local frequent keyword w; server party inputs $\{x_i, num_i\}_{i \in [n]}$, all x_i's are distinct

Output: Client party gets document number $number_i$ if $w = x_i$, nothing otherwise; server party: nothing

1. The server party defines L bins and maps the n items into the L bins using a random, publicly known hash function H with a range of size L. H is applied to the database's frequent keywords, frequent keyword x_i is mapped to bin $H(x_i)$. Let m be a bound such that, with high probability, at most m items are mapped to any single bin.

2. For every bin j, the server party defines two polynomials: P_j and Q_j of degree $(m-1)$. The polynomials are defined such that for every pair (x_i, num_i) mapped to bin j, it holds that $P_j(x_i) = 0$ and $Q_j(x_i) = (num_i|0^l)$, where l is a statistical security parameter.

3. For each bin j, the server party picks a new random value r_j and defines the polynomial $Z_j(w) = r_j \cdot P_j(w) + Q_j(w)$.

4. The two parties run an OPE protocol in which the server evaluates all L polynomials at the searchword w.

5. The client party learns the result of $Z_{H(w)}(w)$, i.e., of the polynomial associated with the bin $H(w)$. If this value is of the form $number_i|0^l$, the client party gets the $number_i$.

Our construction uses an OPE method based on homomorphic encryption, such as Paillier's system [27], in the following way.

◾ The server party's input is a polynomial of degree m, where the polynomial $P(x) = \sum_{i=0}^{m} a_i x^i$. The client party's input is a keyword represented w as a value.

- The client party sends to the server party homomorphic encryptions of the powers of w up to the m-th power, i.e., $Enc(w)$, $Enc(w^2)$, ..., $Enc(w^m)$.
- The server party uses the homomorphic properties to compute the following:

$$\prod_{i=0}^{m} Enc(a_i w^i) = \sum_{i=0}^{m} Enc(a_i w^i) = Enc(P(w)).$$

The client party sends this result back to the server party.

To prevent a client from cheating in OPE, the server party can ask the client party to produce zero knowledge proof of $Enc(w_i)$ before the construction in terms of a single database bin. We can use Damgård and Jurik's scheme proposed in [6] to prove that the input is the encryption of w_i without disclosing the keyword w.

The document-selecting protocol preserves a client party's privacy because the server cannot distinguish between any two of a client party's inputs w, w'. The protocol also protects the server party's privacy if a polynomial Z with fresh randomness is prepared for every query on every bin, then the result of the client party's query w is random if w is not a root of P, and the malicious input of a client party can be prevented by using the zero knowledge proof of the frequent keyword w.

Lemma 10.2. (Client party's privacy is preserved). If the encryption scheme is semantically secure, then the views of client for any two inputs are indistinguishable. (The proof uses the fact mentioned above that the only information that the server party receives consists of semantically secure encryptions.)

Lemma 10.2. (Sever party's privacy is preserved). For C', which operates in the real model, there is a client C operating in the ideal model, such that for every input X of Bob, the views of Bob in the ideal model is indistinguishable from the views in the real model. (The proof is that a polynomial Z with fresh randomness is prepared for every query on every bin, then the result of the client's query w is random if w is not a root of P.)

Private Cluster Inclusion Test. After the local computation of document clustering, there may be overlaps among each party's local result. So, we have to combine such overlap and make a cluster to be unique in the global result. Every cluster can be represented as a binary string according to the documents' order from Party A to Party B, such as Doc_A^1, Doc_A^2..., Doc_B^m. Each bit of the string corresponds to a document; there is 1 in the entry i if and only if the cluster contains the party 1's document Doc_1^i;

if the document doesn't exist, there is 0. Client party i has a set $C_i \subseteq D$, server party j has a set $C_j \subseteq D$, and the two parties must establish whether $C_i \subseteq C_j$ or if either of the parties obtain any additional information. More precisely, the protocols must satisfy client privacy and server privacy. We assume that the client has n words in his database. Our basic idea is based on the fact that if for two clusters C_i and C_j satisfying $C_i \in C_j$, we have $|C_i \cap C_j| = |C_j|$.

Below, we modify the matrix-based private inclusion scheme [21] into a new scheme, which can deal with binary string to construct our private cluster merging protocol. We implement this with the homomorphic cryptosystem, which is proved to be secure in the sense of IND-CPA under reasonable complexity assumptions.

Private Cluster Inclusion Test Protocol

Private Input: Client party: cluster C_i, sever party: cluster C_j.
Private Output: Client party knows whether $C_i \subseteq C_j$; if yes, outputs $CD_i \cap CD_j$.

1. Client party generates a new key pair $(sk, pk) \longleftarrow G$. Send pk to server party. For any $i \in [n]$, generate a new nonce $r_i \overset{r}{\longleftarrow} R$. Send $e_i \longleftarrow E_{pk}(C_i; r_i)$ to server party.
2. Server party draws $s \overset{r}{\longleftarrow} P$, $r \overset{r}{\longleftarrow} R$ uniformly at random. Set $e \longleftarrow (\prod_{t=1}^{l} C_i[t]/C_j[t])^s \cdot E_{pk}(0; r)$, where l is the last l_{th} bit of 1. Send e to client party.
3. Client party sets $d \longleftarrow D_{sk}(e)$. Accept that $C_i \subseteq C_j$ iff $d = 0$ and send the result to server party.
4. Sever party returns the cluster C_j as a merged cluster and outputs the $CD_j = CD_i \cap CD_j$.

After this process, the flat clusters for the agglomerative document clustering are generated and only the cluster descriptions are output. All the parties can use those cluster descriptions to group their documents. By using zero-knowledge proofs, client party can prove that the correctness of (a) pk is a valid public key and that (b) every bit of C_i encrypts either 0 or 1.

Lemma 10.2. Private cluster inclusion testing protocol is a privacy-preserving protocol.   Computational client privacy follows directly from the IND-CPA security. So, an adversary can learn nothing about the plaintext corresponding to a given ciphertext, even when the adversary is allowed to obtain the plaintext corresponding to ciphertexts of its choice. As server party sees only ciphertexts of encrypted clusters, his privacy is guaranteed as the second step depends only on whether $C_i \in C_j$ or not.

Private Measurement of Similarity. To measure the similarity of the cluster, we consider that two clusters, which have the most overlap of documents, have the most similarity. Such two clusters, that contain most documents in common should be merged into a cluster in the agglomerative clustering process. We use Hamming distance to measure that similarity of two clusters. The Hamming distance is the number of positions in two strings of equal length for which the corresponding elements are different. Every cluster can be represented by a binary string as the same as in the private inclusion cluster merging protocol. To compute the Hamming distance privately, we use the private-sample-XOR protocol proposed by Feigenbaum [11] as following:

Notions: In this protocol, $d_h(a, b)$ denote the Hamming distance between (a, b), for any $x \in \{0, 1\}^n$ $r \in [n]$ and $m \in \{0, 1\}^n$, we denote by $x << r$ a cyclic shift of x by r bits to the left, and by $x \oplus m$ the string whose i-th bit is $x_i \oplus m_i$.

Private Approximation of Hamming Distance

1. Party A generates a random mask $m_A \xleftarrow{R} \{0, 1\}^n$ and a random shift amount $r_A \xleftarrow{R} [n]$. And he computes the n-bit string $d \stackrel{def}{=} (a << r_A) \oplus m_A$. Symmetrically, Party B generates $m_B \xleftarrow{R} \{0, 1\}^n$ and $r_B \xleftarrow{R} [n]$, and computes $b' \stackrel{def}{=} (b << r_B) \oplus m_B$.
2. A and B invoke in parallel two $\binom{n}{1}$-OT protocols:
   - A retrieves $z_A \stackrel{def}{=} b'_{r_A}$ from B;
   - B retrieves $z_B \stackrel{def}{=} a'_{r_B}$ from A.
3. A sends $z'_A \stackrel{def}{=} z_A \oplus m_A$ to B. B sends $z'_B \stackrel{def}{=} z_B \oplus m_B$ to A. Both parties locally output $z'_A \oplus z'_B$.

After executing the protocol, we can get the approximate result of similarity of the two clusters. The smaller the Hamming distance, the more similar the two clusters, and the most similar two clusters' cluster descriptions will be joined into an intersection, i.e., $CD_A \cap CD_B$.

Lemma 10.2. (Both parties' privacy is preserved.)

Proof: The privacy can be formally argued by describing a simulator for each party. Alice's random inputs m_A, r_A in the real protocol are independent of the inputs (a, b) and the output z and are, thus, distributed in the simulated view as they should. And the output z_A received from $\binom{n}{1}$-OT protocol in the real model is independent of a, b, m_A, r_A, z, as in the simulated view. As in an ideal model, a simulator for Alice's view, based on the input d and output

$z'_A \oplus z'_B$, is computational indistinguishable with the view in a real model. A simulator for Bob's view may be obtained similarly.

Performance evaluation during the private keyword search: We assume that client party assigns the n items to L bins arbitrarily and evenly, ensuring that L items are assigned to every bin; thus, $L = \sqrt{n}$. The server party's message during the OPE consists of $L = O(\sqrt{n})$ homomorphic encryptions; he evaluates L polynomials by performing n homomorphic multiplications and replies with the $L = \sqrt{n}$ results. This protocol has a communication overhead of $O(\sqrt{n})$, $O(n)$ computation overhead at the client party's side, and $O(\sqrt{n})$ computation overhead at the server party's side. In private cluster inclusion test protocol, the server party does not perform any precomputations when server party gets client party's query as an encrypted binary string, the communication of this protocol is $len(|d|)$ bits. For computation of similarity of clusters, we use a $\binom{n}{1}$-OT protocol (in the semihonest model) as a subprotocol. Then, the round complexity of the protocol for approximating the hamming distance $dh(a, b)$ is $OT + 1$, here OT denotes the number of rounds required for OT computation. Hamming distance function can be privately ϵ-approximated with communication complexity $O(n^{1/2}/\epsilon)$ and three rounds of interaction.

10.3.2.4   Security Analysis of the Whole Protocols

Except for the three interactive subprotocols above, other computation processes in our protocol are done locally by the two parties, so under the semihonest model, only one party gets the information based on his own frequent keywords, and any probabilistic polynomial time adversary cannot distinguish the responding output in real model from the one in the ideal model with any party's private input. By using the zero knowledge proof, our protocol also can be secure against a malicious party, but the computational and communication complexity will increase.

Theorem 10.3   Security of approximation protocol: The document clustering protocol is privacy-preserving against the semihonest adversary.

Proof: Our protocol is privacy-preserving as a whole as one can see. Intuitively, the privacy of the protocol follows from the fact that, in all processes of obtaining the output, no party learns any additional information, which is not published by the other party. According to the privacy definition in section 10.3.1, we provide the privacy proof as following.

From Lemma 10.1 and Lemma 10.2, we know that in private documents selection, the security of the subprotocol is based on the assumptions used for proving the security of the homomorphic encryption system. Since the server receives semantically secure homomorphic encryptions and the sub-protocol protects the privacy of the client, the subprotocol ensures the client party's privacy because the server cannot distinguish between any two of a client party's inputs w, w'. For server party, if w is not a frequent key-word, the output is just a random number. It means that the adversary's views of both parties in both real model and ideal model is computation-ally indistinguishable. Each party only learns that w is a common frequent keyword.

During the private cluster inclusion test, computational client privacy also follows directly the security of the homomorphic encryption system, which ensures that e is a random encryption of zero if $C_i \subset C_j$, or a random encryption of a random plain text if $C_i \subseteq C_j$. According to Lemma 10.3, the server party sees only ciphertexts, so any adversary that can distinguish two vectors of ciphertexts can be used for distinguishing only two ciphertexts. Each party only learns whether $C_i \subset C_j$ or not.

When computing the private approximation of Hamming distance be-tween the inputs a and b, the view of each party in these invocations can be simulated from its input and $d_h(a, b)$. Summarizing, we have a simulator S such that $S(d_h(a, b))$ and the output $d_h(a, b)$ are identically distributed according to Lemma 10.4's security proof, so that no probabilistic poly-nomial time adversary can distinguish $S(d_h(a, b))$ and $d_h(a, b)$. Thus, the whole protocol is privacy-preserving against the probabilistic polynomial time adversary under semihonest model.

10.4   Concluding Remarks

This chapter presents some suggestions for defining and measuring privacy preservation. We have shown how these relate to both privacy policy and practice in the wider community, and to techniques in privacy-preserving data mining. We apply the privacy-preserving statistical databases tech-niques and cryptographic protocols to a scheme to preserve the privacy of a dataset when executing distributed density estimation-based clustering. It was inspired by the combination of the computational power of ran-dom data perturbation techniques of secure evaluation of density in the distributed environment. For preventing the random matrix-based filtering attack, we employ the linear transformation, which can change the origi-nal distribution of eigenvalues while preserving some statistical parameter used in clustering. We have shown that our scheme can prevent the random matrix-based filtering attack by altering the distribution of eigenvalues. We have proposed a new scheme based on secure approximation for privacy-preserving k-means clustering and solved the security problems in existing schemes [31] [16] [15] and the result of our scheme is without the correct-ness problem as in [17]. And we have shown that our scheme is more efficient with low communication and computation complexity compared to the existing schemes. We also proposed a divide-and-merge method in distributed document clustering and produced a framework to preserve the privacy of participants.

The inability to generalize the results for classes of categories of data-mining algorithms might be a tentative threat for disclosing information. The key insight is to trade off computation and communication cost for accuracy and improving efficiency over the generic secure multiparty computation method. Currently, assembling these into efficient privacy-preserving data-mining algorithms, and proving them secure, is a challenging task. We demonstrated how to combine the existing techniques to implement a standard data-mining algorithm with provable privacy and information disclosure properties. Our hope is that as the library of primitives and known means for using them grow, standard methods will be developed to ease the task of developing privacy-preserving data-mining techniques. Privacy-preserving data-mining has the potential to increase the reach and benefits of data-mining technology.

References

[1] R. Agrawal and R. Srikant. *Privacy-Preserving Data Mining*, Proceedings, ACMSIGMOD Conference, Edmonton, Alberta, Canada, 2000.

[2] J. Bar-Ilan and D. Beaver. *Non-cryptographic Fault-Tolerant Computing in Constant Number of Rounds of Interaction.* Annual ACM Symposium on Principles of Distributed Computing, Edmonton, Alberta, Canada, pp. 201–209, 1989.

[3] F. Beil, M. Ester, and X. Xu. *Frequent Term-Based Text Clustering*, Proceedings of the 8th Int. Conf. on Knowledge Discovery and Data Mining, Edmonton, Alberta, Canada, 2002.

[4] B. Chor, S. Goldwasser, S. Micali, and B. Awerbuch. *Verifiable Secret Sharing and Achieving Simultaneity in the Presence of Faults.* In Proceedings of the 26th Annual IEEE Symposium on Foundations of Computer Science, Portland, OR, pp. 383–395, 1985.

[5] D.R. Cutting, D.R. Karger, J.O. Pedersen, and J.W. Tukey, *Scatter/Gather: A Cluster-Based Approach to Browsing Large Document Collections.* pp. 318–329, Proc. ACM SIGIR 92, Copenhagen, Denmark, 1992.

[6] I. Damgård and M. Jurik. *Client/Server Tradeoffs for Online Elections.* vol. 2274 of Lecture Notes in Computer Science, pp. 125–140, PKC2002, New York, 2002.

[7] W. Du and M. Atallah. *Privacy-Preserving Cooperative Statistical Analysis.* In 17th ACSAC, pp. 102–112, Nova Scotia, Canada, 2001.

[8] C. Dwork, K. Kenthapadi, F. McSherry, I. Mironov, and M. Naor. *Our Data, Ourselves: Privacy Via Distributed Noise Generation.* EUROCRYPT2006, St. Petersburg, Russia, 2006.

[9] C. Dwork, F. McSherry, K. Nissim, and A. Smith. *Calibrating Noise to Sensitivity in Private Data Analysis.* In Proceedings of the 3rd Theory of Cryptography Conference, Banff, Alberta, Canada, 2006.

[10] M. Ester, H.P. Kriegel, J. Sander, and X. Xu, *A Density-Based Algorithm for Discovering Clusters in Large Spatial Databases with Noise.* Proceedings of the 2nd International Conference on Knowledge Discovery and Data Mining, Portland, OR, 1996.

[11] J. Feigenbaum, Y. Ishai, T. Malkin, K. Nissim, R. Wright, and M. Strauss. *Secure Multiparty Computation of Approximations.* ACM Transactions on Algorithms, 2, 435–372, 2006.

[12] M.J. Freedman, Y. Ishai, B. Pinkas, and O. Reingold. *Keyword Search and Oblivious Pseudorandom Functions.* Second Theory of Cryptography Conference, TCC 2005, Cambridge, MA, 2005.

[13] B. Goethals, S. Laur, H. Lipmaa, and T. Mielikainen. *On Secure Product Computation for Privacy-Preserving Data Mining.* In 7th Annual International Conf. in Information Security and Cryptology, Seoul, Korea, 2004.

[14] O. Goldreich, S. Micali, and A. Wigderson. *How to Play Any Mental Game.* In Proceedings of the 19th Annual ACM Symposium on Theory of Computing, New York, 1987.

[15] G. Jagannathan, K. Pillaipakkamnatt, R. Wright. *A New Privacy-Preserving Distributed k-Clustering Algorithm.* Proceedings of the 2006 SIAM International Conference on Data Mining (SDM), Bethesda, MD, 2006.

[16] G. Jagannathan and R. Wright. *Privacy-Preserving Distributed k-Means Clustering over Arbitrarily Partitioned Data.* Proceedings of the 11th ACM SIGKDD International Conference on Knowledge Discovery and Data Mining (KDD), Chicago, IL, 2005.

[17] S. Jha, L. Kruger, and P. McDaniel. *Privacy Preserving Clustering.* 10th European Symposium on Research in Computer Security, Milan, Italy, 2005.

[18] H. Kargupta, S. Datta, Q. Wang, and K. Sivakumar. *Random Data Perturbation Techniques and Privacy Preserving Data Mining.* 2003 IEEE International Conference on Data Mining, Melbourne, FL, 2003.

[19] E. Kiltz, G. Leander, and J. Malone-Lee. *Secure Computation of the Mean and Related Statistics,* Theory of Cryptography Conference, Cambridge, MA, 2005.

[20] M. Klusch, S. Lodi, and G. Moro. *Distributed Clustering Based on Sampling Local Density Estimates.* Proc. Intl. Joint Conference on Artificial Intelligence (IJCAI 2003), Acapulo, Mexico, 2003.

[21] S. Laur, H. Lipmaa, and T. Mielikainen. *Private Itemset Support Counting,* vol. 3783 of Lecture Notes in Computer Science, pp. 97–111, Beijing, China, 2005.

[22] Y. Lindell and B. Pinkas. *Privacy Preserving Data Mining.* In Advances in Cryptology—CRYPTO '00, vol. 1880 of Lecture Notes in Computer Science, pp. 36–54. Springer-Verlag, Heidelberg, Germany, 2000.

[23] H. Lipmaa. *An Oblivious Transfer Protocol with Log-Squared Total Communication.* Technical Report 2004/063, International Association for Cryptologic Research, 2004.

[24] J. MacQueen. *Some Methods for Classification and Analysis of Multivariate Observations.* Proceedings of the Fifth Berkeley Symposium on Mathematical Statistics and Probability, vol. 1, pp. 281–297, Berkeley, CA. University of California Press, 1967.

[25] M. Naor and B. Pinkas. *Oblivious Transfer and Polynomial Evaluation.* In 31st ACM Symposium on Theory of Computing, pp. 245–254. ACM Press, New York, 1999.

[26] T. Okamoto and S. Uchiyama. *A New Public-Key Cryptosystem as Secure as Factoring.* In Advances in Cryptology—Eurocrypt98, LNCS 1403, pp. 308–318. Springer-Verlag, Heidelberg, Germany, 1998.

[27] P. Paillier. *Public-Key Cryptosystems Based on Composite Degree Residue Classes.* EUROCRYPT 99, Prague, Czech Republic, 1999.

[28] E. Schikuta. *Grid-Clustering: An Efficient Hierarchical Clustering Method for Very Large Data Sets.* Proceedings of the 13th International Conference on Pattern Recognition, 1996.

[29] M. Steinbach, G. Karypis, and V. Kumar. *A Comparison of Document Clustering Techniques.* In KDD Workshop on Text Mining, Boston, MA, 2000.

[30] C. Su, J. Zhou, F. Bao, T. Takagi, and K. Sakurai. *Two Party Privacy-Preserving Agglomerative Document Clustering.* The 3rd Information Security Practice and Experience Conference 2007, to be appear in Lecture Notes in Computer Science, Proceedings, LNCS 4464, pp. 193–208, Hong Kong, 2007.

[31] J. Vaidya and C. Clifton. *Privacy-Preserving k-Means Clustering Over Vertically Partitioned Data.* In Proc. of the 9th ACM SIGKDD Intl. Conf. on Knowledge Discovery and Data Mining, Washington, D.C., 2003.

[32] A.C. Yao, *Protocols for Secure Computation.* In 23rd FOCS, New York, 1982.

[33] O. Zamir and O. Etzioni, *Web Document Clustering: A Feasibility Demonstration.* Proc. of 21st ACM SIGIR on Research and Development in Information Retrieval, pp. 46–54, Melbourne, Australia, 1998.

USER PRIVACY

Chapter 11

HCI Designs for Privacy-Enhancing Identity Management

Simone Fischer-Hübner, John Sören Pettersson,
Mike Bergmann, Marit Hansen, Siani Pearson,
and Marco Casassa Mont

Contents

11.1 Introduction 230
11.2 Related Work.. 231
    11.2.1 The PISA Project 231
    11.2.2 Art. 29 Working Party Recommendations 232
11.3 Prime UI Paradigms... 232
    11.3.1 Role-Centered Paradigm 233
    11.3.2 Relationship-Centered Paradigm 233
    11.3.3 TownMap-Based Paradigm 235
    11.3.4 Data Track.. 238
11.4 From Legal Privacy Requirements to Prime UI Proposals 239
    11.4.1 Information to Be Provided to Individuals.............. 240
    11.4.2 Obtaining Consent from Individuals 241
        11.4.2.1 A Dialogue Box for Informed
                 Click-Through 241
        11.4.2.2 Consent via Menu Selection 242
        11.4.2.3 Consent by Drag-and-Drop Agreements 243

11.4.3 Support of the Individual in Exercising
Privacy Rights 244
11.5 Trust and Assurance HCI 246
11.5.1 Lack of Trust 246
11.5.2 Means for Enhancing Trust 246
11.5.2.1 Assurance Control 247
11.5.2.2 Obligation Management 248
11.6 Conclusions 249
Acknowledgments 249
References 249

11.1 Introduction

In today's information society, users have lost effective control over their personal spheres. Emerging pervasive computing technologies, where individuals are usually unaware of a constant data collection and processing in their surroundings, will even heighten this problem. It is, however critical, to our society and to democracy to retain and maintain an individual's autonomy and, thus, to protect privacy and particularly the individual's right to informational self-determination. Powerful tools for technically enforcing user control and informational self-determination as well as the privacy principle of data minimization can be provided by privacy-enhancing identity management systems, as currently developed within the European Union 6th Framework Program (EU FP6) integrated project PRIME (Privacy and Identity Management for Europe*).

With PRIME, all interactions are *a priori* anonymous, and individuals can choose to act under different pseudonyms with respect to communication partners or activities, and also have control over whether or not interactions and pseudonyms can be linked with each other or not. Moreover, PRIME provides tools that help individuals to define who has the right to do what under which conditions with their personal data, as well as tools providing transparency about who has received what personal data related to them and possibilities to trace personal data being passed on. However, PRIME technologies will only be successful if they are accepted and applied by the end users. For this reason, the PRIME project has also placed emphasis on human–computer interaction (HCI) research on new user interface (UI) solutions and paradigms for privacy-enhancing identity management.

This chapter will present results from the PRIME HCI research activity and is partly based on [20]. It will first present related work on which we have partly based our research for PRIME UI solutions. It will then discuss UI paradigms for privacy-enhancing identity management (IDM) elaborated

---

* https://www.prime-project.eu/

within PRIME as well as the mapping of related legal privacy principles to specific UI design solutions. Finally, we discuss how the UI functions can contribute to increasing trust in privacy-enhancing identity management systems. Some pertinent results from usability evaluations are reported as well.

11.2   Related Work

In the recent years, some work has been done in the area of usability and privacy, including work on the usability of the Platform Privacy Preferences Project (P3P) user agents [7], the presentation of online privacy notices [12,14], and user perception and trust issues [25,26,15].

In the following sections, we briefly summarize the related work that is most relevant in the context of our work in PRIME, namely the research work of the EU FP5 PISA (Privacy Incorporated Software Agent) project [16,17] and recommendations of the Art. 29 Working Party concerning the content and structuring of information to be provided to users [2], which we used as a basis for our HCI design proposals and HCI research in the PRIME project.

11.2.1   The PISA Project

Important domain-specific HCI requirements can be derived from privacy legislation. In the PISA project, it has been studied in detail how privacy principles derived from the EU Data Protection Directive 95/46/EC [8] can be translated into HCI requirements and what are possible design solutions to meet those requirements [16,17]. The derived HCI requirements were grouped into the four categories of comprehension (to understand, or know), consciousness (be aware or informed), control (to manipulate, or be empowered), and consent (to agree). In the PRIME project, we have used and extended these privacy principles and HCI requirements from the PISA project to derive proposed UI design solutions for PRIME (see also section 11.4 and [19]). The PISA project also investigated, in particular, user agreements for obtaining informed user consent and introduced the concept of "Just-In-Time-Click-Through Agreements" (JITCTAs). "The main feature of a JITCTA is not to provide a large, complete list of service terms, but instead to confirm the understanding or consent on an as-needed basis. These small agreements are easier for the user to read and process, and facilitate a better understanding of the decision being made in-context" [16]. The concept of a JITCTA was also used for the PRIME HCI proposals using the "Send Data?" dialogue boxes (see [19]), which will be discussed in section 11.4.2.1.

11.2.2 Art. 29 Working Party Recommendations

The Article 29 Data Protection Working Party [2] has also investigated what information should be provided in what form to users in order to fulfill all legal provisions of the EU Data Protection Directive 95/46/EC for ensuring that individuals are informed of their rights to data protection [5]. The Art. 29 Working Party recommends providing information in a "multilayered format under which each layer should offer individuals the information needed to understand their position and make decisions." They suggest three layers of information provided to individuals:

- The short notice (layer 1) must offer individuals the core information required under Article 10 of the Directive 95/46/EC, which includes at least the identity of the controller and the purpose of processing. In addition, a clear indication must be given as to how the individual can access additional information.
- The condensed notice (layer 2) includes, in addition, all other relevant information required by Art. 10 of the Directive, such as the recipients or categories of recipients, whether replies to questions are obligatory or voluntary, and information about the individual's rights.
- The full notice (layer 3) includes, in addition to layers 1 and 2, the "national legal requirements and specificities."

The Art. 29 Working Party sees short privacy notices as legally acceptable within a multilayered structure that, in its totality, offers compliance. JITC-TAs as defined in the PISA project, in fact, are corresponding to such short privacy notices. Within PRIME, we have followed the Working Party's recommendations to use multilayered privacy notices in its design proposals (see [19] and below).

11.3 Prime UI Paradigms

In this section, we will present the main characteristics of alternative UI paradigms for identity management that have been elaborated and tested by the PRIME HCI work package.

A particular feature prominent in all these attempts was the bundling of personal data and preference settings with different electronic pseudonyms. The bundles were called *roles* or *areas* in the three main UI paradigms, namely the role-centered, the relationship-centered, and the TownMap-based paradigm.

The first two paradigms are traditionally styled, while the third one is based on the metaphor of a townmap and is an attempt to make preference settings more accessible and, hopefully, understandable to users. On the other hand, the latter two share a common approach to the use of preference settings, namely that the selection among the different preference settings (roles and areas, respectively) is implicit when connecting to each service provider. A user has different privacy needs as regards different communication partners and predefined selection of roles should facilitate this a great deal.

The three paradigms are presented below. The UI paradigms have been embodied in an early prototype for IDM [6] and in some mockups and prototypes produced for the PRIME project (in the PRIME integrated prototype Version 2 of the year 2007, the word *role* is replaced by "PreSet" to avoid confusion with other uses of "role" in applications that include the PRIME kernel).

11.3.1   Role-Centered Paradigm

Role-centered means that user control of data disclosure is primarily carried out via the roles described above that function like identity cards that allow for pseudonymous contacts. Within a role, the user can set and utilize different disclosure preferences for different data types. The user then has to select the role he will be acting under when contacting service providers, and whenever he thinks that this role is inappropriate, he has to select one of his other roles. The UI paradigm was embodied in an early user-side prototype called DRIM (Dresden Identity Management [6]) where the IDM functions were displayed in side bars of an ordinary Internet browser (Mozilla Firefox). This UI paradigm also figures in one of the PRIME mockups where the IDM functions were integrated in an ordinary browser (Microsoft Internet Explorer) to explore toolbar designs (although this mockup was never tested with users).

11.3.2   Relationship-Centered Paradigm

An alternative approach could be to define different privacy preferences in relation to each communication partner. In the *relationship-centered* UI paradigm embodied in PRIME mockups, the identity management controls are integrated in the same way as in the role-centered mockup, but in addition, the ordinary bookmarks ("Favorites" in Explorer) have roles attached to them. By default, a predefined role based on transactional pseudonyms* called "Anonymous" is activated. Further kinds of roles could be defined by the user and added as alternative start-roles for any of the bookmarks. In this way, during ordinary Web browsing, there is no extra step of selecting roles. By using transactional pseudonyms as default, the relationship-centered

---

* That is, when a new pseudonym is created for each transaction [23].

Figure 11.1   Bookmark list with role icons.

approach allows the privacy-enhancing functions to be switched on from the start even if the user is not prepared to actively select among them.

In fact, in the PRIME mockups, we decided to always have the icon for the anonymous role ready in the bookmark list, so that anonymous "entrance" to all bookmarked Web sites could always be made—one can hypothesize that even a user, who sets the role of a "registered customer" as the default for a specific Web site, does not always want to be recognized when visiting that Web site. In Figure 11.1, the anonymous role is selected by clicking the masked man for each bookmark while the two other icons stand for roles that can be alternatively activated and might be recognizable by the service provider via the pseudonym that the role is acting under and/or by some released personal data (if the service provider requests such and if the user has agreed to it). Clicking on the name of a bookmark implies selecting the left-most role if there is more than one icon.

The solution described above works when a user accesses Web sites via bookmarks. On the other hand, when the user enters a Web address in the address field of his browser, *the system should find* the default role for that site, if the user has defined one; otherwise, the anonymous role should be used because this is the standard setting and applies to all Web sites if nothing else has been set by the user.

More problematic is that users might find it hard to select the anonymous role when it is not a default; the "Go" button of the Web browser could have alternatives, as in Figure 11.2, even if users presumably would use the "Enter" key if they have keyed in an address. The role icon to the left of the address field shows the current role.

The role-centered and the relationship-centered approaches differ by what is the primary action by the user: either selecting a role (and only secondly or implicitly communication partner) or selecting a communication partner (and implicitly the role = privacy setting).

The primary action of the relationship-centered UI supports the user's primary goals, namely accessing service providers. It should also be noted that while the user interface has to be somewhat more elaborated, this UI

Figure 11.2   Traditional "Go" button and address field with two "Gos."

proposal does not introduce any extra actions during ordinary browsing, while on the other hand, a role-centered UI would force the user to repeatedly change roles (or change Web sites if roles have default start sites, while making a role list with a lot of alternative start pages only begs the question of why to reinvent the ordinary bookmark list).

11.3.3   TownMap-Based Paradigm

In the *TownMap-based* UI paradigm, the roles are replaced by areas visualizing privacy protection concepts with default privacy settings. Predefined areas were the Neighborhood (where relationship pseudonymity* is used by default), the Public area (where transactional pseudonymity is used by default), and the Work area (where relationship pseudonymity is used) with different default privacy preference settings for another set of personal data than for private use.

The approach to use different default "roles" for different areas within a town should make it easier for a novice to see the options available once he has grasped the TownMap metaphor. Individual bookmarks or lists with bookmark menus are symbolized by houses. The user also has his own house in the map (a prominent house at the baseline). Of course, the map display has to vanish or be reduced when the user encounters one of the service providers.

---

* That is, a pseudonym chosen in regard to a specific communication partner (see [23]).

Figure 11.3   TownMap with building tools visible.

In Figure 11.3, the user wants to add a shortcut link (similar to dragging a Web site icon from a present-day browser's address field to the desktop). The user has clicked on the button "Show Tools" and picked a house to place somewhere. This will make it possible not only to put a new bookmark in the TownMap, but also to put an alternative privacy preference definition: If a Web site is already listed in the public space, now the user adds an access point to the same site, but in his neighborhood to indicate that he should be recognized when accessing the Web site this way.

Figure 11.4 shows a view when the user is browsing a site. The user has clicked on the TownMap symbol in the browser bar and can now see a tilted TownMap and all or some of his shortcut links (in this figure, only five houses have been placed on the map). This could be refined—just compare the "Looking Glass" UI paradigm presented by SUN Microsystems*—but in any event, it allows using the spatial relationships with which the user has become acquainted: The way between the user's house and the bank, for instance, can be used for indicating data flow and even for letting the user show preferred data flows.

A preference test (with $N = 34$ test persons) was made by using user interface animations where groups of test participants could see identity management carried out in the traditionally styled user interface and also in the TownMap. Afterward, participants individually filled in a form with questions about their impression and preferences. Then a third design was shown, a simplified map. Swedish university students aged 20 and above, some being older than 45, participated in the preference test; all had used Internet Explorer and only some had used other browsers, as well. Our traditionally styled alternative was based on an Internet Explorer mockup. The traditionally styled browser got a positive response in general: More than half of the answers gave positive descriptions of it. The maps, on the other hand, were considered by many to be messy. One should bear in

---

* "Project Looking Glass," http://www.sun.com/software/looking_glass.

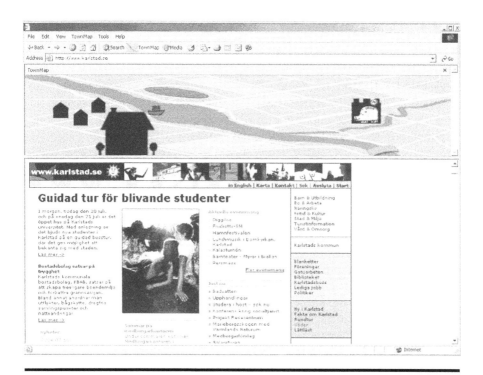

Figure 11.4   Tilted TownMap visible.

mind that the maps were populated from the beginning, while a new user would have found his own map empty (like the bookmark list in an unused copy of a browser). (For more discussion of the test set-up, see [3].)

On the question concerning their impression of the display of data and money transaction, nineteen answered that it "facilitates," while eleven ticked "superfluous." Nine of these eleven persons also ticked "looks childish;" fifteen in all ticked "looks OK." This result speaks in favor of using animation in explanations.

When ranking the alternatives, twenty-four persons put the traditional browser as their primary choice. Seven preferred the realistic TownMap and three preferred the simplified map. Two-fifths of the participants answered that they would like to be able to switch between designs. The test has been replicated in the United States with twenty-seven (young) university students. The results were, in the main, similar to the test conducted in Sweden, although a majority of the American subjects wanted to be able to toggle between designs. Comparing with the age groups among the Swedish participants, one can see a clear trend: Young Internet users generally are in favor of the more graphical user interface represented by the TownMap.

11.3.4 Data Track

The data track is a function available in all three UI paradigms and is for this reason briefly presented in this section. Being able to track what data is disclosed, when, to whom, and how the data is further processed, is an important feature to provide transparency of personal data processing.

Within PRIME, the data track function allows users to remember what personal data they have released to other sites via data records logged at the end user's side. The data track is currently also extended to advise users about their rights and enable them to exercise their basic rights to access data, or to rectify and request their deletion online (see section 11.4.3), and help them to check on agreed obligations or to set obligations (see 11.5.2.2). The data track stores transaction records comprising personal data sent, including pseudonyms, and used for transactions and credentials that were disclosed, date of transmission, purpose of data collection, recipient, and all further details of the privacy policy that the user and recipient have agreed upon (see also [21]). The privacy policy constitutes a valuable document in case that a user feels that something is wrong with how his data has been used. The data track also needs to store the pseudonyms used for transaction to allow a user to identify himself as a previous contact in case he wants to exercise his rights to access, rectification, blocking, or deletion (see Section 11.4.3) while still remaining pseudonymous.

As people engage in many transactions, which may involve multiple providers simultaneously, the implementation of a usable data track is difficult from an HCI perspective. Providing users with easy tools to find relevant data disclosure records is one example. In PRIME, several ways are considered and are discussed in this section.

Two search methods are quite straightforward and might appear as the obvious choices: (1) Sorting step-wise by categories, such as "Personal data" and "Receivers," and (2) Simple search box. However, these two approaches seem unsatisfactory because users are unaware of what the system does as revealed in user tests performed by the PRIME group.

More suitable methods that are currently pilot-tested include: (1) Template sentences that put search boxes within meaningful frames: "Who has received my [drop-down list with data]?" and (2) A scrollable transaction track that shows all the records at once. The records are shown in abbreviated form as small pages stacked along a timeline (see Figure 11.5). A slider provides the possibility to highlight an individual page in the stack. In this way, users could browse through the records without having to understand sorting or to articulate refined search requests. Obviously, this method seems more appropriate for the beginner whose amount of transaction records will be limited. With an increasing amount of transactions it becomes more and more difficult to find the desired record(s). For the

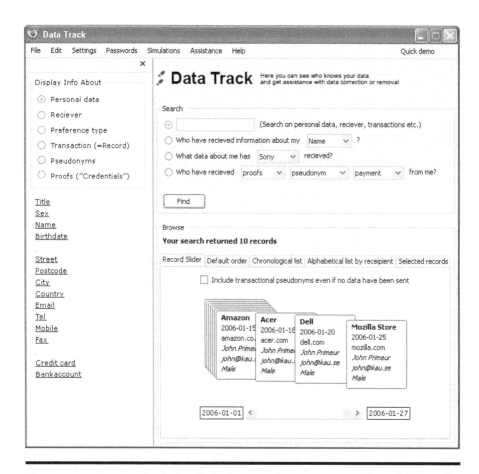

Figure 11.5 Data track window including template sentences and scrollable tracks.

more advanced user, combinations of methods have to be explored and developed (see also [21]).

11.4 From Legal Privacy Requirements to PRIME UI Proposals

As pointed out in section 11.2.1, the PISA project has conducted important research on how to map legal privacy principles to HCI requirements and possible HCI design solutions [17]. The HCI research within the PRIME project has built on these PISA project results by using and extending the privacy principles and corresponding HCI requirements and proposing corresponding PRIME UI solutions (see also Chapter 4 in [19]). In this section, we restrict the discusson to the mapping of some important legal requirements to PRIME UI solutions, namely provisions for informing the individuals, for obtaining consent as a legitimization for data processing and on rights of the individuals to access/rectify/block/erase their data.

11.4.1 Information to Be Provided to Individuals

Art. 10 of the EU Data Protection Directive 95/46/EC requires that individuals from whom personal data will be collected have to be informed about the identity of the controller, the purposes of the data processing—except when individuals are already aware—and about further information in so far as such information is necessary, having regard for the specific circumstances in which the data is collected, to guarantee fair data processing. Web sites of data controllers within the EU have to provide privacy notices or links to privacy notices that display this information. This is, however, not necessarily required for non-European Web sites. Besides, those privacy statements usually contain long legal texts that are usually not read or noticed, and are usually not easily comprehensible by most end users (see, for instance, [12]). As elaborated in [17], the legal privacy principles of information provision and transparency translate to the HCI requirement that users must *know* (i.e., comprehend) who is controlling their data and for what purposes.

Each PRIME-enabled server side should make a complete privacy policy for that side available in computer-readable form (e.g., in XML format). The server side's privacy policy will be retrievable from the PRIME application at any time. We suggest that the information contained in the server side's privacy policy should be displayed in the PRIME interface in the form of privacy notices by following an approach of multilayered privacy notices as suggested by the Article 29 Data Protecting Working Party (see [2] and section 11.2.2 above). A link to the full privacy notice displaying all information required by EU Directive 95/46/EC and other applicable laws (such as Art.4 of Directive 97/7/EC on the protection of the consumers in respect to distance contracts) should be placed at a prominent place in the PRIME user interface (such as plug-in menus found in tool bars in a browser). The computer-readable form furthermore permits that the display will be in a language chosen by the user.

Figure 11.6 shows a dialogue box (the so-called "Send data?" dialogue), which is opened in the traditionally styled PRIME UI if user consent for disclosing personal data is requested. This "Send data?" dialog window can be reduced to only contain short and easily comprehensible text, but must contain the core information that is required under Art. 10 of EU Directive 95/46/EC. Besides, it must include a link to the full or condensed privacy notice.

Figure 11.6   One design of the "Send data?"dialog window.

11.4.2   Obtaining Consent from Individuals

"Unambiguous," "explicit," or "informed" consent by the individual is often a prerequisite for the lawful data processing (see, for instance, Art. 7.a EU Directive 95/46/C or Art. 9 EU Directive 2002/58/EC). Informed user consent is also seen as a HCI requirement in [17].

11.4.2.1   A Dialogue Box for Informed Click-Through

JITCTAs as defined in the PISA project constitute a possible solution for obtaining consent by the user. Also two-clicks (i.e., one click to confirm that one is aware of the proposed processing, and a further one to consent to it) or ticking a box have been suggested by different European legal experts and data commissioners as a means for representing the individual's consent (see also Chapter 2 in [10]).

The "Send data?" window used in PRIME (illustrated in Figure 11.6) corresponds with its form and content to a JITCTA and is following the approach of multilayered privacy notices.

The problem of click-throughs, however, is that having to click *OK* or *Cancel* in the ever-present confirmation boxes of today's user interfaces makes most people react by automated actions, often clicking the right alternative, but sometimes getting it wrong. An observation well known within psychology is that people tend to automate behaviors so that the individual parts of an action are executed without conscious reflection. For example, Raskin ([24], p. 216) explains that "a set of actions that forms a sequence also becomes clumped into a single action; once you start a sequence that takes less than 1 or 2 seconds to complete, you will not be able to stop the sequence, but will continue executing the action until you complete that clump." Raskin uses this observation to argue against dialog boxes asking for confirmation from users. Because such boxes pop up frequently in certain situations, users will become accustomed in such situations to simply click any *OK* button. The (alleged) confirmation is then executed subconsciously and is not really trustworthy.

11.4.2.2 Consent via Menu Selection

Presenting data items in cascading menus to select data or credentials has the effect that the user must read the text for making the menu choices, which means that, in this case, he should make more conscious selections. This form of consent via menu selection suggested by PRIME partner IBM Zurich Labs can be useful as long as the number of data items or credentials is limited. Naturally, such menus would then need to also include the other information that is relevant for data disclosures (data receiver, purpose of data collection, etc.—as explained above). Figure 11.7 illustrates cascading context menus that are following the Art. 29 WP recommendation for a multilayered structuring of privacy policies. Clicking "Privacy Notice" in the main menu (in the center in Figure 11.7) will open the more detailed policy information.

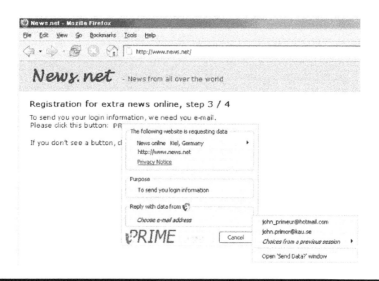

Figure 11.7   Context menus (shaded fields) appearing in conjunction with a button on a Web page.

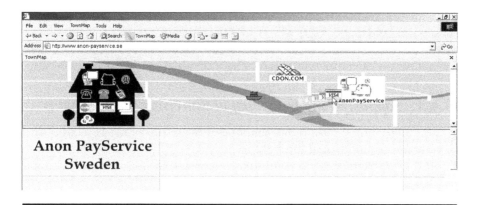

Figure 11.8 DADA to send credit card information (upper part of a screenshot).

11.4.2.3 Consent by Drag-and-Drop Agreements

Drag-and-drop agreements (DADAs) could be a way of avoiding such automation of behavior. DADAs were introduced in the TownMap-based UI proposals as an alternative way for users to express consent, by moving graphic representations of their data to receivers' locations on the Town-Map. In such a construction, the user not only has to pick a set of predefined data (which would be much like clicking "Agree" on a pop-up window), but choose the right personal data symbol(s) and drop them on the right receiver symbol (Figure 11.8). Thereby, the system can to some extent check that the user has understood the request (in contrast to JITCTAs or two-clicks, where users are still tempted to automatically press buttons without clearly reading the text). So-called ToolTips, displaying the specific data content for each data icon, can accompany the drag-and-drop actions. The number of drag-and-drop operations needed to agree varies depending on how much information is contained in a symbol (e.g., a credit card icon could contain card number but also expiration date and holder's name).

The system's check mentioned above requires that the information is already requested by the service provider, so that the drag-and-drop action really is an act of *confirming*, and not an act of stating conditions (a text corresponding to a JITCTA is appearing and requesting the user to agree to the data transaction by drag and drop of the right personal data symbol to the right receiver symbol). Drag-and-drops can be mistakenly performed and would need a final confirmation if they are used to *state* the conditions of an agreement.

Dragging and dropping an item on the computer desktop constitutes an action of the user that is similar to actions, such as ticking a box, that have been legally acknowledged as a way of expressing user consent. Hence, it can be assumed that drag and drop also can express a user's consent. Potentially, this interaction paradigm could be used, not only in the TownMap, but also in schematic form within traditional user interfaces. A graphical representation of the user, the service provider, and third parties could then allow for direct manipulation of its individual graphical constituents.

11.4.3 Support of the Individual in Exercising Privacy Rights

In addition to information rights guaranteed by Art. 10 of the Directive, Art. 12 grants every individual the right to access, i.e., the right to obtain from the data controller, without constraint at reasonable intervals and without excessive delay or expense, a confirmation as to whether data relating to him is being processed, as well as information at least as to the purposes of the processing, the data concerned, and possible recipients or categories of recipients. Moreover, pursuant to Art. 12 each individual has the right to ask for rectification, erasure, or blocking of data concerning him as far as the processing does not comply with the requirements of the directive, in particular when the data is incomplete or inaccurate. Furthermore, Art. 14 ensures that individuals can object, on request and free of charge, to the processing of their personal data, e.g., for direct marketing.

Users must know what rights they have and understand them in order to exercise these rights. In the PISA project, the privacy principles were translated to the HCI requirements that users are *conscious* of their rights, and that they *understand* and *can exercise* their rights.

Our usability tests and other surveys [9] have shown that many individuals are not aware of their privacy rights. But even if they are, they rarely exercise them because it means a great deal of bureaucratic effort to find out whom to address, to compile a letter, often to be personally signed on paper, to send it, wait for an answer, write reminders, etc. When using pseudonyms (e.g., from an identity management system), this may even be more complicated because the data controller needs a proof that he communicates with the specific pseudonym holder.

Information about the individual's rights has to appear in the privacy notices (i.e., if multilayered notices are used, it should appear in the condensed privacy notice or in the short notice if this is necessary for guaranteeing a fair data processing). Furthermore, the interface should provide obvious tools for exercising the individual's rights. It should be possible for the individuals to exercise these rights both online and at the physical address of the controller (see also Chapter 2 of [10]), which has to be provided in the privacy notices and can be used by the individuals as a fall-back solution in case the online functions do not work.

As mentioned in section 11.3.4, the data track function also informs the users about their rights and is currently extended to provide access to online functions helping users to exercise these rights. Once the user has "tracked" specific transaction records, the data track user interface provides buttons that the user can click for activating such online functions. Access to online functions is also provided via the "Assistance" menu within the data track window (see menu bar in Figure 11.5).

When exercising privacy rights, the requests have to be sent to the data controller. If there isn't an answer or any satisfying answer, the next level of escalation is the supervisory authority, which has to be established according to Art. 28 of the directive. This is typically a national or regional data protection authority (DPA) (see also Figure 11.9). Within a fully

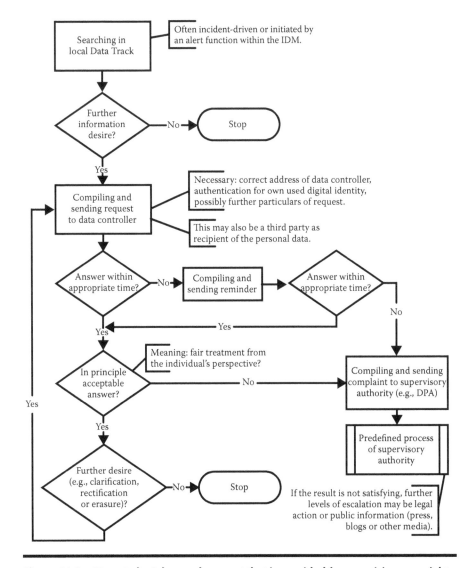

Figure 11.9 **Steps to be taken and support that is provided for exercising user rights.**

PRIME-enabled scenario, the right to access, rectification, etc., even under (authenticated) pseudonyms could be realized online. But, without the automatic service support, the identity management system could at least help in finding out about the address of the data controller (from the privacy policy), generating request letters, giving the needed authentication (even if a pseudonym is used), monitoring the complaint status, compiling reminders, and—in case of problems—addressing the supervisory authority in charge (Figure 11.9).

11.5 Trust and Assurance HCI

11.5.1 Lack of Trust

"Trust is important because if a person is to use a system to its full potential, be it an *E*-commerce site or a computer program, it is essential for him to trust the system," Johnston et al. assert [13]. Our usability tests of early PRIME prototypes have shown that there are problems in making people trust the claims about the privacy-enhancing features of the systems (see [10,20]). Similar findings of a lack of trust were also recently reported by Günther et al. [11] in a study on the perception of user control with privacy-enhancing identity management solutions for radio frequency identification (RFID) environments, even though the test users considered the privacy-enhancing technologies (PETs) in this study fairly easy to use. Our HCI research in PRIME also investigates the challenges of communicating to a user trustworthiness (of a client and services-side systems) and assurance (of services-side services) used to process personal identifying information (PII). For approaching this problem, an interdisciplinary approach has been taken to investigate not only the technical options, but also the social factors and HCI aspects for influencing trust (see Andersson et al. in [1]).

11.5.2 Means for Enhancing Trust

The model of social factors of trust, which was developed by social science researchers in PRIME and presented in [1], suggests that trust in a service provider can be increased if procedures are transparent, reversible, and—in case of breaches of trust—there are means of redress.

Transparency for end users is provided by the data track, with which the user side IDM system keeps records about data disclosures (see section 11.3.4). Moreover, the data track also incorporates features that help raise user awareness of the rights to access data and to request the rectification/deletion/blocking of users' data and help them actively effectuate these rights (see above) and also provide them with updated information on consumer organizations and data protection authorities that can help with legal issues.

The social studies on trust factors have also shown that trust in a service provider can be increased if the user feels in control of the application. Besides, on the so-called institutional layer, trust can indeed be influenced by compliance check functions that allow users to make judgments about the trustworthiness of the service side's information technology (IT) system based on evidence, such as privacy seals issued by trusted independent parties or reputation metrics. Within PRIME, we have developed and evaluated UI proposals for obligation management for increased end user control and compliance checks for verifying whether the receiving service side still has a "good reputation" as well as a "good" privacy seal. The results of this work are briefly presented below.

11.5.2.1   Assurance Control

In order to provide users with greater choice and control, we believe it is beneficial to offer users the option to check the degree of evidence that the service provider can provide and that they can be trusted to process the user's PII in a privacy-friendly manner. To this end, we have implemented an "assurance control" component within the PRIME framework [18]. Its scope goes beyond what end users may digest—it could, in principle, provide service providers with advanced tools for checking out subcontractors, and also certification authorities can use it to check certified services. For ordinary people, however, the assurance control has been slimmed down to rely partly on other parties performing the more advanced checks. In a usability test, we simplified it to a "privacy functionality check" as seen in Figure 11.10 (edited; the test was performed in Swedish). Of course, the check of the service-side system could be varied (third category in the figure), but, in principle, it should conduct capability tests to verify statements made in the service policy (and/or covered by the privacy seals).

In a pilot test (with $N = 12$ test persons), this design was framed by five different Web vendor scenarios. In principle, the test participants like the idea of the functionality check even if well-known brand names and nonforeign vendors were clearly preferred in the tests. The requests for credit card details by a native, non-PRIME-enabled gambling site, however, was denied by all participants. Being able to get third-party judgments on an unknown site was appreciated; e.g., concerning an unknown native book shop, one participant said that in spite of a foreign blacklisting of this site, "If they hadn't had the Functionality Check, they would not have been trustworthy. But there I could see that they were more trustworthy than I thought before."

Figure 11.10   A simplified assurance control for end users.

11.5.2.2   Obligation Management

Obligations are means for dictating constraints, expectations, and duties to enterprises on how they must deal with personal data, in terms of retention, deletion, notifications, data transformation, etc. The obligation management system developed by HP Labs within PRIME [4,5] allows to explicitly collect end-users' privacy preferences (e.g., on deletion of their data or notification preferences) and use this information to customize the enforcement of obligation policies on their personal data, by dictating specific, subjective constraints. It, thus, allows actively involving individuals in the management of their data, and by this enhancing end user control.

We discuss the limits of this prospect in [22] based on design work, which has included smaller user tests among which one rather full-scale mockup test (with $N = 18$ test persons) had the participants set conditions for data use when they provided personal data via the Web. The question was whether ordinary Internet users would be able to use an obligation management system, and indeed whether they would *like* to use such a function, which actually increases complexity. To summarize the test results, the experiment showed that Internet users can be interested in such a function; it seemed to give the test participants a sense of being in control. From this, one may venture to speculate further. First, one may admit that many subscription-based services would probably use standard settings for the conditions. Such standards would make people less prone to set conditions themselves. However, there might still be reasons for people to look up afterward to see what information about them is still in use and also to actively seek to stop uses they do not allow any longer. For people to really do this, it is good if the user interface for setting conditions (at the time when they release their data) is not an obstacle and the idea behind our mockup was generally liked by the participants in our test. A positive attitude to obligation setting should, we hope, provide the ground for a positive attitude to use PRIME for doing follow-up actions.

11.6   Conclusions

This chapter has given a comprehensive presentation of research on human–computer interaction (HCI), especially as regards new user interface solutions for many of the privacy-enhancing identity management functions that have been considered in the PRIME project. User interfaces for privacy-enhancing identity management, as well as for PETs in general, have to meet several objectives, which we addressed in this chapter. These objectives have to be tackled by an interdisciplinary approach involving HCI and PET specialists as well as legal and social scientists. In the first two years of the PRIME project, our HCI research has focused on the objective that the PRIME UIs have to be simple to use and intuitive while at the same time meeting relevant legal privacy requirements by elaborating different UI paradigms for privacy-enhancing IDM along with guidelines on how to reach legal compliance with European data protection legislation. However, the usability evaluations of our early PRIME prototypes have shown that another severe problem needs to be addressed, namely the problem that many end users lack trust in privacy-enhancing technologies. Hence, another objective of the HCI work in PRIME has become the mediation of trust to the end users, and, as a first step, we have investigated how far UI functions for assurance control and obligation management can enhance trust. In the future, we will elaborate further user-friendly online functions, which support end users in exercising their privacy rights. The overall goal is to develop user interfaces that are not only privacy-compliant, but that also enhance the users' understanding, awareness, and control by actively promoting legal privacy principles.

Acknowledgments

The work reported in this chapter was supported by the IST PRIME project. The PRIME project receives research funding from the Community's Sixth Framework Program (Contract No. 507591) and the Swiss Federal Office for Education and Science. We would like to thank other PRIME colleagues who contributed ideas and input to the work presented in this chapter, especially Abhi Shelat (IBM Zurich Labs), Jan Möller and Henri Krasemann (ICPP), Ninni Danielsson, Jenny Nilsson, and Nina Rönntorp (Karlstad University).

References

[1] Andersson, C., Camenisch, J., Crane, S., Fischer-Hübner, S., Leenes, R., Pearson, S., Pettersson, J.S., and Sommer, D., Trust in PRIME, in *Proceedings of the 5th IEEE Int. Symposium on Signal Processing and IT*, December 18–21, 2005, Athens, Greece.

[2] Article 29 Data Protection Working Party, Opinion on More Harmonised Information Provisions, 11987/04/EN WP 100, November 25, 2004. http://ec.europa.eu/justice_home/fsj/privacy/docs/wpdocs/2004/wp100_en.pdf.

[3] Bermann, M., Rost, M., and Pettersson, J.S. Exploring the Feasibility of a Spatial User Interface Paradigm for Privacy-Enhancing Technology, *Proceedings of the Fourteenth International Conference on Information Systems Development* (ISD'2005), Karlstad, Sweden, August 2005. *Advances in Information Systems Development*, Springer-Verlag, Heidelberg, Germany, 2006. 437–448.

[4] Casassa Mont, M., Dealing with Privacy Obligations: Important Aspects and Technical Approaches, in *Proceedings of TrustBus'04*, 2004.

[5] Casassa Mont, M., A System to Handle Privacy Obligations in Enterprises, HP Labs Technical Report, Bristol, HPL-2005-180, 2005.

[6] Clauß, S. and Kriegelstein, T., Datenschutzfreundliches Identitätsmanagement, *Datenschutz und Datensicherheit* 27, 297, 2003.

[7] Cranor, L.F., Guduru, P., and Arjula, M., User Interfaces for Privacy Agents, *ACM Transactions on Computer-Human Interaction* 13(2), June 2006.

[8] Directive 95/46/EC of the European Parliament and of the Council of 24 October 1995 on the protection of individuals with regard to the processing of personal data and on the free movement of such data, *Official Journal L*, No. 281, 23.11.1995.

[9] Eurobarometer (2003) http://ec.europa.eu/public_opinion/index_en.htm, *especially*: http://ec.europa.eu/public_opinion/archives/ebs/ebs_196_data_protection.pdf

[10] Fischer-Hübner, S. and Pettersson, J.S. (Eds.), *Evaluation of Early Proto-types, PRIME deliverable D6.1.b*, 1 December 2004. https://www.prime-project.eu/prime_products/reports/eval.

[11] Günther, O. and Spiekermann, S., RFID and the perception of control: The consumer's view, *Communications of the ACM* 48(9): 73–76, September 2005.

[12] Jensen, C. and Potts, J., Privacy policies as decision-making tools: An eval-uation of online privacy notices, *CHI 2004*, 6, 471–478, 2004.

[13] Johnston, J., Eloff, J.H.P., and Labuschagne L., Security and human com-puter interfaces, *Computers & Security*, vol. 22 (8), 675, 2003.

[14] Karat, C.-M., Karat, J., Brodie, C., and Feng, J., Evaluating Interfaces for Privacy Policy Rule Authoring, in *Proceedings of the SIGCHI Conference on Human Factors in Computing Systems CHI 2006*, April 22–27, 2006, Montreal, Canada.

[15] Kobsa, A., Personalized Hypermedia and International Privacy, *Communi-cations of the ACM* 45(5), 64–67, 2002.

[16] Patrick, A.S. and Kenny, S., From Privacy Legislation to Interface Design: Implementing Information Privacy in Human-Computer Interaction, *Pro-ceedings of the Privacy Enhancing Technologies Workshop (PET 2003)*, Dresden, Germany, 2003.

[17] Patrick, A.S., Kenny, S., Holmes, C., and van Breukelen, M., Human Com-puter Interaction, in *Handbook for Privacy and Privacy-Enhancing Tech-nologies*, PISA project, van Blarkom, Borking, Olk, Eds., 2002, chap. 12. http://www.andrewpatrick.ca/pisa/handbook/handbook.html

[18] Pearson, S., Towards Automated Evaluation of Trust Constraints, in *Trust Management*, LNCS 3986, Springer, Berlin/Heidelberg, 252–266, 2006.

[19] Pettersson, J.S., Ed., HCI guidance and proposals, PRIME deliverable D6.1.c, 11 February 2005. https://www.prime-project.eu/prime_products/reports/arch/

[20] Pettersson, J.S., Fischer-Hübner, S., Danielsson, N., Nilsson, J., Bergmann, M., Kriegelstein, T., Clauss, S., and Krasemann, H., Making PRIME Usable, in *Proceedings of the Symposium of Usable Privacy and Security (SOUPS)*, 4–6 June 2005, Carnegie Mellon University, Pittsburg, PA, ACM Digital Library.

[21] Pettersson, J.S., Fischer-Hübner, S., and Bergmann, M., Outlining Data Track: Privacy-Friendly Data Maintenance for End-Users, in *Proceedings of the 15th International Conference on Information Systems Development (ISD 2006)*, Budapest, 31 August–2 September 2006, Springer Scientific Publishers, Heidelberg, Germany.

[22] Pettersson J.S., Fischer-Hübner, S., Pearsson, P., Casassa Mont, M., How Ordinary Internet Users Can Have a Chance to Influence Privacy Poli-cies, Short paper at *Proceedings of the 4th Nordic Conference on Human-Computer Interaction—NordiCHI 2006*, Oslo, 14–18 October 2006, ACM Press, New York.

[23] Pfitzmann, A., and Hansen, M., Anonymity, Unobservability, Pseudonymity, and Identity Management—A Consolidated Proposal for Terminology, v0.28, 29 May 2006. http://dud.inf.tu-dresden.de/Anon_Terminology.shtml

[24] Raskin, J., *The Humane Interface—New Directions for Designing Interactive Systems,* ACM Press, New York, 2000.

[25] Turner, C.W., How do consumers form their judgment of the security of e-commerce Web sites? *Workshop on Human-Computer Interaction and Security Systems,* CHI2003, April 5–10, 2003, Fort Lauderdale, FL.

[26] Turner, C.W., Zavod, M., and Yurcik, W., Factors That Affect the Perception of Security and Privacy of e-commerce Web Sites, in *Proceedings of the Fourth International Conference on Electronic Commerce Research,* Dallas, TX, November 2001.

Chapter 12

Privacy Perceptions among Members of Online Communities

Maria Karyda and Spyros Kokolakis

Contents

12.1 Introduction 254
12.2 Online Communities 255
    12.2.1 Defining Online Communities 255
    12.2.2 Members of Online Communities 256
12.3 Privacy in Online Communities 257
    12.3.1 Types of Privacy 258
12.4 Case Study: Privacy Concerns among Members
    of Online Communities 258
    12.4.1 Case Study Background 258
    12.4.2 Research Approach 259
    12.4.3 Case Study Findings.................................. 261
    12.4.4 Conclusions from the Case Study 263
        12.4.4.1 Online Community Members' Privacy
                Concerns....................................... 263
        12.4.4.2 Emphasis on Trust Relations 263
        12.4.4.3 Use of Deception............................. 264
        12.4.4.4 Distinguishing Different Types of Privacy..... 264
12.5 Conclusions and Further Research 264
Acknowledgments 265
References.. 265

12.1   Introduction

Internet-based information and communication technologies have enabled the emergence of new types of communicative practices. Traditionally, establishing a community entails live interaction and people meeting face to face. Digital communities (also known as online communities or virtual communities or social networks) are groups of people who share common interests and interact with each other. The term "online community" and its synonyms are used to connote communities in which electronic media facilitates communication and, in particular, for communities where interaction takes place over the Internet. Probably the most well-known definition has been provided by Rheingold, who defines virtual communities as "...social aggregations that emerge from the Net when enough people carry on those public discussions long enough, with sufficient human feeling, to form webs of personal relationships in cyberspace" [1]. Contrary to physical communities, which are usually confined to one location, virtual communities supersede geographical constraints. Physical communities are usually much smaller than digital ones. In recent years, online social networks have experienced exponential growth in membership; the user population in some of them is in the tens of thousands.

Since virtual communities depend upon social interaction and exchange between online members, the unwritten social contract among community members and the specific culture characterizing each community dictate accepted behavior and shape relationships between users. Online relationships develop in a different manner than face-to-face interactions: The lack of physical co-presence allows individuals to change their identity and reduce the influence of norms on individual behavior that typically designates social relationships. To mitigate these traits, most communities employ such means as moderated discussion forums, security and confidentiality rules, codes of conduct, and governance policies.

Online community members typically share personal information and, depending on the nature of the community, they may post extremely self-revealing information (such as health or family problems, sexual preferences, inner thoughts, etc.). Given the fact that privacy concerns are found to be high among Internet users [2] and have been identified as among the basic deterrents that obstruct the proliferation of e-commerce, this relatively new phenomenon of individuals exchanging personal information over the Internet with people unknown to them, requires closer examination. Moreover, the ability for groups and individuals to interact at great distances raises interesting issues for further investigation, such as the protection of personal identity.

Does the exponential membership growth in cyber spaces, like MySpace. com, indicate that online community members do not have any privacy concerns? Or, if they do have, what do these concerns entail? How do online community members perceive privacy risks and what means do they employ in order to mitigate these risks?

This chapter explores privacy concerns among online community members, aiming to contribute to the very limited literature on this subject. It specifically aims to identify research issues pertaining to privacy perceptions in online communities that will enable the formation of a research agenda. It presents the findings of a case study, where members of one of the largest community spaces, MySpace.com, have been interviewed about their attitude toward their privacy. The rest of the chapter is structured as follows: The next section (12.2) elaborates on privacy communities, their members, and the primary incentives for joining a community. Section 12.3 discusses privacy perceptions and the different types of privacy. Section 12.4 describes the case study, the findings, and the conclusions derived from it. Finally, the last section (12.5) presents the overall conclusions.

12.2   Online Communities

12.2.1   Defining Online Communities

Online communities are often characterized as not real but imagined, due to the lack of physical co-presence of the members. The term "imagined community" was coined by Anderson [3] who argued that (imagined) community members hold in their minds a mental image of their affinity and "…will never know most of their fellow members, meet them, or even hear of them, yet in the minds of each lives the image of their communion." Lately, however, the argument that co-presence is a necessity for a community to exist has been questioned and is no longer considered important, thus, research in the area of digital communities is thriving and it is expected to be augmented even more.

What, then, defines a community? Many possible answers have been proposed to this question. The classification proposed by Hagel and Armstrong [4] identifies four distinct types of digital communities: (1) communities of transactions, (2) communities of interest, (3) communities of practice (or relations), and (4) communities of fantasy. *Communities of transactions* mainly comprise buyers and sellers in the area of electronic commerce, whereas the members of a *community of interest* share a common interest or passion, such as a sport, music, gardening. They exchange ideas about their common interest and may know little more than that about each other. A *community of practice* generally refers to a group of like-minded people (often professionals) whose purpose is to support each other, to learn, and to promote their understanding via electronic collaboration in a group [5]. These communities allow members to establish a bond of common experience and build networks that are often continued offline.

Finally, members of a *community of fantasy* share a common interest in fantasy and science fiction. Multi-user gaming is a special case of the latter, where MMORPGs' (massively multiplayer online role-playing games) expansion is so big that the developer company of one of the most popular MMORPGs recently announced that its subscription base counted 8 million players worldwide [6].

There are also other types of communities, including *communities of purpose*, whose members are people going through the same process or trying to achieve a similar objective, e.g., antique collectors. This type of community provides its members with shared experience and exchange of information. There are also *development communities*, whose members collaborate to produce open source software. Furthermore, one can distinguish *communities of circumstance*; members of these communities tend to be personally focused around life-changing experiences, such as death, illness, or divorce. *Blogs* are considered the latest advent to digital communities. We may also consider other types of social experience, such as user-generated content (e.g., Wikipedia) and virtual environments.

From the point of view of computer-mediated communication, the most important elements of an online community are shared resources, common values, and reciprocal behavior. Over time, social, political, technical, and economic aspects of online communities have been explored [4, 5, 7, 8]. Other issues of interest for research include membership incentives and interaction, relations of trust among members, use of deception, identity management, and the issue of digital divide. It was not until very recently that privacy perceptions of online community members attracted researchers' interest [9]. This chapter contributes to the limited literature on privacy attitudes among online community members, by exploring privacy-related concerns.

12.2.2 Members of Online Communities

From a communication point of view, all members in a digital community are able to communicate with each other and participate in communication on an equal basis (i.e., a peer-to-peer architecture is adopted). The peer-to-peer architecture provided by the Internet gives members the ability to initiate communication to anybody connected to the network and also to publish and retrieve information. Different virtual communities have different levels of interaction and participation among their members. At the same time, different members have a different level of engagement with the community. This ranges from adding comments to a blog to competing against other people in online video games. Not unlike traditional social groups or clubs, virtual communities often divide themselves into cliques or even split to form new communities.

A number of different reasons for joining a community have been identified in relevant literature. People join a community, whether physical or digital, primarily for gaining what is called a *"sense of community."* Moreover, people contribute information to the community expecting that they will receive useful help and information in return (*anticipated reciprocity*). Kollock [10] argues that active participants in online communities get more responses to questions and faster than unknown participants. *Recognition* is also a common factor that drives individuals to join an online community. An interesting finding illustrating the power of this incentive is presented in Meyer and Thomas' study of the computer underground [11]: People involved in illegal computer activities often keep the same pseudonym in order to retain the status associated with their nickname, despite knowing that this practice may actually help authorities trace them.

12.3   Privacy in Online Communities

The concept of *perceived privacy* indicates the degree to which members of an online community perceive their messages and other personal information to be private within members of the community. But, for many scholars, the notion of privacy is not compatible with the one the community holds. If the major drive for joining a digital community is the need people have to be part of some "community," thus replacing the absent public spaces in their lives, then where do privacy concerns fit in? Is (and, if yes, to which degree) privacy desirable by online community members? To answer these questions, one must consider the relationship between individuals and the community. If community members consider the community as a means to receive certain services and/or achieve certain goals, then privacy is highly desirable. But, if the community is considered not merely as an enabling infrastructure, but as part of their social life, then they may not wish to shelter themselves from it. This could explain the fact that membership in digital communities is exponentially growing and, at the same time, privacy is among the primary concerns Internet users have.

A recent survey [9] found that nonmembers of a community under study were more conscious of their privacy compared to nonusers; they did not find, however, that privacy concerns prohibit users from joining online communities. In a different context, relating to e-commerce, a 1999 survey [12] found that the value and convenience provided by online services can outweigh privacy concerns.

It should not go without reference that there is a difference between how people perceive risk and actual risk [14]. According to Schnier [13], this difference could explain security trade-offs by Internet users. Gilbert [15] names the following set of reasons that explain why people would overestimate or underestimate risks: people tend to (1) overreact to intentional actions and underreact to accidents, abstract events, and natural phenomena; (2) overreact to things that offend their morals; (3) overreact to immediate threats and underreact to long-term threats; and (4) underreact to changes that occur slowly and over time.

12.3.1   Types of Privacy

Research on privacy indicates that it is a comprehensive concept. One can distinguish several types of privacy [2]:

- *Physical privacy* (also known as *solitude*) is the state of privacy in which persons are free from unwanted intrusion or observation.
- *Informational privacy* (also known as *anonymity*) is the desire to have control over the conditions under which personal data is released.
- *Psychological privacy* is defined as the control over release or retention of personal information to guard one's cognitions and affects.
- *Interactional privacy* (also known as *intimacy*) is relevant to relationships in social units as it preserves meaningful communication between individuals and among group members.

12.4   Case Study: Privacy Concerns among Members of Online Communities

12.4.1   Case Study Background

To explore privacy perceptions and attitudes among online communities' members, we constructed a questionnaire comprising both open and closed questions. We used this questionnaire to interview fourteen individuals, all members of MySpace.com, which is one of the most popular online communities. Its members use the facilities of this virtual place to construct their own social network of friends around the world, to share information, to join groups of their interest, and to post comments, photographs, videos, etc. A new member joining MySpace.com can, free of charge, create his/her profile by posting personal data, upload pictures, send e-mails and messages, and write blog entries. Then, a user can invite his friends to join the network and can also receive messages from other members of the community who do not belong to his network.

Members interact by sending messages to other users; e-mail is not used and, typically, the users' e-mail is not among their personal information that can be viewed by other members (other personal information often shown includes a personal photograph of the user, age, physical characteristics,

Table 12.1   Participants' Details

Demographics of Case Study Participants

Number of interviewees	14
Age	16 to 27 years
Sex	4 male, 10 female
Country	U.K., Australia, Lithuania, Greece, Lebanon, Peru, U.S., the Netherlands, Romania, Uruguay

such as height, weight, color of eyes/hair, hometown, type of music preferred, favorite artists, zodiac sign, etc.). At the time when the case study took place (December 2006), more than 50 million people from almost all countries around the world had registered accounts. MySpace features a privacy policy (a link to the policy is provided in the first page) and declares its concern about its members' privacy.

Participants of the case study were chosen on a voluntary basis. Using the messaging service, we contacted one hundred members, who had been randomly chosen (including both sexes, all age ranges, and most origins). Sixteen individuals responded, among which fourteen agreed to participate in the study; two replied negatively and opposed the fact that we had disturbed them. The data of the case study participants are provided in Table 12.1.

One interesting fact that caught our attention was that strikingly more female than male members chose to take part in the study. This could have occurred accidentally, or could be attributed to the fact that women are more sensitive to privacy issues, or even to the fact that the sender of the message inviting them to participate in the study was male.

12.4.2   Research Approach

To explore the privacy concerns among members of online communities, conducting an Internet survey is the obvious approach. Stanton [16] found that data collected from a sample of participants via the Internet produced results similar to those obtained from a sample that completed the same questionnaire in the traditional paper-and-pencil form. However, online surveys have low response rates and, at times, have been accused of being unwanted mail or spam. Moreover, the aim of this research was to explore the issues pertaining to the privacy attitudes that members of online communities have. For these reasons, the approach of an online interview was chosen. The list of questions asked during the interviews is presented in Table 12.2.

Table 12.2   Case Study Questionnaire

Questions Asked during the Interviews

1. Did you check the privacy policy before you edit your current profile?
2. Do you feel any fear or insecurity about how your uploaded personal information could be used?
3. Do you feel insecure about any of your profile entries?

    A. No
    B. Yes, about my photos and/or videos
    C. Yes, about my age
    D. Yes, about my location
    E. Yes, about my . . . (please explain)

4. If you answered yes in the previous question, please name the most important reasons for which you feel insecure.
5. What do you do when you have to upload some of your personal information about which you feel troubled?

    A. You provide the information that really represents you
    B. You provide false information
    C. You don't provide any information at all
    D. You do something else (please explain)

6. What would make you provide false information about one of your profile's entries?
7. To what degree do you feel insecure about potential misuse of your uploaded personal information?

    A. High
    B. Medium
    C. Low
    D. I do not feel insecure

8. In which way you think someone could misuse your uploaded personal information?
9. If it came to your attention that another user had misused your personal information, what would you do?

    A. Report this user using the site's relevant service
    B. Delete your current profile and withdraw from the community/group
    C. Delete your current profile and create a new one
    D. Something else (please explain)

10. Do you believe that you can protect your uploaded personal information following any of the actions below?

    A. By carefully choosing your friends network
    B. By maintaining a low number of friends
    C. By other means (please explain)

12.4.3 Case Study Findings

Although all participants were aware that the host site had a privacy policy, only four of them reported having read it before joining the community/editing their profile (question #1). One of them, in a later question about the privacy protection means she would find appropriate (question #10) replied: "...always read the privacy policy before you sign up, virus protection on the pc must always have the latest updates." It is interesting, however, that most of the respondents were not interested in reading the privacy policy before joining the community.

Most of the respondents (eleven out of fourteen) said that they do not feel insecure about how their personal information could be used (question #2). When asked, however, whether they feel insecure about any of their profile entries specifically (question #3), two of the individuals who had previously declined having any fear said that they did have some concerns on how their personal photos, videos, and blog entries could be used. Three interviewees, who had previously answered positively about having privacy concerns, named their location and Internet protocol (IP) address as their primary sources of concern. It is interesting that one interviewee, although responding positively to the question about privacy concerns, when asked about her specific personal data included in her online profile, answered that she didn't have any particular concerns and that she "...didn't answer truthfully on location."

As most important reasons for feeling insecure with regard to their privacy (question #4), three respondents mentioned potential misuse by other people, while one commented "...but my main fear is that people will get the wrong impression of me." One interviewee added that her insecurity primarily resulted from the fact "...that I'm not really an expert on internet issues." Finally, one of the interviewees said that she felt people cannot be trusted in general.

When asked what they do when having doubts about how a piece of personal information could be used (question #5), most interviewees (ten of them) answered that they would avoid putting this information on the Internet, whereas one said that she would provide false information. Interestingly, though, three respondents claimed that they would always provide accurate information about themselves even if having doubts.

When asked about what would make them provide false information about their profile's entries (question #6), three interviewees answered that they are always honest about their personal data. Four of the respondents suggested that to avoid spam, stalking, and other potential threats, they would provide false information on their age and location. The youngest of the persons interviewed reported that she would provide false information about herself "...until you get to know them better."

Some of the respondents referred to privacy incidents. One, in particular, mentioned an identity theft incident, when she discovered her personal photos used in other people's profiles. However, the same person said that "...we take this risk and I think most people are aware that there will always be people that way inclined." However, none of the interviewees responded that they felt *highly* insecure about a potential misuse of their personal information. Seven replied that they didn't feel any insecurity, while the rest graded their privacy concerns as *medium* (four interviewees) or *low* (three interviewees) (question #7). It is worth noting that the individual who had experienced an identity theft incident ("...people can pretend to be you by using your pictures and opening a new profile...I have found two on AAAA.com of me!") rated her privacy concerns as low, while the person who reported having suffered stalking in the past, placed her privacy concerns at a medium level.

Answering the question: In which way you think someone could misuse your uploaded personal information? (question #8), interviewees named the following: defacement, identity theft, other people publishing their photos, receiving spam, stalking, harassment. One person commented that "I'm careful what I upload and the information I give out, so I don't think anyone can misuse anything with me," whereas another person reported being afraid that she might be taken hostage. Six of the respondents chose not to answer this question. Compared to the fact that eleven interviewees had answered negatively about having privacy concerns (question #2), it is interesting to note that some interviewees named threat scenarios even though stating that they do not feel insecure.

When asked what they would do in case their personal data were misused (question #9), all interviewees answered that their first action would be to report the ill-willed user to the site's relevant service; one of them added that she would also explore the possibility of taking legal actions, while two said that they would delete their current profiles. An interesting point is that only one person expressed her intention to leave the community in case a threat scenario was likely to happen. It is also worth noting that during the interviews, two individuals reported having fallen victims of privacy-related incidents (one of them mentioned stalking and the other, identity theft); however, none of them expressed their intention of leaving the community in their answers. They both answered that they would report the user. This fact could indicate that, for these users, participation in the community prevails over their perception of privacy risks.

When asked about what means they would employ to protect their privacy (question #10), eight people replied that they do so by selecting their friends; furthermore, three of them added that they also select carefully the information they upload. Three other interviewees answered that they rely on setting their profile to private (a feature available to members of this community; users have the option to grant access to their personal data to their personal network of friends by setting their profile to private, not all sites support this feature). Two interviewees expressed the opinion that taking privacy-protection measures is futile. One of them (the oldest among the interviewees) stated that there is no way one can effectively protect one's privacy on the Internet, while the other argued that "[i]f anyone wants your personal information that badly, they could probably get it."

12.4.4   Conclusions from the Case Study

The conclusions drawn from the analysis of the answers given by the interviewees are elaborated below.

12.4.4.1   Online Community Members' Privacy Concerns

Despite the fact that most interviewees gave a negative answer when asked if they feel insecure about the privacy of their personal data, most of them did describe a scenario of potential misuse of their data. Combined with the fact that nobody expressed his intention to leave the community in case such a scenario actually took place, we presume that (1) these community members do have privacy concerns, but (2) their perceptions of privacy risks are low. This finding highlights the fact that further examination is needed with regard to the issues that balance privacy concerns, specifically since some of the interviewees reported privacy violation incidents that had happened to them. However, we should also point out that, to some extent, privacy concerns seem to affect members' behavior, since it may entail withholding personal information, as many interviewees suggested, or posting false information about oneself. Finally, respondents identified as sources of concern with regard to their privacy the following elements:

- Blogs
- Photos/videos
- IP address—location
- Age

12.4.4.2   Emphasis on Trust Relations

Many answers suggest that the interviewees feel that few threats originate from their fellow community members, thus, they mostly depend on trust relations to preserve their privacy. Among the most characteristic answers we received was the following: "... wait until you get to know the people you are talking to and then tell them your personal information." The majority of the people interviewed reported that selecting the people who participate in the network is the best way to protect oneself. However, it is not straightforward how this can be accomplished, since it entails long-term interaction with one's online acquaintances and depends on the specific culture of the community. The distinction between the insiders (members of the community) and the outsiders is implicit in almost all answers.

12.4.4.3 Use of Deception

Generally, the concept of deception implies either purposeful misinformation or lack of full disclosure. Members of online communities report that they do both of the above as a way to protect themselves from Internet-related threats, such as stalking. It seems, thus, that community members would use "justifiable lies" to protect their privacy against possible online offenders.

12.4.4.4 Distinguishing Different Types of Privacy

Based on the answers received, online community members have concerns about the *physical privacy* (consequently, some would provide false information about their location). *Informational privacy* does not seem to affect them a lot, since the vast majority responded that they carefully select their network of friends and that they control the information they upload to their private space. *Psychological privacy* is another concern, since some respondents were thoughtful about the impression that their information would convey to other people. *Interactional privacy* seems also important for community members who rely on schemes featured by the site's infrastructure to restrict access to members of their social network.

12.5 Conclusions and Further Research

Exploring privacy perceptions among members of online communities is an important issue, since social communities are now regarded, not only as a social phenomenon, but also as a business model [8]. Although the assertion that Internet users are deeply concerned about their privacy is treated, de facto, as true, nevertheless no research has been published on what exactly are these privacy concerns. The case study described in this chapter explored privacy concerns among members of an online community. The overall conclusion this research arrives at is that privacy is perceived differently by Internet users. Different groups of users, such as members of a community, have different perceptions of what poses a threat to their privacy and they employ different methods to protect it. It is evident, therefore, that different approaches to safeguarding security are needed, both at an organizational and a technical level. Among the different topics highlighted by the case study, the most important issues are the following:

1. Online community members have privacy concerns in varying degrees and for different elements: Some reported that they do not have any fears with regard to their privacy, and many expressed

a moderate degree of concern (but referred to different objects of concerns). Their major sources of concern reported are location, age, photos/videos, and blog entries.

2. It is important to identify the different types of privacy, which are considered important by community members. Protecting physical and interactional privacy seems to prevail over psychological and informational privacy.

3. Deception is not only a threat to the users, but is also often employed by them in their attempt to protect their privacy.

These issues require further examination. Findings of the case study presented here support relevant research findings [9] that members of online communities do exhibit privacy concerns, but are not deterred by them from joining the community. Furthermore, our research distinguished between different types of privacy, which are desired by community members.

The research agenda in the area of privacy in online communities should also include another issue, which has been, thus far, overlooked: Personal privacy is associated with a specific individual. Given the fact that people in online communities can and often have multiple (virtual) identities or profiles, how is the concept of privacy protection affected?

It is important to note that the aim of this study has been exploratory; by using semistructured questions, we aimed to catch respondents' feelings and attitudes toward the issue of privacy. In many cases, the interviewees' responses were more detailed and conveyed their overall *weltanschauung* (world view). Due to the limited number of participants and the fact that interviewees were actually self-selected, conclusions drawn by this case study cannot, and should not, be considered as representative of MySpace.com members, or members of any other community. These conclusions, however, provide insight and have enabled us to bring to the foreground some not-so-well-known issues about privacy and online community members.

Acknowledgments

The authors would like to thank George Gampierakis for his support at contacting and interviewing the case study participants. We would also like to thank all of the MySpace.com members who responded to our questions.

References

[1] Rheingold, H., *The Virtual Community: Homesteading on the Electronic Frontier*, Addison-Wesley, Reading, MA, 1993.

[2] Cho, H. and Larose, R., Privacy issues in Internet surveys, *Soc. Sci. Comp. Rev.*, 17, 4, 421–434, 1999.

[3] Anderson, B., *Imagined Communities: Reflections on the Origin and Spread of Nationalism*, Verso, New York, 1991.

[4] Hagel III, J. and Armstrong, A., *Net Gain: Expanding Markets Through Virtual Communities*, Harvard Business School Press, Cambridge, MA, 1997.

[5] Preece, J., Sociability and usability in online communities: Determining and measuring success, *Behav. Inform. Technol.*, 20, 5:347–356, 2001.

[6] http://www.blizzard.com, *World of Warcraft Reaches 8 Million Players Worldwide*, published on January 11, 2007.

[7] Wilson, S.M. and Peterson, L.C., The anthropology of online communities, *Annu. Rev. Anthropol.*, 31:449–67, 2002.

[8] Hummel, J. and Lechner, U., Communities—the role of technology, in *Proc. the 9th European Conference on Information Systems*, Bled, Slovenia, pp. 1264–1275, 2001.

[9] Acquisti, A. and Gross, R., Imagined Communities: Awareness, Information Sharing, and Privacy on the Facebook, in G. Danezis and P. Golle (Eds.): *PET 2006*, LNCS 4258, Cambridge, U.K., pp. 36–58, 2006.

[10] Kollock, P., The economies of online cooperation: Gifts and public goods in cyberspace, in Smith M. and Kollock P. (Eds.), *Communities in Cyberspace*, London, Routledge, 1999.

[11] Meyer, G. and Thomas, J., A postmodernist interpretation of the computer underground, in F. Schmalleger (Ed.), *Computers in Criminal Justice*, Lima, OH: Wyndham Hall, 1991.

[12] NetZero, *Concerns don't slow e-commerce,* available online from http://cyberatlas.internet.com

[13] Schneier, B., *Beyond Fear*, Copernicus Books, New York, 2003.

[14] Slovic P., Perception of risk, *Science*, 236, 280–285, 1987.

[15] Gilbert, D., *Stumbling on Happiness,* Knopf, New York, 2007.

[16] Stanton, J.M., An empirical assessment of data collection using the Internet, *Pers. Psychol.*, 51, 709–725, 1998.

Chapter 13

Perceived Control: Scales for Privacy in Ubiquitous Computing

Sarah Spiekermann

Contents

13.1   Introduction 267
13.2   Loss of Privacy through Loss of Control 269
13.3   Perceived Control in PETs in UC Environments 270
      13.3.1   Perceived Control 270
      13.3.2   PETs for Perceived Control over RFID Technology 271
13.4   Scale Development and Testing 272
      13.4.1   Control Definition and Initial Item Development 272
      13.4.2   Empirical Item Testing 272
      13.4.3   Internal Consistency and Reliability of Control Items . . . 274
13.5   Applying Control Scales to RFID Scenarios 277
13.6   Conclusion 279
References 279

13.1   Introduction

Privacy is a construct widely investigated in the information systems world, both in the context of e-commerce as well as in the context of ubiquitous computing (UC). What has been missing in information security (IS) research, except for a few articles, is a thorough framing and defining of what privacy is, including empirical testing of its building blocks based on properly defined scales. As a result of this lack of research, privacy definitions appear in different forms and facets, misconceptions not excluded. Consequently, when researching privacy for a ubiquitous computing context today, there is little common ground to build on.

Ubiquitous computing refers to environments where most physical objects are enhanced with digital qualities. It implies "tiny, wirelessly interconnected computers that are embedded almost invisibly into just about any kind of everyday object" [1]. Thus, people buy and use products that can be automatically recognized, tracked, addressed, and, potentially, trigger activities or services. Because of these properties, UC and especially one of its core technologies, radio frequency identification (RFID), have stirred some debates about privacy being at risk.*

Yet, a misconception of privacy is actually articulated already in one of the most widely cited articles on ubiquitous computing, notably Mark Weiser's "The Computer for the 21st Century" [2]. Commenting on social challenges arising from UC, Weiser wrote: "The [social] problem [associated with UC], while often couched in terms of privacy, is really one of control." While Weiser was right to point out that UC raises control issues reaching beyond privacy alone, it should be noted that privacy has actually for decades been defined in terms of control. Altman [3], for example, one of the main sociological privacy scholars in the Western Hemisphere, defined privacy in 1975 as "the selective control of access to the self or to one's group." Schoeman [4] saw privacy as "the control an individual has over information about himself or herself," and Margulis [5] reflected on several decades of privacy research when writing: "Privacy, as a whole or in part, represents control over transactions between person(s) and other(s), the ultimate aim of which is to enhance autonomy and/or minimize vulnerability." Summing up, privacy cannot be seen as separate from control. Instead, it is deeply intertwined with it.

Unfortunately, IS research has seen few works building upon this fundamental insight. For this reason, we want to investigate privacy systematically with a view to its inherent control character. More specifically, we want to develop scales that are able to measure *perceived* privacy governance on the basis of perceived control over access to the self. UC, and in particular RFID technology, serves as the context in which privacy is sought.

---

* RFID chips (tags) are embedded into the fabric of products and emit a unique product number once addressed by a reader. The reader feeds the number into a backend information infrastructure where the nature of the product and potentially its owner is identified. Based on this information, further services are being triggered.

13.2   Loss of Privacy through Loss of Control

Loss of privacy in UC environments can really be due to two distinct reasons: The first one is relating to what we want to call *people losing control over being accessed*. In classical privacy literature, researchers relate to this aspect of privacy when they discuss the *collection* of data by marketers and other institutions [6], i.e., via e-commerce Web sites or customer loyalty programs. For UC environments, it is typically assumed that sensor and RFID infrastructures will be ubiquitous. The so-called "intelligent infrastructure" seeks to automatically adapt to people moving through space and for this it needs to establish connections with peoples' objects. People carrying RFID-tagged objects are envisaged to be read out by RFID readers from a distance or be tracked by other technologies. Building on Altman [3], Boyle refers to this privacy aspect in UC as the need "to control the *attention* of the Ubicomp environments" [7]. This control can be exercised through privacy-enhancing technologies (PETs). PETs—according to current research—are supposed to enable users to protect themselves from being accessed against their will. PETs proposed for RFID-enabled environments are blocker tags [8], the Privacy Awareness System (pawS) [9], or authentication-based protection schemes [10–12].

The second factor impacting privacy in UC is a *lack of control over information use and maintenance* once people (or their objects) have been accessed. This concern about unauthorized secondary use is actually a historical one in privacy research [6]. However, UC adds a new dimension of relevance to this aspect of privacy because much more data is being collected. Ubiquitous multimedia environments can, for example, lead to a more prevalent risk of disembodiment or disassociation as discussed by Belotti and Sellen [13]. Tracking of whereabouts and social network analysis suddenly gain a "physical" dimension [14]. And, unique item identification inherent in new numbering standards, such as the electronic product code (EPC) embedded in RFID tags or IPv6 can lead to a degree of personal attribution and potential surveillance unseen before.

Still, this secondary use (and potential abuse) of information is not possible if there has not been access in the first place. This implies that controlling access is a crucial part of the privacy equation in UC. We, therefore, focus on the first dimension of privacy in UC: Perceived control over the *access* that intelligent RFID infrastructures may gain to individuals via their objects.

In section 13.3, we introduce the reader to the main theories and dimensions of perceived control. These are deducted from psychological research and have served as a basis to develop scales for perceived control measurement. In section 13.4, we comment on two main privacy-enhancing technologies envisioned to create control over RFID technology. Based on these two introductory parts, we describe the development of scales, which are able to measure perceived control over RFID readouts as people use PET solutions (section 13.4). We then apply these scales to two RFID uses and protection scenarios.

13.3   Perceived Control in PETs in UC Environments

13.3.1   Perceived Control

Perceived control is a concept investigated in psychology since the 1960s [15]. One of the first investigations of control as a behavioral construct can be found in Seligman's work on *learned helplessness* [16]. Learned helplessness was considered by Seligman as the opposite of being in control. Together with Abramson et al. [17], he defined helplessness as "cases in which the individual...does not possess controlling responses" (p. 51). People enter into a stage of numbness where they feel that their activity really does not impact the course of activities around them. In the context of RFID (or other UC environments), this would imply that people have given up on protecting their privacy as they believe protection efforts to be in vain anyway, e.g., protection efforts against the read-outs of RFID tags embedded in personal belongings.

Related to this feeling, but somewhat weaker in emotional strength, is the notion of control as a means to achieve a desired outcome. Seligman propagated this aspect noting that "a person has control when a desired outcome's occurrence is dependent on the person's responses" [18]. In psychological research this position has mostly been referred to as *contingency* [19].

While Seligman and his peers' research focused on response contingency, Langer [18] propagated that people can only perceive control over situations if they are aware that they can influence these through their *choices*: "...control ... is the active belief that one has a choice among responses that are differentially effective in achieving the desired outcome." In a UC environment, this choice aspect would imply that people can easily opt out of being accessed by the intelligent infrastructure.

In order to make choices, one needs properly informed about one's options. As Fiske and Taylor [20] put it: "...a sense of control ... is achieved when the self obtains or is provided with information about a noxious event" (p. 201). Skinner [15] calls this type of control "information control." In a RFID context, *information control* would mean that people are made aware of being read out understanding when an why readouts are taking place. Moreover, there is a *power* aspect to control, which has been considered by Rodin, who wrote: "[perceived control is] ...the expectation of having the power to participate in making decisions in order to obtain desirable consequences and a sense of personal competence in a given situation" [21]. In fact, power is an important notion also recognized in the motivation literature. When people feel empowered, they may be motivated to make more rigorous use of a technology.

Yet, Rodin also referred here to another notion of control, which is one's feeling of competence. If people feel competent to master a situation, they feel in control. Bandura [22] is one of the scholars focusing on this aspect of control, which is referred to as self-efficacy: "People's beliefs about their capabilities to exercise control over events that affect their lives." Researchers in technology acceptance found the construct of *ease-of-use* is strongly impacted by self-efficacy beliefs [23, 24].

13.3.2 PETs for Perceived Control over RFID Technology

The goal of this article is to document the development of scales, which are able to measure the degree to which privacy-enhancing technologies (PETs) are able to induce a perception of control in people. We assume that if people perceive control over RFID technology through their PETs then they will also perceive themselves exercising their right to privacy. Before delving into the details of scale development, it is important to describe available PETs for RFID in more detail and to give the reader a perspective on the type of PETs used to test the control scales reported on hereafter.

Based on RFID PET research, we consider two types of privacy-enhancing technologies. We term these two alternative PET approaches the "user model" and the "agent model." The user model implies that users exert full control over RFID tags by means of appropriate authentication mechanisms. Objects do not *a priori* respond to network requests. Instead the user self-initiates the use of intelligent services if they are available and useful in the respective context. The context decision when and how the use of tags is appropriate, is thus taken by the object owner [10–12, 25]. If the owner of an object gains some benefit from reviving an object's RFID tag, she can do so by authenticating herself by using a password. We expect the user model to induce a high level of control with users since the intelligent infrastructure cannot act autonomously, but only in response to the user having provided her password.

In contrast, an *agent model* is based on the idea that RFID tags are, by default, answering to network requests. Access control in this scenario is delegated to an agent who negotiates privacy preferences with the network before the latter is allowed to access tag information. This agent system takes a context-sensitive decision for the object owner when to answer network requests based on the purposes specified by the network owner [9, 26]. The user trusts that his agent and the network interacting with it adhere to his privacy preferences.

13.4 Scale Development and Testing

13.4.1 Control Definition and Initial Item Development

Based on the control literature described in section 13.3.1, we developed scales that would be able to test people's perceived control over being accessed by an intelligent infrastructure. Helplessness, contingency, choice, power, information, and ease-of-use described above served as the basic categories to frame the construct (see Table 13.1).

Following the guidelines of proper scale development [27], the first step was the development of a proper definition of the perceived control construct. Based on an expert discussion, we formulated the following definition: "Perceived control [in a UC environment] is the belief of a person in the electronic environment acting only in such ways as explicitly allowed for by the individual." We then developed fourteen question items capturing the different control categories identified above. To assess the relatedness of these items with the control construct definition, we conducted interviews with twenty-five participants (mostly students). Participants ranked the fourteen questions in an order of decreasing relatedness to the control definition. Ten participants, furthermore, categorized the items into meaningful categories. Based on this ranking and classifying, we were able to identify three questions being the least related to the definition and we excluded them from further research. The resulting eleven questions promised a high degree of content validity and they also matched the control classification we had hoped to capture. Their importance ranking with regards to the control definition and their respective categories are presented in Table 13.1. The table also includes four questions adjusted from the technology acceptance model on ease-of-use [23, 24]. Even though perceived ease-of-use is not a direct measure of perceived control it is an important part of the construct under study because it allows consideration of self-efficacy beliefs in interaction with the technology.

The next step was to test whether these categories would indeed show and be internally consistent when applied to PETs.

13.4.2 Empirical Item Testing

One hundred and twenty-eight subjects were invited by a market research agency to participate in a study on tomorrow's shopping environments. Sociodemographics of the participants were close to the German population: 47 percent were female and 53 percent male; 36 percent were below 30 years of age, 21 percent were 30 to 39, and 43 percent were 40 years or older. Forty percent had no A-levels and only 25 percent went to university; 81 percent had an income below € 30,000 (euros).

Table 13.1   Control Items and Categories

Rank	Index	Question Text	Category
1	POW 1	I feel that I can steer the intelligent environment in a way I feel is right	Power
2	POW 2	Thanks to <the PET> the electronic environment and its reading devices, I will have to subdue to my will	
5	POW 3	Due to <the PET>, I perceive perfect control over the activity of my chips	
3	CON 1	Thanks to <the PET>, I could determine myself whether or not I'll interact with the intelligent environment	Contingency
7	CON 2	Through <the PET>, services are put at my disposition when I want them	
6	H 2	I could imagine that if the electronic environment set out to scan me, it would be able to do so despite <the PET>	Helplessness
10	H 1	<The PET> will finally not be able to effectively protect me from being read by the electronic environment	
8	COI 1	Due to <the PET>, it is still my decision whether or not the intelligent environment recognizes me	Choice
4	COI 2	Through <the PET>, I finally have the choice whether or not I am being scanned or not	
9	IC 1	Through <the PET>, I would always be informed of whether and in what form the electronic environment recognizes me	Information
11	IC 2	Using <the PET>, I would always know when and by whom I have been read out	
*	EUP 1	To learn to use <the PET> would be easy for me	Ease-of-use
*	EUP 2	It would be easy for me to learn skillful use of <the PET>	
*	EUP 3	I would find <the PET> easy to use	
*	EUP 4	Due to <the PET>, the information exchange between my chips and reading devices would be clearly defined	

Note: 1 = fully agree to 5 = do not agree at all.

The participants were split into two random groups. Group 1 contained seventy-four subjects, Group 2 had fifty-four participants. Both groups were presented with a film on future shopping environments in which RFID technology would be used. RFID technology, representing the UC environment here, was explained neutrally. Its benefits and drawbacks were commented on without bias. After-sales benefits of RFID were described on the basis of two services: an intelligent refrigerator and product returns without need for a receipt. The film was mostly identical for both groups but different in one respect: the privacy-enhancing technology (the PET) available to the consumer to control his privacy. In Group 1, the film briefing was such that RFID chips would all be switched off at the supermarket exit, but could be turned on again with the help of a personal password if after-sales services (fridge, product exchange) would require it (user model). In Group 2, the film briefing was such that chips would all be left on at the supermarket exit, but could only be accessed by readers for after-sales purposes if the reading purpose would match a person's privacy preference (agent model). Before and after seeing the film participants answered a battery of questions. The fifteen control items were passed among other questions after the film. As depicted in Table 13.1, they were answered on a 5-point scale tested by Rohrman [28].

13.4.3 Internal Consistency and Reliability of Control Items

To understand whether the six control categories would really be reflected in the fifteen control-related questions, we first conducted a factor analysis. Assuming that there could be correlations between factors, we chose oblimin rotation. Very few missing items were replaced by mean values. Principal component analysis was employed. Factor analysis was first conducted for Group 1 (user model) and then analyzed whether the results would replicate for Group 2 (agent model). This first round of analysis showed that only eight out of the fifteen questions would consistently load for both treatments. Three factors with factor loadings above .6 could be identified. Two items, one ease-of-use question and one question on contingency, saw low loadings for both treatments and, therefore, were eliminated from the item set. Five remaining questions, notably those on power and choice, would not load consistently on the separate factors. In fact, for Group 1, power- and choice-related questions loaded together with information and contingency items. Group 2 listed power and choice loading with helplessness. We, therefore, concluded that the items developed for power and choice would not be suited to reliably distinguish between factors and we opted to eliminate them from the list of questions, well recognizing that content validity of leftover scales would suffer due to this step. The remaining eight questions were used again to first run factor analysis for Group 1 and then (to confirm reliability) for Group 2. In this step, three factors explaining the perceived control construct could clearly be identified for both PET samples (see Table 13.2).

Factor 1 is clearly related to the category "ease-of-use" of the PET. The three questions (EUP 1, EUP 2, EUP 3) measure to what extent one feels control over RFID because one feels that the PET protecting one's privacy is easy to use. Factor 3 is characterized by two highly loading items referring to "helplessness" (H1, H2). Factor 2 is characterized by the items classified as

Table 13.2   Final Factor Loadings for the Two PET Treatments

Password PET (Group 1): Pattern Matrix[a]

	Component		
	1	*2*	*3*
EUP 2	0.954	− 0.048	− 0.021
EUP 1	0.881	− 0.065	− 0.094
EUP 3	0.854	0.162	0.088
IC 2	− 0.114	0.918	− 0.046
IC 1	0.077	0.855	0.067
CON 1	0.068	0.822	− 0.025
H 2	0.109	− 0.014	0.905
H 1	− 0.165	0.001	0.800

Note: Rotation Method: Oblimin with Kaiser Normalization.
[a] Rotation converged in five iterations.

Agent PET (Group 2): Pattern Matrix[a]

	Component		
	1	*2*	*3*
EUP 2	0.937	0.042	− 0.028
EUP 1	0.925	− 0.056	− 0.045
EUP 3	0.905	0.047	0.074
IC 2	− 0.069	0.880	− 0.024
IC 1	0.026	0.872	0.004
CON 1	0.082	0.847	0.023
H 2	0.062	− 0.159	0.877
H 1	− 0.068	0.180	0.801

Note: Rotation Method: Oblimin with Kaiser Normalization.
[a] Rotation converged in four iterations.

Table 13.3   Control Scales Group 1 (Password), Reliability Statistics

Control Scales	Item	Cron. α	Culm. Variance Explained	Corr. (r)	Corr. (r)	Corr. (r)
Ease-of-Use of the PET	EUP 1 EUP 2 EUP 3	.881	38.33%			−.214
Information Control	CON 1 IC 1 IC 2	.837	64.30%	.243		
Helplessness	H 1 H 2	.650	78.63%		.110	

"information control" as well as one question treating contingency (CON 1). Looking into the question text for the contingency item, we interpreted the loading as respondents' perception of their PET as an information source to determine further steps. Therefore, we regarded Factor 2 as a dimension of control, which measures the extent to which one perceives control as a consequence of being informed.

Tables 13.3 and 13.4 show that the cumulative variance explained by these three factors is above 78 percent for both PET conditions. Also, the three factors are not quite correlated, which implies that they can be considered independent dimensions of perceived control.

The final step was to investigate the internal consistency of the three scales thus identified. For this purpose, we calculated each item set's Cronbach α. The threshold of .8 was passed by the ease-of-use construct as well as the information control construct. The two items on helplessness displayed a rather weak Cronbach α of around .6. Potentially, these questions

Table 13.4   Control Scales Group 2 (Agent), Reliability Statistics

Control Scales	Item	Cron. α	Culm. Variance Explained	Corr. (r)	Corr. (r)	Corr. (r)
Ease-of-Use of the PET	EUP 1 EUP 2 EUP 3	.915	34.70%			.050
Information Control	CON 1 IC 1 IC 2	.836	61.91%	0.92		
Helplessness	H 1 H 2	.579	78.99%		.118	

would need to be retested in future research and be complemented with other items to form a better scale.

13.5   Applying Control Scales to RFID Scenarios

Typically, scales identified on the basis of one sample should not be applied to the same sample for the report of actual findings. Still, in order to add practical meaning to the control scales discussed in this chapter, we apply them here to demonstrate their usefulness.

As outlined above, we use the scales to measure people's perceived control over UC technology once they have a PET to protect their privacy. Thus, we measure how people perceive exercising privacy with the help of a PET. As described in section 13.4.2, 128 subjects answered to the control scales described above upon seeing a film on RFID deployments in retail and at home. Group 1 and 2, however, differed with respect to the PET displayed in the film stimulus. With this experimental setup, it became possible to test whether people perceive different levels of control depending on the type of PET used. Recall that in the user model, people would get immediate control over when to access the intelligent infrastructure. Only upon reception of a personal password would the intelligent infrastructure be able to read out people's RFID chips. On the other hand, the agent model proposed a PET residing on a mobile network and operating automatically on the basis of privacy preferences specified in advance of transactions. Here, control would be delegated to an agent. The hypothesis we made upon designing the experiment was that participating subjects would perceive more control in the user model and less control in the agent model, thus, producing an argument for more research efforts in UC technology designs, putting control physically into peoples' hands.

People's perception of control on the basis of having one of the two PETs at their disposition is displayed in Table 13.5. It turns out that—against expectations—perceived control is similar for both PET technologies. More specifically, people report to feel helpless (out of control) no matter what PET is at hand. This is despite the fact that they consider both PETs to be rather easy to use. The degree to which they feel informed to actively control the environment is judged as medium. The mean control judgements indicate that the password scheme may be slightly easier to use, but this difference is statistically nonsignificant. The conclusion that can be drawn from these results is that *no* PET presented to participants in the current study seems to induce a perception of control. The proposal of either PET solution must be questioned, seeing that people do not feel in control with any one of the two and, therefore, may question the ability to effectively protect their privacy with either of them.

Table 13.5 Control Scales and Mean Answers Applied to Two RFID PETs

Control Scale	Questions	Mean (User Model)	Mean (Agent Model)
Ease-of-Use of the PET	To learn to use <the PET> would be easy for me	1.65	2.02
	It would be easy for me to learn skillful use of <the PET>	1.92	2.15
	I find <the PET> easy to use	2.16	2.44
Information Control	Using <the PET>, I would always know when and by whom I have been read out	2.96	2.85
	Through <the PET>, I would always be informed of whether and how the intelligent environment recognizes me	2.72	2.51
	Thanks to <the PET>, I could determine myself whether or not I'll interact with the intelligent environment	2.49	2.44
Helplessness	I could imagine that if the intelligent environment set out to scan me, it would be able to do so despite <the PET>	1.57	1.53
	Eventually <the PET> will not be able to effectively protect me from being read by the intelligent environment	1.92	1.78

Note: 1 = Full agree, 5 = do not agree at all.

13.6 Conclusion

The current article documents the development of three scales that are able to measure people's perception of control over being accessed when moving in RFID-enabled environments and having a PET to protect their privacy. Control is measured with a view to whether people feel informed and are able to use the PET. Furthermore, loss of control is considered by the degree of helplessness perceived by users. When researchers of UC today conceive technologies that impact people's privacy, they may want to test whether the environments they envision induce a positive feeling of control. The scales presented here may serve this purpose. The two factors relating to ease-of-use and information control especially could be used as design guidelines for UC developers.

Applying the control scales to two PET scenarios envisioned by UC scholars show that both of them do not win people's trust. More precisely, they do not induce a feeling of control and, thus, privacy. Since they are broadly the most prevalent PET options for RFID technology thought of today, this may cause designers of RFID technology to potentially rethink the marketability of the privacy processes they currently envision.

References

[1] Mattern, F. "The Vision and Technical Foundations of Ubiquitous Computing." *Upgrade* 2, 5 (2001): 2–6.

[2] Weiser, M. "The Computer for the 21st Century." *Scientific American,* September 1991, 94–104.

[3] Altman, I. *The Environment and Social Behavior: Privacy, Personal Space, Territory, Crowding.* Monterey, CA: Brooks/Cole, 1975.

[4] Schoeman, F. *Philosophical Dimensions of Privacy.* Cambridge, U.K.: Cambridge University Press, 1984.

[5] Margulis, S. "Privacy as a Social Issue and Behavioral Concept." *Journal of Social Issues* 59, 2 (2003): 243–61.

[6] Smith, J. H., Milberg, S., and Burke, S. "Information Privacy: Measuring Individuals' Concerns about Organizational Practices." *MIS Quarterly* 20, 2 (1996): 167–96.

[7] Boyle, M. "A Shared Vocabulary for Privacy." Paper presented at the Fifth International Conference on Ubiquitous Computing, Seattle, WA, 2003.

[8] Juels, A., Rivest, R., and Szydlo, M. "The Blocker Tag: Selective Blocking of Rfid Tags for Consumer Privacy." Paper presented at the 10th Annual ACM CCS, Washington, D.C., May 16, 2003.

[9] Langheinrich, M. "A Privacy Awareness System for Ubiquitous Computing Environments." Paper presented at the 4th International Conference on Ubiquitous Computing, UbiComp2002, Göteborg, Sweden, September 29–October 1, 2003.

[10] Engels, D., Rivest, R., Sarma, S., and Weis, S. "Security and Privacy Aspects of Low-Cost Radio Frequency Identification Systems." Paper presented at the First International Conference on Security in Pervasive Computing, SPC 2003, Boppard, Germany, March 2003.

[11] Engberg, S., Harning, M., and Damsgaard Jensen, C. "Zero-Knowledge Device Authentication: Privacy and Security Enhanced Rfid Preserving Business Value and Consumer Convenience." Paper presented at the Second Annual Conference on Privacy, Security and Trust, Fredericton, New Brunswick, Canada, October 13–15, 2004.

[12] Spiekermann, S., and Berthold, O. "Maintaining Privacy in Rfid Enabled Environments—Proposal for a Disable-Model." In *Privacy, Security and Trust within the Context of Pervasive Computing*, P. Robinson, H. Vogt and Wagealla, W. Eds., Vienna, Austria: Springer-Verlag, 2004.

[13] Bellotti, V., and Sellen, A. "Design for Privacy in Ubiquitous Computing Environments." Paper presented at the 3rd European Conference on Computer Supported Cooperative Work ECSCW'93, Milan, Italy, 1993.

[14] Spiekermann, S., and Ziekow, H. "Rfid: A 7-Point Plan to Ensure Privacy." Paper presented at the 13th European Conference on Information Systems (ECIS), Regensburg, Germany, 2005.

[15] Skinner, E. "A Guide to Constructs of Control." *Journal of Personality and Social Psychology* 71, 3 (1996): 549–70.

[16] Seligman, M.E.P. *Helplessness: On Depression, Development, and Death.* San Francisco: Freeman, 1975.

[17] Abramson, L.Y., Seligman, M.E.P., and Teasdale, J.D. "Learned Helplessness in Humans." *Journal of Abnormal Psychology* 87, 1 (1978): 49–74.

[18] Langer, E. *The Psychology of Control.* Beverly Hills: Sage Publications, 1983.

[19] Heckhausen, H. *Motivation and Action.* Berlin: Springer-Verlag, 1991.

[20] Fiske, S., and Taylor, S. *Social Cognition.* New York: McGraw-Hill, 1991.

[21] Rodin, J. "Control By Any Other Name: Definitions, Concepts and Processes." In *Self-Directedness: Cause and Effects Throughout the Life Course*, J. Rodin, C. Schooler, and K.W. Schaie, Eds., 1–15. Hillsdale, US: Erlbaum, 1990.

[22] Bandura, A. "Human Agency in Social Cognitive Theory." *American Psychologist* 44, 9 (1989): 1175–84.

[23] Davis, F. "Perceived Usefulness, Perceived Ease of Use, and User Acceptance of Information Technology." *MIS Quarterly* 13, 3 (1989): 319–34.

[24] Venkatesh, V. "Determinants of Perceived Ease of Use: Integrating Control, Intrinsic Motivation, and Emotion into the Technology Acceptance Model." *Information Systems Research* 11, 4 (2000): 342–65.

[25] Inoue, Y. "Rfid Privacy Using User-Controllable Uniqueness." Paper presented at the RFID Privacy Workshop, Massachusetts Institute of Technology, Cambridge, MA, February 2004.

[26] Floerkemeier, C., Schneider, R., and Langheinrich, M. "Scanning with a Purpose — Supporting the Fair Information Principles in Rfid Protocols." In *Ubiquitous Computing Systems. Revised Selected Papers from the 2nd International Symposium on Ubiquitous Computing Systems*, H. Murakami,

H. Nakashima, H. Tokuda, and M. Yasumura, Eds., Tokyo, Japan: Springer-Verlag, 2004.

[27] Churchill, G., and Iacobucci, D. *Marketing Research: Methodological Foundations*: 8th ed. Southwestern College Pub, Mason, OH, 2001.

[28] Rohrmann, B. "Empirische Studien Zur Entwicklung Von Antwortskalen Für Die Sozialwissenschaftliche Forschung." *Zeitschrift für Sozialpsychologie* 9 (1978): 222–45.

PRIVACY IN UBIQUITOUS COMPUTING

Chapter 14

RFID: Technological Issues and Privacy Concerns

Pablo Najera and Javier Lopez

Contents

14.1 Introduction 286
14.2 RFID Technology Applications 288
14.3 Threats to Anonymity and Privacy 290
    14.3.1 A Double-Edged Sword.................................... 290
        14.3.1.1 No Tag Presence Awareness 290
        14.3.1.2 No Reader Presence Awareness 290
        14.3.1.3 Silent Readings 290
        14.3.1.4 Line of Sight 290
        14.3.1.5 ID Disclosure and Public Identification 290
        14.3.1.6 Unique Identification.......................... 291
        14.3.1.7 Global Database 291
        14.3.1.8 No Human Intervention........................ 292
        14.3.1.9 Lifetime 292
    14.3.2 Privacy Threats 292
        14.3.2.1 Product Information Leakage 292
        14.3.2.2 Association 292
        14.3.2.3 Individual's Tracking 293
        14.3.2.4 Corporation's Privacy Threat.................. 293

14.3.3 Organizations Position on RFID 294
14.3.4 Real-Life Scenarios 295
14.4 Technology-Based Solutions 296
14.4.1 Security Mechanisms in Actual RFID Standards.......... 296
14.4.1.1 Kill Command 297
14.4.2 Proposed Solutions 298
14.4.2.1 Out-of-Tag Privacy Mechanisms 298
14.4.2.2 Noncryptographic Tags 299
14.4.2.3 Tags with Cryptographic Circuits 301
14.5 Policy and Legal Solutions... 301
14.5.1 Fair Information Practices 302
14.6 Conclusions 304
References.. 304

14.1 Introduction

RFID (radio frequency identification) is a type of automatic identification system: Portable tags that are stuck on any kind of product (clothes, smartcards, currency) transmit data wirelessly to readers, which are often connected to computer networks, facilitating the transfer of data to databases and software applications that process the data according to the needs of a particular use.

The data stored by the tag may provide identification or location of the product it is attached to, or specific characteristics about the product tagged, such as price, color, or date of purchase.

As can be seen in Figure 14.1, a basic RFID system consists of two main components:

1. Tag: Attached to or embedded in the object to be identified. It typically contains a coupling element so that it can communicate with readers and an integrated circuit used to manipulate and store the data.
2. Reader: The device that communicates with tags and is able to read or write their memories. It contains an antenna and a control unit to manipulate the data and is connected to a communication network to transfer a tag's identity and data to the central system.

There are two kinds of tags: *passive* and *active*. The passive tags lack an independent power source and need to harvest energy from the reader's signal before they can communicate with it. Their range of readability is quite reduced (up to distances of five meters). An example of a Gen2 UHF passive tag is shown in Figure 14.2. The *active* tags have onboard batteries that dramatically increase their read range and functionality.

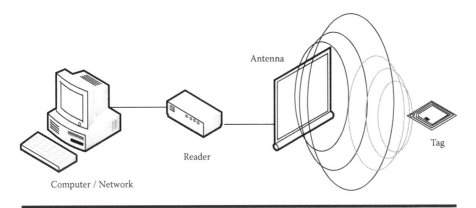

Figure 14.1   Diagram of a basic RFID system.

The most typical data that a tag stores is a code to uniquely identify the physical object it is attached to. Since passive tags (the most widespread type of tags) can only work in presence of a reader, they store the data that a reader writes onto it or the data that was originally stored at the factory. Such information is usually limited to basic aspects of the object. The reading of a tag usually lasts a fraction of a second, and its storage capacity ranges from no memory to 128 kilobytes of data.

There is a wide variety of RFID systems that work on nearly any frequency range from LF (e.g., automobile immobilizer systems) to microwave (e.g., toll collection systems), but leading applications work in HF (e.g., contactless smart cards) and UHF (e.g., supply chain management).

As barcodes, RFID tags can provide product identification, and due to this fact, they are often said to be a new and improved generation of barcodes. However, there are some important differences between barcodes and RFID tags. While barcodes are identical for every unit of the same product, RFID tags provide for unique identification of each tagged unit. Also, their storage and capacity for interactive communication and their read/write capability make them much more powerful. The ability to perform nonline of sight reading at production speeds is one of its best advantages.

Figure 14.2   Alien Technology Gen2 EPCGlobal tag based on UHF frequency.

Tags implement low to moderate security features like memory write protection and basic encryption schemes. As for the price, it depends on their functionality and sophistication. While tags with advanced security measures, as those used in bank applications, have an approximate value of ten Euros, most typical tags with basic features used in supply chain and logistics cost a few Euro cents.

14.2 RFID Technology Applications

Based on essential developments in technology, such as the transistor, the integrated circuit, and communication networks, RFID technology appeared during the second half of the twentieth century. The first RFID [1,2] use was in the 1960s, when Checkpoint Systems and Sensomatic were founded and began developing the Electronic Article Surveillance (EAS) equipment to counter theft. It could detect the presence or absence of a tag attached to an object, but it could not determine the identity of the tag. After that, in the 1970s both the private and public sectors were involved in RFID technology. During this decade, applications for factory automation, and animal and vehicle tracking came up. The 1980s were a decade of different RFID implementations around the world. While in Europe the main interest was in short-range systems for animal and industrial applications, in the United States, transportation, personnel access, and animal tracking were of interest. During the 1990s, different systems for electronic toll collection proliferated in the United States, which allowed vehicles be driven without having to stop at toll collection points.

The beginning of the twenty-first century is becoming the breaking point for RFID technology development, where international standards are being finally set and cost is rapidly decreasing, showing a promising future for technology adoption. One of the leading applications of this technology is said to be in supply chain management [3], providing automation to the warehouse and manufacturing process. Thanks to RFID, it is possible to track trailer and merchandise shipments from suppliers to stores. This technology helps to streamline the receiving/check-in process, tracking trailers and associated merchandise, and providing visibility at any point. This improves customer experience through out-of-stock reductions, as well as benefiting retailers in reducing on-hand inventory and less use of "safety stock." It also increases potential for sales generation, inventory visibility, and internal inventory management, and increases store, manufacturing, and distribution operational efficiency. It even reduces shrink and theft in the supply chain due to the enhanced control of the goods.

The technology also can help customers through easier identification on recalls and on high-cost goods, using it for warranty information or for software upgrades, and it can also be used to reverse the supply chain (if a product is returned, the tag can be used to track the product to supplier for repair and resale or for destruction). Improved product selection and freshness of dated goods are also other useful advantages.

Most product identification uses require a unique code stored in the RFID tag. These codes are managed by EPCglobal [4]. EPCglobal, which was formed in November 2003, is a joint venture of the Uniform Code Council (UCC) and EAN International. Taking the Electronic Product Code (EPC) from its development at the MIT Auto-ID Center to the global marketplace, its mission is to create global standards for the EPCglobal Network.

However, there is a wide variety of application areas other than in the supply chain management that benefit from the wireless identification provided by RFID systems. These predominant application types include electronic payment (at banks, mass transportation, or by means of automatic toll collection systems), access control systems (controlling building access or implemented as automobile immobilizers), animal tracking, and prevention of counterfeiting.

One of the emerging fields where RFID technology is being widely implemented is in the medical field. RFID tags fit into many healthcare scenarios [5], for example, in tasks such as detecting pill expiration dates or preventing mismedication. The information provided by the tag can identify the expiration date of a product, and the software that receives the data from the reader can check it with the actual date and issue a warning if it is wrong. Also, using the identification data of the medicine, the reader can query a database about contraindications and instructions, and warn the doctor of potential problems. With the aid of larger readers, it can be used in hospital to find doctors or a chart at any given time. It can be a useful tool in assessing medical school students and, in the long term, help doctors and nurses proactively through their jobs. Thanks to the tracking ability that RFID technology provides, it is possible to infer Activities of Daily Living (ADL), including dispensed medication, which can help doctors in supervising their patients. It is also being used in test tube tracking, ensuring accuracy and tube identification, and protecting patient safety.

The range of options that RFID offers for tomorrow's uses is endless: smart appliances, refrigerators that automatically create shopping lists, closets that tell you what clothes you have available and searching the Web for advice on current styles, aids for the physically and cognitively impaired, environmental care, and recycling help, such as plastics that sort themselves, and so on. However, not every use of RFID provides an advantage to clients or citizens, and important privacy and anonymity threats are on the rise with the use of this new technology.

14.3 Threats to Anonymity and Privacy

14.3.1 A Double-Edged Sword

RFID is a promising technology whose ability to provide automatic identification in nearly any scenario is revolutionizing many industrial fields. However, it has several features that working together can turn it into a double-edged sword and threaten privacy and civil liberties. Below, we analyze these features.

14.3.1.1 No Tag Presence Awareness

Current miniaturization level allows the manufacture of RFID tags embedded in any object type without being noticed. Integrated circuits' size is comparable to a grain of salt, and antennas that need a few square centimeters surface can now be printed with conductive ink, making them nearly imperceptible. As a result, product owners may not be aware of the tag's presence.

14.3.1.2 No Reader Presence Awareness

RFID readers can be installed invisibly in all kinds of objects as well as embedded in walls, doorways, floor tiles, carpeting, vehicles, roads, sidewalks, furniture, etc. Some manufacturers also distribute handheld devices with readers integrated or in Compact Flash format.

14.3.1.3 Silent Readings

Due to lack of contact needed to read tags, they can be accessed from a distance in a virtually silent and invisible way because humans cannot sense RF radiation. Therefore, readings can be performed without an individual's knowledge or consent.

14.3.1.4 Line of Sight

With RFID, direct line of sight is not required to identify and access data stored in a tag. As a consequence, private items kept out of view (i.e., in a wallet, pocket, backpack, or car trunk) are not protected against an evil reader.

14.3.1.5 ID Disclosure and Public Identification

Prior to any reader tag data transmission, the RFID label needs to be recognized, therefore, its unique code is sent to the reader. Even if a tag implements security measures or a cryptographic co-processor (which is not present in EPC tags used in consumer products), they usually provide authentication and encryption for the tag's stored data reading and writing once the tag's identification has been completed. Accordingly, any (authorized or unauthorized) reader can obtain the tag's electronic code. If no security features are implemented (as in ISO/IEC 15693 tags with no on-board encryption or authentication and only optional protection on write command), even stored data can be accessed and modified.

14.3.1.6 Unique Identification

A tag's electronic code is a globally unique ID number (except for ISO 11784 and ISO 11785 tags used in animal tracking, where serial numbers can collide). A label's ID does not provide identification at product-type level (i.e., barcodes), but it does at item level. Consequently, data inferred from a positive identification surpasses owner's anonymity.

14.3.1.7 Global Database

EPC provides a unique link to individual product data. The data is stored in the object name service (ONS), a globally distributed, but centrally managed, electronic database. Tag readers in remote physical locations can connect to the ONS via the Internet to read and modify the item's ONS dossier throughout its lifecycle. From a query to the EPC network, using a tag's serial number it is possible to know the manufacturer and product type that the serial number identifies. Due to the nature of RFID tags, the number does not identify only the product type, but identifies it as a unique item.

A specific reader not only would be able to identify tags that belong to its own database, but, due to the worldwide standard of identification codes managed by EPCglobal, it would be possible to identify any tag that a person would be carring if he is near enough (i.e., which products he has, even if they are inside a bag; when they were bought and how much they cost).

This multi-identification ability is not a dream according to Jack Grasso from EPCglobal, "Companies would 'join the EPCglobal universe,' which means they would get an identification number, and they would have access to the network where all of the codes would be stored." This system is already at work. Candidates for associating with the tag (in EPCglobal database or in particular databases) include date of purchase, name of the individual, date of sale, price of the sale, warranty, and many other possibilities.

Even the company that manages this database is not completely trustworthy: Verisign was chosen to manage the name service due to its similarity with the domain name service (DNS), for which it had already provided some top-level domains. In 2003, Verisign used its control over DNS servers to promote their own services, redirecting mistyped URLs during Web browsing, an activity that meant a lawsuit from Internet Corporation of

Assigned Names and Numbers (ICANN). E-mail servers were also redirected to their own servers, which implied a potential risk for consumers' privacy.

14.3.1.8 No Human Intervention

Detection and identification of tags in a reader's perimeter is triggered automatically. Also, data processing and database updating can be made without the need of any human intervention. Due to this fact, the amount of data that can be automatically gathered for subsequent data mining increases noticeably. At the same time, the chance to be under observation in any circumstance is remarkably higher.

So, an RFID infrastructure that identifies, compiles, stores, and analyzes the vast amounts of data generated as tagged products make their way from factory to the point of sale and, perhaps, beyond could be deployed [6].

14.3.1.9 Lifetime

In contrast to active or battery-assisted tags that require an external power source with a maximum lifetime of ten years, passive tags operate with no power source (gathering reader's radiation) and contain no mechanical parts offering a virtually unlimited operational lifetime. Therefore, an item embedded with a live RFID tag can be tracked during its entire life span.

14.3.2 Privacy Threats

Due to the particular aspects of RFID technology, a wide range of potential privacy and anonymity threats appear for both individuals and organizations. They are analyzed below.

14.3.2.1 Product Information Leakage

Without a security mechanism to conceal a tag's ID, any unauthorized reader can obtain its unique electronic code. In the case of an EPC code, the EPCglobal product info database can be queried all around the world to know the connection between the tag and the product. It does not contain information about the owner, but allows a reader to know the manufacturer and product type. If the tag provides no protection on the read command (authentication protocol or password-based access), not only the identity, but data stored in the tag also can be compromised.

Added to no line of sight requirements technology offers a stranger a kind of x-ray vision to identify items an individual is wearing or carrying. In a classical example, a thief could target victims based on their belongings.

14.3.2.2 Association

RFID tags are embedded in items to allow objects' automatic identification, but these unique IDs can also be associated with their owners' identity (e.g., at checkout) causing a privacy threat. Associations between users and tagged objects created by organizations or governments could cause future problems or inconveniences to items owners. Consumers may not be aware of the tag embedded in the object or that their identity has been associated with it. As a result, the owner could get rid of the object without destroying the tag first or requesting to update the databases. If any dishonest act is performed when carrying these objects in the future, the original owner would be under suspicion. Keeping track of which objects contains tags and which databases link these items with their identities would be a heavy burden for consumers, if even possible.

14.3.2.3   Individual's Tracking

Because tagged objects contain a globally unique identifier, virtually un-limited operational lifetime and permanent association between tags and owner, an individual can be tracked based on his possessions. As a consequence, the following threats arise:

- *Location information:* If a product ID is uniquely associated to an individual (i.e., tagged items like shoes, glasses, or wallets), it is possible to track the person's movements and obtain his physical location. In fact, it is not necessary that an individual carries the same RFID tag all of the time to establish his electronic identifier, not even if the tagged objects he uses belong to him exclusively. An individual's electronic signature can be derived from the cloud of tags usually carried by him. The identification of some tags related to the set would denote an individual's presence.
- *Individual's profiling:*   Linking item-level data on the tag with per-sonally identifiable information generates a risk of creating a com-prehensive infrastructure for individual profiling. Consumer profiles can be generated by means of compiling and analyzing informa-tion provided by working tags. Tracking a person's movements over an extended period would allow organizations to determine which products a consumer purchases and make inferential assumptions about a consumer's lifestyle, income, health, and buying habits. For instance, a retailer may use the purchase database going beyond po-lite uses and rank individuals based on previous purchase history. At shop entrance, consumers would be silently identified, restricting customer support to valuable clients.

14.3.2.4   Corporation's Privacy Threat

Not only individuals, but any entity related with RFID can suffer from privacy threats [20] derived from controversial technology applications.

As a side effect of using RFID in the supply chain and stores, organizations can suffer industrial espionage. Readers strategically placed and hidden by competitors (e.g., readers concealed at a shop entrance and supply doors) could gather data about product flow, inferring internal business operation knowledge, such as stocks, rate of sales, or consumer profiles and preferences.

Another threat that is not a privacy threat, but a potential attack is due to the nature of RFID technology where radio frequency signals can be easily jammed. In fact, this jamming procedure is one of the options to protect consumer privacy, but used by dishonest third parties can cause malfunctioning or even render the network nonfunctional. Such kind of denial-of-service attack oriented to a business infrastructure could cause big losses.

In conclusion, tagged items can be easily tracked at business levels to infer internal operation of organizations. In addition, tags can be associated with personally identifiable information to provide tracing of individuals and profiling of consumers. Due to these dishonest uses of the technology, potential threats for abuses of consumers' data and the privacy of individuals arise providing individual tracing and consumers' profiling creating a potential for abuses of consumer data and individual privacy.

14.3.3 Organizations Position on RFID

Perhaps killing RFID tags attached to consumer products once the products are sold would reduce privacy threats, but there is evidence that shows that companies are not interested in killing them [7].

Wired magazine wrote in April 2004 [8] that "P&G and other companies suggested they want to keep RFID tags active after checkout, rather than disabling them with so-called 'kill machines.' The companies also want to match the unique codes emitted by RFID tags to shoppers' personal information," reporting on statements made by Sandy Hughes in Chicago at the RFID Journal Live conference.

According to Wal-Mart, the United States' largest retailer, "Consumers may wish to keep RFID tags on packaging to facilitate returns and warranty servicing," so individuals may not be able to choose whether they want to keep live tags on their purchased products or not without sacrificing reliable customer support.

Privacy advocates even argue that forcing companies to kill tags would not give an assurance that it has been really done. According to CASPIAN [9] in its Position Statement on Use of RFID on Consumer Products [10], "Stores would only pretend to kill a tag, when in reality they would make it dormant and then later reactivate it to track you." Also, Cedric Laurent, from EPIC [11] said that "government would prevent stores from killing them, thereby creating a surveillance society."

People in favor of RFID technology have stated that the privacy community has intentionally exaggerated the threats to privacy to stop RFID rollout. Much of what privacy advocates warn will happen is already standard practice in commerce with few or no privacy or consumer issues occurring.

Meeting the concerns of the privacy advocates is not cost-free, and because RFID is only in its initial stages, it is obvious that legislation and regulation is premature as of yet, but, examining the results of a survey carried out by the Direct Marketing Association, which found out that nowadays 62 % of companies gather personal information without telling customers, and 75 % use customers' personal data without asking permission, we can conclude that the threat really exists.

14.3.4   Real-Life Scenarios

There are already several examples that prove that companies are using RFID technology or analogous devices to track customer behavior without warnings. The Path Tracker system is a good example of this. Path Tracker records the coordinates of a shopper from the time they enter the store and select their shopping cart until checkout. Each shopping cart is fitted with an emitter that sends a uniquely coded signal to an array of antennae every four seconds. Using state-of-the-art technology, the path taken and stops made (location and duration) become a database for each shopper who is tracked. In addition, every actual purchase made can be tied to the specific shopper's path, allowing analysis on a specific brand and item level. All kind of stores are now using this technology (i.e., Wal-Mart Stores, Best Buy, CompUSA, and Office Depot).

Another brand that has already used RFID technology in a controversial application is Gillette. At the MIT Auto-ID Center, the razor manufacturer developed an RF-enabled shelf that was oriented to theft prediction and deterrence. The smart shelf detected when inventory had been reduced or gone below a threshold and triggered a hidden camera to take close-up photographs of the shopper's face suggesting a possible theft in progress. A second picture was taken as the person paid for the razors at checkout. After testing the monitoring system at a British Telco store, Caspian launched a boycott campaign against Gillette products [12].

A similar experiment was conducted by Wal-Mart and Proctor & Gamble [13]. They embedded RFID tags in Max Factor Lipfinity products and mounted cameras near the shelves to keep watch on costumers and to track lipsticks leaving the shelves. A sign at the display alerted customers that closed-circuit television and electronic merchandise security systems were in place in the store.

Therefore, it is obvious that RFID raises security problems, most of them based on tracking of personal information and loss of anonymity and privacy. A situation described by Barry Steinhardt, director of the American

Civil Liberties Union Program on Technology and Liberty, shows a man walking around the city stopped in front of a sex shop for a moment to look at the curious items in the store windows. The shop is equipped with a radio customer identification system based on chips in credit cards. A few weeks later the man receives at his home advertisements of sex material. This scenario is not so unlikely.

14.4 Technology-Based Solutions

14.4.1 Security Mechanisms in Actual RFID Standards

A wide range of RFID systems are available nowadays to fulfill the needs of each type of application depending on users' needs. Features include attenuation from water resistance, minimum read range, improved read accuracy, fast read rate, low tag's cost, or high-security features. As a result, a variety of RFID product categories have been defined, such as passive, active, semipassive, or semiactive, based on different frequency ranges (i.e., LF, HF, UHF, or microwave) that implement particular onboard features.

Each RFID standard has being focused on a different set of requirements and implements a particular trade-off between tag's characteristics, performance, and security features. In fact, security mechanisms such as encryption or authentication, on the one hand, increase the tag's cost and latency of read and write processes, and, on the other hand, reduce onboard storage capacity and the number of tag reads per second.

Most of the RFID standards include security features [14] to provide some level of confidentiality or integrity. Mechanisms used to provide confidentiality include password protection on read commands (e.g., ISO/IEC 18000-3), tags addressed by random numbers (e.g., EPC Class 1 Gen 2, ISO 11784-11785 and 10536), masked reader to tag communications (e.g., EPC Class 1 Gen 2 and ISO 10536), "reader-talks-first" protocol (e.g., ISO/IEC 18000-2 and 18000-3), and "quiet mode" (ISO 18000-3, 11784-11785, and 10536). Integrity is addressed by means of protection on write commands (e.g., ISO/IEC 18000-3 Mode 2, optional in ISO 15693) and CRC error detection.

A particularly noteworthy example addressing security issues is the ISO 14443 designed for proximity smart cards that includes cryptographic challenge-response authentication and triple-DES, AES, and SHA-1 algorithms. These proximity cards have been used in environments such as gas stations, public transport services, and banks as a contactless payment method. Most commercial cards belong to proprietary specifications based on the standard, such as Philips' Mifare or Calypso family products. The recent adoption of the ePassport, an internationally accepted Machine Readable Travel Document (MRTD), is based on the International Civil Airation Organization (ICAO) standards that specify the use of the ISO 14443.

Countries such as Germany, Holland, Belgium, and the United States have started issuing these electronic passports containing RFID tags. Unfortunately, secret keys needed to access information on the RFID chips are derived from basic personal information (passport holder's birth date, passport number, and expiration date) that can be read from the data page or hacked [15], enabling a way to clone ePassports [16].

EPC standards apply to supply chain and logistical applications. Main design goals focus on low tag cost and fast read rate. As a result, EPC tags lack the computational resources to implement strong cryptographic encryption or authentication. EPC Class 0 and EPC Class 1 Generation 1 tags did not implement any security feature to provide privacy protection. Due to the tag-sorting protocol used in Gen 1, which is based on a binary tree algorithm, Generation 1 required the transmission of an entire tag's EPC code (96 bits) in order for readers to singulate a unique tag before communication begins. Therefore, identification and tracing on EPC Gen 1 tags is possible, raising several privacy threats. EPC Generation 2 uses a new tag-sorting protocol called "Q" algorithm that does not require the communication of an entire tag code over the air until secure communication is established. Instead, a pair of randomly generated numbers is used for tag singulation. This approach prevents eavesdropping data by a third-party device on tag-reader communications, although it does not address direct EPC code identification requesting. EPC Generation 2 specifications are being adopted in ISO standardization as ISO 18000-6c.

Most privacy threats are caused by unauthorized readers being able to identify RFID tags, even if they are not able to access the data stored inside. At the same time, most security features implemented in tags today focus on authentication schemes to prevent read, write, or lock commands on a tag's memory and provide encryption once the tag has been singulated and identified. In fact, readers usually need to know the tag's ID in order to select the right keys or password. Actual standards lack from the definition of a coherent key management infrastructure designed for environments full of RFID tags. Consequently, real-life applications resort to the use of the same password for all the tags or weak and predictable ones (e.g., ePassports). This inappropriate security architecture entails poor protection to organizations and individual's privacy.

Several privacy-protection schemes have been proposed to prevent RFID tag identification from unauthorized devices. The range of approaches extends from out-of-tag mechanisms to tags with lightweight cryptographic circuits, all the way up to basic tags with simple modifications.

14.4.1.1 Kill Command

EPCglobal standards approach, which provides permanent consumer's privacy protection, does not require any advanced security framework or onboard cryptographic circuits. It uses a simple, but effective solution—killing the tag. The kill command is a function that must be implemented in EPC tags that allows permanently deactivating a tag. It can be used at the point-of-sale preventing any malicious (or legitimate) applications. To execute a successful kill command, a weak 8-bit password is used for EPC Class 1 Gen 1 tags; however, a tag locks out after several incorrect queries. In EPC Class 1 Gen 2, a stronger 32-bit password is necessary.

At first sight, this scheme can provide complete consumer privacy protection, but there are some drawbacks. First, privacy is not protected until the tag is deactivated; thus, it does not address organizational privacy threats or in-store tracking. Second, it is a manual process that adds a burden to shop assistants or consumers; some proposals suggest the placement of kiosks in stores where individuals could deactivate their tags, but this could leave a high ratio of live RFID tags due to unaware customers. Third, deactivating the tags avoids any further legitimate use of them as envisioned by ubiquitous computing environments, home automation systems, or future post-sale services. In the field of emerging services based on live RFID tags, due to the lack of an appropriate key management infrastructure, the same password is usually required to kill any tag used in identical applications, opening a gap for a kind of permanent denial-of-service attack.

14.4.2 Proposed Solutions

14.4.2.1 Out-of-Tag Privacy Mechanisms

ID disclosure can be avoided without modifying a tag's design. Thus, in normal tag operations, its specifications remain the same (e.g., privacy protection does not suppose any alteration of read rate speed or onboard storage capacity) and the most appealing factor, cost of the tag, is not changed. Two main approaches remain in this category.

14.4.2.1.1 Faraday Cage

This solution appears to block the output from a tag by means of an enclosure that avoids the establishment of any reader–tag communication. Metal materials and water that come in contact with or in the proximity of a RFID tag can attenuate radio frequency waves shielding it against any unauthorized reading. Sensitive level depends on the frequency range. For example, UHF tags in contact with a human body cannot be read, but HF tags are still functional. ePassports issued in some countries, such as the United States, are adopting this shielding solution by embedding a web of metal fibers in the front cover so that passports cannot reveal their presence, at least until they are physically opened. In this scheme, individuals need to ensure that a Faraday cage is protecting every RFID tag they own in order to be "safe." So, in most scenarios, this is not a practical solution and human error is possible. Finally, it also blocks any ubiquitous computing application.

14.4.2.1.2   Active Jamming

Based on the same idea as the Faraday cage, a device, in this case, is used to broadcast a signal that prevents unauthorized readers from accessing the RFID tag.

- *Blocker tag.* A noteworthy example is the blocker tag scheme [17], an RFID tag that identifies itself with all possible tag IDs, thus avoiding a malicious reader knowing which tags are really present. The classic blocker tag implementation takes advantage of the tree-sorting protocol used to singulate a tag. Using this algorithm, a reader needs to travel across the binary tree of a tag's codes (where each leaf represents an entire tag's ID and intermediate nodes correspond to an identifier prefix). At the root's state, no bit prefix of any present RFID tag is known; therefore, the reader asks for the first bit value of the tags in the reader's perimeter. From this point on, a recursive search is conducted based on tags' responses. A blocker's tag strategy is to broadcast both values for each reader's request, simulating that all possible tags are present. Under these circumstances, the reader would get hung up trying to scan the complete tree. A selective blocker tag would only disrupt a reader's search if it goes deep into a predefined subtree, for instance, a privacy zone.
- *Soft blocking* [18]. Instead of misleading a reader's search, a soft blocking alternative approach leans to warning the reader about the presence of private tags, thus requiring the reader to give up the search. In order to achieve this, a special prefix that identifies "blocker tags" could be defined and commercial readers' firmware would need to be tested to carry out the policy. The threat of a rogue reader would always exist.

Any of these active jamming solutions entail the same drawbacks suggested for the Faraday cage approach—they add a burden on individuals and suffer from scalability problems.

14.4.2.2   Noncryptographic Tags

In most proposed privacy schemes [19,20], tags themselves need to provide specific features in order to prevent unauthorized identification by third-party readers. At the same time, these solutions do not avoid tag identification and communication with legitimate readers, solving one of the problems of out-of-tag solutions.

- *Tags with rewritable memory* [21–24]. At a minimum requirement level, tags that only implement rewritable memory can be used without needing any onboard cryptographic circuit. In this scenario, tags store encrypted versions of their serial numbers preventing third-party readers from knowing their real IDs. As static encrypted serial numbers can also be traced by malicious devices, the legitimate readers are in charge of refreshing the encrypted serial number versions as often as possible. A central server accessible by the authorized devices is queried to obtain decrypted versions of tag IDs and, optionally, a new encrypted ID to update a tag's memory. Thus, servers are a critical infrastructure resource and can turn into a bottleneck. Since a tag's encrypted ID can be traced until it is refreshed, the level of privacy protection achieved depends on the frequency of update. On the positive side, low-cost tags can be used.

- *Tag pseudonyms* [23]. This solution can be seen as an improved version of the previous one. In this case, a tag contains not one, but a set of pseudonyms or encrypted versions of the original ID and implements a policy for pseudonym selection. Each time a tag's identifier is requested, one from the set is provided, thus making it harder to trace a real tag's identity for unauthorized readers. In a hostile environment, an insistent reader could obtain all available pseudonyms by repeating the identification process multiple times. To prevent this, the pseudonym selection policy could use a kind of time control before cycling pseudonyms. Unfortunately, passive tags lack onboard clocks. As in the previous solution, updating the set of alternative IDs as often as possible improves the security level.

- *Tags with antenna energy analysis* [25]. In this case, a tag tries to guess which readers are legitimate based on the quality of the signal received. For this distinction, two special considerations are made. First, an unauthorized reader usually queries the tag from a longer distance than does an authorized one. Second, signal-to-noise ratio increases as the reader gets closer to the tag. Based on this, a tag can measure this value and decrease the amount of information provided as the reader gets farther away (such as providing a generic product type instead of its unique identifier code). Although this approach is error-prone, it can be implemented as a complement to other solutions.

- *Password checking tags.* In order to provide any private data, including its unique electronic code, a tag could request a password from the reader. At a negligible cost, this solution could provide privacy protection because onboard circuitry that is needed to check a password is inexpensive. This scheme is already being used in some implementations to control read/write operations on data stored in the tag, but it does not address ID disclosure: A reader needs to know a tag's identity in order to provide the right password. As a workaround, in controlled contexts where every tag could be programmed to share the same secret key (e.g., a consumer's home), ID publication could also be addressed by this scheme.

14.4.2.3 Tags with Cryptographic Circuits

In this category, tags are equipped with cryptographic circuits to perform onboard operations, such as encrypting their IDs. The implementation of cryptographic primitives may have a negative impact on other tag's specifications (as has already been commented on) as well as increase the tag's cost. Envisioned applications of RFID technology require tagging products at item level regardless of the cost. As a result, a tag's price needs to be nearly zero-cost. For these reasons, only minimalist and lightweight cryptographic operations are acceptable on most RFID tags. Instead of static encrypted versions of stored electronic codes, as provided by rewritable memory tags, these tags can perform their own encryption functions and generate dynamic identifiers, which avoids tracking from malicious readers.

■ *Hash-chain scheme* [26]. A noticeable example is the hash-chain scheme where two hash functions are implemented in the tag. Hash functions are known for meeting cryptographic properties as preimage resistance (known h) the tag also contains rewritable memory that stores the last key used to generate a new identifier. The secret key s is shared with a central server that knows the link between the key and the real ID. The first hash function G is used to generate the next identifier based on the actual key s (the output value is broadcast to the reader), while the second has h function H is used to update the key (the output value overwrites the last key in memory). Even if the secret value is hacked, due to the one-way nature of hash functions, the past tag history is not compromised.

14.5 Policy and Legal Solutions

Technological solutions alone may not be enough to alleviate privacy threats that arise by radio frequency identification. It is necessary to mitigate possible abuses by means of regulations and law.

It is known that individuals value anonymity and do not trust companies to administer personal data, and fear both private sector and government abuses of privacy. Also, users want to know how their personal information is collected, used, and with whom it is shared.

According to an American survey, the public considers opt-in (the principle that a company must have the consumer's permission prior to gather or use personally identifiable information) as one of the most important privacy rights. Laws must ensure that unscrupulous companies do not take advantage of the ability of RFID technology to identify customers and produce interesting data by means of spy readings of tags the company owns. Companies need to be forced to follow a set of "fair-play" guidelines that ensures that evil uses of RFID do not take place [27]. A good starting point in the regulation of the use of personal information is the use of the U.S. Fair Information Practices.

14.5.1 Fair Information Practices

In 1972, the U.S. Department of Health Education and Welfare proposed a Code of Fair Information Practices in a report on Automated Personal Data Systems, exploring the impact of computerized record keeping on individuals. These principles were the basis for the Privacy Act of 1974 that recommended a series of information practices to protect the use of personal data addressing issues of privacy and accuracy. These principles have been widely accepted and are the basis for many privacy laws in the United States, Canada, Europe, and other parts of the world. All of these documents share five core principles of privacy protection: awareness of data recopilation, consent, access, integrity and data security, and, finally, remedy.

In 1980, the OECD (Organization for Economic Cooperation and Development) rearticulated the Fair Information Practices in its Guidelines for the Protection of Privacy and Transborder Flows of Personal Data [28] as a set of eight principles, which cover the collection of data, security, data quality, and use limitation. These principles have been used as the baseline for evaluating data protection and privacy initiatives.

Specific guidelines that consider the unique aspects of RFID have been derived from Fair Information Practices and OECD principles. In 2002, Simson Garfinkel authored "An RFID Bill of Rights" [29] as a framework of guidelines that companies could voluntary and publicly adopt. In 2003, Caspian introduced the "RFID Right to Know Act of 2003" [31], a proposed legislation to mandate labeling of RFID-enabled products and consumer privacy protections. In 2004, Electronic Privacy Information Center (EPIC) rearticulated Fair Information Practices as guidelines [30] that guide the use of RFID technology to protect consumer privacy from private enterprises and enterprise interests at the same time.

According to these guides, Table 14.1 illustrates practices that companies must follow in order to mitigate possible abuses of privacy.

EPIC guidelines (Table 14.2) also establish the requirements that must be satisfied if personal information is collected and associated with tag data.

Nowadays, state of laws protecting personal information is not homogeneous all around the globe. In particular, Europe has enacted two data

Table 14.1   Industrial Practices to Mitigate Possible Abuses to Privacy

Practice Issue	Description
Consent	Individual's written consent should be obtained before associating any personal data with RFID tags
RFID system presence	Any tagged item or location equipped with readers should be clearly identifiable by means of labels or logos; information displayed should reference the nature of the system and be easily understood
Removal	Individuals should decide if they want live tags in the products they own, so tags must be attached in a way that they can be easily removed or permanently deactivated by the customer
Reading awareness	Any reading activity must be clearly identifiable through a recognized signal (i.e., a tone or light); individuals must know when tags are being read, by whom, and why
No coerce	RFID-enabled services should be accessible without RFID tags; in particular, customers should not be forced to keep tags for the benefits of warranty tracking
Data access	Personally identifiable data collected through an RFID system should be accessible to the individual including tag's data and information stored in databases
Data association	Corporations should not link personal information with tag's data if there are alternatives that achieve the same goal
Profiling or tracking	Tagged items should not be used to create a customer's profile by obtaining individual shopping habits or tracking location

Table 14.2   Requirements for Personal Data Collection and Association According to EPIC Guidelines

Requirement	Description
Purpose	Prior to obtaining consent, individuals must be informed of the purpose of the data association
Use limitation	Data should not be used out of the original scope and kept only as long as is necessary
No third-party disclosure	Data should not be disclosed to third parties
Data quality	Data used in approved applications must be kept accurate and updated
Security	Appropriate security measures must be used in data transmission, storing, and accessing
Openness	Policies and practices applied to RFID systems must be easily accessible for individuals

protection directives (in 1995 [32] and 2002 [33]) that defend individuals against personal information processing by adopting the Fair Information Practices with modifications. Therefore, controversial applications of RFID technology, such as association of data with personal identification or individual tracking, are already regulated and involve a number of data protection obligations. The directives grant data subjects a series of important rights including the right of access to personal data, the right to know where data originated, and the right to withhold permission to use the data. In particular, location data requires consumer's permission prior to collecting or using information; without consent, data should be anonymous.

Consequently, the development of technical measures that prevent privacy abuses and the establishment of regulations that ensure consumer rights is a must.

14.6   Conclusions

It is possible that potential risks and abuses arisen by RFID technology have been exaggerated by privacy advocates. However, alarms and suspicions raised have helped in preventing potential problems and treating them during the technology development phase. They are being considered during the design of new standards that include security measures to alleviate privacy threats. Measures to control privacy threats created by this technology need to be understood both in technology and legal ways, but citizens must also be informed, to warn them about possible troubles that this technology can cause, without generating an irrational alarm and fear that can curb the development of this promising technology.

Nevertheless, an irrational fear of possible consequences due to technology adoption in our lifetime could cause massive consumer rejection that would hamper further technology development or force tags to implement excessive security measures incompatible with the tag's purpose and target scenario (e.g., high-cost tags or crippled features, such as reduced operational reading distance or speed). Privacy threats caused by this emerging technology are a reality, therefore a trade-off allowing for an adequate and safe use of RFID is necessary.

References

[1]   Jeremy Landt, "The History of RFID," *IEEE Potentials*, Oct/Nov, 2005, 8–11.
[2]   Cedric Laurent, Workshop comment on "Radio Frequency Identification: Applications and Implications for Consumers," Electronic Privacy Information Center, Washington, D.C., 2004.

[3] Wal-Mart RFID presentation, *FTC RFID Conference*, Washington, D.C., June 21, 2004.

[4] EPCglobal homepage: http://www.epcglobalinc.org/ Accessed in January 2007.

[5] Ken Fishkin, "RFID for Healthcare: Some Current and Anticipated Uses," *Radio Frequency Identification: Applications and Implications for Consumers*, Washington, D.C., June 21, 2004.

[6] Declan McCullagh, "RFID Tags: Big Brother in Small Packages," Cnet News, January 13, 2003: http://news.com.com/2010-1069-980325.html

[7] Zombie Jo Best, "Zombie RFID tags may never die," ZDNet News, May 18, 2004: http://zdnet.com.com/2100-1103_2-5214648.html.

[8] Mark Baard, "Watchdogs Push for RFID Laws," http://www.wired.com/news/privacy/0,1848,62922,00.html

[9] CASPIAN (Consumers Against Super Market Privacy Invasion and Numbering) homepage: http://www.nocards.org Accessed in January 2007.

[10] CASPIAN, RFID Position Statement of Consumer Privacy and Civil Liberties Organizations, Privacy Rights Clearinghouse, San Diego, CA, November 20, 2003.

[11] EPIC (Electronic Privacy Information Center) homepage: http://www.epic.org/ Accessed in January 2007.

[12] Boycott Gillette campaign: www.boycottgillette.com Accessed in January 2007.

[13] WorldNetDaily, "Wal-Mart Used Microchip to Track Customers," November 15, 2003, http://worldnetdaily.com/news/article.asp?ARTICLE_ID=35629 http://worldnetdaily.com/news/article.asp?ARTICLE_ID=35629

[14] T. Phillips, T. Karygiannis, and R. Kuhn, "Security Standards for the RFID Market," *IEEE Security & Privacy*, 85–89, 2005.

[15] Harko Robroch, "ePassport privacy attack," *11th Annual Cards Asia*, Singapore, April 26, 2006, http://www.riscure.com/2_news/200604%20Cards AsiaSing%20ePassport%20Privacy.pdf

[16] Kim Zetter, "Hackers Clone E-Passports," http://www.wired.com/news/technology/0,71521-1.html

[17] A. Juels, R. Rivest, and M. Szydlo, The blocker tag: Selective blocking of RFID tags for consumer privacy, In Proceedings of the 10th ACM Conference on Computer and Communications Security, Oct. 27–30, 2003, ACM Press, New York, 103–111.

[18] A. Juels and J. Brainard, "Soft blocking: Flexible blocker tags on the cheap," Workshop on Privacy in the Electronic Society, ACM Press, New York, 2004, 1–7.

[19] M. Ohkubo, K. Suzuki, and S. Kinoshita, "RFID Privacy Sigues and Technical Challenges," *Communications of the ACM*, 48, 9, pp. 66–71, Sept. 2005.

[20] S. Garfinkel and A. Juels, "RFID Privacy: An Overview of Problems and Proposed Solutions," *IEEE Security & Privacy*, 34–43, 2005.

[21] A. Juels and R. Pappu, "Squealing Euros: Privacy protection in RFID-enabled banknotes," In Proceedings of Financial Cryptography, Gosier, Guadeloupe, Jan. 27–30, Springer-Verlag, Heidelberg, Germany, 2003.

[22] S. Kinoshita, F. Hoshino, T. Komuro, A. Fujimura, and M. Ohkubo, Low-cost RFID privacy protection scheme, *IPS Journal* 45, 8: 2007–2021 Aug. 2004 (in Japanese).

[23] A. Juels, "Minimalist Cryptography for RFID Tags," 4th Conf. Security in Comm. Networks, C. Blundo and S. Cimato, Eds., Springer-Verlag, Heidelberg, Germany, 2004, 149–164.

[24] P. Golle et al., "Universal Re-encryption for Mixnets," Proc. RSA Conference Cryptographer's Track, T. Okamoto, Ed., Springer-Verlag, Heidelberg, Germany, 2004, 163–178.

[25] K.P. Fishkin and S. Roy, "Enhancing RFID Privacy via Antenna Energy Analysis," IRS-TR-03 -012, Intel Research, Seattle, WA, 2003.

[26] M. Ohkubo, K. Suzuki, and S. Kinoshita, "A cryptographic approach to 'privacy-friendly' tags," RFID Privacy Workshop, Cambridge, MA, Nov. 15, 2003.

[27] Eduardo Ustaran, "Data Protection and RFID systems," *Privacy and Data Protection*, 3, 6–7, 2004.

[28] OECD Guidelines on the Protection of Privacy and Transborder Flows of Personal Data, OECD Publications Service, Paris, France, 2001.

[29] Simson Garfinkel, "An RFID Bill of Rights," *MIT Enterprise Technology Review*, October 2002, http://www.simson.net/clips/2002/2002.TR.10. RFID_Bill_Of_Rights.htm

[30] Epic, "Guidelines on Commercial Use of RFID Technology," Electronic Privacy Information Center, Washington, D.C. July 9, 2004.

[31] K. Albrecht and Zoe Davidson, "RFID Right to Know Act of 2003," CASPIAN, http://www.nocards.org/rfid/rfidbill.shtml

[32] Directive 95/46/EC of the European Parliament and of the Council, "Protection of individuals with regard to the processing of personal data and on the free movement of such data," October 24, 1995.

[33] Directive 2002/58/EC of the European Parliament and of the Council, "Directive on privacy and electronic communications," July 12, 2002.

Chapter 15

Privacy-Enhanced Location Services Information

Claudio A. Ardagna, Marco Cremonini, Ernesto Damiani,
Sabrina De Capitani di Vimercati, and Pierangela Samarati

Contents

15.1 Introduction 307
15.2 Basic Concepts and Scenario 309
    15.2.1 Positioning Systems 310
    15.2.2 Location-Based Services 312
15.3 Location Privacy 313
15.4 Techniques for Location Privacy Protection 314
    15.4.1 Anonymity-Based Techniques 315
    15.4.2 Obfuscation-Based Techniques......................... 318
    15.4.3 Policy-Based Techniques 320
15.5 Conclusions and Discussion 321
Acknowledgments 322
References 323

15.1 Introduction

In today pervasive environments, access to location information is achieved through a variety of sensor technologies, which recently enjoyed a relevant boost in terms of precision and reliability, and through the widespread diffusion of mobile communication devices. Location information is therefore becoming easily available and can be processed to provide services for business, social, or informational purposes [1]. In particular, location information allows the development of a new category of applications, generally called *location-based services* (LBSs), which use the physical position of individuals to offer additional services. For instance, customer-oriented applications, social networks, and monitoring services can be greatly enriched with data describing where people are, how they are moving, or whether they are close to specific locations. Several commercial and enterprise-oriented LBSs are already offered and have gained popularity [2,3]. However, despite the tremendous success of mobile computing, as witnessed by the exponential growth of advanced mobile devices like smart phones and handheld computers, location-based computing also brings a number of privacy concerns. It is not a surprise that personal privacy, which is already the center of many concerns for the risks brought by current online services [2,4], is considered seriously threatened by LBSs. Such concerns call for more sophisticated solutions for preserving the privacy of users when dealing with location information.

In addition, the publicity gained by recent security incidents that have targeted the privacy of individuals has focused the attention of the media and revealed faulty data management practices and unauthorized trading of personal information of users (including ID thefts and unauthorized profiling). For instance, some legal cases have been reported, when rental companies used GPS technology to track their cars and charge users for agreement infringements [5], or when an organization that used a "friend finder" service to track its own employees [6]. Furthermore, research on privacy issues has gained a relevant boost since providers of online and mobile services, often largely exceeded in collecting personal information as a requirement for service provision. In this context, the protection of location privacy of the users is today one of the hottest and most critical research topics.

Interestingly, privacy issues in online services have been analyzed from different perspectives and by several scientific disciplines. Many sociological studies of the privacy problem [2,7] have been conducted to reach a better understanding of the concerns perceived by users in adopting a location-based service. In particular, Barkhuus and Dey [2] present an experimental case analyzing location privacy concerns and how they are related to a service nature and characteristics. The study is focused on *location-tracking services*, where locations of users are tracked by third parties, and on *position-aware services*, where mobile and portable devices are aware of their own position. The result of this research, which examined a location-tracking service and a position-aware service, is that users perceived the latter as more respectful of their privacy and, therefore, were more likely to subscribe to it rather than to the location-tracking service. However, although location-tracking services are considered more critical with respect to privacy, they represent a promising application class that could have a large success, if users were provided with a simple and intuitive means to protect their location privacy.

From a technological point of view, most of the current research on LBS privacy focuses on providing anonymity or support for partial identities to online and mobile services that do not require the personal identification of a user for their provision [8–11]. Although important, anonymity or partial identification are not always viable options for the provision of online services [12,13]. To a certain extent, anonymity and complete knowledge of location information are the opposite endpoints of all possible degrees of knowledge of personal information bound to identities. Location information is just one class of personal information that sometimes can be associated with anonymous entities, but that often must be bound to user identity. When identification of users is required and, consequently, anonymity is not suitable, a viable solution to protect users privacy is to decrease the accuracy of personal information bound to identities [14–16]. For several online services, in fact, personal information associated with identities does not need to be as accurate as possible to guarantee a certain service quality. This is often the case of location-based information that, in many real applications, can be dealt with suboptimal accuracy levels while offering an acceptable quality of service to the final users.

In this chapter, we review the main techniques used for protecting the location privacy of users in online services. The remainder of this chapter is organized as follows. Section 15.2 discusses the basic concepts of current positioning systems and of location-based services. Section 15.3 provides an overview of the location privacy issues discussing different categories of location privacy that must be preserved depending on the scenarios and on the requirements. Section 15.4 presents some techniques that can be used to protect location privacy, analyzing their characteristics and applicability. Finally, Section 15.5 presents our conclusions and an outline of future research directions.

15.2   Basic Concepts and Scenario

Recent enhancements in positioning technologies have been fostering the development of many location-based services that guarantee a high quality of service in any environment. Figure 15.1 illustrates a typical scenario where a user submits a request to a location-based service and the service provider interacts with a positioning system to obtain the user location. Before analyzing the main location privacy issues, we review some of the existing positioning technologies and introduce some notable location-based services based on them.

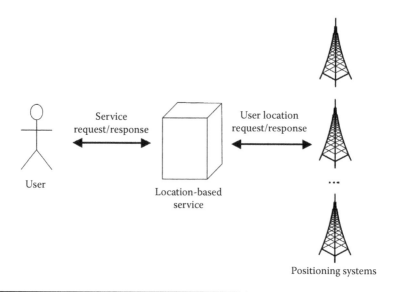

Figure 15.1 Basic scenario.

15.2.1 Positioning Systems

Positioning systems measure the location of users carrying mobile devices. Several location technologies (e.g., GSM/3G technology, GPS, WiFi, and RFID) have been developed to compute location information, each enjoying a relevant boost in terms of precision and reliability. Performance-related properties (e.g., quality of service) of a location service largely depend on the underlying technologies. Technologies like 802.11 WiFi and AGPS/GPS [17,18] can be exploited, even if their applicability is limited. WiFi, for example, has a limited coverage and its usage is restricted to indoor environments (e.g., buildings, airports, malls) and urban areas covered by hotspots. By contrast, GPS does not work indoors, or in narrow spaces; however, it has no coverage limitation, a feature that makes it an ideal location technology for open, outdoor environments.

The improved location capabilities of GSM/3G technologies and the widespread adoption of their mobile devices make GSM/3G positioning systems the most suitable technology for the delivery of services based on physical locations of users. For service provisioning, the location-based service collects the user location by querying one or more positioning systems. Today, most people always carry a mobile phone, a habit that makes it straightforward to gather their location position. Also, several location techniques have been studied and developed for achieving a good level of performance and reliability in any environment with few limitations.

Among the techniques used by GSM/3G technology for location purposes, the most important and already standardized are the following.

- *Cell Identification.* This is the simplest technique and is based on the identification of the mobile terminal serving cell. The spatial coordinates of the cell provide a broad estimation of a user position, which depends on the radius of the cell, where the radius can be between 200 m and 2.5 km. In urban areas, cells are much smaller than in the countryside.
- *Signal Level.* This measures the signal attenuation between the mobile terminal and the base station to calculate a user's position. Unless advanced and computationally heavy ray-tracing algorithms are used, the signal level technique is not well-suited for indoor or urban areas.
- *Angle of Arrival (AoA).* This assumes that more than one single base station for signal reception is available. A user's position can be calculated by computing the angle of arrival at two base stations. It should be noted, however, that if there is no line-of-sight between the mobile terminal and the base stations, the calculated angles do not correspond with the actual directional vector from the base stations to the mobile.
- *Time of Arrival (ToA).* This calculates the distance between a base station and a mobile phone by measuring the time for a signal to complete a round trip between the two endpoints. Signal arrival can be delayed by walls or natural obstacles, decreasing location accuracy.
- *Time Difference of Arrival (TDoA).* This computes the time difference between station-to-terminal propagation, with the purpose of increasing the location accuracy. It can be realized by measuring the differences of arrival time of a certain burst sent by the mobile to several base stations or by recording the time differences of impinging signals at the mobile.

Several papers describe and discuss different location technologies and the best accuracy that can be achieved [19, 20], observing, in particular, that technological improvements in positioning systems can reduce a location error to a few meters, regardless of the particular environment (e.g., urban, suburban, rural, outdoor, or indoor). This location accuracy of sensing technology, combined with the widespread diffusion of GPS, WiFi, and cellular phones, calls for an urgent and careful consideration of users privacy concerns. Such concerns are even more critical if we consider that user mobile devices are not able to define restrictions on location data scattering or to stop the data flow (unless the mobile devices are switched off). The worst-case scenario that some analysts have foreseen as a consequence of an unrestricted and unregulated availability of location technologies recalls the well-known "Big Brother" stereotype: a society where the secondary effect of location technologies, whose primary effect is to enable the development of innovative and useful services, is a form of implicit total surveillance of individuals.

15.2.2 Location-Based Services

The great amount of location information now available gives a considerable boost to location-based services development and deployment. The research efforts result in the definition of many location-based services for business, social, or informational purposes [21]. There are different types of location-based services, as listed below.

- *Nearby-Information Services.* These provide information about the environment surrounding the location of a user (e.g., point of interest, advertisement, or weather and traffic alerts). A user, after subscribing to these services, receives real-time information through a mobile device.
- *"Locate-Me" Services.* These give information about the position of users. They should be used when authorized third parties need to know positions of users. In particular, a locate-me service is well suited for location-based access control (LBAC) services that use the location of users to evaluate and enforce access requests submitted by the users themselves [22].
- *Tracking Services.* These offer information about user movements, such as her path when entering or leaving some areas, her velocity, direction, and so on. It could be used by online services that provide vehicles tracking, tracking of children or employees, warning about dangerous areas, and so on.
- *Locate-Friends and Nearby-Friends Services.* These give information to subscribers about the real-time location or proximity of other subscribers. They could be used, for example, to provide services in the context of social networks.
- *Personal-Navigator Services.* These provide information about the path that has to be followed to reach a target location from the current user's location. The services rely on tracking services to gather the position of a user moving on the field.

The cost of integrating location technologies in existing telecommunication infrastructures can be economically sustained by most companies. Many projects offering locate-me, locate-friends, tracking, personal-navigator, or nearby-information services have been developed. Examples of such projects are *"Teen Arrive Alive"* [23], *uLocate* [24], *CellSpotting* [25], and *Mologogo* [26]. In addition, many other services have been developed, for example, for touristic purposes, such as *Guide Project* [27] that provides tourists with context-aware tourist guides, for children, or for elderly safety [28].

To conclude this brief description of the main application areas that are currently exploiting location technologies, it is important to highlight that LBSs can be useful in critical contexts, where the availability of a precise location can help in protecting human live. For instance, operators, like the enhanced 911 in North America [29], can immediately dispatch emergency services (e.g., emergency medical services, police, or firefighters) where they are needed, reducing the margins of error.

15.3   Location Privacy

User privacy has been considered a fundamental right, internationally recognized in Article 12 of the United Nations Universal Declaration of Human Rights [30]. In particular, location privacy can be defined as the right of the users to decide how, when, and for which purposes their location information could be released to other counterparts. Location privacy receives much consideration due to the exponential availability of reliable location technologies and location-based services. In this context, privacy issues have gained great relevance only recently.

Failure in protecting the location privacy of users could be exploited by malicious users to enforce different attacks such as [31]:

■ Unsolicited advertising of products and services available nearby users position
■ Physical attacks or harassment
■ Users profiling and inferences of personal information, such as state of health, point of interests, hobbies, and so on

Location privacy can assume several meanings and pursue different objectives, depending on the scenario in which the users are moving and on the services with which the users are interacting. Location privacy protection can be aimed either at preserving the privacy of the user identity, the single user location measurement, or the location movement of the user monitored in a certain period of time. The following categories of location privacy can then be identified.

■ *Identity privacy.* The main goal is to protect users' identities associated with or inferable from location information. For instance, many online services provide a person with the ability to establish a relationship with some other entities without her personal identity being disclosed to those entities. In this case, the best possible location measurement can be provided to the others entities, but the identity of the users must be preserved.

■ *Position privacy.* The main goal is to perturb locations of the users to protect the positions of individual users. In particular, this type of location privacy is suitable for environments where users' identities are required for a successful service provisioning. An example of a technique that most solutions either explicitly or implicitly exploit consists of scaling a location to a coarser granularity (e.g., from meters to hundreds of meters, from a city block to the whole town, etc.).

■ *Path privacy.* The main goal is to protect the privacy of the users who are monitored during a certain period of time. The location-based services will no longer receive a single location measurement, but they will gather many samples allowing them to track users. In particular, path privacy can be guaranteed by adapting the techniques used for identity and position privacy to preserve the privacy of a user who is continuously monitored.

These categories of location privacy pose different requirements that are guaranteed by different privacy technologies, which we will analyze in the following section. Note that no technique is able to provide a general solution satisfying all the privacy requirements.

15.4 Techniques for Location Privacy Protection

With respect to the different categories of location privacy described in section 15.3, we describe the main location privacy protection techniques that can be classified as anonymity-, obfuscation-, and policy-based. In particular, anonymity-based and obfuscation-based techniques are dual categories. While anonymity-based techniques have been primarily defined to protect identity privacy and are less suitable for protecting the position privacy, obfuscation-based techniques are well-suited for position protection and less integrable with identity protection. Regarding path protection, both anonymity-based and obfuscation-based techniques are well-suited and able to provide the required degree of protection. Nevertheless, more studies and proposals have been focused on anonymity-based rather than on obfuscation-based techniques. Concerning policy-based techniques, at first sight, they can seem the most suitable solution because they are more flexible and, in general, well-suited for all the location privacy categories. However, policy-based techniques can be difficult to understand and manage for end users.

15.4.1 Anonymity-Based Techniques

An important line of research in location privacy protection relies on the notion of *anonymity* [8–11]. Anonymity typically refers to an individual, and it states that an individual (i.e., the identity or personally identifiable information of an individual) should not be identifiable.

Beresford and Stajano [8,32] propose a method called *Mix zones* that uses an anonymity service based on an infrastructure that delays and re-orders messages from subscribers within predefined zones. The Mix zone model is based on the concepts of *application zone* and *Mix zones*. An application zone represents homogeneous application interests in a specific geographic area, while a Mix zone represents an area where a user cannot be tracked. In particular, within Mix zones, a user is anonymous in the sense that the identities of all users coexisting in the same zone are mixed and become indiscernible. The Mix zone model is managed by a trusted middleware that lies between the positioning systems and the third party applications and is responsible for limiting the information collected by applications. Furthermore, the infrastructure makes a user entering the Mix zone unlinkable from other users leaving it. The authors also provide an analysis of an attacker behavior by defining and calculating the *anonymity level* assured to the users, i.e., the degree of privacy protection in terms of uncertainty. They show that the success of an attack aimed at recovering users identities is an inverse measure of the anonymity provided by the privacy service.

The authors argue that an attacker aiming to reduce the anonymity level within a Mix zone can determine the mapping between ingress and egress paths that exhibit the highest probability. It is also necessary to measure how the probability of the selected mapping varies when this mapping is compared with all the other possible mappings. The anonymity level is then calculated by measuring the level of *uncertainty* of the selected mapping between inbound and outbound paths. The uncertainty is computed through traditional Shannon's entropy measure [33]. If the entropy is equal to b bits, 2^b users are indistinguishable. Also, a lower bound to the level of anonymity of a user u is calculated as the level of anonymity provided by assuming that all users exit the Mix zones from the location that has the highest probability. To conclude, the Mix zones model is aimed at protecting long-term user movements while still allowing the interaction with many location-based services. However, Mix zones effectiveness is strongly dependent on the number of users joining the anonymity service and, in particular, on the number of users physically co-located in the same Mix zone at the same time.

Bettini et al. [9] discuss privacy issues raised by a location-based service scenario. Their paper proposes a framework able to evaluate the risk of sensitive, location-based information dissemination, and introduces a technique aimed at supporting *k*-anonymity [15,16]. The concept of *k*-anonymity tries to capture a traditional requirement followed by statistical agencies according to which the released data should be indistinguishably related to no less than a certain number (*k*) of users. Traditionally, *k*-anonymity is based on the definition of *quasi-identifier*, which is a set of attributes exploitable for linking. The *k*-anonymity requirement then states that each release of data must be such that every combination of values of quasi-identifiers can be indistinctly matched to at least *k* individuals.

The proposal in [9], therefore, puts forward the idea that the geo-localized history of the requests submitted by a user can be considered as a quasi-identifier that can be used to discover sensitive information about the user. For instance, a user tracked during working days is likely to commute from her house to the workplace in a specific time frame in the morning and to come back in another specific time frame in the evening. This information could be used to reidentify the user. In the framework proposed in [9], based on the concepts of quasi-identifier and historical *k*-anonymity, the service provider, which gather both the users' requests for services and the sequence of updates to users' locations, should never be able to link a subset of requests to a single user. To make this possible, there must exist *k* users having a personal history of locations *consistent with* the set of requests that has been issued. Intuitively, a personal locations history of a user is consistent with a set of service requests when, for each request, there exists a location in the personal history of locations where the user could have made the request. The kind of solution is highly dependent on the actual availability of indistinguishable histories of locations: If *k* indistinguishable histories do not exist, *k*-anonymity cannot be preserved. The worst case scenario is when a given user has a history different from all the others, meaning that the user cannot be anonymized and she is always identifiable.

Other works [10,11] are based on the concept of location *k*-anonymity, meaning that a user is indistinguishable by other *k* − 1 users in a given location area or temporal interval. Gruteser and Grunwald [11] define *k*-anonymity in the context of location obfuscation. They propose a middleware architecture and an adaptive algorithm to adjust location information resolution, in spatial or temporal dimensions, to comply with the specified anonymity requirements. To this purpose, the authors propose the concepts of *spatial* and *temporal cloaking* used to transform a user's location to comply with the requested level of anonymity. Spatial cloaking guarantees the *k*-anonymity required by the users by enlarging the area where a user is located until the area contains *k* indistinguishable users. The same reasoning could be applied to temporal cloaking, which is an orthogonal process with respect to the spatial one. Temporal cloaking could provide spatial coordinates with higher accuracy, but it reduces the accuracy in time.

The key feature of the adaptive cloaking algorithm is that the required level of anonymity can be achieved for any location.

Gedik and Liu [10] describe another *k*-anonymity model aimed at protecting location privacy against various privacy threats, and provide a framework supporting location *k*-anonymity. Each user is able to define the minimum level of anonymity and the maximum acceptable temporal and spatial resolution for her location measurement. A message perturbation engine provides location anonymization of request messages sent by users through identity removal and spatio-temporal obfuscation of location information. This engine is composed of four major components that process each incoming message: (1) the *zoom-in component* identifies all pending messages, (2) the *detection component* identifies the *k* messages that can be used in the anonymization process, (3) the *perturbation component* applies a perturbation algorithm on messages identified by the detection component and forwards the generated messages to the location-based service, and (4) the *expiration component* deletes all expired messages. The suitability of this method depends on the number of messages received by the location protection component, which is responsible for message perturbation, and on the message expiration. If the expiration timeout is too short, many messages will be dropped; if it is too long, many useless messages will be processed. A drawback common to all solutions based on *k*-anonymity is that their applicability and performances depend on the number of users physically located in a particular area.

Another line of research that relies on the concept of anonymity is aimed at protecting the *path privacy* of the users [34–36]. In particular, path privacy involves the protection of users that are continuously monitored during a time interval. This research area is particularly relevant for location tracking applications designed and developed for devices with limited capabilities (e.g., cellular phones), where data about users moving in a particular area are collected by external services, such as navigation systems, which use them to provide their services effectively. Gruteser et al. [34] propose a solution to path privacy protection by means of path anonymization. A path is anonymized by associating a pseudonym with a user's location. However, an attacker that gains access to this information is able to associate a path and a pseudonym with a single user by looking at path information, such as the place in which the user stays during the night. To the purpose of strengthening the anonymity, multiple pseudonyms, which change over time, can be associated with a single user. The authors also argue that it is difficult to provide strong anonymity for path protection because it would require the existence of several users traveling along the same path at the same time, an assumption that often cannot be satisfied in a real-world scenario. Hence, Gruteser et al. provide two techniques for weaker anonymity: *path segmentation* and *minutiae suppression*. With weaker anonymity, users could potentially be linked to their identities, but this requires huge efforts. Path segmentation partitions a user's path into a set of smaller paths, and at the same time changes the associated pseudonym. Path segmentation is usually implemented by defining a segment duration and mean pause. After the segment duration time, location updates are suppressed for the given pause period. Minutiae suppression suppresses instead those parts of a path that are more distinctive and could bring an easy association between a path and an identity. The suitability of these techniques is highly dependent on the density of users in the area in which the adversary collects location samples. In areas with low density of users, an adversary has a good likelihood of tracking individuals, whereas in areas with many overlapping paths, linking segments to identities can be extremely difficult.

Other relevant works consider path protection as a process whose outcome must be managed by a service provider. To this aim, privacy techniques also have to preserve a given level of accuracy to permit a good quality-of-service provisioning. Gruteser and Liu [35] present a solution based on the definition of a *sensitivity map* composed of sensitive and insensitive zones. The work defines three algorithms aimed at path privacy protection: *base, bounded-rate*, and *k*-area. The *base* algorithm is the simplest algorithm; it releases location updates that belong to insensitive areas only, without considering possible inferences made by adversaries. The *bounded-rate* algorithm permits the customization of location updates frequency to reduce the amount of information released near a sensitive zone and to make the adversary process more difficult. Finally, the *k*-area algorithm is built on top of sensitivity maps that are composed of areas containing *k* sensitive zones. Location updates of a user entering a region with *k* sensitive areas are temporarily stored and not released. If a user leaving that region has visited at least one of the *k* sensitive areas, location updates are suppressed, otherwise they are released. Experiments show that the *k*-area algorithm gives the best performance in terms of privacy, also minimizing the number of location updates suppression. Ho and Gruteser [36] introduce a path confusion algorithm. This algorithm is aimed at creating cross paths of at least two users. In this case, the attacker cannot recognize which path has followed a specific user.

In summary, anonymity-based techniques are suitable for all those contexts that do not need knowledge of the identity of the users.

15.4.2 Obfuscation-Based Techniques

Obfuscation is the process of degrading the accuracy of the location information to provide privacy protection. Different from anonymity-based techniques, the main goal of obfuscation-based techniques is to perturb the location information still maintaining a binding with the identities of users.

Duckham and Kulik [14] define a framework that provides a mechanism for balancing the individual needs for high-quality information services and for location privacy. The proposed solution is based on the *imprecision concept*, which indicates the lack of specificity of location information (e.g., a user located in Milan is said to be in Italy). The authors propose to degrade location information quality and to provide obfuscation features by adding n points, at the same probability, to the real user position. The algorithm assumes a graph-based representation of the environment. When a user accesses a service asking for proximity information (e.g., asking for the closest restaurant), her location is perturbed by releasing a set O of points containing the real user position. The service receiving the request calculates the query result that is returned to the user: in the best case the user receives a single response, in other cases, depending also on the degree of obfuscation, it could receive a set of closest points of interest. Duckham and Kulik [37] present some obfuscation methods that are validated and evaluated through a set of simulations. The results show that obfuscation can provide at the same time both high quality of service and high privacy level.

Other proposals are based on the definition of a gateway that mediates between location providers and location-based applications. Openwave [38], for example, includes a location gateway that obtains users location information from multiple sources and delivers it, possibly modified according to privacy requirements, to other parties. Openwave assumes that users specify their privacy preferences in terms of a minimum distance representing the maximum accuracy they are willing to provide. Bellavista et al. [39] present a solution based on a middleware that balances the level of privacy requested by users and the needs of service precision. The location information is then provided at a proper level of granularity depending on privacy/efficiency requirements negotiated by the parties. Hence, downscaled location information (with lower precision and lower geographical granularity) is returned instead of exact user positions. This solution only considers a context based on points of interest, and it relies on the adoption of symbolic location granularity (e.g., city, country, and so on), forcing the privacy level to the predefined choices.

In summary, although obfuscation-based techniques are compatible with users specifying their privacy preferences in a common and intuitive manner (i.e., as a *minimum distance*), they present several common drawbacks. First, they do not provide a quantitative estimation of the provided privacy level, making them difficult to integrate into a full-fledged, location-based application scenario [22]. Second, they implement a single obfuscation technique according to which obfuscation is obtained by scaling (i.e., enlarging) the location area. An issue that is often neglected by traditional location obfuscation solutions is the possibility of defining and composing different obfuscation techniques to increase their robustness with respect to possible de-obfuscation attempts performed by adversaries. Finally, they are meaningful in a specific application context only. With respect to the minimum distance specification, the value, "100 meters" is only meaningful when it is a good trade-off between ensuring a sufficient level of privacy to the user and allowing location-based applications to provide their services effectively. For instance, the value "100 meters" could be well suited to applications that provide touristic or commercial information to a user walking in a city center. By contrast, applications working in smaller contexts (e.g., inside an industrial department) are likely to require granularities much finer than 100 meters. Also, 100 meters can be largely insufficient for preserving user privacy in highly sensitive contexts.

15.4.3 Policy-Based Techniques

Another research field aimed at protecting location privacy is based on the definition of *privacy policies*. Privacy policies define restrictions that must be followed when the locations of users are used by or released to third parties.

Hauser and Kabatnik [40] address the location privacy problem in a privacy-aware architecture for a global location service, which allows users to define rules that will be evaluated to regulate access to location information. By means of these rules, a user can define the entities allowed to access her location data at a specified granularity level. The Internet Engineering Task Force (IETF) Geopriv working group [41] addresses privacy and security issues related to the disclosure of location information over the Internet. The main goal is to define an environment (i.e., an architecture, protocols, and policies) supporting both location information and policy data. Geopriv defines the Presence Information Data Format Location Object (PIDF-LO) [42] as an extension of the XML-based PIDF that provides presence information about a person (e.g., if a user is online or offline, busy or idle, away from communication devices or nearby). PIDF-LO is used to carry a *location object*, that is, location information associated with the privacy policies within PIDF. The Geopriv infrastructure relies on both *authorization policies* and *privacy rules*. Authorization policies pose restrictions on location management and access by defining conditions, actions, and transformations. In particular, a transformation specifies how the location information should be modified before its release, by customizing the location granularity (e.g., city neighborhood, country, and so on), or by defining the altitude, latitude, and longitude resolution. Privacy rules are instead associated with the location information and define restrictions on how the information can be managed. For instance, an authorization can state that a recipient is allowed to share a piece of location information that is associated with an expiration time.

Other works used the Platform for Privacy Preferences Project (P3P) [43] to encode users privacy preferences. P3P enables Web sites to define their privacy practices in an XML-based format, defining how data gathered from the counterparts will be managed (e.g., the purposes for which the information is collected, the retention time, and the third parties to whom the information will be released). A user then can check the privacy practices of the Web site she is visiting and, therefore, decide whether the data practices are compatible with her privacy preferences. Usually, the process of comparing user preferences and server practices is performed by agents. Although P3P is not intended to provide location privacy functionalities, it can be easily extended for this purpose. Hong et al. [44] provide an extension to P3P for representing user privacy preferences for context-aware applications. Langheinrich [45] proposes the *pawS* system that provides a privacy-enabling technology for end users. The pawS system allows data collectors, on the one side, to state and implement data-usage policies based on P3P, and, on the other side, to provide data owners with technical means to manage and check their personal information. Hengartner and Steenkiste [46] describe a method of using digital certificates combined with rule-based policies to protect location information.

In summary, policy-based techniques allow the definition of policies that simply can be adapted to the user's needs restricting the location management and disclosure. However, although the adoption of policies-based preferences is probably, from a privacy point of view, the most powerful and flexible technique, it can be very complex and unmanageable for end users. Often, users are not willing to directly manage complex policies and refuse participation in pervasive environments. Also, users remain unaware of the consequences of potential side effects in policy evaluation.

15.5 Conclusions and Discussion

Location privacy is a challenging research topic that involves both technological, legislative, and sociological issues. This chapter has described the technological context in which location privacy is increasingly becoming an important issue and whose management is critical for the diffusion of location-based services. Also, the chapter has presented the main techniques aimed at protecting location privacy in different contexts.

Several open issues still remain unsolved. A first requirement to be fulfilled in the near future is to find a privacy solution able to balance the need of privacy protection required by users and the need of accuracy required by service providers. Location privacy techniques, which are focused on users' needs, could make the service provisioning impossible in practice due to the excessively degradation of location measurement accuracy. A possible direction to avoid excessive degradation is the definition of an estimator of the accuracy of location information (abstracting from any physical attribute of sensing technology) that permits to quantitatively evaluate both the degree of privacy introduced into a location measurement and the location accuracy requested by a service provider. Both quality of online services and location privacy could then be adjusted, negotiated, or specified as contractual terms. A first solution to the definition of a formal estimator of location accuracy, in the context of obfuscation-based techniques, has been provided in [47,48]. The estimator, named *relevance*, is validated in the context of a privacy-aware location-based access control (LBAC) [22] that provides access control functionality based on user location information.

A second issue that calls for consideration is the dynamicity of location information that often is erroneously considered and treated as static information. However, location information changes over time and can be exploited to infer sensitive information of the users. The definition of solutions able to reduce the amount of inference provided by location information is a subject of growing research efforts [9].

A third aspect that needs to be considered is the development of techniques to determine and counteract possible attacks aimed at reversing location privacy techniques and retrieving original sensitive information. In fact, if an attacker can reduce the effects of location privacy techniques, the privacy guaranteed to the users is reduced. For instance, in location path anonymization, trajectories of users enable an attacker to follow users' footsteps by exploiting the high spatial correlation between subsequent location samples. *Multi-target tracking* (MTT) algorithms [49] are used to link subsequent location samples to users who periodically report anonymized location information. By contrast, location obfuscation by scaling the location area can be simply bypassed by reducing the area of a reasonable percentage depending on the context.

To conclude, location information represents an important resource that can be used in different environments and whose usage could offer huge benefits to online services. However, the possible indiscriminated disclosure of location information can evoke a scenario in which location data are abused. We can expect that future research will integrate existing location privacy techniques to provide a more flexible and powerful solution.

Acknowledgments

This work was supported in part by the European Union under contract IST-2002-507591, by the Italian Ministry of Research Fund for Basic Research (FIRB) under project RBNE05FKZ2, and by the Italian MIUR under project 2006099978.

References

[1] Varshney, U., Location management for mobile commerce applications in wireless internet environment. *ACM Transactions on Internet Technology*, 3(3): 236–255, August 2003.

[2] Barkhuus, L. and Dey, A., Location-based services for mobile telephony: A study of user's privacy concerns. In *Proc. of the 9th IFIP TC13 International Conference on Human-Computer Interaction (INTERACT 2003)*, pp. 709–712, Zurich, Switzerland, September 2003.

[3] D'Roza, T. and Bilchev, G., An overview of location-based services. *BT Technology Journal*, 21(1): 20–27, January 2003.

[4] Privacy Rights Clearinghouse/UCAN. *A Chronology of Data Breaches*, 2006. http://www.privacyrights.org/ar/ChronDataBreaches.htm

[5] *Chicago Tribune*, "Rental Firm Uses GPS in Speeding Fine" Associated Press: Chicago, Tribune, July 2, 2001, p. 9.

[6] Lee, J-W., *Location-tracing sparks privacy concerns.* Korea Times. http://times.hankooki.com, 16 November 2004. Accessed 22 December 2006.

[7] Colbert, M., A diary study of rendezvousing: Implications for position-aware computing and communications for the general public. In *Proc. of the International 2001 ACM SIGGROUP Conference on Supporting Groupwork*, pp. 15–23, Boulder, CO, September–October, 2001.

[8] Beresford, A.R. and Stajano, F., Location privacy in pervasive computing. *IEEE Pervasive Computing*, 2(1): 46–55, 2003.

[9] Bettini, C., Wang, X.S., and Jajodia, S., Protecting privacy against location-based personal identification. In Jonker, W. and Petkovic, M., Eds., *Proc. of the 2nd VLDB Workshop on Secure Data Management*, pp. 185–199, LNCS 3674, Springer-Verlag, Heidelberg, Germany, 2005.

[10] Gedik, B. and Liu, L., Location privacy in mobile systems: A personalized anonymization model. In *Proc. of the 25th International Conference on Distributed Computing Systems (IEEE ICDCS 2005)*, pp. 620–629, Columbus, OH, June 2005.

[11] Gruteser, M. and Grunwald, D., Anonymous usage of location-based services through spatial and temporal cloaking. In *Proc. of the First ACM/USENIX International Conference on Mobile Systems, Applications, and Services (MobiSys 2003)*, San Francisco, CA, May 2003.

[12] Hong, J.I. and Landay, J.A., An architecture for privacy-sensitive ubiquitous computing. In *Proc. of the 2nd International Conference on Mobile Systems, Applications, and Services (MobiSys 2004)*, pp. 177–189, Boston, MA, June 2004.

[13] Langheinrich, M., Privacy by design-principles of privacy-aware ubiquitous systems. In *Ubicomp 2001, Ubiquitous Computing, vol. 2201 of Lecture Notes in Computer Science*, pp. 273–291, Springer, Heidelberg, Germany, 2001.

[14] Duckham, M. and Kulik, L., A formal model of obfuscation and negotiation for location privacy. In Gellersen, H-W., Want, R., and Schmidt, A., Eds., *Proc. of the Third International Conference PERVASIVE 2005*, Munich, Germany, May 2005.

[15] V. Ciriani, S. De Capitani di Vimercati, S. Foresti, and P. Samarati. *Security in Decentralized Data Management*, Chap. K-Anonymity. Springer, Heidelberg, Germany, 2007.

[16] Samarati, P., Protecting respondents' identities in microdata release. *IEEE Transactions on Knowledge and Data Engineering*, 13(6): 1010–1027, 2001.

[17] Getting, I., The global positioning system. *IEEE Spectrum*, 30(12): 36–47, December 1993.

[18] Parkinson, B. et al., *Global Positioning System: Theory and Application, vol. II*, Progress in Austronautics and Aerounautics Series, V-164. American Institute of Astronautics and Aeronautics (AIAA), Reston, VA, 1996.

[19] Gustafsson, F. and Gunnarsson, F., Mobile positioning using wireless networks: Possibilities and fundamental limitations based on available wireless network measurements. *IEEE Signal Processing Magazine*, pp. 41–53, July 2005.

[20] Sun, G. et al., Signal processing techniques in network-aided positioning: A survey of state-of-the-art positioning designs. *IEEE Signal Processing Magazine*, pp. 12–23, July 2005.

[21] Hengartner, U., *Enhancing user privacy in location-based services*. Technical Report CACR 2006–27, Centre for Applied Cryptographic Research, 2006.

[22] Ardagna, C.A. et al., Supporting location-based conditions in access control policies. In Lin, F-C., Lee, D-T., Lin, B-S, Shieh, S., and Jajodia, S., Eds., *Proc. of the ACM Symposium on Information, Computer and Communications Security (ASIACCS'06)*, pp. 212–222, Taipei, Taiwan, March 2006.

[23] *Teen Arrive Alive*. http://www.teenarrivealive.com

[24] *uLocate*. http://www.ulocate.com

[25] *CellSpotting.com*. http://www.cellspotting.com

[26] *Mologogo*. http://mologogo.com

[27] Cheverst, K. et al., Experiences of developing and deploying a context-aware tourist guide: The guide project. In *Proc. of the 6th Annual International Conference on Mobile Computing and Networking (MOBICOM-00)*, pp. 20–31, Boston, MA, August 2000.

[28] Marmasse, N. and Schmandt, C., Safe and sound a wireless leash. In Cockton, G. and Korhonen, P., Eds., *Proc. of ACM Conference on Human Factors in Computing Systems (CHI 2003)*, pp. 726–727, Ft. Lauderdale, FL, April 2003.

[29] *Enhanced 911—Wireless Services*. http://www.fcc.gov/911/enhanced/

[30] General Assembly of the United Nations. "Universal Declaration of Human Rights." United Nations Resolution 217 A (III). December 1948.

[31] Duckham, M. and Kulik, L., *Location privacy and location-aware computing*. In Drummond, J., Billen, R., and Joao, E., Eds., *Dynamic and Mobile GIS: Investigating Change in Space and Time*, Taylor & Francis, Boca Raton, FL, 2007.

[32] Beresford, A.R. and Stajano, F., Mix zones: User privacy in location-aware services. In *Proc. of the 2nd IEEE Annual Conf. on Pervasive Computing and Communications Workshops (PERCOM 2004)*, pp. 127–131, Orlando, FL, March 2004.

[33] Shannon, C.E., A mathematical theory of communication. *Bell System Technical Journal*, 27(379–423): 623–656, July, October 1948.

[34] Gruteser, M., Bredin, J., and Grunwald, D., Path privacy in location-aware computing. In *Proc. of the Second International Conference on Mobile Systems, Application and Services (MobiSys2004)*, Boston, MA, June 2004.

[35] Gruteser, M. and Liu, X., Protecting privacy in continuous location-tracking applications. *IEEE Security & Privacy Magazine*, 2(2): 28–34, March–April 2004.

[36] Ho, B. and Gruteser, M., Protecting location privacy through path confusion. In *Proc. of the IEEE/CreateNet International Conference on Security and Privacy for Emerging Areas in Communication Networks (SecureComm)*, Athens, Greece, 2005.

[37] Duckham, M. and Kulik, L., Simulation of obfuscation and negotiation for location privacy. In Cohn, A.G. and Mark, D.M., Eds., *Proc. of the COSIT 2005*, pp. 31–48, Ellicottville, NY, September 2005.

[38] Openwave. *Openwave Location Manager*, 2006. http://www.openwave. com/

[39] Bellavista, P., Corradi, A., and Giannelli, C., Efficiently managing location information with privacy requirements in wi-fi networks: A middleware approach. In *Proc. of the International Symposium on Wireless Communication Systems (ISWCS'05)*, pp. 1–8, Siena, Italy, September 2005.

[40] Hauser, C., and Kabatnik, M., Towards privacy support in a global location service. In *Proc. of the IFIP Workshop on IP and ATM Traffic Management (WATM/EUNICE 2001)*, Paris, France, 2001.

[41] Geographic Location/Privacy (geopriv). September 2006. http://www. ietf.org/html.charters/geopriv-charter.html

[42] Peterson, J., *A Presence-based GEOPRIV Location Object Format*, December 2005. Request for comments (RFC) 4119. http://www.RFC-editor.org/rfc/ rfc4119.txt.

[43] W3C. *Platform for privacy preferences (p3p) project*, April 2002. http:// www.w3.org/TR/P3P/

[44] Hong, D., Yuan, M., and Shen, V.Y., Dynamic privacy management: A plug-in service for the middleware in pervasive computing. In Tscheligi, M., Bernhaupt, R., and Mihalic, K., Eds., *Proc. of the 7th International Conference on Human Computer Interaction with Mobile Devices and Services (MobileHCI'05)*, pp. 1–8, Salzburg, Austria, September 2005.

[45] Langheinrich, M., A privacy awareness system for ubiquitous computing environments. In Borriello, G. and Holmquist, L.E., Eds., *Proc. of the 4th International Conference on Ubiquitous Computing (Ubicomp 2002)*, pp. 237–245, Göteborg, Sweden, September 2002.

[46] Hengartner, U. and Steenkiste, P., Protecting access to people location information. In Hutter, D., Müller, G., Stephan, W., and Ullmann, M., Eds., *Proc. of First International Conference on Security in Pervasive Computing*, pp. 25–38, Boppard, Germany, March 2003.

[47] Ardagna, C.A. et al., A middleware architecture for integrating privacy preferences and location accuracy. In *Proc. of 22nd IFIP TC 11 International*

Information Security Conference (IFIP SEC2007), Sandton, Gauteng, South Africa, May 2007.

[48] Ardagna, C.A. et al., Managing Privacy in LBAC Systems. In *Proc. of the Second IEEE International Symposium on Pervasive Computing and Ad Hoc Communications (PCAC-07)*, Niagara Falls, Ontario, Canada, May 2007.

[49] Reid, D.B., An algorithm for tracking multiple targets. *IEEE Transactions on Automatic Control*, 24(6): 843–854, December 1979.

Chapter 16

Beyond Consent: Privacy in Ubiquitous Computing (Ubicomp)

Jean Camp and Kay Connelly

Contents

16.1 Introduction 327
16.2 Privacy: A Contested Value 328
16.3 Data Protection and Fair Information Practices.................. 329
16.4 Privacy as Autonomy 330
16.5 Alternative Concepts of Privacy 331
16.6 Privacy and Value-Sensitive Design 334
16.7 The Perfect Privacy Storm 336
16.8 Limits of Subject-Driven Design 338
16.9 Conclusions 339
Acknowledgments 340
References.. 340

16.1 Introduction

Privacy is a socially constructed value that differs significantly across environments and age cohorts of individuals. The impact of ubiquitous computing (ubicomp) on privacy will be the most intense in home-based healthcare. Value-sensitive design has the potential to make this transformational change less disruptive in terms of personal autonomy and individual boundaries by integrating privacy into ubicomp home health-care. Yet value-sensitive design must be predicated upon a shared concept of the particular value under consideration.

Currently, design for privacy in this space requires a user who under-stands the social implications of ubicomp technology, demands a design that respects privacy, and articulates specific technical design requirements. Design for pervasive privacy also requires a ubicomp designer with mastery of privacy-enhancing technologies, security mechanisms, and a complete understanding of privacy. Data protection and fair information practices require a transactional approach to data management, where users make discrete decisions about data flows that are then integrated. None of these is an adequate approach to the myriad problems in privacy in ubicomp. Nei-ther individual scientists nor individual citizens have the capacity to make such designs, nor can any person handle such intensity of transactions.

In this chapter, we provide a high-level overview of the competing con-cepts of privacy. We critique each of these concepts in terms of its appli-cability to the specific domain of home-based healthcare. We also critique privacy as constructed in home-based ubicomp systems, and in ubicomp systems that present themselves as privacy-enhancing. We introduce the strengths and weaknesses of value-sensitive design for the case of ubi-comp, particularly in the home. We enumerate the possible interactions between home-based ubicomp, various privacy regimes, and design for values.

We conclude that not only is no single theory of privacy applicable, but also that the knowledge of both the technology and the privacy risks is an unreasonable requirement for ubicomp designers. We argue that intimacy of the technology, the continuity of the data flow, and the invisibility of the risk in ubicomp limits the efficacy of data protection and fair information practices. Data protection must be augmented by more subtle mechanisms, and standards of care in privacy design should be developed before the Or-wellian default becomes an installed base. We propose that what is needed is not only a minimal set of best practices, but also a design process that is centered on the subject of the technology.

16.2 Privacy: A Contested Value

Ubicomp has the potential to serve the needs of the aging population, yet current trends in ubicomp design have yet to substantively address the in-herent privacy challenges. A reason for ignoring the privacy issue to date is that elders lose considerable privacy if they move into a nursing home, but relatively less privacy to ubicomp or other home healthcare technol-ogy [36]. It is likely when threatened with the loss of their independence, most elders will choose the lesser evil: The loss of privacy that comes with modern monitoring technologies.

Privacy versus ubicomp is a Hobson's choice.* The ubicomp projects in this area claim that technology will help family members decide when an elder must be moved to an assisted-living facility. So by definition, the technology is being introduced before the elder is faced with the above either–or choice. In addition, the technology is presented in its entirety, with potentially privacy-influencing design choices embedded and without the possibility of the participant's examination. As such, it is essential that research in this area address the issues of privacy surrounding sensing and monitoring technologies in the home.

Implementing value-sensitive design requires understanding of what a particular value (in this case, privacy) means in the design context [9,18]. The sheer complexity of understanding a value as amorphous as security, which is itself better specified than privacy, has been a serious difficulty in applying value-sensitive design [16]. There is no monolithic perspective on privacy. There are multiple stakeholders in any instantiation of ubicomp, particularly in healthcare. These include participants and the network of informal caregivers (typically family and friends), each perhaps with distinct and often competing conceptualizations of privacy. While some argue that disambiguation of privacy is required [7], we argue for assisting subjects to communicate using a full range of privacy conceptions.

In the following sections, we describe a subset of the current theories about the nature of privacy, and how these distinct views of privacy alter technical design. We will utilize these theories to a construct privacy framework.

16.3 Data Protection and Fair Information Practices

Data Protection and Fair Information Practices are widely accepted as the mechanisms by which privacy can be protected in practice. A popular evaluation is that when data is protected, privacy takes care of itself. In this section, we look at data protection and its interaction with ubicomp.

The earliest instantiation of privacy protection through careful information practices is based in the Code of Fair Information Practice. The Code was offered by the U.S. Office of Technology Assessment in 1986 and is a foundation on which subsequent data protection practices have been constructed. The Code (and the related data-protection requirements) has as its core transparency, consent, and correction.

---

* Hobson's choice: No choice at all; the only option being the one that is offered to you.

In terms of privacy, these generally are seen as a reasonable minimum. However, in the case of designing for home-based ubicomp, even the Code, which is far more simple than the European or Canadian data-protection regimes, is problematic. Transparency requires that no data compilation be secret. Consent includes not only the existence of data in sorted form, but also the uses of that data. Consent implies that data can be deleted or corrected when desired by the subject. However, in the case of home-based ubicomp, some combination of caregiver and care recipient action may be necessary. For example, individuals may attempt to hide any increase in impairment by deleting data or increasing filtering to the point where the data is no longer illustrative.

The capacity to alter data, included in the requirement that individuals are allowed to ensure data is correct, obviously has distinct implications when the data is stored locally and the individual may not perceive correct data as being in his or her own interest. Furthermore, the interpretation and, therefore, correction of medical data may require personnel about whom there are other privacy concerns.

16.4   Privacy as Autonomy

Privacy is a form of autonomy because a person under surveillance is not free. In the United States, Constitutional definitions of privacy are based on autonomy, not seclusion. These decisions have provided both sexual autonomy and, in the case of postal mail and library records, a tradition of information autonomy. (This concept of information autonomy was altered under the USA PATRIOT Act.)

In technical systems, privacy as autonomy is usually implemented as strong anonymity. Yet, in installations where there are medical providers, family members, and medical payment providers, anonymity will inevitably be limited. Clearly, with a browser button that says, "Where is Dad," the parent is not seeking anonymity from the monitoring adult offspring.

Autonomy requires the ability to act freely. Elements of autonomy include freedom of speech and freedom of religion, both of which are practiced in the home. Some data will inevitably provide religious information; for example the household that turns off all sensor data from Friday sunset to sunset Saturday is likely to be following the precepts of Orthodox Judaism. This then could be used to target the residents with customized frauds, or target the home for robbery during local Orthodox services.

Certainly, real-time videos showing meals will indicate any religion followed, given the distinct traditions of blessing mealtimes. In-home video-taping is not currently legally protected, as shown by the use of home video without subject consent on the television show *Shocking Events*. That show consists entirely of selections from private surveillance videos.

Autonomy also requires privacy in the right to association [43], and the right to read anonymously [14]. The right to association is explicitly threatened by those in-home surveillance systems that detect visitors, and alert monitors of portal interactions (e.g., door monitoring). Portal interaction monitoring is critical in home-based ubicomp to address the risk for senile, dementia suffering, or simply confused individuals who may wander from the home at considerable risk to themselves. Monitoring of entities in the house may also be needed, as otherwise functional elderly are disproportionately targeted for high-pressure scams or frauds.

There exists a minimal level of privacy that is required for physically vulnerable or frail individuals to maintain their autonomy, and even security. Identification of vulnerable individuals on the network as being vulnerable has the potential to significantly change their risk profile. Section 16.9 describes the risks and minimal response in more detail.

16.5   Alternative Concepts of Privacy

Autonomy is among the most infrequently used definitions of privacy. Autonomy is too subtle to be addressed via a single computational mechanism. There are a large set of alternatives, indeed one paper identifies as many as 16 different perspectives [40].

Privacy can also be considered a property right and, as such, control over privacy can yield economic advantage to select stakeholders [5,31]. For example, ubicomp that provides demographic information and, thus, enables price discrimination can violate this dimension of privacy. In this case, the data is economically valuable and, thus, centralized authorities will have economic incentives to share this data [34].

Privacy can be a right to seclusion—"the right to be let alone" [49]. Privacy as seclusion is the underlying theory of privacy tort rights. A constant video ubicomp environment would violate the right to seclusion, potentially even when the system allows for the preservation of anonymity. Consider, for example, ubicomp in a bathroom. Accurate depictions would violate privacy in the sense of seclusion even without the association of a unique name to any user. Yet ubicomp in such a location may be necessary in a home healthcare system; for example, the bathroom is a common location for falls. Some activities that need monitoring are necessarily (e.g., hygiene) or commonly (e.g., taking medication) localized to the bathroom.

Most often, privacy in ubiquitous computing is spatial, conceived of as an issue of boundaries [6,21,25,27]. Many ubicomp designers have adopted a concept of contested social spaces as articulated in the concept of privacy as process [3]. The idea of contested space is particularly useful in public spaces where there is an issue of privacy in public, often examined under the rubric of social privacy. As our area of focus is home-based ubicomp, social privacy plays a correspondingly smaller role, with the primary issue of social privacy being on data compiled on guests in the social area of a home.

The boundary concept strongly parallels the early work on regulation of speech on the Internet, in which legal and policy scholars disputed the nature of cyberspaces, e.g., [32,44]. In the academic realm, legal scholars have never overcome the historical definitions of privacy as four torts: intrusion, false light, publicity of private facts, and appropriation.

Intrusion upon seclusion is the intentional intrusion upon the solitude or seclusion of another, not an accidental wandering into a private space. The civil concept is also a criminal one in some states; for example, Stephanie's Law in New York, which prohibited "surreptitious surveillance without consent and disseminating and unlawful recording thereof," under New York Section Ch 29, Sec 8: 250. Civil remedies usually require the intrusion to be grossly offensive or extreme.

False light is defamation, whereby a person knowingly publishes incorrect private facts about another. Publicity of private facts is the most difficult to prove, as it only applies when the facts are not newsworthy and are not availably publicly in some manner. For example, there is a distinction between an assault in a public area as opposed to publicizing a matter in confidential records.

Appropriation is the privacy tort only available to the already famous. Appropriation is the use of a person's name, image, or likeness for commercial gain.

Publicity of private facts requires that there be some expectation of privacy and confidentiality; a design document that clarifies that expectation could be useful were the data from a ubicomp systems misappropriated. For example, the resale of video from home surveillance for entertainment is a very real threat of video-based ubicomp.

The use of privacy violations in civil court (e.g., under tort, not criminal law) is problematic. A tort normally has four elements: duty, breach, causation, and harm. In some cases, such as medical or commercial records, there is clearly a duty. But in other cases, establishing a duty is quite difficult, e.g., what is the duty of care for a grocer when he obtains medical and lifestyle information as a result of a frequent buyer card program? Breaches are far easier to prove now that 35 states have disclosure laws requiring that subjects of data be notified when there is a breach. However, causation and harm are both difficult to prove. Connecting a particular bit of fraud or identity theft to an individual loss of data is problematic.

In the policy realm, the physical space versus media type debate [13] was settled when Internet service providers obtained a safe harbor provision in the Digital Millennium Copyright Act. This safe harbor provision delineated appropriate Internet service providers (ISP) behavior with regards to copyright (a most troublesome modern speech/property conflict) and expression.

In both pervasive computing and the regulation of speech in digital realms, spatial metaphors are useful because of the potential power of the heuristic. Spatial metaphors offer great subtlety. Like the speech debate, the spatial ubicomp privacy discourse has integrated issues of social, natural, and temporal spaces [27]. Again, mirroring the speech debate, ubicomp researchers are finding that while spatial metaphors offer insight, they offer little practical design guidance.

One way of conceptualizing the privacy differences between virtual and physical spaces is essentially the nature of the boundaries that divide them. Virtual boundaries are distinct in three dimensions: simultaneity, permeability, and exclusivity [11]. Simultaneity refers to the ability of a person to be two places at once: at work and at a train ticket booth. Permeability is the capacity of information and communications technologies (ICTs) to make spatial, organizational, or functional barriers less powerful or even invisible. The permeability of the work/home barrier is most clearly illustrated with telecommuting. Exclusivity, in contrast, is the ability of ICTs to create spaces that are impermeable, or even imperceptible, to others. Intranets may offer exclusive access through a variety of access control mechanisms, and the creation of databases that are invisible to the subjects clearly illustrates the capacity for exclusivity. In the physical sphere, the walled private developments offer an excellent example of exclusivity, yet it is not possible to make physical spaces so exclusive as to be invisible. Technologies redefine the nature of space, and digital networked technologies alter the nature of boundaries [37].

Different technologies implement different concepts of privacy. Making the concept(s) of privacy that are embedded into privacy-enhancing technology explicit can assist the subjects of ubicomp systems define their own privacy requirements; for example, the Zero-Knowledge System (ZKS), a privacy services company that offered complete data privacy even from the servers at the company itself. ZKS offered autonomy through anonymity and required trust only in the underlying technology, while iPrivacy concentrated trust in its corporate parent [12]. ZKS allowed people to participate with cryptographically secure pseudonyms. Onion routing as implemented in Tor (an anonymous Internet communication system) enables individuals to obtain limited anonymity by obscuring the IP address of a subject originator from any node knowing the destination and the destination from any node knowing the originator. The privacy implications of a particular sensor might vary according to the application and environment, with the designer and the subjects bringing their own subtleties to an understanding of privacy.

16.6 Privacy and Value-Sensitive Design

Value-sensitive design is a method whereby an initial design is accompanied by a values statement, which guides the choices of privacy-enhancing technologies and documents privacy implications during the development. The values statement is explicitly not a software development impact statement [22] because, while values choices can be made in design, value choices can also emerge during use.

Design for values as a method embeds explicit values choices, documents those choices, and thus, enables adoption and alteration of technologies to be explicit choices made in a larger social context. Design for values is not exclusively technologically deterministic.

The technologically deterministic [15,30], socially constructed [17], and dynamic iterative [26] models of technological development have clear parallels in, respectively, the technical, preexisting, and emergent models proposed for computing systems in design for values [20].

Technical bias is that which is inherent in or determined by the technology. Preexisting bias is that bias which has been previously socially constructed and is integrated into the technology. Emergent bias develops as a system and is used and developed in a specific social context. The goal in value-sensitive design is not to create omniscient designers, but rather ethical design (within the designers informational space) that enhances social discourse about any specific technological artifact.

In other cases, innovative security work expands the options in ubicomp, but in doing so creates a new set of risks. For example, one design for security in ubicomp is the mother duckling model [41]. In this model, a device is imprinted by a central device upon initiation (waking) and responds only to that device, as a duckling is imprinted by its mother. The ability to reinitialize a device (e.g., resurrect a duckling) creates some security risks through denial of service via resource exhaustion. Such a denial-of-service attack may be particularly problematic in a medical monitoring system where reliability concerns may trump security concerns. In one situation, it may be better for a device to fail and the failure brought to the attention of a responsible party than to risk device hijacking by reinitialization. In another situation, it may be better for there to be a loss of privacy than a loss of functionality, so security risks are rejected over resource loss.

In fact, some work on security in ubicomp has been in direct opposition to privacy [10]. For example, in one design, the addition of access control to location systems concentrated data rights by creating a centralized authority. This removed the right of the individual to control his or her own information by having institutional policies apply to individuals, and having spatial policies that override personal policies. Indeed, the potential privacy and personal security threats are exacerbated in this system because the individual requesting data is anonymous while the person whose location information is provided is both identified and incapable of knowing when he or she is identified [23]. By implementing a narrow concept of centralized access control as security, this system has increased exposure of personally identifiable information, prohibited opt-out, and decreased individual autonomy. The stated goal of these designers was to add security, so that control could be increased. Yet ignoring privacy resulted in a mutual-surveillance panopticon.*

Privacy by design, as in the Cricket system, enables both location services and individual privacy [38]. In this case, the location offers relevant information that can be requested by users. The only authorization required is physical location. Therefore, by using verifiable assertion of location, the location service can determine the authorization required for data access, and the default is anonymity of the party requesting information. In this case, the data is public (e.g., relative location, available nearby services, such as food). The individual is able to access information based on the relevant information (i.e., location) without losing privacy. The Cricket system implemented an autonomy model of user interaction where users could be anonymous and still access data. The Cricket designers did not use an explicit value-sensitive design approach, but did effectively and explicitly design to value privacy.

Privacy and security are obviously aligned in the case of confidentiality. In terms of medical information and monitoring, privacy can also enhance the integrity of data. At Indiana University, the dietary intake monitoring application (DIMA) projects [39] illustrate that self-reported data can result in more reliable data than daily self-recall. In this case, handheld devices were used by a population with diabetes and with low computer literacy. When the details of consumption were private, e.g., not provided to health providers or any other party, the subjects were more forthcoming with information.

Fear of censure or even loss of benefits can encourage misuse or subversion of ubicomp. By providing minimal high-level medical data (e.g., one's use of insulin) rather than detailed behavioral data (e.g., had a milkshake and waffles, thus required insulin), subjects may be more cooperative. More cooperative subjects can result in data that is more reliable, and more effective technology. Privacy can enhance data reliability in pervasive computing by aligning technology with the interests of the patients.

While there is no known predictable method for making an absolute assertion about the privacy implications of a given default in a particular feature for a generic system, clearly predictions can be made about the potential for privacy violations created in a particular technology [8,28].

---

* Panopticon: An area where everything is visible.

Although much research on privacy is applicable to ubiquitous computing and there are nearly 150 privacy-enhancing technologies on the market, as well as many tens of innovations submitted every year to the Privacy Enhancing Technologies Workshop, there has been almost no work on examining these issues in the context of home-based ubicomp for caregiving, potentially one of the most extreme cases in terms of privacy. An exception is Intel's CareNet project, which performed extensive user studies that included examining the issues surrounding privacy with home-based ubicomp. Unfortunately, they simulated the sensor network and, thus, privacy issues that may have emerged during deployment could not be considered.

16.7   The Perfect Privacy Storm

The implications of ubicomp in terms of privacy will be of particular importance in another area of transformational change—the rapidly aging population. As the number of elders increases, so will the need for healthcare. Home-based healthcare takes on increased importance as a major part of the U.S. healthcare system. The U.S. Government Accountability Office estimates that informal care (e.g., visits, chores, reminders, help with medicines, errands) accounts for more than 85 percent of all elder care [47]. The amount of informal care given to elders is likely to increase as the baby boom generation starts to use, and threatens to overwhelm, current formal healthcare systems. Indeed, the number of people over the age of 65 in the United States is projected to double in the year 2030 to over 69 million, an increase from 8 to 22 percent of the U.S. population [48].

The combination of a vulnerable population, embedded computing, and inadequate privacy regimes may lead to a digital perfect storm. An obvious threat is financial fraud enabled by the combination of cross-border data flows (legal or otherwise) and international financial opportunities.

Loss of privacy and detailed data surveillance is not a requirement for ubicomp if the designers are aware of the reason for the technology and design accordingly. For example, consider a pressure sensor. What elder home health issues can be aided by such a sensor (e.g., identifying falls)? What filters are available that de-identify individuals (e.g., removing detailed gait information), count events (e.g., mild balance loss) without detailed recording, and obscure exact timestamps with time periods?

The concept of privacy as autonomy brings forward the right to act without surveillance. If seclusion is the right to choose not to participate, autonomy demands participation without identification. Autonomy is often seen as implying protection of other data that could be embedded; for example, even a combination of blurred timestamps with gait-identifying pressure sensors could indicate sexual orientation in a fully active house. Autonomy is a unique challenge, as in asking, "What exactly is it you do not want us to learn?" is inane in any case, but in privacy research, such a question is a particular oxymoron.

From the paradigm of privacy as seclusion comes the right to be let alone, leading to the questions: does the elder want to be able to turn the technology off, or have it always on? Should someone (i.e., an informal caregiver) be notified if it is off for a higher level of checking? For example, gait identification in the home may be something that comforts the elder in the evening by identifying thumps in the night as the caregiver or the cat, but not desirable during more social daylight hours. The privacy as property paradigm brings forward not only the alienable nature of data, but the idea of the right to exclude.

Spatial questions can serve to bring autonomy to the fore by assisting users in defining sensitive or personal spaces. For example, an elder may not want tracking of those coming in and out of his bedroom. The framework as a whole must embed the understanding that removing the data from only the bedroom would be meaningless if the person disappeared off the house map into the bedroom only to reappear in the hall at a specified later time. Thus, the questions would be translated to indicate rough spatial filtering in and out of the home only; better or worse balance in a given time period. Spatial questions can also assist in defining data boundaries. Should the elder know whenever a caregiver "drops in" or checks the data? Should the ubicomp monitoring system "reach out" to the caregiver for periodic checks? Does the elder want to actively manage his or her own data boundaries, or allow them to be highly permeable at all times? And if so, who should be included, bringing back the details of property-like exclusion.

Some elements of data protection bring rise to questions that address both privacy and ease of use: Will elders want to review and interact with the data? Do they prefer visible ubicomp or embedded (invisible) designs? The data protection emphasis on visibility may not be appropriate for livable home-based ubicomp, as people may become tired of consciously interacting with the technology on a day-to-day basis. Other questions from data protection demand the reasons for data compilation and a firm deletion date.

Recognizing that these models of privacy exist is not to dictate design specifics. Privacy as the right to seclusion fits under the boundaries model. Privacy as property in ubicomp would require either too much contractual overhead or a ubiquitous digital currency with very low computation requirements. Yet, each of these perspectives can assist in informing designers about privacy implications and help participants articulate privacy concerns.

Consider the case of medication adherence, which can indicate cognitive well-being. Failure to adhere to guidelines for taking medications can result in personal, emotional, and financial harm for elders and their caregivers.

In an invisible design, sensors placed where medicine is kept and taken can detect if a person did not follow all the instructions, took the incorrect dosage, took doses at the wrong time, or in the wrong combination. In a visible design, users can indicate how and when they have taken medication by pressing buttons on a personal handheld device [42].

Ubicomp can be used to monitor symptoms of actions as opposed to merely actions. For example, a changed heart rate can be associated with dehydration, infection, wrong medication, overdose of medication, or some form of stress. A heart rate monitor can be used to measure this aspect of physical well being. One design might place the heart rate monitor in a television remote, thereby measuring an elder's heart rate invisibly whenever they use the remote. Another design may place a heart rate monitor in a button that the elder is reminded to push every morning when he or she is fixing breakfast. The second design is visible, the first is integrated.

What is user-centered privacy and how does it relate to larger social/demographic changes in society? How should we elicit and design for individual needs for privacy and embed them in the tools and systems we design? How do we evaluate these tools for their privacy-enhancing potential and capabilities? How do we describe and present data to caregivers, participants, and others in a way that enhances privacy, minimizes confusion, and maximizes utility?

16.8   Limits of Subject-Driven Design

The use of design for values is unlikely to address all security and privacy threats because individuals often have inappropriate mental models of security [4], are unaware of the full range of risks [19], and greatly, increasingly over time, discount privacy risks [1]. There is a need for a minimal set of privacy requirements, as depending on the expertise of subjects for privacy definition may leave significant security risks. Current regulation of information is inadequate to protect security requirements for ubicomp [33], much less in-home ubicomp.

Confidentiality of health data is required under the Health Insurance Portability and Accountability Act (HIPAA) [45]. Under HIPAA, health information can be shared under conditions of consent, as required under necessary business practices, and for medical care. These exceptions are sufficient to cover a ubicomp system that sends a consistent stream of encrypted information to a centralized facility. To the extent that the data is not strictly medical data (e.g., the observation of movements of an individual with Alzheimer's is not strictly medical data), the data is not protected Therefore, movement, habit, and location information are not protected.

There are fundamental issues of safety that are obvious to any technologist who considers the possibility of broadcasting streams of ubicomp data across the public networks. However, the commercialization of the technologies does not address these threats, and the end user may not even be able to imagine them.

Applications have distinct signatures [2]. To the extent that home-based ubicomp applications also have unique signatures, each application will indicate a particular population: mentally disabled, frail elderly, or even the more targeted, such as schizophrenics.* The addressing information can be correlated with physical addresses. Nontechnical individuals are unlikely to identify traffic analysis and application identification as legitimate threats. Surveys of individuals about smart homes, for example, did not give rise to traffic analysis as an issue [35].

Man-in-the-middle attacks for domestic information are both the least and most vulnerable. Recall that the Trojan Horse scandal that struck Israel in 2005 was initiated as a domestic attack, targeted at the ex-wife of the male author of the malware [24]. Domestic information can be targeted both at the source of information and the recipient, in order to cause distress to either. The market for home surveillance is also driven by parents seeking oversight for childcare providers and spouses seeking surveillance on each other.

Minimal security standards indicate that confidentiality of address and content, integrity of data, anonymity to data compilers, and reliability of the system are most critical. To some extent these are the most traditional subjects of security technology. Those threats least obvious to the layperson are more obvious to the technologist; thus, design for values integrated with a set of best practices offers a possible way forward.

16.9 Conclusions

Ubicomp is going to change concepts of privacy in a fundamental way: Transactional approaches will no longer be adequate. The impact of ubicomp as a large-scale transformational change will be the greatest in terms of privacy in home-based healthcare. Value-sensitive design has the potential to make this transformational change less disruptive in terms of personal autonomy and individual boundaries by integrating privacy into ubicomp

---

* Particular mental disorders create vulnerability to different types of fraud. For example, financial capacity is often a critical issue in treatment of schizophrenics, who have difficulty in evaluating other people and in understanding the nature of financial instruments [29]. Cognitively impaired seniors are at risk for being targeted for fraud [46].

home healthcare. Yet value-sensitive design must be predicated upon a shared concept of the particular value under consideration. We posit that a single framework built on the technology and the various concepts of privacy inform both designers, for value-sensitive design, and participants, for their own autonomy.

There are numerous sensors and as many combinations of risks and applications as there are elders. It will require more than the law or technologists alone to develop a meaningful framework that provides a cooperative, elder-informed understanding of the concerns of caregivers and participants for sensors in each space, for each risk set, and for each application. Technologists and lawyers must begin now to examine ubicomp as it is being developed and designed.

Demographic changes, longer life spans, and advances in medical care that make previously fatal injuries or birth defects into manageable life-long disabilities can be predicted to increase the need for home healthcare. The demand for home healthcare will be increased by social changes, in particular, the movement toward the mainstreaming of and community living for the chronically ill and disabled. Cost containment policies by insurers and hospitals have also contributed in that these policies lead to earlier discharge of chronically ill patients into the care of their families. Simultaneously, other demographic changes (e.g., families living farther away from each other, increased necessary participation of women in the paid workforce) have complicated informal caregiving.

Ubicomp holds promise for the development of easy-to-use technologies that enhance the ability of caregivers to monitor those in their care, but most extant technologies have not been developed with a socially aware, privacy-sensitive design method.

Acknowledgments

We wish to acknowledge Lesa Lorenzen–Huber and Kalpana Shankar for their contributions to this work.

References

[1] A. Acquisti. Privacy in electronic commerce and the economics of immediate gratification. In *EC '04: Proceedings of the 5th ACM Conference on Electronic Commerce*, pp. 21–29, New York, 2004, ACM Press.

[2] R.K. Ahuja, T.L. Magnanti, and J.B. Orlin. *Network Flows: Theory, Algorithms, and Applications.* Prentice-Hall, Upper Saddle River, NJ, 1993.

[3] I. Altman. *The Environment and Social Behavior.* Brooks/Cole, Monterey, CA, 1975.

[4]   F. Asgharpour and D. Liu. Risk communication in computer security using mental models. Usable security. In *Usable Security (USEC'07)*. IFCA, Trinidad, 2007.

[5]   E. Bloustein. Privacy as an aspect of human dignity: an answer to dean prosser. *New York University Law Review*, pp. 962–970, New York, 1968.

[6]   M. Boyle. A shared vocabulary for privacy. In *Fifth Annual Intl. Conf. on Ubiquitous Computing: Privacy in Ubicomp*, Seattle, WA, 2003.

[7]   M. Boyle and S. Greenberg. The language of privacy: Learning from video media space analysis and design. *ACM Trans. Comput.-Hum. Interact.*, 12(2): 328–370, 2005.

[8]   L.J. Camp. *Trust and Risk in Electronic Commerce*. The MIT Press, Cambridge, MA, 2001.

[9]   L.J. Camp. Design for trust. In R. Falcone, Ed., *Trust, Reputation, and Security: Theories and Practice*. Springer-Verlag, Heidelberg, Germany, 2003.

[10] L.J. Camp. Digital identity. *IEEE Technology and Society*, 23 (3), 34–41, IEEE, New York, 2004.

[11] L.J. Camp and Y.T. Chien. The Internet as public space: Concepts, issues and implications in public policy. In R. Spinello and H. Tavani, Eds., *Readings in Cyberethics*. Jones and Bartlett Publishers, Sudbury, MA, 2001.

[12] L.J. Camp and C. Osorio. Privacy enhancing technologies for Internet commerce. In Rino Falcone, Ed., *Trust in the Network Economy*. Springer-Verlag, Heidelberg, Germany, 2003.

[13] L.J. Camp and D. Riley. Bedrooms, barrooms and board rooms on the Internet: The failure of media types in cyberspaces. *Selected Papers from the 1996 Telecommunications Policy Research Conference, Alexandria, VA*, Earlbaum, Mahweh, 1997.

[14] J. Cohen. A right to read anonymously: A closer look at copyright management in cyberspace. *Conn. Law Review*, pp. 981–1011, 1996.

[15] E. Eisenstein. *The Printing Press as an Agent of Change: Communications and Cultural Transformations in Early Modern Europe*, Cambridge University Press, Cambridge, U.K., 1979.

[16] E. Felton, H. Nissenbaum, and B. Friedman. Computer security: Competing concepts. In *The 30th Research Conference on Communication, Information and Internet Policy*, MIT Press, Cambridge, MA, September 2002.

[17] C.S. Fischer. America calling: A social history of the telephone to 1940. 1994.

[18] B. Friedman. *Human Values and the Design of Computer Technology*. University of Chicago Press, Chicago, IL, 2001.

[19] B. Friedman, D. Hurley, D.C. Howe, H. Nissenbaum, and E. Felten. Users' conceptions of risks and harms on the Web: A comparative study. In *CHI '02: CHI '02 extended abstracts on human factors in computing systems*, pp. 614–615, New York, 2002, ACM Press.

[20] B. Friedman and H. Nissenbaum. Bias in computer systems. *ACM Transactions on Information Systems (TOIS)*, 14(3), 330–347, ACM Press, New York, 1996.

[21] J. Geraci. Community and boundary in the age of mobile computing: Ubicomp in the urban frontier. In *Privacy in Ubicomp Workshop*, New Nottingham, U.K., 2004. http://www.cs.berkeley.edu/~jfc/ubicomp-privacy2004/

[22] D.H. Gleason. Should the system do this? *Handbook of Business Strategy*, 5(1), 299–305, Emerald Group, West Yorkshire, U.K., 2004.

[23] U. Hengartner and P. Steenkiste. Implementing access control to people location information. In *9th Symposium on Access Control Models and Technologies*, Yorktown Heights, NY, 2004.

[24] D. Izenberg. Trojan horse couple pleads guilty. In *Jerusalem Post*, March 14, 2006.

[25] X. Jiang. Safeguard privacy in ubiquitous computing with decentralized information spaces, *Privacy in Ubicomp '2002*, Göteborg Sweden, 2002.

[26] J. Kesan and R. Shah. Establishing software defaults: Perspectives from law, computer science, and behavioral economics. *The Notre Dame Law Review*, 82(2), 583–634, 2006.

[27] M. Langheinrich. Privacy invasions in ubiquitous computing. 2002.

[28] L. Lessig. *Code and Other Basic Laws of Cyberspace*. Basic Books, New York, 1999.

[29] D.C. Marson, R. Savage, and J. Phillips. Financial capacity in persons with schizophrenia. *Schizophrenia Bulletin*, 32(1), 89–91, 2006.

[30] M. McLuhan. *The Gutenberg Galaxy*. University of Toronto Press, Toronto, 1977.

[31] P. Mell. Seeking shade in a land of perpetual sunlight: Privacy as property in the electronic wilderness. *Berkeley Technology Law Journal*, 11(1), 11–92, 1996.

[32] E.J. Naughton. Is cyberspace a public forum? Computer bulletin boards, free speech and state action. *Georgetown Law Journal*, 81(2), 409–441, 1992.

[33] E.M. Newton, L. Sweeney, and B. Malin. Preserving privacy by de-identifying face images. *IEEE Transactions on Knowledge and Data Engineering*, 17(2), 232–243, 2005.

[34] A. Odlyzko. Privacy, economics and price discrimination on the Internet. In L. Jean Camp and Stephen Lewis, Eds., *Economics of Information Security*, vol. 12, *Advances in Information Security*, pp. 187–212, Springer, New York, 2004.

[35] R. Carsten, Maddy D. Janse, Nathalie Portolan, and Norbert Streitz. User requirements for intelligent home environments: A scenario-driven approach and empirical cross-cultural study. In *EUSAI '05: Proceedings of the 2005 Joint Conference on Smart Objects and Ambient Intelligence*, pp. 111–116, ACM Press, New York, 2005.

[36] P.E. Ross. Managing care through the air. *IEEE Spectrum*, 41(12), 26–31, 2004.

[37] S. Shapiro. Places and space: The historical interaction of technology, home, and privacy. *The Information Society*, 14(4), 275–284, 1998.

[38] E. Shekita and M. Zwilling. Cricket: A mapped, persistent object store. *Proceedings Fourth International Workshop on Persistent Objects*, September 1990, Martha's Vineyard, MA. University of Wisconsin, Madison, 1990.

[39] K.A. Siek, Y. Rogers, and K.H. Connelly. Fat finger worries: How older and younger users physically interact with pdas. *Proceedings of Interact, LNCS*, pp. 267–280, 2005.

[40] D. Solove. A taxonomy of privacy. *Fordham Law Review*, 154(3) 477–517, 2006.

[41] F. Stajano. The resurrecting duckling. *Proceedings 7th International Workshop on Security Protocols*, Springer-Verlag, London, pp. 204–214, 2000.

[42] A. Sterns. Curriculum design and program to train older adults to use personal digital assistants. *The Gerontologist*, 45(6), 828–834, 2005.

[43] K.J. Strandburg. Surveillance of emergent associations: Freedom of association in a network society. *DIMACS Economics of Information Security Workshop*, Piscatway, NJ, 2007.

[44] C. Sunstein. The first amendment in cyberspace. *Yale Law Journal*, 104(7), 1757–1804.

[45] P.P. Swire and L. Steinfeld. Security and privacy after September 11: The health care example. *SSRN eLibrary*.

[46] M.C. Tierney, J. Charles, and G. Naglie. Risk factors for harm in cognitively impaired seniors who live alone. *JAGS*, pp. 1435–1441, 2004.

[47] U.S. Government Accountability Office. Long-term care: Diverse, growing population includes Americans of all ages. Technical report, Washington, D.C., 1998.

[48] U.S. Administration on Aging. Profile of Older Americans. U.S. Department on Health and Human Services, Washington, D.C., 1999.

[49] S. Warren and L. Brandeis. The right to privacy. *Harvard Law Review*, Cambridge, MA, 4(5), 193–220, 1890.

THE ECONOMICS OF PRIVACY

Chapter 17

A Risk Model for Privacy Insurance

Athanassios N. Yannacopoulos, Sokratis Katsikas,
Stefanos Gritzalis, Costas Lambrinoudakis,
and Stelios Z. Xanthopoulos

Contents

17.1 Introduction 348
17.2 Modeling the Possible Claim of an Individual j for
Revealing Private Data D_m 350
  17.2.1 A Random Utility Model 350
  17.2.2 Model Construction 352
17.3 The Collective Risk Model 353
17.4 Inhomogeneity of the Population and Disclosure
of More than One Piece of Data 355
17.5 Use of the Collective Risk Model for the Insurance
and Risk Management of an IT Business Dealing
with Personal Data 357
  17.5.1 Insurance of an IT Business Handling Private Data 357
  17.5.2 Risk Management of the IT Firm 359
  17.5.3 Other Applications 359
17.6 Conclusions 360
References 360

17.1 Introduction

The value of privacy is by no means a trivial issue. Privacy incidents are, in a sense, unique as to the loss they can incur, as opposed to other security incidents whose impact may be objectively valued. For example, if due to some security incident the Internet site of a company is unavailable for an hour, then it is quite possible to estimate the financial value of this incident in an objective manner by estimating the possible number of clients and their potential buys within this period. The situation is more difficult when it comes to privacy. For instance, when somebody's telephone number is disclosed, then it is rather subjective whether one should care or not. When a bank uses the credit history of a client without her consent in order to issue a presigned credit card, then it is subjective whether the client will feel upset about it and press charges for breach of the Personal Data Act or not. In fact, banks may issue hundreds of presigned credit cards, but only one customer may decide to press charges and ask for compensation. And, given that this has actually happened, what is the likely amount of the compensation? Again, this is a very personal thing (no matter whether the court grants the compensation or not) and somehow should be related to how much the particular client values her privacy.

If we want to study the risk that a firm is undergoing by possible privacy incidents that a client may have caused, a means is definitely needed that will allow one to find out how much individuals subjectively value their privacy.

Since this chapter is a first attempt at this extremely complicated task and we also wish to keep it as free as possible from technicalities so as to concentrate on the basic conceptual issues related to this important problem, we start with the simplest possible model. This model incorporates the personalized view of whether individuals perceive a possible privacy incident as a loss and, if so, how much they value this loss.

Privacy is the right of someone to be left alone. Information privacy is the right of the individual to decide what personal information should be communicated to others and under what circumstances [10], or, in short, the ability to control one's personal information. Loss of information privacy may lead to loss of privacy in the contexts defined above. Information technology and particularly the expansion of the Internet have raised public concern about information privacy. This concern has been evidenced by various surveys and experiments [25–28]. However, differences in sensitivity about secondary use of information and cultural values seem to have a significant effect on the level of privacy concerns [4,23,24].

In Smith et al. [2], four dimensions of privacy concerns about organizational information privacy practices have been identified. These are (1) the collection and storage of large amounts of personal information data, (2) the unauthorized secondary use of personal data, (3) the errors in collected data, and (4) the improper access to personal data due to managerial negligence. The first two, particularly the second one, seem to have been identified as the most important aspects of privacy concern [3, 5–7].

Regarding online privacy preferences, individuals are classified in Ackerman et al. [8] in three basic classes:

1. *The Privacy Fundamentalists* who almost always refuse to provide personal information even in the presence of privacy protection measures.

2. *The Pragmatic Majority* who constitute the majority of the Internet users, who exhibit privacy concerns, but not as strongly as the Privacy Fundamentalists.

3. *The Marginally Concerned* who almost always are willing to reveal their personal data. Furthermore, in Spickermann et al. [9], it is shown that the Pragmatic Majority class contains two "subclasses," namely those whose main concern lies in revealing personal data, such as name, address, etc., and those whose main concern is about providing information concerning their personal profile (health, interests, etc.).

It should be noted, though, that these studies do not claim that individuals will actually behave according to their stated preferences. In fact, it has been shown that a deviation exists between stated information privacy preferences and actual behavior when individuals need to make a privacy-related decision [9,11,13,21]. An analysis of the drivers and inconsistencies of privacy decision-making behavior can be found in [13,19,20].

However, there is strong evidence that people are willing to exchange personal information for economic benefits or personalized services [11,12,15]. In [16] techniques of experimental economics are applied in order to provide a foundation for estimating the values that consumers place on privacy. In Hann et al. [11], in particular, an attempt is made to estimate the monetary value of privacy concerns to individuals. Interestingly, this is found to be much less than the cost of proposed privacy legislation estimated in Hann [22]. This willingness to trade off privacy concerns in exchange for economic benefits supports proposals like that of Lauden [14] for regulation of privacy through national information markets, where personal information can be bought and sold at market prices. Furthermore, in [18] the free market critique of privacy regulation is scrutinized.

Finally, the impact of a company's privacy incidents on its stock market value is explored and analyzed in Acquisti [17].

The remainder of the chapter is organized as follows: In Section 17.2, we present a model of the possible claim of an individual when private data is disclosed. Section 17.3 extends this model to multiple claims. Section 17.4 further extends the model to cover numerous claims by multiple, diverse individuals. Section 17.5 discusses how the model may be used to design the company's insurance and risk management policies. Finally, Section 17.6 summarizes and concludes the chapter.

17.2 Modeling the Possible Claim of an Individual j for Revealing Private Data D_m

In this section, we consider the following first step toward modeling the risk process that an information technology (IT) firm may face as a result of disclosure of private data. We consider the case that a private data D_m disclosure has occurred and we wish to answer the question: "How much would an individual j claim as compensation for the above mentioned privacy breach?" Closely related to this is the question: "How much would an individual be willing to pay in order to achieve better protection against privacy violations?" Rephrasing this question leads to asking: "How much would a privacy-concerned individual be willing to pay in order to avoid the burden of asking for compensation that would seem appropriate for this individual, should some privacy violation occur?" In this work, we will deal with the first question.

17.2.1 A Random Utility Model

As stated above, the very nature of the incident calls for a personalized modeling of the individual's preferences. The basic framework used is the random utility model (RUM) that has been used in the past in the modeling of personalized decisions and nonmarket valuation. According to this model, we assume that the individual j may be in two different states. State 0 is the status quo state that, in our context, is the state where no personal data is disclosed. State 1 is the state where personal data has been disclosed. For the simplicity of the model, we first assume that there is only one sort of data that may be kept secret or disclosed. This is an oversimplification, which is made now for the sake of presentation of the model and can later be removed.

The level of satisfaction of individual j in state 1 is given by the random utility function

$$u_{1,j}(y, z) + \varepsilon_{1,j}$$

where y is the income (wealth) of the individual, z is a vector related to the characteristics of the individual, (e.g., age, occupation, whether she is technology averse or not, etc.). This vector may be, for instance, a vector containing entries of 1 and 0 in specific slots, depending on whether an answer of "yes" or "no" occurs in a particular question describing the individual's characteristics. The term $\varepsilon_{1,j}$ is a term that will be considered as a random variable and models the personalized features of the individual j.

This term takes into account contingent effects, for instance, the same individual may consider a privacy violation as annoying, whereas another time she may not bother with it at all. This term introduces the random features to the model and is essential for its subjective nature. Similarly, the level of satisfaction of the same individual j in state 0 is given by the random utility function $u_{0,j}(y, z) + \varepsilon_{0,j}$, where the various terms have similar meaning.

State 1, the state of privacy loss, will be disturbing to individual j as long as $u_{1,j}(y, z) + \varepsilon_{1,j} < u_{0,j}(y, z) + \varepsilon_{0,j}$. This may happen with probability $P(\varepsilon_{1,j} - \varepsilon_{0,j} < u_{0,j}(y, z) - u_{1,j}(y, z))$.

This is the probability that an individual will be bothered by a privacy violation and may be calculated as long as we know the distribution of the error term. This also will depend on the general characteristics of the individual through z as well as on her income y. The particular dependence can be deduced through statistical tests, which will be sketched briefly in the following.

Given that an individual j is bothered by a privacy violation, how much would she value this privacy violation, and how much would she like to be compensated? If the compensation is C_j, then this would satisfy the random equation $u_{1,j}(y + C_j, z) + \varepsilon_{1,j} = u_{0,j}(y, z) + \varepsilon_{0,j}$, the solution to which will yield a random variable C_j. This is the (random) compensation that an individual may ask for a privacy violation. The distribution of the compensation will depend on the distribution of the error terms $\varepsilon_{i,j}$, as well as on the functional form of the deterministic part of the utility function.

The following two cases are quite common.

1. $u_{i,j}(y, z) = a_i y + b_i z$, linear utility function. We may also assume that a_i is the same in both states $i = 0$ and $i = 1$. Then the random compensation is given by the formula

$$C_j = Bz + \varepsilon_j$$

where $B = \frac{1}{a_1}(b_0 - b_1)$ and $\varepsilon_j = \frac{1}{a_1}(\varepsilon_0 - \varepsilon_1)$. Then (since B is a deterministic vector), the distribution of the compensation C_j is the distribution of the random variable ε_j. A common assumption is that ε_j is normally distributed. This leads to a normally distributed compensation, and forms the basis of the well-known class of econometric models called *probit models* [29]. Another common assumption is that the random variable ε_j is distributed by a logistic distribution. This forms the basis of the well-known class of econometric models called *logit models* [29]. Note that the linearity of the utility function in the income makes the compensation independent of the income.

2. $u_{i,j}(y, z) = a_i \ln(y) + b_i z$, i.e., the utility function is log linear in income. In this case, the compensation may easily be calculated to be equal to the random variable

$$C_j = y \exp(Bz + \varepsilon_j) - y$$

when $a_0 = a_1$ and where B and ε_j are again defined as in 1. above. The distribution of the compensation is determined by the distribution of the error term ε_j. Normally distributed errors will lead to a probit model, whereas errors following a logistic distribution will lead to a logit model.

The models mentioned above, in principle, may lead to unbounded claims, though with diminishing probability. In an attempt to remedy this situation, we may resort to bound logit or probit models. Such models have been used with great success in the literature for valuation of environmental and natural resources [30]. An example of such a model is given by

$$C_j = \frac{y_j}{1 + \exp(-z_j\gamma - \varepsilon)}$$

where the error may be taken to follow either a logistic or a normal distribution.

17.2.2 Model Construction

Such models may be constructed using appropriately designed questionnaires in order to obtain enough data for the proposed claims so that a logit or probit distribution may be fit into them. An appropriate question could be, for instance: "Would you be ready to accept a sum of t euros in order to reveal this data (e.g., telephone number, credit card number, etc.)?" The test is made for a vector of ts and the answer is in the form of "yes (1)" and "no (0)." The answers to the test provide estimates for the probability that $P(C_j > t)$. These results then are fitted into a logit or probit model using standard statistical procedures, which are now well implemented in commercial packages. A possible procedure for the model construction is, for instance, a maximum likelihood method, where the likelihood of the observed answers to the survey is computed as a function of the parameters of the model obtained by the random utility model and then the parameter values are chosen to be such that the likelihood is maximized. For the random utility models described above, i.e., the logit and the probit model, there exist analytic formulae for the likelihood, thus facilitating the maximization. Having completed the model construction, we have a good approximation of the probability distribution of the claims that may be made by an individual j with characteristics z_j and income y_j for disclosure of some private data D_m.

In order to get a better feeling of the practical aspects of the above discussion, following are some examples of individual claims. Four models (M1, M2, M3, and M4) are considered. For each, a Monte Carlo simulation is performed. The four models represent individuals with income $y = 20{,}000$

and $z = (1, 1, 1, 1, 1, 0, 0, 0, 0, 0)$. The models should be constructed as follows:

M1: Linear utility function, such that $a_0 = a_1 = 1$, $b_0 - b_1 = (200, 200, 200, 200, 200, 200, 200, 200, 200, 200)$ and error term $\varepsilon = \varepsilon_0 - \varepsilon_1$ that is normally distributed with mean 0 and standard deviation 1.

M2: Linear utility function, such that $a_0 = a_1 = 1$, $b_0 - b_1 = (200, 200, 200, 200, 200, 200, 200, 200, 200, 200)$ and error term $\varepsilon = \varepsilon_0 - \varepsilon_1$ that is logistically distributed with mean 0 and standard deviation 1.

M3: Loglinear utility function, such that $a_0 = a_1 = 1$, $b_0 - b_1 = (1\%, 1\%, 1\%, 1\%, 1\%, 1\%, 1\%, 1\%, 1\%, 1\%)$ and error term $\varepsilon = \varepsilon_0 - \varepsilon_1$ that is normally distributed with mean 0 and standard deviation 1%.

M4: Loglinear utility function, such that $a_0 = a_1 = 1$, $b_0 - b_1 = (1\%, 1\%, 1\%, 1\%, 1\%, 1\%, 1\%, 1\%, 1\%, 1\%)$ and error term $\varepsilon = \varepsilon_0 - \varepsilon_1$ that is logistically distributed with mean 0 and standard deviation 1%.

The respective distributions of the individual claims are shown in Figure 17.1.

17.3   The Collective Risk Model

We now assume that within a specified time period t, a random number $N(t)$ of claims $C_1, \ldots, C_{N(t)}$ arrive. Each of these claims is distributed with a distribution as determined by the random utility model described above. The distribution of the random number of claims will be modeled as a Poisson distribution $\text{Pois}(\lambda)$ or as a geometric distribution. Then, assuming that the claims $C_1, \ldots, C_{N(t)}$ are independent and identically distributed, the total claim up to time t will be given by the random sum

$$L(t) = \sum_{i=0}^{N(t)} C_i)$$

This is a compound random variable and forms the basis of the model of collective risk in actuarial mathematics. The distribution of $L(t)$ depends on the distribution of the C_is. Assuming independence of the number of claims $N(t)$ with their size C_i, the characteristic function for the total claim distribution will be given by the formula

$$\phi(s) = \exp(-\lambda(1 - \phi_{C_i}(s)))$$

for real s. Another choice of model for the claims arrival times may be that the claims arrive with a geometric distribution with parameter $p \in (0, 1)$.

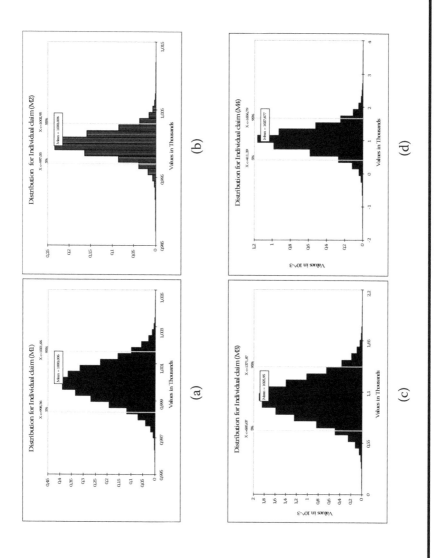

Figure 17.1   Distribution of the individual claim for models M1 (a), M2 (b), M3 (c), and M4 (d).

Furthermore, we may calculate the expected total claim as $E[L(t)] = E[N(t)]E[C_i]$ and the variance of the claim as

$$\text{var}(L(t)) = \text{var}(N(t))(E[C_i])^2 + E[N(t)]\text{var}(C_i)$$

Well-founded techniques from the theory of actuarial mathematics [31] may be used for the analytical approximation of the total claim as well as for its numerical simulation. In the following, we present some results from the numerical simulation of the total claim. Let us assume that we have 100 clients who all share the same characteristics as in the previous example; that is, they all have the same y and z. Suppose also that we have estimated that the number of claims from these clients follows a Poisson distribution with $\lambda = 50$. Then, each of the models M1 to M4 (defined in the example of the previous section) will produce the distributions for the total claims as seen in Figure 17.2.

17.4 Inhomogeneity of the Population and Disclosure of More than One Piece of Data

In the above collective risk model, we assumed that the population of clients that may claim charges for a privacy violation is homogeneous; in the sense that they all share the same characteristics, such as income, level of computer literacy, etc. This may simplify the analysis of the model, but it is rarely a realistic assumption.

It is now assumed that the IT firm has a collection of clients, whose income is distributed by a probability distribution of income $F(y)$ and whose characteristics z are distributed by a probability distribution $G(z)$. Then a possible claim will be a random variable, which depends on parameters that are random variables themselves and follow some probability distribution, which is either known objectively and treated as some sort of statistical probability, or can be thought of as a subjective belief concerning the composition of the population, which may be treated using the methodology of Bayesian statistics. If we then assume a logit or probit model with income y and parameters z, the possible claim will be a random variable C, such that

$$E[C|Y = y, \; Z = z] = C(y, z) \sim \text{Logit}(y, z)$$

or

$$E[C|Y = y, \; Z = z] = C(y, z) \sim \text{Probit}(y, z)$$

respectively.

This is valid for a single claim. We now model the claims coming for compensation at different times as coming from different individuals

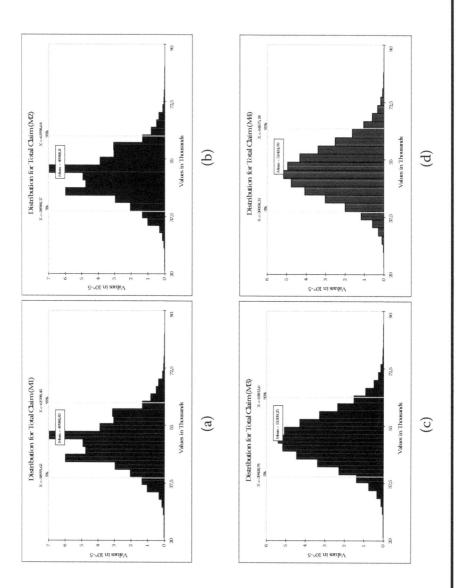

Figure 17.2   Distribution of total claim for models M1 (a), M2 (b), M3 (c), and M4 (d).

(clients) with different characteristics. Therefore, the collective claim will be

$$L(t) = \sum_{i=0}^{N(t)} C(Y_i, Z_i)$$

where the random variables Y_i and Z_i represent draws from the distribution $F(y)$ and $G(z)$, respectively, at the times where the point process $N(t)$ takes the values $N(t) = i$, i.e., at the times when the claims occur. The simulation of the inhomogeneous population model will give more realistic estimates on the possible distribution of claims. Following are results from some simulations.

The histograms in Figure 17.3 extend and enrich our previous examples and show the distribution of total claims, assuming now that each client has income y drawn from a Pareto distribution having mean 20,000, mode 10,000, and Pareto index 3. Moreover, the coordinates of her vector z can take values equal to either 1 or 0, each value occurring with probability 0.5.

17.5   Use of the Collective Risk Model for the Insurance and Risk Management of an IT Business Dealing with Personal Data

The proposed collective risk model may be used for the insurance and risk management of an IT business that deals with personal data. The case of insurance is described first.

17.5.1   Insurance of an IT Business Handling Private Data

Assume that the IT business enters into a contract with an insurance firm that undertakes the total amount of claims X that its clients may ask for as a consequence of privacy breaches. This, of course, should be done at the expense of a premium paid by the IT business to the insurer. How much should this premium be?

This is an important question that has been dealt with in the past in Gritzalis et al. [1]. The minimum premium charged by the insurer will be calculated in such a way that the insurer will not face any losses on average. In some sense, the premium should be such that the insurer is in the mean safe. Certain premium calculations are $\pi(X) = (1 + a)E[X]$, where a is a strictly positive number chosen by the insurer to ensure that ruin is avoided and is called the safety loading factor, $\pi(X) = E[X] + f(\text{var}(X))$, where the usual choices for $f(x)$ are $f(x) = ax$ or $f(x) = a\sqrt{x}$ or $\pi(X) = \frac{1}{a}\ln(E[e^{aX}])$. All these are easily calculated by the properties of the collective risk model introduced above.

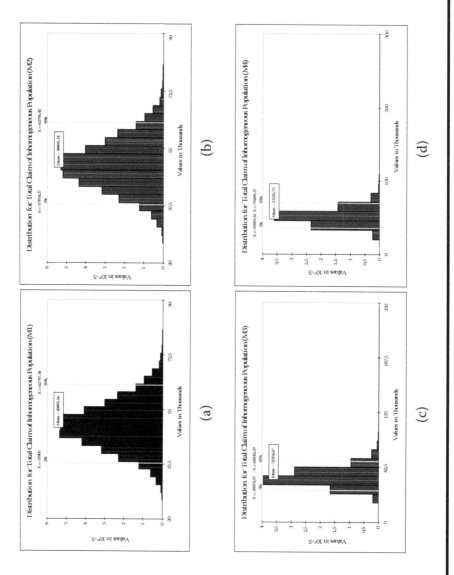

Figure 17.3   Distribution of claims for inhomogeneous populations with model M1 (a), M2 (b), M3 (c), and M4 (d).

17.5.2   Risk Management of the IT Firm

For the risk management of an IT business handling personal data, we may ask ourselves, "What is the sum that is in danger at time i for the business at some certainty level α?" This is the value at risk (VaR) for the IT firm, which is defined through the quantile of the random variable X_i. More precisely, the value at risk of the firm at time i with confidence level α is

$$VaR(X_i ; \alpha) = x$$

where

$$P(X_i > x) = \alpha$$

for some $\alpha \in (0, 1)$. This corresponds to the largest sum that the firm is jeopardizing at time i with a confidence level α. This quantity, which is very important for the financial decisions of the firm can be calculated or approximated through our collective risk model. Following are some simulations of the value at risk of an IT business due to possible privacy breaches using the inhomogeneous collective model proposed above. For example, under the assumptions of the examples presented in the last four diagrams, the 95 percent confidence VaR of the IT firm due to possible privacy breaches can be read in the diagrams above the line indicated as 95 percent. For example, according to models M1 and M2, the firm expects with 95 percent confidence that the total claims will not exceed 63,000 euros as can be seen in Figure 17.3. Similarly, Figure 17.3 shows that according to models M3 and M4 there is only a 5 percent chance that the total claims will exceed 70,000 euros.

17.5.3   Other Applications

In the above, we have only mentioned two possible applications of our collective risk model in the study of insurance and risk management of IT firms handling personal data. Its applicability, however, is by no means limited to these applications. One additional possible application is the use of the risk model proposed here to the design of contract structures between different firms handling data related to privacy, or between such firms and insurers so as to allow the optimal risk transfer and the best possible coverage. Thus, one may define the analogs of credit swaps or other credit derivatives that will effectuate the optimal risk transfer.

Another interesting application is the application of the risk model to study the optimal insurance contract that will offer the best possible coverage for two firms A and B, where firm A is assumed to be a contractor, subcontracting a project to firm B, which may be of questionable credibility.

As such, firm B may deliberately disclose private data of the clients of A for her own interest, thus exposing A to possible claims from her clients.

One possible way for A to cover herself against this situation is to enter into a joint insurance contract to optimally cover her possible losses. In Gritzalis et al. [1], we have studied the design of the optimal contract for this situation, taking for granted the possible loss L for a security violation or privacy breach. The collective risk model proposed in this work may be used within the context of [1] for the better modeling of the subcontracting situation in the case of privacy data.

17.6   Conclusions

A risk model that models the risk that an IT firm is exposed to, as a result of privacy violation and possible disclosure of personal data of its clients, has been proposed. The basis of the model is a random utility model, which aims at capturing the subjective nature of the value of privacy. A collective risk model has also been proposed that models the exposure of the firm over a certain time period for homogeneous and inhomogeneous client populations. The model has been used for the valuation and design of insurance contracts that optimally cover the firm, or for risk management purposes of the firm. The model may be used in other interesting applications as well.

References

[1]   S. Gritzalis, A.N. Yannacopoulos, C. Lambrinoudakis, P. Hatzopoulos, and S.K. Katsikas, "A probabilistic model for optimal insurance contracts against security risks and privacy violations in IT outsourcing environments," *International Journal of Information Security*, 6(4), 197–211, (2007).

[2]   J. Smith, S. Milberg, and S. Burke, "Information privacy: Measuring individuals' concerns about organizational practices," *MIS Quarterly*, 20, 167–196, (1996).

[3]   K.B. Sheehan and M.G. Hoy, "Dimensions of privacy concern among online customers," *Journal of Public Policy & Marketing*, 19(1), 62–73, (2000).

[4]   M.J. Culnan, "How did they get my name?: An exploratory investigation of consumer attitudes toward secondary information use," *MIS Quarterly*, 17, 341–343, (1993).

[5]   G.S. Dhillon and T.T. Moores, "Internet privacy: Interpreting key issues," *Information Resources Management Journal*, 14(4), 33–37, (2001).

[6]   L.F. Cranor, J. Reagle, and M.S. Ackerman, "Beyond concern: Understanding net user's attitudes about online privacy," AT&T Labs —Research Technical Report TR 99.4.3, (1999).

[7] H. Wang, M.K.O. Lee, and C. Wang, "Consumer privacy concerns about Internet marketing," *Communications of the ACM*, 41 (3), 63–70, (1998).

[8] M.S. Ackerman, L.F. Cranor, and J. Reagle, "Privacy in e-commerce: Examining user scenarios and privacy preferences," *Proceedings of the First ACM Conference on Electronic Commerce*, 1–8, Denver, CO, (1999).

[9] S. Spiekermann, J. Grossklags, and B. Berendt, "E-privacy in 2nd generation e-commerce: Privacy preferences versus actual behavior," *Proceedings of the 3rd ACM Conference on Electronic Commerce*, Tampa, FL, 38–47, (2001).

[10] A.F. Westin, *Privacy and Freedom*, Atheneum, New York, (1967).

[11] I. Hann, K.L. Hui, T.S. Lee, and I.P.L. Png, "Online information privacy: Measuring the cost-benefit tradeoffs," *Proceedings of the Twenty-Third International Conference on Information Systems*, Barcelona, Spain, 1–10 (2002).

[12] S. Faja, "Privacy in e-commerce: Understanding user trade-offs," *Issues in Information Systems*, VI(2), 83–89, (2005).

[13] A. Acquisti and J. Grossklags, "Uncertainty, ambiguity and privacy," *4th Annual Workshop on Economics and Information Security* (WEIS), Harvard University, (2005).

[14] K.C. Laudon, "Markets and privacy," *Communications of the ACM*, 39(9), 92–104, (September 1996).

[15] E.C. Tam, K.L. Hui, and B.C. Tan, "What do they want? Motivating consumers to disclose personal information to Internet businesses," *Proceedings of International Conference on Information Systems* (ICIS), Barcelona, (2002).

[16] D.L. Baumer, J.B. Earp, and J.C. Poindexter, "Quantifying privacy choices with experimental economics," Law and Economics Category, *2005 Workshop on the Economics of Information Security (WEIS)*, Harvard University, (2005).

[17] A. Acquisti, A. Friedman, and R. Telang, "Is there a cost to privacy breaches? An event study," *Workshop on the Economics of Information Security (WEIS)*, Cambridge University, (2006).

[18] K. Hui, and I.P.L. Png, "The economics of privacy," in Terry Hendershott, Ed., *Handbook of Information Systems and Economics*, Elsevier, Amsterdom (2006).

[19] A. Acquisti and J. Grossklags, "Losses, gains, and hyperbolic discounting: An experimental approach to information security attitudes and behavior," in *2nd Annual Workshop on Economics and Information Security (WEIS)*, College Park, MD, (2003).

[20] A. Acquisti and J. Grossklags, "Privacy and rationality in individual decision making," *IEEE Security and Privacy*, 3(1), 26–33, (2005).

[21] R.K. Chellappa and R. Sin, "Personalization versus privacy: An empirical examination of the online consumer's dilemma," *Information Technology and Management*, 6(2–3), (2005).

[22] R. Hahn, "An Assessment of the Costs of Proposed Online Privacy Legislation," Working Paper, AEI Brookings Joint Center for Regulatory Studies, Washington, D.C., (2001).

[23] S.J. Milberg, H.J. Smith, and S.J. Burke, "Information privacy: Corporate management and national regulation," *Organization Science*, 11(1), 35–57, (2000).

[24] H.J. Smith, "Information privacy and marketing: What the U.S. should (and shouldn't) learn from Europe," *California Management Review*, 43(2), 8–33, (2001).

[25] J. Phelps, G. Nowak, and E. Ferrell, "Privacy concerns and consumer willingness to provide personal information," *Journal of Public Policy and Marketing*, 19(1), 27–41, (2000).

[26] S. Fox, "Trust and privacy online: Why Americans want to rewrite the rules," Technical Report, The Pew Internet and American Life Project, Washington, D.C., (2000).

[27] M.J. Culnan and G.R. Milne, "The Culnan–Milne Survey on Consumers and Online Privacy Notices: Summary of Responses," December 2001: (http://www.ftc.gov/bcp/workshops/glb/supporting/culnanmilne.pdf).

[28] D.L. Hoffman, T.P. Novak, and M.A. Peralta, "Building Consumer Trust Online," *Communications of the ACM*, 42(4), 80–85, (1999).

[29] P. Kennedy, *A Guide to Econometrics*, 5th ed., Blackwell, Oxford, U.K., (2004).

[30] T.C. Haab and K.E. McConnell, *Valuing Environmental and Natural Resources: The Econometrics of Non-Market Valuation*, New Horizons in Environmental Economics Series, Edward Elgar, Cheltenham, U.K., (2003).

[31] T. MiKosh, *Non-Life Insurance Mathematics, An Introduction with Stochastic Processes*, 2nd ed. Springer, New York (2006).

Chapter 18

What Can Behavioral Economics Teach Us about Privacy?

Alessandro Acquisti and Jens Grossklags

Contents

18.1 Introduction 363
18.2 Privacy and Incomplete Information 364
    18.2.1 The Classical Distinction between Risk
        and Uncertainty 366
    18.2.2 Privacy as a Problem of Risk or Uncertainty? 367
18.3 Behavioral Economics and Privacy.............................. 368
    18.3.1 Helping Individuals Understand Risk
        and Deal with Bounded Rationality 369
    18.3.2 Framing and Heuristics 370
    18.3.3 Other Systematic Biases 372
18.4 How to Research the Privacy Phenomenon 374
References... 374

18.1 Introduction

Privacy is a complex decision problem resulting in opinions, attitudes, and behaviors that differ substantially from one individual to another [1]. Subjective perceptions of threats and potential damages, psychological needs, and actual personal economic returns all play a role in affecting our decisions to protect or to share personal information. Thus, inconsistencies or even contradictions emerge in individual behavior: Sometimes we feel entitled to protection of information about ourselves that we do not control and end up trading away that same information for small rewards. Sometimes we worry about personal intrusions of little significance, but overlook those that may cause significant damages. In previous works [1–4], we have highlighted a number of difficulties that distance individual actual privacy decision making from that prescribed by classical rational choice theory.* First, privacy choices are affected by *incomplete information* and, in particular, *asymmetric information* [5]: Data subjects often know less than data holders about the magnitude of data collection and use of (un)willingly or (un)knowingly shared or collected personal data; they also know little about associated consequences. Second, the complex life cycle of personal data in modern information societies can result in a multitude of consequences that individuals are hardly able to consider in their entirety (as human beings, because of our innate *bounded rationality* [6], we often replace rational decision-making methods with simplified mental models and heuristics). Third, even with access to complete information and cognitive power to process it exhaustively, various behavioral anomalies and biases could lead individuals to take actions that are systematically different from those predicted by rational choice theory [7]. In this chapter, we present an overview of those difficulties, and highlight how research on behavioral economics may improve our understanding of individuals' everyday privacy behavior. In section 18.2, we consider the role of asymmetric and incomplete information in privacy scenarios and how information asymmetries determine risk, uncertainty, and ambiguity in decision making. We argue that, due to the prevalence of these informational complications, individuals' privacy relevant behavior may be best understood in terms of bounded rationality [6], and behavioral biases. Specifically, in section 18.3, we discuss how insights from the behavioral economic literature may cast a light on the often confusing observations drawn from privacy decision making. In section 18.4, we comment on a number of possible paths that privacy research can follow based on these insights.

18.2 Privacy and Incomplete Information

The occurrence of incomplete information is relevant to privacy for two reasons.** The first and perhaps most obvious reason is inherent to the very concept of privacy: An individual has some control on the level of

---

* According to a straw version of the classical view, individuals would be maximizing their utility over time, using all available information, Bayesian updating, and consistent preferences.
** This section is based on "Uncertainty, Ambiguity and Privacy," Alessandro Acquisti and Jens Grossklags, presented at the WEIS 2005 Workshop.

access that other entities can gain on her personal sphere. For example, a subject's personal data may be concealed from other people's knowledge. Others, thus, will rely only on incomplete information when interacting with the subject. This is the interpretation of privacy as "concealment" (of job-relevant skills, valuation for a product, creditworthiness, etc.) that Posner and most subsequent formal economic models have recognized [8].

However, incomplete information relates to privacy also in a second sense. It affects the data subject whenever her control on her personal or informational sphere is limited or not clearly determinable. For example, information asymmetries often prevent a subject from knowing when another entity has gained access to or used her personal information; in addition, the subject may not be aware of the potential personal consequences of such intrusions. The associated difficulties to exercise adequate control over private information have been amplified in highly networked, digitized, and interconnected information societies. The release and exchange of personal information has become ubiquitous and often invisible. For example, Varian noted that an individual has little or no control on the secondary use of her personal information and, hence, may be subject to externalities whenever other parties transact her personal data [9].

This second sense, in which incomplete information creates uncertainties relating to privacy, is not new in the economic or legal literature on privacy. However, links between that literature and economic research on incomplete information have been surprisingly limited. So have been formal or empirical analyses of the impact of risk, uncertainty, or ambiguity on privacy decision making.

Incomplete information complicates privacy decision making because of the resulting mathematical complexity of (evaluating) privacy costs and benefits of transactions. For example, individuals would have to consider multiple layers of outcomes and associated probabilities rather than purely deterministic outcomes. The complexity of the privacy decision environment leads individuals to arrive at highly imprecise estimates of the likelihood and consequences of adverse events, and altogether ignore privacy threats and modes of protection [1].

In the following sections, we restrict the discussion to the role of incomplete information about outcomes and probabilities associated with these outcomes. In particular, we relate the problem of privacy decision making to the research literature in the field of risk, uncertainty, and ambiguity.*

---

* Before we proceed, we want to note that economists, psychologists, and marketers often use terms like *risk* and *uncertainty* in different ways. Even within the same discipline, researchers disagree on the interpretation given to terms, such as *uncertainty.*

18.2.1 The Classical Distinction between Risk and Uncertainty

The distinction between risk and uncertainty in economics dates back to Knight [10] (although earlier discussions of the relations between risk, uncertainty, and utility may be recognized in Bernoulli [11] and then Menger [12]). Knight proposed to distinguish situations characterized by risk (in which the possible random outcomes of a certain event have known associated probabilities) from those characterized by uncertainty or ambiguity (in which the randomness cannot be expressed in terms of mathematical probabilities, and the probabilities themselves are *unknown*). For example, the expected utility theory [13] is based on objectively knowable probabilities (what Knight would have referred to as *risk*).

This distinction has not gone unchallenged by economic theorists and statisticians. A large body of literature suggests that individuals are always able to assign reasonable probabilities to random events. These probabilities could objectively exists in the world [13] and could be used to calculate expected utilities. Or, these probabilities could be *subjective* [14]. Savage adapted expected utility theory into a theory of subjective expected utility, in which, under certain assumptions, people will have personal beliefs about the possible states of nature.*

Behavioral economists and psychologists have worked on modifications of the theories of risk and uncertainty to produce satisfactory descriptive models of human decision making under incomplete information.** For example, Hogarth [16] suggests focusing on subjective weights associated to the various possible outcomes of a certain event—where the weights do not have the same mathematical properties as probabilities. In fact, Hogarth proposes that decision weights may be obtained by the individual through a process of anchoring and adjustment. First, an individual may anchor her value on an initial estimate of probabilities over outcomes. Then, she would adjust such an estimate after mentally simulating alternative values. This adjustment may be influenced by the degree of ambiguity and by the size of the outcome (e.g., whether the gain or loss is large or small).

---

* The concept of subjective probabilities establishes a bridge between the concept of risk and uncertainty, since the known probability (of a risk) is set on par with a subjective belief. Prescriptively, decision theory and mainstream economic theory of expected utility have incorporated the idea that knowledge (or subjective belief) of the actual risks associated with different events and decisions will drive the actions of an economic agent. An economic agent will consider a set of possible actions with different outcomes, probabilities over these outcomes, and associated utilities. He will then choose a strategy consisting of a series of actions leading to the highest expected utility.
** Experimental evidence and formal modeling work on ambiguity is reviewed in Camerer and Weber [15] in great detail.

The debate outlined above is instrumental in the understanding of decision making under uncertainty in both the descriptive and the normative sense. It is also important to the theory of privacy decision making. In particular, we favor the view that in numerous privacy-sensitive situations it is unrealistic to assume existence of known or knowable probabilities or complete (subjective) beliefs for probabilities over all possible outcomes.

18.2.2 Privacy as a Problem of Risk or Uncertainty?

When presented with a privacy-related problem, consumers often face two major unknowns: (1) what privacy-relevant outcomes may occur under different contexts, and (2) with what consequences [1]. Implicit in these two major unknowns are, however, layers of additional uncertainties, which are briefly described below.

First, an individual has often only vague and limited knowledge of the actions she can take to protect (or give away) her personal information. She also has limited knowledge of the possible or actual actions undertaken by other entities (e.g., a marketer's purpose and means to collect information).

Second, actions taken by the individual (whether as an attempt to protect or trade information) or another party have often hardly predictable consequences. For example, it is often unknown whether provided contact information will be used for unwanted communication or whether past consumption data is input for price discrimination strategies.

Third, possible relevant states of nature (with associated additional actions and consequences) may be unknowable in advance because they depend on future, unforeseeable events and environmental changes (e.g., a technology development, such as private information retrieval [17]; or Google caching, making old Usenet archives searchable).

Fourth, certain desirable actions and information may not be available (see research on asymmetric information and hidden action). Most importantly, consumers often cannot regain control over information formerly released to commercial entities or other individuals.*

Fifth, we observed in prior work that individuals iteratively uncover additional layers of a privacy choice situation that reveal further actions and outcomes, with their sets of associated (possible) values and (possible) probabilities. For example, in [1] we describe how people change their perception on which parties have access to their credit card transactional data if they are prompted with this topic repeatedly. We show that individuals sometimes ignore both privacy risks and forms of protection, and even

---

* There are substantial differences between United States and European Union data protection legislation concerning the legal rights to gain knowledge of, correct, and delete commercial data records about an individual.

when they are aware of them, often miscalculate their probability of occurrence and their numerical outcome in terms of financial magnitude. This carelessness or ignorance might be justifiable if one considers the effort needed to evaluate everyday privacy choices carefully.

Sixth, privacy protection or invasion are often by-products of other (and sometimes unrelated) transactions. The privacy "good" is often attached to other goods in complex bundles—or, in other words, trade-offs involving privacy are often trade-offs between heterogeneous goods. For example, when an individual purchases a book online (thus saving the time she would have to spend going to the bookstore and paying in cash), she will often reveal her credit card details to the online merchant, which may lead to an increased risk of identity theft. Or, in order to receive a monetary discount from the grocery store, she will reveal her buying patterns by using a loyalty card, which may increase her probability of receiving junk mail or undesired commercial offers.

Comparisons between these different goods are difficult because of their combinatorial aspects, but may be further complicated if the offers are uncertain or ambiguous. The marketing literature has long been interested in scenarios where the underlying values are incommensurate. In particular, Nunes and Park [18] consider how different forms of wealth are difficult to "convert into any meaningful common unit of measurement." For example, they study a promotion that is presented in nonmonetary terms (e.g., an umbrella). Under these conditions, the marginal value of the nonmonetary, incremental benefits becomes difficult to evaluate for the individual, in relation to the focal product or its price. Note that privacy-related benefits and costs are rarely monetary and often immaterial.

Because of these intertwined layers of complexity, we conclude that an individual who is facing privacy-sensitive scenarios may be uncertain about the values of possible outcomes and their probability of occurrence, and that sometimes she may not even be able to form beliefs about those values and those probabilities. In fact, she may have no knowledge of the possible *outcomes* of a certain situation since the states of nature may be unknown or unknowable in advance. As a result, individuals may sometimes ignore both privacy risks and forms of protection.

18.3 Behavioral Economics and Privacy

Due to the uncertainties, ambiguities, and complexities that characterize privacy choices, individuals are likely influenced by a number of cognitive limitations and behavioral biases that have been discussed in the literature on behavioral economics.

Behavioral economics studies how individual, social, cognitive, and emotional biases influence economic decisions. This research is predominantly based on neoclassical models of economic behavior, but aims to integrate rational choice theory with convincing evidence from individual, cognitive, and social psychology. Behavioral economic models often abandon some of the tenets of rational choice theory: that agents possess consistent preferences between alternatives, choose the utility maximizing option, discount future events consistently, and act upon complete information or known probability distributions for all possible events. In fact, behavioral models expand the economic modeling toolkit by addressing many empirical phenomena, such as how our innate *bounded rationality* limits our ability to exhaustively search for the best alternative and how the *framing* of a scenario or a question may influence an individual's reaction to it. It also addresses how *heuristics* often replace rational searches for the best possible alternative and how *biases* and other anomalies affect the way we compare alternatives, perceive risks, or discount values over time [7,19]. In this section, we present a number of themes analyzed in the behavioral literature and discuss their relevance to privacy research, either by making reference to current results or by proposing possible paths of research.

18.3.1 Helping Individuals Understand Risk and Deal with Bounded Rationality

Consumers will often be overwhelmed with the task of identifying possible outcomes related to privacy threats and means of protection. Even more so, they will face difficulties in assigning accurate likelihoods to those states. Policymakers often suggest that providing more information to consumers will help them make better decisions and avoid those impediments. Such additional information may be provided by commercials entities (e.g., antispyware vendors), by consumer advocacy groups, or by peers.

However, even if individuals had access to complete information, they would often be unable to process and act optimally on large amounts of data. Especially in the presence of complex, ramified consequences associated with the protection or release of personal information, our innate bounded rationality limits our ability to acquire, memorize, and process all relevant information, and it makes us rely on simplified mental models, approximate strategies, and heuristics.

Bounded problem solving is usually neither unreasonable nor irrational, and it doesn't need to be inferior to rational utility maximization. However, these strategies replace theoretical quantitative approaches with qualitative evaluations and "aspirational" solutions that stop short of perfect (numerical) optimization. In [1], we found some evidence of simplified mental models of privacy in a survey about individual privacy attitudes and behavior: A number of survey participants combined together security and privacy issues when they reported feeling that their privacy was protected by merchants who offered Secure Sockets Layer (SSL) connections to complete online payments. Similarly, the presence of a privacy policy may be taken by many to represent privacy protection regardless of its content [20]; or a privacy seal may be interpreted as a guarantee of a trustworthy Web site [21].

Consumer advocates might suggest that providing individuals with clearly phrased advice or preprocessed information (e.g., to avoid a certain product or activity) will help overcome problems of information overload and bounded decision making. Nevertheless, consumers may still use this data in ways that are different from that of expected utility maximization or contradict their own best interest. In a recent study, Good et al. found evidence that even well-presented notices of dangerous behaviors of computer programs (e.g., spyware) may not always lead individuals to abort installations or to feel regret about completed installations [22]. Similarly, Spiekermann et al. found individuals' behavior in an interactive online shopping episode was not significantly affected as the privacy statement of the Web site was modified substantially [23]. Through these studies, we learn that individuals are influenced by additional factors that add to the complexity of determining risks and uncertainties associated with privacy threats.

18.3.2 Framing and Heuristics

Tversky and Kahneman have shown that the way a problem or question is *framed* affects how individuals respond to it [24]. Acquisti and Grossklags [25] discuss experimental evidence from a survey study detailing the impact on the willingness to accept or reject a marketer's privacy related offer, when the consequences of the offer are reframed in uncertain and highly ambiguous terms. Anecdotal evidence also suggests that it is a safer strategy to convince consumers *ex ante* to provide personal information (even in exchange for small benefits or rewards) than to allow for revelation of privacy-intrusive practices after the fact. In addition, Good et al. describe preliminary experimental results suggesting that potentially unwanted privacy and security practices discussed in a privacy notice written in vague language might be considered less intrusive by consumers compared to more detailed descriptions of possible dangers [26].

Tversky, Kahneman, and others have also highlighted a number of *heuristics* that guide individual decision making more than rational choice processes. In this context, an heuristic is some technique—often simple and efficient—that helps learning or problem solving. As an example, individuals often *anchor* on a specific valuation of a goods or service, and then adjust that valuation when new information becomes known. However, the process of initial anchoring may be arbitrary [27], and may create persistent bias in the evaluation process [?]. The value that individuals assign to their own personal information, in fact, may be assigned through anchoring on a focal and possibly arbitrary value: it is very difficult for an individual to "price" her own information. However, once a price has been found (perhaps completely arbitrarily or perhaps by anchoring it to the reward received by a merchant in exchange for that information) it is likely that the consumer's valuation of her own personal data, thereafter, will orbit around that value.*

Other heuristics may also be found in privacy decision making. For example, individuals may tend to discount as improbable those events that are difficult to picture mentally, such as identity theft (the simulation heuristic [30]); or may associate trustworthy behavior with the neat appearance and design of a Web site (an example for the representativeness heuristic [31]).

One of the most influential theories in this context is prospect theory [32] that provides an interpretation of how individuals evaluate and compare uncertain gains and losses. Kahneman and Tversky showed that individuals' evaluations around losses and gains can be represented as starting from a reference point, with an S-shaped value function passing through that point. Because of this shape, the same variation in absolute value has larger impact as a loss than as a gain. In other words, this representation reveals how individuals tend to be loss averse, by preferring avoiding losses to acquiring gains. An outcome of the theory is the so-called "pseudocertainty effect": individuals tend to make risk-averse choices in the presence of positive expected payoffs, but risk-seeking choices in the presence of negative expected payoffs. In addition, individuals are often not only risk averse, but also *ambiguity averse* [15]. Given the choice between a certain outcome (e.g., $10) and a lottery outcome (e.g., $0 with 50% likelihood and X with 50% likelihood), individuals prefer the certain choice unless they are offered a premium in the lottery so that the expected value of the lottery is greater than the certain outcome (e.g., X strictly greater than $20). Furthermore, there is evidence that competence and knowledge affect individuals' choices. People prefer to bet on events they know more about, even when their beliefs are held constant [33].

The role of these effects on privacy decision making is likely to be significant, although by no means clear, since many competing hypotheses can be formulated. Individuals who do not adopt free and readily available privacy technologies to protect their data, or accept small rewards in exchange for providing their information to parties they know little about, may have simply no interest in keep personal information private or, in fact, may be displaying both ambiguity love (rather than aversion) or little consideration of future risks. Individuals' low *ex ante* valuation of risks could also be due to a lack of faith about the power of protective solutions to noticeable decrease risks.

---

* See [28] and [29] for survey and experimental evidence on the valuation of personal information.

Related to prospect theory is also the so-called endowment effect that suggests that individuals value goods more when they already have them in their possession [34]. In the privacy arena, we found preliminary evidence that individuals tend to assign a higher "sell" value to their personal information (the amount they request from others to give them their information) than the "buy" value (the amount they are willing to spend to make sure that the same information is not released to others) [1]. This happens even for pieces of information that would not appear to have financial consequences when released.

18.3.3 Other Systematic Biases

Individuals tend to sometimes make paradoxical, surprising, and seemingly contradictory decisions (see, for example, [35] and [36]).

In the privacy arena, a bias that has been an object of attention is hyperbolic discounting. Hyperbolic discounting refers to the idea that people do not discount distant and close events in a consistent way. These inconsistencies could lead to phenomena, such as addiction and self-control biases [37]. In [3], we presented a model of privacy behavior grounded on some of those distortions, in particular, the tendency to trade-off privacy costs and benefits in ways that may be inconsistent with individuals' initial plans leading to damages of the future selves in favor of immediate gratification [38].

Several other deviations from rationality also may affect the way consumers decide whether to protect or to reveal personal information. Below is a list of topics for ongoing and future research.

> *Valence effect.* The valence effect of prediction refers to the tendency to overestimate the likelihood of favorable events. In the form of a *self-serving bias*, individuals tend to overestimate the likelihood of favorable events happening to them relative to *other* individuals. In preliminary analysis of users of an online social network, Acquisti and Gross found that online social network users believe that providing personal information publicly on social networks could cause privacy problems to other users, although the same respondents are not particularly concerned about *their* own privacy on those networks [39].
>
> *Overconfidence.* Overconfidence refers to the tendency to be more confident in one's knowledge or abilities than what would be warranted by facts. Examples of overconfidence can be easily found in different arenas, especially in scenarios where probabilities are difficult to predict. In [1], we found evidence of overconfidence in estimating exposure to a number of privacy risks.

Rational ignorance. Ignorance can be considered rational when the cost of learning about a situation enough to inform a rational decision would be higher than the potential benefit one may derive from that decision. Individuals may avoid assessing their privacy risks for similar reasons; for instance, they may disregard reading a data holder's privacy policy as they believe that the time cost associated with inspecting the notice would not be compensated by the expected benefit (for a related model, see [40]).

Status quo bias. It also could be that individuals choose not to look for solutions or alternatives to deal with their personal information because they prefer, on average, for things to stay relatively the same (the so-called *status quo* bias [41]). In a study of online social networks, we found that the vast majority of users do not change their default (and very permeable) privacy settings [39]. Further research in this area could investigate the relative importance of the *status quo* bias compared to individuals' desire to avoid learning and transaction costs involved in changing existing settings.

Reciprocity and fairness. Reciprocity and fairness have been studied in social psychology and economics [42]. This literature considers the innate desire to act fairly in transactions with other individuals, but also to retaliate or reward others' behavior when deemed appropriate. We believe that such social phenomena are also of relevance to privacy behavior. It is well known, for example, that survey takers are more likely to respond to a survey when the interviewer sends in money even before the survey has been completed. Web sites that ask for registration even before providing any service in return, instead, may end up receiving incorrect or no data at all.

Inequity aversion. Related to the aforementioned concept is the idea of inequity aversion.* Because of it, individuals reject offers or express discontent with scenarios in which they feel that *others* are unfairly getting better rewards than the individual, or in which they feel that *they* are getting rewards they do not deserve [43]. In the privacy arena, it is possible that individuals are particularly sensitive to privacy invasions of companies when they feel companies are unfairly gaining from the use of their personal data without offering adequate consideration to the individual. Or, vice versa, users of social networks may find it natural and fair that, in exchange for the free service they offer, hosting Web sites end up learning and using information about the individual users [39].

---

* This concept should not be confused with economic inequality, which typically refers to inequality among individuals or entities within a larger group or society.

18.4   How to Research the Privacy Phenomenon

Privacy decision making is subject to several environmental constraints. Because of the complexities and the influence of uncertainty and ambiguity, providing more privacy information, while helpful, may not be always beneficial to the individual, as it may lead to more cognitive costs, heuristics, and biases.

Heuristics are not necessarily risky strategies. They can be good or bad guides to decision making. Similarly, biases and anomalies that affect privacy behavior are not necessarily damaging. Even *ex post*, only few of the consequences of privacy decisions are actually quantifiable; *ex ante*, fewer yet are. Accordingly, economic actors and observers will find it difficult to judge the optimality of a certain privacy-related choice in economic terms.

It follows that one of the contributions that behavioral economics can offer to privacy research is not necessarily a set of lessons to let consumers avoid *all* costly mistakes, but rather a number of tools to better understand privacy decision making and behavior.

One of the main challenges in this process lies in the fact that several layers of difficulties are intertwined in the privacy phenomenon: incomplete information, framing and heuristics, anomalies, and biases may all play interdependent roles, yet by no means are all of them always present. It is hard, both theoretically and empirically, to separate the impact of any of these layers from the others. Understanding privacy decisions, therefore, requires a delicate balance between two types of studies: those that cover privacy holistically in its richness, and those consisting of controlled analyses of specific aspects. Combing the recent wave of theoretical models (like [44], [45], or [46]), surveys (like [47], [48], or [1]), and experiments (in the lab [4], [28], or [29]; and in the field [39]) with behavioral economics and newer approaches (such as neuroeconomics [49]) may help us cast light on the intricacies and surprising observations with respect to privacy valuations and actions. The above research can improve policy decision making and technology design for end users and data-holding entities. The works and directions discussed in this chapter point at an exciting research agenda.

References

[1]   Acquisti, A., Grossklags, J.: Privacy and rationality in decision making. *IEEE Security & Privacy*, January–February (2005) 24–30.

[2]   Acquisti, A.: Privacy and security of personal information: Economic incentives and technological solutions. In Camp, J., Lewis, S., Eds.: The Economics of Information Security. (2004) Originally presented at the *2002 Workshop on Economics and Information Security (WEIS '02)*, University of California, Berkeley.

[3]   Acquisti, A.: Privacy in electronic commerce and the economics of immediate gratification. In *Proceedings of the ACM Conference on Electronic Commerce (EC '04)*. (2004) New York, 21–29.

[4]   Acquisti, A., Grossklags, J.: Losses, gains, and hyperbolic discounting: An experimental approach to information security attitudes and behavior. In Camp, J., Lewis, S., Eds.: The Economics of Information Security. (2004). Originally presented at the *2003 Workshop on Economics and Information Security (WEIS '03)* University of Maryland, College Park.

[5]   Akerlof, G.A.: The market for 'lemons': Quality uncertainty and the market mechanism. *Quarterly Journal of Economics* 84(3) (1970) 488–500.

[6]   Simon, H.A.: Models of bounded rationality. MIT Press, Cambridge, MA (1982).

[7]   Camerer, C., Lowenstein, G.: Behavioral economics: Past, present, future. In *Advances in Behavioral Economics*. (2003) 3–51.

[8]   Posner, R.A.: An economic theory of privacy. *Regulation* May–June (1978) 19–26.

[9]   Varian, H.R.: Economic aspects of personal privacy. In *Privacy and Self-Regulation in the Information Age*, National Telecommunications and Information Administration (1996).

[10] Knight, F.H.: *Risk, Uncertainty, and Profit*. Hart, Schaffner & Marx; Houghton Mifflin Company, Boston, MA (1921).

[11] Bernoulli, D.: Specimen theoriae novae de mensura sortis. Commentarii Academiae Scientiarum Imperialis Petropolitannae (1738). Translated and published as "Exposition of a New Theory on the Measurement of Risk" in *Econometrica* 22(1): 23–36, January 1954.

[12] Menger, C.: *Principles of Economics*. New York University Press, New York, (1981 edition), (1871).

[13] von Neumann, J., Morgenstern, O.: *Theory of Games and Economic Behavior*. Princeton University Press (1953 ed.), Princeton, NJ (1944).

[14] Savage, L.J.: *The Foundations of Statistics*. Dover (1972 ed.), New York (1954).

[15] Camerer, C., Weber, M.: Recent developments in modeling preferences: Uncertainty and ambiguity. *The Journal of Risk and Uncertainty* 5 (1992) 325–370.

[16] Hogarth, R.M., Kunreuther, H.: Decision making under uncertainty: The effects of role and ambiguity. In Heller, F., Ed.: *Decision Making and Leadership*, Cambridge, U.K.: Cambridge University Press (1992) 189–212.

[17] Chor, B., Goldreich, O., Kushilevitz, E., Sudan, M.: Private information retrieval. In *IEEE Symposium on Foundations of Computer Science*. (1995) Santa Fe, NM, 41–50.

[18] Nunes, J.C., Park, C.W.: Incommensurate resources: Not just more of the same. *Journal of Marketing Research* 40 (2003) 26–38.

[19] Shefrin, H.: *Beyond Greed and Fear: Understanding Behavioral Finance and the Psychology of Investing*. Oxford University Press, Oxford, U.K., (2002).

[20] Turow, J., Hoofnagle, C.J., Mulligan, D., Good, N., Grossklags, J.: The FTC and Consumer Privacy in the Coming Decade. Samuelson Law, Technology and Public Policy Clinic report. University of California, Berkeley (2006).

[21] Moores, T.: Do Consumers understand the role of privacy seals in e-commerce? *Communications of the ACM* 48(3) (2005) 86–91.

[22] Good, N., Grossklags, J., Mulligan, D., Konstan, J.: Noticing notice: A large-scale experiment on the timing of software license agreements. *Proceedings of SIGCHI Conference on Human Factors in Computing Systems (CHI'07)*, San Jose, CA, (2007).

[23] Spiekermann, S., Grossklags, J., Berendt, B.: E-privacy in 2nd generation e-commerce: Privacy preferences versus actual behavior. In *Proceedings of the ACM Conference on Electronic Commerce (EC '01)*. (2001) Tampa, FL, 38–47.

[24] Tversky, A., Kahneman, D.: The framing of decisions and the psychology of choice. *Science* 211 (1981) 453–458.

[25] Acquisti, A., Grossklags, J.: Uncertainty, ambiguity and privacy. In *Workshop on Economics and Information Security (WEIS '05)*. Boston, MA, (2005).

[26] Good, N., Grossklags, J., Thaw, D., Perzanowski, A., Mulligan, D., Konstan, J.: User choices and regret: Understanding users' decision process about consensually acquired spyware. *I/S: A Journal of Law and Policy for the Information Society* 2 (2) (2006) 283–344.

[27] Ariely, D., Loewenstein, G., Prelec, D.: Coherent arbitrariness: Stable demand curves without stable preferences. *Quarterly Journal of Economics* 118 (2003) 73–106.

[28] Hann, I.H., Hui, K.L., Lee, T.S., Png, I.P.L.: Online information privacy: Measuring the cost-benefit trade-off. In *23rd International Conference on Information Systems*, Barcelona, Spain, (2002).

[29] Huberman, B., Adar, E., Fine, L.R.: Valuating Privacy. IEEE Security of Privacy, September–October (2005), 22–25.

[30] Kahneman, D., Tversky, A.: The simulation heuristic. In Kahneman, D., Slovic, P., Tversky, A., Eds. Judgment under uncertainty: Heuristics and biases. Cambridge, U.K.: Cambridge University Press (1982) 201–210.

[31] Kahneman, D., Tversky, A.: On the psychology of prediction. *Psychological Review* 80 (1973) 237–251.

[32] Kahneman, D., Tversky, A.: Prospect theory: An analysis of decision under risk. *Econometrica* 47(2) (1979) 263–269.

[33] Heath, C., Tversky, A.: Preference and belief: Ambiguity and competence in choice under uncertainty. *Journal of Risk and Uncertainty* 4 (1991) 5–28.

[34] Thaler, R.: Towards a positive theory of consumer choice. *Journal of Economic Behavior and Organization* 1 (1980) 39–60.

[35] Kahneman, D., Tversky, A.: *Choices, Values, and Frames*. University Press, Cambridge, MA, (2000).

[36] Ellsberg, D.: *Risk, Ambiguity, and Decision*. Garland Publishing, New York and London (2001).

[37] Lowenstein, G., Prelac, D.: *Choices Over Time*. Russell Sage Foundation: New York (1992).

[38] Rabin, M., O'Donoghue, T.: The economics of immediate gratification. *Journal of Behavioral Decision Making* 13(2) (2000) 233–250.

[39] Acquisti, A., Gross, R.: Imagined communities: Awareness, information sharing, and privacy on the facebook. Carnegie Mellon University, Pittsburgh, PA (2006).

[40] Vila, T., Greenstadt, R., Molnar, D.: Why we can't be bothered to read privacy policies: Models of privacy economics as a lemons market. In *2003 Workshop on Economics and Information Security* (WEIS '03). University of Maryland, College Park, (2003).

[41] W. Samuelson, Zeckhauser, R.J.: Status quo bias in decision making. *Journal of Risk and Uncertainty* 1 (1988) 7–59.

[42] Fehr, E., Gächter, S.: Fairness and retaliation: The economics of reciprocity. *Journal of Economic Perspectives* 14(3) (2000) 159–181.

[43] Fehr, E., Schmidt, K.M.: A theory of fairness, competition, and cooperation. *The Quarterly Journal of Economics* 114 (1999) 817–868.

[44] Taylor, C.R.: Private demands and demands for privacy: Dynamic pricing and the market for customer information. Technical report, Duke University, Durham, N.C., Economics Department (2002).

[45] Acquisti, A., Varian, H.R.: Conditioning prices on purchase history. *Marketing Science* 24(3) (2005) 1–15.

[46] Calzolari, G., Pavan, A.: Optimal design of privacy policies. Technical report, Gremaq, University of Toulouse, Toulouse, France, (2001).

[47] Ackerman, M., Cranor, L., Reagle, J.: Privacy in e-commerce: Examining user scenarios and privacy preferences. In *Proceedings of the ACM Conference on Electronic Commerce* (EC '99). (1999) Denver, CO, 1–8.

[48] Federal Trade Commission: Privacy online: Fair information practices in the electronic marketplace (2000) http://www.ftc.gov/reports/privacy2000/privacy2000.pdf

[49] Camerer, C., Loewenstein, G., Prelec, D.: Neuroeconomics: How neuroscience can inform economics. *Journal of Economic Literature* 43(1) (2005) 9–64.

PRIVACY AND POLICY

Chapter 19

Privacy of Outsourced Data

Sabrina De Capitani di Vimercati, Sara Foresti,
Stefano Paraboschi, and Pierangela Samarati

Contents

19.1 Introduction 382
19.2 Basic Scenario and Data Organization 383
    19.2.1 Parties Involved 383
    19.2.2 Data Organization.. 384
    19.2.3 Interactions 386
19.3 Querying Encrypted Data 387
    19.3.1 Bucket-Based Index....................................... 387
    19.3.2 Hash-Based Index.. 389
    19.3.3 B + Trees Index 390
    19.3.4 Other Approaches 392
    19.3.5 Evaluation of Inference Exposure 394
19.4 Security Issues 396
    19.4.1 Access Control Enforcement.............................. 396
        19.4.1.1 Selective Encryption............................ 397
        19.4.1.2 Other Approaches.............................. 403
19.5 Conclusions 404
Acknowledgments 404
References.. 405

19.1   Introduction

The amount of information held by organizations' databases is increasing rapidly. To respond to this demand, organizations can either add data storage and skilled administrative personnel (at a high rate) or, a solution becoming increasingly popular, delegate database management to an external service provider (*database outsourcing*). In database outsourcing, usually referred to as *Database As a Service* (DAS), an external service provider provides mechanisms for clients to access the outsourced databases. A major advantage of database outsourcing is related to the high costs of in-house versus outsourced hosting. Outsourcing provides significant cost savings and promises higher availability and more effective disaster protection than in-house operations. On the other hand, database outsourcing poses a major security problem, due to the fact that the external service provider, who is relied upon for ensuring high availability of the outsourced database, cannot always be trusted with the confidentiality of database content.

Besides well-known risks of confidentiality and privacy breaks, threats to outsourced data include improper use of database information: the server could extract, resell, or commercially use parts of a collection of data gathered and organized by the data owner, potentially harming the data owner's market for any product or service that incorporates that collection of information. Traditional database access control techniques cannot prevent the server itself from making unauthorized access to the data stored in the database. Alternatively, to protect against "honest but curious" servers, a protective layer of encryption can be wrapped around specific sensitive data, preventing outside attacks as well as infiltration from the server itself [1]. Data encryption, however, raises the problem of efficiently querying the outsourced database (now encrypted). Since confidentiality demands that data decryption must be possible only at the client side, techniques have been proposed, which enable external servers to directly execute queries on encrypted data. Typically, these solutions consist mainly of adding a piece of information, called *index*, to the encrypted data. An index is computed based on the plaintext data and it preserves some of the original characteristics of the data.

Several approaches have been proposed for encrypting and indexing outsourced databases and for querying them. Also, these proposals assume all users have complete access to the entire database. This assumption does not fit current scenarios where different users may need to see different portions of the data, that is, where selective access needs to be enforced. Adding a traditional authorization layer to the current outsourcing scenarios requires that, when a client poses a query, both the query and its result have to be filtered by the data owner (who is in charge of enforcing the access control policy), a solution however that is not applicable in a real-life scenario. More recent research has addressed the problem of enforcing selective access on the outsourced encrypted data by combining cryptography with authorizations, thus enforcing access control via *selective encryption*. Basically, the idea is to use different keys for encrypting different portions of the database. These keys are then distributed to users according to their access rights. The challenge is then to limit the amount of cryptographic information that needs to be stored and managed.

In this chapter, we survey the main proposals addressing the data access and security issues arising in the database outsourcing scenario. Section 19.2 gives an overview of the entities involved in the DAS scenario and of their typical interactions. Section 19.3 describes the main indexing methods proposed in the literature for supporting queries over encrypted data. Section 19.4 presents the main proposals for enforcing selective access on the outsourced data. Finally, section 19.5 summarizes the conclusion.

19.2 Basic Scenario and Data Organization

Described below are the entities involved in the DAS scenario, how data is organized in the outsourced database, and the interaction among the entities for query execution.

19.2.1 Parties Involved

There are four distinct entities interacting in the DAS scenario (Figure 19.1):

- *Data owner* (person or organization) who produces and outsources resources to make them available for controlled external release.
- *User* (human entity) who presents requests (queries) to the system.
- *Client* front-end transforms the queries posed by users into equivalent queries operating on the encrypted data stored on the server.
- *Server* that receives the encrypted data from one or more data owners and makes them available for distribution to clients.

Clients and data owners, when outsourcing data, are assumed to trust the server to faithfully maintain outsourced data. The server is then relied upon for the availability of outsourced data, so the data owner and clients can access data whenever requested. However, the server (which can be "honest but curious") is not trusted with the confidentiality of the actual database content, as outsourced data may contain sensitive information that the data owner wants to release only to authorized users. Consequently, it is necessary to preserve the server from making unauthorized access to the database available. To this purpose, the data owner encrypts her data with a key known only to trusted clients, and sends the encrypted database to the server for storage.

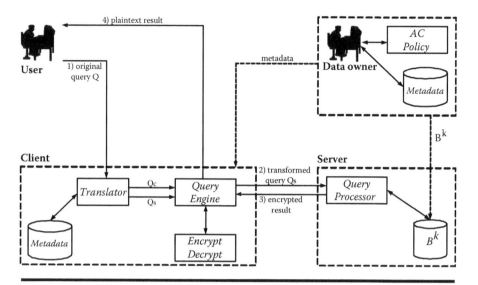

Figure 19.1   DAS scenario.

19.2.2   Data Organization

A database can be encrypted according to different strategies. In principle, both symmetric and asymmetric encryption can be used at different granularity levels. Symmetric encryption, being cheaper than asymmetric encryption, is usually adopted. The granularity level at which database encryption is performed can depend on the data that need to be accessed. Encryption can then be at the finer grain of [2,3]:

■ *Table*: Each table in the plaintext database is represented through a single encrypted value in the encrypted database. Consequently, tuples and attributes are indistinguishable in the released data and cannot be specified in a query on the encrypted database.

■ *Attribute*: Each column (attribute) in the plaintext table is represented by a single encrypted value in the encrypted table.

■ *Tuple*: Each tuple in the plaintext table is represented by a single encrypted value in the encrypted table.

■ *Element*: Each cell in the plaintext table is represented by a single encrypted value in the encrypted table.

Both table level and attribute level encryption imply the communication to the requesting client of the whole table involved in a query, as it is not possible to extract any subset of the tuples in the encrypted representation of the table. On the other hand, encrypting at the element level would require an excessive workload for data owners and clients in encrypting/decrypting data. For balancing client workload and query execution efficiency, most proposals assume that the database is encrypted at the tuple level.

While database encryption provides an adequate level of protection for data, it makes it impossible for the server to directly execute the users' queries on the encrypted database. Upon receiving a query, the server can only send to the requestor the encrypted tables involved in the query; the client can then decrypt such tables and execute the query on them. To allow the server to select a set of tuples to be returned in response to a query, a set of indexes can be associated with the encrypted table. In this case, the server stores an encrypted table with an index for each attribute on which conditions may need to be evaluated. For simplicity, we assume there is an index for each attribute in each table of the database. Different kinds of indexes can be defined, depending on the clauses and conditions that need to be remotely evaluated for the different attributes. Given a plaintext database $\mathcal{B}$, each table r_i over schema $R_i(A_{i1}, A_{i2}, \ldots, A_{in})$ in $\mathcal{B}$ is mapped onto a table r_i^k over schema $R_i^k(\texttt{Counter}, \texttt{Etuple}, I_1, I_2, \ldots, I_n)$ in the corresponding encrypted database $\mathcal{B}^k$. Here, $\texttt{Counter}$ is a numerical attribute added as a primary key of the encrypted table; $\texttt{Etuple}$ is the attribute containing the encrypted tuple whose value is obtained by applying an encryption function E_k to the plaintext tuple, where k is the secret key; and I_j is the index associated with the j-th attribute in R_i. While we assume encrypted tuples and indexes to be in the same relation, we note that indexes can be stored in a separate table [4].

To illustrate, consider table $\texttt{Employee}$ in Figure 19.2(a). The corresponding encrypted table is shown in Figure 19.2(b), where index values are conventionally represented with Greek letters. The encrypted table has exactly the same number of tuples as the original table. For the sake of readability, the tuples in the encrypted table are listed in the order in which they appear in the corresponding plaintext table. The same happens for the order of indexes, which are listed in the same order as the plaintext attributes to which they refer.

Employee						Employee^k					
Emp-Id	Name	YoB	Dept	Salary		Counter	Etuple	I_1	I_2	I_3	I_4	I_5
P01	Ann	1980	Production	10		1	ite6*+8wc	π	α	γ	ε	λ
R01	Bob	1975	R&D	15		2	8(nfeua4!=	φ	β	δ	θ	λ
F01	Bob	1985	Financial	10		3	Q73gnew321*/	φ	β	γ	μ	λ
P02	Carol	1980	Production	20		4	-1vs9e892s	π	α	γ	ε	ρ
F02	Ann	1980	Financial	15		5	e32rfs4+@	π	α	γ	μ	λ
R02	David	1978	R&D	15		6	r43arg*5[)	φ	β	δ	θ	λ

(a)   (b)

Figure 19.2 An example of plaintext (a) and encrypted (b) table.

19.2.3 Interactions

The introduction of indexes allows partial evaluation of any query Q at the server-side, provided it is previously translated in an equivalent query operating on the encrypted database. Figure 19.1 summarizes the most important steps necessary for the evaluation of a query submitted by a user.

1. The user submits her query Q referring to the schema of the plaintext database B, and passes it to the client front-end. The user need not be aware that data has been outsourced to a third party.
2. The client maps the user's query onto: (1) an equivalent query Q_s, working on the encrypted tables through indexes, and (2) an additional query Q_c working on the results of Q_s. Query Q_s is then passed on to the remote server. Note that the client is the unique entity in the system who knows the structure of both B and B^k and can translate the queries the user may submit.
3. The remote server executes the received query Q_s on the encrypted database and returns the result (i.e., a set of encrypted tuples) to the client.
4. The client decrypts the tuples received and eventually discards spurious tuples (i.e., tuples that do not satisfy the query submitted by the user). These spurious tuples are removed by executing query Q_c. The final plaintext result is then returned to the user.

Since a client may have a limited storage and computation capacity, one of the primary goals of the query execution process is to minimize the workload at the client-side, while maximizing the operations that can be computed at the server-side [2,3,5,6].

Iyer et al. [2,3] present a solution for minimizing the client workload that is based on a graphical representation of queries as trees. The tree representing a query is split in two parts: the lower part includes all the operations that can be executed by the server, while the upper part contains all the operations that cannot be delegated to the server and, therefore, needs to be executed by the client. In particular, since a query can be represented with different, but equivalent, trees by simply pushing down selections and postponing projections, the basic idea of the proposed solution is to determine an equivalent tree representation of the query, where the operations that only the client can execute are in the highest levels of the tree. For instance, if there are two ANDed conditions in the query and only one can be evaluated on the server-side, the selection operation is split in such a way that one condition is evaluated server-side and the other client-side.

Hacigümüs et al. [5] show a method for splitting the query Q_s to be executed on the encrypted data into two subqueries, Q_{s1} and Q_{s2}, where Q_{s1} returns only tuples that will belong to the final result, and query Q_{s2} may contain also spurious tuples. This distinction allows the execution of Q_c over the result of Q_{s2} only, while tuples returned by Q_{s1} can be immediately decrypted. To further reduce the client's workload, Damiani et al. [6] propose an architecture that minimizes storage for the client and introduce the idea of selective decryption of Q_s. With selective decryption, the client decrypts the portion of the tuples needed for evaluating Q_c, while complete decryption is executed only for tuples that belong to the final result and that will be returned to the final user. The approach is based on a block-cipher encryption algorithm, operating at tuple level, that allows the detection of the blocks containing the attributes necessary to evaluate the conditions in Q_c, which are the only ones that need decryption.

It is important to note that the process of transforming Q in Q_s and Q_c greatly depends both on the indexing method adopted and on the kind of query Q. There are operations that need to be executed by the client, since the indexing method adopted does not support the specific operations (e.g., range queries are not supported by all types of indexes) and the server is not allowed to decrypt data. Also, there are operations that the server could execute over the index, but that require a precomputation that only the client can perform and, therefore, must be postponed in Q_c (e.g., the evaluation of a condition in the having clause, which needs a grouping over an attribute whose corresponding index has been created by using a method that does not support the group by clause).

19.3 Querying Encrypted Data

When designing a solution for querying encrypted data, one of the most important goals is to minimize the computation at the client-side and to reduce communication overhead. The server, therefore, should be responsible for the majority of the work. Different index approaches allow the execution of different types of queries at server-side.

We now describe in more detail the methods initially proposed to efficiently execute simple queries at the server-side, and we give an overview of more recent methods that improve the server's ability to query encrypted data.

19.3.1 *Bucket-Based Index*

Hacigümüs et al. [7] propose the first method to query encrypted data, which is based on the definition of a number of *buckets* on the attribute domain.

Let r_i be a plaintext relation over schema $R_i(A_{i1}, A_{i2}, \ldots, A_{in})$ and r_i^k be the corresponding encrypted relation over schema $R_i^k(\texttt{Counter}, \texttt{Etuple})$. Considering an arbitrary plaintext attribute A_{ij} in R_i, with domain D_{ij}, bucket-based indexing methods partition D_{ij} in a number of

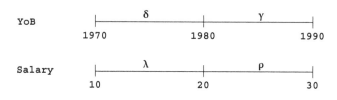

Figure 19.3   An example of bucketization.

nonoverlapping subsets of values, called *buckets*, containing contiguous values. This process, called *bucketization*, usually generates buckets that are all of the same size.

Each bucket is then associated with a unique value and the set of these values is the domain for index I_j associated with A_{ij}. Given a plaintext tuple t in r_i, the value of attribute A_{ij} for t belongs to a bucket. The corresponding index value is then the unique value associated with the bucket to which the plaintext value $t[A_{ij}]$ belongs. It is important to note that, for better preserving data secrecy, the domain of index I_j may not follow the same order as the one of the plaintext attribute A_{ij}. Attributes I_3 and I_5 in Figure 19.2(b) are the indexes obtained by applying the bucketization method described in Figure 19.3 to attributes YoB and Salary in Figure 19.2(a).

Bucket-based indexing methods allow the server-side evaluation of equality conditions appearing in the where clause, as these conditions can be mapped into equivalent conditions operating on indexes. Given a plaintext condition of the form $A_{ij} = v$, where v is a constant value, the corresponding condition operating on index I_j is $I_j = \beta$, where β is the value associated with the bucket containing v. As an example, with reference to Figure 19.3, condition YoB $= 1985$ is transformed into $I_3 = \gamma$. Also, equality conditions involving attributes defined on the same domain can be evaluated by the server, provided that attributes are indexed using the same bucketization. In particular, a plaintext condition of the form $A_{ij} = A_{ik}$ is translated into condition $I_j = I_k$ operating on indexes.

Bucket-based methods do not easily support range queries. Since the index domain does not necessarily preserve the plaintext domain ordering, a range condition of the form $A_{ij} \geq v$, where v is a constant value, must be mapped into a series of equality conditions operating on index I_j of the form $I_j = \beta_1$ or $I_j = \beta_2$ or ... or $I_j = \beta_k$, where $\beta_1, \ldots, \beta_k$ are the values associated with buckets that correspond to plaintext values greater than or equal to v. As an example, with reference to Figure 19.3, condition YoB > 1977 must be translated into $I_3 = \gamma$ or $I_3 = \delta$, as both values represent years greater than 1977.

Since the same index value is associated with more than one plaintext value, bucket-based indexing usually produces spurious tuples that need to be filtered out by the client front-end. Spurious tuples are tuples that satisfy the condition over the indexes, but that do not satisfy the original plaintext condition. For instance, with reference to the tables in Figure 19.2, query "select * from **Employee** where **YoB** = 1985" is translated into "select **Etuple** from **Employee**^{k} where $I_3 = \gamma$." The result of the query executed by the server contains tuples 1, 3, 4, and 5; however, only tuple 3 satisfies the original condition as written by the user. Tuples 1, 4, and 5 are spurious and must be discarded by the client.

Hore et al. [8] propose an improvement to bucket-based index methods by introducing an efficient way for partitioning the domain of attributes. Given an attribute and a query profile of it, the authors present a method for building an efficient index, which tries to minimize the number of spurious tuples in the result of range and equality queries.

One of the main disadvantages of bucket-based indexing methods is that they expose data to inference attacks (see section 19.3.5).

19.3.2   Hash-Based Index

Hash-based index methods are similar to bucket-based methods and are based on the concept of the *one-way hash function* [4]. Let r_i be a plaintext relation over schema $R_i(A_{i1}, A_{i2}, \ldots, A_{in})$ and r_i^k be the corresponding encrypted relation over schema $R_i^k(\text{Counter}, \text{Etuple})$. For each attribute A_{ij} in R_i to be indexed, a secure one-way hash function $b : D_{ij} \rightarrow B_{ij}$ is defined, where D_{ij} is the domain of A_{ij} and B_{ij} is the domain of index I_j associated with A_{ij}.

Given a plaintext tuple t in r_i, the index value corresponding to attribute A_{ij} for t is computed by applying function b to the plaintext value $t[A_{ij}]$.

An important property of any secure hash function b is its *determinism*; formally, $\forall x, y \in D_{ij} : x = y \Rightarrow b(x) = b(y)$. Another interesting property of secure hash functions is that the codomain of b is smaller than its domain, so there is the possibility of *collisions*; a collision happens when given two values $x, y \in D_{ij}$ with $x \neq y$, we have that $b(x) = b(y)$. A further property is that b must produce a strong mixing, that is, given two distinct but near values x, y ($| x - y | < \epsilon$) chosen randomly in D_{ij}, the discrete probability distribution of the difference $b(x) - b(y)$ is uniform (the results of the hash function can be arbitrarily different, even for very similar input values). A consequence of strong mixing is that the hash function does not preserve the domain order of the attribute on which it is applied. As an example, consider the relations in Figure 19.2. Here the indexes corresponding to attributes **Emp-Id**, **Name**, and **Dept** in relation **Employee** are computed by applying a hash-based method. The values of attribute **Name** have been mapped onto two distinct values, namely α and β; the values of attribute **Emp-Id** have been mapped onto two distinct values, namely π and ϕ; and the values of attribute `Dept` have been mapped onto three distinct values, namely ε, θ, and μ. Like for bucket-based methods, hash-based methods allow an efficient evaluation of equality conditions of the form $A_{ij} = v$, where v is a constant value. Each condition $A_{ij} = v$ is transformed into a condition $I_j = h(v)$, where I_j is the index corresponding to A_{ij} in the encrypted table. For instance, condition `Name` = "Alice" is transformed into $I_2 = \alpha$.

Also, equality conditions involving attributes defined on the same domain can be evaluated by the server, provided that these attributes are indexed using the same hash function. The main drawback of hash-based methods is that they do not support range queries, for which a solution similar to the one adopted for bucket-based methods is not viable; colliding values, in general, are not contiguous in the plaintext domain. Index collisions produce spurious tuples in the result. A collision-free hash function guarantees absence of spurious tuples, but may expose data to inference (see section 19.3.5). For instance, assuming that the hash function adopted for attribute `Dept` is collision-free, condition `Dept` = "Financial" is translated into $I_4 = \mu$, that will return only the tuples (in our example, tuples 3 and 5) that belong to the result set of the query that contains the corresponding plaintext condition.

19.3.3 B+ Trees Index

Both bucket- and hash-based indexing methods do not easily support range queries, since both of these solutions are not order-preserving. However, there is frequently the need for range queries. Damiani et al. [4] propose an indexing method that, while granting data privacy, preserves the order of plaintext data. This indexing method exploits the traditional B+ tree data structure used by relational database management systems (DBMSs) for physically indexing data. A B+ tree with fan-out n is a tree where every vertex can store up to $n - 1$ search key values and n pointers and, except for the root and leaf vertices, has at least $\lceil n/2 \rceil$ children. Given an internal vertex storing p key values $k_1, \ldots, k_p$ with $p \leq n - 1$, each k_i is followed by a pointer a_i, and k_1 is preceded by a pointer a_0. Pointer a_0 points to the subtree that contains keys with values lower than k_1, a_p points to the subtree that contains keys with values greater than or equal to k_p, and each a_i points to the subtree that contains keys with values included in the interval $[k_i, k_{i+1})$. Internal vertices do not directly refer to tuples in the database, but merely point to other vertices in the structure; on the contrary, leaf vertices do not contain pointers, but directly refer to the tuples in the database having a specific value for the indexed attribute. Leaf vertices are linked in a chain that allows the efficient execution of range queries. As an example, Figure 19.4(a) represents the B+ tree index built for attribute `Name` of table `Employee` in Figure 19.2(a). To access a tuple with key

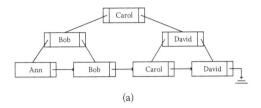

(a)

Id	VertexContent
1	2, Carol, 3
2	4, Bob, 5
3	6, David, 7
4	Ann, 5, 1, 5
5	Bob, 6, 2, 3
6	Carol, 7, 4
7	David, nil , 6

(b)

Id	C
1	gtem945/*c
2	8dq59wq*d'
3	ue63/);w
4	8/*5sym,p
5	mw39wio[
6	=wco21!ps
7	oieb5(p8*

(c)

Figure 19.4 An example of B+ tree indexing structure.

value k, value k is first searched in the root vertex of the B+ tree. The tree is then traversed by using the following scheme: If $k < k_1$, pointer a_0 is chosen; if $k \geq k_p$, pointer a_p is chosen, otherwise if $k_i \leq k < k_{i+1}$, pointer a_i is chosen. The process continues until a leaf vertex has been examined. If k is not found in any leaf vertex, then the table does not contain tuple where the indexed attribute has value k.

A B+ tree index can be usefully adopted for each attribute A_{ij} in schema R_i and defined over a partially ordered domain. The index is built by the client over the plaintext values of the attribute, and then stored on the remote server, together with the encrypted database. To this purpose, the B+ tree structure is translated into a specific table with just two attributes: the vertex identifier and the vertex content. The table has a row for each vertex in the tree and pointers are represented through cross references from the vertex content to other vertex identifiers in the table. For instance, the B+ tree structure depicted in Figure 19.4(a) is represented in the encrypted database by the relation in Figure 19.4(b).

Since the relation representing the B+ tree contains sensitive information (i.e., the plaintext values of the attribute on which the B+ tree is built), this relation has to be protected by encrypting its content. To this purpose, encryption is also applied at the level of vertex to protect the order relationship between plaintext and index values. The corresponding encrypted table, therefore, has two attributes: attribute **Id** that, as before, is the identifier of the vertex, and attribute C that is the encrypted vertex. Figure 19.4(c) illustrates the encrypted B+ tree table that corresponds to the plaintext B+ tree table in Figure 19.4(b).

The B+ tree-based indexing method allows the evaluation of both equality and range conditions appearing in the where clause. Moreover, being order preserving, it also allows the evaluation of order by and group by clauses, and, of most of the aggregate operators, directly on the encrypted database.

Given the plaintext condition $A_{ij} > v$, where v is a constant value, the client needs to traverse the B+ tree stored on the server to find out the leaf vertex representing v. To this purpose, the client queries the B+ tree table to retrieve the root, which is the tuple with *Id* equal to 1. It then decrypts it, evaluates its content, and, according to the search process mentioned, above queries again the remote server to retrieve the next vertex that has to be checked. The search process continues until a leaf vertex containing v is found (if any). The client then follows the chain of leaf vertices starting from the retrieved leaf. As an example, consider the B+ tree in Figure 19.4(a) defined for attribute Name. A query asking for tuples where the value of attribute Name follows Bob in the lexicographic order is evaluated as follows. First, the root is retrieved and evaluated: since Bob precedes Carol, the first pointer is chosen and vertex 2 evaluated. Since Bob is then equal to the value in the vertex, the second pointer is chosen and vertex 5 evaluated. Vertex 5 is a leaf, and all tuples in vertices 5, 6, and 7 are returned to the final user.

It is important to note that B+ tree indexes do not produce spurious tuples when executing a query, but the evaluation of conditions is much more expensive for the client with respect to bucket- and hash-based methods. For this reason, it may be advisable to combine the B+ tree method with either hash-based or bucket-based indexing, and use B+ tree only for evaluating conditions based on intervals. Compared with traditional B+ tree structures used in DBMSs, the vertices do not have to be of the same size as a disk block; a cost model then can be used to optimize the number of children of a vertex, potentially producing vertices with a large number of children and trees with limited depth. Finally, we note that since the B+ tree content is encrypted, the method is secure against inference attacks.

19.3.4 Other Approaches

In addition to the three main indexing methods previously presented, many other solutions have been proposed to support queries on encrypted data. These methods try to better support SQL (structure query language) clauses or to reduce the amount of spurious tuples in the result produced by the remote server.

Wang et al. [9,10] propose a new indexing method, specific for attributes whose domain is a set of characters, which adapts the hash-based indexing methods to permit direct evaluation of like conditions. The index value associated with any string s, composed of n characters $c_1 c_2 \ldots c_n$, is obtained by applying a secure hash function to each couple of subsequent characters in s. Specifically, given a string $s = c_1 c_2 \ldots c_n = s_1 s_2 \ldots s_{n/2}$, where $s_i = c_{2i} c_{2i+1}$, the corresponding index is $i = h(s_1) h(s_2) \ldots h(s_{n/2})$.

Hacigümüs et al. [5] study a method to remotely support aggregation operators, such as count, sum, avg, min, and max. The method is based on the concept of *privacy homomorphism* [11,12], which exploits properties of modular algebra to allow the execution over index values of sum, subtraction, and product, while not preserving domain ordering. Evdokimov et al. [13] formally analyze the security of the method based on privacy homomorphism with respect to the degree of confidentiality assigned to the remote server. Specifically, a definition of intrinsic security is given for encrypted databases, and it is proved that almost all indexing methods are not intrinsically secure; in particular, methods that do not cause spurious tuples to belong to the result of a query inevitably are exposed to attacks coming from a malicious third party or from the service provider.

The *Partition Plaintext and Ciphertext* (PPC) is a new model for storing server-side outsourced data [3]. This model proposes outsourcing of both plaintext and encrypted information, which need to be stored on the remote server. In this model, only sensitive attributes are encrypted and indexed, while the other attributes are released in plaintext form. The authors propose an efficient architecture for the DBMS to store together, and specifically in the same page of memory, both plaintext and encrypted data.

To support equality and range queries over encrypted data without adopting B+ tree structures, Agrawal et al. [14] present an *Order Preserving Encryption Schema* (OPES). An OPES function has the advantage of flattening the frequency spectrum of index values, thanks to the introduction of new buckets when needed. It is important to note here that queries executed over this kind of indexes do not return spurious tuples. Also, OPES provides data secrecy only if the intruder does not know the plaintext database or the domain of original attributes.

Aggarwal et al. [15] discuss a new solution for querying remotely stored data, while preserving their privacy. The authors assume that some security constraints are defined on outsourced data, specifying which sets of attributes cannot be released together and which attributes cannot appear in plaintext. To guarantee constraint satisfaction, the authors propose to vertically fragment the universal relation R, decomposing the database into two fragments that are then stored on two different servers. The method is based on the assumption that the two servers do not exchange information and that all the constraints can be satisfied by encrypting just a few attributes in each fragment.

Index	Query		
	Equality	Range	Aggregation
Bucket-based [7]	•	○	–
Hash-based [4]	•	–	○
B+ Tree [4]	•	•	•
Character oriented [9,10]	•	○	–
Privacy homomorphism [5]	•	–	•
PPC [3]	•	•	•
OPES [14]	•	•	○
Secure index data structures [16–20]	•	○	–
Fragmentation based [15]	•	•	•

• fully supported; ○ partially supported; – not supported

Figure 19.5 Indexing methods supporting queries.

Different working groups [16–20] introduce other approaches for searching keywords in encrypted documents. These methods are based on the definition of a *secure index data structure*. The secure index data structure allows the server to retrieve all documents containing a particular keyword without the need to know any other information. This is possible because a trap door is introduced when encrypting data, and such a trap door is then exploited by the client when querying data. Other similar proposals are based on *identity-based encryption* techniques for the definition of secure indexing methods. Boneh and Franklin [21] present an encryption method allowing searches over ciphertext data, while not revealing anything about the original data. This method is shown to be secure through rigorous proofs. Although these methods for searching keywords over encrypted data have been originally proposed for searching over audit logs or e-mail repositories, they are also well suited for indexing data in the outsourced database scenario.

To summarize, Figure 19.5 shows, for each indexing method discussed, what type of query is supported. Here, a hyphen means that the query is not supported, a black circle means that the query is supported, and a white circle means that the query is partially supported.

19.3.5 Evaluation of Inference Exposure

Given a plaintext relation r over schema $R(A_1, A_2, \ldots, A_n)$, it is necessary to decide which attributes need to be indexed and how the corresponding indexes can be defined. In particular, when defining the indexing method for an attribute, it is important to consider two conflicting requirements: on one side, the indexing information should be related with the data well enough to provide for an effective query execution mechanism; on the other side, the relationship between indexes and data should not open the door to *inference* and *linking attacks* that can compromise the protection granted by encryption. Different indexing methods can provide a different trade-off between query execution efficiency and data protection from inference. Therefore, it is necessary to define a measure of the risk of exposure due to the publication of indexes on the remote server.

Although many techniques to support various types of queries in the DAS scenario have been developed, a deep analysis of the level of protection provided by all these methods against inference and linking attacks is missing. In particular, only inference exposure of a few indexing methods has been evaluated [4,8,22,23].

Hore et al. [8] analyze the security issues related to the use of bucket-based indexing methods. The authors consider data exposure problems in two situations: (1) the release of a single attribute and (2) the publication of all the indexes associated with a relation. To measure the protection degree granted to the original data by the specific indexing method, the authors propose to exploit two different measures. The first measure is the *variance* of the distribution of values within a bucket *b*. The second measure is the *entropy* of the distribution of values within a bucket *b*. The higher the variance, the higher the protection level granted to the data. Therefore, the data owner should maximize, for each bucket in the relation, the corresponding variance. Analogously, the higher the entropy of a bucket, the higher is the protection level of the relation. The optimization problem that the data owner has to solve, while planning the bucketization process on a table, is the *maximization of minimum variance and minimum entropy*, while maximizing query efficiency. Since such an optimization problem is *NP-hard*, Hore et al. [8] propose an approximation method, which fixes a maximum allowed performance degradation. The objective of the algorithm is then to maximize both minimum variance and entropy, while guaranteeing performances not to follow under an imposed constraint. To the aim of taking into consideration also the risk of exposure due to association, Hore et al. [8] propose to adopt, as a measure of the privacy granted by indexes when posing a multi-attribute range query, the well known *k-anonymity* concept [24].

Ceselli et al. [22] evaluate the exposure to inference due to the adoption of hash-based indexing methods. Inference exposure is measured by taking into account the prior knowledge of the attacker that introduces two different scenarios. In the first scenario, called $Freq + DB^k$, the attacker is supposed to know, in addition to the encrypted database (DB^k), the domains of the plaintext attributes and the distribution of plaintext values (Freq) in the original database. In the second scenario, called $DB + DB^k$, the attacker is supposed to know both the encrypted (DB^k) and the plaintext database (DB). In both scenarios, the exposure measure is computed as the probability for the attacker to correctly map index values onto plaintext attribute values. The authors show that to guarantee a higher degree of protection against inference, it is convenient to use a hash-based method that generates collisions. In case of a hash-based method where the collision factor is equal to 1, meaning that there are no collisions, the inference exposure depends on the number of attributes used for indexing. In the $DB + DB^k$ scenario, the exposure grows as the number of attributes used for indexing grows. In the $Freq + DB^k$ scenario, the attacker can discover the correspondences between plaintext and indexing values by comparing their occurrence profiles. Intuitively, the exposure grows as the number of attributes with a different occurrence profile grows. For instance, considering relation **Employee** in Figure 19.2(a), we can notice that both **Salary** and the corresponding index I_5 have a unique value, that is, 20 and ρ, respectively. We, therefore, can conclude that the index value corresponding to 20 is ρ, and that no other salary value is mapped into ρ as well.

Damiani et al. [23] extend the inference exposure measures presented in [22] to produce an inference measure that can be associated with the whole table instead of with single attributes. Specifically, the authors propose two methods for aggregating the exposure risk measures computed at attribute level. The first method exploits the weighted mean operator and weights each attribute A_i proportionally with the risk connected with the disclosure of the values of A_i. The second one exploits the OWA (ordered weighted averaging) operator, which allows the assignment of different importance values to different sets of attributes, depending on the degree of protection guaranteed by the indexing method adopted for the specific subset of attributes.

19.4 Security Issues

The emerging DAS scenario also introduces numerous research challenges related to data security. Below is the description of the main proposals that aim at ensuring the confidentiality of the outsourced data.

19.4.1 Access Control Enforcement

All the existing proposals for designing and querying encrypted/indexing outsourced databases assume that the client has complete access to the query result. However, this assumption does not fit real-world scenarios, where different users may have different access privileges. A trivial solution for implementing selective access in the DAS scenario consists of explicitly defining authorizations at the data owner site. The main drawback of this method is that the server cannot directly send the result of a query to the client because the data owner first has to remove all the tuples that the final user cannot access (this task cannot be delegated to the remote server, which may not be allowed to know the access control policy defined by the data owner). Such an approach, however, puts much of the work on the data owner by introducing a bottleneck for computation and communication.

A promising direction consists in selectively encrypting data so that users (or groups thereof) can decrypt only the data they are authorized to access. Intuitively, selective encryption means that data is encrypted by using different keys and that users can decrypt only data for which they know the corresponding encryption key. Although it is usually advisable to leave authorization-based access control and cryptographic protections separate, since encryption is traditionally considered a mechanism and should not be adopted in model definition, such a combination proves successful in the DAS scenario [25]. In particular, since neither the data owner nor the remote server can enforce the access control policy, for either security or efficiency reasons, the data need to implement selective access. In the following there is the description of the proposals supporting selective access in more details.

19.4.1.1 Selective Encryption

Given a system composed of a set $\mathcal{U}$ of users and a set $\mathcal{R}$ of resources, the data owner may want to define and enforce a policy, stating which user $u_i \in \mathcal{U}$ is allowed to access which resource $r_j \in \mathcal{R}$ in the outsourced database. In the DAS scenario, a resource may be a table, an attribute, a tuple, or even a cell, depending on the granularity at which the data owner wishes to define her policy. Since existing solutions do not depend on the granularity level to which the access control policy is defined [25], in the remainder of this section, we will continue to use the generic term resource to generically indicate any database element on which authorizations can be specified.

The set of authorizations defined by the data owner are represented through a traditional *access matrix* A having a row for each user in $\mathcal{U}$ and a column for each resource in $\mathcal{R}$. Since only read privileges are considered (the enforcement of write privileges is still an open issue), each cell $A[u_i, r_j]$ may assume two values: 1, if u_i is allowed to access r_j; 0, otherwise. Given an access matrix A over sets $\mathcal{U}$ and $\mathcal{R}$, $acl(r_j)$ denotes the *access control list* of resource r_j (i.e., the set of users that can access r_j), and $cap(u_i)$ denotes the *capability list* of user u_i (i.e., the set of resources that u_i can access). For instance, Figure 19.6 represents an access matrix for a system with four users (A, B, C, and D), and four resources (r_1, r_2, r_3, and r_4). Here, for example, $acl(r_1) = \{B,C\}$ and $cap(B) = \{r_1,r_3\}$.

The naive solution for enforcing access control through selective encryption consists in using a different key for each resource in the system, and in communicating to each user the set of keys associated with the resources she can access. This solution correctly enforces the policy, but it is very

	r_1	r_2	r_3	r_4
A	0	1	1	1
B	1	0	1	0
C	1	1	0	1
D	0	1	1	1

Figure 19.6 An example of access matrix.

expensive since each user needs to keep a number of keys that depends on her privileges. That is, users having many privileges and, probably, often accessing the system, will have a greater number of keys than users having a few privileges and, probably, accessing the system only rarely. To reduce the number of keys a user has to manage, the authors propose using a *key derivation method*. A key derivation method is basically a function that, given a key and a piece of publicly available information, allows the computation of another key. The basic idea is that each user is given a small number of keys from which she can derive all the keys needed to access the resources she is authorized to access.

The aim of using a key derivation method is that it is necessary to define which keys can be derived from another key and how. Key derivation methods proposed in the literature are based on the definition of a *key derivation hierarchy*. Given a set of keys $\mathcal{K}$ in the system and a partial order relation $\preceq$ defined on it, the corresponding key derivation hierarchy is usually represented as a pair $(\mathcal{K}, \preceq)$, where $\forall k_i, k_j \in \mathcal{K}$, $k_j \preceq k_i$ iff k_j is derivable from k_i. Any key derivation hierarchy can be graphically represented through a directed graph, having a vertex for each key in $\mathcal{K}$, and a path from k_i to k_j only if k_j can be derived from k_i. Depending on the partial order relation defined on $\mathcal{K}$, the key derivation hierarchy can be: a *chain* (i.e., $\preceq$ defines a total order relation); a *tree*; or a *directed acyclic graph* (DAG). The different key derivation methods can be classified on the basis of the kind of hierarchy they are able to support, as follows.

- The hierarchy is a *chain of vertices* [26]. Key k_j of a vertex is computed on the basis of key k_i of its (unique) parent (i.e., $k_j = f(k_i)$) and no public information is needed.
- The hierarchy is a *tree* [26–28]. Key k_j of a vertex is computed on the basis of key k_i of its (unique) parent and on the publicly available label l_j associated with k_j (i.e., $k_j = f(k_i, l_j)$).
- The hierarchy is a *DAG* [29–37]. Since each vertex in a DAG can have more than one parent, the derivation methods are, in general, more complex than the methods used for chains or trees. There are many proposals that work on DAGs; typically they exploit a piece of

public information associated with each vertex of the key derivation hierarchy. In [30], Atallah et al. introduce a new class of methods. The method maintains a piece of public information, called *token*, associated with each edge in the hierarchy. Given two keys, k_i and k_j arbitrarily assigned to two vertices, and a public label l_j associated with k_j, a token from k_i to k_j is defined as $T_{i,j} = k_j \oplus h(k_i, l_j)$, where $\oplus$ is the *n*-ary **xor** operator and h is a secure hash function. Given $T_{i,j}$, any user knowing k_i and with access to public label l_j, can compute (derive) k_j. All tokens $T_{i,j}$ in the system are stored in a *public catalog.*

It is important to note that the methods operating on trees can be used for chains of vertices, even if the contrary is not true. Analogously, the methods operating on DAGs can be used for trees and chains, while the reverse is not true.

When choosing a key derivation method for the DAS scenario, it is necessary to take into consideration two different aspects: (1) the client overhead and (2) the cost of managing access control policy updates. The client overhead is mainly the communication and computation time for getting from the server the public information that is needed in the derivation process (e.g., tokens in [30]). The cost of enforcing access control policy updates is the cost of updating the key derivation hierarchy. As we will see later on, the key derivation hierarchy is used to correctly enforce the access control policy specified by the data owner and, therefore, its definition is based on the access control policy itself. Intuitively, since the access control policy is likely to change over time, the hierarchy needs to rearrange accordingly (i.e., insert or delete vertices, and modify keys). An important requirement then is to minimize the amount of reencrypting and rekeying needed in the hierarchy rearrangement. Indeed, any time the key of a vertex is changed, at least the tuples encrypted with that key need to be reencrypted by the data owner, and the new key should be given to all users knowing the old one. By analyzing the most important key derivation methods, we can observe that the key derivation methods operating on trees allow insertion and deletion of leaf vertices without need of changing other keys in the tree. If, instead, an internal vertex v is inserted or deleted, all the keys of the vertices in the subtree rooted at v must be updated accordingly. Similarly, methods operating on DAGs and associating public information with edges in the graph (e.g., Atallah et al. [30]) allow insertion and deletion of vertices without need of rekeying operations. By contrast, all the other key derivation methods operating on DAGs require both to modify all keys derivable from the key that has been changed, and to reencrypt all tuples previously encrypted by using the old keys. Among all the key derivation methods proposed, the key method proposed in [30] seems the method that better suits the DAS scenario.

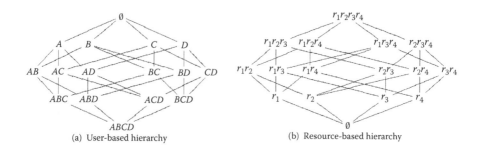

(a) User-based hierarchy   (b) Resource-based hierarchy

Figure 19.7 Examples of key derivation hierarchies.

Key Derivation Hierarchies

We now describe how it is possible to define a key derivation hierarchy that allows the correct enforcement of the access control policy defined by the data owner.

An access control policy $\mathcal{A}$ can be enforced by defining different key derivation hierarchies. In particular, a key derivation hierarchy can be defined according to two different strategies: *user-based* and *resource-based*. In the user-based strategy, the access control policy $\mathcal{A}$ is modeled as a set of access control lists, while in the resource-based strategy, it is modeled as a set of capabilities. A user-based or a resource-based hierarchy can be defined as follows.

A user-based hierarchy, denoted **UH**, is defined as a pair $(P(\mathcal{U}), \preceq)$, where $P(\mathcal{U})$ is the set containing all possible sets of users in the system, and $\preceq$ is the partial order relation induced by the set containment relation $(\subseteq)$. More precisely, $\forall a, b \in P(\mathcal{U})$, $a \preceq b$ if and only if $b \subseteq a$. The user-based hierarchy contains the set of all subsets of $\mathcal{U}$ and the corresponding DAG has $2^{|\mathcal{U}|}$ vertices. For instance, Figure 19.7(a) represents a user-based hierarchy built over a system with four users A, B, C, and D. To correctly enforce the access control policy, each vertex in the hierarchy is associated with a key, each resource in the system is encrypted by using the key of the vertex representing its *acl*, and each user is given the key of the vertex representing herself in the hierarchy. From the key of vertex u_i, user u_i then can derive the keys of the vertices representing groups of users containing u_i and, therefore, she can decrypt all the resources she can access (i.e., belonging to her capability list). Note that the empty set vertex represents a key known only to the data owner, and it is used to encrypt resources that nobody can access. As an example, consider the policy in Figure 19.6 and the hierarchy in Figure 19.7(a). Resource r_1 is encrypted with key k_{BC} of vertex BC, r_2 with k_{ACD}, r_3 with k_{ABD}, and r_4 with k_{ACD}. Each user knows the key associated with the vertex representing herself and there is a path connecting each user's vertex with all the vertices representing a group containing the user. For instance, if we consider user A, from vertex A it is possible to reach vertices AB, AC, AD, ABC, ABD, ACD, and $ABCD$. Consequently, user A can decrypt r_2, r_3, and r_4, which are exactly the resources in her capability list.

A resource-based hierarchy, denoted **RH**, can be built in a dual way. The resource-based hierarchy thus is defined as pair $(P(\mathcal{R}), \preceq)$, where $P(\mathcal{R})$ is the set of all subsets of $\mathcal{R}$, and order relation $\preceq$ is based on the set containment relation $(\subseteq)$. In other words, $\forall a, b \in P(\mathcal{R})$, $a \preceq b$ if and only if $a \subseteq b$. For instance, Figure 19.7(b) represents a resource-based hierarchy built over a system with four resources r_1, r_2, r_3, and r_4. Like for the user-based hierarchy, to correctly enforce the access control policy, each vertex in the hierarchy is associated with a key, each resource in the system is encrypted by using the key of the vertex representing the resource itself in the hierarchy, and each user is given the key of the vertex representing her *capability*. From the key of the vertex corresponding to her capability, each user can compute the keys of the vertices representing resources belonging to her capability list. For instance, consider users B and C and resource r_1. Vertex r_1 can be reached starting from vertices $r_1r_2r_3r_4$, $r_1r_2r_3$, $r_1r_2r_4$, $r_1r_3r_4$, r_1r_2, r_1r_3, and r_1r_4. Users B and C know the key of vertices r_1r_3 and $r_1r_2r_4$, respectively, which are the vertices corresponding to their capability lists. Consequently, since there is a path from the key of B and C to the key used for encrypting r_1, B and C, which are exactly the users in the access control list of r_1, can access r_1.

Both the user-based and the resource-based hierarchies here defined correctly enforce the policy described in the access matrix $\mathcal{A}$, and both of them assign a unique secret key to each user of the system and define a unique key for encrypting each resource in the system. The most important difference between these approaches lays in the *key assignment method*. In a user-based hierarchy, a different key is assigned to each user, while tuples may share the same key (if they have the same access control list). By contrast, with a resource-based hierarchy, a different key is associated with each resource, while users may share the same key (if they have the same capability list). When deciding whether to adopt a user-based or a resource-based hierarchy, it is important to determine whether users can share the same key for accessing the system. It is also important to note that the number of keys in the system depends on the number of users and resources in the system, respectively. Consequently, if the number of users is lower than the number of resources, it may be convenient to adopt **UH**.

Hierarchy Reduction

For simplicity, we now focus our attention on **UH** (however, the following considerations are valid also for the resource-based hierarchy). It is easy to see that the solution described above defines more keys than actually needed and requires the publication of a great amount of information on the remote server, thus causing an expensive key derivation process at the client-side. The higher the number of users, the deeper the key derivation hierarchy (the hierarchy height is equal to the number of users in the system). As an example, consider the user-based hierarchy in Figure 19.7(a) and, in particular, consider user A. To access resource r_3, A has to first derive k_{AD} that, in turn, can be used for deriving k_{ABD}, which is the key needed for decrypting r_3. However, in this case, vertex AD makes only the derivation process longer than needed and, therefore, it can be removed without compromising the correctness of the derivation process.

Since an important goal is to reduce the client's overhead, it is possible to simplify the key derivation hierarchy, removing nonnecessary vertices, while ensuring a correct key derivability. Therefore, instead of representing all the possible groups of users in the DAG, it is sufficient to represent those sets of users whose key is relevant for access control enforcement. Intuitively, these groups are those corresponding either to the *acl* values or singleton sets of users. The vertices corresponding to *acl*s and to users are necessary because their keys are used for resource encryption and allow users to correctly derive all the other keys used for encrypting resources in their capabilities, respectively. This set of vertices needs then to be correctly connected in the hierarchy. In particular, from the key of any user u_i it must be possible to derive the keys of all those vertices representing a group that contains u_i. Since Damiani et al. [25] propose using a user-based hierarchy in combination with Atallah et al.'s key derivation method, it is not advisable to connect each user's key directly with each group containing the user itself. Indeed, any time a client needs to derive a key, it queries the remote server to gain the tokens necessary for derivation. Another important observation is that when building the key derivation hierarchy, other vertices can be inserted, which are useful for reducing the size of the public catalog, even if their keys are not used for derivation. As an example, consider a system with five users and three *acl* values: ACD, ABD, and ADE. If vertices A, B, C, D, and E are connected directly with ACD, ABD, and ADE, the system needs nine tokens. If instead a new vertex AD is inserted and connected with the three *acl* values, A and D do not need an edge connecting them directly to each *acl* value, but they only need an edge connecting them with AD. In this case, the system needs eight tokens. Therefore, any time three or more vertices share a common parent, it is useful to insert such a vertex for saving tokens in the public catalog. Figure 19.8 illustrates the hierarchy corresponding to the access control policy in Figure 19.6 and containing only the vertices needed for a correct enforcement of the policy. The problem of correctly enforcing a policy through a key derivation graph while minimizing the number of

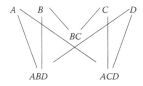

Figure 19.8   An example of reduced hierarchy enforcing the access control policy in Figure 19.6.

edges in the DAG, however, is *NP-hard*. In [25], Damiani et al. have solved this problem through an approximation algorithm.

19.4.1.2   Other Approaches

Damiani et al. [25] propose a method based on key derivation methods operating on trees and transform the original user-based hierarchy in a tree enforcing the same policy. In this case, each user has to manage more than one key. They propose an approximation algorithm to the aim of limiting the average number of keys assigned to each user in the system.

Zych and Petkovic [38] propose an alternative access control enforcement method for outsourced databases, which exploits the Diffie–Hellman key generation scheme and asymmetric encryption. They define a user-based hierarchy that is then transformed into a *V-graph*. For each vertex in the V-graph, the number of incoming edges is either 2 or 0, and for any two vertices, there is at most one common parent vertex. The resulting structure is a *binary tree*, whose leaves represent singleton sets of users, and whose root represents the group containing all the users in the system. Here, the key derivation process goes from leaf vertices to the root. Each user is given the private key of the vertex representing herself in the hierarchy, while each resource is encrypted with the public key of the vertex representing its *acl*. Consequently, each user can compute, through derivation, the keys necessary to decrypt the resources she is authorized to access. This method requires: $O(E)$ public space, where E is the set of edges in the tree; $O(N)$ private space on clients, where N is the number of cells equal to 1 in the access matrix; and $O(n)$ derivation time, where n is the number of users in the system.

Key derivation hierarchies also have been adopted for access control enforcement in contexts different from the one introduced in this chapter. For instance, pay TV systems usually adopt selective encryption for selective access enforcement and key hierarchies to easily distribute encryption keys [39–43]. Although these applications have some similarities with the

DAS scenario, there are important differences that do not make them applicable in the DAS scenario. First, in the DAS scenario, we need to protect stored data, while in the pay TV scenario, streams of data are the resources that need to be protected. Second, in the DAS scenario key derivation hierarchies are used to reduce the number of keys each user has to keep secret, while in the pay TV scenario, a key derivation hierarchy is exploited for session key distribution.

To guarantee security in the DAS scenario, physical devices have also been studied, both operating client-side [44] and server-side [45]. However, the usage of smart cards for clients and of secure co-processors for the remote server has not been deeply studied. These methods can be adopted together with the security and querying solutions presented in this chapter.

19.5 Conclusions

Database outsourcing is becoming an emerging data management paradigm that introduces many research challenges. In this chapter, we focused on the problems related to query execution and access control enforcement. For query execution, different indexing methods have been discussed. These methods mainly focus on supporting a specific kind of condition or a specific SQL clause and on minimizing the client burden in query execution. Access control enforcement is instead a new issue for the DAS scenario and has not been deeply studied yet. The most important proposal for enforcing selective access on outsourced encrypted data is based on selective encryption. This method exploits cryptography for access control enforcement by using different keys to protect data. Each user is then given the set of keys allowing her to access exactly the resources belonging to her capability list.

There are, however, many other issues that need to be investigated further. The identification of techniques able to enforce updates that can modify the set of users, the set of resources, or their authorizations while maintaining a limited cost in terms of key reassignment or decryption/encryption is again an open issue. Another interesting issue is related to the management of write privileges; although there are solutions that provide data integrity by detecting nonauthorized modifications of database content, these solutions do not prevent unauthorized modifications.

Acknowledgments

This work was supported in part by the European Union under contract IST-2002-507591, by the Italian Ministry of Research Fund for Basic Research (FIRB) under project RBNE05FKZ2, and by the Italian MIUR under project 2006099978.

References

[1] Davida, G., Wells, D., and Kam, J., A database encryption system with subkeys. *ACM Transactions on Database Systems*, 6: 312, 1981.

[2] Hacigümüs, H., Iyer, B., and Mehrotra, S., Providing database as a service. In *Proc. of the 18th International Conference on Data Engineering*, San Jose, CA. IEEE Computer Society, Washington, D.C., 2002, 29.

[3] Iyer, B. et al., A framework for efficient storage security in RDBMS. In Bertino, E. et al., Eds., *Proc. of the International Conference on Extending Database Technology (EDBT 2004)*, vol. 2992 of *Lecture Notes in Computer Science*, Crete, Greece. Springer, Heidelberg, Germany, 2004, 147.

[4] Damiani, E. et al., Balancing confidentiality and efficiency in untrusted relational DBMSs. In Jajodia, S., Atluri, V., and Jaeger, T., Eds., *Proc. of the 10th ACM Conference on Computer and Communications Security (CCS03)*, Washington, D.C., ACM Press, New York, 2003, 93.

[5] Hacigümüs, H., Iyer, B., and Mehrotra, S., Efficient execution of aggregation queries over encrypted relational databases. In Lee, J., Li, J., Wndhang, K., and Lee, D., Eds., *Proc. of the 9th International Conference on Database Systems for Advanced Applications*, vol. 2973 of *Lecture Notes in Computer Science*, Jeju Island, Korea. Springer, Heidelberg, Germany, 2004, 125.

[6] Damiani, E. et al., Implementation of a storage mechanism for untrusted DBMSs. In *Proc. of the Second International IEEE Security in Storage Workshop*, Washington, D.C., IEEE Computer Society, Washington, D.C., 2003, 38.

[7] Hacigümüs, H. et al., Executing SQL over encrypted data in the database-service-provider model. In *Proc. of the ACM SIGMOD 2002*, Madison, WI, ACM Press, New York, 2002, 216.

[8] Hore, B., Mehrotra, S., and Tsudik, G., A privacy-preserving index for range queries. In Nascimento, M. et al., Eds., *Proc. of the 30th International Conference on Very Large Data Bases*, Toronto, Canada. Morgan Kaufmann, San Francisco, CA, 2004, 720.

[9] Wang, Z. et al., Fast query over encrypted character data in database. *Communications in Information and Systems*, 4: 289, 2004.

[10] Wang, Z., Wang, W., and Shi, B., Storage and query over encrypted character and numerical data in database. In *Proc. of the Fifth International Conference on Computer and Information Technology (CIT'05)*, Shanghai, China. IEEE Computer Society, Washington, D.C., 2005, 77.

[11] Boyens, C. and Gunter, O., Using online services in untrusted environments—a privacy-preserving architecture. In *Proc. of the 11th European Conference on Information Systems (ECIS '03)*, Naples, Italy, 2003.

[12] Domingo-Ferrer, J. A new privacy homomorphism and applications, Information Processing Letters, 6:5, 1996.

[13] Evdokimov, S., Fischmann, M., and Gunther, O., Provable security for outsourcing database operations. In Liu, L., Reuter, A., Whang, K., and Zhang, J., Eds., *Proc. of the 22nd International Conference on Data Engineering (ICDE '06)*, Atlanta, GA, IEEE Computer Society, Washington, D.C., 2006, 117.

[14] Agrawal, R. et al., Order preserving encryption for numeric data. In Weikum, G., König, A., and Deßloch, S., Eds., *Proc. of the ACM SIGMOD 2004*, Paris, France. ACM Press, New York, 2004, 563.

[15] Aggarwal, G. et al., Two can keep a secret: A distributed architecture for secure database services. In *Proc. of the Second Biennal Conference on Innovative Data Systems Research (CIDR 2005)*, Asilomar, CA, 2005, 186.

[16] Boneh, D. et al., Public-key encryption with keyword search. In *Proc. of the Eurocrypt 2004*, vol. 3027 of *Lecture Notes in Computer Science*, Interlaken, Switzerland. Springer, Heidelberg, Germany, 2004, 506.

[17] Brinkman, R., Doumen, J., and Jonker, W., Using secret sharing for searching in encrypted data. In Jonker, W. and Petkovic, M., Eds., *Proc. of the Secure Data Management Workshop*, vol. 3178 of *Lecture Notes in Computer Science*, Toronto, Canada. Springer, Heidelberg, Germany, 2004, 18.

[18] Goh, E., *Secure indexes.* http://eprint.iacr.org/2003/216/, 2003.

[19] Song, D., Wagner, D., and Perrig, A., Practical techniques for searches on encrypted data. In *Proc. of the 21st IEEE Computer Society Symposium on Research in Security and Privacy*, Berkeley, CA, IEEE Computer Society, Washington, D.C., 2000, 44.

[20] Waters, B. et al., Building an encrypted and searchable audit log. In *Proc. of the 11th Annual Network and Distributed System Security Symposium*, San Diego, CA. Internet Society, Washington, D.C., 2004.

[21] Boneh, D. and Franklin, M., Identity-based encryption from the weil pairing. *SIAM Journal on Computing*, 32: 586, 2003.

[22] Ceselli, A. et al., Modeling and assessing inference exposure in encrypted databases. *ACM Transactions on Information and System Security (TISSEC)*, 8: 119, 2005.

[23] Damiani, E. et al., Measuring inference exposure in outsourced encrypted databases. In Gollmann, D., Massacci, F., and Yautsiukhin, A., Eds., *Proc. of the First Workshop on Quality of Protection*, vol. 23 of *Advances in Information Security*, Milan, Italy. Springer, Heidelberg, Germany, 2005.

[24] Samarati, P., Protecting respondents' identities in microdata release. *IEEE Transactions on Knowledge and Data Engineering*, 13: 1010, 2001.

[25] Damiani, E. et al., Selective data encryption in outsourced dynamic environments. In *Proc. of the Second International Workshop on Views on Designing Complex Architectures (VODCA 2006)*, Electronic Notes in Theoretical Computer Science, Bertinoro, Italy. Elsevier, Amsterdam, the Netherlands, 2006.

[26] Sandhu, R., On some cryptographic solutions for access control in a tree hierarchy. In *Proc. of the 1987 Fall Joint Computer Conference on Exploring Technology: Today and Tomorrow*, Dallas, TX. IEEE Computer Society, Washington, D.C., 1987, 405.

[27] Gudes, E., The design of a cryptography-based secure file system. *IEEE Transactions on Software Engineering*, 6: 411, 1980.

[28] Sandhu, R., Cryptographic implementation of a tree hierarchy for access control. *Information Processing Letters*, 27: 95, 1988.

[29] Akl, S. and Taylor, P., Cryptographic solution to a problem of access control in a hierarchy. *ACM Transactions on Computer System*, 1: 239, 1983.

[30] Atallah, M., Frikken, K., and Blanton, M., Dynamic and efficient key management for access hierarchies. In Atluri, V., Meadows, C., and Juels, A., Eds., *Proc. of the 12th ACM Conference on Computer and Communications Security (CCS05)*, Alexandria, VA, ACM SIGSAC, 2005, 190.

[31] De Santis, A., Ferrara, A.L., and Masucci, B., Cryptographic key assignment schemes for any access control policy. *Inf. Process. Lett.*, 92(4): 199–205, 2004.

[32] Harn, L. and Lin, H., A cryptographic key generation scheme for multilevel data security. *Computers and Security*, 9: 539, 1990.

[33] Hwang, M. and Yang, W., Controlling access in large partially ordered hierarchies using cryptographic keys. *The Journal of Systems and Software*, 67: 99, 2003.

[34] Liaw, H., Wang, S., and Lei, C., On the design of a single-key-lock mechanism based on Newton's interpolating polynomial. *IEEE Transaction on Software Engineering*, 15: 1135, 1989.

[35] MacKinnon, S. et al., An optimal algorithm for assigning cryptographic keys to control access in a hierarchy. *IEEE Transactions on Computers*, 34: 797, 1985.

[36] Shen, V. and Chen, T., A novel key management scheme based on discrete logarithms and polynomial interpolations. *Computer and Security*, 21: 164, 2002.

[37] Crampton, J., Martin, K., and Wild, P., On key assignment for hierarchical access control. In *Proc. of the 19th IEEE Computer Security Foundations Workshop (CSFW'06)*, Los Alamitos, CA. IEEE Computer Society, Washington, D.C., 2006, 98.

[38] Zych, A. and Petkovic, M., Key management method for cryptographically enforced access control. In *Proc. of the 1st Benelux Workshop on Information and System Security*, Antwerpen, Belgium, 2006.

[39] Birget, J. et al., Hierarchy-based access control in distributed environments. In *Proc. of the IEEE International Conference on Communications*, vol. 1, Helsinki, Finland. IEEE Computer Society, Washington, D.C., 2002, 229.

[40] Ray, I., Ray, I., and Narasimhamurthi, N., A cryptographic solution to implement access control in a hierarchy and more. In *Proc. of the 11th ACM Symposium on Access Control Models and Technologies (SACMAT'02)*, Monterey, CA. ACM Press, New York, 2002, 65.

[41] Tsai, H. and Chang, C., A cryptographic implementation for dynamic access control in a user hierarchy. *Computer and Security*, 14: 159, 1995.

[42] Wong, C., Gouda, M., and Lam, S., Secure group communications using key graphs. *IEEE/ACM Transactions on Networking*, 8: 16, 2000.

[43] Sun, Y. and Liu, K., Scalable hierarchical access control in secure group communications. In *Proc. of the IEEE Infocom*, vol. 2, Hong Kong, China. IEEE Computer Society, Washington, D.C., 2004, 1296.

[44] Bouganim, L. and Pucheral, P., Chip-secured data access: Confidential data on untrusted servers. In Bernstein, P. et al., Eds., *Proc. of the 28th International Conference on Very Large Data Bases*, Hong Kong, China. Morgan Kaufmann, San Francisco, CA, 2002, 131.

[45] Bouganim, L. et al., Chip-secured data access: Reconciling access rights with data encryption. In Freytag, J., Lockemann, P., Abiteboul, S., Carey, M., Selinger, P., and Heuer, A., Eds., *Proc. of the 29th VLDB Conference*, Berlin, Germany. Morgan Kaufmann, San Francisco, CA, 2003, 1133.

Chapter 20

Communications Data Retention: A Pandora's Box for Rights and Liberties?

Lilian Mitrou

Contents

20.1   A New Age for Surveillance and Liberties? 410
20.2   Data Retention as a (Valuable?) Surveillance Tool 411
     20.2.1   Communications and Traffic Data 412
     20.2.2   Interception, Preservation, and Retention 413
20.3   European Regulatory Framework 414
     20.3.1   Cybercrime Convention of the Council of Europe 414
     20.3.2   Privacy and Electronic Communications Law
           in the European Union 415
          20.3.2.1   The E-Privacy Directive: Data Retention
                  as an Option 415
          20.3.2.2   Mandatory, Routine Data Retention:
                  The New Directive 416
     20.3.3   Data Retention as Interference with the Right
          to the Respect of (Communicational) Privacy 418
20.4   Privacy and Electronic Communications Law
     in the United States 419

20.4.1 The Legal Framework: The Electronic
Communications Privacy Act 419
20.4.2 The Fourth Amendment and the "(Un)reasonable"
Expectation of Communicational Privacy 420
20.5 New Challenges, Old Instruments: The Shortcoming
of "Content-Envelope" Distinction 422
20.5.1 The Blurring Lines of "Content" and "Envelope" 422
20.5.2 A False Distinction? 423
20.6 Data Retention versus Fundamental Freedoms 424
20.6.1 An Unnecessary and Disproportionate Measure? 424
20.6.1.1 Criteria of "Acceptable" Interference 424
20.6.1.2 A Disproportionate "Dataveillance" 425
20.6.2 Communications Surveillance as Interference into
the Rights of Anonymity and Freedom of Expression ... 426
20.6.3 The Question of Independent and Adequate
Oversight 427
20.6.4 Common Information Pools for Public
and Private Sector 428
20.7 An Information-Based (Pre)prevention of Risks
or a Threat to Democracy 429
References 430

20.1 A New Age for Surveillance and Liberties?

The internationally increased attention on organized crime, cyber-crime, as well as terrorism—reinforced by the terrorist attacks, especially in New York, Madrid, and London—have created a fertile ground for governments and international organizations to speed up the adoption of legislation that will strengthen the investigation and prosecution powers of enforcement authorities. The shock of terrorist attacks puts the subject of "security" thoroughly back on the political agenda and the public debate. In the wake of each attack, earlier proposals, which had "no chance to be accepted" [25,27], were reintroduced, and new policies with similar objectives were drafted to extend state surveillance authority. In the past five years, the legal and political landscapes have shifted significantly in many countries and at the international level, in order to face the new risks and threats and, in general, the problems that arise from the changing nature and type of criminal activity and terrorism.

The legal apparatus reflects new powers, investigative methods, and procedures that are supported, when not created, by a new technological environment. Technology has always been used to safeguard collective and individual security. However, new sophisticated technologies have led to a profound increase in law enforcement surveillance, as they have given governments an unprecedented ability to engage in powerful mass surveillance [43]. The events of September 11 have facilitated and accelerated the move toward an intelligence-gathering form of policing [27]. The so-called "soft security measures" mainly seek to exploit the interactivity of information communication technologies in order to identify the risk-posing individuals and their networks [31].

The freedom of the individual and the security of all, i.e., the state's tasks of guaranteeing individual, constitutionally protected freedoms, and of attending to and providing for the community's security, are inevitably in a relationship marked by tension and even contradiction [17]. Surveillance measures raise significant concerns in relation to the respect of privacy and other fundamental rights and freedoms. This contribution deals with the question of data retention as a method of mass communications surveillance. In this chapter, I discuss the retention of communications data as a security measure, which interferes with the right to privacy. Privacy is perceived not as merely a right possessed by individuals, but as a prerequisite for making autonomous decisions, freely communicating with other persons, and being included in a participation society.

In Section 20.2, I examine communications monitoring as a law enforcement tool, by presenting the notions of interception of content, data retention, and data preservation. I consider critically the choices of legislators in the European Union and the United States (Sections 20.3 and 20.4), by referring to the legal framework and assessing the respective jurisprudence. Emphasis is given on the recently (2006) adopted EU Data Retention Directive and its effects on freedom of communication and privacy. In Section 20.5, assessed is the distinction of content and communications data, which forms the groundwork for the legislative options and judicial approaches. Further, I examine in Section 20.6 whether, and to what extent, the new legal landscape takes into account the values and fundamental rights deeply embedded in democratic societies and legal orders. Section 20.7 concludes the chapter by considering the far-reaching effects of mass surveillance on the relationship and the adjustment of freedom and security and consequently on the nature of state and society.

20.2 Data Retention as a (Valuable?) Surveillance Tool

Access to communications data and its content has always been one of the most commonly used ways of gathering information for criminal investigations and the activities of intelligence services. In the emerging information society, more and more social interaction as well as business relationships are conducted via electronic communications networks. As a result, traditional procedural measures of information collection through law enforcement authorities, such as search and seizure, have to be adapted to the dynamic nature of data and information flows and more generally to the new technological and societal environment [13].

If communications content is intercepted only in exceptional and specific cases, providers store the communications or transactional data routinely for the purposes of conveying and billing of communications. In the context of prevention, investigation, detection, and prosecution of criminal offenses and/or terrorist attacks (committed or supported by means of electronic communication networks), data relating to the use of communications are valuable in tracing and locating the source and the route of information as well as collecting and securing evidence. The retention of this data is pivotal to reactive investigations into serious crimes and the development of proactive intelligence on matters affecting not only organized criminal activity, but also national security [8].

20.2.1   Communications and Traffic Data

A lot of confusion exists about the notion of this data, as the definitions in various national and/or international legal texts are quite different [12]. The provisions of the EU e-Privacy Directive relate to "traffic data" as "any data processed for the purpose of the conveyance of a communication on an electronic communications network or for the billing thereof" (Art. 2 b). The e-Privacy Directive covers all traffic data "in a technology neutral way," i.e., those of traditional circuit-switched telephony as well as packet-switched Internet transmission. Different communications infrastructures give rise to different forms of transactional data [37]. "Traffic data, among other things, may consists of data referring to the routing, duration, time, or volume of a communication; to the protocol used; to the location of the terminal equipment of the sender or recipient (location data); to the network on which the communication originates or terminates; to the beginning, end, or duration of a connection. It may also consist of the format in which the communication is conveyed by the network" (2002/58/EC Recital 15). However, the European Data Retention Directive refers not only to "traffic data," but also to any related data necessary to identify the subscriber or user (data necessary to identify the source and the destination of a communication, such as the name and address of the subscriber or registered user). To the extent that this data is relating to an identified or identifiable natural person, it is deemed to be "personal data," as defined in the Data Protection Framework Directive (Art. 2 a).

The Convention of the Council of Europe on Cybercrime, assigning "traffic data" to a specific legal regime, defines it as "any computer data relating to a communication by means of a computer system, generated by a computer system that formed a part in the chain of communication, indicating the communication's origin, destination, route, time, date, size, duration, or type of underlying service" (Art. 1 d). This definition lists exhaustively the categories of traffic data that is treated by a specific regime in this convention (Explanatory Report, 30). The basic idea of this definition is that traffic data is data used by the telecommunications service providers to allow them to supervise the network. This type of data does not need to be personal [33].

In United States law (Stored Communications Act), "transactional" data lists certain customer record information: the customers name, address, phone numbers, billing records, and types of services the customer utilizes. The USA PATRIOT Act (2001) expanded this list to include "records of session times and durations," any temporarily assigned network address, and "any credit card or bank account number" used for payment [43,34].

20.2.2 *Interception, Preservation, and Retention*

Traditionally, the interception and collection of content data (i.e., the meaning or purport of the communication, or the message or information being conveyed by the communication) has been a useful tool for law enforcement authorities. Telecommunications interception is defined as a third party acquiring knowledge of the content and/or data relating to private telecommunications between two or more correspondents and, in particular, of traffic data concerning the use of telecommunications activities [2]. American courts have uniformly concluded that an interception of an electronic communication occurs only when the communication is seized during its transmission and before it becomes available to the subscriber [7].

Highly important for law enforcement purposes is to further the measures of data preservation and data retention. As underlined in the Explanatory Report of the Cybercrime Convention of the Council of Europe, traffic data might last only ephemerally, which would make it necessary to order its expeditious preservation. In the language of the Cybercrime Convention, data preservation is the procedure of keeping stored data secure and safe. "Data preservation" must be distinguished from "data retention." The preservation measures apply also to computer data that "has been stored by means of a computer system," which presupposes that the data already exists, has already been collected, and is stored. Expedited data preservation claims, within the framework of a specific investigation or proceeding, the right for the relevant authorities to compel a provider (already in possession of certain data on a specific subscriber/user) to conserve it against the possibility of disappearing.

The so-called "fast-freeze-quick-thaw" model [5], adopted by the Council of Europe and the United States (1986), targets principally the communications of a specific individual, who is already under investigation. As noted by Crump, data preservation "demonstrates the utility of Internet traffic data as evidence of criminal wrongdoing;" whether data retention, "by making it easier to link acts to actors," aims at the change of the communication context [15].

20.3 European Regulatory Framework

20.3.1 Cybercrime Convention of the Council of Europe

The Council of Europe (CoE) adopted, in November 2001, the first international legal text on cyber-crime. The CoE aimed at adapting the substantive and procedural criminal law "to technological developments, which offer highly sophisticated opportunities for misusing facilities of the cyberspace and causing damage to legitimate interests." Given the cross-border nature of information networks, a "binding international instrument" was deemed necessary in order to "ensure... efficiency in the fight against these new phenomena" [13]. The convention was originally open to the members of the CoE and to countries that were involved in its development like the United States, Canada, Japan, and South Africa and came into force on January 7, 2004, once it was ratified by five signatory states, all of which are members of the CoE.

The convention provides for the criminalization of certain online-conducted activities. Included are offenses against the confidentiality, integrity, and availability of computer data and systems (e.g., unauthorized access, etc.), computer-related fraud and forgery, content-related offenses of unlawful production or distribution of child pornography, and offenses related to infringements of copyright and related rights. The convention sets out procedural powers to be adopted by the signing states: expedited preservation of stored data; expedited preservation and partial disclosure of traffic data; production order; search and seizure of computer data; real-time collection of traffic data; interception of content data, which will apply to any offense committed by means of a computer system or the evidence of which is in electronic form. The Convention also contains provisions concerning traditional and computer crime-related mutual assistance as well as extradition rules.

Article 16 of the Cybercrime Convention envisages the rapid conservation as being for a maximum, though renewable, term of 90 days. It aims at ensuring that competent national authorities are able to order or similarly obtain the expedited preservation of provisory stored computer data in connection with a specific criminal investigation or proceeding. The convention establishes specific obligations in relation to the preservation of traffic data and provides for expeditious disclosure of some traffic data so as to identify that other service providers were involved in the transmission of the specified communications.

The measures in Articles 16 and 17 apply to stored data that has already been collected and retained by data holders, such as service providers. They do not apply to the real-time collection and retention of future traffic data or to real-time access to the content of communications. The Convention neither requires nor authorizes the signing States to impose supplementary data conservation obligations upon providers and certainly not to operate such conservation as a general regime for all uses of their services [35]. However, Articles 20 and 21 provide for the real-time collection of traffic data and the real-time interception of content data associated with specified communications transmitted by a computer system.

The first drafts of the convention were strongly criticized, as they initially introduced a general surveillance obligation consisting of the routine retention of all traffic data, an approach abandoned "due to the lack of consensus" [13]. The Art. 29 Data Protection Working Party (DPWP), a committee composed of representatives of supervisory authorities designated by EU Member States (Art. 29 of the Framework Data Protection Directive), had expressed serious concerns regarding the vague and confusing wording of the Convention [3]. However, the DPWP had recognized that the Convention's preservation model, by contrast to the mandatory, routine data retention, is "entirely adequate for the prevention or prosecution of criminal offenses" [4].

20.3.2 Privacy and Electronic Communications Law in the European Union

20.3.2.1 The E-Privacy Directive: Data Retention as an Option

While the content of communications has already been recognized as deserving protection under constitutional laws, traffic data because of its sensitivity, was considered as "external elements of communication," even if it reflected a level of interaction between the individual and the environment that rests on similar grounds like the "message" itself. The provision of the Directive 2002/58/EC on privacy and electronic communications (E-privacy Directive) has led to a big improvement on the principle of confidentiality and anonymity by extending the scope of Art. 5 to include not just the content of the communication, but also the related traffic data. Through the new wording, all traffic data generated during the transmission of a communication should enjoy the same confidentiality as provided for the content communications. Electronic communications providers must not disclose any information on contents or data traffic except for the purposes of telecommunications or where explicit law requires it [33].

According to the directive, traffic data generated in the course of an electronic communication should be erased when it is no longer necessary for the purpose of the transmission of the communication. Exemptions to this principle are limited to a small number of specific purposes, such as billing purposes (Art. 6). A "general obligation concerning data retention and any form of systematic interception" would be "contrary to the proportionality principle" [21]. The vigorous debate about the mandatory retention of traffic data ended in 2002 with a compromise solution: Member states were allowed to adopt legislative measures for the retention of data for a limited period, if these are necessary to safeguard national security, defense, public security, and the prevention, investigation, detection, and prosecution of criminal offenses, etc. (Art. 15 § 1). Such measures were required to be "necessary, appropriate, and proportionate within a democratic society" and, explicitly, "to comply with the general principles of Community law," e.g., those recognized by the Charter of Fundamental Rights of the EU (right to privacy, protection of personal data, freedom of expression, and communication) as well as with the fundamental rights guaranteed by the European Convention for the Protection of Human Rights and Fundamental Freedoms of the Council of Europe (ECHR).

Even if this provision was supposed to constitute an exception to the rules established by the E-privacy directive, "the ability of governments to oblige communication providers to store all data of all of their subscribers could hardly be construed as an exception to be narrowly interpreted" [37]. Furthermore, this provision was widely drafted and it was criticized for making "little distinction between the action, which may be taken in response to extreme terrorist activity and more routine criminal behaviour" [38].

20.3.2.2 Mandatory, Routine Data Retention: The New Directive

Four years later, the permissive language of the E-privacy directive has been transformed into an obligation on EU Member States. The "Directive 2006/24/EC on the retention of data generated or processed in connection with the provision of publicly available electronic communication services or of public communication networks and amending Directive 2002/58/EC" (Data Retention Directive) introduced the EU-wide obligation to compel "the providers of publicly available electronic communications services or public communications networks" to retain "certain data, which is generated or processed by them, in order to ensure that "the data is available for the purpose of the investigation, detection, and prosecution of serious crime, as defined by each Member State in its national law (Art. 1)."

The exclusion of—the initially included—"prevention" of crime from the scope of the directive was the fruit of a privacy-enhancing approach of the European Parliament. However, the reference to undetermined "serious crime" (instead of the initial proposal's reference to "fight against terrorism and organized crime") leaves a very wide margin of appreciation [6], allowing extending the scope of measures, which might not have been taken outside the specific context of terrorism [26]. According to DPWP, "serious crime" should be "clearly defined and delineated" in order to comply with the principle of "finality" (purpose limitation) laid down in all relevant data protection legislative texts [6].

Providers are required to retain data necessary to identify and trace the identity of the source and the destination of a communication, the date, time, duration, type of the communication, as well as data necessary to identify the communication equipment and its location. Covered also is data relating to unsuccessful call attempts, if the relevant data is already stored or logged. The directive requires that the providers "retain only such data as is generated or processed in the process of supplying their communications services. . . It is not intended to merge the technology for retaining data. . . " (Recital 23). The directive is applicable to electronic communication services offered via the Internet, but "it does not apply to the content of the communications" (Art. 5). Article 29 DPWP considers that since the content is excluded from the scope of the directive, "specific guarantees should be introduced in order to ensure a stringent, effective distinction between content and traffic data—both for the Internet and for telephony" [5]. If such a distinction is feasible is a highly controversial issue.

By no later than September 15, 2007, EU member states have to adopt legislative measures to ensure that the data retained is provided to the competent national authorities in specific cases and in accordance with national law, while member states are allowed to postpone until March 15, 2009, the application of the directive to Internet access, Internet telephony, and Internet e-mail. National legislators have to specify the procedures to be followed and the conditions to be fulfilled in order to gain access to retained data "in accordance with necessity and proportionality requirements"(Art. 4). These requirements have to be taken into account especially for the designation of law enforcement authorities, who will have access to the retained data.

With regard to the retention period, the directive requires member states to ensure the data is retained for a minimum of six months and a maximum of two years from the date of the communication (Art. 6). Member states facing "particular circumstances" are allowed to extend the maximum retention period, provided that the commission approves the national measures that deviate from the directive's provision (Art. 12), a possibility that raises significant concerns relating to the harmonized application [48,28] and mainly to the power afforded to a community institution lacking democratic legitimization.

20.3.3 Data Retention as Interference with the Right to the Respect of (Communicational) Privacy

Communications data retention interferes with the right to confidential communications guaranteed to individuals by Art. 8 of the European Convention on Human Rights (ECHR), which states that "everyone has the right to respect for his private and family life, his home, and his correspondence." The convention establishes basic rules regarding fundamental rights and liberties that are applicable throughout the contracting states. According to Art. 6 (2) of the Treaty on European Union, the ECHR is binding not only for member states, but also for the European Union as well. The right to the protection of privacy is recognized also by Art. 7 of the Charter of Fundamental Rights of the European Union.

The notion of privacy could be defined as freedom of unwarranted and arbitrary interference from public authorities or private actors/bodies into activities that society recognizes as belonging to the realm of individual autonomy (private sphere) [23]. The European approach to privacy is largely grounded to the dignity of the person, who operates in self-determination as a member of a free society. (German Federal Constitutional Court, *Census case*, 1983). Dignity as related to privacy is a concept summarizing principles, such as protection of individual's personality, noncommodification of the individual, noninterference with other's life choices, and the possibility to act autonomously and freely in society [36,16].

The European Court of Human Rights has not viewed privacy only as a condition of "total secrecy" and/or "separateness." On the contrary, the court has clearly interpreted the reference to "private life" expansively. In its jurisprudence, the court admitted that the scope of Art. 8 extends to the right of the individual "to establish and develop relationships with other human beings" (Court of Human Rights, *P.G. v. United Kingdom, Niemitz v. Germany*). The Court considers the mere storing of personal information as an interference with the right of privacy, whether or not the state subsequently uses the data against the individual (Court of Human Rights, *Amann v. Switzerland*). Even "public information (i.e., public available information about an individual) can fall within the scope of private life where it is systematically collected and stored by public authorities" (Court of Human Rights, *Rotaru v. Romania*).

The communication with others as well as the use of communication services falls within the zone of (communicational) privacy [14]. In the case *Malone v. UK*, the court asserted that traffic data is an "integral element on the communications made" by telephone. Therefore, the metering (use of a device that registers automatically the numbers dialed, time, and duration) of traffic data without the consent of the subscriber constitutes an interference with Art. 8 [12]. Traffic data retention, as laid down by the Data Retention Directive, interferes with the fundamental right to confidential communications [5]. The fact that the data is retained by private parties (providers) is not decisive. Significant for the classification as interference, it remains that the authorities have the right, as specified by domestic law, to access the data at any time [8,28].

20.4 Privacy and Electronic Communications Law in the United States

20.4.1 The Legal Framework: The Electronic Communications Privacy Act

Electronic surveillance in the United States emerged as early as the use of telegraph during the Civil War, with Congress attempting to obtain telegraph messages maintained by Western Union; an attempt that raised "quite an outcry" [43]. The current framework of communications surveillance is dominated by the "strong sense of vulnerability" to the terrorist threat. The latter reinforced the orientation of the government to strengthen the hand of law enforcement agencies, enabling them to trace electronic communications. The USA PATRIOT Act emerged as a response to the September 11 attacks, but undoubtedly the significant problems concerning communications surveillance and intelligence gathering predate the recently adopted framework.

Electronic surveillance law is comprised of the statutory regimes introduced by the Electronic Communications Privacy Act (ECPA) of 1986. Congress amended Title III of the Omnibus Crime Control and Safe Streets Act of 1968 in order to extend the prohibitions on interception to electronic communications and to craft new guarantees for stored communications and records. ECPA covers wire, oral, and electronic communications and is structured into three titles: (1) the Wiretap Act, (2) the Stored Communications Act, and (3) the Pen Register Act.

The Wiretap Act deals with the interception of communications while in transmission, "even if they are briefly stored" (U.S. Courts of Appeals, *U.S. v. Councilman*). Law enforcement agencies are required to obtain a "warrant-like order," e.g., a special and specific order issued by a judge on probable cause. The Wiretap Act extended the scope of protection to the in-transit interception of wireless voice communications and to nonvoice electronic communications (e-mail, etc.).

The Stored Communications Act governs communications in "electronic storage," e.g., any temporary intermediate storage...incidental to the electronic transmission thereof, as well as any storage...for purposes of backup protection. It also allows law enforcement agencies—by merely demonstrating relevance to an ongoing criminal investigation and issuing a subpoena to the Internet service provider (ISP)—to access subscriber-identifying information, transactional data, and the content of electronic communications that are maintained either incident to transmission or stored in the account.

The Pen Register Act regulates the government's use of pen registers and trap and trace devices, which create lists of one's outgoing and incoming phone calls. A pen register is a device that records the numbers of one's outgoing phone calls (numbers, date, time, and duration). The Patriot Act amended the definition of pen register to include information on e-mails and IP addresses [43,7]. The court must issue an order permitting the installation of such a register based upon a certification of the government office that the information likely to be obtained is relevant to an ongoing criminal investigation [34].

All three statutes generally prohibit unauthorized interception and/or access to communications and information, and provide for prospective and retrospective surveillance, permitting specified exceptions [34]. Preliminarily, it is interesting to note that, although President George Bush encouraged the president of the European Commission to "[r]evise draft privacy directives that call for mandatory destruction to permit the retention of critical data for a reasonable period" (Letter of January 16, 2001), U.S. statutory provisions permit data retention only in respect to specific investigations that are already underway.

20.4.2   The Fourth Amendment and the "(Un)reasonable" Expectation of Communicational Privacy

The legal array relating to the surveillance of electronic communications has been adopted "against a backdrop of constitutional uncertainty" [7]. In the United States there is no express right to privacy embedded in the Constitution and—with the exception of several highly specific regulations (as ECPA, the Genetic Privacy Act, or the Video Privacy Act)—there is no comprehensive legal framework providing for the protection of privacy. However, in certain situations, the Supreme Court has interpreted the Constitution to protect the privacy of the individuals: In the 1960s and 1970s, the Court reasoned that the Constitution protected a "zone of privacy" that safeguarded individual autonomy in making certain decisions, traditionally left to individual choice, such as whether to have children (Supreme Court, *Row v. Wade*). In *Whalen v. Roe* (1977), the Court held that the zone of privacy extends to the independence in making certain kinds of decision and the individual interest in avoiding disclosure of personal matters. Several U.S. scholars have maintained that privacy is a form of freedom built into social structure and—subsequently—inadequate protection of privacy threatens deliberative democracy by inhibiting people from engaging in democratic activities [44,40,47].

The critical constitutional framework for communicational privacy consists of the Fourth Amendment and its interpretation by the courts, mainly the U.S. Supreme Court. The Fourth Amendment affirms the right of the people to be secure in their persons, homes, papers, and effects, against unreasonable searches and seizure. It generally prohibits searches or seizures without a warrant. A first important issue concerns the notion of search for Fourth Amendment purposes in relation to the framing question, whether a subscriber/person has a "reasonable expectation of privacy" in data transmitted and retained by providers.

In *Katz v. U.S.* (1967), the "lodestar" of Supreme Court surveillance cases, Justice Harlan articulated the two-part requirement for a government action to be considered a search: "First, that a person have exhibited an actual (subjective) expectation of privacy and, second, that the expectation be one that society is prepared to recognize as 'reasonable'." In Katz, the Supreme Court decided that an electronic eavesdropping device, commonly referred to as a "wiretap," placed on the outside of a public phone booth to detect the contents of the phone conversation implicated the Fourth Amendment and was presumptively unreasonable without a warrant. Departing from its previous narrow definition of a search, the Court stated that protected are "people, not places." According to the Court, also protected are "communications, which the individual seeks to protect as private, even in an area accessible to the public."

However, since the end of the Warren Court era (1969), the Supreme Court, generating exceptions and exclusions, has interpreted the Fourth Amendment in a way that leaves communications surveillance largely free from constitutional restrictions [24,39]. Twelve years after Katz, in *Smith v. Maryland* (1979), the Court reasoned that there is no Fourth Amendment interest in the telephone numbers one dials: A first argument, set out already in another famous case (*United States v. Miller*), concerns the "nonprivate" character of data retained: A person has no reasonable expectation of privacy in information voluntarily revealed to a third party and conveyed by it to a public authority, "even if the information is revealed on the assumption that it will be used only for a limited purpose." Since people "know that they must convey numerical information to the phone company" and that the phone company records this information for billing purposes, people cannot "harbour any general expectation that the numbers they dial will remain secret" (*Smith v. Maryland*). The underlying principle is that technological possibilities determine the reasonableness of privacy expectations. Furthermore, the Supreme Court subdivides a technologically enhanced communication into content and other parts, which are not protected under the Fourth Amendment: "[A] pen register differs significantly from the listening device employed in Katz, for pen registers do not acquire the contents of communications... These devices do not hear sound..." [24,44,39].

One particularly insidious characteristic of the reasonable expectation of privacy approach is that the more individuals rely on technology, the more government intrusion into personal information seems "reasonable." "If we remain isolated in our homes, with the curtains tightly drawn, the phone and the computer unplugged, we are within the core of Fourth Amendment protection" [10]. It is highly questionable if the Fourth Amendment and the statutory provisions, as currently interpreted, continue to be an adequate regulatory tool for privacy protection in the Internet space and era.

20.5 New Challenges, Old Instruments: The Shortcoming of "Content-Envelope" Distinction

By adapting "traditional" procedural requirements to new technological environments, a critical question concerns the terms used to define and regulate the communications surveillance. The choice of "appropriate terminology" has profound impacts on the extent of power granted to state authorities and respectively on the level of protection afforded to citizens. By failing to provide specific definitions or guidance, the law could lead to major interpretation problems relating to the provisions, guarantees, and checks applied, leaving the public authorities a wide discretion to opt for the convenient legal instrument [42]. This remark, among others, refers to the notion of search and seizure, to the differences of transmission and storage, but mainly it concerns the basis distinction of "content" and "traffic/transactional" data.

Both the European and the American regulatory approaches rely on the traditional distinction of "content" and "envelope." While recognizing that both types of data may have associated privacy interests, the dominant assumption, explicitly or implicitly shared by legislators and courts, is that the privacy interests in respect to content data are greater due to the nature of the communication content or message [13]. However, in the modern network environment, this separation is not quite as obvious. Moreover this distinction does not reflect necessarily a distinction between "sensitive" and "innocuous" information [43].

20.5.1 The Blurring Lines of "Content" and "Envelope"

Whereas in the context of traditional telephone communications it is quite easy to distinguish dialing, routing, signaling, or billing information and content, in the landscape of electronic communications the frontiers are blurring. There are numerous network services that cannot easily be categorized in a mere distinction between content and traffic data. The ambiguity of separation is particularly acute in the context of the Internet. It is highly uncertain whether e-mail, instant messaging, and other online activities analogous to "speaking" could be covered by the traditional concepts.

E-mail messages contain information sequences that include both address and content [42]. An e-mail's subject line and the name of the file attached (e.g., "Communist manifesto.doc" or "BinLaden. doc") are also arguably content [15].

Content and traffic data are often generated simultaneously. A fundamental question relates to the nature of URLs: even in the basic level a domain name (such as *www.aegean.edu* or *www.aryan-nations.org*) provides information on the content of what the user will find on the Web page [19,7]. In the case of a request operated with a search engine, such as Google or Altavista, a result like *http://www.google.com/sites/web?q=aids+medical+treatment* reveals not only data necessary for the conveyance of an electronic communication, but also elements of content, indicating at least the interests of the user [12], and information that is automatically logged together with the IP address of the user and the time of the search [28].

20.5.2 A False Distinction?

Apart from the difficulties of establishing clear distinctions between content and traffic data, it is disputable if—under the changing technological circumstances—the surveillance of content remains more privacy invasive than the retention of/and access to traffic data. It is argued that "the information value and usability of traffic data is extremely high and at least equals that of content," as this data can be analyzed automatically, combined with other data, searched for specific patterns, and sorted according to certain criteria [8].

Justice Stewart, dissenting in *Smith v. United States*, expressed the opinion that "even the phone numbers one dials have some content, in that a list of the phone numbers a person dials easily could reveal the identities of the persons and the places called, and thus reveal the most intimate details of a person's life." The German Federal Constitutional Court in the "Connection Capture" decision, the German equivalent of American "pen registers," found that also protected are the "specific circumstances of the telecommunications relationship," including "the fact that a call has been attempted" [39]. Privacy relevant can be proved also location information generated by mobile communications infrastructure [32].

The distinction between traffic/transactional data and content becomes more difficult in the case of communications over the Internet, as the latter relies on "packet switching": To obtain e-mail addresses and session times, providers and law enforcement officers have to separate the address from the content of the message [42]. Moreover, even the "to" and "from" lines of an e-mail can be classified as traffic data as they provide more information than a phone number; they, in general, tend to be more person-specific than phone numbers or they may also have other affiliations, such as an employer in the domain name [15,19].

Technological changes transform rapidly the parameters of the distinction of content and external communication elements: Voice over Internet Protocol (VoIP), relying on Internet's packet-switched network, creates the potential for telephone conversations to be trivially stored by the parties involved as well as at the network level [7]. The imminent growth of VoIP is likely to have profound implications on the content-traffic data approach. Such a routine storage would result in the restriction of user's privacy protection, especially where the access to stored data and communications requires less procedural and substantial guarantees as the interception of content. As Swire [46] points out, the spread of VoIP and pervasive caching of telephone communications could create a *reductio ad absurdum* (reduction to absurdity), in which the "reasonable expectation of privacy" would concern "only a few telephone calls that do not happen to be stored anywhere" [46]. This last remark relates to a major challenge, which lawmakers and courts have to meet in the information era, which is to keep pace with the advance of surveillance technologies, practices, and purposes of the—respectively changing—societal needs and expectations.

20.6 Data Retention versus Fundamental Freedoms

Given the expanding use of the Internet and the creation of a new (cyber) "space," individuals have a both subjectively and objectively reasonable expectation of privacy and a claim to control the acquisition or release of personal information, which statutes such as ECPA or the Data Retention Directive fail to reflect, let alone to protect. Quite the reverse. Their—mostly vaguely formulated—provisions constitute a threat to the right to privacy. The new communication surveillance measures, adopted both in the European Union and in the United States, have been strongly criticized by parliamentarians, academics, and privacy advocates. Criticism in Europe has put strong emphasis on the disproportionality of measures adopted in relation to the rights and liberties affected [8,38], while in the United States, the criticism has been largely focused on inadequate and insufficient judicial oversight of communication surveillance procedures and measures, partly as a result of the restrictive approach to "reasonable expectation of privacy" [43,24].

20.6.1 An Unnecessary and Disproportionate Measure

20.6.1.1 Criteria of "Acceptable" Interference

According to the ECHR, communications surveillance is unacceptable, unless it fulfills three fundamental criteria set in Art. 8 (2): (1) a legal basis, (2) the need/necessity of the measure in a democratic society, and (3) the conformity of the measure with the legitimate interests of national security, public safety, or the economic well-being of a country, prevention or disorder of crime, protection of health or morals, or protection of the rights and freedoms of the others. The provision reflects the tension between individual and community and the need to take into account the interests of society without infringing upon the intrinsic value of privacy in a democratic society.

The catalog of justified restrictions on the right to privacy seems to be extensively large. However, the European Court of Human Rights in its case law has specified the requirements to be met. The law authorizing the interference in the communicational privacy has to meet the standards of accessibility and foreseeability inherent in the concept of the rule of law, so that persons can regulate their conduct according to the law (Court of Human Rights, *Malone v. U.K., Kruslin v. France*). Conditions, safeguards for the individuals, and implementation modalities must be sufficiently summarized, in order to succeed the "quality of law" test [12,15].

Proportionality, a key principle in European constitutional law, requires a further assessment of the necessity of the measure and its suitability to achieve its aims. Even if "necessary is not synonymous with indispensable... it implies a pressing social need" (Court of Human Rights, *Handyside v. U.K.*). The objective pursued must be balanced against the seriousness if the interference, which is to be judged taking into account, inter alia, the number and nature of persons affected and the intensiveness of the negative effects [8]. Restrictions must be limited to a strict minimum: Legislators are required to minimize the interference by trying to achieve their aims in the least onerous way (Court of Human Rights, *Hatton v. U.K.*). The necessity and proportionality have to be clearly demonstrated by considering that privacy is not only an individual right of control over one's information, but moreover a key element of a democratic constitutional order (German Constitutional Court, *Census Decision*).

20.6.1.2 A Disproportionate "Dataveillance"

Considerable doubts are expressed about whether the above-mentioned criteria are fulfilled in the EU Data Retention Directive. A first significant objection concerned the necessity of the general data retention. The new framework was adopted without demonstrating that "the (pre)existing legal framework does not offer the instruments that are needed to protect physical security" [20] and this large-scale surveillance potential was the only feasible option for combating crime. Serious concerns have been expressed about the proportionality of means, ends, and—provable—security gains. According to a research of T-Online (a big German provider), only 0.0004% of traffic data retained is needed for law enforcement purposes [9]. However, this framework will apply to all persons who use

European-based electronic communications. The comprehensive storage of all traffic data gives rise to an indefinite and ongoing interference with the privacy rights of all users, not just those who are suspected of committing a crime [14,12,18]. It makes surveillance that is authorized in exceptional circumstances, the "rule" [5]. Additionally, generalized data retention conflicts with the proportionality, fair use, and specificity requirements of data protection regulation: Personal data may not be collected, processed, or transmitted with the sole purpose of providing a future speculative data resource. The adoption of such an invasive measure could result in opening a Pandora's box of universal surveillance, where every person is treated as a potential criminal [33].

The generalized storing of communication/traffic data is wildly disproportionate to the law enforcement objectives and, therefore, could not be deemed as necessary in a democratic society. Routine retention of traffic and location data concerning all kinds of communications (i.e., mobile phones, SMS, faxes, e-mails, chatrooms, and other uses of the Internet) for purposes varying from national security to law enforcement constitutes what Clarke [11] refers to as "dataveillance," i.e., the routine, systematic, and focused use of personal data systems in the investigation or monitoring of the actions or communications of one or more persons. Considering the increased use of electronic communications in daily life and the fact that, especially, the Internet is unprecedented in the degree of information that can be stored and revealed, the storage of this data could be seen as an "extended logbook" of a person's behavior and life [12]. Encroaching into the daily life of every person, routine data retention "may endanger the fundamental values and freedoms that all (European) citizens enjoy and cherish" [6].

20.6.2 Communications Surveillance as Interference into the Rights of Anonymity and Freedom of Expression

The feature of the electronic communication networks and the interactive use of networks increase the amount of transactional/traffic data generated [1]. As electronic communications leave a lot of "digital traces," communication surveillance impedes or even eliminates the right to anonymity [43,15]. The ability to maintain one's anonymity in certain contexts, as in using technology without having to reveal one's name forms part of privacy [10]. Anonymity has to be assessed not only as a component of private sphere and intimacy, but also and mainly in the context of its significance for the right to freedom of expression, which includes "the right to receive and impart information and ideas without interference by public authorities" (Art. 10 of the European Convention of Human Rights).

According to the landmark decision of the German Federal Constitutional Court on the census law, unrestricted access to personal data imperils virtually every constitutionally guaranteed right: Neither freedom of speech nor freedom of association nor freedom of assembly can be fully exercised as long as it remains uncertain whether, under what circumstances, and for what purposes, personal information is collected and processed. Blanket data retention, by making communication activity potentially traceable, has a disturbing effect on the willingness to voice critical and constructive ideas, and on the free exchange of information and ideas, which is of paramount importance in a democratic society [8,29]. Identification and fear of reprisal might discourage participation to public debate (U.S. Supreme Court, *Talley v. California*). On the contrary, anonymity allows information and ideas to be disseminated and considered without bias. The U.S. Supreme Court has found that the Constitution protects the right to receive information and ideas and, more specifically, that the First Amendment extends to anonymous speech activity.

The claim to anonymity, inherent in the right to privacy, is essential to freedom of communication via electronic networks, but, at the same time, it runs against public policy objectives. From a law enforcement perspective, anonymity is perceived as the main reason for increasing cyber-criminal activity [12]. However, there is no sustainable argument for abandoning the principle that where a choice of offline anonymity exists, it should also be preserved in the online world (*Ministerial Declaration of the Ministerial Conference on Global Information Networks*, Bonn, 1997). Proportionate restrictions to this right, in order to face the specific nature and risks of cyberspace activities, must be permitted in limited and specified circumstances. The Supreme Court, acknowledging the instrumental value of anonymity in enriching public discussion and maximizing freedom of (anonymous) association [15], has held that this constitutionally guaranteed right must be reconciled with compelling public interests. According to the Court, identification is held to be constitutional only if there is no other effective way for the government to achieve law enforcement objectives (*Buckley v. Valeo*).

20.6.3   The Question of Independent and Adequate Oversight

As a counterpart to restrictions of freedoms that governments adopt to respond to public security threats, adequate safeguards and remedies must be provided that can counter possible abuse by the administration and specifically by the law enforcement authorities [22]. The involvement of independent oversight mechanisms is a crucial element in order to ensure the lawful access to communications data and records and guarantee that the consequences for individuals and their rights and freedoms are limited to the strict minimum necessary.

Following the opinion of the DPWP, access to data, in principle, should be duly authorized by a judicial authority, who, where appropriate, should specify the particular data required for the specific cases at hand. Effective controls on the original and any further use should be provided: (1) by judicial authorities within and for the purposes of a criminal procedure and (2) by data protection authorities concerning data protection, regardless of the existence of a judicial proceeding [5,6]. Independent supervisory authorities have become an essential component of the data protection supervisory system in the EU. The Data Retention Directive requires member states to designate one or more public authorities, acting with complete independence. However, in this case, the EU legislators have a narrow perception of their competence, as it seems to be restricted to "monitoring the application of the national law provisions adopted by Member States regarding the security of the stored data" (Art. 9).

In the United States, the Wiretap Act requires the government to meet very high standards in order to obtain authorization to intercept communications (specific description, type, duration, etc.). However, the most significant deficiency is that the majority of the statutes permits governmental access to third-party records with only a court order or subpoena, which falls short of the Fourth Amendment's requirement for warrants supported by probable cause and issued by a neutral and detached judge. Regular warrants are required only to obtain the contents of electronic communications in electronic storage for 180 days or less. If they are stored over 180 days, the government can access them with an administrative subpoena, a grand jury subpoena, a trial subpoena, or a court order. In the case of the Pen Registers Act, the courts must take the government's certification that the information is relevant to an ongoing investigation. Judges are not required to review the evidence and assess the factual predicate for the government's certification. Several scholars have stressed the need for a higher threshold to obtain the court order and for the guarantee of judicial review of the government's application [43]. Another point of criticism has been the fact that the ECPA contains no statutory exclusionary rule for wrongfully acquired electronic communications, which means that it does not prohibit the use as evidence of any communications obtained in violation of these requirements [7].

20.6.4 Common Information Pools for Public and Private Sector

Systematic data retention is a paradigm for (recently enhanced) policies, which aim at enabling and promoting increased data sharing between the public and the private domain, particularly for prevention and law enforcement purposes. The exploding collection of consumer information by private sector actors has produced enormous pools of information, which can be adapted to domestic surveillance [44,29]. Especially in the aftermath of September 11, data flows (increasingly and often internationally) from the private sector, ranging from banks and insurances (SWIFT case, Choice-Point case) to airlines (EU–USA PNR data case), to governmental agencies. Privatization and diversification of traditionally state-controlled sectors (like telecommunications), interoperability, and technological synergy have as consequence the so-called "function creep," which can result in a "mission creep" [37]. "For example, not only are the same data-mining techniques developed for profiling consumers being used by security and intelligence services to profile potential terrorists, often the very data from which these profiles are created is the same" [45].

Regardless, the national rules being developed to regulate access to traffic data by law enforcement agencies, will mean that mandatory retention would effectively create a massive database, putting at the disposal of the state an unprecedented amount of information about the everyday activities of—indiscriminately—each and every user. The increasing amount of personal information flowing to the government poses significant problems with far-reaching effects [44]. The (even potential) availability and accessibility of vast amounts of data, collected by private entities for entirely other purposes, constitutes a threat to informational self-determination and it can chill not only politics-related, but also personal activities.

20.7 An Information-Based (Pre)prevention of Risks or a Threat to Democracy

The terrorist attacks in the United States, Europe, and elsewhere, and the expansion of organized crime/cyber-crime, have altered the balance of security interests and freedom in a way that deeply affects the fundamental values, which form the basis of democratic and constitutional states. Surveillance-susceptible infrastructures and data-retention schemes supply the governments with new privacy-intrusive surveillance tools. As life in the information society depends upon information and communication, data retention extends beyond a potential search basis: Not only does "it rigidifies one's past" [43], but it records citizen's behavior and social interaction [34,8]. Pervasive surveillance affects the self-determination and the personality of individuals, inclining their choices toward the mainstream [41,43]. "Potential knowledge is present power," emphasizes the Report of the [U.S. Department of Defense] Technology and Privacy Advisory Committee, adding, "awareness that government may analyze activity is likely to alter behavior" as "people act differently if they know their conduct could be observed" [49]. Data retention symbolizes the "disappearance of the disappearance," which seems to become a defining characteristic of the information age [31]. In this sense, the "freedom of movement," another historically fundamental freedom right, is currently jeopardized in virtual "spaces."

The decision to routinely retain communications data for law enforcement purposes is "an unprecedented one with a historical dimension" [6]. It reflects the transformation from the traditional constitutional model of gathering conclusive evidence of wrongdoing of suspect individuals toward intelligence gathering, which may be carried out against individuals at random [31,17]. The individual itself "is no longer perceived as a principally law-abiding citizen, rather as a potential threat" or "as an exchangeable element in a principally dangerous environment" [30]. Further, even after the deletion of "prevention" from the aims allowing access to retained data according to EU law, generalized, and indiscriminate data retention, as such, mirrors the shift from a constitutional state guarding against the threat of specific risks in specific situations toward a security-orientated preventive [17] or even prepreventive state, which acts operatively and proactively. The imperative to fight new threats through preprevention measures and policies "blows up the cornerstones of the rule of law state" [25].

The rapid reaction to the expectation of the people that the government will keep the "security promise," reveals certainly the state's readiness to suspend freedom [26], merely catalyzed, yet not caused, by the latest terrorist acts. The "invention" of a "fundamental right to security" did nothing to resolve the problems of security, but was only used as an argument to justify everwider powers of state intervention [17,26]. Prevention and removal of risks have become a social and political imperative in the risk society. Curtailment of rights and reduction of scrutiny seems to be in large extent tolerated by majorities [15]. A decisive question is if and to what extent the society is ready to take risks in freedom's interest.

Governments must respond to the new challenge in a way that effectively meets the citizens' expectations without undermining individual human rights "or even destroying democracy on the ground of defending it" (European Court, *Klass v. Germany*). Absolute security could not exist because it could be achieved only at the price of freedom. The legitimization of the democratic state depends upon its success in balancing the various public objectives, i.e., freedom and security, under the terms and within the limits of core democratic values. Levi and Wall [31] propose as "guidance for future directions or thoughts" Benjamin Franklin's famous quote: "Any society that would give up a little liberty to gain a little security will deserve neither and lose both."

References

[1] Article 29, Data Protection Working Party, Recommendation 3/97 Anonymity on the Internet, December 1997.

[2] Article 29, Data Protection Working Party, Recommendation 2/99 on the respect of privacy in the context of interception of telecommunications, May 1999.

[3] Article 29, Data Protection Working Party, Opinion 4/2001 on the Council of Europe's Draft Convention on Cyber-Crime, March 2001.

[4] Article 29, Data Protection Working Party, Opinion 9/2004 on a draft Framework Decision on the storage of data processed and retained for the purpose of providing electronic public communications services or data available in public communication networks with a view to the prevention, investigation, detection and prosecution of criminal acts, including terrorism, November 2004.

[5] Article 29, Data Protection Working Party, Opinion 113/2005 on the Proposal for a Directive on the retention of data processed in connection with the Provision of Public Electronic Communication services and amending Directive 2002/58/EC, October 2005.

[6] Article 29, Data Protection Working Party, Opinion 3/2006 on the Directive on the retention of data generated or processed in connection with the provision of publicly available electronic communication services or of public communications networks and amending Directive 2002/58/EC, March 2006.

[7] Bellia, P.L., The Fourth Amendment and Emerging Communications Technologies, *IEEE Security and Privacy*, 20, 2006.

[8] Breyer, P., Telecommunications Data Retention and Human Rights: The Compatibility of Blanket Traffic Data Retention with the ECHR, *European Law Journal*, 11, 365, 2005.

[9] Breyer, P., Bürgerrechte und TKG-Novelle—Datenschutzrechtliche Auswirkungen der Neufassung des Telekommunikationsgesetzes, *Recht der Datenverarbeitung*, 20, 147, 2004.

[10] Cheh, M., Technology and privacy: creating the conditions for preserving personal privacy, in *Scientific and Technological Developments and Human Rights*, Sicilianos, L.A. and Gavouneli, M., Eds., Ant. Sakkoulas Publishers, Athens, 2001, 99.

[11] Clark, R., Introduction to dataveillance and information privacy [2006 (1997)]: http://www.anu.edu.au/people/Roger.Clarke/DV/Intro#DV

[12] Coemans, C. and Dumortier, J., Enforcement issues—Mandatory retention of traffic data in the EU: Possible impact on privacy and on-line anonymity, in *Digital Anonymity and the Law*, Nicoll, C. Prince J.E.J., and van Dellen, J.M., Eds., TMC Asser Press, The Hague, the Netherlands, 2003, 161.

[13] Council of Europe, Convention on Cybercrime—Explanatory report, 2001.

[14] Covington and Burling LLP, Memorandum of laws concerning the legality of data retention with regard to the rights guaranteed by the European Convention on Human Rights, Memorandum prepared for Privacy International (October 10, 2003): http://www.privacyinternational.org/issues/terrorism/

[15] Crump, C., Data retention—Privacy, anonymity, and accountability online, *StanfordLaw Review*, 56, 191, 2003.

[16] De Hert, P. Balancing security and liberty within the European Human Rights Framework. A critical reading of the Court's case law in the light of surveillance and criminal law enforcement strategies after 9/11, *Utrecht Law Review*, 1, 68, 2005.

[17] Denninger, E., Freiheit durch Sicherheit? Wie viel Schutz der inneren Sicherheit verlangt und verträgt das deutsche Grundgesetz?, *Kritische Justiz*, 35, 467, 2002.

[18] Deutscher Bundestag–Wissenschaftliche Dienste (Sierck, G., Schöning, F., and Pöhl, M.), *Zulässigkeit der Vorratsdatenspeicherung nach europäischem und deutschem Recht—Ausarbeitung*, Berlin, 2006.

[19] Ditzion, R., Electronic surveillance in the Internet age: The strange case of Pen Registers, *American Criminal Law Review*, 41, 1321, 2004.

[20] European Data Protection Supervisor, Opinion on the Proposal for a Directive on the retention of data processed in connection with the provision of public electronic communication services and amending Directive 2002/58/EC.

[21] European Parliament, Recommendation on the strategy for creating a safer information society by improving the security of information infrastructures and combating computer-related crime, C 72 E/323-329 *Official Journal of EC*, March 31, 2002.

[22] EU Network of Independent Experts in Fundamental Rights—CRF-DF, Comment, *The Balance between Freedom and Security in the Response by the EU and Its MS to the Terrorist Threat*, 2003.

[23] EU Network of Independent Experts on Fundamental Rights—CRF-DF, Commentary of the Charter of Fundamental Rights of the European Union, June 2006.

[24] Herman, S.N., The USA PATRIOT Act and the submajoritarian Fourth Amendment, *Harvard Civil Rights–Civil Liberties Law Review*, 41, 67, 2006.

[25] Hoffmann-Riem, W., Freiheit und Sicherheit im Angesicht terroristischer Anschläge, *Zeitschrift für Rechtspolitik*, 35, 497, 2002.

[26] Hustinx, P.J. (European Data Protection Supervisor), Human rights and public security: Chance for a compromise or continuity of safeguards? in *Conference on Public Security and Data Protection*, Warsaw, 2006.

[27] Institute For Prospective Technological Studies, *Security and Privacy for the Citizen in the Post-September 11 Digital Age: A Prospective Overview*. Report to the European Parliament Committee on Citizens Freedoms and Rights, Justice and Home Affairs, European Communities, 2003.

[28] Kosta, E. and Valcke, P., Retaining the data retention directive, *Computer Law & Security Report*, 22, 370, 2006.

[29] Kreimer, S.F., Watching the watchers: Surveillance, transparency and political freedom in the war on terror, *University of Pennsylvania Journal of Constitutional Law*, 7, 133, 2004.

[30] Lepsius, O., Liberty, security and terrorism: The legal position in Germany, Part 2, *German Law Journal*, 5, 435, 2004.

[31] Levi, M. and Wall, D.S., Technologies, security and privacy in the Post-9/11 European Information Society, *Journal of Law and Society*, 31, 194, 2004.

[32] McPhie, D., Almost private: Pen registers, packet sniffers, and privacy at the margin, *Stanford Technology Law Review*, 1, 2005.

[33] Mitrou, E. and Moulinos, K., Privacy and Data Protection in Electronic Communications, in *Proc. Int. Workshop Computer Network Security*, Gorodetsky, V., Popyack, L., and Skormin, V., Eds., Springer, Berlin-Heidelberg, 2003, 432.

[34] Mulligan, D.K., Reasonable expectations in electronic communications: A critical perspective on the Electronic Communications Privacy Act, *George Washington Law Review*, 72, 1557, 2004.

[35] Poullet, Y., The fight against crime and/or the protection of privacy: A thorny debate, *International Review of Law Computers & Technology*, 18, 251, 2004.

[36] Rodota, S., Privacy, freedom and dignity, closing remarks at the 26th *International Conference on Privacy and Personal Data Protection*, Wroclaw, Poland, September 16, 2004.

[37] Rotenberg, M. et al. Privacy and human rights 2005—An international survey of privacy laws and developments, Electronic Privacy Information Center, Privacy International, http://www.privacyinternational.org/index/ September 7, 2006.

[38] Rowland, D., Data retention and the war against terrorism—A considered and proportionate response? *The Journal of Information, Law and Technology*, (3) 2004, www2.warwick.ac.uk/fac/soc/law/elj/jilt/2004_3/

[39] Schwartz, P.M., German and U.S. telecommunications privacy law: Legal regulation of domestic law enforcement surveillance, *Hastings Law Journal*, 54, 751, 2003.

[40] Schwartz, P.M. and Reidenberg, J.R., *Data Privacy Law—A Study of United States Data Protection*, Michie Law Publishers, Charlottesville, VA, 1996.

[41] Simitis, S., Reviewing privacy in an Information Society, *University of Pennsylvania Law Review*, 135, 707, 1987.

[42] Smith, J.C., The USA PATRIOT Act: Violating reasonable expectations of privacy protected by the Fourth Amendment without advancing national security, *North Carolina Law Review*, 82, 412, 2003.

[43] Solove, D.J., Reconstructing the electronic surveillance law, *The George Washington Law Review*, 72, 1701, 2004.

[44] Solove, D.J., Digital dossiers and the dissipation of Fourth Amendment Privacy, *Southern California Law Review*, 75, 1084, 2002.

[45] Surveillance Studies Network (Wood, D.M., Ed.), A report on the Surveillance Society for the (UK) Information Commissioner, September 2006.

[46] Swire, P.P., Katz is dead. Long live Katz, *Michigan Law Review*, 102, 904, 2004.

[47] Taipale, K.A., Technology, security and privacy: The fear of Frankenstein, the mythology of privacy and the lessons of King Ludd, *Yale Journal of Law and Technology*, 7, 123, 2004–2005.

[48] Taylor, M., The EU Data Retention Directive, *Computer Law and Security Report*, 22, 309, 2006.

[49] U.S. Department of Defense, Report from the Technology and Privacy Advisory Committee Safeguarding Privacy in the Fight Against Terrorism, March 2004, available at http://www.sainc.com/tapac/finalReport.htm

Surveillance of Emergent Associations: Freedom of Association in a Network Society

Katherine J. Strandburg

Contents

21.1 Introduction 436
21.2 The Increasing Importance of Emergent Association............ 437
21.3 The Rise in Relational Surveillance............................. 438
    21.3.1 The Availability of Relational Data 438
    21.3.2 Evolving Uses of Relational Data and Social
            Network Analysis 439
21.4 The Failure of Existing Legal Paradigms to Protect
    Emergent Association 442
    21.4.1 The Fourth Amendment and Relational Surveillance 442
    21.4.2 Low Protection for Relational Data under
            Surveillance Statutes 443
    21.4.3 Relational Surveillance and the First Amendment 445
21.5 Where to Go from Here 449
    21.5.1 The First Amendment Is the Primary Barrier
            against Overbroad Relational Surveillance 449
    21.5.2 Principles for Adapting to Technological
            Change Derived from Fourth Amendment Law.......... 450

21.5.2.1 Pattern-Based Network Analysis............... 452
21.5.2.2 Targeted Link Analysis 453
21.5.2.3 Access to Communications Traffic Data
outside the Network Analysis Context 454
21.6 Conclusions 454
Acknowledgments 455
References.. 455

21.1 Introduction

Recent events have combined to bring the prospect of using communications traffic data to ferret out suspect groups and investigate their membership and structure to the forefront of debate. While such "relational surveillance" has been around for years, efforts are being made to update traffic analysis to incorporate insights from "social network analysis"—a means of analyzing relational structures developed by sociologists [1–13]. Interest in employing social network analysis for law enforcement purposes was given a huge boost after September 11, 2001, when attention focused on tracking terrorist networks [5,7,9,11,12,14–17]. Traffic data, when stored, aggregated, and analyzed using sophisticated computer algorithms, contains far more "information" than is commonly appreciated. Increasing computational capabilities make it possible to apply computerized analysis to larger and larger sets of traffic data and raise the possibility of employing data-mining techniques to uncover "suspicious" patterns of association. Increasing use of the Internet and other digital communications means that traffic data is increasingly recorded by communication intermediaries. The availability of this data facilitates relational surveillance [1,11,18–22].

The Internet, wireless communication, and locational technology have also transformed the ways in which civic and political associations operate [23–30]. More and more political and civic "work" is performed, not by traditional face-to-face associations with well-defined members, policies, and goals, but by decentralized, often transient, networks of individuals associating primarily electronically and with policies and goals defined synergistically with the formation of the emergent association itself. Relational surveillance, particularly in the form of a search for "suspicious" patterns of association, has great potential to chill this increasingly important type of associational activity.

Historically, both Fourth Amendment and statutory protections from government surveillance have been strongest for communication content, offering significantly decreased protection for traffic data, which reveals who is talking to whom [19,20–22,31–37]. Freedom of association doctrine has the potential to provide strong protection against overreaching relational surveillance, but so far has focused on protecting the rights of traditional associations [38–41]. This chapter considers how relational surveillance must be regulated to preserve the growing role of emergent associations in politics and civic society. It concludes that First Amendment freedom of association provides the strongest basis for such regulation [40,42], and extends the First Amendment analysis into the age of electronic communications by extracting principles from Fourth Amendment doctrine about how surveillance regulation must respond to technological change.

21.2 The Increasing Importance of Emergent Association

The Internet, embodied in the World Wide Web, electronic mail, chat rooms, weblogs, and instant messaging, is revolutionizing the organization of grassroots political movements [28–30]. The speed and asynchronous nature of Internet communication make it an ideal tool for rapidly mobilizing a group of like-minded citizens. The Internet facilitates broad-based recruiting and, through the ease of e-mail forwarding and hyperlinking, allows associations to organize and adapt quickly, using highly connective social networks, to operate without a central command and control strategy. Newer technologies, combining Internet communication with location information, promise even more flexible tools for association [27].

Digital technology has lowered the costs of collective activity and decreased the importance of geographical proximity. Associations emerge on all size scales and can be geographically local or dispersed. They can form around specific issues and then die out quickly. They can remain loosely connected or coalesce into more traditional forms of organization with paid staff, centralized decision making, and so forth. In an emergent association, strategies, issues, and positions can be selected democratically or imposed by a central leadership, but also can self-organize out of the independent actions of individuals. The low cost and many-to-many structures of modern communication technology facilitates experimentation and cooperation between different groups. Internet communication opens the door to more effective exercise of political power by groups without significant material resources. It facilitates the aggregation of financial resources from many individuals as an alternative to more traditional fundraising, which must focus on the well-heeled. Internet pseudonymity also facilitates the emergence of groups whose members might otherwise have been deterred from joining until a threshold number of others was seen participating.

Comprehensive relational surveillance would be especially likely to nip in the bud the very emergent associations that modern technology has just begun to produce. The threads of Internet organization are invisible in the physical world, but can be traced all too easily in cyberspace. Not only can surveillance of emergent associations be more complete because of their cyberspace "tracks," but network analysis has the potential to expose these associations to government or public scrutiny at a much earlier stage than would be possible for a traditional, "real space" organization. Long before there is a name for the association, a platform, or a membership list, the associational pattern is recorded in the relational data. Associations may be evident even before the participants are aware that they have formed a collective enterprise and certainly before participants have made the kind of intentional "joining" decision that is typical for traditional organizations. Minimal activities, such as participating in e-mail campaigns or subscribing to an informational listserve, could mark an individual as a "member" of an emergent association.

Fear that digital communication technology may enhance the effectiveness of malevolent associations drives government efforts in relational surveillance [7–11]. Because the Internet and related digital communication technologies are useful not only to legitimate political and civic groups but also to criminal and terrorist groups, a difficult policy question arises as to how to regulate relational surveillance so that it can be used when appropriate, but not used or abused at too great a cost in liberty [14,17].

21.3   The Rise in Relational Surveillance

21.3.1   The Availability of Relational Data

In May 2006, news media reported that the National Security Agency had been secretly amassing a huge database of phone call records obtained from many of the nation's leading telephone companies [15]. The reported aim of the database is to facilitate "network analysis" presumably for purposes of relational surveillance. The program is the subject of a lawsuit alleging that AT&T broke the law when it provided the government access to the database.

Internet service providers, which do not bill on a per-transaction basis, need not save traffic data for very long, yet some law enforcement officials would like to ensure the availability of Internet traffic logs. Proposals to require traffic data retention have been floated through Congress, though none have been passed [21]. As more communications involve mobile devices, maintaining geographical communication records becomes easier. Location may be inferred from call tower data or obtained from GPS tracking technology that is meant to facilitate emergency response or to provide services such as local restaurant reviews or "yellow pages" [1,42].

The exploding availability of traffic data is a by-product of modern communication technologies, social practices that increasingly rely on communication carried by intermediaries, and the fact that data storage is now plentiful and cheap. The era when most communications and associations were shielded by practical obscurity is over. Policymakers must grapple with the question of how a nearly comprehensive communication record should be regulated and used.

21.3.2 Evolving Uses of Relational Data and Social Network Analysis

The use of traffic data by law enforcement agencies and the military has a long history [5]. In World War I, military officials analyzed the Earth returns near telegraph transmitting stations to obtain traffic data. In 1941, communication traffic data was used by the British to reconstruct the network structure of the German Air Force, thus allowing a more accurate estimate of German military strength [5]. These historical precursors differ from today's uses of relational data in both kind and degree, however. The extent to which traffic data is automatically recorded today means that there is no need to intercept traffic data in real-time or to identify targets in advance. Advanced computational capability, combined with the availability of complete records, profoundly changes the nature of relational surveillance and permits detailed mapping of associations.

Social network analysis uses various metrics to compare networks and to analyze the positions of individuals in a network [2,4,13]. For example, an individual's role can be measured by "degree" (the number of associates the individual has) or "betweenness" (the extent to which relationships between other members of the network go "through" a particular individual). Additionally, networks can be characterized by reciprocity (the extent to which relationships "go both ways") and transitivity (the extent to which an individual's associates associate with each other). There are several ways in which social network metrics might be employed in a law enforcement context. Associational patterns within a known network might be used to identify key players and form strategies to undermine the networks. "Link analysis" targeted at a suspected individual might be used to determine the associative groups to which that individual belongs. Finally, network models of malevolent associations might be developed and data-mining techniques used for "pattern analysis" in hopes of identifying terrorist or malevolent networks [3,8,10,16]. Social networks are structured such that most individuals are connected by a surprisingly small number of associative links (the so-called "small world property") [2,13]. Targeted link analysis and pattern analysis, which rely on entire networks of communications patterns, thus have the potential to sweep in a very large number of individuals and their associations in short order.

A targeted "link analysis" begins with a particular "suspicious" individual and uses the communications traffic data of that individual, his or her contacts, their contacts, and so forth, to map out the web of relationships in which that individual is embedded. Its goal is to identify the associational groups to which that individual belongs. For example, a suspected terrorist may communicate with three groups of people—his family, a church group, and a terrorist organization. There may be no way to distinguish the members of these groups based on his traffic data records alone, but it may be possible to separate them using the traffic data of his associates: Family members may all contact one another, but only the central individual contacts both family members and members of the terrorist organization. Of course, the analysis may not always be cut and dried (different groups may have overlapping memberships), but the point remains that the more traffic data obtained, the more accurate a link analysis is likely to be in separating out the various groups to which the target individual belongs.

Link analysis is likely to expose and analyze many legitimate, innocent associations. It thus has potential to chill free association because it may expose a particular individual's association with groups that are socially disfavored or simply discordant with that individual's public persona. Accuracy is also an issue with link analysis, as the data itself may give an inaccurate picture of the relationships (it is not always clear who is actually using a particular phone number or Internet account, for example) and the network analysis algorithm will not always partition associations accurately and can cast unwarranted suspicion by misinterpreting relationships to the targeted individual. If a targeted individual belongs to terrorist, political, and religious organizations, for example, the network analysis might mistakenly categorize a contact who is a member of the legitimate political organization as a member of the terrorist organization.

Pattern-based network analysis is a version of data mining seeking to identify patterns within a large dataset using information implicit in the data. One of the most well-known uses of data mining is to identify credit card fraud [21]. Data mining finds patterns of transactions (such as a rapid string of expensive purchases) associated with fraud. Credit card companies have a lot of experience with fraud, so models of fraudulent purchasing behavior used in the analysis can be reasonably accurate. In addition, incentives are aligned well for appropriate use of data mining in the credit card fraud context. Credit card companies generally pay the cost of false negatives (failure to identify fraud) by reimbursing the victims for fraudulent purchases. False positives, on the other hand, are generally resolved simply by contacting the card holder and verifying the suspect transactions. The ramifications of a false positive are minimal in this context.

Attempts to identify criminal or terrorist networks through pattern-based data mining are likely to be far less effective and have far worse consequences. The first stage of pattern-based network analysis seeks to identify associated groups in a traffic data network using a clustering-type algorithm. A second stage looks for "signatures" of a particular type of group (such as a criminal or terrorist network) either by analyzing previous examples or using a theoretical model. Once such signatures are identified, existing networks can be probed for "matching" associations. The accuracy of pattern-based analysis of a network depends on the accuracy of the clustering algorithm used to map out associational groups within a network of traffic data and the accuracy of the pattern or model used to identify suspicious or malevolent groups.

Network analysis can provide the equivalent of association membership lists. Clustering algorithms will reveal vast numbers of legitimate associational groups along with any malevolent groups. Some of these will be associations that have, for perfectly legitimate reasons, decided not to publicly identify themselves. Clustering algorithms may also expose individuals who prefer to keep their associations with particular groups confidential. Algorithms for clustering large networks are not particularly accurate and are computationally expensive and slow. To some extent these difficulties are inherent in the closely connected structure of social networks, which renders associations difficult to disentangle and mistaken identifications inevitable.

Once associative groups are identified, there remains the need to distinguish malevolent from legitimate associations. Here the problems run quite deep. Terrorist events, for example, are thankfully rare. This means, however, that coming up with accurate "patterns" for terrorist networks is a difficult, if not impossible, task. Even if a set of model network properties fit most possible terrorist networks (thus, minimizing the problem of false negatives), there would likely be a huge problem with false positives. There is little reason to assume that terrorist networks have inherently different relational structures than legitimate social networks. To the extent that the network structure of terrorist networks reflects their most obvious difference from typical social networks—their covert nature—it may very well be similar to the structures of the most sensitive of political networks involving unpopular ideas or disfavored groups. Pattern-based analysis is likely to be plagued with false positives and false negatives to an unacceptable degree.

Despite these problems, law enforcement entities may seek to employ these methods prematurely. Law enforcement entities are likely to internalize the costs of false negatives (failure to identify a malevolent network), but not the costs of false positives. Unlike in the credit card fraud case, the costs of false positives to those brought under suspicion would be large [21]. Unfortunately, those costs might well be concentrated on disfavored groups rather than imposed on the officials who decide whether or not to use the methods. The costs of unnecessary and intrusive investigations might not cause sufficient discomfort to the majority to result in a political rejection of flawed network analysis methods. False positives, in the form either of inaccurate inclusions in malevolent groups or of inaccurate characterization of groups as illegitimate, thus have a high potential to chill association, especially association of the emergent sort that is increasingly important in the current technological milieu. Even uncovering the membership and structure of legitimate, but unpopular, groups has the potential to chill expressive association significantly. In the Internet context, network analysis may even expose associations that are unknown to anyone—including the individuals involved.

21.4   The Failure of Existing Legal Paradigms to Protect Emergent Association

Surveillance law, as embodied in the Fourth Amendment and in a complicated associated statutory regime, provides its lowest protection to noncontent, traffic data that is in third-party hands. Under First Amendment freedom of association doctrine, courts strictly scrutinize government requirements that expressive groups turn over their membership lists. This existing protection is no longer sufficient to uphold the right to associational freedom, however. Relational surveillance threatens to undermine the potential of technologically facilitated emergent association by giving the government means to evade the legal strictures on direct inquiry that protect traditional associations, leaving a major gap in protection of the right to freedom of association.

21.4.1   The Fourth Amendment and Relational Surveillance

The Fourth Amendment protects "[t]he right of the people to be secure in their persons, houses, papers, and effects against unreasonable searches and seizures." The inquiry as to whether there has been an "unreasonable search" begins with a determination as to whether a "search" has occurred. The law holds that there has been no search cognizable under the Fourth Amendment unless the government has intruded into a "reasonable expectation of privacy" (*Katz v. U.S.*, 389 U.S. 347 (1967)). Once there has been a search, the Fourth Amendment by default requires a warrant based on probable cause, though the case law provides exceptions to the warrant requirement based on factors such as exigency and administrative necessity.

The Fourth Amendment, as thus far applied, provides little protection against relational surveillance. Current Fourth Amendment doctrine provides virtually no protection to information in third-party hands. In the seminal case of *U.S. v. Miller*, 425 U.S. 435 (1976), the Court determined that an individual had no Fourth Amendment interest in his bank records, which were deemed "business records of the banks." The Court, unswayed by bank confidentiality obligations, reasoned that the information was regularly exposed to bank employees in the ordinary course of business and that depositors "assume the risk" that employees might convey it to the government. Concluding that the subject of bank records need not even be notified of a subpoena to the bank, the Court summarized its view that "[w]hen a person communicates information to a third party even on the understanding that the communication is confidential, he cannot object if the third party conveys that information or records thereof to law enforcement authorities." Particularly troubling was the Court's refusal to take into account the fact that the Bank Secrecy Act *required* banks to maintain the records involved.

A few years later, in *Smith v. Maryland*, 442 U.S. 735 (1979), the Supreme Court considered whether installation of a "pen register" to record telephone numbers dialed from a suspect's home was a Fourth Amendment "search." Again the Court found no "reasonable expectation of privacy" and, hence, no search. The Court noted that telephone users "know that they must convey numerical information to the phone company; that the phone company has facilities for recording this information; and that the phone company, in fact, does record this information for a variety of legitimate business purposes" and held that the petitioner "voluntarily 'exposed' [the phone numbers] to [the phone company's] equipment in the ordinary course of business" and, thus, "assumed the risk that the company would reveal to police the numbers he dialed."

The doctrine that information conveyed to a third party loses Fourth Amendment protection has been criticized in light of the extent to which communications are routinely handled (and recorded) by intermediaries in the age of digital technology [20–22,31–32,36]. Outside the communications context, the Fourth Amendment protects physical property even when it has been entrusted to third parties for storage or transport [31]. Arguably, the third-party doctrine should be limited so that owners of computer files and e-mail archives retain Fourth Amendment interests in their contents. Indeed, one appellate court recently has held that an individual retains a reasonable expectation of privacy in e-mail sent through a commercial ISPB (*Warshak V. U.S.*, No. 06–4042) (6th Cir. June 18, 2007).

Even if courts agree that the *contents* of electronic files maintained by third parties are protected by the Fourth Amendment, courts are less likely to find a reasonable expectation of privacy in traffic data, which is conveyed to intermediaries *for use* in the ordinary course of business. In denying Fourth Amendment protection for dialed phone numbers, the Court relied in part on the fact that pen register data does not disclose conversation content. Courts have applied a similar analysis to Internet subscriber data. In *U.S. v. Forrester*, No. 05–60410 (9th Cir. July 6, 2007), the court opined that "[e]mail and Internet users have no expectation of privacy in the to/from addresses of their messages. . . because they should know that these messages are sent. . . through the equipment of their Internet server providers. . . . "

21.4.2 Low Protection for Relational Data under Surveillance Statutes

Congress has supplemented the Fourth Amendment with a statutory regime. That regime follows a tiered scheme in which the level of protection is keyed to the third party and content/noncontent distinctions, along with a further distinction between real-time interception and obtaining stored records. Surveillance statutes also distinguish law enforcement and foreign intelligence contexts. Foreign intelligence surveillance is overseen by a special court under the Foreign Intelligence Surveillance Act (FISA).

Traffic data has only minimal protection in either context. Real-time acquisition of traffic data for law enforcement purposes is governed by 18 U.S.C. §3121, known as the "pen register" statute because of its origins as a means of regulating that technology. In its current incarnation, the statute defines "pen register" broadly to encompass any "device or process which records or decodes dialing, routing, addressing, or signaling information transmitted by an instrument or facility from which a wire or electronic communication is transmitted, provided, however, that such information shall not include the contents of any communication..." (18 U.S.C. §3127). A pen register may not be used without a court order based upon a certification "that the information likely to be obtained is relevant to an ongoing criminal investigation" (18 U.S.C. §3122). Upon receiving an appropriate application, a court *must* issue the order (18 U.S.C. §3123). A pen register order also may be obtained "upon certification that the information [to be obtained]" is "relevant to an ongoing investigation to protect against international terrorism" as long as the investigation is not "solely upon the basis of activities protected by the First Amendment" (50 U.S.C. §1842).

The most likely source of traffic data for network analysis is communications carrier records. Telephone companies and Internet service providers can maintain vast databases recording communications traffic almost indefinitely. Service providers are prohibited from voluntarily disclosing such data in most circumstances (18 U.S.C. §2702), but electronic communications records may be obtained by government officials pursuant to a court order based on "specific and articulable facts showing that there are reasonable grounds to believe that the ... records or other information sought, are relevant and material to an ongoing criminal investigation." Certain records also may be disclosed pursuant to an administrative, grand jury, or trial subpoena (18 U.S.C. §2703). In the national security context, toll billing records may be requested using a "national security letter" issued without judicial oversight by certain FBI officials, who certify that the records are "relevant to an authorized investigation to protect against international terrorism ... not conducted solely on the basis of activities protected by the First Amendment" (18 U.S.C. §2709). Alternatively, FISA provides that certain FBI officials may apply "for an order requiring the production of any tangible things (including books, records, papers, documents, and other items) for an investigation ... to protect against international terrorism ..., provided that such investigation ... is not conducted solely upon the basis of activities protected by the first Amendment" (50 U.S.C. §1861). The application must include "a statement of facts showing that there are reasonable grounds to believe that the tangible things sought are relevant to an authorized investigation ... to protect against international terrorism ...."

In general, traffic data may be obtained by the government upon a showing of mere "relevance" (sometimes augmented by "materiality") to a law enforcement or international terrorism investigation. Oversight is minimal. Courts often are required to issue these orders as long as the proper attestations are made and, in some cases, no court order is required. Persons to whom the orders pertain often are given no notice of the requests and third-party data holders are often prohibited from disclosing that they received such requests. The potential First Amendment implications of disclosing traffic data are barely recognized by FISA's limitations on investigations "conducted solely upon the basis of activities protected by the First Amendment."

Relational surveillance based on network analysis sits uncomfortably in this statutory scheme. Moreover, a recent audit of the FBI's use of national security letters uncovered more than 1,000 cases in which agents violated laws or regulations.

How many "links" away in the network of communication must an individual be before her traffic data is no longer "relevant" or "material" to an investigation that begins with suspicion of some central individual? Does the answer to this question depend on the algorithm that law enforcement officials employ? How large a sample of the network is needed if the goal of a link analysis is to understand the role a target individual plays in her associational network? If a pattern analysis is intended, how complete must the network be before patterns can be classified in a meaningful way? Arguably, the accuracy of any large-scale data analysis algorithm is improved by including more data. The scope of relevance could be argued to extend quite far.

21.4.3   *Relational Surveillance and the First Amendment*

While the First Amendment is not usually applied to surveillance using traffic data, freedom of expression jurisprudence robustly protects expressive associations and recognizes that citizens must be able to associate without government inquiry into association membership. These protections must be adapted to today's associational paradigms and surveillance technologies.

The right of assembly to petition the government is explicit in the Constitution. The more general right to freedom of association is implicit, but longstanding and strong. Recently, the Supreme Court stressed the right of "expressive associations" to determine their own membership requirements and policies, observing that "[t]his right is crucial in preventing the majority from imposing its views on groups that would rather express other, perhaps unpopular, ideas" (*Boy Scouts of America v. Dale*, 530 U.S. 640 (2000)). The Court defines "expressive association" broadly: "[A]ssociations do not have to associate for the 'purpose' of disseminating a certain message in order to be entitled to the protections of the First Amendment. An association must merely engage in expressive activity that could be impaired in order to be entitled to protection." In *Dale*, freedom of association trumped state interests in addressing discrimination against gays despite quite weak evidence that the Boy Scouts had intended to express a position on homosexuality. The Court "accept[ed] the Boy Scouts' assertion [that it sought to teach against homosexuality]." The Court not only "give[s] deference to an association's assertions regarding the nature of its expression, [but] also give[s] deference to an association's view of what would impair its expression." Once an association meets this deferential standard for asserting that its rights to expressive association would be impaired by government action, the action is allowed only if it is "adopted to serve compelling state interests, unrelated to the suppression of ideas, that cannot be achieved through means significantly less restrictive of associational freedoms." Expressive association, broadly defined, thus is afforded the highest protection under the First Amendment.

It is not immediately clear, however, how this protection applies to the emergent association that concerns us here. Emergent associations may not have well-defined "positions" or a well-defined hierarchy or membership to determine who can assert the group's rights. Moreover, relational surveillance does not directly regulate the messages that groups can express, but merely attempts to determine association membership and structure. Nonetheless, relational surveillance implicates the associational interests recognized in *Dale*. The burdens imposed by relational surveillance in the form of network analysis are of at least three types:

1. Chilling of association by revealing its existence, structure, and membership.
2. Chilling of association because of the potential for network analysis to mistake legitimate association for illegitimate.
3. Harms to self-determination and chilling of exploratory associations because of the potential for network analysis to treat individuals as "members" of a group with which they did not want to associate themselves.

These are the types of harms addressed by a line of freedom-of-association cases dealing with government requests for association membership lists. Beginning in the 1950s, the Supreme Court has recognized that compelled disclosure of group membership to or at the behest of government may be an unconstitutional infringement on the right of association. In *NAACP v. Alabama*, 357 U.S. 449 (1958), the Court struck down an Alabama statute requiring disclosure of association membership lists, noting that:

Effective advocacy of both public and private points of view, particularly controversial ones, is undeniably enhanced by group association .... It is beyond debate that freedom to engage in association for the advancement of beliefs and ideas is an inseparable
aspect of the "liberty" assured by the Due Process Clause ....
[I]t is immaterial whether the beliefs sought to be advanced by
association pertain to political, economic, religious or cultural matters, and state action which may have the effect of curtailing the
freedom to associate is subject to the closest scrutiny.

The Court also stated that "[i]nviolability of privacy in group association
may, in many circumstances, be indispensable to preservation of freedom
of association ...."

Freedom of association is not absolute, of course. Identities of group
members must sometimes be disclosed in response to compelling government interests. In *Buckley v. Valeo*, 424 U.S. 1 (1976), the Court considered
the required disclosure of certain campaign contribution information that
inherently disclosed political associations. The Court emphasized that:

We long have recognized that significant encroachments on First
Amendment rights of the sort that compelled disclosure imposes
cannot be justified by a mere showing of some legitimate governmental interest. [S]ubordinating interests of the State must survive
exacting scrutiny. We also have insisted that there be a "relevant
correlation" or "substantial relation" between the governmental
interest and the information required to be disclosed. This type
of scrutiny is necessary even if any deterrent effect on the exercise of First Amendment rights arises, not through direct government action, but indirectly as an unintended but inevitable result
of ... requiring disclosure.

The Court further recognized that "[i]t is undoubtedly true that public disclosure of contributions to candidates and political parties will deter some
individuals who otherwise might contribute. In some instances, disclosure
may even expose contributors to harassment or retaliation. These are not
insignificant burdens on individual rights, and they must be weighed carefully against the interests which Congress has sought to promote by this
legislation."

Upholding the requirements nonetheless, the Court relied on the fact
that the petitioners had conceded that the disclosure requirements were the
"least restrictive means" of advancing the compelling government interests
in the "free functioning of our national institutions" addressed by the legislation, challenging them only as to certain minority parties and candidates.
The Court determined that speculative allegations of harm to those parties
and candidates were outweighed by the substantial public interest in the

disclosures. In *Brown v. Socialist Workers '74 Campaign Committee*, 459 U.S. 87 (1982), on the other hand, the Court struck down disclosure requirements of a state campaign finance law where a minor party presented "substantial evidence of both governmental and private hostility [ ] and harassment." The Court explained: "The right to privacy in one's political associations and beliefs will yield only to a 'subordinating interest of the State [that is] compelling,' and then only if there is a 'substantial relation between the information sought and [an] overriding and compelling state interest'."

In considering whether to compel disclosure of association membership information, courts scrutinize the extent to which the disclosure request is tailored to governmental objectives. When the requested disclosure is too broad, it is unconstitutional. Thus, in *Shelton v. Tucker*, 364 U.S. 479 (1960), the Court struck down a requirement that teachers list every organization to which they had belonged within the preceding five years, noting that "even though the governmental purpose be legitimate and substantial, that purpose cannot be pursued by means that broadly stifle fundamental personal liberties when the end can be more narrowly achieved." In *Britt v. Superior Court*, 574 P.2d 766 (Cal. 1978), the court similarly blocked a discovery request for disclosure of associational affiliations where "[i]n view of the sweeping scope of the discovery order at issue, we think it clear that such order 'is likely to pose a substantial restraint upon the exercise of First Amendment rights.'" The court noted that the protections of freedom of association were not limited to membership in unpopular organizations. Similarly, in upholding a subpoena to produce a Ku Klux Klan membership list, the court noted the Klan's history of racially motivated violence and the close connection of the context of the subpoena, which was the investigation of an arson in which Klan emblems were found on the lawn of a burned home, to the membership disclosure (*Marshall v. Bramer*, 828 F.2d 355 (6th Cir. 1987)).

In the discovery context, some courts require an initial showing of "some probability" of harm before shifting the burden to the requestor to establish that the request goes to the "heart of the matter" and that there is no other means to obtain the information (*Snedigar v. Hoddersen*, 786 P.2d 781 (Wash. 1990)). Those courts recognize, however, that concrete evidence of chilling effects is not needed and that a "common sense approach," assuming that disclosure of membership information will chill association, is sometimes appropriate.

Obtaining information from a third party does not avoid First Amendment strictures "because the constitutionally protected right, freedom to associate freely and anonymously, will be chilled equally whether the associational information is compelled from the organization itself or from third parties" (*In re First National Bank*, 701 F.2d 115 (10th Cir. 1983)).

21.5   Where to Go from Here

Because the First Amendment is not grounded primarily in privacy and protects groups' membership data even when it is in third-party hands, it provides a sounder basis than the Fourth Amendment for regulating relational surveillance. Nonetheless, Fourth Amendment precedent is instructive as to how to adapt freedom of association doctrine in light of technological evolution affecting associational behavior and surveillance methods.

21.5.1   *The First Amendment Is the Primary Barrier against Overbroad Relational Surveillance*

Because of the case law's crabbed approach to "reasonable expectations of privacy," which are destroyed by disclosure to third-party intermediaries, and surveillance law's emphasis on protecting content and guarding against real-time interception, network analysis of traffic data will not easily be brought within the ambit of the Fourth Amendment's protections. The Supreme Court has opined that Fourth Amendment procedures must be applied with "scrupulous exactitude" when seizing books and other First Amendment materials (*Zurcher v. The Stanford Daily,* 436 U.S. 547 (1978)). However, case law does not resolve the question of what to do when government information-gathering has First Amendment implications, yet falls outside of the Fourth Amendment because there is no "reasonable expectation of privacy" in the information. Amar [43] has argued that the permissibility of a search under the Fourth Amendment should be determined by a general inquiry into reasonableness and that the First Amendment significance of the information acquired should inform the reasonableness of a search under the Fourth Amendment. Solove [40] suggests that whether a search "implicates" the First Amendment could be an alternative basis to "reasonable expectation of privacy" for Fourth Amendment application.

The awkward fit between freedom of association interests and "reasonable expectations of privacy" suggests that direct resort to the First Amendment provides the best basis for regulating relational surveillance. This chapter thus agrees with Solove that the First Amendment should "provide an independent source of criminal procedure" [40]. Existing doctrine tells us much about how to evaluate the constitutional permissibility of government attempts to obtain associational information. Such attempts must be driven by a compelling government interest and there must be a substantial relation between the specific information and that interest. Even where an association is not unpopular or disfavored, courts can employ a "common sense" presumption that overly broad disclosures impose an impermissible burden upon freedom of association.

21.5.2 Principles for Adapting to Technological Change Derived from Fourth Amendment Law

Fourth Amendment doctrine has often confronted new technological realities. In this respect, freedom of association doctrine lags behind. Case law to date deals essentially exclusively with membership information compiled by traditional organizations. What should be done when technology shifts the locus of important associational activity away from traditional organizations and the means of data acquisition away from traditional document requests? Fourth Amendment jurisprudence exemplifies three specific principles that can inform the extension of freedom of association doctrine to new technological circumstances. First, surveillance doctrine must be responsive to technological change that transforms significant social practice. Second, surveillance doctrine must recognize that new means of analyzing available data can change the constitutional balance. Finally, surveillance doctrine must be sensitive to the extent to which a particular surveillance technology discriminates between innocent and illegal behavior.

In *Katz*, the Court held unconstitutional a search using an electronic listening device attached outside a telephone booth and made its now famous statement that "the Fourth Amendment protects people, not places. What a person knowingly exposes to the public … is not a subject of Fourth Amendment protection. But what he seeks to preserve as private, even in an area accessible to the public, may be constitutionally protected." Since individuals increasingly held private conversations by telephone and telephone booths were designed to facilitate such conversations away from the home, it would be unreasonable to permit warrantless government surveillance of such conversations. Recognizing that surveillance doctrine must adapt to technology-driven social change, the Court stated that "[t]o read the Constitution more narrowly is to ignore the vital role that the public telephone has come to play in private communication."

In *Kyllo v. U.S.*, 533 U.S. 27 (2001), the Court dealt with a technological change not in locus of social activity, but in means of surveillance. Thermal imaging technology necessitated interpreting the Fourth Amendment such that "obtaining by sense-enhancing technology any information regarding the home's interior that could not otherwise have been obtained without physical 'intrusion into a constitutionally protected area,' constitutes a search—at least where (as here) the technology in question is not in general public use." The Court noted that "[t]he question we confront today is what limits there are upon this power of technology to shrink the realm of guaranteed privacy." This question is directly relevant to whether the Constitution protects against data mining and network analysis technology. Like a thermal imager analyzing heat radiating from a house, network analysis of traffic data produces knowledge that is embedded in accessible data, yet not observable without using advanced technology. Advances in surveillance technology may involve either ways to obtain more data or ways to obtain more information from available data. From the perspective of controlling government intrusion, there is no distinction. Legal recognition that a technology for analyzing available data can change the constitutional balance is a critical bulwark against the intrusive power of advancing technology.

Finally, the Court has considered the extent to which surveillance technology exposes legitimate behavior in determining whether there has been an unconstitutional government intrusion. In *Illinois v. Caballes*, 543 U.S. 405 (2005), the Court held that a "dog sniff" for drugs during a routine traffic stop was not a search because "governmental conduct that only reveals the possession of contraband 'compromises no legitimate privacy interest.'" Contrasting "dog sniffs" with thermal imaging, the Court noted that "[c]ritical to [the *Kyllo*] decision was the fact that the device was capable of detecting lawful activity." Regardless of the validity of the assertion that dog sniffs only detect contraband (an assertion strongly disputed by Justice Souter's dissent), the point remains: The constitutionality of a surveillance technology depends on the extent to which it exposes both legitimate and illegitimate activity and its accuracy in distinguishing the two.

The three principles identified above provide guidance for updating freedom of association doctrine in the context of modern day relational surveillance. First, just as telephones expanded the *situs* of private life, digital communications technology has moved a large fraction of socially significant expressive association to informal, emergent groups. Because network analysis discloses membership simultaneously with identifying associations, one can no longer wait until an association is identified as "expressive" before determining whether it is protected from disclosing its membership. Courts should assume that, just as broad disclosure of associational memberships has a reasonable probability of chilling protected association, an insufficiently targeted social network analysis of relational data will likely chill expressive association.

Second, First Amendment protections must be extended to government use of sophisticated network analysis algorithms, which evade traditional prohibitions on compelling disclosure of associational information yet produce equivalently intrusive information. The correlations uncovered by network analysis are not like the simple lists of numbers dialed involved in *Smith*. Communications intermediaries could not "see" these implicit structures in the course of ordinary business uses of traffic data. Indeed, the pseudonymous and nonhierarchical nature of emergent association means that there may be no one—not even an association's participants—who has a list of participants in an emergent association until a network analysis is performed.

Third, the extent to which surveillance technology unacceptably intrudes upon freedom of association depends on how well it distinguishes associations related to the relevant compelling government interest from other associations. A technique that is likely to disclose significant protected activity is similarly likely to burden freedom of association.

In sum, the standard of constitutionality of relational surveillance based on analysis of traffic data should be this: Does the surveillance serve a legitimate and compelling government interest? Is the analysis sufficiently accurate and sufficiently closely related to that interest in light of the extent to which it is likely to expose protected expressive and intimate associations? We can illustrate this analysis by applying it to three types of relational surveillance.

21.5.2.1 Pattern-Based Network Analysis

Assume that a compelling government interest motivates a pattern-based network analysis. Its constitutionality then depends critically on the accuracy of the analysis algorithm and its ability to discriminate between associations relevant to the compelling government interest and other associations. An algorithm's ability to identify a particular type of organization depends on having a sufficiently accurate pattern that can be "matched" against available traffic data. The pattern must be sufficiently well specified that it will not "match" large numbers of other types of associations—book groups, political organizations, and so forth. Furthermore, there must be a sufficiently unique pattern to be found. If, for example, book groups and terrorist organizations have similar traffic data patterns, no network analysis algorithm will ever distinguish them. Similarly, if various terrorist organizations have significantly different traffic data patterns, an attempt to identify them using a known pattern may be substantially underinclusive.

Social network analysis is still in its infancy. It is highly unlikely that a pattern-based analysis of traffic data could be sufficiently well tailored to identify a particular type of illegitimate organization as distinguished from numerous legitimate organizations. This is particularly true with respect to organizations, such as terrorist networks, which are sufficiently rare as not to have been studied in statistically relevant numbers. Thus, it is implausible that First Amendment standards would be met for pattern-based analysis. Congress, therefore, should prohibit the use of pattern-based network analysis for relational surveillance. If specific pattern-based analysis programs are ever to be authorized, they should be vetted publicly, preferably through legislative hearings or at least by an administrative process, to sets standards of technical accuracy and associational privacy sufficient to meet First Amendment requirements. Since pattern-based network analysis cannot meet First Amendment standards at present (and may be inherently unable to do so), there is no legitimate need for a government to acquire large, indiscriminate databases of traffic data, such as AT&T's call record database. Congress should reinforce current restrictions on access to communication records and clarify that possible use in network analysis is insufficient justification for acquiring traffic data.

21.5.2.2 Targeted Link Analysis

Targeted link analysis uses traffic data from a target individual, those individuals with whom the target has communicated, those with whom they have communicated, and so on, to investigate the target's associations. Because link analysis employs second and even higher order connections to categorize a target individual's associates into groups and to determine such things as the structure of a group or a particular individual's role in the group, it is more intrusive to the target than a mere list of direct links or numbers dialed. It also intrudes into the associations of untargeted individuals. Link analysis can expose a large fraction of the target's group affiliations. As established in *Shelton v. Tucker* (1960), wide-ranging inquiry into associations is precluded unless First Amendment standards are met. One way to satisfy freedom-of-association requirements with respect to the target would be to require a warrant based on probable cause that the targeted individual either has committed a crime or is involved in a criminal or terrorist enterprise. To ensure a substantial relationship between the inquiry into associations and a compelling government interest, the crime involved should be sufficiently serious.

A more difficult question is what standard to impose for obtaining communications traffic records of those who have communicated with the target of a link analysis. Because the use of one individual's traffic data in conjunction with a link analysis focused on another is not intended to reveal the broad sweep of the second individual's associations, the freedom of association burden on such secondary individuals is less than would be imposed by an analysis focused on them. On the other hand, because a link analysis will tend to be more accurate if it includes more data about higher order associations, the present standard of mere "relevance" might permit intrusions into the associations of a large number of innocent individuals. This is particularly true because social networks are often closely connected. Going just a few links out from any particular individual is likely to sweep in a large number of others whose innocent associations will unavoidably be exposed. The more attenuated the links to the target individual become, the less useful traffic data about these remotely connected individuals will be in sorting out the associations of the target person. A mere showing of traffic data relevance is insufficient freedom of association protection for untargeted individuals. The standard must account for the First Amendment balance between relationship to the link analysis and degree of imposition on associational rights. A requirement that officials detail grounds for reasonable suspicion that the untargeted individual is a member of a criminal enterprise involving the target would be appropriate. Given the probable cause standard for initiating the link analysis (and in the absence of supplemental information to the contrary), this standard is likely to permit officials to obtain traffic data for most who have direct communication links to the target individual. It is less likely to be met with respect to those more tenuously linked to the target individual.

21.5.2.3 Access to Communications Traffic Data outside the Network Analysis Context

Even if it is not used in a network analysis and even though it is not equivalent to a detailed disclosure of association memberships, a list of an individual's communications traffic data may potentially burden expressive association. In some cases the burden may be quite great (consider the case, discussed by Solove, of data pertaining to the office phone of an unpopular expressive association or the case where traffic data discloses repeated calls by an individual to an unpopular expressive association) [40]. Where, as in Solove's example, there is an evident potential to burden expressive association, a probable cause warrant should perhaps be required. In other cases, at a minimum, a court order should be required to obtain traffic data. Applicants for such orders should be required to articulate specific facts based upon which the court can assess the First Amendment issues. In determining whether to issue such an order, courts should consider the potential burden on protected association and not simply whether the investigation is "conducted solely upon the basis of activities protected by the First Amendment."

21.6 Conclusions

We are at an important crossroads for the future of free association. Law enforcement officials charged with preventing terrorism understandably seek to exploit relational data for that purpose, leading to pressure to expand the availability of traffic data to government. There are calls to require Internet service providers and others to retain more and more traffic data. It is critical that these calls for increased relational surveillance be balanced by careful analysis both of what is really possible with these new computational technologies and of what is at stake for democratic society, in light of the increasing importance of technologically mediated emergent association.

The right to freedom of association limits legitimate government use and acquisition of communications traffic data based on the extent to which the government data use amounts to a disclosure of expressive associations.

These limitations are in addition to, and independent of, any limitations arguably deriving from the Fourth Amendment and require higher barriers to government acquisition and use of traffic data than current surveillance statutes impose.

Acknowledgments

This work was generously supported by the DePaul University College of Law and by the DePaul University Research Council. Excellent research assistance from J.D. student Elizabeth Levine is also gratefully acknowledged.

References

[1] Ball, K. et al., A Report on the Surveillance Society, prepared for Information Commissioner of the United Kingdom, 2006.

[2] Barabasi, A.-L., *Linked: The New Science of Networks*, Perseus Group, New York, 2002.

[3] Carley, K., Lee, J.-.S., and Krackhardt, D., *Destabilizing networks*, Connections, 24, 79, 2002.

[4] Carrington, P.J., Scott, J., and Wasserman, S., *Models and Methods in Social Network Analysis*, Cambridge University Press, New York, 2005.

[5] Danezis, G. and Clayton, R., Introducing Traffic Analysis, Chapter 5, this volume.

[6] Danezis, G. and Wittenben, B., The Economics of Mass Surveillance and the Questionable Value of Anonymous Communications, WEIS 2006.

[7] Keefe, P.R., "Can Network Theory Thwart Terrorists?" *New York Times*, March 12, 2006.

[8] Kolda, T. et al., Report of DHS Workshop on Data Sciences, Data Sciences Technology for Homeland Security Information Management and Knowledge Discovery, Sandia Report SAND2004-6648, Los Alamos, NM, 2004.

[9] Memon, N. and Larsen, H.L., Practical approaches for analysis, visualization and destabilizing terrorist networks, *Proceedings of the First International Conference on Availability*, Reliability and Security (ARES '06), Vienna, Austria, 2006.

[10] Seifert, J.W., Data Mining And Homeland Security: An Overview, CRS Report RL31798, Washington, D.C., 2006.

[11] Taipale, K.A., *Whispering wires and warrantless wiretaps: data mining and foreign intelligence surveillance*, N.Y.U. Rev. L. & Security, Supl. Bull. On L. & Sec., 7, Spring 2006.

[12] Van Meter, K.M., *Terrorist/Liberators: researching and dealing with adversary social networks*, Connections, 24, 66, 2002.

[13] Watts, D., *Six Degrees: The Science of a Connected Age*, W.W. Norton & Co., New York, 2003.

[14] Garfinkel, S.L., *Leaderless resistance today*, First Monday, 8, March 2003.

[15] Gellman, B. and Mohammed, A., "Data on Phone Calls Monitored," *Washington Post*, May 12, 2006.

[16] Klerks, P., *The network paradigm applied to criminal organisations*, Connections 24(3), 2001.

[17] Margulies, P., *The clear and present Internet: terrorism, cyberspace, and the First Amendment*, UCLA Journal of Law and Technology, Los Angeles, 2004, 4, 2004.

[18] Fulda, J.S., *Data mining and privacy*, Albany Law Journal of Science and Technology, Albany, NY, 11, 105, 2000.

[19] Kreimer, S.F., *Watching the watchers: surveillance, transparency, and political freedom in the war on terror*, University of Pennsylvania Journal of Constitutional Law, Philadelphia, 7, 133, 2004.

[20] Slobogin, C., *Transaction surveillance by the government*, Mississippi Law Journal, Oxford, 75, 139, 2005.

[21] Swire, P., *Privacy and information sharing in the war on terrorism*, Villanova Law Review, Philadelphia, 51, 951, 2006.

[22] Zittrain, J., *Searches and seizures in a networked world*, Harvard Law Review Forum, Cambridge, MA, 119, 83, 2006.

[23] Benkler, Y., *The Wealth of networks: How social production transforms markets and freedom*, Yale University Press, New Haven, CT, 2006.

[24] Madison, M.J., *Social software, groups, and governance*, Michigan State Law Review, East Lansing, 1, 153, 2006.

[25] McCaughey, M. and Ayers, M.D., Eds., *Cyberactivism: Online Activism in Theory and Practice*, Routledge, New York, 2003.

[26] Noveck, B.S., *A democracy of groups*, First Monday, 10, 2005.

[27] Rheingold, Howard, *Smart Mobs: The Next Social Revolution*, Basic Books, New York, 2002.

[28] Saco, D., *Cybering Democracy: Public Space and the Internet*, University of Minnesota Press, Minneapolis, 2002.

[29] Shane, P.M., Ed., *Democracy Online: The Prospects for Political Renewal Through the Internet*, Routledge, New York, 2004.

[30] Van de Donk, W. et al., Eds., *Cyberprotest: New Media, Citizens, and Social Movements*, Routledge, New York, 2004.

[31] Bellia, P., *Surveillance law through cyberlaw's lens*, George Washington Law Review, Washington, D.C., 72, 1375, 2004.

[32] Henderson, S.E., *Learning from all fifty states: how to apply the Fourth Amendment and its state analogs to protect third party information from unreasonable search*, Catholic University Law Review, Washington, D.C., 55, 373, 2006.

[33] Kerr, O.S., *The Fourth Amendment and new technologies: constitutional myths and the case for caution*, Michigan Law Review, Ann Arbor, 102, 801, 2004.

[34] Rosenzweig, P., *Civil liberty and the response to terrorism*, Duquesne Law Review, Greenburg, PA, 42, 663, 2004.

[35] Rosenzweig, P., *Privacy and consequences: legal and policy structures for implementing new counter-terrorism technologies and protecting civil liberty*, in *Emergent Information Technologies and Enabling Policies for*

Counter-Terrorism, Popp, R. and Yen, J., Eds., John Wiley & Sons, Hoboken, NJ, 2004.

[36] Swire, P., *Katz is dead, long live Katz*, Michigon Law Review, Ann Arbor, 102, 904, 2004.

[37] Thai, J.T., *Is data mining ever a search under Justice Stevens's Fourth Amendment?* Fordham Law Review, New York, NY, 74, 1731, 2006.

[38] Farber, D.A., *Speaking in the first person plural: expressive associations and the First Amendment*, Minnesota Law Review, Minneapolis, 85, 1483, 2001.

[39] Fisher, L.E., *Guilt by expressive association: political profiling, surveillance and the privacy of groups*, Arizona Law Review, Tucson, 46, 621, 2004.

[40] Solove, D.J., *The First Amendment as criminal procedure*, New York University Law Review, New York, 82, 2007.

[41] Gutmann, A., Ed., *Freedom of Association*, Princeton University Press, Princeton, NJ, 1998.

[42] Zick, T., *Clouds, cameras, and computers: The First Amendment and networked public places*, Florida Law Review, Gainesville, 59, 1, 2007.

[43] Amar, A.R., *Fourth Amendment first principles*, Harvard Law Review, Cambridge, MA, 107, 757, 1994.

Index

A

acceptable data retention interference, 442–425

access control. *See* obfuscation; passwords

active adversary, 76

active jamming of RFID tags, 299

Activities of Daily Living (ADL), 289

additive splitting, 57

Adium X, 12

ADL. *See* Activities of Daily Living

ADSL. *See* Asymmetric Digital Subscriber Line

adversary angel, 79–80

adversary facade, 79–80

Advogato, 101

agency collaboration, 191

AIP. *See* Anonymous Internet Proxies

airport security, 190–191

    profiling, 118–119

Amann v. Switzerland, 418

American Civil Liberties Union Program on Technology and Liberty, 295–296

AN.ON project, 42

anonymity, 20–21

anonymity and pseudonymity systems, interactive, 7–10

    See also privacy-enhancing technologies

    Anonymizer.com, 8

    Freedom Network, 8–9

    Java Anon Proxy, 9

    Onion Routing, 8

    Tor, 9–10

anonymity system adversary angels, 79–80

anonymity system adversary facades, 79–80

anonymity systems

    about, 74–75, 80–81

    path compromise, 78–79

    See also anonymity systems and MorphMix; Byzantine attacks on anonymity systems

anonymity systems and MorphMix

    node selection, 82

    path construction, 81–82

    See also MorphMix simulation attacks

anonymity systems compromise attacks, countermeasures, 89–91

Anonymizer.com, 8

anonymous communications, traffic analysis, 107–110

Anonymous Internet Proxies (AIP), 9

anti-phishing tools, 13–14

appropriation privacy tort, 332

Art. 29 Working Party recommendations, 232, 415

    legal privacy requirements and PRIME proposals, 239–246

Asymmetric Digital Subscriber Line (ADSL), 99

asymmetric information, 364

attribute-based access control, 62–64

auctions, 51–52, 59

autonomy as privacy, 330–331

B

Babel, 76

benchmarking, 52–53

BFT. *See* Byzantine fault tolerance

BGP. *See* Border Gateway Protocol

bidding, 51–52

binary tree, 403

blocker tags, 269, 299
Bluetooth, 107
Border Gateway Protocol (BGP), 101
bounded-rate algorithm, 318
bounded rationality, 364, 369–370
Boy Scouts of America v. Dale, 446
Brandeis, L., ix
Brewer, 4
Britt v. Superior Court, 448
Broadcast, 25–26
*Brown v. Socialist Workers '74 Campaign
    Committee,* 448
Buckley v. Valeo, 427, 447
buses, 28–30
Bush, George W., 420
Byzantine adversary, 78
Byzantine agreement and malicious model
    schemes, 56
Byzantine attacks on anonymity systems
    about, 75
    common threats, 76–77
    participating adversary, 77–78
    Sybil attacks, 80–81
Byzantine failure model, 78
Byzantine fault tolerance (BFT),
    89–91

C

cable modems, 99
CALEA. *See* Communication Assistance for
    Law Enforcement Act
Calypso products, 296
CAPPS II prescreening, 119
CAPPS prescreening, 119
CareNet project, 336
Cashmere, 88–89
catching, 103–104, 424
CDMA. *See* Code Division Multiple Access
CD protection technologies, 157–158
CellSpotting, 312–313
censorship-resistant publishing, 10
Charter of Fundamental Rights of the
    European Union, ix
Chaum, David, 74, 108
Checkpoint Systems and Sensomatic, 288
Choicepoint, 4
client, 383
clock skew, 104
Cloudmark Anti-Fraud Toolbar, 14
cluster analysis in marketing
    buyer behavior, 122
    general, 123–124
    new product opportunities, 123
    reducing data, 123

segmenting, 122
    test markets, 123
cluster inclusion test, protocol, 220
clustering algorithm of divide phase, 216
cluster update computation, 209–210
Code Division Multiple Access
    (CDMA), 99
CoE. *See* Council of Europe
collective risk model for privacy insurance
    assumptions, 353–355
    example application in IT business,
        357–359
    other applications, 359–360
    population inhomogeneity and data
        disclosure, 355–357
Communication Assistance for Law
    Enforcement Act (CALEA), 111
communities
    of purpose, 256
    of transactions, 255
computational outsourcing, 64–65
computational puzzles, 80
coNP-hard, 182
constitutional rights, 411, 420–422
    First Amendment, 445–448
    Fourth Amendment, 419–422, 428,
        436–437, 442–443, 450–454
    importance of to overboard relational
        surveillance, 450
    See also Fourth Amendment
content data, 422–423
contested spaces, 331–332
contract negotiations, 53–54
copy and digital rights protection, 414
    obfuscation, 157–158
correlation distance, 203
Council of Europe (CoE), 414–415
credential privacy systems, 12–13, 62–63
Cricket system, 335
criminal intelligence
    data retention, 110–112
    false light, 332
    RFID tags, 292–293
    social network analysis, 100–101
    See also data retention; emergent
        association surveillance
Crowds, 24–25
cryptographic obfuscation. *See* obfuscation
cryptographic primitives, 204–205, 214
cryptographic protocol, applied
    attribute-based access control, 62–64
    computational outsourcing, 64–65
    nearest neighbor, 60–62
    scalar product, 60
    trust negotiation, 62–64

cryptographic protocol results in practice
  extending scrambled circuit, 56–57
  two-party honest-but-curious scrambled
    circuit, 55–56
cryptographic protocols
  auction bidding, 51–52
  collaborative benchmarking, 52–53
  contract negotiations, 53–54
  database querying, 50–51
  data mining, 52
  definition, 48–50
  distributed voting, 51
  forecasting, 52–53
  participant behavior, 54–55
cryptographic protocol technique
  encrypted value computing, 58
  input quality problems, 59–60
  splitting techniques, 57–58
cryptography, obfuscation, 159–162
cryptography-based methodologies, data
    mining and privacy-preserving
    techniques, 199–201
cypherpunk remailers, 5–6

D

DAG. *See* directed acyclic graph
DAS. *See* Database As a Service
DAS scenario
  about, 382
  data organization, 384–385
  interactions, 386–387
  parties involved, 383–384
Database As a Service (DAS), 382
database organization, 384–385
database outsourcing, 382
database privacy, 158–159, 162–164
  computationally infeasibility, 164
  uncircumventable, 164
  See also passwords
database querying, 50–51
data brokers, dossier effect, 4
data mining, 52, 183
  about, 188
  cryptography-based methodologies,
    199–201
  cryptography-based methods of
    issues, 203–205
    privacy definition under secure
      multiparty computations,
      199–201
    privacy-preserving document
      clustering, 213–223
  document clustering, 213–223
  inductive learning, 188–189

information requiring privacy,
    190–191
  machine learning, 190
  pattern analysis, 439, 440
  perturbation methods of. *See* random
    data perturbation methods of data
    mining
  and privacy, 127–128
  random data perturbation methods,
    192–199
  statistics, 189–190
  See also data mining, cryptography-based
    methods of; random data
    perturbation methods of data
    mining
data modulation, 106
data owner, 383
data preservation, 111, 413, 414
data privacy, obfuscation, 158–159
data protection and Code of Fair
    Information Practice, 329–330
Data Retention Directive, 111, 428
data retention (Europe)
  Cybercrime Convention of the Council of
    Europe, 414–415
  as interference with right to the respect of
    communicational privacy, 418–419
  mandatory and routine, 416–417
  privacy and communications law,
    415–417
  traffic analysis, 110–112
data retention (general)
  about, 410–411
  distinguishing content and traffic data,
    423–424
  interception, 413–414
  preservation, 413–414
  retention, 413–414
  retention period, 414, 416, 417
  as a surveillance tool, 411–412
  traffic analysis, 110–112
  traffic data, 412–413
data retention (United States)
  The Electronic Communications Privacy
    Act, 419–420
  Fourth Amendment, 420–423
  traffic analysis, 110–112
data retention *vs.* fundamental freedoms
  criteria of "Acceptable" interference,
    424–425
  "Dataveillance," 425–426
  interference into rights of anonymity and
    freedom of expression, 426–427
  oversight of data retention methods,
    427–428

shared public and private sector
information, 428–429
threats to Democracy, 429–430
data standardization, 206–207
data track functions, 238–239
DC-Network. *See Di*ning *C*ryptogrphers
network
DDC. *See* distributed data clustering
deniability in OTR, 12
denial-of-service (DoS)
about, 84
attacks on Mixminion, 86–88
attacks on Tor, 84–86
countermeasures, 89–91
reliability improvement options,
88–89
density estimation-based clustering, 193
density reconstruction, 196–197
deployability in useful security and privacy
technologies, 15
Desert Storm, 97
dietary intake monitoring application, 335
Digital Millennium Copyright Act, 332
digital rights management (DRM), 157–158,
329–330, 332, 414
digital rights protection (DRP), 157–158
*Di*ning *C*ryptographers network
(DC-Network), 31–33
directed-access database, 165–166
directed acyclic graph (DAG), 62
Direct Sequence Spread Spectrum (DSSS),
98
disclosure attacks, 108
distance measuring, 202–203, 208–209
distributed data clustering (DDC), 194
distributed environments, 197–198
distributed voting, 51
document clustering
about, 213
cluster inclusion test, 219–220
cryptographic primitives, 214
divide phase, 215–216
implementing, 217–219
initialization, 215
merge phase, 216–217
preliminaries, 214
problem definition, 213–214
protocol, 214–215
dominant equilibrium, 54
DoS. *See* denial-of-service
dossier effect, 4
Dresden Identity Management (DRIM), 233
DRIM. *See* Dresden Identity Management
DRM. *See* digital rights management
DRP. *See* digital rights protection

DSSS. See Direct Sequence Spread Spectrum
dummy traffic, 38, 44

E

EAS. *See* Electronic Article Surveillance
eBay, 120
Account Guard, 14
See also Vickrey auctions
effectiveness in useful security and privacy
technologies, 15
Electronic Article Surveillance (EAS), 288
Electronic Communications Privacy Act
(ECPA), 419, 420
Electronic Product Code (EPC), 289,
291–292
e-mail anonymity
defined, 5
type-III remailers, 7
type-I remailers, 5–6
type-II remailers, 6–7
type-0 remailers, 5
e-mail pseudonymity systems, 5
emergent association surveillance
about, 436–437
failure of existing legal paradigms,
442–448
future directions, 449–454
importance of, 437–438
relational data and social network
analysis, 439–442
relational data availability, 438–439 (*See
also* constitutional rights)
encoding-based splitting, 58
encrypted values, computing with, 58
encryption
e-mail, 6
homomorphic, 58, 203
selective, 383, 397–401
Enterprise Privacy Authorization Language
(EPAL)
about, 135–136, 144–145
applicable rules (7.8), 143
compatible vocabulary (7.12), 145
condition language (7.4), 141
condition vocabulary (7.3), 140–141
hierarchy (7.1), 139–140
Lemma 7.1, 148–149
Lemma 7.2, 149–150, 150–151
Lemma 7.3, 150–151
Lemma 7.4, 151
Lemma 7.5, 152
obligation model (7.2), 140
overview and issues involved, 136
policies, 136–137, 139

policy conjunction (7.19), 149–150
policy disjunction (7.19), 150–151
policy equivalence (7.16), 146
policy refinement (7.15), 145–146
precedence range (7.10), 143–144
refinement and equivalence of
    obligations (7.14), 145
request (7.7), 142–143
ruleset and privacy policy (7.6),
    141–142
semantics (7.11), 144
suitability of use, 137–138
unfolded rules (7.8), 143
union of vocabularies (7.13), 145
vocabulary (7.5), 141
weak policy equivalence (7.16), 146
well-founded policy (7.18), 148
Enterprise Privacy Authorization Language
    (EPAL) algebraic properties of the
    Operators
about, 151
Lemma 7.4, 151–152
Lemma 7.5, 152
Enterprise Privacy Authorization Language
    (EPAL) composition
about, 147–148
well-founded policy (7.18), 148
Enterprise Privacy Authorization Language
    (EPAL) definition of conjunction and
    disjunction of privacy policies
about, Lemma 7.1, 148–149
policy conjunction (7.19), Lemma 7.2,
    149–150
policy disjunction (7.19)
    Lemma 7.2, 150–151
    Lemma 7.3, 150–151
Enterprise Privacy Authorization Language
    (EPAL) policies
hierarchy (7.1), 139–140
obligation model (7.2), 140
Enterprise Privacy Authorization Language
    (EPAL) refinement and policies
about, 144–145
compatible vocabulary (7.12), 145
policy equivalence (7.16), 146
policy refinement (7.15), 145–146
refinement and equivalence of
    obligations (7.14), 145
union of vocabularies (7.13), 145
weak policy equivalence (7.16), 146
Enterprise Privacy Authorization Language
    semantics of policies
applicable rules (7.8), 143
precedence range (7.10), 143–144
request (7.7), 142–143

semantics (7.11), 144
unfolded rules (7.8), 143
Enterprise Privacy Authorization Language
    syntax and semantics
condition language (7.4), 141
condition vocabulary (7.3), 140–141
Enterprise Privacy Authorization Language
    syntax of policies
ruleset and privacy policy (7.6),
    141–142
vocabulary (7.5), 141
EPAL. *See* Enterprise Privacy Policies and
    Languages
ePassport, 296, 298
EPC. *See* Electronic Product Code
EPCglobal, 289, 291, 297
e-Privacy Directive. *See* European Union
    e-privacy Directive
Euclidean distance, 202
European Union, 111
    Charter of Fundamental Rights of the
        European Union, ix
    Convention of Human Rights,
        426–427
    data protection compared with United
        States, 367
    Data Retention Directive, 411, 412–413
    e-privacy Directive, 412, 415–417
    MRTD use, 296–297
    Privacy and Identity Management for
        Europe, 230–231
expressive associations, 445
extending scrambled circuit evaluation,
    56–57

F

false light, 332
Faraday Cage protection of RFID tags,
    298–299
"fast-freeze-quick-thaw" model, 413–414
Federal Aviation Administration, 118–119
Felten attack, 104
First Amendment, 445–448
    importance of to overboard relational
        surveillance, 449
forecasting, 52–53
Foreign Intelligence Surveillance Act (FISA),
    444
Fourth Amendment, 419–422, 428, 436–437,
    442–443, 450–454
framing, 370–372
Freedom Network, 8–9
"function creep" *vs.* "mission creep," 429

G

Garfinkel, Simson, 302
Gates, Bill, 156
Genetic Privacy Act, 420
Geopriv, 320
German Constitutional Court, 425, 426–427
German Federal Constitutional Court, 423
Gillette Corporation, 295
global passive adversary model, 76–77
Global Positioning System (GPS, 99, 308
GNU Privacy Guard (GnuPG), 11
GnuPG. *See* GNU Privacy Guard
Google caching, 367
Google PageRank, 101
Google Safe Browsing, 14
GPS. *See* Global Positioning System
    See also location services, privacy
        enhanced
Grasso, Jack, 291
GSM/3G techniques, 310–312
GSM phones, 97, 98
Guide Project, 313

H

Hacker's-at-Large (HAL), 106
HAL. *See* Hacker's-at-Large
hammering distance, private
    approximation, 221
Handyside v. U.K., 425
hash-chain scheme used with RFID, 301
Hatton v. U.K., 425
HCI designs for identity management
    about, 230–231
    PRIME UI paradigms, 232–239
    PRIME UI proposals and legal privacy
        requirements, 239–246
    related work in PRIME context, 231–232
    trust and assurance HCI, 246–249
HCI. *See* human-computer interaction
HCI trust and assurance
    assurance control, 247–248
    enhancing trust, 246–247
    lack of, 246
    obligation management, 248–249
health care and privacy issues. *See* health
        care computing; Ubicomp, privacy
        issues
health care computing
    benchmarking and forecasting, 52–53
    See also Enterprise Privacy Authorization
        Language (EPAL)
Health Insurance Portability and
        Accountability Act (HIPPA), 338–339

Herman, Michael, 96
heuristics, 370–372
hiding information. *See* obfuscation
HIPPA. *See* Health Insurance Portability and
        Accountability Act
Hobson's choice, 329
Homo economicus, 54–55
homomorphic encryption, 58, 203
honest-but-curious adversary model, 49
    extending scrambled circuit evaluation,
        56–57
Hughes, Sandy, 294
human-computer interaction (HCI), 230
Hushmail, 11
Hussein, Saddam, 100
Hydra-Onions, 88–89
hyperbolic discounting, 372

I

ICAO. *See* International Civil Airation
        Organization)
ID3 classification, 127
identity-based encryption, 394
identity privacy and location privacy,
        313–314
Illinois v. Caballes, 451
incentive compatible process, 59
incomplete information and privacy
    behavioral economics, 368–369
    consumer education with bounded
        rationality, 369–370
    framing, 370–372
    heuristics, 370–372
    incomplete information, 364–365
    individual subjectivity of opinion,
        363–364
    researching the privacy phenomenon,
        374
    risk and uncertainty determination,
        367–368
    risk and uncertainty distinctions, 366–367
    systematic biases, 372–373
index
    B+ trees, 390–392
    bucket based, 387–389
    database, 382, 386–387
    hash-based, 389–390
index data structure, secure, 394
Indiana University, 335
indistinguishability and privacy networks
    about, 178
    k–indistinguishability (9.4), 180–182
    solutions, 181–182
    symmetricity (9.3), 178–180

inductive learning, data mining and
    privacy-preserving techniques,
    188–189
inductive learning in data mining, 188–189
inequity aversion, 373
inference control, 182–183
inference exposure, 394–396
information control, 270
information requiring privacy, data mining
    and privacy-preserving techniques,
    190–191
information security (IS), 267–268
informed user consent, 241
    consent via menu selection, 242
    drag-and-drop agreements, 243–244
    JITCTAs ("Just-In-Time-Click-Through
    Agreements"), 241–242
instant messaging, 11–12
    See also peer-to-peer structures
Intelligence Power in Peace and War
    (Herman), 96
Intel Research, 107
International Civil Airation Organization
    (ICAO), 296–297
International Covenant on Civil and
    Political Rights, ix
Internet Engineering Task Force (IETF), 320
Internet Protocol (IP), 20
invisible implicit addressing, 26
IPID fields, 105
IPSec, 109
IPv6 protocol, 105
IS. *See* information security
iteration stopping, 210, 211

J

JAP (Java Anon Proxy), 9
Java Anon Proxy, 9
JITCTAs. *See* "Just-In-Time-Click-Through
    Agreements"
jondo, 24–25
"Just-In-Time-Click-Through Agreements"
    (JITCTAs) , 231, 241–242

K

k, 181
k-anonymity, 126, 174
k-anonymity and location-based
    information models, 316–318
Katz v. U.S., 421, 442, 450
keyboards and keystrokes, 102
key compromise attacks, 7
key derivation hierarchy, 398, 400–401

key derivation hierarchy reduction, 401–403
key derivation method, 398–399
k-indistinguishability (9.4), 180–182
Klass v. Germany, 430
k-means clustering, 201–203
k-means clustering over two parties,
    201–213
    data mining and privacy-preserving
    techniques, 201–213
Kruslin v. France, 425
k-uncertainty (9.2), 177–178, 181–182
Kyllo v. U.S., 450, 451

L

Laurent, Cedric, 294
LBS. *See* location-based services
Leaderless Resistance model, 100
learned helplessness, 270
Lemma 10.1, 210–211
Lemma 10.2, 211, 219, 220, 221–222
Lindell-Pinkas method, 52
linear utility function, 351–352
link analysis, 439, 440, 453–454
local proxies, 23
local superposing, 31
locate-friends and nearby-friends services,
    312
"Locate-Me" services, 312
location-based services (LBS), 125, 308
location services, privacy enhanced
    about, 307–309, 314
    anonymity-based, 315–318
    location-based services, 312–313
    location privacy, 313–314
    nearest neighbor, 60–62
    obfuscation-based, 318–320
    policy-based, 320–322
    positioning systems, 310–312
London, England, 110
long-term intersection attacks, 108

M

machine learning, 190
Machine Readable Travel Document
    (MRTD), 296–297
Madrid, Spain, 110, 410
Malone v. UK, 418, 425
man-in-the-middle attacks, 339
marginally concerned individuals, 349
Marshall v. Bramer, 448
Media Access-Control (MAC), 20
mental disorders, 339
merge phase algorithm, 217

military traffic analysis, 96–99
MIT Reality Mining project, 107
Mix cascades, 34, 75
Mix channels, 40–41
Mixes, 33–43
    functionality, 35
    message transformation, 36–41
    topologies, 33–35
mixing, type-I remailers, 6
Mixmaster remailers, 7, 42
Mixminion
    attack countermeasures, 89–91
    DoS (denial-of-service) attack, 86–88
    reliability improvement options, 88–89
Mixminion remailers, 7, 41, 76
Mix systems (existing)
    general principles, 44–45
    high latency, 41–42
    low latency, 42–43
    private information retrieval, 43–44
Mix zone anonymity service model, 315
Mologogo, 313
MorphMix, 10, 79
MorphMix simulation attacks
    about, 81–82
    attack execution, 82–83
    countermeasures, 83–84
    See also anonymity systems and
        MorphMix
MRTD. *See* machine readable travel
        document
MTT. *See* Multi-target tracking applications
multiplicative splitting, 57
Multi-target tracking (MTT) applications,
        322
MySpace.com, 254–255

N

NAACP v. Alabama, 446
NAT (Network Address Translation), 105
(n - 1) attack, 40
nearby-information services, 312
nearest neighbor, 60–62
Netscape, 11
Network Address Translation (NAT), 105
Network device identification and mapping,
        traffic analysis, 104–106
Network Time Protocol (NTP), 104
Niemitz v. Germany, 418
nmap, 105
node discovery, 80–84
nodes, AIP, 9
noise generation, 197
NTP. *See* Network Time Protocol

O

obfuscation
    about, 156
    for access control, 164–167
    for access control for group privacy,
        167–170
    applications, 162–164
    copy and digital rights protection,
        157–158
    cryptography, 159–162
    data privacy, 158–159
    self-composing, 167
    "White-box" cryptography, 156–157
Oblivious Polynomial Evaluation (OPE),
        204–205
OECD. *See* Organization for Economic
        Cooperation and Development
OECD Declaration on the Protection of
        Privacy of Global Networks,
        302–304, ix
Off-the-Record Messaging (OTR),
        11–12
Omnibus Crime Control and Safe Streets,
        419
Onion routing, 8
online communities
    about, 254–255
    defining characteristics, 255–256
    members, 256–257
online communities and privacy
    perceived *vs.* actual privacy, 257–258
    types of privacy, 258
online communities privacy case study
    background, 258–259
    conclusions, 263–264
    findings, 261–263
    further research, 264–265
    research approach, 259–260
online community types
    blogs, 256, 263
    of circumstance, 256
    development, 25
    of fantasy, 256
    of interest, 255
    of practice, 255
    of purpose, 256
open proxies, 23
Openwave, 319
OPE. *See* Oblivious Polynomial Evaluation
OPES. *See* Order Preserving Encryption
        Schema
Oracle protocol, 205
Order Preserving Encryption Schema
        (OPES), 393

Organization for Economic Cooperation
and Development (OECD), 302–304
OTR. *See* Off-The-Record Messaging
outsourced data privacy
about, 382–383
DAS scenario, 383–387
DAS security issues, 396–404
inference exposure, 394–396
other indexing methods, 392–394
querying encrypted data, 387–392
outsourcing, computational, 64–65
overconfidence, 372

P

P3P. *See* Platform Privacy Preferences
Project
packet switching, 423
panopticon, 335
partial persistent storage, 127
participating adversary model, 77–78
Partition Plaintext and Ciphertext (PPC),
393
password-hashing procedure, 164–167
passwords, 159
and SSH protocol, 102
Pastry routing, 88–89
path compromise attacks, 78
path privacy, 314, 317–318
Path Tracker system, 295
pattern analysis, 439, 452–453
pawS (Privacy Awareness System), 269, 321
payment privacy systems, 12–13
Pearl Harbor, 97
peer-to-peer structures, 75
long-lived nodes, 80
See also MorphMix
Pen Register Act, 419, 420, 443, 444
perceived control and scales for privacy
about, 267–268
applying control scales to RFID
scenarios, 277–279
control definition, 272
perceived control in PETS in UC, 270–271
scale development and testing, 272–277
See also Ubicomp, privacy issues
perfect forward secrecy in OTR, 12
personal information protection, 190
personal navigation systems, 312
P.G. v. United Kingdom, 418
PGP. *See* Pretty Good Privacy
Philips' Milfare, 296
phishing, 13–14
"PipeNet," 7–8

PIR. *See* private information retrieval
PISA project, 231–232
Platform Privacy Preferences Project (P3P),
136, 231, 321
basic classes, 349
point function, 164
positioning systems, 310–312
See also location services, privacy
enhanced
position privacy, 314
power law networks. *See* social networks
PPC. *See* Partition Plaintext and Ciphertext
pragmatic majority, 349
Pretty Good Privacy (PGP), 11
pricing via processing, 168
PRIME. *See* Privacy and Identity
Management for Europe)
See also HCI designs for identity
management
privacy
alternate concepts, 331–333
of community members, 257–258
defined by EU Court of Human Rights,
418
defined by U.S. Supreme Court, 420–422
definition, ix
individual's interest in, 261–263, 349
individual subjectivity, 363–364
personal perception, 348–349 (*See also*
risk model for privacy insurance)
types, 258, 264, 333
unawareness of RFID tags, 290–292
Privacy and Identity Management for
Europe (PRIME), 230–231
privacy and targeted marketing,
122–127
Privacy Awareness System (pawS), 269
privacy-enhancing identity management.
See HCI designs for identity
management
privacy-enhancing technologies (PETS), 4
OTR (Off-The-Record Messaging), 11–12
PGP (Pretty Good Privacy), 11
SSL (Secure Sockets Layers), 11
TLS (Transport Layer Security), 11
See also anonymity and pseudonymity
systems, interactive
privacy fundamentalists, 349
privacy homomorphism, 393
privacy loss through loss of control,
269–270
See also perceived control and scales for
privacy; radio frequency
identification
privacy metrics, 173–176

privacy policy enforcement via
   cryptographic obfuscation. *See*
   obfuscation
privacy protection with uncertainty and
   indistinguishability
   about, 174–176
   (α, κ)—anonymity, 182–183
   challenges, 181–182
   indistinguishability
      about, 178
      k–indistinguishability (9.4), 180–181
      symmetricity (9.3), 178–180
   solutions, 181–182
   uncertainty, 176–177
      association cover (9.1), 177
private data standardization, 203, 207–208
private distancing measuring, 203, 212–213
private information retrieval (PIR), 43–44,
   50–51
private payments, 12–13
Proctor & Gamble Corporation, 294, 295
profiling
   individual's, 293
   privacy-preserving, 118–122
prospect theory, 371–372
proxies
   about, 20–22
   simple, 22–24
proxy chains, 22, 23–24
pseudonymity, 5
pseudonymity systems. *See* anonymity and
   pseudonymity systems, interactive
publicity of private facts, 332–333
public-key cryptography, 156

Q

querying encrypted data
   B+ trees index, 390–392
   bucket-based index, 387–389
   hash-based index, 389–390

R

radio communications, 97
radio frequency identification (RFID)
   about, 286–288
   applications, 288–289
   cryptographic circuit tags, 301
   kill command, 297–298
   noncryptographic tags, 299–301
   policy and legal solutions, 301–304
   real-life scenarios, 295–296
   security mechanisms in RFID standards,
      296–298

solutions to ID disclosure, 298–301
   threats to anonymity and privacy,
      290–294
   views on RFID technology, 294–295
random data perturbation (RDP), 194–195
random data perturbation (RDP) based on
   linear transformation, 195–196
random data perturbation (RDP) methods
   of data mining
   clustering based on RDP techniques,
      193–199
   density estimation-based clustering,
      193–199
   distribution function from perturbed data
      set, 192–193
random oracle model, 164–165
random utility model risk model for privacy
   insurance, 350–353
rational and selfish participants, 54–55
rational ignorance, 373
RDP. *See* random data perturbation
recipient anonymity, 20, 44
reciprocity and fairness, 373
relational data. *See* emergent association
   surveillance
relationship anonymity, 20
relationship-centered UI paradigm, 233–235
relay path, 75
remailers, 5–7
Renesys Corporation, 101
replay attacks, 6, 37–38
return addresses, untraceable, 38–40
RFID chips, 268, 286
RFID. *See* radio frequency identification
RFID readers, 286
Ring-Network, 27–28
risk, 365
risk model for possible claim of individual
   j for revealing private data D_m
   model construction, 352–353
   random utility model, 350–352
risk model for privacy insurance, collective
   risk model, 353–360
robustness in useful security and privacy
   technologies, 15
role-centered UI paradigm, 233
Rotaru v. Romania, 418
Row v. Wade, 420

S

scalar product, 60
scalar product protocol, 208
seclusion as privacy, 337
seclusion intrusion, 332

seclusion right, 331
secure approximation construction, 207
Secure Function Evaluation (SFE), 49
secure multiparty computation, 199–201
Secure Multiparty Computation (SMC),
    49–50, 56–57
Secure Shell protocol (SSH), 102
Secure Shell protocol (SSH), traffic analysis,
    102
Secure Sockets Layer (SSL), 11
Secure Sockets Layer (SSL), traffic analysis,
    103
selective encryption, 397–401
selfish and rational participants, 54–55
semantic security, 162
"Send Data" dialogue boxes, 231, 240
sender anonymity, 20, 44
sensitive information protection,
    190–191
September 11, 410, 411, 436
server, 383
SFE. *See* Secure Function Evaluation
Shocking Events (TV show), 330
Signals Intelligence (Sigint), 98
Simon, Herbert, 54
simple proxies, 22–24
size correlation attacks, 6
SMC. *See* Secure Multiparty Computation
Smith v. Maryland, 421, 443, 451
Smith v. United States, 423
Snedigar v. Hoddersen, 448
snort, 105
Social Network Analysis, 99–101
social networks, 99
soft blocking, 299
soft security measures, 411
spatial cloaking, 316
S^{PPF}-tree, 127
PR-tree index structure, 126–127
SSH. *See* Secure Shell protocol
SSL. *See* Secure Sockets Layer
statistics and data mining, 189–190
status quo bias, 373
Steinhardt, Barry, 295–296
Stephanie's Law, 332
stepping stones, 106
Stored Communications Act (U.S.),
    413, 419
subjective probabilities, 366
superposed sending, 31
supervised learning, 189
surfing, 103
surveillance society, 294
Sybil attacks, 80–81
SYM binary relations, 174

T

Talley v. California, 427
targeted marketing and privacy
    mobile users, 125–127
    static users, 122–124
Tarzan network, 42–43
    Sybil attacks, 81
technical bias, 334
Teen Arrive Alive, 312
telecommunications databases, 444
telecommunications interception, 413
telecommunications rights, 421
temporal cloaking, 316
timing correlation attacks, 6
TLS. *See* Transport Layer Security
T-Online, 425–426
Tor, 9–10, 42
    anonymity and pseudonymity systems,
        interactive, 9–10
Torbutton, 10
Tor network, 8, 75, 79
    attack countermeasures, 89–91, 109
    DoS (denial-of-service) attacks, 84–86
    reliability improvement options, 88–89
TownMap-based UI paradigm, 235–237
tracking, individual's, 293
tracking services, 312
traffic analysis
    about, 76, 95–96
    anonymous communications, 107–110
    in civilian sectors, 95–96, 99–101
    data retention, 110–112
    in military settings, 96–99
    Network device identification and
        mapping, 104–106
    Secure Shell protocol (SSH), 102
    Secure Sockets Layer (SSL), 103
    social networks, 99–101
    stepping stones, 106
    Transport Layer Security (TLS), 103
    used as surveillance (*see* criminal
        intelligence; data retention)
    used for social network analysis,
        439–442
    web privacy, 103–104
    wireless location data, 106–107
Transport Layer Security (TLS), 11, 109
    traffic analysis, 103
Trent, 48–49
Trojan Horse scandal, 339
trust negotiation, 62–64
two-party honest-but-curious scrambled
    circuit, cryptographic protocol
    results in practice, 55–56

two-party honest-but-curious scrambled
circuit evaluation, 55–56
two party *k*-means clustering over two
parties, 201–213
two-party scrambled circuit evaluation,
honest-but-curious adversary model,
55–56
type-III remailers, 7
type-I remailers, 5–6
type-II remailers, 6–7, 42
type-0 remailers, 5

U

Ubicomp. *See* ubiquitous computing
Ubicomp, privacy issues
about, 327–328
alternative concepts of privacy, 331–333
a contested value, 328–329
Data Protection and Fair Information
Practices, 329–330
implications, 336–338, 339–340
privacy a form of autonomy, 330–331
subject-driven design limitations,
338–340
value-sensitive design, 334–336
ubiquitous computing (ubicomp), 327
UI (user interface), 230
uncertainty, 365
uncertainty and privacy metrics
association cover (9.1), 177
example scenario, 176–177
k–uncertainty (9.2), 177–178
United States v. Miller, 421
Unix operating systems, 164
unsupervised learning, 189
U.S. Army Counterinsurgency Manual, 100
U.S. DARPA Agency, 110
U.S. Department of Defense Technology
and Privacy Advisory Committee,
429
U.S. Department of Homeland Security, 119
U.S. Fair Information Practices, 302–304,
329–330
U.S. Government Accountability Office, 336
U.S. National Security Agency, 98
U.S. Naval Research Lab, 8
U.S. v. Councilman, 419
U.S. v. Forrester, 443
U.S. v. Miller, 442
USA PATRIOT Act, 330, 413, 419

useful security and privacy technologies,
14–15
Usenet archives, 367
user (human), 383
user interface (UI), 230
user right to know, 244–246

V

valence effect, 372
verifiable secret sharing (VSS), 195
Vickrey auctions, 52, 59
Vidalia, 10
Video Privacy Act, 420
VIEW $_{mean}$, 212
virtual black box, 160–162
visible implicit address, 26
Voice over IP, 110, 424
VSS. *See* verifiable secret sharing

W

Wagner, 4
Wal-Mart stores, 294, 295
Warshak v. U.S., 443
web privacy, 136
traffic analysis, 103–104
web site-based proxies, 22–23
Web site-based proxy, 22
Wei Dai, 7–8
Weiser, Mark, 268
Whalen v. Roe, 420
"White-box" cryptography, 156–157
WiFi, 310
wireless communications, 426
privacy ensuring, 125–127
wireless location data, traffic analysis,
106–107
Wiretap Act, 419, 428

X

XOR operation, 32, 43

Z

Zendian Problem, 98
Zero-Footprint, 22
zero-knowledge proofs, 56
Zero-Knowledge Systems (ZKS), 8, 333
ZKS. *See* Zero-Knowledge Systems
Zurcher v. The Stanford Daily, 449